Effective Financial Management in Public and Nonprofit Agencies

Effective Financial Management in Public and Nonprofit Agencies

Fourth Edition

Jerome B. McKinney

 PRAEGER

AN IMPRINT OF ABC-CLIO, LLC
Santa Barbara, California • Denver, Colorado • Oxford, England

Library of Congress Cataloging-in-Publication Data

McKinney, Jerome B.
    Effective financial management in public and nonprofit agencies / Jerome B. McKinney. — Fourth edition.
       pages cm
    Revised edition of the author's Effective financial management in public and nonprofit agencies, 3rd ed., published in 2004.
    Includes bibliographical references.
       ISBN 978-1-4408-3122-5 (hardback) — ISBN 978-1-4408-3123-2 (e-book)   1. Finance, Public. 2. Nonprofit organizations—Finance. I. Title.
    HJ197.M35 2015
    658.15—dc23   2014040021

ISBN: 978-1-4408-3122-5
EISBN: 978-1-4408-3123-2

19 18 17 16 15   1 2 3 4 5

This book is also available on the World Wide Web as an eBook.
Visit www.abc-clio.com for details.

Praeger
An Imprint of ABC-CLIO, LLC

ABC-CLIO, LLC
130 Cremona Drive, P.O. Box 1911
Santa Barbara, California 93116-1911

This book is printed on acid-free paper ∞

Manufactured in the United States of America

Contents

About the Fourth Edition

Public and other nonprofit financial management systems have been going through profound change during the past two decades. We are passing through a period in which the public is demanding more and better services while demonstrating an unwillingness to pay higher taxes or fees. Access to government and nonprofit sources of funding have been made more difficult since the Great Recession of 2008–09. Accordingly, public and private officials hold the view that public and other nonprofit agencies can and must find new ways to cut costs while improving efficiency, effectiveness, transparency, and accountability. This edition is an important means to achieve these goals.

Even more so than in the past, effective management of financial resources is critical to the success and survival of public and other nonprofit agencies. While the nonfinancial manager will not be expected to be an accountant/ bookkeeper or an auditor, any lack of familiarity with the concepts of accounting and other financial processes will limit the manager's ability to ask the critical questions and to effectively monitor and evaluate fiscal activities. This text is written to be understandable to those who are not "experts" but to those who are or may become managers.

Every chapter of this fourth edition is updated with the most recent developments, maintaining simplicity and practicality. Special emphasis is focused on sustainability as a unifying means to address a wide array of public and nonprofit fiscal management issues, especially the demand for greater transparency and accountability and the pursuit of the "sweet spot" in the triple bottom line (TBL) approach to sustainability. Attention is given to the Treadway Commission, or Committee on Sponsoring Organization (COSO), study on internal control, including its widely accepted recommendations aimed at maximizing the achievement of an organization's mission and goals. Next, recent developments to minimize organizations' vulnerability to fraud, waste, and abuse (FWA), including the triangle versus the diamond approaches and cloud computing are examined.

Other important areas on which this new edition focuses attention include (1) the recent research on and changing approach to risk management; (2) the government performance and Results Act of 1993, discussion of which has been comprehensively rewritten in 2010, focusing attention on tighter congressional oversight and on greater public transparency and accountability; (3) break-even analysis, introducing a new approach for calculating the result and articulating its linkage and importance to margin of safety, allowing managers to better manage their budgets and resources; (4) ties together the fiscal side (budgeting, financing, and controlling) and the substantive management side (planning, programming, and evaluating) to facilitate the unimpeded flow of required information to the appropriate responsibility centers' decision points in public and nonprofit agencies; (5) it shows how to think about resource needs and translate them into effective budgets; (6) it shows how to obtain and use financial advisory services; and (7) it incorporates the massive changes brought about the Governmental Accounting Standards Board (GASB) in statement number 34.

The author thanks students and practitioners who exchanged ideas and examples. Thanks go to Mary McKinney and my daughter Katie for their continued encouragement and to the memory of Melissian and Octavious McKinney. I also owe thanks to Anita Marchese for typing and editing and the Graduate School of Public and International Affairs of the University of Pittsburgh.

1

Understanding Financial Management

The pursuit of virtually every collective public purpose has financial implications. Undertakings that have no cost seldom bring many benefits. Financial management plays an indispensable role in the achievement of an organization's objectives. It is the fuel that gives life and substance to the engine of public administration. Financial management is the only activity that touches every employee in an organization. The new international economic order has increased competitiveness among every jurisdiction of the world, because each individual must now directly compete against others for goods and services. Inflation has been effectively controlled in the United States from 2004 to 2014. The new competitive environment, the rising cost of governmental programs, and citizens' demands for less bureaucracy and more cost-effective delivery of goods and services are forcing public managers and others in not-for-profit organizations to make creative use of their scarce financial resources. This is happening at a time when taxpayers are demanding greater value creation for resources expended, showing an unwillingness to support increased expenditures on services. Ideally, public and not-for-profit organizations seek to minimize cost, maximize net revenue, and break even financially (revenues equal or exceed costs) in the delivery of goods and services.

Transparency and Accountability. In recent years, these terms have been popularized both in the United States and abroad to mean good, trustworthy, corruption-free, responsive organization in private, public, and other non-profit organizations. Although transparency and accountability are sometimes used interchangeably, they are different—but interrelated.

In government, transparency suggests that reliable, relevant, and timely information about the activities of government is desirable and available to the public. There is an expectation that governments will listen to citizens and interested stakeholders. A transparent public organization not only must have visibility and accessibility, but must also institutionalize a process that responds quickly to requests for information. Additionally, large amounts of information are published without the need to make a specific formal request. Such information is regularly published on organizational Internet sites or in user-friendly leaflets and reports. Also, transparent organizations that respond to large number of requests for information typically create positive benefits through what is sometimes called proactive or communication transparency efficiency. The need for disclosure creates the opportunity for better information organization. This results in reliable data gathering that enhances enhanced fact-based decision making and communication.[1]

In the typical nonprofit agency, a useful way, the provision of easily understandable information, is to make the organization's financial records readily available showing the main programmatic activities and the top officer(s) salary by means of the IRS Federal Form 990. The latter is a major source of information that rating agencies use to make organizational comparisons. Savvy nonprofits put the IRS 990 form on the Internet and use it as an opportunity to market their services and programs.[2]

In the "age of digital technology," citizens at all levels of government and nonprofit agencies are expecting access to information to enable them to make decisions indicative of responsible decisions in a modern democracy.[3]

Accountability. In the Weberian hierarchical decision making model, according to which the typical bureaucracy operates, authority and power flow down the hierarchy and accountability flows upward in the form of information feedback communication and reports. Officials in organizations (public, private, voluntary) are answerable for all their activities. When duties and commitments are not met, appropriate disciplinary action can be initiated. In practice, accountability and transparency are mutually self-reinforcing. Transparency gives citizens the opportunity and resources to have timely access to and availability of relevant information to influence decision making, whereas accountability allows citizens and clientele to call decision makers to account for the outcomes of their decisions. Individuals to whom authority has been granted have the duty to act publicly, predictably, and clearly to encourage participation, enhancing the opportunity to achieve accountability.

This chapter provides a broad overview of the components and processes involved in financial administration. The discussion is presented in seven sections. The first presents a definition of financial management and shows how it has emerged as a critical force in everyday operations and increasing pursuit of sustainability objectives. The second and third examine the federal financial management system and the role of the federal chief financial officer. The fourth compares public and private financial management, indicating the similarities and differences in how articulated objectives are pursued. The fifth discusses the organizational framework in which financial administration takes place.[4] In the sixth, the duties of financial managers are briefly examined and the important roles of accountability and improved financial management are introduced, along with an overview. The seventh introduces the emerging role of sustainability on public financial management. The final section of the chapter contains an overview of the remainder of the book.

The pursuit of environmental sustainability has become a worldwide goal to many private and public organizations. Sustainable practice inevitably leads to ecoefficiency. As a management strategy, it is viewed as creating more value with less resource use. The approach minimizes use of inputs while maximizing generation of competitively priced outputs. The production of goods and services are accomplished while progressively reducing or eliminating negative ecological impact on the environment.[5] As the World Business Council for Sustainable Development (WBCSD) indicates, sustainability is about the creative use of resources that have less environmental impact.[6]

Among the benefits typically linked with sustainable organizations are the following:

- Enhancement of product or service value
- Promotion of efficient use of inputs such as energy and materials
- Maximization of cost savings
- Inducing organizations to be risk/liability-aware by avoiding the use of toxic materials producing toxic waste
- Enhancing organizational and individual productivity
- Recovering and reusing waste materials with positive impact on the environment

When sustainability is viewed as a resource by management, it suggests that finite resources must be managed in a manner that will provide use and service of resources over an extended time horizon. Every organization must maintain continuing health and vitality if it is to achieve balanced and enhanced outputs.

As can be seen from Figure 1.1, the society and economy are subsets of the environment. The economy exists within the society, and both the economy and society are within the environment. Thus, if growth and continued sustainability are to be realized, the society and economy must operate so that their activities are consistent with the operating environment.

Sustainability: The Triple Bottom Line Approach

The triple bottom line (TBL) approach is focused on three pillars (social capital, economic capital, environmental capital) of sustainable development, also referred to as the 3 Ps—people, planet, and profit. Maximum attention is given to the pursuit of both the organization and the common good interest by the financial and nonfinancial stakeholders. There is mutual recognition and acceptance of what is called the common ground known as the sweet spot. It is the point "where the pursuit of profits [for the private sector] blends seamlessly with the pursuit of the common good,"[7] as shown in Figure 1.2.

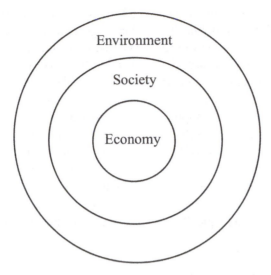

FIGURE 1.1 Showing environmental constraints on society and economy.

Source: See EPA Environmental Management Solutions, The Hows and Whys of Sustainability, www.epa-environmental.com

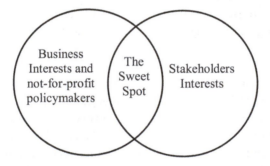

FIGURE 1.2 The sustainability sweet spot.

In the public and not-for-profit sector, the sweet spot is reached when stakeholders and the policymakers accept a program and its prospective outcomes that mutually enhance the common interests of all and the environmental requirements. This sweet spot is the ideal that should propel all organizations. The pursuit and achievement of the sweet spot is what the best run organizations are trying to identify in determining how best they can realize the sweet spot that leads to maximum profit (private) and maximum policy outcome (not-for-profit) organizations. When interdependent social, economic, and environmental aspects are effectively integrated, it enhances quality of life.

Maximum emphasis, as noted earlier, is put on preventing problems and minimizing resource use. Maximum benefits are obtained from each product while minimizing waste generation in the production process, requiring cradle-to-grave analysis. To achieve this objective, continuous measuring of inputs from the point of extraction to the point of complete recycling process is necessary.[8]

Defining Financial Management

Public financial management is the process wherein a governmental unit or agency (1) employs the means to obtain and allocate resources or money based on implied or articulated priorities and (2) uses methods and controls to effectively achieve publicly determined ends. Two important elements are emphasized: efficient raising of resources and wise and accountable usage of funds to achieve end products of the highest possible quality. Though the definition does not stress time and uncertainty (and the literature seldom articulates these concepts), both have particular importance in the field of applied public financial management. So defined, financial management is viewed not as a staff specialty concerned only with controlling the government or agency funds, but rather as an integral part of management.

In general terms, financial management comprises three main activities: (1) It determines the scope and content of fiscal policies. This is a process in which agency, community, or relevant political leaders set forth programs and provide the appropriation or resources required to accomplish them. (Issues such as employment, inflation, borrowing/debt management, taxation, and revenue raising are considered and resolved.) (2) It establishes general guidelines and standards to ensure that funds are spent honestly and wisely to achieve publicly determined purposes. (3) It provides organizational structures and controls to effectively carry out fiscal duties and responsibilities.[9] Traditionally, the main financial management components include budgeting, taxation (revenue raising), accounting, treasury management, purchasing, and auditing. In Figure 1.3, the integrated approach to financial management incorporates an additional set of components, including planning, programming, and evaluating functions. The key to the figure clarifies what is meant by each of these six processes.

Integrative Role

The critical and integrative role that financial management plays in the operation of everyday management can be seen in Figure 1.3. For simplicity, the combination of the two processes may be seen as a set of sequential steps: *planning, programming, budgeting, financing, controlling, evaluating*.

The first of the basic management processes depicted in Figure 1.3 involves the articulation of the goals and objectives to be pursued (*planning*). Their feasibility for implementation is determined and appropriate activities to realize the planned goals selected (*programming*).

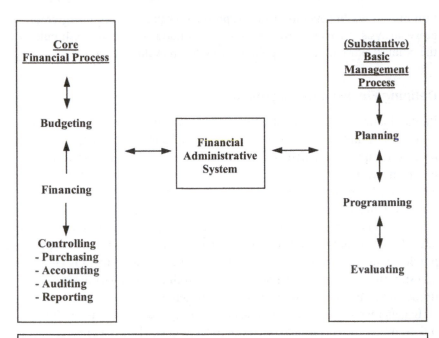

FIGURE 1.3   The integrative role of financial management.

The first action on the "financial process side" is completion of the *budget* (or expenditure plan), which allocates available resources based on these programmed activities and priorities. After the expenditure plan has been developed, financial resources are sought to execute the plan (*financing*). In order to monitor the progress of activities through the execution stages, and thereby to ensure that planned, programmed, and financial objectives are being carried out according to targets and expectations, a system of *controls* is created. Whenever it is determined that progress is not meeting expectations, interventions can be made to redirect the activity toward its target. Returning to the management side, it can be seen that *evaluation* is the final action in the process. This activity determines whether the articulated goals and objectives have been achieved.

Traditionally, financial management has given little attention to the basic management processes of planning, programming, and evaluation. Instead, it has dwelled on the core financial functions, especially the budgeting and controlling activities. However, because of continuing competition for declining financial resources, the basic management processes are beginning to receive more attention, as evidenced by recent literature discussing the subject. Planning, programming, and evaluating require policymakers to observe, understand, and reflect before they enact potentially unwise policies. This changing emphasis will be discussed later in this volume.

The Fragmented Federal Financial Management System

The federal government provides an excellent example of a system that needs greater linkage and integration between the financial and management processes (as shown in Figure 1.2). There are gaps in six principal areas:

- poor quality of financial-management information;
- poor linkage between the phases of the financial management process;
- inadequate attention to monitoring and comparing budgeted activity with results;
- primary emphasis on fund control;
- inadequate disclosure of assets, cost, and liabilities; [and]
- antiquated and fragmented financial-management systems.[10]

In recent years, the federal government has made great strides to bridge the principal management gaps identified in Figure 1.4. The implementation of the Governmental Performance Results Act of 1993 (GPRA), its modernization in 2010 to (GPRAMA) and the Chief Financial Officers (CFO) Act of 1990 are the two most prominent steps that have been taken to overcome these gaps. These and other acts (Government Management Reform Act [GMRA], Information Technology Management Reform Act [also known as the Clinger–Cohen Act], and the Federal Financial Management Improvement Act [FFMIA]) reinforcing the GPRAMA and the CFO Act have been passed.

The Federal Chief Financial Officer: Toward Integrated Management

In 1990, in the CFO Act, dealing with chief financial officers, the federal government enacted legislation to achieve an integrated system of financial management paralleling the approach depicted in Figure 1.4[11] directed at promoting greater accountability. The act aims to promote effective financial management practices in the federal government, to improve each agency's financial management system, and to ensure timely and reliable financial reporting. The CFO Act strengthened the management side of the Office of Management and Budget (OMB) by creating a deputy director of management at executive pay level 3 who reports directly to the OMB director. The new deputy now has equal status with the powerful budget side at OMB. This was a significant upgrading and improvement of the management responsibilities at OMB. Because of the vacuum that had existed on the management side, administrative functions delegated to the Office of Federal Procurement Policy (OFPP) and the Office of Information and Regulatory Affairs (OIRA) overseeing federal paperwork clearance and information resource management activities could not be effectively coordinated and implemented.[12] According to a joint 2011 report, these problems have been significantly mitigated.

To carry out the functions of the CFO Act, the Office of Federal Financial Management (OFFM) was created within the OMB to develop an operating organization based on an eight-part program:

- The CFOs' responsibilities, as well as the authorities of the twenty-three agencies and the council composed of the OFFM (a government-wide chief financial officer officially known as the "controller"), CFOs, and deputy CFOs, were defined. Council participants are charged with advising the OFFM controller on financial matters and to aid in the implementation of financial management efforts.
- The OFFM is required to assess the staff's capability and professional qualifications of the financial management personnel, identify deficiencies, and make recommendations as they relate to qualifications, recruitment, performance, and retention.[13]
- To promote uniformed federal accounting and general-purpose accounting standards, the OMB, U.S. Department of Treasury, and U.S. General Accounting Office (GAO) established the Federal Accounting Standards Advisory Board (FASAB). With the FASAB creation, the OFFM outlined the form and content of agencies' financial statements.
- Agencies were required to establish an integrated financial management system that facilitated agencies' budget request reviews, analysis of plans, and the steps being made in creating a new financial management system.
- Auditors were directed to report on internal control weaknesses and weaknesses identified in financial audits.
- To streamline federal delinquent collections and disbursements to state, vendors, employees, and benefit recipients, state-of-the-art electronic techniques were implemented. To speed up collection, agencies were authorized to use a variety of means, such as income tax refund offset and private collection agencies.

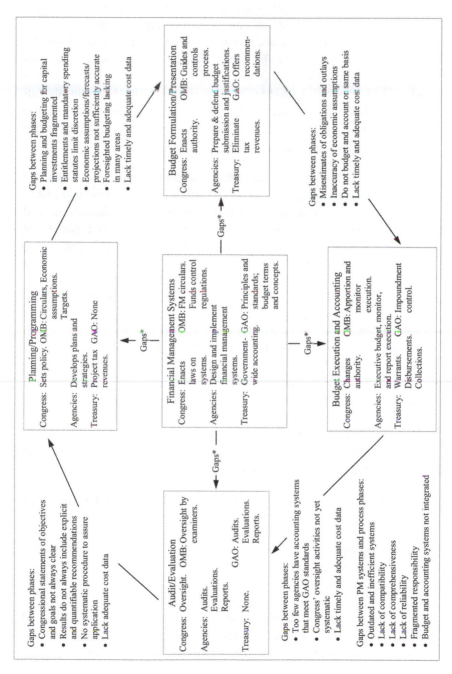

FIGURE 1.4 Observations of government-wide financial management processes and systems.

- Rules relating to federal grant recipients were tightened and improved. Recipients were expected to make greater use of financial audits to enhance their credibility of reported financial information, internal controls, and promotion of better compliance with the grants' requirements.
- The OFFM outlined what audits must contain and how they should be prepared. Additionally, the OFFM recognized that if financial statements are to be maximally useful, they must report on the nature and amount of services provided. To realize this objective, the OFFM requires that all financial statements contain selected program performance measures. The OFFM provides agencies assistance in selecting and presenting performance measures, thus paralleling the objectives of the GPRA Act of 1993.

Perhaps the CFO Act's most important accomplishment has been the acceptance of and greater appreciation of accountability in the management of resources. Focus is placed on the particular individual or organization charged with efficiently and effectively accomplishing and on the timely reporting of results. Several important statutes that have been instrumental in promoting the new mandated orientations include the following:[14]

- GPRAMA requires that agencies define mission goals in their strategic plans, prepare annual performance plans that indicate how goals are to be achieved, and issue annual reports showing achievements.
- The Government Management Reform Act (GMRA) extends the CFO Act to all other federal agencies not covered.
- The Federal Financial Management Improvement Act (FFMIA) defines an agency's information system requirements and the procedure for reporting on the extent to which they have been met.
- The Information Technology Management Reform Act (also known as the Clinger–Cohen Act) requires accountability for the acquisition, use, and disposal of information technology and resources.

Other significant improvements resulting from the CFO Act include the following:

- Financial management systems have been reduced and effectively integrated.
- The FASAB created pursuant to the CFO Act has been accepted by the American Institute of Certified Public Accounts (AICPA) as an instrument capable of issuing generally accepted accounting principles.
- The CFO Act has been instrumental in developing core competencies and effective recruitment and retention policies for financial management personnel, such as accountants, budget analysts, and financial analysts.[15]

In the agencies, the twenty-three CFOs occupy, in name or substance, positions coterminous with that of the principal management official (assistant secretary for management), plus a purely financial management role or portfolio duties. This organization placement and design provides for optimum integration between the naturally interrelated functions of management and finance. The broad responsibilities of each agency's CFO purposely parallel the duties of the U.S. chief financial officer—the OMB deputy director for management and finance, who has been given charge of the functions that include management systems, procurement, human resources, and regulatory affairs.[16]

Because of the decentralized nature of many agencies, whose activities are carried out by bureaus or units that are geographically remote from the direct access and supervision of the central agency, the CFO Act permits the personnel of these units to directly report to the subunit head, with broken-line reporting to the CFO. This approach "recognizes financial management as an integral component of any overall administrative structure and must remain imbedded in that infrastructure for both to be effective."[17] The broken-line model permits the subunit to exercise a chain of command over the financial managers while allowing the CFO authority to be maintained throughout the agency by means of an integrated financial management system.

The CFO Act requires that the twenty-three departments and agencies be given CFOs, who must develop financial management plans and provide annual progress reports to the agency head and to Congress. Based on CFO reports and inspectors general (IGs), Department of Treasury, and GAO, program manager, and private-sector inputs, OMB is required to annually produce a government-wide financial management status report and a projected five-year plan. Clearly defined strategy for generating audited financial statements is prepared and submitted to Congress, identifying agency vulnerabilities and proposed actions for correcting them. Additionally, CFOs must maintain permanently audited financial statements for revolving funds, trust funds, and funds substantially related to commercial activities.[18]

Dual monitoring responsibility for budget execution is given to the OMB's deputy director for management and to the agency CFOs. These latter are also directed to maintain systems that facilitate the integration of accounting and budgeting information aimed at improving policymaking and decision making and enhancing program efficiency. The responsibility is given to the CFO to recruit, select, and train all personnel who carry out the financial functions; this includes "all financial management, personnel activities and operations, including . . . the implementation of agency assets, [as well as] management systems, including systems for cash management, credit management, debt collection, and property and inventory management and control."[19]

In summary, the CFO Act is based on three main premises: (1) Continual improvement in the quality of government financial management systems is possible by effectively linking management programs, budgeting, and accounting into an efficiently operating financial management system (see Figure 1.3);

(2) audited financial statements can be valuable inputs to decision makers; and (3) the production of timely audit reports in accordance with audit recommendations can be facilitated. Thus, the CFO structure is viewed as the best means that could be developed and implemented to appropriately achieve these objectives.[20] In reflecting on the role of the CFOs, one member of Congress stated: "[A] strong, independent statutory CFO who keeps track of how much is being spent will be able to let Congress know what the program is really costing, not keep it hidden until it is too late."[21]

The effectiveness of the CFO greatly depends on the relationship that develops between the office and the head of the agency to which it is attached. Agency heads involve the CFOs in key agency decisions and activities, and the CFO is given an equivalent place with counterpart officers in the making of important decisions.

The CFO Act does not replace the inspectors general (IGs), but rather complements and parallels their functions. The act explicitly requires that the CFO provide federal agencies with systems capability to develop "internal controls adequate to . . . deter fraud, waste and abuse of government resources."[22] Before the CFO Act, the charge to reduce fraud, waste, and abuse was viewed as being in the province of the IGs. Today, both offices work cooperatively to achieve a common objective.

Changes in GPRA to GPRA Modernization Act of 2010

When GPRA, now known as Government Performance Results Act Modernization Act (GPRAMA), was enacted in 1993, it was the first time that Congress established requirements in statute for federal "agencies to set goals, measure performance and report the information to Congress"[23] providing opportunities for exercising its allocation and review responsibilities.

- The agency strategic plan (ASP; formerly known as strategic plan) requires that each agency put its four strategic plan on its public website.
- The agency consults with Congress and nonfederal stakeholders in the development of its four-year agency strategic plan.
- The agency performance plan (APP, known formerly as annual performance plan) is required annually to be put on its public website. The APP is accompanied with the president's agency budget proposal to Congress.

The GPRAMA introduced a number of changes to the 1993 act, including the following:

1. Although it made significant changes to the 1993 Act, it continues the GPRA 1993 three-agency level. As in the 1993 act, the GPRAMA aims to improve the confidence of Americans in the capability of the federal government by specifically identifying mechanisms for holding federal agencies

accountable for achieving results. Stress is put on achieving program effectiveness and public accountability. This is done by promoting a renewed focus on results and service quality and on customer/citizen satisfaction. Motivate and encourage federal managers to improve service delivery by requiring planning to achieve program objectives and by giving them timely information to enable them to realize program results, enhanced service quality and improve internal management.

2. It creates new requirements that focus on goal setting and performance measurement in policy areas that cross agencies.
3. It focuses attention on goals and measures during the policy implementation process.
4. It requires that more information be reported on the public websites.
5. It requires that specific individuals be accountable for priority goals and management tasks implementation.

The GPRAMA timed the changes to coincide with presidential terms and budget proposals. A central role was created for the Office of Management and Budget (OMB) to facilitate coordination with the president's policy preferences and required greater consultation with Congress. Additionally, the law provides for nonfederal stakeholders to give inputs on how agencies and the OMB set goals and evaluate performance.

The GPRAMA attempts to make the agencies more responsive than the GPRA of 1993 by requiring the agencies to report on a number of specific questions:

1. How effective are the relations of OMB and agencies with Congress? Additionally, are the performance assessments reflecting congressional intent?
2. Are the agencies and OMB performances useful and credible to Congress and stakeholders?
3. Are OMB and agencies' implementation of GPRAMA participative and transparent?
4. Are OMB and agencies' focused in minimizing duplication across policy areas?
5. If OMB and agencies are ineffectively implementing GPRAMA, what needs to be done to redirect them?[24]

Agency-Level Functions and Processes Continuing from GPRA 1993

As noted previously, GPRAMA retains the three agency-level functions of GPRA 1993 Act, but were new statutory names with additional requirements.

- *Agency strategic plan (ASP), previously known as strategic plan.* Each agency is required to post its four-year *agency strategic plan* on its website. As in GPRA 1993, the new GPRAMA strategic plan provides goals and objectives for all major functions and a description of the evaluation method used in developing the goals and objectives. The GPRAMA requires that the agency be expected to explain how it is collaborating with other agencies to realize its goals.

As previously explained, the GPRAMA aligns its process of developing and updating its ASP to take place with presidential terms and budget proposals. A revised ASP must be completed immediately after the first year of the president's term, the first Monday in February paralleling the arrival of the president's budget proposal.

Agency consultations with Congress and nonfederal stakeholders with ASP were previously practiced under the GPRA of 1993. GPRAMA requires that there must be consultation with Congress with both the majority and minority appropriation committees of Congress periodically when developing or updating the ASP.[25]

- *Agency performance plan (APP), previously known as annual performance plan.* The GPRAMA requires agencies to annually post the APP on their websites. The APP, covering the agency activities, including indicators such as efficiency, outputs, outcomes, is included with the president's submission to Congress. Each APP must identify and justify programs with low priority designations. Additionally, the APP must identify agency officials known as the "goal leaders," who are responsible for achieving each performance goal.
- *Agency performance update (APU), previously known as program performance report.* The GPRAMA requires that all updates to an agency performance be posted on the agency's public website. As was done under the GPRA in 1993, the APU provides updates to performance indicators comparing stated goals with achieved results. When a past performance goal was not achieved, the APU must explain why and describe ways to realize the goal or explain why the goal is not feasible. Where there is information relating to a program that precedes the annual update, it should be provided if it does not involve undue administrative burden.[26]

New Agency-Level Functions and Processes

Agency Priority Goals (APGs) GPRAMA. Every two years, the GPRAMA requires agencies such as the CFO Act agencies and any OMB-designated agencies to identify a selected number of APP performance goals or "agency priority goals." Each agency is required to identify an official, known as a goal leader, who is accountable for achieving APG goals. These priority goals are identified as the highest priority of the agency, as designated by the agency head.

Quarterly Reviews of Priority Goals. The head and deputy head of the agency are required to conduct quarterly progress reviews during the fiscal year, focusing on how program goals are being realized. The review is not required to be transparent to Congress or the public, though some information on APGs is required to be included on the OMB website.

"Unmet goal" Reports and Plans. Annually, the OMB is required to determine the extent to which agency performance goals in APPs have been met. Depending on the findings, the OMB must develop plan and strategies indicating how it will address the unmet goals.[27]

New Executive Branch–Wide Functions and Processes

The GPRAMA added new requirements for goal setting, plans, implementation reviews, and reports for the executive branch–wide level agencies.

Federal Government Priority Goals (FGPGs). OMB is given the task of assisting agencies to develop long-term "federal government priority goals" (FGPGs). There are two categories of federal government priority goals that must be developed: (1) outcome-oriented goals in selected priority areas, and (2) improvement goals across the federal government.

Federal priority goals coincide with deadlines for submitting the president's budget immediately after the first year. The goals are updated and revised every four years. When the OMB makes adjustments or revisions to FGPGs, it must periodically consult with the majority and minority of the appropriate specific committees.

Quarterly Reviews for FGPGs. OMB is required to conduct a "quarterly priority progress review" indicating the extent to which federal priority goals have been achieved. During its FGPG reviews, OMB is not required to provide transparency about its actions to Congress or the public, though some information about federal government priority goals is required to be put on the OMB developed website.

The OMB Performance Website. is required to be accessible to Congress and the public. There are two kinds of information about two kinds of priority goals and federal priority goals which incorporate the view and suggestions emanating from congressional exchanges. When the president's budget proposal goes to Congress, it must include the federal government performance plan (FGPG), agency-level agency strategic plans (ASPs), and agency performance plans (APPs). Finally, there must be detailed information about each identified agency programs and how each agency defines the term "program."[28]

Institutional Changes

The GPRAMA created new particular positions and outlined their duties and responsibilities.

Chief Operating Officers (COOs). GPRAMA also created deputy COOs. COO duties included the following:

- Improving agency performance
- Assisting the agency in implementing the GPRAMA
- Conducting quarterly review on agency priority goals
- Coordinating efforts to improve mission support functions

Performance Improvement Officers (PIO). The GPRAMA required that each agency head appoint a senior executive as the performance improvement officer (PIO) to manage the performance improvement efforts. The performance improvement officer could be drawn from the career civil service or from the political rank. The main duties of the PIO are to assist the agency head and deputy in areas of goal setting, planning, and performance assessment. Additional duties of the PIO included assistance in developing quarterly review of the progress of APGs, and the development and measurement of personnel performance and appraisals.[29]

The GPRAMA introduces greater legislative control and accountability and puts major emphasis on public agency transparency. The act requires OMB to consult with relevant majority and minority committees and relevant stakeholders. During the development of agency strategic plans (ASPs) and reports, constant exchanges with Congress are required. At every phase of program implementation, including measurement and progress monitoring, information is fed to appropriate congressional committees and executive policymakers in the administrative branch.

Unlike the GPRA of 1993, the GPRAMA created new or renamed officials who are designated to carry out identified functions, such as agency priority goal leader, performance improvement officers, and the chief operating officer (COO). Additionally, the GPRAMA attempts to minimize duplication by facilitating integration of cross-cutting programs.

Strategic Financial Planning

Strategic planning is a continuous process involving decisions on how to combine and employ resources. While emphasis is placed on the systematic approach or analytical techniques that may characterize strategic planning, some components are *irregular*, because opportunities and creative ideas arrive on unpredictable timetables. Strategic plans articulate expected results, as compared to the management control process that allows managers to take specific action to attain desired results. Top managers are the main actors in the strategic planning process. Benefits of the planning process include the following:[30]

- It directs the management team to pursue its objectives on a systematic basis.
- It enhances coordination in the pursuit of organizational objectives.
- It clarifies the roles and responsibilities of participants.
- It promotes the development of monitoring and performance standards.
- It allows management to deal with unexpected changes.

Newman and Wallender draw attention to factors that can and do uniquely influence strategic planning in the not-for-profit agencies. Among the potential impact factors are the following:[31]

- The inability of management to effectively quantify and measure services
- The weak influencing impact of customers
- Strong professionalism that tends to prevail
- Restraint in using reward and punishment
- Impact of a charismatic leader in choice making

Long-Range Financial Planning Process

Financial projection extending over a five-year period is developed similar to the planning programming and budget system (PPBS) found in chapter 14. Projections should be done periodically and linked to the agency's strategic planning process much as in the GPRAMA process outlined in this chapter. The financial planning document should include both existing programs and future programs that have been approved. As the planning process evolves, additions or deletions are integrated into the plan. The long-range plan is structured to achieve the following purposes:

- Development of guiding financial policies (revenue, expenditure, financing) facilitating linkage of the financial resources to the agency's strategic plan
- Preparation of multiyear financial plans, especially outlays for capital expenditures
- Promotion of consistency between multiyear financial plans and yearly budgets
- Projection of future shortfalls or surpluses
- Identifying funding gaps during shortfall periods and potential sources and strategies to overcome the problems
- Providing seasonal and cyclical patterns of cash flow and strategies for meeting expected gaps
- Providing an overall view and analysis of the operating, investing, and financing needs of the agency
- Maintenance of effective communication with credit rating agencies and state and local governments

Failure to undertake long-range financial planning—though important to the public sector—is especially critical to other not-for-profit agencies. Often, these latter do a good job in identifying programs but fail to plan for the financial requirements of the programs.[32]

Changing Orientation in Financial Management

The financial crises experienced by cities such as New York and Cleveland during the 1970s, Detroit in 2012, and state and federal deficits during the 1980s and during the past fifteen years have increased the interest in financial management at all levels of government, and particularly at the local levels. Although traditional emphases on control and compliance (making sure activities conform to laws, rules, and procedures laid down by the purchasing, accounting, auditing, and budget systems) are still important, new, critical concerns have emerged. These can be stated as a series of questions, including the following:

1. What indicators would permit us to assess both fiscal and nonfiscal sustainability of a governmental unit or agency?
2. What is the most effective approach for forecasting revenue and expenditures?
3. What are the best methods for meeting the needs and demands of the community?
4. What methods are used to evaluate the adequacy of financial management systems in: (a) permitting managers to anticipate financial problems and (b) allowing managers to solve these problems before they reach critical limits?
5. What systems, methods, and techniques that must be created to enhance performance, minimize fraud, waste, and abuse, and promote maximum accountability?
6. What performance indicators can be developed to assess managers' performance in promoting maximum transparency and accountability in the delivery of goods and services?
7. What world-class financial practices can be used to benchmark responsibility centers and system performance?
8. How can innovation technology be effectively identified and employed to enhance the financial management processes and system in effectively responding to the needs of stakeholders and clients/customers?

Public versus Private Financial Management

As in the public sector, virtually every key decision made in a firm has financial implications. Managers ask questions such as the following: In an attempt to make the best financial decision, how can risk and the potential return on an investment be balanced? Is sufficient cash or access to funds available to meet daily needs and maturing obligations? What should be the firm's credit policy toward its customers, and what privileges should particular customers be granted? What potential sources of funds may be used to finance investments? How can cash flow be effectively managed to maximize the amount available for investment?

Many of the concepts, objectives, and techniques employed in one sector are also used in the other (as shown in Table 1.1). First, both public and private sectors are concerned with financing ongoing operations and effectively managing the flow of funds. Second, in seeking debt funds, both sectors must go to the same financial markets. Third, large purchases require competitive bidding in the public sector, though to a lesser extent than in the private sector. Fourth, both sectors have systems of employee pension plans. Finally, both have unions that require contract negotiations and wage/salary administration, although unionization is a greater factor in the private sector.

Major differences between the private and public sectors relate to the end objectives and how resources are raised. Ideally, the ultimate objective of the public financial decision makers is to maximize the production and delivery of goods and services. The emphasis is on the provision of socially beneficial services to the community, a large portion of which is distributed on the basis of need. Business decision makers seek to maximize profit or wealth for their stockholders. The private sector depends on the contribution of investors in order to obtain funds to conduct business. The public sector imposes taxes to meet its objectives. These tax resources are typically extracted based on some measure of ability to pay. There are no equity shares that can be traded or sold.

In pure public or nonprofit agencies where the provision of government services is based entirely on need, no individual charges or costs are paid by recipients of the services. Pure public or nonprofit agencies produce collective or indivisible services or goods, such as defense, that cannot be excluded from the simultaneous enjoyment of the service—hence the impossibility of pricing. In between the conceptual poles of purely public and purely private lie a host of quasipublic agencies and organizations. Services provided by such quasipublic or nonprofit agencies are provided on a break-even or partial cost-recovery basis (e.g., school lunches, parking facilities, sewage). However, there are cases in which public policy requires that individuals with incomes below a particular cutoff point be exempted from paying for the provision of services.

Finally, nongovernment/nonprofit agencies experiencing heavy deficits will suffer the same fate as any business unless the leadership of these organizations can find sympathetic ears among the corporate managers or publicly elected officials.

Organizing for Financial Administration

Particularly at the state and local levels of government, checks and balances and separation of powers (functions) have dominated how financial administration is conducted in the United States. The view that honesty can be

TABLE 1.1   Comparing Objectives: Public/Nonprofit and Private Organizations

Activity	Objective	
	Public Nonprofit Organization	**Private**
Resource allocation	Budget and political process.	Market and pricing system.
Resource application	Optimal use provision of goods and services to meet stated objectives.	Optimal use in terms of higher return on investment.
Expenditure/expense	Wise usage of funds to achieve policy objectives.	Wise usage of funds to maximize return on investment.
Finance	Less integrated with management.	Usually integral part of top management.
Mission	Pursuant of public purpose, congruence between achieved results and stated mission.	Clear decision path to make money or profit to increase wealth.
Managing and determining source of funds	From taxation and borrowing; political officials with financial manager's advice; raising additional funds at least cost; ensuring liquidity position to enable entity to meet current maturing obligations and to deliver appropriate goods and services.	From earnings, equity, and borrowing according to financial plans, ensuring liquidity position to meet current and maturing obligations to achieve profit and wealth maximization.
Determining organizational structures	Provision normally is made by legislative or by funding sources; lesser functions determined by practice, convention, and financial necessity to better provide goods and services. Top policy-makers and officials usually are compensated in public but not board members in not-for-profit sector.	Usually by practice, industry, rationality, or pragmatic necessity, to achieve greater profits. Top policy-makers and officials are compensated.
Production of goods- and-services reporting	Dollar accountability (fiscal-stewardship) and operational accountability of managers.	Operational accountability of managers.

promoted by dividing powers among independently elected officers has led to the election of many fiscal officials. Although this value is widely held and the practice is still prevalent, there is little evidence to show that it produces competent and creative officials. On the contrary, it has led at times to fragmented, decentralized, uncoordinated, and ineffective financial systems. This has generated a number of problems: (1) inability to act quickly, (2) competition over policy space and responsibility for financial activities, and (3) multiple clearances and conflicting advice from financial decision makers.

While the particular form of a *decentralized financial decision making model* may vary, financial activities are typically administered by separate officers who are appointed or elected. In each case, a board or individual other than the chief executive is given some powers over the officials, who have insufficient supervisory authority to bring about an integration of the financial management system.

The complexity of modern government and the need to respond quickly to citizens' demands have led to the movement away from the decentralized financial model to the *centralized one*, suggesting a comprehensive scope that allows financial functions to be under the control or guidance of one unit. This model is closely allied with the hierarchical decision making approach and the integrated model of decision making. Both models locate power at the top of the hierarchy, from which authority flows downward and responsibility and accountability flow upward. In this centralized organization, supervisory powers to direct financial officials reside in one individual, who is typically appointed by the chief executive of the governmental unit. This arrangement promotes policy integration, minimizing divided responsibility and making it more likely that plans will be executed according to planned policy intentions. Additionally, the operation of the model must demonstrate independence if it is to maintain the trust and confidence of citizens and the financial community.

The integrated model varies depending on the context in which the governmental unit is imbedded. Especially in large jurisdictions, the head of the finance function may be known as the "director of finance" or the "chief financial officer," much as in the federal model articulated earlier. In some jurisdictions such as Los Angeles, the finance function may be under the chief operating officer (COO), who coordinates all operating departments on behalf of the mayor. Whatever the reporting norm, the finance functions should be grouped to achieve efficiency, minimize duplication, and enhance communication. Similar functions should be grouped and organized in one division.

Four major guidelines have been suggested by Moak and Hillhouse (1975) and GAO to use in organizing for financial administration: (1) standards for effective leadership; (2) guidelines for the efficient operation (e.g., promoting coordination, minimizing duplication, gaps units) and effective use of resources; (3) ways for ensuring accountability to citizens (e.g., exercise of financial discipline, clear lines of responsibility, maintaining capacity to implement policies, and the opportunity for citizens to participate in the budget process);[33] and (4) use of cutting-edge information technology and world-class best financial practices from government and private organizations.[34]

The first of these guidelines, the pursuit of effective leadership, requires that the chief executive be judicious in the delegation of responsibility. This will aid in achieving an appropriate span of control in the administration of financial activities. To facilitate this objective, staff with the capacity to develop alternative financial plans must be available or be trained; a system of controls to ensure that articulated policies are executed as planned and programmed must be developed as well. To promote honesty and integrity, due cognizance should be given to the segregation of duties to minimize the occurrence of errors and make collusion among employees difficult. Additionally, efforts should be made to provide technical assistance to operating managers.

The efficient and effective application of financial resources requires first that provision be made for the specialization and division of labor regarding the main financial functions. There is also a strong need for coordination— namely, through the grouping of related financial activities. This facilitates the establishment of "responsibility centers" to permit a comparison of standards with achieved results. To ensure that resources are used as planned, monetary and nonmonetary control systems are developed to monitor the expenditures and amount of goods or services produced from one time period to the next.

Because of the demand for responsiveness and the need to fix blame or approbation for job performance in governments, concern for accountability (Moak and Hillhouse's third guideline) has particular significance in financial management. This requires that clear lines of authority be set up to identify the duties of executing officers. It is important to establish a system of financial controls leading directly to the chief executive. The identification of financial duties and institutionalization of executive controls set in place the structure needed to obtain an integrated financial reporting system for the organization.

In addition to the internal control system, responsiveness to public concerns typically requires that a system be established that permits citizens to appeal arbitrary financial rules and regulations. Perhaps the means most widely employed to promote accountability of financial activities is the use of the independent postauditor.

Recent Review and Analysis: Structure of Finance Departments

The best way to structure the financial organization to achieve efficiency and effectiveness is not a settled issue. Our examination of this question will focus on the model typically practiced in the local government systems. A recent study has shown that most large U.S. cities employ one or two departments to carry out the financial function. Although some of the largest cities' financial structures are less centralized, the greatest number of cities have become more centralized over time (during the last fifteen years). A majority of all chief financial officers report directly to the chief executive (usually the mayor of the governmental units). Typically (though there are exceptions), the finance function is not headed by an elected official.[35]

It can be argued that a finance organization becomes decentralized and complex as the number of finance offices increases and as financial offices are headed by an elected official (cities with more than one elected official include Milwaukee, Nashville, San Francisco, St. Louis, and Virginia Beach). In a financial organization with multiple offices, less coordination is possible, because decision making authority is dispersed among two or more individuals who can report independently to the mayor or manager.[36] The coordination problem increases significantly if one or more of the offices is elected. Such an arrangement typically creates a lack of linkage between the officers.

There are three basic financial models in practice. The classic integrated model that houses the finance function in a single department is viewed as the simplest structure. The second approach divides the responsibilities into two offices, separated into the budget and finance departments. Third model divides the responsibilities into multiple activities such as accounting, treasury, revenue collection, and budgeting; most often an elected officer heads these functions. Occasionally miscellaneous activities such as cafeteria and neutering cats and dogs are given to finance offices.

Proponents of the single, integrated financial structure side with the National Municipal League, which believes that the centralized model carries out the financial functions most efficiently and effectively. Girard Miller (1984) asserts that "[a]ccountability and professionalism are seldom achieved through fragmented financial offices."[37] Despite the widespread support for the centralized finance structure, the most recent study found that the integrated/centralized model is more efficient, but not necessarily the most effective.

The Digital Revolution and Government

The digital age has brought information technology that permits us to exchange information efficiently and process a multitude of transactions effectively across networks. Digital government allows e-government efforts and e-commerce to operate in a seamless web through the medium of the Internet. Innovative governments are implementing Internet portals, giving citizens and suppliers the opportunity to efficiently access data and information across government agencies.

Electronic bond bidding is now available for municipal issues. Operating websites provide an array of data on municipal bond sales such as sales calendars, municipal news, real-time sales results, winning syndicate (indicating winning and bidding accounts), coupons, rates, yields and concessions, insurance, and ratings. Through the Committee on Uniform Securities Identification Procedures (CUSIP) bureau, the electronic application and receipt of new issues by CUSIP members is now possible.[38]

A number of governmental units have established Internet portals that provide citizens the opportunity to access information and complete functions that were traditionally time-consuming. The following are examples of these types of governmental initiatives:

- The state of Utah is developing a portal to carry out procurement, income and sales tax filing, unemployment, and workforce applications.
- The state of North Carolina portal allows citizens to customize the type of service that they are interested in, such as weather, employee benefits, and school closings. The portal system allows businesses to search for open bids from the state by product area.
- Pennsylvania and twenty-nine other states allow taxpayers to file personal income tax returns electronically.
- "The state of Indiana Department of Workforce Development (DWD) allows job-seekers and employers to access a full range of employment services, including multiple benefits registration and candidate registrations. . . . Job-seekers can operate the system . . . and staff is available to assist with questions or counseling."[39]
- The Ohio treasurer, through its Bid Ohio, conducts a live auction bid of the tax receipt (idle funds) that are not immediately needed and that can be invested to earn interest revenue. The system allows the biggest bank of the state to be efficient, competitive, and up to date, giving the state the opportunity to achieve equal footing among banks regardless of size or geographic location.[40]
- Virginia and Alaska enable eligible drivers to order personalized license plates using the Internet.
- Riverside County, California, uses e-commerce to conduct property sales of delinquent taxpayers' property. Because of the cost-efficiency and instant access of the Internet, the county has been able to conduct auctions more frequently. The media has allowed better marketing and advertising strategies that increase awareness and, accordingly, the number of bidders at auctions.[41]
- Oakland County, Michigan, which is prevented from offering new services due to lack of available resources, got around the state revenue-raising restrictions by charging for an enhanced access fee to inspect or copy important information or public documents through digital means, as allowed by state law.[42]

Duties of Financial Managers

The financial management duties and roles have traditionally been looked upon as mainly a staff specialty function that provides support and advice to line managers.[43] This compartmentalized approach, though still present in some organizations, has given way to the integrated practice in which the financial manager acts as an integral part of the management decision making team. The major functions of financial managers include the following:

1. *Financial planning:* (a) participation in short- and long-range planning and evaluation of various courses of action; (b) interpretation of the financial implications of legislation and regulations; (c) preparation of procedural manuals and instructions to facilitate compliance with such regulations; and (d) definition of programs and activities.
2. *Budget preparation and expenditure control* in which the manager provides (a) a forecast of expenditure and revenue, (b) guidance and assistance in the preparation and submission of budgets, (c) establishment of expenditure classification control, and (d) management of cash requirements.
3. *Accounting system and procedures* for which the manager (a) develops the accounting system to permit an incorporation of budgeting and internal controls in order to meet agency and other mandated needs; (b) develops appropriate cost accounting systems to accommodate agency needs and undertakes special cost and work measurement studies, when necessary, to assist in alternative decision making; (c) advises operating heads on how best to use the accounting system; and (d) periodically reviews agency accounting, budgeting, financial, and statistical reporting systems and procedures, making improvements where required.
4. *Reporting for financial management control performance* by developing agency information systems for timely reporting of financial and other relevant data to operating and supervisory management. This information should indicate variances between the budget and actual performance, showing plans that are not being attained.
5. *Maintenance of an asset control system* by establishing a control procedure for the safekeeping of assets such as inventories, cash, materials, and equipment.
6. *Providing effective investment management* by preserving investment assets and increasing investment income.
7. *Financial liaison* by developing and maintaining an effective liaison with officials (e.g., state auditors general) as well as other agencies whose regulations may require changes in agency financial regulations.
8. *Staff training* by advising and participating in the development of staff training.

9. *Analysis of fiscal health* through the analysis of fiscal conditions. The manager must constantly be able to answer questions such as the following: Can the unit of government or agency pay its own way? Can the unit pay for services and avoid large tax or fee increases? Proper attention to these questions requires an evaluation of the community's fiscal condition; this requires having reliable information on local infrastructure such as roads, bridges, and sewers, as well as on the extent of unfunded obligations for pension liabilities.

The financial manager is expected to sort out key factors affecting the fiscal condition of the community or agency. For example, can it maintain an economic base to meet expenditure demands and revenue expectations? Can the community maintain existing service levels? In addition, the manager must be able to determine the causes of fiscal distress and be able to measure its extent.

It can be seen that the financial manager is a key player in maintaining the viability of an agency. The manager is expected to assist in developing plans and options for keeping and attracting businesses. In the case of an agency, managers must develop, maintain, and/or expand revenue sources. They act as negotiators in union contracts and with community groups seeking goods and services that involve the use of monetary resources. Finally, the manager acts as a controller in all financial activities.

World-Class Financial Management

A world-class financial management organization is one that produces outputs and results, enhancing decision analysis, providing capability to perform ad hoc and long-term alternative analysis, producing cutting-edge solutions, reducing operating costs, and constantly improving the level of performance. To achieve these objectives requires changing the traditional organizational environment to one that is willing to change and adapt to a new culture. There must be a future-oriented and shared vision and mission that guide core values, goals, and strategies. The ultimate aim of the financial management system is the creation of value for the customers or citizens.

The GAO study of nine (six private and three public) world-class financial organizations found leadership to be the most critical factor in bringing about the required cultural changes. Top management must be committed to follow through on their words with action. The leader must ensure that improvements affect every entity through a well-designed system of controls and accountability that links internal line management decision making and external performance reporting. To facilitate and promote the desired organizational culture change, top management must provide continuous and innovative training.[44]

Eleven practices have been identified as being most useful to a world-class financial organization that wishes to maximally achieve its objective:

- Develop a clearly defined control system linking internal decision making and external reporting on management performance to achieve maximum accountability. To realize this objective, the system must use financial reporting and the audit process as a basic management oversight tool. Effective internal controls must be adapted to ensure that efficiency is not sacrificed.
- Exhibit clear, consistent, strong executive leadership that fosters the pervasive role of fiscal management throughout the organization.
- Use training as a strategic means to change organizational culture, especially line managers.
- Continually examine how well the financial organization meets its agreed-upon mission. Additionally, evaluate the organization's mission, measure achieved performance, collect customer feedback, and compare to best practices. Next, identify achievement gaps and indicate the required actions to correct them.
- Streamline day-to-day accounting activities, eliminating inefficient practices, standardizing transaction processes, and exploring the potential for external outsourcing.
- Continually organize the finance function to add value. To aid the achievement of this objective, management must promote consistency and congruency between the financial core function and the substantive management function (see Figure 1.3).
- Design the management information system to link the finance functions with day-to-day line management operations by integrating the general ledger system to support financial reporting control, by implementing the electronic system to accurately measure the cost of products and service activities, and by providing operating line managers with timely financial and nonfinancial information and reports.
- Re-engineer new technology to existing practices so that the financial system could easily adapt to commercial, off-the-shelf software packages (COTS) consistent with "quality assurance, processes which adhere to management's established plans, standards, and procedures."[45]
- Organize financial data according to user information needs. To be most useful, management must design reports around key drivers such as products, services, customers/clients, and present financial information in an understandable, simple format with concise detail.
- Assemble a finance team with appropriate skills and competencies that complement one another.
- Build a finance organization that attracts and retains the best talents by creating clear career path opportunities and developing job rotation and multifinancial career path development.

Accountability and Improved Financial Management

The beginning of the 21st century finds clients and constituents demanding improved goods and services and greater privatization. Taxpayers resist tax increases, and donors demand results for their contribution. Demands are made that public managers and other not-for-profit organizations use available resources wisely. Additionally, there is a growing need for systems to be devised to facilitate greater accountability for the expenditure of public money.

Accountability will require that managers at all organizational levels know specifically to whom and for what they are accountable. This will necessitate that objectives be clearly articulated. Performance operations must be planned and programmed, indicating explicitly what is to be done, what are the (allowable) resources, what methods will be employed, what the required performance is, and how the results will be measured and evaluated. All this requires that an increased emphasis be given to program planning and increased use of innovation technology.

In program planning, each manager has the responsibility to allocate resources in such a way as to achieve the organization's objective with maximum efficiency and effectiveness. Program planning involves prioritizing both the objectives sought and the tasks to achieve them. If fewer resources are allocated to the manager than were anticipated, the manager will need to decide what operations will be pruned or dropped and what combination of resources will be required to achieve the organizational objective.

To improve the use of resources and avoid a hit-or-miss approach to decision making, participants concerned with financial management are expected to assist, engage in, and provide guidance for both short- and long-range financial planning. Elements such as the following must be set forth: (a) clear identification of objectives, (b) proposed plans of action to achieve the objectives, (c) expected results for each unit of time in the plan, (d) alternative plans of action, and (e) measures to judge the efficiency and effectiveness in meeting the objectives.

Accountability requires that there be a constant matching of stated or implied (desired) goals and objectives with achieved results. The difference between the achieved and desired results is the *accountability gap*. The aim is to minimize, and ultimately eliminate, this gap. The integrative role of financial management provides a strategic means in facilitating the achievement of accountability.

Organization of the Text

The first three chapters of this volume provide the reader with an understanding of the scope, nature, and function of modern financial management, stressing the changing focus and important role of accounting and the critical role of internal controls.

Resource management functions are examined in chapters 3 through 8. Nationally successful practices and techniques in revenue administration, purchasing, cash management, and debt and risk management are evaluated. Although some attention is given to theory, the major focus is on how the systems work, indicating their potentials and possible restraints.

Chapters 9 through 19 discuss the management control process as a means of achieving accountability. The reader is shown how linkage may effectively be achieved among the accounting, auditing, reporting, and monitoring systems in financial management. This section also shows how indicators can be developed and used to control day-to-day operations and permit a close watch on the agency or community fiscal health.

Chapters 20 and 21 explore special concerns such as fraud, waste, and abuse (FWA), along with the advising functions that are important to the modern financial manager.

Appendix: The Financial Manager: Some Useful Concepts to Read the Economy

The economic terms and acronyms appearing in the popular media have been growing in number, yet few definitions or primers are provided to aid the reader. The following discussion attempts to briefly describe these terms.

Gross National Product

The gross national product (GNP) is the broadest indicator or measure of economic output and growth in the U.S. economy. It comprises goods and services produced and consumed in the private, public, and international sectors. GNP measures the market value of all goods produced, including those produced outside the United States.

Gross Domestic Product

The gross domestic product (GDP) contrasts with the GNP in that it measures the market value of only those goods that have been solely produced in the United States. GNP and GDP emphasize two components: (1) the demand, identifying the market for goods and services, and (2) the supply, identifying the costs required to produce the goods and services. The U.S. Department of Commerce's Division of the Bureau of Economic Research (BER) publishes GNP/GDP data on a quarterly basis in its monthly magazine, *Survey of Current Business*.

Gross State Product

The gross state product (GSP) is a new concept, the state counterpart to the GDP. The GSP is the gross market value of goods and services relating to labor and property located in a given state. Unlike with the national GNP and GDP, the BER produces the state GSP figures annually. Estimates of the GSP are prepared for sixty-one industries. Four components are included for each industry: (1) employee compensation, (2) business income with adjustment for inventory and capital consumption allowances, (3) indirect business taxes and nontax liability, and (4) other charges, related mainly to capital.

Genuine Progress Indicator

The genuine progress indicator (GPI) measures economic growth of a country from a multifaceted perspective (including economic/financial and nonfinancial components). A number of analysts consider it a replacement for the widely used gross domestic product (GDP) as an indicator of progress. GPI includes the components that constitute GDP. Additionally, GPI adds other costs representing the negative effects generated by economic activity such as crime, ozone depletion, pollution, and cost of resource depletion. Adjustments are made for factors such as income distribution and additions are made for factors such as value for household and voluntary work. GPI nets the positive and negative outputs generated by economic growth to determine the extent to which positive and negative have been created.

GPI has been gaining attention as a better indicator of progress as evidenced by its use in a number of US state governments and nongovernmental organizations worldwide. Proponents say that it is a better tool for assessing sustainable development and planning. GPI allows policymakers at all levels of government to measure how well citizens are doing economically and socially. It is a better tool for assessing sustainable development. GPI documents a more truthful picture of economic and social progress.

Consumer Price Index

The consumer price index (CPI) measures the changes in prices taking place for a fixed basket of consumer goods and services with constant quantity and quality as purchased by average urban consumers. This indicator is a representative reflection of the prices of the goods and services that consumers use for everyday living. The CPI is made up of seven major components: apparel, medical care, housing, food and beverages, transportation, entertainment, and "other goods and services." Eighty-five locations are averaged and weighed, representing the different population groups, and comparisons of the monthly indexes are made. Two CPIs are calculated and published: (1) for all urban consumers (CPI-U), covering 80 percent of the population, and (2) for urban wage earners and clerical workers (CPI-W), covering 32 percent of the population.

The index value of current prices is compared to average prices in an assigned base period with a value of 100. Hence, a CPI of 141 would mean that what cost $100 in the base period now costs $141. (The U.S. Department of Labor's Bureau of Labor Statistics [BLS] provides the data monthly, following the month to which they relate.)

The CPI is widely used as a barometer to chart the direction of the national economy, as well as as an indicator of inflation in decisions relating to future production and consumption. The CPI is widely used in "escalator" clauses in the determination of income payment agreements. This practice is commonly referred to as *indexing*. For this reason, the CPI has figured prominently in collective bargaining agreements for millions of workers. Presently, approximately 50 million Social Security beneficiaries, retired military personnel, civil service employees, food stamp recipients, and others use the CPI to monitor potential changes in their income.

Although many people think of the CPI as the cost of living index, the Bureau of Labor Statistics has often attempted to debunk this interpretation. The CPI is simply a measure of prices, reflecting changes in the purchasing power of the average family. The view is expressed that there is an inherent upward bias notion about the CPI that results in overstating inflation, thus giving rise to demands for wage, benefit, and other increases. Additionally, the CPI does not give recognition to the substitution effects of the fixed basket of goods because of how it treats home ownership.

Predicting the Direction of the Economy: Trend Indicators

Economic trend indicators are classified as *leading*, *coincident*, and *lagging*, describing the result of activities or processes such as employment and unemployment, production, income, consumption, and trade that provide us with clues or insights about present and future economic trends, particularly as they relate to recessions (contractions) and cyclical expansions. Key indicators are grouped and categorized according to their tendency or sensitivity to "change direction before, during, or after the general economy turns from an expansion to a recession or from recession to expansion."[46]

The system of economic indicators is premised on the basis that capitalistic economies are subject to recurring business cycles that depend on the profit outlook. When the profit outlook is favorable, businesses expand. The reverse (contraction) occurs when the profit outlook is negative. Positive advances in the average manufacturing workweek, production, and the financial markets are *leading indicators* and reflect business commitments and expectations. *Coincident indicators* show the existing level of sales and production, whereas *lagging indicators* provide a view of what has happened in the economy. These indicators are all retrospective, because they are used to assess and confirm prior economic activities.

Some General Guidelines for Interpreting Economic Indicators

The indicators have varying economic effects, especially on federal spending and revenue results:

- A change in the economy typically affects federal revenue more than federal spending. Relatedly, a decline in the inflation rate may sometimes have a negative impact on the deficit, as may a rise in unemployment.
- A rise of 1 percentage point in unemployment reduces revenue by $12 billion, whereas the reverse (i.e., a 1 percentage point rise in employment) generates an increase of $5 billion in revenue.
- An increase of 1 percentage point in the inflation rate subsequent to the budget preparation generates an additional $5 billion in revenue and adds $1 billion to the spending side.
- A rise of 1 percentage point in the interest rate adds $2 billion to the spending side and generates $1 in additional revenues.
- A decrease in unemployment by 1 percentage point reduces state and local revenues by approximately $8 billion.
- A reduction of 1 percentage point in unemployment creates an additional 1.45 million jobs.

Notes

1. See www.democracy-international.org/transparency.
2. See www.zimmerman-lehman.com/accounabilityandtransp.htm.
3. See http://www.johnlocke.org/acrobat/policyReports/transparency-guide.pdf.
4. Jerome B. McKinney and Lawrence C. Howard, *Public Administration: Balancing Power and Accountability*, 2nd ed. (Westport, CT: Praeger, 1988), 345–347.
5. See www.epa.gov/sustainability/basicinfo.html.
6. See http://www.wbcsd.org/pages/EDocument/details.aspx=
7. Andrew W. Savitz and Karl Weber, *The Triple Bottom Line* (San Francisco: Jossey-Bass 2006), p. 22.
8. See http://www.epa.gov/sustainability/analytics/life-cycle.htm.
9. U.S. General Accounting Office, *GAO Managing the Cost of Government: Building an Effective Financial Management Structure*, AFMD 83 35A (Washington, DC: GAO, February 1985), p. 11.
10. Ibid., p. 12.
11. Frank Horton, "Insights into the Chief Financial Officers Act of 1990," *Government Accountants Journal 40*, no. 5 (spring 1991): 9.
12. Jill E. Kent, "Organization of the Agency Chief Financial Officers," *Government Accountants Journal 40*, no. 5 (spring 1991): 27.
13. Harold I. Steinberg, "The Chief Financial Officers Act: A Ten Year Progress Report," *Government Accountants Journal 49*, no. 4 (winter 2000): 45.
14. Ibid., 46.
15. Ibid., 46–48.

16. Ibid., 28.

17. Ibid.

18. See CFO Act, Section 205(a); codified at 31 U.S.C 902(a).

19. Frank Hodsoll, "Office of Management and Budget's Plans for Implementation of Chief Financial Officers Act," *Government Accountants Journal 40*, no. 5 (spring 1991): 17.

20. John Conyers Jr., "Vigilance in Government," *Government Accountants Journal 40*, no. 5 (spring 1991): 24.

21. CFO Act, Section 102(b)(2).

22. Ibid.

23. Clinton T. Brass, *Changes to the Government Performance and Results Act (GPRA): An Overview of the New Framework of Products and Processes* (Washington, DC: Congressional Research Service, February 29, 2012).

24. Ibid., p. 3.

25. Ibid., p. 4.

26. Ibid., pp. 5–6.

27. Ibid., p. 8.

28. Ibid., pp. 7–8.

29. Ibid., pp. 13–15.

30. Melville Branch, *The Corporate Planning Process* (New York: American Management Association, 1962).

31. William H. Newman and Harvey Wallender III, "Managing Not-for-Profit Enterprises," *Academy of Management Review 3* (January 1978): 24–31.

32. Regina E. Herzlinger, "Managing the Finances of Non-Profit Organizations," *California Management Review 21*, no. 3 (spring): 60–69.

33. Lennox L. Moak and Albert M. Hillhouse, *Local Government Finance* (Chicago: Municipal Finance Officers Association, 1975), pp. 345–347.

34. See General Accounting Office (GAO), AIMD-00-134: *Creating World-Class Financial Management* (Washington, DC: GAO, April 1, 2001), p. 7; and James L. Chan and Rowan A. Miranda, "Principles of Designing the Finance Organization: A Guide to Reform Effort and Leadership Transitions," *Government Finance Review 14*, no. 3 (June 1998): 16.

35. R. Gregory Michel, "The Organizational Structure of City Finance Offices," *Government Finance Review 16*, no. 3 (June 2000): 21.

36. Ibid.

37. Girard Miller, *An Elected Official's Guide to Government Finance* (Chicago: Government Finance Association, 1984), p. 7.

38. Renata Morgenstern, "Electronic Bidding For Municipal Bonds: Technology Innovation for Competitive Bond Sales," *Government Finance Review 16*, no. 1 (February 2000): 23.

39. Jeff Breen, "At the Dawn of e-Government: The Citizen as Customer," *Government Finance Review 16*, no. 5 (October 2000): 19.

40. Joseph T. Deteri, "Bid Ohio: Using Technology to Earn More for Taxpayers," *Government Finance Review 16*, no. 6 (October 2000): 37.

41. Rochelle Johnson and Tom Muller, "Electronic Auctions for Delinquent Tax Properties: E-Government in Riverside County, California," *Government Finance Review 16*, no. 1 (February 2000): 19.

42. Jeffrey C. Pardee, "Charging a Fee for e-Government: Oakland County, Michigan Enhanced Access Project," *Government Finance Review 16*, no. 1 (February 2000): 49.

43. Line managers are the individuals responsible for the direct delivery of goods and services to the clients and constituents that the agency was created to serve. These persons are known as *doers*, as opposed to staff people, who are known as *advisors*.

44. See General Accounting Office (GAO), *Creating World-Class Financial Management*.

45. Ibid.

46. David Levitan, "How to Read the Economy: A Primer," *Government Finance Review 9*, no. 2 (April 1993): 25.

2

Accounting's Role in Financial Management

In both public and private organizations, accounting has served as a major mechanism of management control. It is important to note that the structure of financial analysis is dependent predominantly on accounting information, the means by which the consequences of the various options available to management are communicated. Management can use accounting information as a control and monitoring tool to assess performance, take corrective action, and mitigate future risk. In public and not-for-profit agencies, decision makers should thus have an understanding of the accounting process as well as of its strengths and weaknesses. Although decision makers need not be accountants, an understanding of the function and structure of accounting systems is necessary for effective fiscal planning and management. To be of maximum use, the accounting system should have a flexible account structure that provides data not only for appropriated expenditures, but also for (1) program elements or activities to aid in budget analysis and presentation, (2) special project details, (3) major organizational and geographical divisions, (4) a common database to facilitate performance measurement, and (5) determination of the full cost of programs and activities.

The purpose of this chapter is to provide the reader who is unfamiliar with accounting with a general overview of the accounting process and its practices and an introduction to sustainability. Those who desire a more extensive and detailed introduction to this subject are directed to any of the standard introductory texts.[1]

Defining Accounting

Accounting translates the economic activities of a business into quantitative terms—dollars (or alternative currency)—as the common unit of measure. Each economic activity or financial transaction is recorded in a book called a *journal* (a chronological record of transactions indicating name, code number, and amount of change in each account). All information in a journal is transferred to a *ledger* (a summary grouping of accounts). Each account systematically groups similar transactions, such as assets, liabilities, revenues, and expenses, allowing account totals to be available as needed. From these account totals, financial statements and reports (balance sheet, revenue and expenditure report, and cash flow analysis) are prepared and communicated to relevant stakeholders and interested parties. Accounting is an instrument of the controlling process directed at collecting, summarizing, recording, ordering, reporting, and analyzing the financial resources and transactions of an organization. Accounting keeps track of the activities of an organization (e.g., governmental unit, hospital, club, family) and facilitates standardizing, monitoring, and use of data. Accounting reduces all transactions into common-denominator monetary terms, allowing for comparison of two or more activities that otherwise would be difficult (the proverbial comparison of "apples to oranges"). *Accounting* is thus a common language that keeps track of transactions occurring within an organization and among other organizations. The accounting system is retrospective in that it records information relating mainly to an organization's past fiscal condition. However, with the emergence of real-time processing (RTP) technology, accounting information systems are able to record a transaction simultaneously as it occurs. Technological advancements, such as RTP, are reducing the retrospective nature of accounting systems.

An effective accounting system should seek to satisfy a number of fundamental objectives:

1. *Control*: As the basic element of the financial control structure, accounting is the most important means for ensuring that public and not-for-profit expenditures are limited to the purposes and amounts that were legally authorized and intended.
2. *Accountability*: The accounting system maintains a set of procedures to ensure that officers and employees are held responsible and accountable for the safeguarding of money and property entrusted or assigned to them. A system of internal controls must be maintained to permit the continual review of commitments in an effort to promote confidence and integrity in the system.
3. *Responsibility accounting*: This plays an integral role in achieving accountability. Responsibility accounting is organized to permit the accumulation of actual budgeting data and accounting records to show the expense or expenditure responsibilities of each manager. This allows top management to hold each manager accountable for the efficient and effective use of resources. However, managers should only be held accountable for the expenditures over which they had control.

4. *Internal and external reporting*: (a) Internal reporting relates to the use of accounting information in the planning and control of routine operations within the organization, whereas (b) external reporting portrays the state and condition of the organization to other administrative officers, government regulatory agencies, various constituencies or client groups, creditors, general public, and other stakeholders.

5. *Information*: The accounting system facilitates the provision of information to appropriate officials, bond raters, and creditors in the form, frequency, and timeliness desired. Information is the single most important product, especially in local governments, in which accounting is the only system that provides comprehensive, detailed, and comparable information on the activities of all agencies. The accounting system also provides information to assist management in the formulation of long-range policy plans and strategies. Unfortunately, this latter aspect is at present more a hope than reality in most governments and not-for-profit agencies. Budgetary shortfalls and political pressures have encouraged many government officials to focus on short-term policies and fiscal solutions.

Financial Accounting

The major objective of *financial accounting* is the preparation of a financial statement, which offers a measurement of past and current financial status mainly to external users (bond holders, taxpayers, the press, creditors, bond raters, the general public, and other interested groups) in conformance with generally accepted accounting principles (GAAP) as they apply to government and not-for-profit organizations.[2] Financial accounting focuses on the recording of financial transactions. Financial statements outline resource flows (revenues and expenses) and assets. GAAP is articulated through the Governmental Accounting Standards Board (GASB) for state and local governments, the Federal Accounting Standards Advisory Board (FASAB) for the federal government, and the American Institute of Certified Public Accountants (AICPA) for not-for-profit agencies.

GAAP provides uniform minimum standards of and guidelines for financial accounting and reporting. Adherence to GAAP ensures that financial statements/reports contain the same statements and similar disclosures for the same categories and types of funds based on the same measurement criteria.[3] All state and local entities maintain their accounting system to comply with all legal and constitutional requirements. Occasionally legal provisions may conflict with GAAP. When such conflicts with the Governmental Accounting Standards Board arise, the statements are prepared on a GAAP basis. To clarify the situation, two different statements should be prepared, one on the GAAP basis and the other on the legal budgeting basis of accounting. A required reconciliation of the two statements under GAAP is then prepared.

By means of a predetermined code or chart of accounts, financial transactions are systematically recorded in accounting ledgers (books containing the summary of account). The data from these ledgers are used periodically to produce required fiscal statements, which provide monetary information and are used for budget preparation, internal control, and adherence to legal and other external reporting requirements. In the private sector, four major reports are typically presented to external users: (1) statement of financial position, or balance sheet, (2) statement of earnings, (3) statement of earnings or equity, and (4) statement of cash flows. In the governmental entity, under the *comprehensive annual financial report* (CAFR) system, there are five required financial statements: (1) combined balance sheet—involving all types of funds and account groups; (2) combined statement of revenues, expenditures, and changes in fund balances—used in all governmental fund types; (3) combined statement of revenues, expenditures, and changes in fund balances—both budgeted and actual—involving both general and special revenues types (and similar governmental fund types for which annual budgets have been legally adopted); (4) combined statement of revenues, expenses, and changes in fund balances (or equity)—involving all propriety fund types; and (5) combined statement of changes in financial position—again, in all proprietary fund types.

Service Efforts and Accomplishments Reporting

In July 2010, the GASB strongly suggested that government entities issue service efforts and accomplishments (SEA) reports in conjunction with the mandated financial statements. SEA reporting is "intended to include information about the services provided and the effect of those services to assist users in assessing the degree to which the government is achieving its program or government-wide goals." Traditional financial statements, such as those mentioned the preceding section, do not provide sufficient information regarding service effectiveness. The focus of those statements continues to be primarily economic. Effective service delivery and increasing the well-being of citizens should be the primary goals of governmental entities; accordingly, there should be information on the progress of meeting those endeavors.

The GASB, after more than twenty years of research and case studies, has established suggested guidelines describing the four essential components of an effective SEA report and the six qualitative characteristics that SEA performance information must possess. The components include:

- *Purpose and scope:* Why is the SEA performance information being reported? To what portion of a government does it relate?
- *Major goals and objectives:* What are the major goals and objectives of the programs and services being reported? What is the government intending to accomplish?

- *Key measures of SEA performance:* What key measures are most important to readers that also reflect the government's achievement, or lack thereof, of its major goals and objectives?
- *Discussion and analysis of results and challenges:* What factors affect the level of achievement of results? What is the government's plan for addressing future challenges?

The six qualitative characteristics include comparability, consistency, relevance, reliability, timeliness, and understandability. Owing to the vast range of governmental services provided, GASB has yet to issue specific standards for each service type but continues to give governmental entities recommendations for preparing SEA reports. To date, SEA reporting remains voluntary but continues to increase in importance as users desire the most relevant information governments can furnish.[4]

Managerial Accounting

The provision of information to aid internal management in improving the effectiveness of programming, decision making, and control is the concern of *managerial accounting*, which uses both financial (historical) data and nonfinancial information. It focuses attention on the organization of information to enable and enhance decision making related to daily operations, activities, programs, or responsibility centers, as well as on the planning of future operations. Distinguishing features of managerial accounting include the following:

- It is future-oriented.
- It aids efficiency analysis.
- It provides data for internal use, management decision making, and internal reporting.
- It focuses on key internal reports, such as the budget, and on cost finding, showing relationships between volume of service, expenses, revenues, cash flows, and units of service costs.
- It is eclectic by not being bound by generally accepted accounting principles, but rather emphasizes the relevance and flexibility of data selection, including data from other disciplines.
- It is driven by decision makers' requests and information needs.
- It places emphasis on nonmonetary data—unlike financial accounting—and provides information very useful in short- and long-range budget preparation.
- It uses variance reports to analyze deviations from planned performance.
- It encourages cost-consciousness by its emphasis on performance standards and unit costs as they relate to responsibility centers. A "responsibility center" is a section or division of an organization (for example, purchasing and

maintenance) that is an individual's assigned responsibility and over which that individual is given control to achieve one or more purposes (objectives) as part of the overall goals of an organization.

- It is audited (if at all) by internal auditors.
- It promotes, by its cost approach, linkages with cost accounting, financial accounting, management control, performance, and program budgeting.
- It acts as a motivating mechanism, holding officials accountable to attain planned results and reward accomplishments.
- It uses an understanding of the past to plan, shape, and redirect the future.[5]

Cost Accounting

The assemblage and recording of all cost elements related to a project or unit of work are the responsibility of *cost accounting*. Expressed in another way, "it is an art of determining the cost of a product, service, or activity."[6] Cost accounting generates information about the cost of an organization and its components; it is the connecting link between financial and managerial accounting. *Financial accounting* provides historical data that may be used in costing out options for management decision making. Table 2.1 shows how a cost accounting system may be used strategically to aid management decision making. Cost information can be used to enhance planning (operations and strategic), budgeting, controlling, evaluating, pricing decisions, and reporting. A major purpose of cost accounting information is to permit managers to *plan* and *control* the activities of the organization. *Planning* provides the organization with the opportunity to optimally achieve its potential, while the *control* process ensures that the opportunity provided is realized. Planning allows optimal opportunities to be selected while avoiding problematic ones. In the not-for-profit sector, decisions will not always be based solely on the accounting information because of public policies and overriding social issues. There are a number of important uses for public and not-for-profit agencies' cost information:

- *Budgeting* provides the basic costing data for preparing the budget, planning, and allocating resources.
- *Cost efficiency analysis* provides information to assess the efficiency of programs and activities.
- *Life cycle costing* furnishes the total cost associated with a long-lived asset, including acquisition, operation, and maintenance costs over the life of assets, such as equipment, less any resale value upon disposal.
- *Avoidable cost* accounts for the amount of expense that would not occur if a given decision were implemented.
- The *contracting out decision* provides a basis to determine whether an activity should be completed in-house or contracted out.

TABLE 2.1 The Costing Matrix

	Direct Cost	Marginal Cost	Fixed Cost	Unit Cost	Variable Cost	Avoidable Cost	Life-Cycle Cost	Total Cost
Eliminate Service			x		x	x		
Reassign Personnel					x	x		
Reduce Service		x			x	x		
Improve Productivity		x		x				
Contract Out						x		
Civilianize the Delivery	x					x		
Substitute Equipment			x	x		x	x	
Charge for Service		x						x
Status Quo	x							x

Source: Joseph T. Kelley, *Costing Government Services: A Guide to Decision-Making* (Washington, DC: Government Research Center, 1984), 36.

- *Fee determination* facilitates the development of a fee schedule and reimbursement costs.
- *Reporting* adds greater cost consciousness to financial statements, as fund accounting does not permit cost and performance analysis.
- *Opportunity cost* shows the maximum value of benefits foregone by selecting one option over another. Opportunity cost is useful when choices must be made among alternative courses of action, which is the case for most financial decisions. For example, if a governmental unit wishes to contract out its garbage collection rather than continue to do it in house, opportunity cost is considered. Unchangeable fixed costs and costs that have already been incurred should not be considered—these are viewed as unavoidable.
- *Differential costs* present the amount of increase or decrease in revenue or expenses that is expected to result from a particular course of action as compared to an alternative. It may also be viewed as the difference between incremental costs at two different levels of activity.
- The *diagnosis-related group* (DRG) is a system that categorizes patients into specific groups based on medical diagnosis or particular characteristics such as age and type of procedure. It is a flat price or rate that U.S. government hospital and other health care managers pay hospitals for Medicare patients, requiring hospitals to modify their accounting system from an actual process measuring system to one that adopts standard costs per product in DRG.
- *Full cost* offers another way of presenting the total or absorption "cost."
- *Responsibility accounting system* provides information that management can use to evaluate the performance of a manager. Managers should only be evaluated on performance measurements over which they have direct control. Accordingly, managerial roles and organizational hierarchy should be clearly defined.
- A *process costing system* produces an average per unit cost by aggregating all relevant costs of a process and dividing it by the units of output produced. For example, in a hospital, all costs related to inpatient care are divided by the total number of days of care, resulting in an average cost per patient day, as depicted in Table 2.2.
- *Direct costs* are clearly and directly associated with a specific cost objective that is typically controllable by the responsibility manager.
- The *cost center* is a unit in an organization that is assigned responsibility for costs.
- The *cost driver* is an activity that causes costs to be incurred. As the cost driver activity increases, costs should increase in a relatively proportional manner.
- *Expired cost or expense* is an asset that is fully or totally consumed.
- *Marginal cost pricing* is the change in cost related to a change in activity. Marginal cost pricing is also referred to as *incremental* or *out-of-pocket cost.*

If added revenue exceeds added costs of counseling an additional client, the organization is better off accepting the additional client. Marginal cost pricing is an acceptable method for making short-term decisions.

- *Activity-based costing* (ABC) is a cost allocation method that focuses on activities performed. It links costs to specific activities and then assigns them to specific objects. The emphasis on linking activity to cost allows management to take specific action to increase benefits or reduce resource consumption. When activities are reduced to a final output without costing individual components, it becomes impossible to determine what contribution each specific activity is making. For example, a department may report the average cost of each course taught at a given figure, omitting any indication that some classes have as many as 200 students and that a quarter of them have fewer than 15 students.[7]

Traditional cost systems have tended to use allocation bases (e.g., square feet of occupancy, direct cost, number of employees) that are not often closely related to the way costs actually occur or that are too broad in scope to be the driver of all the assigned costs. ABC, in contrast, captures costs related to individual activities. Overhead costs are accumulated or collected in homogeneous cost pools (a temporary account that accumulates incurred costs to support an activity), as shown in Table 2.3. The organization then

TABLE 2.2   Calculating Unit Cost

Activity of Process	Costs (A)	Output (B)
Inpatient Care	$50,000	400 patient days
Average cost (A) ÷ (B) = $1,250 per patient day		

TABLE 2.3   Cost Allocation in Activity-Based Costing

Overhead cost	Activity cost pool	Cost driver	Cost object based (e.g., job)
Purchasing } } }	Materials purchasing	Number of purchase orders	Number of orders × unit cost
	Materials handling	Material requisitions/ hours	Labor hours × unit labor cost
Personnel	Personnel processing	Number of employees hired/ laid-off	Number labor hours × unit cost
Maintenance	Building	Number of square feet	Labor hours × unit cost
Inspection: safety	Quantity	Number of inspections	Labor hours or number inspections × unit cost

uses a cost driver (it is both a variable that causes an activity's cost to go up or down and a measurement indicator for allocating unit costs or rate bases) for distributing costs to objects such as clients, procedures, job orders, services, and products. ABC requires a clear understanding of the activities that consume resources. Ideally, information is collected from similar agencies or competitors to aid in benchmarking and identifying non-value-added activities that can be pared or restructured in a manner that generates value.

Cost Behavior

It is important to be able to discern the behavior of various kinds of costs as they relate to managerial decisions. Costs may be categorized according to their behavior patterns at different levels of activity. Based on the changes of the total cost generated by a change in activity level, there are four basic cost relationships, as shown in Figure 2.1.

- *Fixed cost* remains constant, within a relevant range, regardless of the variation in volume of activity. Because the expense does not change as the number of units or products increases, the cost per unit decreases. Yearly rent and insurance premiums are good examples of fixed costs.
- *Semifixed cost* is also known as "step cost." It is fixed for a given level of activity but increases to higher plateaus as activity increases. Supervision is a good example: An additional supervisor is expected to be taken on when the volume of work reaches a specific level of activity.
- *Variable cost* tends to fluctuate according to the variation in the volume of activity. Variable cost increases or decreases directly in proportion to a change in the level of activity. For example, the materials cost for making license plates increases or decreases depending on the number of units produced.
- *Semivariable cost* has both fixed and semivariable characteristics. The predominant element of the cost is variable, but it has some element of fixed costs at either the lower or higher range of activity. The guaranteed minimum wage is a good example of a fixed cost at the lower end of activity, whereas Social Security benefits, unemployment taxes, maintenance, and salary plus commission represent examples of fixed costs at higher levels of activity.[8]

Responsibility Accounting/Centers

These two concepts are intertwined in theory and in practice. *Responsibility accounting* is the mechanism used to provide performance information to the individual who is directly responsible for a particular activity or function (when viewed in this context, the unit, section, department, and division are all considered to be *responsibility centers*). The reporting of results is made

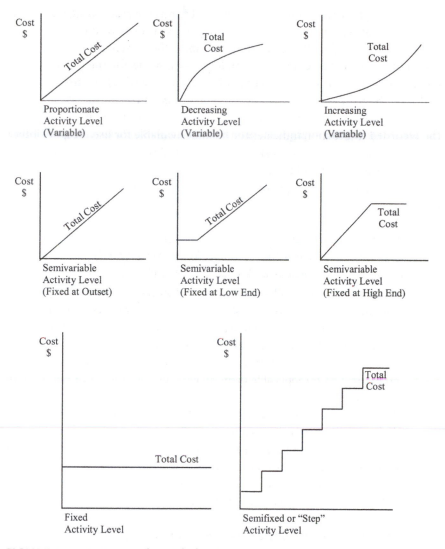

FIGURE 2.1   Patterns of cost behavior.

possible, permitting the identification and fixing of responsibility for allowable or significant variances from planned performance. It permits management to take timely and corrective action. It is particularly noteworthy that responsibility accounting assigns responsibility to those individuals who have control and influence over day-to-day costs, thereby minimizing the potential for "passing the buck." In a county health department, for example, the costs of sanitation, inspection, communicable disease control, environmental control, and community mental health may be reported separately. The county health director, then, could hold each unit, and the manager personally, accountable for the results in its respective responsibility area.

In responsibility accounting, appropriated funds are made available to specific organizational units within an agency. Each unit is responsible for the resources entrusted to it. The responsible unit official may authorize a commitment of expenditure and is ultimately accountable for the actions taken and results achieved. The resources made available are stipulated in the budget and must be recorded in the accounts, wherein each commitment, payment, or refund must be entered. Thus, at any given time, the amount allocated less the recorded transaction indicates the balance available for use. Responsibility costs in monetary terms are costs incurred by, and on behalf of, a responsibility center over a period of time.

Anthony and Young suggested the following procedures in determining and allocating costs:

- Determine the object or unit of goods or services for which cost is being sought. For example, a cost object for a hospital may be a patient day; for a university, a student year. A university may choose to use different cost objects, such as the cost for a classroom or laboratory hour.
- Determine the responsibility cost center (an area over which management is held accountable for inputs and outputs and over which a reasonable degree of control is exercised) from which the cost is to be collected.
- Determine the direct costs (traceable to a specific cost object or cost center) and indirect costs (applicable to more than one cost object or responsibility cost center).
- Allocate service support center costs to the mission (the main purpose for which an agency exists), as shown in Table 2.4. The basis or technique for allocating or apportioning those service center costs is the one that is most appropriate in relation to the experience of the particular agency or individual. It may be the square footage occupied by the mission cost center or the hours of service rendered by the service cost center.[9]

Four types of responsibility centers are common, especially in the private sector. (1) The *cost center* (also known as an *expense center*) is the smallest area of responsibility for which costs or expenses are collected; it does not measure the monetary value of the responsibility center's output. In it resides neither authority nor responsibility for controlling revenues. The main objective is controlling costs. (2) A *revenue center* is charged with the responsibility of achieving some predetermined revenue generation expressed in monetary terms or else in some revenue target or objective. (3) A *profit center* measures the monetary value of the input (expenses) incurred and the output (revenue) produced. The difference between expense and revenue equals profit. (4) The *investment center* measures not only the profit generated but also the amount of capital employed, providing the basis for determining the return on investment (ROI). Investment centers can be viewed as independent entities, with

TABLE 2.4   Responsibility Centers and Programs

Responsibility center	Alcohol detoxification	Drug rehabilitation	Trauma center	Renal dialysis
Mission Centers				
Routine exam	No. days	No. days	No. days	No. days
Surgery	—	—	No. procedures	
Laboratory	No. tests	No. tests	No. tests	No. tests
Radiology	No. procedures	No. procedures	No. procedures	No. procedures
Outpatient care	No. visits	No. visits	No. visits	No. visits
Service Centers				
Housekeeping Dieting Laundry Administration Social Services	Cost distributed to mission centers and programs to determine their full costs.			

many subsidiaries seen in private sector multinational corporations (MNCs) being categorized as such for internal accounting purposes. Because ROI depends specifically on a particular investment project or individual components, it may not always present a clear picture. Return on asset (ROA) presents a clearer picture, because it provides a view of the entire organization or entity.

$$ROI = \frac{Net\ Income}{Investment\ (Project)}$$

$$ROA = \frac{Net\ Income}{Total\ Assets}$$

Of the four types of centers, the cost/expense center is the one most widely used in public and not-for-profit organizations.

Sustainability Accounting

As the information demands of organizational stakeholders shift from purely financial to a more holistic overview, sustainability accounting is becoming a vital reporting component for both private and public sector entities. Sustainability accounting "involves linking sustainability initiatives to company (entity) strategy/mission, evaluating risks and opportunities, and providing measurement, accounting and performance management skills to ensure sustainability is embedded into day-to-day operations of the company."[10]

The focus of this integrated accounting method is referred to as the "triple bottom-line": (1) economic viability, (2) social responsibility, and (3) environmental responsibility. Sustainability accounting reports are often issued in conjunction with corporate social responsibility (CSR) report in the private sector and are intended to demonstrate environmental and social commitments to stakeholders, promote transparency with stakeholder groups, demonstrate relationship-building with communities, enhance risk management, grow shareholder value, and strengthen the entity's public image.

The emerging focus in both private and governmental accounting is to aggressively promote greater emphasis on improving nonfinancial disclosure to enhance transparency and accountability. The aim is to use indicators to assess the extent to which sustainable actions are helping to sustain fiscal resources while simultaneously maintaining or enhancing environmental quality. The GASB Service Efforts and Accomplishments is a step in the direction of sustainability. The focus forces an organization to articulate goals, objectives, and performance indicators that are necessary inputs for strategic planning that assesses an organization's long-term potential to achieve long-term fiscal sustainability.

Organizations such as the Global Reporting Initiative (GRI) and the Sustainability Accounting Standards Board (SASB) have been created to provide sustainability accounting guidance. GRI is a nonprofit global organization assisting organizations to provide uniformed sustainability reporting. The SASB is an American organization that focuses on securities law, environmental law, matrics, and accounting. The SASB is guided by an independent Standards Council that reviews outcomes, compliance with process and compliance with American National Standards Institute (ANSI) guidelines. Sustainability reporting is discussed further in chapter 18.

Basic Accounting Concepts and Principles

Accounting principles are built on a number of important concepts. Accountants habitually apply these concepts in their day-to-day accounting activities (recording, classifying, summarizing, and interpreting data) while seldom making specific reference to them. The following are the major concepts and principles of accounting:

- *Money as a measure:* Accounting recognizes only those activities that can be quantitatively expressed in monetary terms; this gives accounting the power to express heterogeneous activities in a common language. It permits items owned by an agency, such as receivables, equipment, and inventories, to be aggregated as one total unit. A possible shortcoming is that it cannot measure quality improvement in the service delivery or morale of an organization.

- *The entity concept:* Accounting reports are required for each economic or legal organization that uses resources to achieve a common strategic, operating, reporting or compliance goal. A useful distinction is that the accounting system recognizes transactions only as they affect the business, not the individuals who manage the organization.
- *The going concern concept and periodicity:* The assumption is made that a business will continue in existence for an indefinite period. Assets are thus valued according to what is expected to happen to them in the normal course of operations. An implicit assumption is that accounting is a means whereby an organization's value is enhanced over an indefinite time horizon. Like corporations, these organizations are assumed to have perpetual existence. To determine how well managers are performing their resource-enhancing objectives, an arbitrary time period such as a calendar year or a twelve-month fiscal period is identified as the required time to present reports on the organization's accomplishment.
- *Consistency:* The ability to make comparisons is an important requirement in the analysis and use of financial data. In the accumulation and presentation of financial data, the principle of consistency requires that an enterprise follow the same generally accepted accounting practices in the recording and reporting of financial data in succeeding periods. When an independent auditor finds exceptions to these practices, such inconsistencies must be reported.
- *Conservatism and the cost concept:* Given two equally acceptable alternatives, the accountant will typically accept the option that tends to portray an entity in the least optimistic financial position. Given the choice between two or more equally acceptable asset values to record, the one with the least value will be accepted and the larger of two acceptable liability options chosen. The guiding principles relating to the recognition of expense and income suggest that when in doubt, it is better to *overstate expense* and *understate revenue*. The operating view is to anticipate losses but not gains. It is particularly noteworthy that this does not justify the deliberate misinterpretation of the operating results of an enterprise unit. Application of accounting conservatism is also referred to as adherence to the *doctrine of prudence*.
- *Matching:* Under this principle, accountants attempt to match all expenses or expenditures incurred with the revenues generated in the achievement of objectives for a specific period of time. The main aim is to permit an evaluation of the effort–achievement relationship. The matching of *effort* (expenses) with *achievement* (revenue) in determining the operating profit or loss is difficult in the not-for-profit sector because of problems in assigning value to service achievements.
- *Duality concept:* This is a central guiding norm and strength of the accounting system. The principle requires the identification of the source from which

the available resources of an organization are received. The concept generates the following equation: *assets equal liabilities plus equity (or funds)*. It matches assets with liabilities and funds, providing the system with internal checks by relating each inflow to an outflow of an entity. Note that entities that incur liabilities exceeding assets will have a negative equity (fund) balance; in such a case, the entity is considered insolvent.

Generally Accepted Accounting Principles

Until 1984, there were two primary authoritative sources of generally accepted accounting principles (GAAP) applicable to state and local governments: (1) the AICPA *Audit of State and Local Governmental Units* (and related interpretations) and (2) the Government Finance Officers Association (GFOA) *Governmental Accounting, Auditing, and Financial Reporting* (1980) and National Committee on Governmental Accounting (NCGA) *Statement #1: Governmental Accounting and Financial Reporting Principles* (1979). As of 1984, accounting and financial reporting standards for state and local governments were set by the Governmental Accounting Standards Board (GASB), established by the Financial Accounting Foundation. The GASB consults with, and is advised by, the Governmental Accounting Advisory Council (GAAC). This group is comprised of organizations such as the National Association of Counties, U.S. Conference of Mayors, U.S. General Accounting Office, Governmental Finance Officers Association, Health Care Financial Management Association, National Association of College and University Business Office Officers, and American Accounting Association, as well as bond raters, municipal underwriters, and representatives of the Financial Accounting Standards Advisory Council (FASAC), the advisory group to the Financial Accounting Standards Board (FASB). At the federal government level, the Federal Accounting Standards Advisory Board (FASAB) was created (under the CFO Act of 1993) jointly by the General Accounting Office (GAO), Office of Management and Budget (OMB), and Department of the Treasury to establish federal accounting standards.

In the private sector, this is paralleled by the FASB, which has the responsibility for establishing standards for business organizations. Generally Accepted Accounting Principles (GAAP) are applicable to the general-purpose financial statements of entities or activities in the public sector such as hospitals, colleges, universities, utilities, and pension plans. Organizations in the public sector are subject to the FASB standards except in those instances in which the GASB has issued pronouncements applicable to such entities or activities. Existing standards established by the AICPA and NCGA will remain in effect until amended or superseded by the GASB. Other authoritative sources that guide governmental entities include two federal bodies, the GAO and the Office of Management and Budget (OMB).

The GASB and FASB are financed and coordinated by the Financial Accounting Foundation (FAF), representing a consortium of prominent business and professional associations concerned with financial reporting. The FAF is a not-for-profit private organization that carries out its standard-setting activities for the public and private sectors, as shown in Figure 2.2. The FAF's being a private body entity ensures that political considerations do not supersede actions that benefit accounting reporting and compliance.

Nongovernmental not-for-profit agencies rely on AICPA pronouncements and on those by a variety of authoritative bodies, such as the Internal Revenue Service (IRS) and the federal Securities and Exchange Commission (SEC), from which they obtain guidelines for accounting. In the hospital sector, the American Hospital Association sets accounting standards; similarly, in the not-for-profit human service organizations, the United Way acts as an authoritative body (see its *Accounting and Financial Reporting Manual*).

Basis of Accounting

Basis of accounting identifies when revenues, expenditures, expenses, transfers, and liabilities are to be recognized. Stated another way, a *basis of accounting* is the procedure used for indicating specific points in the transaction cycle when resource inflows and outflows are to be recognized. Bases of accounting indicate when to record the measurement of income, expenditure, commitment,

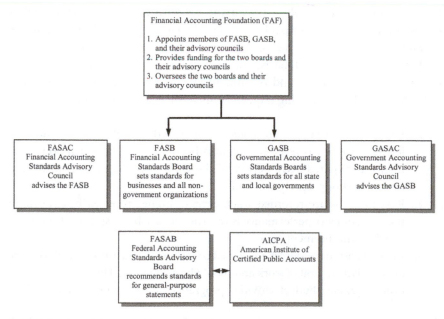

FIGURE 2.2   GASB, FASB, and FASAB.

liability, or transfer. Three bases are generally found in practice: the cash basis, the accrual basis, and the modified cash accrual basis.

Cash Basis

This approach measures and records changes in an entity's books only when cash is paid out or received. Because many nonprofit enterprises predominantly provide socially desirable services, they typically measure only inflows (revenue) and outflows (expenditures) of spendable resources. Likewise, profit-oriented entities that provide services in exchange for fees often use the cash basis of accounting, emphasizing the points of cash receipt and disbursement as opposed to the points at which resources are earned and used (accrual basis). Most individuals maintain their finances on the cash basis. The cash basis is highly desirable because of its simplicity and the low cost to maintain it. A checkbook is the only accounting record that is needed, as the entity needs only to summarize its check stubs to generate financial statements. For entities that transact most operations on a cash basis, this approach can be useful.

Accrual Basis

The accrual basis presents, for a given period, the recognition and recording of all revenues earned, all expenses or expenditures incurred or consumed, all assets purchased, and all liabilities owed or incurred. Stated another way, to accrue means to record an amount in the accounting records in anticipation of future receipt or payment (i.e., cash flow). Accrual accounting is a method that recognizes revenue when earned and expense when incurred regardless of when each is received or paid. The accrual basis is required by GAAP in the private sector because it is accepted as a better measure of assessing enterprise performance than the cash basis. The accrual basis permits a direct matching between expense outflow and revenue inflow in a responsibility center. The GAO has noted the following requirements for accrual accounting:

1. Expenditures accrue when charges are incurred (i.e., when services are performed property is received, amounts become owed for which no performance is required), irrespective of the time when payment is made and invoice and/or property are received.
2. Revenues due are recorded when earned; money received in advance of the government's performance is recorded as a liability as a good/service is owed for this payment.
3. Expired costs or resources consumed constitute the measure of performance of an activity or unit of work and should be accumulated by major organizational segments, budget activities, programs, or responsibility centers.[11]

The accrual concept places emphasis on earning and on that point at which costs expire or resources are consumed, rather than on inflow and outflow, as in the cash basis. Accrual accounting is an example of the matching principle—revenues are matched with expenses incurred in producing said revenues for a specific period of time.

Although accrual accounting is widely practiced in the private sector and in proprietary and fiduciary operations in the not-for-profit sector, difficulties are encountered when attempts are made to apply it to most governmental and not-for-profit agencies. Some revenues, such as property taxes, can be accrued (with reasonable allowance for uncollectible revenues) in those cases in which taxpayers are obligated to pay given amounts when the tax is levied. There are, however, some revenues, such as permits and fees, that are not measurable until the cash is actually collected, because there is no reliable way to determine how much will be collected. The same can be said about the collectability of fees in public and not-for-profit agencies when goods and services are distributed to clients on an as-needed basis. Liability for long-term debt is an example. Although a liability exists on long-term debt at the time of issuance, the principal portion of the liability is not recognized until the period when payment is due, because only then are resources required to meet the liability.

Modified Cash Accrual Basis

This basis presents expenditures other than accrued interest on general long-term debt, inventory, and disbursements, which may be recorded at the time of purchase or when used, and prepaid expenses, which are normally recorded or recognized on the accrual basis at the time the liability is incurred. Revenues are recorded when received, and those that are measurable and available for expenditure are accrued to properly reflect the taxes levied and revenues earned.

Because revenue and expenditure measurements are subject to unique constraints, legal and otherwise, in the not-for-profit sector—and especially in governmental units—the modified cash accrual basis of accounting is used. The modified cash accrual basis also accords with the GASB and the principle of conservatism, which is relevant to not-for-profit organizations. The system permits expenditures to be fully stated—or perhaps overstated—whereas the reverse is true for revenue. This procedure enhances the possibility of creating a surplus and reduces the chances of generating a deficit, as governmental officials are more likely to act in a conservative manner with the entity's resources.

Accounting Bases: Advantages and Disadvantages

Before an agency chooses a basis of accounting, it should evaluate the advantages and disadvantages of each type. The *cash basis* is the simplest method to implement and is widely used in small businesses, small governmental units, and other not-for-profit organizations. The cash basis is also the least expensive to operate. In addition, it requires the least accounting knowledge and experience to operate the system. On the negative side, it provides the least accurate information. For example, revenues and expenses for which cash has not been received or paid are not recognized. Also, it is more difficult for a certified public accountant to express an opinion about the accounting statements.

The *accrual basis* provides the most accurate picture of the financial position of an agency because the method requires the recording of all transactions affecting the agency, whether or not cash changes hands. The accrual basis provides an accurate picture of the organization at any point in time, assuming that accurate and up-to-date records are kept. A disadvantage of the accrual basis is its added cost, because of the extra knowledge, experience, and training needed to implement it. A decision to use the accrual basis should weigh the accuracy to be gained against the cost of implementing it. Businesslike governmental entities, such as enterprise and internal service departments, follow an accrual basis approach to accurately reflect the profit objectives of the entity rather than simply raising enough revenue to meet all necessary expenditures.

The *modified cash accrual basis* is a compromise between the accrual and cash basis options. It increases the accuracy of accounts without all the additional costs associated with the accrual system. This modified basis does, however, require additional personnel, because bookkeeping is slightly more complicated than under the cash basis.

In determining which basis of accounting is best for an organization, recognition should be given to the following factors:

- Technical knowledge of the available personnel
- Sophistication of information required to ensure an efficient and effective operation
- Comparative cost of the basis
- External reporting requirements
- Internal reporting requirements
- GASB recommendations and requirements

In Tables 2.5 and 2.6, the cash and accrual accounting bases are compared in the acquisition and use of an asset.

Contrasting Public and Private Accounting

Not-for-profit organizations, especially government agencies, operate in a different political and economic environment than do business enterprises. Accordingly, governmental accounting standards have developed differently than have business enterprise standards. Even so, many common practices

TABLE 2.5   Cash Basis versus Accrual Basis: Asset Acquisition and Use

Period/Description	1	2	3
Transaction	Asset purchased but not paid for (on credit or account)	Asset consumed or used	Asset purchased (on credit) paid in cash
Accrual Basis	Asset and liability recognized	The use and decrease in asset value recognized	Decrease in liability and cash recognized
Cash Basis	No entry	No entry	Decrease in cash and asset recognized

TABLE 2.6   Cash Basis versus Accrual Basis: Revenue Recognition

Period/Description	1	2	3
Transaction	Service delivered	Bill sent	Bill paid in cash
Accrual Basis	Revenue and accounts receivable Recognized	No entry	Accounts receivable decreased and cash increased
Cash Basis	No entry	No entry	Cash increased and revenue recognized

make governmental and business accounting standards more alike than divergent. Many of the principles and concepts (e.g., controlling, reporting, concern for relevance, comparability, consistency, understandability) enumerated earlier in this volume have applicability in both the not-for-profit and private sectors. The basic differences between the two sectors can be stated as follows:

1. Not-for-profit agencies, especially those in the public sector, require strict adherence to legal and administrative directives. These directives may be logical for legal and administrative purposes but lack relevance for private sector accounting purposes.
2. In the private sector, the income statement (the principal inflow and outflow statement) emphasizes earning and using resources. This inflow and outflow statement shows the extent to which operating objectives have been met, focusing on how resource outflows benefit future periods as well as the current reporting period.

3. Not-for-profit agencies have inflow (revenue) and outflow (expenditure) statements. However, they are concerned with raising and expending resources according to specific budget plans.

4. Not-for-profit agencies are expenditure-oriented rather than expense-oriented. (Expenditure measures the monetary value of resources used in the acquisition of goods and or services.)

5. Emphasis is placed on the sources of revenues and ways in which they are used, so not-for-profit organizations are dollar accountability–oriented. Typical is the expression "Where got? Where gone?"

6. GAAP take precedence in private sector accounting. In a public organization, when GAAP and legal requirements conflict, GAAP give way.

7. Public sector accounting transactions are guided by an inflexible budget plan, whereas the private sector employs a flexible budget that changes as the volume of output changes. This flexible budget helps entities evaluate operational performance and variances.

8. Private sector accounting records are maintained to show the owner's equity in one consolidated account, whereas in the not-for-profit sector, there is no equity accounting, and funds are based on legal requirements.

9. GASB Statement No. 34 divides the public sector financial reporting model into categories: *fund financial statements* and *government-wide financial statements*. Fund financial statements comprise governmental funds, proprietary funds, and fiduciary funds. Government-wide financial statements employ the full accrual basis for long-lived assets and long-term liabilities. Government-wide statements generate two statements: the government-wide statement of net assets (the balance sheet) and the governmental statement of activities (statement of revenue and expenses).

10. Private accounting uses the accrual basis, although not-for-profit accounting may use either the cash basis or modified cash accrual basis.

11. Ideally, private sector accounting reflects the results of economic activities or *operational accountability*, expressing the efficiency with which the profit objective has been achieved. This is made possible by the direct matching of revenues with expenses for a given period and a specific responsibility center. Thus, management can be held operationally accountable to owners, creditors, and other interests.

12. The public and other not-for-profit sectors do not typically have operational accountability or the matching principle as a central objective. Typically, these organizations do not set prices for their goods and services. Most often, little or no revenue is collected from the beneficiaries to whom their activities are mainly directed. Even in hospitals, whose major source of revenues is derived from the sale of health care, services are not entirely market-determined. (Hospitals structure their prices to account for indigent and other nonpaying patients.) Thus, operational

accountability is not entirely reflected in the accounting statement. Because of this reality, the major emphasis in not-for-profit organizations is placed on stewardship or the fiduciary role of administrators. These administrators owe the intended beneficiaries of the not-for-profit services and donors the duties of loyalty and care in regards to entity resources. This requires that management be able to account for the inflow of funds and their expenditure in the pursuit of basic objectives. As noted throughout this volume, this results in financial statements that typically show dollar accountability.

13. Dollar accountability systems emphasize cash inflows (revenues or receipts and outflow expenditures).

Principal Accounting Statements

All accounting transactions are summarized in three principal statements: the *balance sheet*, the *income statement*, and the *statement of changes in financial position*.

Balance Sheets

The *balance sheet* is one of the basic accounting reports indicating the financial assets controlled by an organization and the ways in which they are financed. The main purpose of the balance sheet is to indicate the financial position of an agency at a specific point in time. The financial position shows the available resources (assets) as compared to outstanding obligations (liabilities and fund equity) on a particular date. The balance sheet may be compared to a snapshot: In every moment following the snapshot, the picture is likely to change. Balance sheet accounts are referred to as "real accounts." They are never closed out at the end of a fiscal period and are thus perpetual items. The balance sheet for Bright Hospital is shown in Table 2.7. An examination of its format and categories provides a summary of Bright Hospital's assets, liabilities/obligations, and fund balance or equity.

Two broad categories contained in a balance sheet are *assets* and *liabilities*. Assets are things of value that can be owned. They constitute the resources of an organization measured in monetary terms on a specific date (for example, the resources of Bright Hospital on December 31, 2003). Liabilities are the debts owed by an organization to others outside the organization (for example, claims that outsiders have against the hospital that must be paid at certain known times in the future). When total liabilities are subtracted from total assets, the difference represents the funds or equity invested by contributors or shareholders. Inspection of the asset and liability categories reveals that they are subdivided into current and fixed assets and current and long-term liabilities.

Current assets refer to cash or other assets that may reasonably be expected to be converted or realized in cash, sold, or consumed, usually within a year or less, through the normal operations of a business. This balance sheet in Table 2.7 was simplified for ease in understanding nonprofit institutions typically consisting of several separate divisions such as current funds unrestricted and restricted and fund categories such as construction, building, land, endowment, or other funds, depending on the original source and disposition of capital funds. Each fund has a set of self-balancing accounts. There is no set number of current assets; rather, they vary according to the type and needs of an individual organization. Table 2.7 provides a list of the items frequently found in the current asset subdivision of a balance sheet:

- *Cash*, consisting of money in the form of currency, coin, checks, money orders, banker's drafts on hand or on deposit with an official, and bank deposits that are free for disbursement at any time.
- *Accounts receivable*, claims against customers for amounts owed on open accounts or on credit from private persons, firms, or corporations for the delivery of goods and services. In Table 2.7, *accounts receivable* refers to services rendered to patients. In government organizations, *accounts receivable* does not usually include amounts due from other funds of the same governmental unit. Note that although taxes and assessments receivable are included in the term "receivable," they are reported separately as *taxes receivable* and *special assessments receivable*. In accounts receivable, a provision is made for the uncollectible amount that is likely to prove worthless. The uncollectible amount is denoted as a contra-asset, rather than a liability. This amount is subtracted from the accounts receivable, showing the net amount.
- *Inventory*, items or merchandise for sale in the normal course of business. In not-for-profit organizations, *inventory* has at least two different meanings: (1) supplies not for sale but for use in the delivery of goods or services and (2) a detailed list showing quantities, descriptions, and values of owned property (e.g., desks, cabinets), typically found in the fixed asset account group.

Fixed assets represent assets such as land, buildings, machinery, furniture, and other equipment having a nominal life longer than one year. The purchase price of most fixed assets is reduced by an annual depreciation charge. Fixed assets, less accumulated depreciation, represent the remaining economic and potential productive value of the assets. During each fiscal period, the amount allowed for depreciation is included in the income statement as part of the cost of doing business. The depreciation expense may be viewed as an allowance for capital recovery that may be managed to generate sufficient funds to replace the asset at the end of its useful life.

TABLE 2.7 Bright Hospital: Simplified Consolidated Balance Sheet as of December 31, 2013 and December 31, 2014

ASSETS	2013		2014	
Current Assets				
Cash		$305,000		$225,000
Accounts receivable–patients	$1,200,000		$840,000	
less uncollectible accounts	21,000	1,179,000	15,000	825,600
Marketable securities (market value)		20,000		75,000
Inventories		134,400		115,000
Prepaid expenses		23,000		23,000
Total current assets		1,661,400		1,263,600
Fixed Assets				
Land ($200,000 in 2003)				
Buildings and equipment	6,500,000	250,000 $6,826,400		250,000
less accumulated depreciation	860,000		905,000	
Total net fixed assets		5,640,000		5,921,400
Total assets		$7,571,400		$7,435,000

LIABILITIES	2013		2014	
Current Liabilities				
Accounts payable	$170,000		$120,000	
Taxes payable	6,000		7,000	
Salaries payable	150,000		145,000	
Current loans	400,000		350,000	
Advance payments—third-party contracts	130,000		140,000	
Total current liabilities		856,000		762,000
Long-Term Liabilities				
Long-term loans ($400,000 in1996)	1,397,400		1,300,000	
Bonds ($1,000,000 in 1996)	2,000,000		2,000,000	
Mortgages	350,000		330,000	
Total long-term liabilities		3,747,400		3,630,000
Fund balance		2,968,000		3,043,000
Total liabilities and fund balances		$7,571,400		$7,435,000

Note: This balance sheet was simplified for ease in understanding nonprofit institutions typically consisting of several separate divisions such as current funds unrestricted and restricted and fund categories such as construction, building, land, endowment, or other funds depending on the original source and disposition of capital funds. Each fund would have a set of self-balancing accounts.

Current liabilities comprise those obligations that can be objectively determined, that will come due in a short period of time (usually a year or less), and that will have to be paid out of current assets. Table 2.7 indicates the categories that are classified as current liabilities:

- Accounts payable constitute the claims of vendors or suppliers to the organization.
- Taxes payable are the amount owed but not yet paid.
- Salaries payable represent the salaries that employees have earned but that are still owed by the organization.
- Advance payments on third-party (insurance company) contracts are payments that have been received for which no services were rendered.
- *Current loans* refer to the short-term loans that have been obtained from banks and other financial institutions.
- Deferred revenue indicates the receipt of financial resources that have not yet been earned. This denotes that the entity owes a good or service in the future; accordingly, a liability is recorded.

Long-term liabilities comprise the obligations that are not required to be met for at least a year or more. The following are usually classified as long-term liabilities:

- Long-term loans are funds borrowed from banks and other financial institutions.
- Bonds are a form of interest-bearing note employed by organizations to borrow money on a long-term basis. They are like long-term loans but have more formal requirements. Typically, they are secured by specific assets, except in the case of governmental units and large corporations, which may float some bonds on their general credit. In many cases, governmental bonds are referred to as municipal securities, whereas bonds issued by well-established, highly solvent, corporations are known as commercial paper. In addition, bonds may be traded on exchanges, whereas long-term loans may not. This allows bonds to be issued at lower interest rates than long-term loans, because the liquid nature of security reduces the overall investment risk.
- Mortgages are long-term loans that are usually secured by some identified fixed assets.

Funds in not-for-profit organizations are resources that are available to obtain goods and services. Examples of funds in not-for-profit organizations are unspent resources from taxes, charges, donations, and endowments, which may be restricted or unrestricted. The presence of restricted funds means that the donor or authorizing body (legislature or board) stipulates the conditions regarding the use of the funds; no such conditions apply on the use of unrestricted funds.

Income Statements

The *income statement* is a summary of revenues and expenses or expenditures for a specific period of time. In profit-oriented companies, profits are measured by comparing revenues generated in a given period with expenses incurred to produce those revenues in the same period (this is known as the "matching principle"). Revenues represent the inflow of assets from the sale of products or the delivery of services to customers or clients. Expenses are the sacrifices made or the costs incurred to produce those revenues. When revenue exceeds expense, net income results. If the reverse is true, the organization or business is said to be operating at a loss. All income statement accounts are referred to as "nominal" accounts, meaning that they are always closed out at the end of each fiscal period. Table 2.8 presents the income statement of Bright Hospital for January 1, 2003, to December 31, 2003, and 2004. The income statement typically contains three parts, showing *revenues, expenses,* and *net profit or loss.* The revenues of Bright Hospital were generated mainly from inpatient, ambulatory, and auxiliary services.

Not-for-profit organizations that operate on the cash basis simply compare the total fund's inflow and outflow and accept the result as an adequate measure of the organization's performance. The use of this approach violates the matching principle if some revenues are earned in one period but not recognized until the next, when they are physically received. This is true for expenses as well. When the matching of revenues and expenses does not occur, it may distort the performance assessment. This is the main reason why many not-for-profit organizations are increasing their use of the accrual basis for measuring income. It effectively overcomes the distortion of net income because it matches revenues with expenses for each given period. Bright Hospital is on the accrual basis, so the $75,000 shown as net income or surplus may not be equated with cash. Net income and cash will be exactly the same *only* when all expenses incurred are actually paid and when all revenues earned are received in the period for which the income statement is prepared.

When enterprise or proprietary operations are undertaken in public or not-for-profit organizations, they are similar to such for-profit undertakings in which *assets = liabilities + equity (contributed capital + retained earnings).* Increases in retained earnings result from net income and transfer from prior periods.

Statement of Changes in Financial Position

The *statement of changes in financial position or funds' flow statement* is devoted exclusively to reporting changes in the fiscal position for a specified period of time. This statement identifies the sources from which additional investable funds or cash were derived and the uses to which these funds were put. For this reason, the statement is known variously as a "statement of funds provided and applied," "sources and uses of funds," or "changes in financial position."

TABLE 2.8   Bright Hospital: Income Statement for the Period January 1, 2003 to December 31, 2003 and December 31, 2004

REVENUES*	2003		2004	
Income from:				
Inpatient services	$4,800,000		$4,625,000	
Ambulatory services	400,000		425,000	
Auxiliary income	1,100,000		1,220,000	
Total deductions including free service	300,000		320,000	
Other revenue:				
Sale of radiology equipment	180,000		-0-	
Total revenues (net)		$6,780,000		$6,690,000
EXPENSES**				
Salaries and wages	$4,925,000		$4,625,000	
Supplies	80,000		40,000	
Depreciation	290,000		340,000	
Administrative and general expenses	890,200		1,205,200	
Interest	129,800		60,800	
Miscellaneous and other expenses ($50,000 rate payable)	390,000		297,000	
Total expenses		$6,705,000		$6,568,000
Net Profit (Excess of revenues over expenses)		$ 75,000		$ 123,000
Fund balance at beginning of year		2,968,000		3,043,000
Fund balance at end of year		3,043,000		3,166,000

* Total operating revenues ($6,780,000 less $120,000) from radiology equipment sale.
** While interest expense is not excluded in this calculation of ratios, some analysts do exclude them.

The funds' flow statement has come into general use because of the need to provide information to decision makers relating to finance and investment activities. Information on sources and uses of funds may be obtained from an analysis of the income statement and balance sheet. The principal sources (inflow) and uses (outflow) may be summarized as follows:

Sources

Net cash revenue from operations for the period

Additional investment (e.g., donations and endowment)

Increase in bonds or long-term loans

Uses

Additions to plant and equipment

Expenses during period

Distribution of income

A statement of changes in financial position for Bright Hospital is shown in Table 2.9.

Accounting and Internal Controls

Internal controls are commonly classified as either "administrative controls" or "accounting controls." Internal administrative controls are comprised of procedures and records that assist management in achieving an organization's goals. For example, when poor-quality work occurs in a particular responsibility center, the use of internal controls permits management to better evaluate personnel performance and attempt to improve the quality of the output. Internal accounting controls refer to procedures, records, reports, and physical restrictions that have been designed to safeguard assets and promote the reliability of financial records and reports. For example, guidelines and specific procedures developed to ensure the recording of transactions in accordance with GAAP aid in assuring the reliability of financial records. An important means for safeguarding assets is to limit their access to authorized personnel.

The internal control system varies depending on the size of the not-for-profit organization. In organizations where there are few employees and the manager of the organization provides direct supervision and oversight, few controls are needed. The situation changes as the complexity and size of the organization increase. This requires that management delegate greater authority, making it necessary to place more reliance on the accounting system. Financial institutions, such as large banks and investment firms, are engaged in especially complex business activities and accordingly have extensive and highly complex internal controls in place.

The Fund Accounting System

The universe of not-for-profit organizations using the *fund accounting system* may be classified as follows: (1) voluntary health and welfare organizations, (2) hospitals, (3) colleges and universities, (4) federal state and local governments, and (5) others, including church associations, political parties, museums, and cemeteries.

The "fund" is the basic accounting entity for the public sector and, to a lesser extent, for other not-for-profit organizations. An important objective

TABLE 2.9   Bright Hospital: Statement of Cash Flow Position for Year Ending December 31, 2004

Cash flow from operating activities		
Cash from revenues	$5,200,000	
Less cash expenses	5,150,000	$50,000
Cash flow from investing activities		
Purchase of land	(250,000)	
Purchase of equipment	(1,580,000)	
Sale of equipment	300,000	
Net cash from investing activities		(1,530,000)
Cash flow from financing		
Proceeds from long-term loans	$ 400,000	
Proceeds from bond sale	1,000,000	
Net cash flow from financing		1,400,000
Net cash decrease		(80,000)
Cash balance December 31, 2003		305,000
Cash balance December 31, 2004		$ 225,000

is to ensure that donated and restricted resources are applied in accordance with the authorizing body or donor's wishes. Although the private organization focuses on profitability, the not-for-profit entity focuses on resources—the relationship between inflows and outflows (balanced budget or surplus). In private sector accounting, the entire business or firm is the basic accounting and reporting unit; in government, the fund is the basic unit. Unlike in the not-for-profit sector, there are no restricted funds in the private sector. The fund is referred to as a fiscal and accounting entity, and a system with a set of self-balancing accounts. It is characterized by the following:

- Recording of cash and all other financial resources, related liabilities, and residual balances and charges therein
- Segregation for the purpose of carrying out specific activities or attaining or abiding by particular objectives, special regulations, restrictions, and limitations
- A fund accounting equation: *assets + expenditures = liabilities + receipts + fund balance*

Funds are developed to measure and account for financial resources. Balances at the end of the period are available to be spent (expendable) or appropriated for future periods. "Reserved fund balance" identifies financial assets that are not spendable or available for appropriation. The designation "unreserved fund balance" segregates or "earmarks" financial resources for specified purposes, though unreserved and spendable. The unreserved fund balance is not designed to reflect economic health, but simply identifies the financial resources available for future spending or appropriation: *funds – fund liabilities = fund equity.*

The Fund Balance Requirement

Each fund contains a set of self-balancing accounts. When total revenue exceeds total expenditure, the fund has a surplus balance. Especially in local government, funds are often legally required to be balanced. In a number of governmental jurisdictions, a negative fund balance may have to be erased by increasing revenues during the succeeding periods. The fund balance (net or residual assets) represents the net amount of resources of the fund. It is equivalent to, or a counterpart of, the for-profit organization's retained earnings.

Types of Funds

There are three main categories of funds—*governmental funds, proprietary funds,* and *fiduciary funds*—and funds may be restricted or not. The nature of the activity accounted for determines the category. The following are brief definitions of the funds used in governmental units:

- The *general fund* accounts for all financial resources except those funds that must be accounted for in another fund. Most revenues are accounted for in the general fund. This is usually the largest fund and is created to carry out the basic purposes (services) for which the governmental unit was established. For example, fire, sanitation, and health would be in the general fund, but the construction of a firehouse typically would be accounted for in another fund. Normally, a bond is floated to finance building costs, subject to certain laws and legal requirements.

  The general fund equation looks like the following: *assets (financial, both legally restricted and nonspendable) = liabilities (payable in the near future— year or less) + fund balance (unreserved designated, unreserved undesignated, and reserved balance).* The level of "unreserved fund balance" in the general fund balance is of particular importance to bond raters and some stakeholders. Although there is no specific required amount for the unreserved fund balance level, the "rule of thumb" is that 5 percent of annual operating expenditure is the minimum expectation. Other proponents advocate one month of operating expenditure. Two important considerations that should be kept in mind are the reliability of revenue sources (the predictability) and the timing of cash flows.[12]
- *Special revenue funds* account for proceeds or specific revenue sources (often earmarked) that are restricted to expenditure for specific purposes.

Typically, special revenues exclude special assessments, expendable trusts, and major capital projects.

- *Capital project funds* account for financial resources to be used for the acquisition or construction of capital facilities unless the transactions are handled by special assessment, enterprise, or trust funds.
- *Debt service funds* account for monies accumulated for the payment of general long-term debt principal and interest. There are three basic kinds of long-term debts: (1) term or sinking fund bonds, (2) serial bonds, and (3) notes or time warrants that mature in a year after issuance.
- *Special assessment funds* account for funds used for projects financed from special assessments levied against property owners.
- *Enterprise or proprietary funds* measure income. These funds are designed to reflect the economic health of the fund. Under GASB Statement No. 34, an enterprise fund may account for any activity where a fee is charged to external users for goods or services. Whenever an activity is financed from debt revenue and laws or regulations require that the activity's cost be recovered from fees and charges or when policies dictate pricing to recover costs, an enterprise fund is established. These funds are like commercial or nonexpendable funds used to account for activities that parallel those of a profit-oriented organization. For example, a publicly owned parking garage, transit system, or water or electric utility applying user charges according to services received is similar to a privately operated water utility. The earnings from the enterprise fund may be used for general purposes or other uses when it has been determined that such uses are justified. The enterprise or proprietary fund equation looks like the following: *assets (all) = liabilities (all) + equity (contributed capital, retained earnings reserved and retained earnings unreserved).*
- *Internal service funds* account for the financing of goods and services provided by one department or agency to other departments or agencies of a governmental unit on a cost recovery or reimbursement basis. A motor pool for which each department makes a contribution would be an example. The internal services are provided internally to other units of an organization, while the enterprise fund provides external services primarily to the public on a user charge basis.
- *Plant, property, and equipment funds* maintain records on resources invested in the plant, property, and equipment and account for the payment of debt used to finance these activities.
- *Endowment funds* account for donors' gifts that are to be maintained in perpetuity to produce income that may be expended or be used for either restricted or nonrestricted purposes. Sometimes, quasi-endowments may be restricted by a governing board instead of the owner.
- *Fiduciary funds* account for assets (trust and agency funds) held by a governmental unit in a trustee or agency capacity. A bequest left to a city to

maintain a park would be an example. Both expendable and nonexpendable funds are included in this category. Expendable trust funds account for monies being held that may be totally expended. In the case of nonexpendable funds, only the interest earned may be expended; such funds are accounted for in a manner similar to proprietary funds. Because fiduciary funds are purely custodial, they do not require a measurement of results of the operation, and thus there is no fund balance, only assets and liabilities.

- *Expendable funds* are usable in current operations and consumption, while funds that are dedicated to the maintenance of capital and are self-sustaining are nonexpendable. The expendable fund places emphasis on the flow of resources, focusing on current assets and liabilities and modified accrual on the operating statement. Four funds (the general fund, special revenue funds, capital project funds, and debt service funds) are viewed as "expendable funds" (they are sometimes referred to as "source and disposition funds"). These funds are created to offer services to the public, often without charge or at only a nominal fee. Because all the resources raised are to be expended within a reasonable time period, the accountability system is organized to control cash or dollar accountability. The expendable funds focus only on resources raised to be expended. The "nonexpendable funds" place emphasis on the preservation or maintenance of capital such as property or self-sustaining funds, including enterprise, internal, and trust funds, and permanent funds such as endowments.

- *Restricted funds* and *nonrestricted funds* are categorized based on the restraint or control that governs their use or application. The unrestricted funds typically include all expendable resources that are not constrained by a specific stipulation about their use. Generally, this means that any resources that are unrestricted are available for the general operations of the entity, governmental unit, or organization. Restricted funds include those that can be expended only as the law, regulation, authorizing body, or donor require, consistent with public policy.

Contrasting Public and Not-for-Profit Entities

Not-for-profit entities resemble business enterprise. The FASB requests that not-for-profit agencies classify their net assets into three categories based on donor-imposed restrictions:[13]

- *Unrestricted net assets* are temporarily restricted assets consisting predominantly of resources that must be used for specific purposes (for example, for research or acquisition of plant). Specific periods (for example, a term endowment of a gift that allows only the income to be spent for a specific period) or when some specific events take place (for example, an annuity gift that provides the donor with income until the death of the donor).

- *Governmental Funds* consist of general purpose or governmental funds (major funds), proprietary funds (major funds), and fiduciary funds mandated by the GASB Rule No. 34. The GASB seeks to improve operational accountability, emphasizing the big picture that may be lost in the details of fund accounting. Governmental funds primarily account for the government's tax-supported activities.
- *Fund Accounting Cycle:* The major objective of fund accounting, especially governmental fund accounting, is to show that resources (unrestricted and restricted funds) have been used in accordance with authorized purposes. Accounting records are expected to show data from budgetary authority and transactions relating thereto. Accounting for funds begins as soon as the authority has been granted to obtain and expend resources for specified purposes. The journal entries below indicate entries that might be typical of a fund accounting cycle. Tables 2.10 and 2.11 show the ending balance for the hypothetical city as of the end of 2014. Although small governments reflected in these tables' reporting will not be changed as greatly, for large governments, GASB Rule No. 34, *Basic Financial Statements,* reporting requirements have changed significantly, as discussed below.

TABLE 2.10   City of A: Balance Sheet as of December 31, 2014

Assets		Liabilities, Reserves, and Fund Balance	
Cash	$ 10,000	Vouchers payable	$ 90,000
Taxes receivable	100,000	Due to working capital fund	10,000
			50,000
		Reserve for encumbrances	(40,000)
		Fund balance	
Total assets	$110,000	Total Liabilities, Reserves, and Fund	$110,000

TABLE 2.11   City of A: General Fund Analysis of Changes in Fund Balance for Year Ended December 31, 2014

Beginning fund balance, January 1, 2004 Deduct excess of expenditures and encumbrances over revenues for period ended December 31, 2003		$ -0-
Expenditures	$940,000	
Revenues	900,000	(40,000)
Fund balance		$(40,000)

How GASB Rule No. 34, Basic Financial Statements, Combines Funds: The New Reporting Model

Under the new model mandates, governments prepare two separate sets of financial statements. The *government-wide statements* (net assets or balance sheet) and *government-wide statement of activities* (or operating statements) concentrate on the government as a whole. It consolidates all the government's operations and includes all of the government's economic resources, including long-lived assets. Both governmental and business-type activities' statements are organized on a full accrual basis and reflect the economic measurement focus. The GASB Rule No. 34, for reporting purposes, requires that accruals and amortizations (including depreciation of capital assets) be followed in governmental activities, paralleling those that presently exist in proprietary funds. Tables 2.12 and 2.13 are government-wide statements of Sample City. Note that Table 2.12's statement of net assets has columns for primary governmental activities, business-type activities, combined totals of the two, and a separate column for component units. The difference between the net assets and net liabilities is identified as "net assets" rather than the traditional fund equity designation. Table 2.13 shows that the statement of activities is prepared on a function or program basis. It designates the gross expenses for each program, offset by program revenues (charges for services and grants) and net program expenses. It also shows the extent to which the program is financed by general governmental taxes and other revenue sources.

The second set of statements, *fund financial statements*, shows the government as a collection of separate funds. Government and business-type funds are presented in separate schedules. Governmental funds include one column for the general fund, one each for the major funds, and one that combines all the nonmajor funds. The total of the columns merely combines the funds rather than consolidating them, so interfund items such as receivables and payables or transfers from funds are not eliminated. The focus of these governmental funds' statements is on current resources, reflecting the modified accrual basis, while business-type activity is on the accrual basis as in the past.

GASB's Allowing Fund Level Statements

The government-wide financial statements are accompanied by the *fund level* financial statements, integrated with the governmental statements, through a reconciliation process that is shown in Table 2.15. The fund level continuance reflects the following:

- The financial resources measurement focus and the modified accrual basis accounting, as noted earlier, continues the existing practice.

- The total of governmental funds in the fund level balance sheet is reconciled with the net assets indicated in the governmental activities column of the government-wide statement of net assets. Thus, a review of the fund level balance sheet for governmental funds in Table 2.14 indicates that $123,558,874 is the same as the total assets shown in the governmental activities column of the government-wide statement in Table 2.13.
- The net change in fund balances reported that total governmental funds in the funds level operating statement is reconciled with the change in net assets shown in the governmental activities column of the government-wide statement of activities. Thus, the net deficit change in assets shown in Table 2.13 of $3,114,286 is the same as shown in the reconciliation statement of revenue and expenditure in Table 2.16.
- The differences reflected in the statements are due to the modified accrual basis of accounting used in the fund level statements versus the full accrual basis employed in the government-wide statement.
- Government fund level statements will no longer be prepared by fund type. The GASB requires the inclusion of the general fund, special major funds, a total of other governmental funds, and a total of all governmental funds.
- The proprietary fund level statement continues to be prepared on the full accrual basis. Like the government-wide funds statement, the proprietary fund statement at the fund level includes separate columns for major funds. The proprietary fund statement at the fund level is required to contain balance sheet, statements of revenues, expenses and changes in fund equity, and cash flow.

Fixed Assets and Long-Term Liabilities under the New Gasb Rule No. 34

The new model government-wide statements report both capital assets and long-term liabilities. Neither fixed assets nor long-term liabilities are recognized in the funds, since they employ the modified accrual basis. To overcome this problem, the old model employed the *account group* system. This is, in essence, an off–balance sheet list of assets and liabilities, with accompanying depreciation and amortization schedules. All of the excluded fixed assets of an entity become the general fixed asset account group. These fixed assets are not recognized in the accounts because they were identified as expenditures when they are acquired. The *long-term debt account group*, like the entity's fixed assets, is not recorded in the funds. It is also tracked by a listing system.

TABLE 2.12   Sample City: Government-Wide Statement of Net Assets for Year Ended December 31, 2013

| | Primary Government | | | |
	Governmental Activities	Business-type Activities	Total	Component Units
Assets				
Cash and cash equivalents	$13,597,899	$ 10,279,143	$ 23,877,042	$ 303,935
Investments	27,365,221		27,365,221	7,428,952
Receivables (net)	12,833,132	3,609,615	16,442,747	4,042,290
Internal balances	175,000	(175,000)		
Inventories	322,149	126,674	448,823	83,697
Capital assets, net	170,022,760	151,388,751	321,411,511	37,744,786
Total assets	224,316,161	165,229,183	389,545,344	49,603,660
Liabilities				
Accounts payable	6,783,310	751,430	7,534,740	1,803,332
Deferred revenue	1,435,599		1,435,599	38,911
Noncurrent liabilities				
Due within one year	9,236,000	4,426,286	13,662,286	1,426,639
Due in more than one year	83,302,378	74,482,273	157,784,651	27,106,151
Total Liabilities	100,757,287	79,659,989	180,417,276	30,375,033
Net Assets				
Invested in capital assets, net of related debt	90,701,684	73,088,574	163,790,258	15,906,392
Restricted for:				
Capital projects	24,715,566		24,715,566	492,445
Debt service	3,020,708	1,451,996	4,472,704	
Community development projects	4,811,043		4,811,043	
Other purposes	3,214,302		3,214,304	
Unrestricted (deficit)	(2,904,429)	11,028,624	8,124,195	2,829,790
Total net assets	$123,558,874	$85,569,194	$209,128,068	$19,228,627

Source: Adapted from working papers prepared by the staff of the Governmental Accounting Standards Board.

TABLE 2.13 Sample City: Governmental Statement of Activities for Year Ended December 31, 2013

Functions/Programs	Program Revenues				Net (Expense) Revenue and Changes in Net Assets			
						Primary Government		
	Expenses	Charges for Services	Operating Grants and Contributions	Capital Grants and Contributions	Governmental Activities	Business-Type Activities	Total	Component Units
Primary government:								
Governmental activities:								
General government	$ 9,571,410	$ 3,146,915	$ 843,617		$ (5,580,878)		$ (5,580,878)	
Public safety	34,844,749	1,198,855	1,307,693	$ 62,300	(32,275,901)		(32,275,901)	
Public works	10,128,538	850,000		2,252,615	(7,025,923)		(7,025,923)	
Engineering services	1,299,645	704,793			(594,852)		(594,852)	
Health and sanitation	6,738,672	5,612,267	575,000		(551,405)		(551,405)	
Cemetery	735,866	212,496			(523,370)		(523,370)	
Culture and recreation	11,532,350	3,995,199	2,450,000		(5,087,151)		(5,087,151)	
Community development	2,995,389			2,580,000	(414,389)		(414,389)	
Education (payment to Sample City SD)	21,893,273				(21,893,273)		(21,893,273)	
Interest on long-term debt	6,068,121				(6,068,121)		(6,068,121)	
Total government activities	105,807,013	15,720,525	5,176,310	4,894,915	(80,015,263)		(80,015,263)	
Business-type activities:								
Water	3,595,733	4,159,350		1,159,909		$ 1,723,526	1,723,526	
Sewer	4,912,853	7,170,533		486,010		2,743,690	2,743,690	

	Expenses	Charges for Services	Operating Grants and Contributions	Capital Grants and Contributions	Governmental activities	Business-type activities	Total	Component units
Parking facilities	2,796,283	1,344,087				(1,452,196)	(1,452,196)	
Total business-type activities	11,304,869	12,673,970	1,645,919			3,015,020	3,015,020	
Total primary government	$117,111,882	$28,394,495	$6,540,834	$5,176,310	(80,015,263)	3,015,020	(77,000,243)	
Component units:								
Landfill	$3,382,157	$3,857,858	$11,397					$ 487,098
Public school system	31,186,498	705,765		3,937,083				(26,543,650)
Total component units	$34,568,655	$4,563,623	$11,397	$3,937,083				(26,056,552)
General revenues:								
Taxes:								
Property taxes, levied for general purposes					51,410,478		51,410,478	
Property taxes, levied for debt service					4,726,244		4,726,244	
Franchise and public service taxes					13,308,487		13,308,487	
Payment from Sample City								21,893,273
Grants and contributions not restricted to specific programs					1,457,820		1,457,820	6,461,708
Interest and investment earnings					1,958,144	601,349	2,559,493	881,763
Miscellaneous					884,907	104,925	989,832	22,464
Special item—Gain on sale of park land					2,653,488		2,653,488	
Transfers					501,409	(501,409)		
Total general revenues, special items, and transfers					76,900,977	204,865	77,105,842	29,259,208
Change in net assets					(3,114,286)	3,219,885	105,599	3,202,656
Net assets—beginning					126,673,160	82,349,309	209,022,469	16,025,971
Net assets—ending					$123,558,874	$85,569,194	$209,128,068	$19,228,627

Source: Adapted from working papers prepared by the staff of the Governmental Accounting Standards Board.

TABLE 2.14 Sample City: Governmental Fund Balance Sheets For Year Ending December 31, 2013

	General Fund	HUD Programs	Community Development	Route 7 Construction Fund	Other Governmental Funds	Total Governmental Funds
Assets						
Cash and cash equivalents	$ 3,418,485	$ 1,236,523			$ 5,606,792	$ 10,261,800
Investments			$ 13,262,695	$ 10,467,037	3,485,252	27,214,984
Receivables, net	3,644,561	2,953,438	353,340	11,000	10,221	6,972,560
Receivable from other funds	1,370,757					1,370,757
Receivable from other governments		119,059			1,596,038	1,715,097
Liens receivable	791,926	3,195,745				3,987,671
Inventories	182,821					182,821
Total assets	$ 9,408,550	$ 7,504,765	$ 13,616,035	$ 10,478,037	$ 10,698,303	$ 51,705,690
Liabilities						
Accounts payable	3,408,680	129,975	190,548	1,104,632	1,074,831	5,908,666
Payable to other funds		25,369				25,369
Payable to other governments	94,074					94,074
Deferred revenue	4,250,430	6,273,045	250,000	11,000		10,784,475
Total liabilities	7,753,184	6,428,389	440,548	1,115,632	1,074,831	16,812,584

Fund Balances

Reserved for:

Noncurrent assets	974,747					974,747
Encumbrances	40,292	41,034	119,314	5,792,587	1,814,122	7,807,349
Debt service					3,832,062	3,832,062
Other purposes					1,405,300	1,405,300
Unreserved, reported in:						
General fund	640,327					640,327
Special revenue funds		1,035,342			1,330,718	2,366,060
Capital projects funds			13,056,173	3,569,818	1,241,270	17,867,261
Total fund balances	1,655,366	1,076,376	13,175,487	9,362,405	9,623,472	34,893,106
Total liabilities and fund balances	$9,408,550	$7,504,765	$13,616,035	$10,478,037	$10,698,303	

> "Designations" of unreserved fund balances may be displayed, or disclosed in the notes.

Amounts reported for *governmental activities* in the Statement of Net Assets are different because:

Capital assets used in governmental activities are not financial resources and therefore are not reported in the funds	161,082,708
Other long-term assets are not available to pay for current-period expenditures and therefore are deferred in the funds	9,348,876
Internal service funds are used by management to charge the costs of certain activities, such as insurance and telecommunications to individual funds. The assets and liabilities of the internal service funds are included in governmental activities in the Statement of Net Assets	2,994,691
Long-term liabilities, including bonds payable, are not due and payable in the current period and therefore are not reported in the funds.	(84,760,507)
Net Assets of Governmental Activities	$123,558,874

Source: Adapted from working papers prepared by the staff of the Governmental Accounting Standards Board.

TABLE 2.15 Sample City: Statement of Revenues, Expenditures and Changes in Fund Balances, and Governmental Funds for Year Ended December 31, 2013

	General Fund	HUD Programs	Community Development	Route 7 Construction Fund	Other Governmental Funds	Total Governmental Funds
Revenues						
Property taxes	$ 51,173,436				$ 4,680,192	$ 55,853,628
Other taxes	13,025,392					13,025,392
Fees and fines	606,946					606,946
Licenses and permits	2,287,794					2,287,794
Intergovernmental	6,119,938	$ 2,578,191			2,830,916	11,529,045
Charges for services	11,374,460				30,708	11,405,168
Interest	552,325	87,106	$ 549,489	$ 270,161	364,330	1,823,411
Miscellaneous	881,874	66,176		2,939	94	951,083
Total revenues	86,022,165	2,731,473	549,489	273,100	7,906,240	97,482,467
Expenditures						
Current operating:						
General government	8,630,835		417,814	16,700	121,052	9,186,401
Public safety	33,729,623					33,729,623
Public works	4,975,774				3,721,542	8,697,317
Engineering services	1,299,645					1,299,645
Health and sanitation	6,070,032					6,070,032
Cemetery	706,305					706,305
Culture and recreation	11,411,685					11,411,685
Community development		2,954,389				2,954,389

Education—payment to school district	21,893,273					21,893,273
Debt service:						
Principal					3,450,000	3,450,000
Interest and other charges					5,215,151	5,215,151
Capital outlay			2,246,671	11,281,769	3,190,209	16,718,649
Total expenditures	88,717,173	2,954,389	2,664,485	11,298,469	15,697,954	121,332,470
Excess (deficiency) of revenue over expenditures	(2,695,008)	(222,916)	(2,114,996)	(11,025,369)	(7,791,714)	(23,850,003)
Other Financing Sources (Uses)						
Proceeds of refunding bonds					38,045,000	38,045,000
Proceeds of long-term capital debt			17,529,560		1,300,000	18,829,560
Payment to bond refunding escrow agent					(37,284,144)	(37,284,144)
Transfers in	129,323				5,551,187	5,680,510
Transfers out	(2,163,759)	(348,046)	(2,273,187)		(219,076)	(5,004,068)
Total other financing sources and uses	(2,034,436)	(348,046)	15,256,373		7,392,967	20,266,858
Special Item						
Proceeds from sale of park land	3,476,488					3,476,488
Net change in fund balance	(1,252,956)	(570,962)	13,141,377	(11,025,369)	(398,747)	(106,657)
Fund balances—beginning	2,908,322	1,647,338	34,110	20,387,774	10,022,219	34,999,763
Fund balances—ending	$ 1,655,366	$ 1,076,376	$ 13,175,487	$ 9,362,405	$ 9,623,472	$ 34,893,106

Source: Adapted from working papers prepared by the staff of the Governmental Accounting Standards Board.

TABLE 2.16   Sample City: Reconciliation of the Statement of Revenues, Expenditures, and Changes in Fund Balances of Governmental Funds to the Statement of Activities for Year Ended December 31, 2013

Net change in fund balances—total governmental funds (Table 2.15)	$ (106,657)
Amounts reported for *governmental activities* in the Statement of Activities are different because:	
Governmental funds report capital outlays as expenditures while governmental activities report depreciation expense to allocate those expenditures over the life of the assets. This is the amount by which capital outlays exceeded depreciation in the current period.	14,039,717
In the Statement of Activities, only the *gain* on the sale of the park land is reported, while in the governmental funds, the proceeds from the sale increase financial resources. Thus, the change in net assets differs from the change in fund balance by the cost of the land sold.	(823,000)
Revenues in the Statement of Activities that do not provide current financial resources are not reported as revenues in the funds.	1,920,630
Bond proceeds provide current financial resources to governmental funds, but issuing debt increases long-term liabilities in the Statement of Net Assets. Repayment of bond principal is an expenditure in the governmental funds, but the repayment reduces long-term liabilities in the Statement of Net Assets.	(16,140,416)
Some expenses reported in the Statement of Activities do not require the use of current financial resources and therefore are not reported as expenditures in governmental funds.	(1,245,752)
Internal service funds are used by management to charge the costs of certain activities, such as insurance and telecommunications to individual funds. The net revenue (expense) of the internal service funds is reported with governmental activities.	(758,808)
Change in Net Assets of Governmental Activities (Table 2.13)	$ (3,114,286)

Source: Adapted from working papers prepared by the staff of the Governmental Accounting Standards Board.

Every item listed in the fixed assets and liabilities informal system is offset by an "artificial" counteraccount. The asset counteraccount is typically listed as "investment" in general fixed assets. The liability counter-ccount is identified as some variant of "amounts to be provided from general government resources to repay debt." This double-entry approach enables an entity to incorporate the "lists" into the balance sheets without creating an imbalance in debts and credits.

The account groups are not given recognition in the new GASB Rule No. 34 reporting model. Even so, account groups have not been banished. Although governmental entities continue to maintain their accounting systems on the modified accrual fund basis, most entities find the account group system a useful means for tracking long-lived assets and long-term liabilities. This practice allows government to systematically gather information to incorporate into government-wide statements.

Double-Entry Bookkeeping: Some Basic Mechanics

The convention of debit and credit was designed to show the increases and decreases affecting a financial entity. For every debit, there must be an equal credit, and vice versa, to maintain an absolute balance or equality at all times. Before an entry can be made, all the possible accounts that can be debited or credited for the entity or organization must be known. The following must also be determined: all the asset accounts (things owned by the organization) such as cash, accounts receivable, inventory, and supplies; all the liabilities (claims or obligations others have against the organization) such as accounts payable and loans payable; all the revenue or income accounts such as taxes, donations, and endowments; and all the expenses/expenditures (expired costs, things to be acquired, or obligations against the organization), such as rent, postage, salaries, insurance, and travel.

An Illustration of Governmental Fund Accounting

A simplified example of the fund accounting journalizing and closing of the city of Bright is presented. This illustration includes the general fund, the internal service fund, and the debt service fund. Assume the following balances:

TABLE 2.17 City of Bright: General Fund Statement as of December 31, 2013

Assets		Liabilities and Fund Balance	
Cash	$26,000	Payables	$ 6,000
		Unrestricted fund balance	20,000
	$26,000		$ 26,000

The following transactions took place during the 2004 fiscal year:

1. Budgeted revenues by source:

Property taxes	$ 600,000
Court fines	100,000
Other taxes	300,000
	$1,000,000

Budgeted expenditures by function:

Administration	$ 200,000
Fire/police	300,000
Sanitation	100,000
	$ 600,000

Payments to:

Motor pool fund	$ 40,000
Debt service fund	60,000
Utility fund	90,000
Special assessment fund	100,000
Working capital fund	10,000
Total	$ 900,000
Budgeted fund balance	$ 100,000

2. The tax assessor's office mailed property tax statements to taxpayers amounting to $600,000.
3. Other revenues in the amount of $400,000, including $100,000 of court fines, were collected.
4. Property taxes in the amount of $500,000 were collected.
5. Expenditures for the period are as follows:

Administration	$ 102,000
Fire/police	198,000
Sanitation	100,000

Payments:

Motor pool fund	$ 40,000
Debt service fund	60,000
Utility fund	90,000
Special assessment fund	100,000
Working capital fund	$ 10,000
	$ 700,000

6. A contract in the amount of $250,000 was placed for equipment and supplies.
7. A truck originally costing $10,000 was no longer needed and was sold for $2,000.
8. Receipts of goods and supplies in the amount of $190,000 were delivered relating to encumbrances of $200,000.

9. Vouchers of $790,000 were approved for payment, including $90,000 to the utility fund, $100,000 to the assessment fund, $40,000 to the motor pool fund, and $60,000 to the debt service fund.
10. Payables in the amount of $5,000 were paid.
11. Close the revenue and expenditure accounts.

TABLE 2.18   General Fund Books' Journal

Transaction	Entry	Debit	Credit

1. Adoption of budget for fiscal year ending Dec. 31, 2004, indicating estimated revenues of $1,000,000 and appropriations of $900,000.	Estimated Revenues
	  Appropriations
	  Unrestricted fund balance
		$1,000,000	$900,000
			
			100,000

2. Accrual of income from tax levy.	Taxes receivable Revenues	600,000	600,000
3. To record the receipt of realization of other taxes.	Cash Revenues	400,000	400,000
4. Collection of taxes previously levied.	Cash Taxes receivable	500,000	500,000

5. Expenditures made in accordance with appropriations.	Expenditures
	  Vouchers payable
	  Due to utility fund
	  Due to special assessment fund
	  Due to working capital
	  Due to motor pool fund
	  Due to debtservice fund
		800,000	400,000
			90,000
			
			100,000
			10,000
			
			40,000
			
			60,000

6. Estimates of expenditures for orders placed for supplies and equipment.	Encumbrances Reserve for encumbrances	250,000	250,000
7. Sold truck at auction.	Cash Revenues	2,000	2,000

(Continued)

TABLE 2.18   *(Continued)*

Transaction	Entry	Debit	Credit
8. Liquidation of encumbrances ($200,000) upon receipt of invoices and determination of actual expenditures ($190,000) to record the obligation ($190,000) and approve vouchers to be paid.	Reserve for encumbrances Encumbrances Expenditures Vouchers payable	250,000 190,000	 250,000 190,000
9. Payment of vouchers and billing.	Vouchers payable Due to utility fund Due to assessment fund Due to motor pool fund Due to debt-service fund Due to working capital Cash	500,000 90,000 100,000 40,000 60,000 10,000	 790,000
10. Paid payables in the amount of $5,000.	Payables Cash	5,000	 5,000
11. Closing the accounts.	Revenues Estimated revenues	1,002,000	 1,000,000
To close revenues and estimated revenue accounts at end of fiscal year.	Revenues Fund balance		2,000
To close appropriations, expenditures, and encumbrances at end of fiscal year. To restrict fund balance due to outstanding encumbrances.	Appropriations Fund balance Expenditures Encumbrances	900,000 40,000	 890,000 50,000

Transactions 1 through 10 in the General Fund Books' Journal must be posted into a set of books called the "ledgers" (the place where the summaries of all accounts are recorded on a regular basis—for example, weekly or monthly). The ledgers represent "T" accounts having a debit and credit side. The "T" accounts for transactions 1–10 are as follows:

A. Balance Sheet "T" Accounts

Cash			
*B Bal.	$ 20,000	(9)	$790,000
(3)	400,000	(10)	5,000
(4)	500,000		
(7)	2,000		
E. Bal.	127,000		

Taxes Receivable			
(2)	$600,000	(4)	$500,000
E. Bal.	100,000		

Due to Working Capital Fund			
** E. Bal.		(5)	$10,000

Payables			
(10)	$5,000	B. Bal.	$6,000
		E. Bal.	1,000

Due to Utility Fund			
(8)	$90,000	(5)	$90,000

Reserve for Encumbrances			
(7)	$200,000	(6)	$250,000
E. Bal.			50,000

Vouchers Payable			
(9)	500,000	(5)	400,000
		(8)	190,000
E. Bal.			90,000
E. Bal.			90,000

Fund Balance			
(9)	100,000	B. Bal.	$ 14,000
(C2)	40,000	(1)	100,000
		(C1)	2,000
E. Bal.	24,000		

Due to Special-Assessment Fund			
(8)	$100,000	(5)	$100,000

Due to Motor Pool			
(9)	$40,000	(5)	$40,000

Due to Debt-Service Fund			
(9)	$60,000	(5)	$60,000

*B Bal. means beginning balance.
**E. Bal. means ending balance.

FIGURE 2.3   A. Balance sheet "T" accounts.

Treatment of Encumbrances on the Books

The transactions just shown do not use the restricted and unrestricted fund balance. The alternate way for reflecting the outstanding reserve for encumbrances at the end of the period is as follows: Treat the reserve for encumbrance accounts as a nominal account and close it out as a regular income statement transaction. Thus,

B. Expenditure/Expense and Revenue "T" Accounts

Expenditures			
(5)	$800,000	(C2)	$890,000
(7)	190,000		
	890,000		890,000

Encumbrances			
(6)	$250,000	(8)	200,000
		(C2)	50,000
	250,000		250,000

Estimated Revenues			
(1)	$1,000,000	(9)	$1,000,000
	1,000,000		1,000,000

Appropriations			
(9)	$900,000	(1)	$900,000
	900,000		900,000

Revenues			
(C1)	$1,002,000	(2)	$600,000
		(3)	400,000
		(7)	2,000
	1,002,000		1,002,000

FIGURE 2.4   B. Expenditure/expense and revenue "T" accounts.

TABLE 2.19   Fund Accounting Basis

Fund Type	Fund Categories	Measurement Focus	Basis of Accounting
1. General	Governmental	Spending	Modified Accrual
2. Special Revenue	Governmental	Spending	Modified Accrual
3. Capital Projects	Governmental	Spending	Modified Accrual
4. Debt Service	Governmental	Spending	Modified Accrual
5. Special Assessments	Governmental	Spending	Modified Accrual
6. Enterprise	Proprietary	Capital Maintenance	Accrual
7. Internal Service	Proprietary	Capital Maintenance	Accrual
8. Trust and Agency: Agency	Fiduciary	---	Modified Accrual
Pension Trust	Fiduciary	Capital Maintenance	Accrual
Expendable Trust	Fiduciary	Spending	Modified Accrual
Nonexpendable Trust	Fiduciary	Capital Maintenance	Accrual
9. Permanent Restricted Endowment	Fiduciary	Capital Maintenance	Accrual

Source: Adapted from Paul E. Glick How to Understand Local Government Financial Statements: A User's Guide (Chicago, Ill: Government Finance Officers Association, 1986, p. 11), and Governmental Accounting. http://www.kirkwoodmo.org/mm/files/governmental-accounting.pdf

at the end of the period, the outstanding reserve for the encumbrance amount is closed. For example, in our case, we have a $50,000 encumbrance balance. This amount would be closed on the expenditure side and set up on the balance sheet as follows: (a) Debit the reserve for encumbrance for $50,000 and credit the encumbrance by $50,000, and (b) debit the unrestricted fund balance for $50,000 and credit the restricted fund balance for $50,000, earmarking and reducing the amount available to be spent and showing the amount outstanding and obligated.

Lapsing Assumptions A and B: Legal Provisions

These assumptions are the most frequently used assumptions in public and not-for-profit agencies. This is an important concern that determines how unspent or unused appropriated resources will be reflected in closing entries, and how much discretion and trust are given to the administrators in settling outstanding obligations. Under assumption A, encumbered appropriations do not lapse. The reserve for encumbrance accounts remains on the books as a continuing authorization to spend until the objective of the authorization has been fulfilled. The closing entries recognize whatever the outstanding obligations (amounts) are as expenditure as follows:

Expenditure   xxx (debited);
Encumbrance   xxx (credited)

Under assumption B, the unexpended appropriations lapse and unspent resources are returned to the authorizing body. All outstanding unfilled orders relating to appropriations are closed as follows:

Reserve for encumbrance   xxx (debited);
Encumbrance   xxx (credited)

Unlike assumption A, assumption B does *not* delegate discretion to administrators to liquidate outstanding obligations. Thus, authority to expend funds for past unfilled orders will lapse and must be reauthorized or reappropriated during the following year.

It is important that administrators and vendors dealing with public and other not-for-profit agencies know the assumption under which they are operating when transacting business. Not knowing the operating assumption may create unnecessary problems.

Disclosing and Controlling Supplies Inventories

The balance sheet is designed to reflect the value of appropriable (spendable) resources and identifiable claims against such resources. The present system applies the acquisition approach. An expenditure is charged at the time the purchase is made as follows:

Expenditure (debited);
Vouchers payable or cash (credited)

Because this approach treats inventory supplies on hand as a nonappropriatable resource, they are excluded from the balance sheet or the general fund assets. The principle of full disclosure suggests that the cost of significant supplies on hand should be shown on the balance sheet. This can be done by using a memo entry:

Inventory supplies (debited);
Reserve for inventory supplies (credited)

When this system is used, the memo account is adjusted periodically to account for increases and decreases in the balance of supplies on hand at the end of a fiscal period. If a reduction in the supplies on hand occurs, a reversing memo entry is made. An increase is recorded by another memo.

Important reasons for reflecting the inventory on hand at the end of the period may relate to management's need to increase control over the efficient use of supplies and minimize waste and abuse. By reflecting the inventory in the account, it draws management's attention to the need for a prudent use of supplies. This recognition is likely to make employees more sensitive to misusing or casually removing supplies from the organization. Responsibility managers are not permitted to incrementally increase their budget for supplies without considering what is on hand when this practice is used.

The manipulation of an entity's inventory accounts is a financial statement fraud technique seen frequently in private sector misstatements. Inventory can be subject to high turnover, market valuation fluctuations, and intentional double-counting, making it difficult for auditors to test and verify stated amounts. In the early 1990s, Crazy Eddie, a chain of consumer electronic stores, and the company's family-run management were found guilty of financial statement fraud; this violated the Securities and Exchange Commission Act of 1934.[14] The fraud was achieved by understating cost of goods sold and overstating the company's inventory, thus inflating net income.[15] Through the fraudulent overstatement of this one account, the company was able to increase reported profits and inflate the share price of Crazy Eddie stock. Management collusion was instrumental in this case, so external and internal auditors, even those involved in public audits, should be keenly aware of inventory's susceptibility to manipulation. Effective internal controls and high accountability and reporting transparency standards can mitigate the risk of inventory misstatement.

The misstatement of inventory accounts on a government entity's financial statements would not be intended to inflate profits/share price, but rather to hide the inefficient use of supplies or to overstate assets to appear more financially stable. As municipal, state, and federal government entities come under increasing pressure to operate as efficiently as possible, officials may look to inventory as an account that can be adjusted to create the illusion of superior fiscal performance.

Controlling Subsidiary Entries

This is a means of maintaining a check between what is entered in the subsidiary ledger accounts and the individual details that support the summary totals entered in the controlling ledger account. To record the adoption of the city of Bright's budget, the subsidiary account can be reflected as follows:

TABLE 2.20   City of Bright: Subsidiary Account

Estimated revenues	$ 1,000,000	
Debit revenue subsidiary ledger:		
Property taxes	600,000	
Court fines	100,000	
Other taxes	300,000	
	$ 1,000,000	
Appropriations	$ 900,000	
Fund balance	100,000	
Credit expenditure subsidiary ledger:		
Administration		$ 200,000
Fire/police		300,000
Sanitation		100,000
Motor pool fund		40,000
Debtservice fund		60,000
Utility fund		90,000
Specialassessment fund		100,000
Working capital fund		10,000
		$ 900,000

In order to minimize errors, facilitate tracking and coordination, and maintain the account balance, a system known as a "chart or code of accounts" is used. The following is an example:

1. All asset accounts may be identified as follows:
    22.   Cash
    22.1 Petty Cash

      33.   Accounts Receivable

      33.1 Allowance for Uncollectible Accounts

2. All liabilities and fund balances may be identified as follows:

      40. Accounts Payable

      41. Boards

      42. Long-Term Debt

      50. Fund Balance

3. All revenue and expense and expenditure accounts may be identified as follows:

      60.   Personnel Services

      60.1   Regular Employees

      60.2   Replacement and Overtime

      61.   Contractual Services

      61.1   Utilities

      61.1.1 Fuel

      61.1.2 Water Sewer Fund

      70.   Property Taxes

      71.   Sales Taxes

The number of accounts is limited only by the degree of detail desired by the managers of the organization or enterprise.

Understanding Debits and Credits

According to the system of accounting logic, increases (+) in assets and expense accounts are accumulated on the left and decrease (−) on the right, while whereas, equity (capital), and revenue accounts increases (+) are accumulated place on the right and decrease (−) on the left. By applying this system consistently, the balance in an account can be determined at any given point in time as follows:

FIGURE 2.5   Assets "T" account.

The system is based on the accounting equation *assets (resources) = liabilities (creditors' claims against resources) + owners' equity (owners' claims against resources)*, or

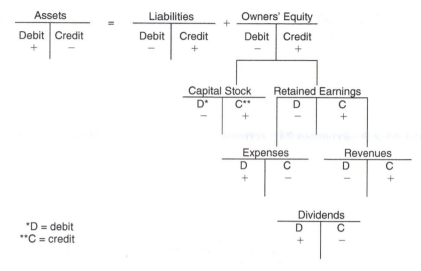

FIGURE 2.6   System is based on the accounting equation.

Again, in applying the accounting equation logic to liabilities and capital accounts, increases (+) are accumulated on the right side and decreases (–) on the left, as follows:

Assets			=	Liabilities			+	Capital	
Debit	Credit			Debit	Credit			Debit	Credit
+	–			–	+			–	+

FIGURE 2.7   "T" accounts showing assets = liabilities + capital.

In accounting, the left side of an account is known as the *debit side,* and the right side is known as the *credit side.* There is no intrinsic value to debit and credit other than what the accounting convention has assigned to them.

So far, we have dealt with items found in the balance sheet (assets, liabilities, and capital). Because the accounts in the balance sheet are not closed out at the end of the period, they are referred to as *real accounts.* The reverse is true for income statement accounts: They are known as *nominal accounts* and are closed out to the capital account at the end of the fiscal period. Thus, the debit/credit analysis of revenues and expenses is related directly to capital. Revenue (credit) increases capital, whereas expenses (debit) decrease capital, as shown in the following:

Revenues	
Debit	Credit
–	+

FIGURE 2.8   Revenues "T" account.

Following the same logic for expenses, an increase (debit) in expense produces a decrease in capital, as follows:

FIGURE 2.9   Expenses "T" account.

By memorizing a few basic rules, the system of debits and credits can be easily applied:

TABLE 2.21

	To Increase Accounts	To Decrease Accounts
Assets	Debit	Credit
Liabilities	Credit	Debit
Revenues	Credit	Debit
Expenditures/expenses	Debit	Credit
Capital/fund balance	Credit	Debit

To determine the net income/loss or net deficit or surplus (in not-for-profit agencies), all revenues are totaled and all expenditures are totaled and subtracted from revenue for each fiscal period.

Break-Even Analysis and Revenue and Expense Estimating

Break-even analysis is a tool that has been widely used in the private sector. Although there are some constraints in applying it to the not-for-profit sector (for example, the assumption that there is a direct relationship between revenues and outputs, which is not typically true), there are opportunities where it may be employed, especially in those agencies that are client-oriented.

Variable and fixed costs are two key elements in determining the break-even point of a project, program, or organization. Fixed costs are those costs that do not change in total as the volume of clients or patients changes, given that the volume occurs over a relevant range; after a certain point, an increase in volume may require an organization to occur additional fixed costs. In Figure 2.10, the fixed cost can be viewed as the horizontal line on the graph.

For any quantity of outputs measured on the horizontal axis, the total cost will amount to $A. Whatever the volume of B measured on the vertical axis, the fixed cost will always be $A, assuming that the activity stays within the

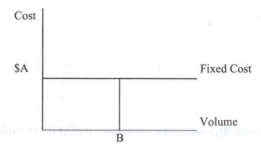

FIGURE 2.10   Graph depicting fixed cost.

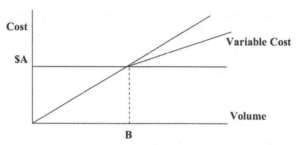

FIGURE 2.11   Graph depicting variable cost.

relevant range (range of volume over which fixed costs and variable costs vary in direct proportion).

Figure 2.11 depicts variable costs. As the volume (indicated by B) rises on the horizontal axis, the variable costs rise on the vertical axis in direct proportion. A greater volume change occurs in B.

Break-even analysis determines the volume whereby a service or program becomes self-sufficient. Any increase in volume, after the break-even point, generates a profit/surplus; alternatively, any decline in volume will produce a loss. Thus, to produce a surplus/profit net revenue, the inflow must always exceed net expenses or outflow. The break-even point can be represented as follows:

$$\text{Revenue} = \text{Fixed Cost} + \text{Variable Cost.}$$

The break-even point is defined as that level of activity whereby total revenues equal total expenses or expired costs. At this level of operation, the organization will neither realize a profit nor incur an operating loss—the ideal operating point for not-for-profit organizations. While break-even analysis can be applied to past periods, it is most helpful when used to aid in future planning/budgeting, and where curtailment of operations is an objective.

Break-even analysis assumes that costs can be broken down into variable and fixed components. The main purpose of this analysis is to determine the level of output whereby revenue includes both fixed and variable costs. The break-even point can be calculated by means of a formula, or it can be determined from a graphic presentation of the relationship among cost, revenue, and the level or volume of productive capacity. Before the break-even sales volume (known as the *equation approach*) can be determined, the following data are required: (1) estimated fixed costs and expenses for a given period, such as a year and (2) total estimated variable costs and expenses for the same period. The second approach is based on the unit contribution margin.

The equation approach is as follows: *sales (number of units × unit price) = variable cost + fixed cost*. Take, as an example, a situation in which the sales price is $2 per unit, variable costs are $1 per unit, and fixed costs are $3,000:

$$\text{Let } Q = \text{ the units at break-even}$$
$$2Q = Q + \$3,000$$
$$Q = 3,000 \text{ units}$$

If we are unsure about additional fixed costs that might be incurred because of an undertaking, we might include an additional expense or "overrecovery" to compensate for the uncertainty. Assuming that the overrecovery cost is predicted to be $50, the equation would then appear as follows:

$$2Q = Q + 3,000 + 50 \text{ (desired overrecovery cushion)}$$
$$2Q - Q = 300 + 50$$
$$Q = 3,050 \text{ units}$$

In the *unit contribution approach*, the unit contribution margin (unit price minus variable cost) is the amount that the extra sale unit provides to cover the fixed costs plus profit. This approach calculates the number of units necessary to cover fixed expenses or any overrecovery. Two break-even formulas are presented. The first provides for break-even in units, the second in dollars.

$$Break\text{-}even \ \ units = \frac{fixed \ \ costs}{unit \ \ contribution \ \ margin} \text{ or } \frac{FC}{SP - VC}$$

Using information in the above example, we solve for break-even in units as follows:

$$Q = \frac{3,000}{(2Q - Q)}$$
$$Q = 3,000 \text{ units}$$

$$Break\text{-}even\ in\ dollars = \frac{Fixed\ Cost}{contribution\ margin\ ratio}$$
$$(unit\ contribution\ margin \div selling\ price\ per\ unit)$$

FIGURE 2.12   Break-even in dollars equation.

Again, using the information in the above example, we solve for break-even in dollars:

$$Break\text{-}even\ dollars = \frac{FC}{(SP-VC)\div(SP)} = \frac{\$3,000}{(1 \div 2)} = \frac{\$3,000}{.50}$$
$$Q = \$1,500$$

The same formula can be used to calculate the revenue per unit fee. Let us assume that a governmental unit wants to know the fee it needs to charge for building inspection that would allow for at least a break-even outcome. If there are 5,000 building inspections that are typically made yearly with $400,000 in fixed costs and variable costs of $80,000, what is the break-even required fee per inspection? It is calculated as follows:

$$Revenue\ per\ inspection = \frac{Fixed\ cost}{Number\ of\ Inspection} + \frac{Variable}{Number\ of\ inspections}$$
$$Revenue\ per\ inspection = \frac{\$400,000}{5,000} + \frac{\$80,000}{5,000}$$
$$= \$96\ per\ building\ inspection$$

FIGURE 2.13   Revenue per inspection equations.

By using the same equation (equating sales with revenue), we can find the surplus or deficit:

$$Net\ surplus\ at\ revenue\ of\ \$15,000\ fixed\ cost = (revenue \times contribution\ margin\ ratio) -$$
$$= (\$15,000 \times .50) - \$3,000$$
$$= \$7,500 - \$3,000)$$
$$= \$4,500$$

$$Find\ the\ revenue\ to\ yield\ a\ surplus\ of\ \$6,000 = \frac{Fixed\ cost + Target\ surplus}{Contribution\ ratio}$$
$$= \frac{\$3,000 + \$6,000}{.50}$$
$$= \$18,000$$

FIGURE 2.14   Find the revenue to yield a surplus of $6,000.

With the information from this above example (the equation approach), a break-even chart can be used to determine the break-even point as shown in Figure 2.15. A break-even chart is developed in the following manner:

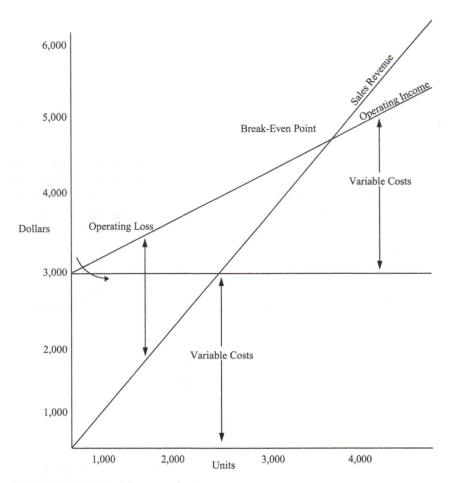

FIGURE 2.15   Break-even chart.

$$Contribution\ Margin(CM) = Selling\ Price - Variable\ Cost$$
$$CM = \$40 - 30 = \$10$$
$$Break\text{-}even\ unit = \frac{Fixed\ cost}{CM}$$
$$= \frac{10,000}{10}$$
$$= 1,000\ units$$

FIGURE 2.16   Contribution Margin (CM) equation.

- The number of units to be produced by an organization is plotted along the horizontal axis, and dollar amounts representing operating data are plotted along the vertical axis.
- A diagonal line representing sales is drawn from the lower left corner to the upper right corner.
- A point representing fixed costs is drawn horizontally, paralleling the horizontal axis.
- The point where sales (revenue) and total costs intersect is the *break-even point*. The areas representing operating income and operating loss are thus identified.

Once the various cost components have been determined, break-even analysis can be innovatively applied to a number of not-for-profit organizations where unit cost information is maintained on the delivery of services. The following indicates an application: A state school for the blind produces knit floor rugs that are very popular. To encourage the development of multiple skills, however, the state sharply reduces its subsidy to rug making beyond the break-even point. It has been determined that the selling price for the rugs is $40, the labor cost is $20, the cost for materials is $10, and the fixed costs are $10,000. What is the break-even point?

Determining Fixed Cost, Selling Price, and Variable Cost and Applying the Break-Even Formula

The formula that is used to determine break-even in units can be used to find any variable. Clinic 5 has fixed costs of $2,200,000, revenue per patient of $225, and variable costs of $105 per patient and operates at a capacity of 15,000 patients. How much would the clinic need to charge per patient to break even? The break-even (BE) formula is applied as follows:

TABLE 2.22   Break-Even Formula as Applied to Clinic Five

$$BE = \frac{FC}{SP - VC}$$

$$15,000 = \frac{\$2,200,000}{P - \$105}$$

15,000	× (SP − $105)	=	$2,200,000
15,000P	− $1,575,000	=	$2,200,000
	15,000P	=	$2,200,000 + $1,575,000
	15,000P	=	$3,775,000
	SP	=	$251.67

If the Clinic 5 is able to collect $251.67 per visit, the clinic would break even. If this fee is imposed, the number of Clinic 5 patients would likely drop sharply, and the clinic would experience a loss. If, however, Clinic 5 wants to keep the patient fee at $150 per visit and the variable cost at $105 per patient, what would be the most the clinic could spend on fixed costs and still break even with 15,000 expected patients?

TABLE 2.23   The Most Clinic Five Could Spend on Fixed Cost and Still Break Even with 15,000 Expected Patients

BE	$=$	$\dfrac{FC}{SP - VC}$
15,000	$=$	$\dfrac{FC}{SP - VC}$
15,000	$\times$ ($150 - $105)	$=$ FC
FC	$=$	15,000 $\times$ ($150 - $105) $=$
FC	$=$	15,000 $\times$ $45
	$=$	$675,000

Clinic 5 would break even if the fixed cost is lowered to $675,000. Assume, however, that the clinic's examination shows that it could not reduce fixed costs below $1,200,000. If Clinic 5 decides to keep revenue per patient at $150 with 15,000 patient visits and fixed cost lowered only to $1,200,000, what is the most the variable cost can be to achieve break-even?

TABLE 2.24   Clinic Five: The Most the Variable Cost Can Be to Achieve Break-Even

BE	$=$	$\dfrac{FC}{SP - VC}$	
15,000	$=$	$\dfrac{\$1,200,000}{\$150 - VC}$	
15,000	$\times$ ($150 - VC)	$=$	$1,200,000
15,000	$\times$ $150 - $15,000 VC	$=$	$1,200,000
$2,250,000	$-$ 15,000 VC	$=$	$1,200,000
$2,250,000	$-$ $1,200,000	$=$	15,000 VC
	$1,050,000	$=$	15,000 VC
	VC	$=$	1,050,000/15,000
	VC	$=$	$70.00

Margin of Safety

All organizations wish to raise more revenue than the break-even level. The excess over the break-even revenue level is called the *margin of safety*. This is the amount that revenue can drop before the agency or governmental unit incurs a loss. The margin of safety can be expressed in units or dollars or as a percentage of the predicted level of revenue. For example, if expected revenues are $100,000, the margin of safety is $20,000 above the break-even revenue of $80,000. As a percent of the margin of safety, it is 20 percent of expected revenue:

$$Margin \ of \ safety = \frac{Expected \ revenues \ - \ Break\text{-}even \ revenue}{Expected \ revenues}$$

$$= \frac{\$100,000 - 80,000}{\$100,000} = 20 \ percent$$

It is important to note that the higher the margin of safety percentage, the greater the leeway that the agency manager or governmental unit has in making decisions that would increase expenses before it will incur a deficit. The margin of safety provides a cushion that management can use as a guide to maintain the break-even level or generate a surplus.

Operating Leverage

The *operating leverage* is especially useful when managers begin the planning process and want to predict outcomes for alternative strategies. These strategies may entail changes in revenue, fixed costs, and variable costs. Managers would like to know the effects of some or all of these factors.

A major goal of all managers is to obtain the maximum benefit from fixed costs. The objective is to use 100 percent of fixed cost capacity so that the unit fixed cost will be as low as possible, within the relevant range. The magnitude of fixed costs in the total cost structure, so in relation to variable and semi-variable costs, is known as *operating leverage*. When an agency has a higher proportion of fixed costs in its total cost structure, it is viewed as "operating on higher leverage," such as an agency that automates and increases its fixed costs and lowers its variable costs. Operating leverage is a useful managerial measure that can help assess the effect of surplus/deficit on the *degree of operating leverage* (DOL), defined as follows:

Total contribution margin (in dollars) ÷ surplus.

Assume that a social counseling agency has 1,200 client visits, with clients paying $45 per visit; variable costs of $15 per unit; and fixed costs of $24,000. The total margin contribution is $36,000 (1,200 visits × $30 contribution margin per unit). After subtracting fixed costs of $24,000, the projected surplus is $12,000 ($36,000 − 24,000). The degree of operating leverage for the social agency is 3.0. It is computed as the contribution margin divided by projected surplus ($35,000 ÷ 12,000). We can use the DOL to assess the effect of changes on the level of revenue required to produce the surplus. If the social counseling agency increases revenue by 10 percent, it will generate a 30 percent increase in surplus. Generally, the higher the DOL, the higher the risk of shortfalls, because it requires more revenue to cover a larger proportion fixed costs; conversely, once the break-even revenue point has been obtained, a larger surplus will result, as only a relatively small portion of variable costs must then be covered.

Alternative Break-Even Method

An alternate method may be employed to obtain the break-even point, indicated as follows:

$$(FR - FC) = (VRPU - VCPU) \times SV, \text{ where}$$

$$FR = \text{fixed revenue}$$

$$FC = \text{fixed costs}$$

$$VRPU = \text{variable revenue per unit}$$

$$VCPU = \text{variable costs per unit}$$

$$SV = \text{service volume}$$

This formula emphasizes the difference between fixed revenue and fixed costs. When fixed revenue exceeds fixed costs, a net fixed surplus is generated. Likewise, when fixed costs exceed fixed revenue, a deficit is produced. We can determine the contribution margin per unit of service by subtracting the variable cost per unit of service from the variable revenue per unit of service. This can be restated by the following break-even formula:

$$NFS/D = CMPU \times SV, \text{ where}$$

$$NFS/D = \text{net fixed surplus/deficit}$$

$$CMPU = \text{contribution margin per unit}$$

$$SV = \text{service volume}$$

The total contribution margin can hence be obtained for the following nonprofit case: in the program, Prevention of Teenage Drug and Alcohol Abuse, the contribution margin per unit of service is $4 ($14 − 10). The contribution margin percentage times the volume of service produces the total contribution margin. In the example, there are 8,000 client sessions, so the total contribution is $32,000 ($4 × 8,000).

Because of the above restatement, a single measure can be used to determine the net benefits from volume changes. For example, in the not-for-profit program, Prevention of Teenage Drug and Alcohol Abuse, the purpose of the service is to counsel teenagers between the ages of 12 and 17. The fees are set to permit most high-risk teenagers to avail themselves of the services, because the fees are based on family income. (This was stipulated by a foundation that provided a six-year annual grant of $40,000.) The 1996 client sessions numbered 8,000. Each client revenue intake averages $14. The operating fixed cost is $60,000 per year, whereas the variable fixed cost is $10 per session.

When fixed revenues and variable revenues are combined, they produce a revenue forecasting formula as follows:

$$TR = FR + (VCPS \times NCS), \text{ where}$$

$$TR = \text{total revenue}$$

$$FR = \text{fixed revenue}$$

$$VCPS = \text{variable cost per session}$$

$$NCS = \text{number of client sessions}$$

TABLE 2.25   Operating Statement for Year Ending 1996 as Reflected in the Program Data

Fixed components:		
Fixed revenues	$ 40,000	
Fixed expenses		$ (60,000)
Net fixed deficit		($20,000)
Variable components:		
Variable revenues		14
Variable expenses		(10)
Contribution margin per unit		$ 4
Total contribution margin ($4 x 8,000)		$32,000
Surplus		$12,000

The application of the formula permits us to estimate the revenues at a given volume. Thus, if Prevention of Teenage Drug and Alcohol Abuse estimates 7,200 client sessions, the projected revenues would be $140,800 (or $40,000 + [$14 × 7,200]). This flexible budget for revenue generates the following formula:

$$Total \ revenue = a + b(x), \text{ where}$$

$$a = \text{fixed revenue}$$

$$b = \text{variable revenue per service unit}$$

$$x = \text{volume or level of service produced}$$

On the cost side, applying the same reasoning and analysis as was done for revenues and assuming projected units of 7,000 per client session, the following formula expresses the relationships between total cost due to changes in the volume of service:

$$TC = FC + (VCPS \times NCS), \text{ where}$$

$$TC = \text{total cost}$$

$$FC = \text{fixed costs}$$

$$VCPS = \text{variable cost per session}$$

$$NCS = \text{number of client sessions}$$

It generates the following formula:

$$Total\ Costs = a + b(x), \text{ where}$$

$$a = \text{total fixed cost}$$

$$b = \text{variable cost per service unit}$$

$$x = \text{volume or level of service produced}$$

Again, applying the flexible budget cost approach, the projected cost for an estimated volume of 7,000 client sessions would be $123,000 (or $60,000 + [$9 × 7,000]).

Figure 2.17 provides a graphic alternate way for determining the break-even point of Prevention of Teenage Drug and Alcohol Abuse. It clearly indicates the fixed and variable costs and revenues. The break-even point shows the volume of service units at 6,000 on the × axis, whereas the y axis shows $124,000. If the existing relationships remain, the greater the number of sessions handled beyond the break-even point, the larger the surplus will be. The reverse is also true: As the number of client sessions declines, the deficit will increase. Whenever revenue decreases, whether fixed or variable, achieving the break-even point becomes harder.

Break-Even Analysis for Multiple Services

In a number of services, there are many activities whereby multiple rate payers are charged varying rates for different service procedures within the same responsibility center. In the health care area, Diagnosis-Related Groups (DRGs) are grouped and applied uniformly to each type of procedure or visit to a physician. To obtain a meaningful and close approximation to the true

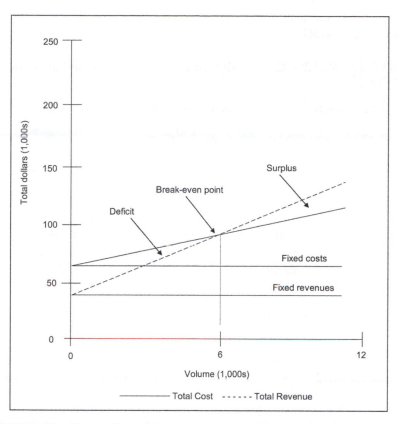

FIGURE 2.17 Prevention of teenage drug and alcohol abuse program cost volume.

break-even point, it is necessary to calculate an average weighted price and cost for the participating patients in each of the DRGs. The following are the patient and rate distributions for which the weighted average price must be determined. This can be calculated as follows:[16]

TABLE 2.26 Patient and Rate Distributions for Which the Weighted Average Price Must Be Determined

Weight of Patients %		Rate $		Weighted Revenue $
DRG 1 20	×	400	=	80
DRG 2 37	×	3,000	=	1,110
DRG 3 43	×	900	=	387
		Weighted Average Price		$ 1,577

we need to calculate the variable costs weighted for the proportion of patient in each DRG:

TABLE 2.27   Variable Costs Weighted for the Proportion of Patient in Each DRG

Percent of Patients %		Variable Cost $		Weighted Revenue $
DRG1 20	×	250	=	50
DRG2 37	×	2,000	=	740
DRG3 43	×	700	=	301
		Weighted Variable Cost		$ 1,091

Let us now calculate the break-even volume of admission for the appropriate fixed cost as shown in Table 2.27. We must find the cost for the entire hospital, plus the program's specific fixed costs and the hospital-wide joint costs:

$$Q = \frac{FC}{SP - VC} = \frac{\$660,000}{\$1,577 - \$1,091} = 1,358 \text{ patients}$$

To find the break-even volume of patients for the hospital as a whole, we have to include not only the fixed program-specific costs, but also the joint costs, as shown in Table 2.27. The fixed costs thus become $660,000. The 1,358 patients are the volume required for break-even admissions, which consists of 20 percent for DRG1 patients, 37 percent for DRG2 patients, and 43 percent for DRG3 patients. Obviously, if the required break-even for each DRG was calculated by using only the program-specific fixed costs, the volume of patients would be lower. However, when the joint and specific fixed costs shown in Table 2.27 are included in the fixed costs, the patients required for break-even would have to be increased. The break-even for the social functions at the Montrose Hospital is calculated as shown in Table 2.28.

TABLE 2.28   Montrose Hospital Data for Multiple Types of Patients

Type of Service	% of Patients in this DRG $	Rate of Reimbursement $	Program-Specific Fixed Costs $	Variable Cost $
DRG1	20	400	40,000	250
DRG2	37	3,000	90,000	2,000
DRG3	43	990	130,000	700
	100	Joint Costs	400,000	
			660,000	

Source: Adapted from Steven A. Finkler and David Ward, *Essentials of Cost Accounting for Health Care Organizations,* 2nd ed. (Gaithersburg, MD, 1999), p. 109.

Financial Ratios

The Private Sector

The dynamic and changing environment and complexity of modern for-profit-oriented business requires the use of well-developed information systems for reporting and analysis. Accounting lies at the heart of such systems. Recently there has been a trend in the private sector to adopt enterprise resource planning (ERP) information systems, which allow companies to integrate, analyze, and report on information from all segments of the organization. Accounting techniques can provide a condensed, internally consistent picture of the firm. The *balance sheet* gives us a capsule summary of the financial status of a business at a particular point in time, usually at the end of a company's fiscal year. During the period between two balance sheets, the *income statement* summarizes the firm's operations and financial performance. Financial ratio analysis provides a useful means for interpreting these accounting statements, as it examines the relationships between the different accounting totals. Ratios are calculated and interpreted in order to answer questions such as the following: How liquid is the entity? How well does it use its resources? Is the entity's debt financing reasonable given the industry and current economic conditions? Are the profits reasonable for the sales level and resources invested?

Financial Ratios as Predictors of Default

Typically, when funds are borrowed, debt contracts state the minimum compliance conditions, referred to as covenants, in terms of balance sheet ratios. There are important reasons why ratios have been found to be useful predictors of financial distress and bankruptcy. The most useful ratio predictors have been (1) cash flow to total debt, (2) net income to total sales, (3) total debt to total assets, (4) working capital to total assets, and (5) current ratio.

Ratios and Credit Quality

The key financial ratios that bond rating agencies, banks, insurance companies, and trade credit suppliers often use in assessing a firm's credit quality fall into four categories: (1) *profitability*—the ability of a firm to earn income by analyzing the ratios of net income to sales, earnings of operations to sales, and return on equity; (2) *activity*—with creditors and owners assessing the ability of management to use the assets at its disposal by examining the ratios of a firm's sales per dollar of average investment for specific asset categories and the ratio of sales to the firm's average total assets (asset turnover such as receivable turnover, inventory turnover, and total asset turnover); (3) *liquidity*—estimating the ability of a firm to generate cash from assets to meet obligations, assessing the acid test ratio (cash, marketable securities, short-term notes, and receivables divided by current liabilities), current ratio (current assets divided by current liabilities), and the ratio of cash flow to total debt (earnings plus depreciation plus additions to the deferred charge divided by the total of short- and long-term debt and deferred income taxes); and (4) *leverage*—assessing the degree to which a firm's earnings must go to pay debt, obtaining ratios of total debt to equity, long-term debt to equity, total balance sheet and off–balance sheet debt to equity, net income to net interest payments, and coverage on earnings before income taxes (EBIT) to interest payments.

The Public and Not-for-Profit Sectors: Ratios

Financial ratios provide us with relative measures of public and not-for-profit agencies' financial position. Ratios may give us insight about (1) the agency's or governmental unit's historic financial record, (2) the relative financial strength that an agency or governmental unit has at a given point in time, and (3) how the agency or governmental unit compares with similar and approximate size organizations.

Unlike private firms whose main purpose is profitability and increasing shareholder wealth, the not-for-profit agency's goal is service delivery. The pursuit of surpluses, not the accumulation of resources, is the typical indicator of success. Resource accumulations should be made mainly to enhance future delivery of goods or services or mitigate potential budget shortfalls. From a historical perspective, the analysis of not-for-profit statements is likely to yield minimal benefits. As will be shown in chapter 11, the amount of money expended on a given program or activity may tell us very little about the quality, quantity, adequacy, or sustainability of results.

Not-for-profit ratios should be used only in the context of a given agency's mission, goals, and objectives (as they respond to the clientele, constituency, and political and legal environments) to provide useful clues about the efficiency and effectiveness of an agency's use of the resources entrusted to it. As in the for-profit sector, ratios may indicate potential financial dangers and be used to assess the credit worthiness of public and other not-for-profit agencies (see chapter 19). Ratios provide relationships only between components within the agency. While there are no absolutes in ratios, careful and judicious interpretations and use can sometimes provide insights into internal agency operations and interagency comparisons in the application of resources. The maximum utility and meaning of ratios will result from the use of financial ratios only in cases where the analyst is thoroughly aware of an agency's total operations. In some cases, the analyst may have to modify or construct new ratios to fit particular agency situations.

Not-for-profit organizations should exercise caution when interpreting and using financial analysis. Interpreting relates to the matching of the organizational goals with its available financial resources. There must be a continuing watch to ensure that programmatic commitments do not exceed organizational capability. To ignore this reality postpones a future day of reckoning, as was done during the 1970s following the boom years of the previous decade, when government and not for profit agencies overexpanded (cities such as New York and Cleveland became bankrupt, and not-for-profit entities such as public libraries and universities had to undertake major budget reductions). During the latter part of the 1970s, and especially into the 1980s, massive retrenchment was required to bring programmatic expenditures into line with resource inflow.

Currently, an increasing number of municipalities across the United States are experiencing large budget deficits from growing expenditures and revenue declines. This economic reality can be variously attributed, but one expenditure is proving to be a common burden amongst these local governments, the growing cost of pension funding. Municipal accountants have been accused of straying from the practice of conservatism by overestimating anticipated pension fund returns, especially during the recent U.S. housing market bubble. Municipal officials used this information to justify decreasing direct payment amounts to the pension funds. With the crash of the housing market, the anticipated returns never materialized, and municipal pension funds for firefighters, police officers, and other governmental personnel have become tremendously underfunded. The underfunded status of some pension funds has gotten to the point at which unfortunate municipalities have had to declare bankruptcy.

No city epitomizes the current U.S. municipality pension funding crisis more than Detroit, Michigan. Declining revenue due to population flight, depressed property values, and business relocations have limited Detroit's ability to pay for the most basic operating expenses. As a result of these financial shortfalls, the city has seen infrastructure deterioration, a reduction in the number of police and firefighter personnel, and slow response to virtually all citizen complaints and requests. Like other U.S. municipalities, the city relied on investment returns to fund its pension obligations, setting aside only a fraction of the revenue required. The recent financial crisis of 2007–2009 evaporated anticipated pension fund investment gains and has left the city with extensive fund obligations that it has no ability to fulfill. In total, the mismanagement of revenues and expenditures, primarily involving Detroit's pension fund, has led to $18.2 billion in debt liabilities (approximately $26,000 per resident) and to the city's declaring bankruptcy in 2013.

Municipal officials must be prudent with revenues and expenditures, ensuring that shortfalls are corrected, through increases in revenue and decreases in expenditures, so that bankruptcy never presents itself as the necessary fiscal option.[17]

The second caution focuses on the maintenance of intergenerational equity. The emphasis here is placed on balancing spending for the generation today without robbing future generations of the benefits they should enjoy. Massive federal long-term borrowing increases the national debt and not only serves to deny posterity its future benefits, but also requires that tomorrow's citizen shoulder the financial burden of the benefits that Americans enjoy today. This practice has always been frowned upon because it allows long-term-debt creation to be used to satisfy short-term maintenance needs. This practice was followed in a number of public health schools during the 1960s and 1970s. Short-term grant money allowed faculty to be hired and be given tenure. As the grants were reduced or ended, however, resources had to be reallocated from other priorities to meet tenure commitments.

Another concern is the excessive dependence on one or only a few sources of revenue/funding to maintain an agency. When problems with one source develop, it places the agency's viability at risk. When reduction in Medicare health insurance reimbursements for the elderly occurred, it created major problems for a number of health care agencies because of their heavy dependence on federal inflows. Of course, it goes without saying that an overdiversified agency may have to contend with increased coordination and administrative costs.

In examining profitability in the not-for-profit sector, profit is viewed as an excess of revenues over expenses, or surplus. However, in not-for-profit organizations (particularly those that are nongovernmental), viability requires the generation of a profit. Among the reasons included are (a) the need to replace assets that are recorded at cost rather than at market or replacement value, (b) the need to finance expansion or expected service delivery cost increases, and (c) the need to build up reserves to ensure against uncertainties and the unpredictability of earnings. When not-for-profit organizations fail to generate adequate surplus (profit) or return, they must use the current fund balance built up over prior years to maintain their existing purchasing power. Accordingly, it is useful to keep a close watch on important ratios/groups such as liquidation ratios, long-term solvency ratios, revenue–expense–assets ratios, and asset management ratios.

The Revenue–Expense–Assets Ratio

Ratios falling into this category are also commonly referred to as "profitability measures" because they provide indicators of an organizations' ability to generate funds from operations. The *operating margin* is a popular ratio. The operating margins for Bright Hospital (see Table 2.29) are as follows:

$$Operating\ margin = \frac{Net\ operating\ surplus}{Total\ operating\ revenues}$$

$$2012 = \frac{75,000}{6,780,000} = .011$$

$$2013 = \frac{123,000}{6,690,000} = .018$$

(Industry average = .018)

FIGURE 2.18   Operating margins for Bright Hospital.

The operating margins indicate stability with respect to the excess of revenues over expenses. In 2012, Bright Hospital generated an operating margin of .011 (below the industry average); results improved in 2013, with an operating margin of .018 (equaling the industry average).

Return on assets (ROA) is widely used in profit-oriented firms to assess how well management has used its available assets to generate profits. Although this indicator is important to private and some not-for-profit agencies such as hospitals (for example, Bright Hospital), it has little relevance to public sector agencies. For Bright Hospital, the return on assets is as follows:

$$ROA = \frac{Annual\ surplus/Deficit}{Total\ assets}$$

$$2012 = \frac{\$75,000}{\$7,571,400} = .018$$

$$2013 = \frac{123,000}{7,435,000} = .020$$

(Industry average = .027)

FIGURE 2.19   Bright Hospital return on assets.

Although there was improvement from 2012 to 2013 on Bright Hospital's ROA, both years were still below the industry average. These results may suggest that revenue has been declining: Either a change in the revenue–expenses relationship has been taking place, or assets have not been employed productively.

TABLE 2.29 Deriving the Break-Even Level for Social Service Centers

	Service A			Service B			Total		
	Units	Rate	Total	Units	Rate	Total	Units	Rate	Total
Revenues	1000	$ 90	$90,000	800	30	$240,000	9000	36.11	330,000
Variable Cost	1000	50	50,000	800	10	80,000	9000	14.44	130,000
Contribution Margins	1000	$ 40	$40,000	800	20	160,000	900	21.67	200,000
Contribution Margin Ratio	$40,000	÷ $90,000	= 44.74	$160,000	÷ 240,000	= 66.66	200,000	÷ 330,000	= 60.06

Break-even   FC ÷ Contribution margin ratio = $330,000 ÷ 60.06

= $549,450.54

Return on fund balances (ROFB) provides another measure to assess the return that an agency is internally generating from its invested resources in terms of fund balances. This ratio for Bright Hospital is as follows:

$$\text{ROFB} = \frac{\text{Annual surplus/deficit}}{\text{Total fund balances}}$$

$$2012 = \frac{75,000}{2,968,000} = .019$$

$$2013 = \frac{123,000}{3,043,000} = .040$$

(Industry average = .070)

FIGURE 2.20   Ratio for Bright Hospital.

Again, the ratio for 2013 shows considerable improvement, but both are still below industry averages. The ROFB indicates the extent to which the unspent surplus of prior years has been preserved and enhanced. It may also provide early clues regarding prospective problems in revenue generation (earnings). When the ratios are rising faster than industry averages or a target historical average for the agency, the pricing structure of the fees needs to be modified. The increasing ratio average provides management with greater options to enhance the agency's capital base, setting the stage for greater stability, growth, and profitability.

Other expense-related ratios that may provide some useful input for analysis include the following:

$$\textit{Fund balance reserve ratio} = \frac{\textit{Fund balance}}{\textit{Total expenses}}$$

which reveals how much cushion of permanent financing is being maintained relative to annual expenses. The fund balance relative to expense provides a view of operating risk. The larger the fund balance reserve ratio, the less risky the operating environment.

$$\textit{Program expense ratio} = \frac{\textit{Program expenses}}{\textit{Total expenses}}$$

which attempts to determine the amount of resources necessary to achieve the program mission of the agency. It may also suggest whether the agency is allocating too much of resources to overhead, preventing it from realizing its main objective of delivering services to clients.

$$\textit{Contribution ratio} = \frac{\textit{Total contribution or donated revenue}}{\textit{Total revenue}}$$

The higher this ratio is, the greater the need for quick turnaround plans because of its predictor of a significant fall in donations. Churches' heavy reliance on donations make them most vulnerable (donations are 90 percent or above of total revenue, especially in the case of foreign missions) to this indicator, whereas most colleges tend to be at the lower end (about 38 percent).

$$Target\ liquidity\ level = cash + cash\ equivalents + short\ term\ investments$$
$$- short\ term\ loans$$

reveals the extent to which the goal of liquid resources has been reached. It shows how much liquidity is had at any given point in time and the amount needed to be arranged for to maintain the target liquidity level.

Asset Management Ratios

These ratios are called *activity* or *turnover* ratios. They provide insights relative to the effectiveness with which total assets are being used to generate revenues. Asset management ratios involve four calculations: current turnover, current asset turnover, inventory turnover, and long-term assets turnover. The Bright Hospital turnover ratios are as follows:

$$Current\ asset\ turnover = \frac{Total\ operating\ revenues}{Total\ current\ assets}$$
$$2012 = \frac{6,780,000}{1,661,400} = 4.80$$
$$2013 = \frac{6,690,000}{1,263,600} = 5.29$$
$$(Industry\ average = 3.98)$$

FIGURE 2.21   Bright Hospital turnover ratios.

Both 2012 and 2013 show excellent ratios. The latter high one may suggest that management is doing an excellent job in collecting its receivable, investing cash and managing inventory.

The total asset turnover ratio is calculated as follows:

$$Current\ asset\ turnover = \frac{Total\ operating\ revenues}{Total\ assets}$$
$$2012 = \frac{6,600,000}{7,552,000} = .87$$
$$2013 = \frac{6,590,000}{7,435,000} = .89$$
$$(Industry\ average = .95)$$

FIGURE 2.22   Total asset turnover ratio calculation.

For each dollar invested, management generated $.87 revenue in 2012 and $.89 in 2013, respectively. Both indicators are slightly below the industry average, although 2013 indicates improvement. The below industry average turnover rate suggests that assets are idle or, alternatively, that there was a relative drop in revenue. Bright Hospital's turnover problem relates to an increase in prepaid expenses and new investment in equipment that has not generated the expected improved productivity.

The *long-term* or *fixed asset turnover ratio* comprises mainly net property, plant, and equipment. For Bright Hospital, it is calculated as follows:

$$Long\text{-}term\ asset\ turnover = \frac{Total\ operating\ revenues}{Net\ long\text{-}term\ assets}$$

$$2012 = \frac{\$6{,}780{,}000}{\$5{,}640{,}000} = 1.20$$

$$2013 = \frac{\$6{,}590{,}000}{\$5{,}900{,}000} = 1.13$$

(Industry average $= 1.42)$

FIGURE 2.23   Bright Hospital long-term asset turnover calculation.

Both the 2012 and 2013 ratios are below average, indicating that the hospital is not using its assets effectively in generating revenue. Although the 2013 ratio suggests an improved delinquency collection rate, assets used to generate revenues—perhaps due mainly to new equipment—has not generated the efficiency that was expected.

The *inventory turnover ratio* provides management with information about the acceptable or desirable levels of inventory necessary to generate required revenues. A large ratio indicates that a lesser need is required to generate greater revenues. Conversely, a small ratio may suggest excess or higher levels of inventory than necessary.

Liquidity Ratios

Liquidity ratios provide indicators that reveal the extent of an agency's ability to meet current and maturing obligations. Liquidity measures the gap between the current need for cash and the agency's ability to convert noncash assets into cash to settle outstanding obligations as they become due. The Bright Hospital current liquidity ratio is calculated as follows:

The 2012 Bright Hospital current liquidity ratio shows that it has $1.94 of assets for every liability request that is currently being made. This strong liquidity position is above the industry standards. In 2013, the ratio fell below the industry average. When the ratio falls to a point where current obligations cannot be met as they come due, the organization is placed in a precarious position (which must be avoided). When the amounts of noncash items such

$$Current\ liquidity\ ratio = \frac{Current\ assets}{Current\ liabilities}$$

$$2012 = \frac{1,661,000}{856,000} = 1.94$$

$$2013 = \frac{1,285,000}{762,000} = 1.66$$

(Industry average = 1.78)

FIGURE 2.24   Bright Hospital current liquidity ratio calculation.

as receivables becomes too high, better management of the receivables may be required.

The *quick ratio* (also known as the *acid test ratio*) is a stringent test of an agency's short-term bill-paying ability. The quick ratio excludes inventories and prepaid expenses from the current asset base. When problems arise concerning an agency's ability to convert inventories into cash in a timely manner, the quick ratio is typically used. For Bright Hospital, the quick ratio is calculated as follows:

$$Quick\ ratio = \frac{Cash + short\text{-}term\ investment + receivables}{Current\ liabilities}$$

$$2012 = \frac{\$305 + \$20 + \$1,179}{\$856} = 1.76$$

$$2013 = \frac{\$225 + \$825 + \$75}{\$762} = 1.48$$

(Industry average = 1.47)

FIGURE 2.25   Bright Hospital quick ratio calculation.

Its 2012 and 2013 quick ratios are above the industry average. Accounts payable and current loan declines are two factors that played a role in improving the ratios, especially in 2013.

The number of days' revenue in net receivables is another liquidity ratio that measures the ability of an agency to collect its outstanding accounts receivable. The Bright Hospital ratio for this is calculated as follows:

$$Number\ of\ days'\ revenue\text{-}Net\ accounts\ receivable = \frac{Net\ accounts\ receivable}{Net\ patient\ revenue\ /\ 365}$$

$$2012 = \frac{\$1,179,000}{\$4,800,000\ /\ 365} = 89.70$$

$$2013 = \frac{\$825,000}{\$4,625,000\ /\ 365} = 65.16$$

(Industry average = 61.20)

FIGURE 2.26   Bright Hospital number of days' revenue calculation.

Bright Hospital appears to have a problem with slower collection than the industry average. Although the figure in 2013 represents a significant improvement from the previous year, additional improvement is still desirable. When the ratio is restated so that the dollar amount of net patient revenues is divided by net outstanding receivables, the receivable turnover ratio is produced. The 2012 ratio is 4.1 ($4,800,000/1,179,000)—or, on average, account receivables has a turnover rate of 4.1 per year.

Additional insight may be obtained by making comparison between years (what is typically referred to as *horizontal analysis*). These useful ratios may be obtained as follows:

$$Percent\ decrease\ of\ accounts\ receivable = \frac{\$1,179 - 8.25}{\$11,179} = 30.05\ (30\%)$$

$$Percent\ decrease\ of\ estimated\ uncollectible\ accounts = \frac{\$20,400 - 15,000}{\$20,000} = .27\ (27\%)$$

$$Percent\ decrease\ of\ net\ patient\ revenues = \frac{\$4,800 - 4,625}{\$4,800} = .036\ (3.6\%)$$

FIGURE 2.27   Calculation of horizontal analysis ratios.

Bright Hospital's 30 percent decrease in accounts receivable suggests a significant increase in the collection of outstanding accounts receivable. Uncollectibles have improved 25 percent, indicating that the quality of the patient receivables is improving. Although revenue inflow is being reduced by 3.6 percent, it does not seem to present a problem at this time.

Long-Term Solvency Ratios

Long-term solvency goes beyond the short-term ability of an organization to meet obligations as they come due. Stress is placed on the organization's ability to meet future payments on principal and interest on long-term debt, whatever the source of the outstanding commitment or obligation. The focus is on the entity's ability to generate sufficient cash flow to meet scheduled payments (coverage). *Long term solvency ratios* are often used as indicators to assess long-term solvency as in ratios of total debt to fund balances, fund balances to long-term financing, and total asset to fund balances.

The *total debt–fund balance ratio* is a useful indicator of how externally borrowed funds are used to supplement internally generated funds. The ratio for Bright Hospital is calculated as follows:

The *fund–financing ratio* places emphasis on the percentage of assets that have been obtained from funds that were internally generated. The Bright Hospital fund–financing ratio is calculated as follows:

$$Total\ debt : fund\ balance = \frac{Current\ liabilities + Long-term\ liabilities}{Fund\ balance}$$

$$2012 = \frac{\$856 + 3,747}{\$2,968} = 1.55$$

$$2013 = \frac{\$762 + 3,630}{\$3,043} = 1.44$$

(Industry average = 1.10)

FIGURE 2.28   Bright Hospital total debt to fund balance ratio.

$$Fund : Financing\ ratio = \frac{Fund\ balance}{Total\ assets}$$

$$2012 = \frac{\$2,968}{\$7,571} = .39\ (50\%)$$

$$2013 = \frac{\$3,043}{\$7,435} = .41\ (41\%)$$

(Industry average = 42%)

FIGURE 2.29   Bright Hospital fund to financing ratio.

A conservative capital structure generates a high percentage, indicating that most debt financing comes from internal sources. Conversely, a low ratio would suggest that most of the asset financing is obtained through debt, which must be paid off in the future. Lending agencies are more disposed to those organizations that have a healthy fund balance, which leads to lower interest rates for those organizations. The amount and percentage of fund balance serve as leverage in attracting external funds.

Concluding Observations

The importance of the accounting system cannot be overemphasized in public and other not-for-profit organizations. In many governmental units, it may be the only mechanism capable of bringing a semblance of coordination to the financial management system. By means of the accounting system, a number of important accountability and control objectives may be achieved. After the budget is passed, the breakdown of the component parts is recorded by means of a chart or code of accounts directly linking and identifying the division of authority and the responsibility centers within the organization. This operation facilitates responsibility accounting whereby individual units can be held answerable for the appropriated funds made available to it.

Accounting has multiple applications depending on the objectives being sought for the organization, including accounting for funds, control, and compliance with financial accounting. When the emphasis is placed on improvement in efficiency and internal decision making, managerial accounting may be effectively applied. When the organization requires the costing out of programs, activities, and special projects, a cost accounting capacity may be developed to generate the data. Based on the accounting data, balance sheets and income statements can be projected for future operations. Recently, public and other not-for-profit organizations have started to employ break-even analysis to aid in making projections, especially those long-term assets.

Notes

1. See, for example, W. Steve Albrecht, James I. Stice, Earl K. Stice, and K. Fred Skousen, *Financial Accounting*, 8th ed. (Cincinnati: Southwestern Publishing/Thomson Learning, 2002); Kermit D. Larson, John J. Wild, and Barbara Chiappetta, *Fundamentals of Accounting Principles* (Boston: Irwin McGraw-Hill, 1999); Robert W. Ingraham and Bruce A. Baldwin, *Financial Accounting*, 4th ed. (Cincinnati: South-Western College Publishing/Thomson Learning, 2001); and Michael H. Granof, *Government and Not-For-Profit Accounting*, 2nd ed. (New York: John Wiley & Sons, 1998).

2. Leo Herbert, Larry N. Killough, and Alan Walter Steiss, *Governmental Accounting and Control* (Monterey, CA: Brooks/Cole Publishing, 1984), p. 5.

3. See: *Codification of Governmental Accounting and Financial Reporting Standards*, Governmental Accounting Standards Board., Sec. 122.101.

4. Source: "Basic Facts about Service Efforts and Accomplishments Reporting." *Basic Facts about Service Efforts and Accomplishments Reporting*. Governmental Accounting Standards Board, n.d. http://www.gasb.org/resources/ccurl/530/819/SEAFactsheet-2010-07DBLPKDMMDRBRHA.pdf.

5. See Robert Simons, "Strategic Orientation and Top Management Attention to Central Systems," *Strategic Management Journal*, 12 (1991): 49–62.

6. Herbert, Killough, and Steiss, *Governmental Accounting and Control*, p. 5.

7. Bridget M. Anderson, "Using Activity-Based Costing for Efficiency and Quality," *Government Finance Review* 9, no. 3 (June 1993): 7–10; Robin H. Cooper and Robert S. Kaplan, "Profit Priorities from Activity-Based Costing," *Harvard Business Review*, 69 (May/June 1991): 130–135.

8. Edward S. Lynn and Robert Freeman, *Fund Accounting Theory and Practices*, 2nd ed. (Englewood Cliffs, NJ: Prentice-Hall, 1983), pp. 627–628.

9. Robert N. Anthony and David W. Young, *Management Control in Nonprofit Organizations* (Homewood, IL: Richard D. Irwin, 1984), pp. 17, 141.

10. "Sustainability Accounting." *Sustainability*. AICPA, n.d. http://www.aicpa.org/InterestAreas/BusinessIndustryAndGovernment/Resources/Sustainability/Pages/Sustainability%20Accounting.aspx.

11. U.S. General Accounting Office, *Accounting Manual for Guidance of Federal Agencies*, revised, Title 2 (Washington, DC: U.S. General Accounting Office, 1978).

12. Stephen J. Gauthier, *Fund Balance: An Elected Official Guide* (Chicago: Government Finance Officers Association, 1991), p. 17.

13. See FASB Statement #117, *Financial Statements of Not-for-Profit Organizations*, 1993.

14. Jeanne B. Pinder, "Crazy Eddie Founder Guilty of Fraud." *The New York Times*. http://www.nytimes.com/1993/07/21/business/crazy-eddie-founder-guilty-of-fraud.html. The New York Times, July 21, 1993.

15. Paul M. Clikeman, *Called to Account: Fourteen Financial Frauds That Shaped the American Accounting Profession*. New York: Routledge, 2009.

16. For an excellent discussion, see Stephen A. Finkler and David M. Ward, *Essentials of Accounting for Health Care Organizations*, 2nd ed. (Gaithersburg, MD: Aspen Systems, 1999), p. 109.

17. Source: Richard J. Riordian, and Tim Rutten. "A Plan to Avert the Pension Crisis." http://mobile.nytimes.com/comments/2013/08/05/opinion/a-plan-to-avert-the-pension-crisis.html?from=opinion.

3

Internal Control Management

Public and not-for-profit agencies are constantly seeking ways to effectively accomplish the organizational mission, goals, and objectives, leading to enhanced accountability. Internal control is a key factor in helping organizations minimize operational problems and achieve desired outcomes. In an ever-changing environment with ever-evolving demands, effective internal controls help an organization cope and make necessary adjustments to produce optimal outcomes. The Performance and Results Act of 1993 and the Government Performance and Results Modernization Act of 2010 (GPRAMA) have significantly aided the internal control function by requiring that organizations articulate goals and performance measures.[1]

Controls are part of our everyday experience. Laws are enacted to guide our behavior, such as those passed to control our driving speed on highways to promote traffic safety. When we charge items on our credit cards, we keep receipts of our transactions to compare with our monthly credit-card statements. Likewise, we keep records of checks we write against which to verify the accuracy of our monthly bank statements. Banks give us identification numbers for our credit and debit cards as a control against unauthorized use. And when a prudent consumer buys milk, the first thing he or she does is check the sell-by date; dairy owners use this dating system as a control indicator to prevent us from drinking sour milk.

Internal control and information processing methods are important to effective accounting. Internal control consists of the policies and procedures used to protect an organization's assets from improper use, to maintain accurate information, and to ensure adherence to laws and regulations. The processing methods used to collect, summarize, and report accounting information may be manual or computerized. Many accounting systems use computerized systems, employing technology to rapidly accomplish the job previously performed using manual accounting systems.

Computer Software Basics

Programs (or "software") issue a computer instructions. The two major types of computer programs are *operating systems* and *applications*. The *operating system* provides instructions for the operation of the computer. An operating system is essential to all computers. Microsoft Windows, in its various releases, is the most popular operating system globally. Among the tasks that *applications* perform include: word processing, spreadsheets, and accounting. Applications are myriad and can perform tasks to accommodate almost any need. Examples of popular applications include the following:

TABLE 3.1   Popular Software Applications

Type	Example
Accounting	QuickBooks®, Peachtree®, Account Pro, BS/I Small Business, BS/I Professional Business, Design Solution Accounting, Expense Reports Pro, Invoiceit!, Smart Accounting
Spreadsheet	Excel, Lotus 1, 2, 3®, Spread Pro, Investment and Business Valuation
Web broker	Netscape® Navigator, Microsoft Internet Explorer
Word processing	WordPerfect®, Letter Art, As-U-Type, Letter Writer, PolyEdit, Open Office.org

This brief introduction provides the foundation for our discussions of internal control systems, but a comprehensive presentation and description of computerized accounting is beyond the scope of this book.

Despite the critical role that internal control plays in every phase of management, only minimal attention is typically devoted to it. This lack of attention is due, among other things, to the general view that internal control is purely or mainly a financial function to be managed by those charged to control finance. This is an inaccurate perspective of the true function of internal controls. Small governments and nonprofit agencies believe that they cannot afford a system of internal controls. However, evidence indicates that internal controls are indispensable to agencies of all sizes.[2]

In small establishments, especially socially oriented not-for-profit agencies, managers are reluctant to implement internal controls because of the feelings of trust and camaraderie that exist among fellow workers. This view misconstrues the special importance of internal controls, which are established to "keep honest people honest." Although it may be proper to assume that all employees are honest, it is unfair to permit weaknesses in the internal system to tempt individuals toward dishonesty. This guiding perspective aids the generation of data; the resulting information is likely to prevent or minimize human error. Each employee in each responsibility area should be made aware of proper internal control procedures related to his or her specific job function. Effective internal controls protect employees against unwarranted allegations by fixing responsibility and removing causes of employee temptation. A strong internal control system is very helpful to the independent auditor. The degree of confidence placed in the internal control system directly bears on the extent of the detailed checking required to assess the reliability of an agency's records. A sound internal control system requires the independent auditor to carry out fewer tests and less checking of an agency's records, thereby reducing the time and cost of auditing. A sound internal control system invigorates procedures, minimizes avoidable errors, and remove easy temptation.

We should bear in mind that when organizational fraud occurs, it is perpetrated by someone in whom the organization has placed its trust. It is never a good practice to rely on only one individual, yet too often, small social agencies and businesses tend to put their trust in long-time, loyal employees. Often such employees are viewed as being above reproach. However, it is important to note that employee circumstances *do* change in ways that may take precedence over employee–employer relationships. Individual circumstances may change because of things such as family illness and gambling debts, which create conditions that may tempt otherwise loyal and incorruptible individuals. Therefore, it is seldom wise to place complete trust in one employee without also relying on checks or constraints. Because no one system is foolproof, it is always the greatest part of wisdom to obtain an insurance policy on all employees who are entrusted with cash or valuable assets. By taking out fidelity bonds, the agency hedges against the possibility of an occasional failure of the internal control system.

It cannot be overstressed that careful hiring practices and extensive and continuous on-the-job training are critical factors to reducing ethical lapses. Particular attention should be given to the internal control system when personnel changes are taking place, because this is the time when it is most vulnerable to errors and irregularities.

After a system of internal controls has been implemented, it requires monitoring to ensure that objectives are being effectively achieved. The literature is replete with the failures of organizations viewing internal control systems as self-executing or self-guiding. For example, even with the Phar-Mor Corporation's internal control system in place, most the company's assets were stolen. The president and a staff member (the controller) were charged with absconding with more than 50 percent of the entity's assets—because the system was not being carefully monitored and controlled.

This chapter examines the principles and practices of internal control management in public and not-for-profit agencies. Six sections are included, in which (1) principles and structure of internal controls are reviewed, showing how they strategically facilitate the achievement of an agency's programmatic accountability; (2) the different types of internal controls are examined; (3) the importance of documentation and the audit trail are examined, showing how they provide the essential linkage that fixes accountability for actions taken; (4) the internal control system of authorizations is discussed; (5) the cost–benefit justification of internal controls is reviewed; and (6) designing and evaluating the internal control system are discussed.

Understanding the Internal Control Structure and Its Relation to Accountability

Internal control encompasses every aspect (financial and nonfinancial) of an organization. There are three main objectives that an internal control system must provide: (1) reasonable assurance that assets are safeguarded and used for organizational purposes; (2) additional assurance that agency accounting information is accurate and staff members comply with rules, regulations, and procedures; and (3) the promotion of efficient operations. An effective internal control system is the nerve center of an organization and hence is critical to the achievement of both short- and long-term organizational mission, goals, and objectives. The survival of an organization is tied to the effective design, implementation, maintenance, and monitoring of such a system. The elements of an internal control system include (1) the control system environment; (2) risk assessment; (3) control procedures; (4) effective monitoring and follow-up on internal auditing recommendations; (5) the general oversight system, such as the legislature, the board, or the audit committee of the governing board overseeing regular independent reviews; (6) division of responsibility for related transactions; (7) bonding of key employees; and (8) separation of record-keeping from custody of funds. Furthermore, there are five standards for internal control:

- Control environment
- Risk assessment
- Control activities
- Information and communications
- Monitoring

These standards require the development of detailed policies, procedures, and practices to fit each organization's operations.

The Control System Environment

A strong control environment is indispensable for a well-functioning internal control system. The control environmental standard provides discipline, structure, and climate affecting the quality of internal control. The *control system environment* has a pervasive influence on the activities of an organization in terms of how the organization is structured, objectives are established, risks assessed, information and communication, and monitoring systems operate. An effectively operating control environment mitigates the risk of fraud; alternatively, its failure negatively affects all other internal control components.[3]

Five guiding principles describe the functions (discipline, process and structure) of the control environment:

- Demonstration of commitment to integrity and ethical values
- Demonstration of effective oversight of the performance of the internal control
- Establishment of oversight structures reporting lines in pursuit of the organization's objective
- Demonstration of commitment to attract, develop and retain competent employees
- Demonstration of ability to hold employees accountable for their internal control responsibilities[4]

The control environment is the component that indicates the degree of control-consciousness within an organization. The organization's control environment reflects the general attitude of management and employees about the importance of controls. A major influence of such an environment is management's philosophy and operating style. Management must not only *articulate* rules but also *follow* them; to do otherwise will encourage employees to likewise ignore them. Controls must be viewed as an essential and integral activity in the provision of goods and services.[5]

A well-defined organizational structure provides a clear framework for planning and controlling the operations that affect the control environment. Each responsibility manager must have authority to establish and implement the organization's control environment expectations.

Personnel policies impact directly on the control environment. Policies relating to training, compensation, and promotion of employees must be implemented with an understanding of how they impact the control environment. An incentive system must be established and continuously monitored for discrepancies between expected and actual performance to avoid unintended consequences. The New York State Employment Agency's employees failed to adhere to state policies because bonuses were paid to employees simply for the number of people who could be easily hired, without closely monitoring whether reasonable efforts were given to all participants who applied without regard to race or national origin. A similar Sears & Roebuck auto service bonus system during the 1990s that paid employees' incentives based on the dollar amount of work done influenced managers to overstate the amount customers paid for such work.

In summary, a number of critical or key factors constitute the control environment in public, nonprofit and business organizations:

- The maintenance and demonstration of integrity and ethical values
- A requirement that all personnel possess the competence to accomplish their assigned talks and duties
- Management's philosophy and operating style, especially relating to willingness to take risks and acceptance of performance-based management
- Organizational structure, facilitation, planning, directing, and controlling operations working to achieve organizational objectives
- The manner of delegation of authority and responsibility throughout the organization
- Good human capital policies, including in hiring, orienting, training, evaluating, counseling, promoting, compensating, disciplining, and supervising
- Agency relationship with legislative and central oversight agencies

Risk Assessment

Risks are anything that could negatively affect an organization's ability to realize its operational objectives. Management must have the ability to identify, analyze, and manage risks that could impede the organization from accomplishing its objectives. Typically an organization is most vulnerable to risks during change of personnel. A precondition to risk assessment requires a clear and consistent articulation of agency objectives. Risks are present in all organizations. Ideally, *risk assessment* is a continuous process that seeks to maintain an organization's ability to safely create maximum value.[6] Stated differently, it is the identification and analysis (which includes estimating a risk's significance and likelihood of occurrence) of potential problems, such as fraud, associated with achieving an objective and determining how it may be prevented or mitigated. Risk identification methods may include quantitative and qualitative ranking of activities management conference, forecasting, and strategic planning. Importantly, the organization should identify and assess pending changes that could significantly affect or alter the internal control system. In public and other not-for-profit agencies, examples of risk include changes in economic factors that affect tax intake and donations, public reaction to scandal, and employee violation of agency policies and procedures. The ability to recognize risks provides management with the power to assess risks' potential effects and to determine the possibility of their occurring. Action can then be taken to eliminate or minimize such risks.

Risk may be classified in terms of five different types:[7]

- *Strategic* risk could makes it difficult or prevent entirely the achievement of an organization's mission/goal.

- *Financial* risk could increase an organization's expenditures or reduce its revenues.
- *Regulatory or compliance* risk could subject the organization to fines and penalties from a regulatory agency for lack of compliance with laws and regulations.
- *Reputational* risk could expose the organization to negative publicity.
- *Operational* risk could impede an organization from operating effectively and efficiently.

Control Activities

The internal control structure is another way of viewing the operations of an organization. It is a perspective that focuses on doing the right things the right way. There are three main guiding principles relating to the control activities:

1. Select and develop control activities that mitigate risks.
2. Select and develop control activities to align technology with organizational objectives.
3. Develop control activities to maximally achieve stated policies.[8]

Policies and procedures ensure that an organization's goals and objectives are realized.[9] Control is used both as a preventative measure and as a monitoring device to safeguard goal achievement; ideally, it should be an integral part of substantive management (everyday decision making) and the accounting system. Effective control requires the hiring of competent personnel, the rotation of duties, and mandatory vacation policies. To ensure that personnel perform the functions entrusted to them, management must not only hire competent people but also have an ongoing training program to keep up with internal and professional changes. Rotation of duties, training, and mandatory vacations allow personnel to be versatile and remain challenged while providing the opportunity for replacements to uncover errors, whether intentional or unintentional.

To improve efficiency and minimize errors and fraud, related functions should be divided among two or more individuals, known as separation of duties. Functions such as purchasing, receiving, and disbursement for supplies should be divided among different areas. When dividing functions, attention should be given to separating specific duties to avoid duplication. Effective internal control requires the *definitive establishment of responsibilities* to ensure that responsibility centers are held accountable. In a simple example of this, if more than one cashier has to use the same machine, management can obtain a register with separate drawers.

Proofs and security measures should be employed to safeguard assets and ensure reliable accounting data. Control procedures should apply to authorizations and reconciliation procedures. For example, employees who travel should be required to obtain their superior's approval before traveling. Indeed, a small local government in the state of Washington illustrates the negative consequences that can result when appropriate checks and balances are not in place. In Bremertown, an auditor discovered $4,000 missing from the municipal court for traffic citation receipts. Because three basic control check procedures were not followed, the cashier stole the funds—there was no requirement that receipts be made out for cash received.

Examples of control activities include the following:

- Top management review of actual performance
- Review by management at the functional activity level
- Controls over information processing
- Segregation of duties
- Accurate and timely recording of transactions
- Appropriate documentation of transactions and internal control
- Physical control over vulnerable assets

Monitoring and Independent Reviews

Monitoring is a key instrument used to periodically review controls that have been put in place to ensure that they are effective and are working as intended. This can be done by ongoing monitoring and focused evaluations on internal controls. Monitoring is the process that locates weaknesses, allowing management to take appropriate action to intervene and improve control effectiveness. Monitoring is used to assess the design and operation of the internal control components to determine how well they are being used to assess the organization's risk.[10] Changes in personnel, stress of time pressures, and technological developments present opportunities for shortcuts and lapses. To overcome problems, periodic reviews of internal control systems should be undertaken by internal auditors to ensure that procedures are being followed. These reviews should be conducted by internal auditors who are *not* directly involved with the operating activities.

The evaluation of internal control function can be quite useful when focused directly on the controls' effectiveness at specific points in time. The frequency and parameters of separate internal control evaluation will depend on risk assessment and the effectiveness of the feedback on the monitoring of existing procedures. Problem identified during monitoring evaluation or from audits and other reviews should be resolved promptly.[11] The resolution process is initiated when audit or other reviews have been communicated to management.

In business, but less so in government and other not-for-profit agencies, outside external audits are brought in to review the internal control systems. Additionally, before external auditors commence their annual audit of an organization, they review the internal control systems. An understanding of the internal control environment enables the auditor to evaluate whether controls have been appropriately designed to identify misstatements and risks and whether the tests required to detect them are being performed.

A basic first step involves the evaluation of the internal control system. This assessment is not only helpful to the external auditors, but also to the client agency, because it will highlight the system's strengths and weaknesses. This internal control review also provides the auditors with inputs that they can use to determine the extent of its testing and the parameters for the cost of the audit to be conducted. Among other signs that should raise alarms are (1) missing documents or gaps in transaction numbers, (2) excessive increases in refunds, and (3) a backlog in recording transactions. The audit or financial review committee ideally provides its results to a legislative or governing board.

Bonding Key Employees

Effective internal controls require that assets be adequately insured against casualty and that all employees handling cash and negotiable assets be bonded. Although *bonding* does not eliminate risks, it reduces the potential for loss occurring from theft. Bonding discourages theft—employees know that bonding agencies will be relentless in their pursuit of violators.

Separation of Record-Keeping from Custody of Assets

Separate incompatible functions such as authorization, record-keeping, and custody of assets. An employee who controls or has access to assets should not be allowed to maintain the related accounting records. This practice prevents an employee from being able to both commit and conceal an irregularity. Additionally, it reduces the risk of theft or waste, because the person with control over the assets knows that another employee keeps the records—the assumption being that the record-keeper who has no access to the assets does not have reason to falsify records. With this setup, if a theft occurs, at least two parties must be involved in committing the fraud, a situation known as "collusion."

Information and Communications

Information and communication (known also as information, communication and technology, or ICT) is vital to making effective decision making. It is an important responsibility: Organizations must ensure that there are adequate ways of communication with and obtaining information from external stakeholders that may significantly affect how the agency achieves its goals.[12] Thus, to be most useful, information must be recorded and communicated to management decision points reliably and timely, in a form that enables management to carry out internal control responsibilities. Information allows managers to both manage and control the organization.

The ICT is an integral part of the organization enabling management to accomplish its objectives. Additionally, ICT clarifies how decisions are made, indicating who provides the inputs and who is accountable for particular actions. This ensures that key stakeholders take on the appropriate role and responsibilities to clearly guide management in directing activities and control the organization's resources.

For many organizations, email is the principle means of communication among employees, suppliers and customers, providing a simple, inexpensive means of communication. To facilitate and enhance the communication process a number of tools have been developed:

- Live chat
- Online meeting
- Video conferencing
- Voiceover telephone (VOIP)

Technology and Internal Controls

The most significant effect of technology on internal controls is that it facilitates quicker access to databases and information. Hence, technology can be an important means of improving management's ability to monitor and control public and other not-for-profit organizations. There are a number of positive services that technology can offer to enhance these internal controls:

- It can reduce information processing errors if the proper software and data are correct.
- It provides the opportunity for more extensive review of records. Unlike in a manual system, large samples or even complete data files can be quickly reviewed and analyzed.
- It links the evidence needed for processing, because fewer hard copies of documentary evidence will be necessary for reviewing. The system record information (a password being required for entry) identifies the person making particular entries, noting date, time, and source of entry. This allows the internal controls to depend more on the design and operation of its system and less on the resulting documents.
- It affects the separation of duties. There is an opportunity for job elimination and consolidation, thus creating the potential for decreasing the separation of responsibilities, which is a basic check on the system. Because advanced-technology personnel need special technical skills, their close monitoring is essential to minimize error and fraud. Ideally, the designer of the system should not be allowed to operate it. With or without technology, in smaller

agencies it is difficult to maintain the separation of duties due to cost. One possible solution to this problem is to institute a system whereby some type of spot check is done from time to time.

The Voucher System as an Internal Control Feature

The *voucher system* is a set of procedures and approvals designed to control cash disbursements and acceptance of obligations. The voucher system is used for verifying, approving, and recording obligations for eventual cash disbursement and for issuing checks in payment of verified, approved, and recorded obligations. As was shown in chapter 2, the voucher system is an integral part of the public financial management system, involving commitment and out-flows of resources. Typically a voucher system uses (1) vouchers, along with (2) a file for unpaid vouchers and (3) a file for paid vouchers.

The accounting department normally prepares the voucher after all required supporting documents have been received. Before a voucher can be paid in exchange for a good or service, the purchase order and receiving report for that good or service must be attached, with the employee in charge of accounts payable verifying the quantity, price, and mathematical accuracy of the sup-porting documents. The voucher is then given to the appropriate official for approval and returned to the accounting department, where it is recorded in the account and placed in an unpaid file by due date, allowing for all purchase discounts to be taken. The voucher is removed from the unpaid file when pay-ment is received; on the back of the voucher, the date received, as well as check number and amount, are entered. Following payment, vouchers are marked "paid" and filed, typically in numerical order in a paid voucher file.

Magnitude and Extent of Controls

The internal control system varies depending on the size of the not-for-profit organization. In organizations with few employees and in which the manager of the organization provides direct supervision and oversight, few controls are needed. The situation changes as the complexity and size of the organization increases, but this requires that management delegate greater authority, mak-ing it necessary to place more reliance on the accounting system.

Accounting and Internal Control

After an agency has decided on its goals and objectives, it must directly link each type of accountability with its internal control system. This requires the iden-tification of all important decision points in each responsibility center within the organization. For each control decision point, quantitative and qualitative measurement indicators must be clearly defined. Next, the process necessary to realize each measurement indicator must be established and understood by all concerned. After goals, objectives, decision points, and the measurement indicators have been defined, the type of accountability that the internal control system is seeking can easily be indicated and linked. The internal control system must be an organic and functional instrument if it is to be maximally useful in achieving the organization's financial and nonfinancial goals.

Defining Internal Controls

An internal control system is an organizational structure and the sum of the methods and measures that are used to accomplish the internal control objectives. The internal control system is a set of guidelines and parameters used to maintain control over the operations of the programs and functions that are undertaken by an agency. Internal control is an integral component of an agency's management system that provides reasonable assurance that the following are being achieved:

- effectiveness and efficiency of operations,
- reliability of financial reporting, and
- compliance with applicable laws and regulations.[13]

Stated another way, internal controls are plans, methods, and procedures used to realize mission, goals, and objectives and, accordingly, to support performance-based management. Internal control is a built-in component of management that serves as the first line of defense in protecting/safeguarding and detecting errors and fraud.[14] In Table 3.2, the Office of Management and Budget provides an overview of the internal control evaluation, improvement, and reporting process:

TABLE 3.2   Overview of Internal Control Evaluation, Improvement, and Reporting

Organize the Process
1. Assign responsibilities to ensure efficient evaluation, improvement, and reporting of internal controls.
2. Give key consideration to responsibility assignment for internal reporting, documentation, personnel supervision, and scheduling the evaluation process, including vulnerability assessments and internal control reviews.
Segment the Agency
1. Divide the agency into components, programs, and administrative functions to facilitate the evaluation of internal control and vulnerability assessment.

2. Consider the following factors in identifying assessable units: existing organizational structure, special programs, administrative functions, agency size, number of programs and subprograms, the organization's operating programs, uniqueness of the operating systems, extent of centralization or decentralization, budget allocations, and number of personnel.

Conduct Vulnerability Assessments

1. Develop criteria and guidelines to determine program/functions that are susceptible to waste, loss, and unauthorized use or misappropriation.

2. Assess the potential existence of the following: lack of compliance of obligations and cost with applicable laws; lack of adequate safeguards of funds, property, and assets and exposure to waste, loss, or unauthorized use; and lack of properly recorded and accounted for revenues and expenditures that generate unreliable financial reports and unreliable accountability over assets.

3. Vulnerability assessments comprise these important steps:

   - Analysis of the control environment, including management's attitude as expressed in a written commitment to the maintenance of a strong internal control system; organizational structures delineating necessary functions and the required reporting relationships; competent, motivated, and loyal personnel; policies and procedures disseminated to all employees showing how functions/activities are to be performed; budget-reporting practices; and utilization of clearly defined organizational checks and balances, indicating the strengths and potential weaknesses inherent in the system.

   - Evaluation of potential and/or inherent risks, with an assessment of the potential waste, loss, and unauthorized use or misappropriation of each.

   - Preliminary assessment of agency safeguards, making preliminary judgments about the existence and adequacy of internal control over selected programs and administrative functions. (This is not an in-depth evaluation. It is a judgment of the evaluator's knowledge regarding the satisfactory functioning of safeguards to protect the agency from waste, loss, and unauthorized use or mismanagement.)

Development Plans for Subsequent Actions

1. Summarize the vulnerability-assessment results to determine actions that may be necessary. (The objective at this stage is to strengthen the internal control system to achieve a more cost-effective result.)

2. Classify the identified program/function vulnerability exposure, providing each with direction attention to achieve a timely and best outcome and enhance the internal control system.

3. Pursue the following actions that may bring about enhancing remedial action: scheduling and implementing, required internal control reviews; recommending that auditing be initiated; setting in place improved monitoring procedures; carrying out staff training programs; issuing clearly defined instructions; and modifying existing procedures and documents.

(Continued)

TABLE 3.2 *(Continued)*

Conduct Internal Control Reviews

1. *Defining the event cycle.* It is the focal point of reference for the review of internal control. The event cycle consists of a series of steps that are required to be taken to carry out a specific task, activity, or function. For example, in an entitlement program, a cycle of events is as follows: informationgathering and verificationobtaining, eligibilitydetermination information, informationprocessing and recordkeeping, payment and monitoring. An administrativefunction event cycle might involve payroll, supplies, and materials procurement, and letter writing/correspondence handling.

2. *Analyze the general control environment.* This involves the management attitude, organizational structure, personnel, extent and type of delegation of authority, policies and procedures, budgeting and reporting practices, and the extent, type, and quality of organizational checks and balances.

3. *Documenting the event cycle.* This provides an understanding of how activities, events, or functions operate. It requires the review of individuals in the event cycle, documentation and observation of the events, and the preparation of a narrative explanation or a flowchart to provide sufficient detail to assess the adequacy of the internal control system.

4. *Evaluation of internal controls.* Assess the internal control event cycle to determine how the internal control objectives are being met, thus minimizing the potential for waste, loss, unauthorized use, or misappropriation. Attempt to determine from written documentation whether the internal control system as defined provides reasonable and adequate assurance that obligations and costs are in compliance with the law. Appropriate safeguards must be in place to protect the agency's funds, property, assets, and revenue. Expenditures are recorded to permit and facilitate the preparation of accounts and reliable financial statements.

5. *Testing internal controls.* Determine if control objectives are being carried out as intended. This can be done by various sampling techniques, including making observations and reviewing documentation. This review should clearly identify problems that exist of control techniques that are not functioning as planned.

Prepare Report on Internal Controls

Preparing two types of reports. The final report, suggesting corrective action, is prepared for program managers. The second report goes to the agency head or the chief executive. Reports should detail weaknesses in the system and reasonable ways to rectify them. Recommendations for economy and efficiency should be made. Particular attention should focus on the following:

1. To what extent is the overall control system efficient in providing the required facilitative atmosphere for effective functioning of internal controls?

2. In what areas are the required control techniques nonexistent?

3. In what areas are the internal controls functioning as planned?
4. In what areas are control techniques excessive and creating inefficiencies?
5. Are there executive and/or legislative requirements that are excessive and creating inefficiencies?

Source: Adapted from U.S. Office of Management and Budget, *Internal Control Guidelines* (Washington, DC: OMB, 1982).

1. Organize process to permit the assignment of key responsibilities in the organization.
2. Facilitate the division of the organization into component programs or responsibility centers to be evaluated.
3. Conduct vulnerability assessment of the internal control system.
4. Develop plans to remedy vulnerability controls problems.
5. Conduct periodic review of the internal control system to determine how well it is enabling management to realize organizational goals and objectives.
6. Recommend how the organization can most efficiently and effectively achieve its goals and objectives.

The following is a segmenting example. The Department of Health and Human Services (HHS) might be divided or segmented into the Social Security Administration, the Health Care and Finance Administration, and other, smaller units. Similarly, the Social Security Administration can be segmented into the Supplemental Security Income Program, the Old Age, Survivors, and Disability Insurance Program, and smaller administrative functions such as eligibility determination systems, benefit payment systems, and quality controls. Internal controls facilitate the carrying out of a vulnerability assessment to determine an agency's greatest potential exposure to waste, loss, unauthorized use, and misappropriation of funds or other assets by identifying risk-creating factors in the environment.

Preparing for Internal Control

Internal control comprises a clear-cut organizational plan, method, and procedures designed to produce accurate data, providing assurance that the agency's objectives will be accomplished and that assets and resources will be safeguarded. The internal control plan should provide for (1) the definite identification of responsibility, with a clear division of duties between authorization and record-keeping so that the activities of one employee act as a check on another; (2) the use of forms, documents, and procedures that facilitate control and provide for proper approval; and (3) the facilitation of compliance with policies and procedures. Alternatively, internal control involves compliance with a combination of policies, standards, and procedures that, when applied collectively, will minimize, prevent, or detect illegal or unauthorized acts and preserve the assets and integrity of the agency. This senior-management responsibility should not be carelessly delegated, yet most internal control activities must be assigned to specific individuals who will carry out the day-to-day operations. Keep in mind that the pursuit of the internal control objective must be balanced with the benefits to be achieved and the costs incurred and risks involved. The paramount internal control aim is ensuring that assets are used as efficiently and effectively as possible, as directed by an authorizing body such as a legislature or governing board and enforced by top administrators.

The design of the internal control plan delineates the duties under which employees are expected to operate. Under the system of internal control, duties are assigned to make it possible to exercise effective control over assets, liabilities, and expenditures. A summary of requirements of the major objectives of the internal control system includes determining the following:

1. Obligations, commitments, and costs are in compliance with applicable laws.
2. Funds, property, and other assets are safeguarded against waste, loss, unauthorized use, and misappropriation.
3. Revenues and expenditures applicable to agency operations are properly recorded and accounted for to permit reliable preparation of accounts and financial and statistical reports and as a means of maintaining accountability over assets.
4. Timely and accurate reports are provided to the different constituencies and users of information.
5. High priority is given to the development of professional integrity and maintenance of the most affordable level of competence to enable employees to efficiently and effectively accomplish their assigned duties and responsibilities in accordance with an internal control system tailored to maximize the achievement of agency objectives.
6. Due cognizance is given to the encouragement, facilitation, and maintenance of a supportive employee attitude toward internal controls.
7. Internal control objectives are identified for each decision point in each responsibility center.
8. Key duties and responsibilities, such as authorizing, processing, recording, and reviewing transactions, are separated.
9. Effective and continuous supervision is provided to ensure that internal control objectives are being promptly and efficiently achieved.
10. Access to resources and periodic reviews of resources and records are limited to specifically authorized individuals, and the accountability for oversight, custody, and use of resources is specifically assigned and maintained.

11. Managers promptly evaluate audit findings and take necessary action in response to findings and recommendations, instituting corrective actions as required. When prompt resolution cannot be achieved, the matter is brought to the attention of senior management or the board of directors.
12. Personal accountability is clearly defined.
13. Accurate and reliable records are available from which financial statements can be prepared in accordance with generally accepted accounting principles (GAAP).

Classifying Internal Controls

Internal controls are commonly classified as *accounting controls* and *administrative controls*. *Accounting controls* are procedures, records, and reports that have been designed to safeguard assets and promote the reliability of financial accounting records and reports. They enable the management of an organization to ascertain that expenditures are properly authorized and made in accordance with appropriate laws and regulations. The accounting controls provide guidelines and specific procedures for the recording of transactions in accordance with GAAP, thereby ensuring the reliability of financial records. In other words, accounting controls relate to management's responsibility for maintaining the assets entrusted to it and for providing accurate information on the financial condition and results of the organization's operation.

Internal *administrative controls* comprise procedures and records that assist management in achieving the organization's goals. For example, when poor-quality work occurs in a particular responsibility center, the use of internal controls permits management to better evaluate personnel performance and attempt to improve the quality of the output.

Some General Principles of Internal Control

The following are broad principles of internal control that should be considered:

1. Competent personnel and rotation of duties:
   a. Employees should be adequately trained and supervised.
   b. Clerical personnel should be rotated periodically from job to job. This broadens the understanding of the employees and is helpful in uncovering any irregularities.
   c. Annual vacations and reassignments of jobs to others during such absences should be encouraged.
2. Assignment of responsibility:
   a. Clearly defined responsibility is a prerequisite for the efficient execution of assigned duties.

    b. To facilitate sound internal controls, an agency should have a formal plan of organization that fixes responsibility for the functions to be performed with the necessary authority to carry them out.

    c. Overlapping and undefined responsibility areas should be avoided. Responsibility and authority for a given function should not be shared, to avoid both duplicating effort and jobs' being left undone when each responsible individual thinks the other is performing the assignment. When one person has responsibility for the function, praise and blame can be clearly assigned for specific results.

3. Segregation of responsibility for related duties:

    a. Plan the organizational controls so that one individual is prevented from having complete control over a sequence of related transactions. A premise underlying effective control is that if collusion is necessary to permit a fraud, such action will be deterred. Thus, the desired separation of the core duties of authorization, accounting, and custody is required.

    b. Divide related duties or operating responsibilities among two or more individuals to minimize the possibility of error, fraud, collusion, and inefficiency. For example, a single individual should not be permitted to not only extend credit on account to customers, but also record the account and collect the payment. Individuals who receive and approve time reports of employees should not prepare or sign payroll checks. Employees who prepare the general ledger's trial balance should not be allowed to approve general ledger activities or prepare monthly statements. Similarly, the employee who reconciles the bank account should not also prepare withdrawals or deposits.

    c. Provide for checks and balances by distributing the responsibility over a number of departments. This requires that work in one department and its accompanying documents be compared with and agree with what is prepared in other departments. Similarly, when purchase orders and receiving reports are processed by different individuals, a third individual can compare the order, the receiving reports, and the vendor's invoice before payment is approved. This practice reduces the likelihood of the fictitious conversion of goods. (Improper separation of duties increases the probability of fraud, carelessness, and unreliable record-keeping.)

4. Separation of operations and accounting:

    a. Authorizing transactions, accounting transactions, and custody over assets should be segregated.

    b. There should be separation of responsibility for the maintenance of the accounting records from those engaging in business transactions and from those with the custody of the agency's assets. For example, the employees who handle cash payments should not have access to the journals or ledgers, thereby reducing the possibility of error and embezzlement.

5. Proofs of security measures:
   a. Various techniques include separate bank accounts, provisions for the safekeeping of cash and other valuable documents, and encouragement of possible observance and acceptance of printed receipts from clerks.
   b. Fidelity insurance can be used to ensure against losses caused by fraud arising in response to shortcomings in the internal control system.
   c. An independent review of the internal control system should be carried out periodically to determine whether internal procedures are being followed.
6. Proper accounting for transactions:
   a. The system should ensure that all transactions are accurately and appropriately classified and timely recorded.
   b. All subsidiary ledgers must regularly be reconciled with the general ledger.
7. Adequate safeguarding of assets:
   a. The internal control system should ensure that assets are physically protected from fire, natural disaster, theft, and other problems.
   b. Both direct and indirect access to assets should be restricted.
   c. There should be an inventory of assets to reconcile the actual counts to the accounting records.
   d. Differences between actual assets and accounting records should be promptly investigated.

Documentation and the Audit Trail

The *audit trail* is an important means of tracing source documents through the accounting system and identifying individuals who are charged with the execution of particular duties. For example, as an employee authorizes a transaction, the document is typically initiated or signed to indicate authorization, while the individual requesting the custody of the assets or performance of an activity normally submits a *requisition form*. As the maintainer of the institutional memory, an accounting department employee puts an identifying mark on the document to indicate that it has been checked for mathematical accuracy, reconciled with invoices or receiving reports, and been subjected to some specific action to guard and protect against improper use and loss of assets. When computers are involved, an audit trail may be automatically created. In this context, particular software may be used to identify user passwords that indicate how long each person accesses the system and show whether particular files have been read or changed. By means of the audit trail, the controller of the system has the ability to assess the effectiveness of the internal control system.

Authorization Systems

Every activity and transaction of a governmental unit should be authorized by statutes, ordinances, rules, or procedures. Examples of authorizations include advance approval, written documentation, appropriate authorization level, and compliance with the organization's approved policies and with legal restrictions. Authorizations determine by whom the conditions, functions, or duties of the agency will be carried out. It is by means of these conditions that a facilitative environment is established. As conditions, needs, and situations change, authorizations should be examined for workability and utility. The review of authorizations provides an opportunity to assess the adequacy of their required documentation and the efficiency with which they are being communicated.[15]

Ideally, every transaction should be authorized by an individual who (1) has no interest in the transaction; (2) possess authority and sufficient knowledge of the transaction, its purpose, and its legal ramifications; and (3) is at the appropriate level of the organization to issue the authorization and understand the procedures required to discharge the responsibilities involved. As an operating norm, the persons who are permitted to authorize transactions should have limits set on what they can authorize, and authorizations should be made in writing.

Authorizations may be either general or specific. General authorizations are set forth by laws, regulations, and basic management policies. Individuals are expected to execute general authorizations as prescribed by laws, regulations, or policies of the governing board. Examples of general authorizations include tax rates, user charges, wage rates, and acquisition policies. The primary vehicle for general authorizations in governmental units is the budget, under which most transactions are processed.

Some transactions require specific authorizations. Typically, these are made on a case-by-case basis. They are nonroutine transactions that are established by the responsible official of a governing unit or agency. Examples include the purchase of capital assets and the issuance of bonds. Most specific authorizations are set forth by law or the policies of the governing board.

Designing and Evaluating Internal Controls

Risk assessment is the process of identifying and analyzing potentially negative factors that impede the achievement of objectives. Risks may be internal or external events and circumstances, including an agency's operating environment and the construction of a new information system. In every organization, management must determine the level of risk it is willing to accept and implement the necessary steps to not exceed this limit.[16]

Risk exposure is the focal point in designing and evaluating an internal control system. A number of critical questions should be answered, among them the following: (1) What things are likely to go wrong? (2) What specific components in the internal control system are designed to prevent problems? (3) What components in the internal control system are designed to detect problems if they occur? (4) What specific consequences of a problem might continue or remain after the implementation of the prevention, detection, and control system?

Preventive controls are the most cost-effective means for avoiding or minimizing risks in a responsibility center, because they are intended to prevent problems from occurring. For example, credit profiles of students requesting government loans may be checked before the loans are advanced, and only those fitting the acceptable profile will be granted. Dual check signing is another example of preventive control in which two individuals are required to review the supporting documents before expenditure authorization. *Detective control* is initiated only after errors and irregularities have occurred. A good example is the reconciliation of bank statements, whereby the book balance is matched with the reported bank statement balance. Detective control is also used in watching for the theft of inventory supplies.

The design of an internal control system should give due cognizance to its cost, which must be compared to the benefits that the system will reasonably generate in reducing risks. Sensitivity to cost–benefit considerations requires that each internal control system be tailored to the particular agency, governmental unit, or entity. This involves recognizing the size of the entity, the complexity of operations, and the extent of computer use, as well as building in the flexibility to permit management to take appropriate action as each situation dictates.

Preventive control is likely to provide greater protection against risks than detective control. To obtain the best outcome (and prevent losses from occurring) will necessitate the application of controls on all transactions. By comparison, detective control can be applied effectively to samples of transactions. Of particular note is that the very nature of most transactions in organizations precludes the use of preventive internal controls such as bank reconciliation or dual authorization. Therefore, in most instances, detective control is the most cost-effective means of reducing risks.

Designing Internal Controls with Employees in Mind

The *employee* represents both ends of the same control continuum. At one end, the employee is the most important ingredient for the achievement of effective internal control; at the other, the employee poses potentially the greatest risk to the agency. To promote employees' best contributions, the organization must design a control system that integrates incentives in such a way that participants find it easy and attractive to help enforce their internal control duties. One way of achieving the internal control objective requires that employee responsibilities and duties be tied directly to the agency's performance evaluation system. Hence, raises, bonuses, and promotions should incorporate the standards of both operating performance and compliance with the internal control system. The extent of the rewards should be commensurate with the quality with which the internal control functions have been executed. The linkage of these two important activities (control and operating duties) indicates the seriousness and priority that management assigns to the control function. Sound management principles—including planning, budgeting, clearly defined responsibility, and timely followthrough action—convey important signals and cues to employees that management is fully supportive and committed to excellence.

Internal Control and Flowcharts

Flowcharts are important means for tracing the paths of transactions. They provide a graphic representation of information flows that indicate transactions, activities, processes, and interrelated decisions. They show lines of communication from the initiating point to terminus. A flowchart is a shorthand way of depicting and simplifying complex relationships and can easily be achieved by using organizational charts or procedure manuals.

The system flowchart, representing the data throughout the system under review, is the most widely used technique for identifying information gaps, bottlenecks, redundancies, inefficient use of personnel, and poorly operating routing systems. Because the flowchart identifies sources of information, decision points, storage points, and information flow direction, it can easily identify the individuals responsible for processing data.

If flowcharts are to be maximally useful, the individual preparer must have direct knowledge of activities as they actually exist. This demands a keen understanding of the organization and sequencing of operations. Figure 3.1 provides the standard flowchart symbols. Figure 3.2 illustrates the flow of information for the purchasing function in a small nonprofit agency.

Concluding Observations

Internal control has achieved greater visibility because its strategic role is gradually being recognized. Revelations of major deficits in internal control has led to significant losses in organizations in both the public and private sectors. When sound internal controls are maintained and effectively monitored, they are an essential aid in enhancing productivity and effectiveness. Furthermore, they are a vital means for "keeping honest people honest."

Process – Manual, mechanical, or automated changes in data. For example, document preparation generating a computer run, recording accounting entries, proofing totals on an adding machine.

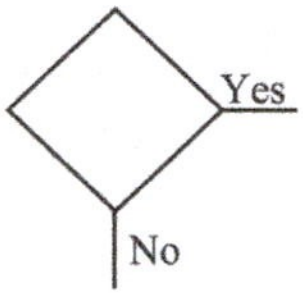

Decision – Involving two alternate procedures, solutions, answers, etc.

Yes

No

Document – Example of a record that supports an operation. This may be a form, report, computer printout, correspondence, accounting record, etc.

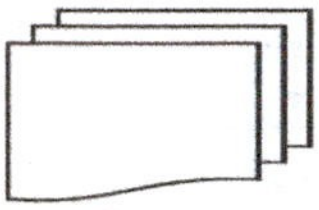

Multiple Documents – To identify disposition of copies, number each separately. Provide an additional document symbol to indicate any remaining copies.

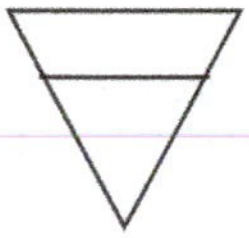

Storage or File – Any media such as correspondence files, computer tapes, etc., used to retain information while it is not being processed. Notations such as "T" for temporary or "A" for alphabetical order may be made within the symbol.

Punched Card – A card with holes punched that signify information; used in data processing.

Terminal – Beginning or end of flow.

Information Flow – Indicating the direction of flow of information.

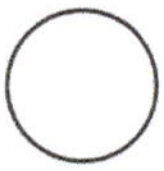

Connector – Indication of information existing in one part of the chart but reentering at another point. Maintain continuity by entering the same number or letter from one connector to the next..

FIGURE 3.1   Standard flowchart symbols.

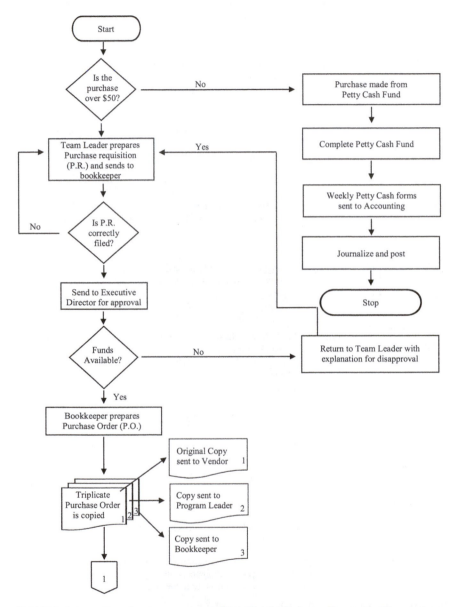

FIGURE 3.2a **Purchasing process flowchart of a small nonprofit agency.**

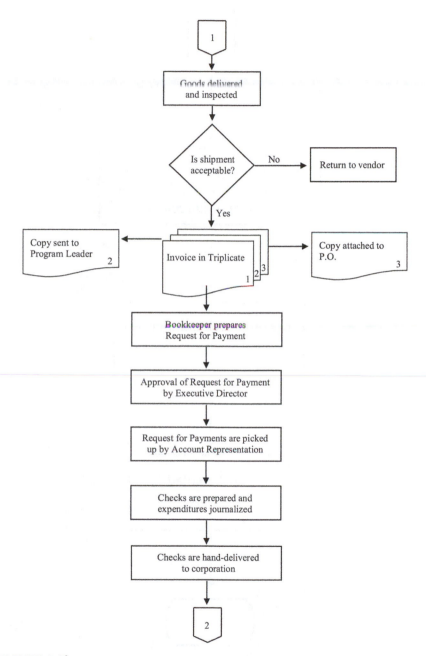

FIGURE 3.2b

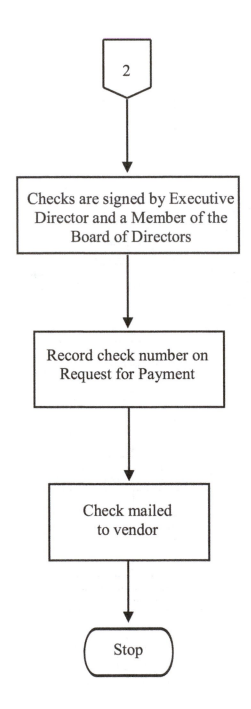

FIGURE 3.2c

TABLE 3.3 Appendix: Internal Control Questionnaire

General

1.	Is there a policy and procedures manual?	Yes	No
2.	Are there periodic physical inventories of supplies and equipment?	Yes	No

Control Over Checks

3.	Are all disbursements, except petty cash, made by check?	Yes	No
4.	Is the signing of checks in advance prohibited?	Yes	No
5.	Is the practice of drawing checks to "cash" or "bearer" prohibited?	Yes	No
6.	Are checks drawn limited to payrolls and/or pettycash reimbursements?	Yes	No
7.	Are the bank accounts independently reconciled by someone other than the employee who keeps the case records?	Yes	No
8.	Is the sequence of check numbers accounted for when reconciling the bank accounts?	Yes	No
9.	Are checks ever issued on the basis of verbal authority only?	Yes	No
10.	Is proper inventory control maintained over blank checks and voided checks?	Yes	No
11.	Are agency funds from major programs kept in a separate bank account?	Yes	No
12.	Are surprise counts made of the petty-cash fund?	Yes	No
13.	Are vouchers or other supporting documents presented together with the checks submitted for signature?	Yes	No
14.	Are the supporting documents stamped with a "paid" stamp or other mark so as to prevent their use for duplicate payment?	Yes	No
15.	Are cash receipts recorded and deposited daily?	Yes	No
16.	Are checks issued in blank prohibited?	Yes	No
17.	Are alterations of checks or bank transfers prohibited?	Yes	No
18.	Are check protection machines used where appropriate and feasible?	Yes	No
19.	Is protective paper used?	Yes	No

Control Concerning Cash Receipts

20.	Is a surety bond required for employees handling cash?	Yes	No
21.	Are bank accounts authorized by the treasurer?	Yes	No
22.	Is the person performing the mail-opening function kept from making deposits?	Yes	No

(Continued)

TABLE 3.3 *(Continued)*

23.	Is the person opening the mail required to give receipts in detail?	Yes	No
24.	Is comparison made with the cashier's record and mail receipts by an independent person?	Yes	No
25.	Is there a system to independently control miscellaneous cash receipts?	Yes	No
26.	Are bank duplicate deposit tickets compared with cash receipts?	Yes	No
27.	Are postdated checks protected in a secure place?	Yes	No
28.	Are postdated checks required to be reported or logged in?	Yes	No
29.	Do people handling the cashier function engage in collection activities?	Yes	No
30.	Are vacations mandatory for people handling cash?	Yes	No

Control Concerning Cash Disbursements

31.	Is a system in place that accounts for all prenumbered checks?	Yes	No
32.	Are spoiled checks mutilated and secured to prevent reuse?	Yes	No
33.	Is there a system that controls unused checks?	Yes	No
34.	Are people who sign checks prohibited from:		
	a) Handling cash?	Yes	No
	b) Approving disbursements?	Yes	No
	c) Recording cash receipts?	Yes	No
	d) Posting ledger accounts?	Yes	No
35.	Are signature facsimiles in use adequately controlled?	Yes	No
36.	Is there a system for countersigning checks?	Yes	No
37.	Are documents supporting payments destroyed or stamped "paid" when payment is made?	Yes	No
38.	Is the checkpreparation function and the approval of invoices separated?	Yes	No
39.	Are bank statements reconciled monthly?	Yes	No
40.	Is there a system to control and promptly record transfers from one bank to another?	Yes	No
41.	Are those charged with investing funds separated from:		
	a) Recording investments?	Yes	No
	b) Issuing confirmation of purchases?	Yes	No
	c) Matching securities purchases with broker, dealer, or institutional confirmation?	Yes	No
	d) Preparing bank reconciliation and periodic reports?	Yes	No

Control Over Payroll

42.	Are payroll checks issued prior to receiving time and attendance reports?	Yes	No
43.	Is proper authorization and documentation made in the hiring of additional staff and/or granting salary increases?	Yes	No

44. Is official documentation presented to the payroll clerk to support the payroll?	Yes	No
45. Is the payment of overtime properly approved?	Yes	No
46. Are there procedural controls over the use of overtime?	Yes	No
47. Are time and attendance reports countersigned by an individual in authority?	Yes	No
48. Is a complete current record maintained on personnel and rates?	Yes	No

Control Over Purchases

49. Is a separate bank account maintained for payroll funds? (If the answer is "yes," is a monthly reconciliation of the payroll bank account made by an employee who is independent of payroll preparation and accounting functions?)	Yes	No
50. Are payment vouchers or invoices approved by a responsible official?	Yes	No
51. Does he/she have a record of the individuals' signatures?	Yes	No
52. Are there proper safeguards over undistributed or unclaimed checks?	Yes	No
53. Are payroll checks distributed by someone other than the personnel preparing the checks?	Yes	No
54. Are employees' names, salary rates, etc., checked against payroll by someone other than the payroll clerk on a test-check basis?	Yes	No
55. Are all invoices matched to the purchase order and/ or approved by someone in authority, indicating that the item was in fact received or the services were in fact performed prior to the preparation of the check in payment?	Yes	No
56. Are all invoices examined to verify that the items, price, and quantity invoiced are proper and as ordered?	Yes	No
57. Does the financial officer or department have a list of the individuals who are authorized to sign purchase requisitions, purchase orders, receiving reports, time and attendance cards, etc.?	Yes	No
58. Are all requisitions for purchases approved by a properly designated individual?	Yes	No
59. Are all purchase requisitions checked against the budget to verify that a budget line exists authorizing such purchases?	Yes	No
60. Are purchase orders used to indicate receipt of all merchandise?	Yes	No
61. Are receiving reports used to indicate receipt of all merchandise?	Yes	No
62. Are purchase orders properly signed by someone in authority?	Yes	No

(Continued)

TABLE 3.3 *(Continued)*

Overall Organization of the Agency Operations

63.	Is the overall management and departmental structure of the agency, including duties, lines of responsibility, and accountability or key employees, defined in organization charts and job descriptions?	Yes	No
64.	Are the organization charts and written descriptions reviewed periodically to determine if they are up to date?	Yes	No
65.	Are the duties, lines of responsibility, and accountability of the accounting staff adequately defined in organization charts or job descriptions?	Yes	No
66.	Are the organization charts and written job descriptions reviewed periodically to determine whether they are appropriate and up-to-date?	Yes	No
67.	Are there written policies regarding personnel that relate to delegation of duties when personnel are absent?	Yes	No
68.	Are annual vacations for all personnel enforced?	Yes	No
69.	Are the accounting policies reviewed periodically to determine whether they are appropriate?	Yes	No
70.	Is there an up-to-date manual of accounting procedures?	Yes	No
71.	Is there a list of account codes (charts of accounts)?	Yes	No
72.	Are there written policies relating to the physical safeguarding of critical accounting forms, records, transactionprocessing areas, and procedural manuals?	Yes	No

Computer Department

73.	Are the duties, lines of responsibility, and accountability of the computer-department staff adequately defined in organization charts and written job descriptions?	Yes	No
74.	Are the organization charts and written job descriptions reviewed periodically to determine whether they are appropriate and up-to-date?	Yes	Yes
75.	Are the organization charts and written job descriptions approved by appropriate levels of management?	Yes	No
76.	Are there written policies regarding computer staff that relate to the delegation of duties when staff members are absent?	Yes	No
77.	Are annual vacations for all computer staff enforced?	Yes	No

Fidelity Insurance

78.	Are there written policies with respect to insurance coverage and employee fidelity bonds?	Yes	No

79. Does the agency take appropriate steps to confirm the adequacy of its insurance coverage (e.g., by ensuring that the coverage is regularly reviewed by a knowledgeable person who strives to make a professional evaluation)?   Yes   No

80. Does the agency carry fidelitybond coverage of the appropriate type and amount?   Yes   No

Notes

1. See Government Accounting Office (GAO), GAO/AIMD-00-21.3.1: *Standards for Internal Control in the Federal Government* (Washington, DC: GAO, 1999), pp. 1–2; also, Clinton T. Bass, *Changes to the Government Performance and Results Act (GPRA): Overview of the New Framework of Products and Processes* (Washington, DC: Congressional Research Service, February 29, 2012).

2. See Jack D. Bakker and John Marts, "Internal Controls," *Small Business Forum* (fall 1990): 29–31.

3. Vincent O'Reilly, Barry N. Winograd, James S. Gerson, and Henry R. Jaenicke, *Montgomery's Auditing*, 12th ed. (New York: John Wiley & Sons, 1999), p. 195.

4. Committee of Sponsoring Organizations (COSO), *The Internal Controls Integrated Framework* (December 2011), p. 11.

5. Stephen J. Gauthier, *An Elected Official's Guide to Internal Controls and Fraud Prevention* (Chicago: Government Finance Officers Association, 1974), p. 5.

6. Timothy Bell, Frank Marrs, Ira Solomon, and Howard Thomas, *Auditing Organizations through a Strategic-System Lens: The KPMG Business Measurement Process* (New York: Peat Marwick LLP, 1997), p. 31.

7. See *Internal Controls for Local Governments: A Training Presentation for City of Tampa's Leaders* (Tampa, FL: City of Tampa, Florida, n.d.).

8. COSO, *The Internal Controls Integrated Framework*, p. 13.

9. Michael C. Knapp, *Financial Accounting: A Focus on Decision Making*, 2nd ed. (Cincinnati, OH: Southwestern College Publishing, 1998), p. 82; and Statement of Auditing Standards No. 78, "Consideration of Internal Control in a Financial Statement Audit: An Amendment to SAS No. 55" (New York: American Institute of Certified Public Accountants, 1996), paragraph 6.

10. Knapp, *Financial Accounting*, p. 82.

11. GAO, *Standards for Internal Control in the Federal Government*, p. 20.

12. Ibid., p. 19.

13. Ibid., p. 4.

14. Ibid.

15. Irwin T. David, *How to Evaluate and Improve Internal Controls in Governmental Units* (Chicago: Municipal Finance Officers Association, 1981), p. 19.

16. Ibid., p. 180.

4

Revenue Management

Governments have the responsibility for providing an array of public and quasipublic goods and services that are expressed through the expenditure process—the governmental budget, which identifies who gets what portions as well as when and how much of the available community resources go into that portion. An important factor to keep in mind is that a budget reveals simply the other side of the coin. Thus every expenditure of dollars requires an equal amount of revenues to be withdrawn from the public. This results in a reduction of private consumption and a transfer of private savings to the public sector. Taxation is a fundamental component of government's fiscal base that significantly influences the direction of the economy on a day-to-day basis.[1]

Unlike the private sector, revenue in the public and, to a lesser extent, the not-for-profit sectors is not indicative of demand for goods and services. An increase in taxes tells us nothing about the quality and quantity of the services. Hence, the conventional financial statements cannot supply information about the demand for goods and services. There is no direct link between revenue and expenditures. Like revenues, expenditures are not linked to client/customer constituents. Donors may continue to increase their giving to not-for-profit agencies, but these are not reflected in increased services. The matching concept that is central to financial accounting—requiring the paring of revenue to expenditures—is missing. There is typically no matching of costs with the generation of revenue. This is an important observation that must be kept in mind.

While there are numerous spending categories, typically fewer categories are employed in collecting taxes. Especially in larger units of governments and other not-for-profit organizations, revenues are seldom subject to earmarking (resources designated to be spent for specific program or activities such as education or old age pensions) except in those cases where funds are transferred in from other governmental units. Moreover, revenue inflows and sources tend to be relatively stable in contrast to expenditures. For these reasons, among others, revenue raising has seldom attracted a great amount of political attention. Additionally, politicians are loath to talk about revenues, because they involve extracting resources from the public rather than in giving them, as is the case with expenditure programs. The advent of California Proposition 13 in 1976 departed significantly from this norm and provided the impetus for a successful antitax movement throughout the country. This movement is still negatively affecting governments' tax raising opportunities.

Unlike the expenditure process, revenue policies typically have a number of legal constraints. This is true for all levels of government and other not-for-profit organizations. The problem is particularly evident at the local levels of government. Constraints take such forms as uniform assessments, maximum rates, and specified accounting procedures. Other not-for-profit agencies, especially those participating as United Way members, are restricted in whom they may solicit and in when such solicitations may take place.

This chapter presents the different meanings and concepts of revenue, discusses the economics of revenue raising, and explains the determination and administration of a revenue plan. An analysis of selected methods for forecasting revenues is then presented.

Articulating Revenue Policies

Although level of wealth or revenue capacity and political philosophy influence revenue policies, there are many other significant factors that help to determine the revenue structure and policies. Especially in democracies such as the United States, revenue policies are shaped by citizens' attitudes, such as a perceived fairness of the revenue structure. "Fairness" suggests that both the tax revenue and public service benefits should be equitably distributed. Because the demand for goods and services typically does not parallel revenue capacity and willingness to pay for the services desired, administrators are constantly involved in budget balancing acts.[2]

Criteria of a Good Tax System

Adam Smith articulated four criteria that can be considered indicative of a good tax system in financial absences, referred to as "canons of taxation," in 1776:[3]

1. The citizens of a state should contribute to the government as nearly as possible according to their respective abilities.
2. The obligated tax that each individual is required to pay should be certain and not arbitrary, based on clearly articulated rules and procedures.
3. The levying of the tax should be at a time and the manner that make it easy and convenient to pay.

4. The tax law should be enacted so as to equal only the amount necessary to carry out the functions of the government.

It is useful here to summarize the goals of revenue policies. The following ones are not mutually exclusive, thus the conflict among them, and the need for tradeoffs is unavoidable. These following are "impact" goals:

- *Political acceptability* involves review and analysis of the environment, citizens' attitudes, review of existing tax revenue capacity, and comparative benchmarking with other jurisdictions. After this is done, proposed tax changes must be clearly explained, showing how tax burdens are being fairly distributed.
- *Revenue yield (adequacy) and stability* are overriding objectives. Revenue sources must be structured to provide sufficient resources to finance required and desirable services. The revenue yield should be responsive to important changes in population and income, allowing analysts to reasonably predict revenue results. The predictability of tax sources allows the government to plan its budgets effectively.
- *Political accountability* suggests that revenues should be the product of direct legislative action and not a system structured to automatically hike tax rates. For example, the Allegheny County, Pennsylvania, reassessment system allows some jurisdictions to significantly increase their revenues without legislative action. To minimize the impact of the reassessment system, state law requires that municipalities whose taxes rise above 5 percent must return the difference to taxpayers.
- *International implications.* Especially at the national level, attention must be given to trading partners comparisons are not out of step. This is particularly important in the existing international economic free market system being advocated. Taxing policies cannot be viewed only from internal country perspective.

To help in making the governmental administrator's job less difficult, it is important that revenue policies be clearly articulated. Policy statements should set forth the explicit assumptions on which the expected revenue is based, indicating the percentage of increase or decrease, and providing clear guidelines for all stakeholders and interested parties. In most of the rest of the not-for-profit sector, the concern about fairness and balancing the revenue burden with the distribution of goods and services receives less attention. The revenue inflow sources differ significantly. Important sources of revenue in most not-for-profit organizations are made up of endowments, invested capital, and receipts from the sale of services. These revenue inflow sources are heavily dependent on endowment investment decisions and the pricing decisions for services.[4]

Revenue and Sustainability

In the short term, we tend to think of sustainability as meaning current practices that can maintain our existing lifestyle. We want to know whether we have enough income flow to pay for the goods and services to which we are accustomed. Similarly, a government uses many revenue sources that generate resources adequate to continue expected level of services. This short-term emphasis focuses on viability or the ability to generate enough revenue to meet current operating payments, including debt commitments.

Sustainability takes a long-term perspective. Revenue sources (capacity) must be capable of providing sufficient inflow for an extended time horizon in the future, allowing the government to meet expected financial requirements without the need to make significant changes or adjustments to revenues and expenditures. This articulation of revenue sustainability is largely useful only as it relates to expenditure.[5] The congruence between revenue inflows and expenditure outflow determines whether there is a surplus or there is a deficit. Thus revenue and expenditure projection and assessment are viewed from fiscal policy perspective where revenue and expenditure are linked. The fiscal policy is said to be sustainable if the present value of future primary surplus equals the current debt (known as intertemporal budget constraint). To the extent that government debt matches the generated surplus excessive debt is avoided. This allows government to roll over its debt. Sustainability indicators resulting from long-term fiscal policy (taxes and expenditures) could provide useful lead time and aid to detect unsustainable policies, preempting costs associated with fiscal correction.[6]

The primary gap as shown in the equation below indicates the distance from the sustainable primary balance. Although the primary gap is a very useful indicator, it does not fully account for the tensions that may arise from the expenditure—for example, as a result of an aging populace. "The tax gap expenses the difference between the actions and the sustainable revenue-to-GDP ratio. The sustainable revenue ratio is such that [it] enables future spending to be financed. In terms of signaling the magnitude of the required fiscal correction, the tax gap is a more appropriate indicator. The primary gap and the tax gap can be calculated for different time horizons from one year to an infinite horizon."[7]

Sustainability and Environmental Taxes

If sustainability and environmental goals are to be achieved, appropriate taxes must be implemented. In business, environmental taxes affect the heart of business decision making, being likely to gain the attention of the financial officials by acting as a catalyst for enhancing environmental performance. To be successful, these taxes must achieve the buy in of the affected business and

stakeholders. Businesses need to see the taxes not as unnecessary cost, but as a short and long-term instrument to improve efficiency and competitiveness.
Environmental taxes have several goals:

- There should be explicit leverage to governmental environmental objectives.
- Each tax must be designed to positively change environmental behavior, consistent with policy objectives.
- The taxes should be structured in relation to environmental objectives so that the tax is levied according to the damage to the environment—for example, the greater the pollution, the greater the fine.

A formula for the intertemporal tax gap (ITGAP) was developed by the European Commission to indicate the infinite horizon tax gap or fiscal sustainability gap indicator:

$$ITGAP = \frac{(r-g)\left(b_t - \sum_{i=1}^{\infty}\left(\frac{1+g}{1+r}\right)ipb_{t+i}\right)}{1+g}$$

where b_t is the debt to GDP ratio, r is the interest rate on government debt, g is the government growth rate of the economy, and pb_t is the primary balance to GDP ratio.

The infinite tax gap provides the adjustment necessary to accommodate the intertemporal budget constraint, giving the one-time change to achieve the primary balance to meet the required GDP ratio. Assuming that ITGAP is 8 percent, the primary balance will have to be greater than the projected 8 percent of GDP in each future year.[8]

Defining Revenues

Revenues are inflows or receipts (excluding cash in kind) from all external sources, less refunds, debt issuances, and the liquidation of investments. This parallels the *net revenues* line item used in private industry reporting to define economic benefits obtained, less certain expenses and discounts, from a business transaction. All levels of government and other not-for-profit organizations classify revenues by source. These entities also use the term *receipts* synonymously with *cash collections*, whereas the term *revenue* is also typically equated with the accrual of funds (earned but not yet received). The types of revenues vary among the different levels of government and among other not-for-profit agencies. Although the process for assessing, levying, and collecting taxes is similar in all forms of government, it differs significantly from the revenue process in other not-for-profit organizations. Both by law and by tradition, there is greater reliance on certain kinds of taxes at different levels of government. For example, real and personal property are viewed almost exclusively as a local tax source, whereas at the state levels and—especially—federal levels, income taxes, both corporate and individual, are important. Additionally, sales and excise taxes provide a significant source of revenue for states.

Meaning of Revenue: Federal Level

The General Accounting Office (GAO) has defined *revenue* as referring to the increase in assets or reduction in liabilities resulting from operations. The GAO identified three important ways by which revenues could be generated:

- When the government performs services for which money is due
- When tangible goods and other tangible property are delivered to purchasers from whom payment is expected
- When the government is owed amounts for which no current performance is required

At the federal government level, the Treasury Department (meaning predominantly the Internal Revenue Service and the Bureau of Customs) is charged with the main responsibility for the collection of receipts:

- Individual income taxes
- Corporate income taxes
- Social insurance taxes and contributions
- Excise taxes
- Custom duties
- Miscellaneous receipts[9]

Meaning of Revenue and Receipts: State and Local

The federal meaning of revenue and receipts differs somewhat at the lower levels of government. Thus, *revenue* may be defined as the inflow or receipt of money by a governmental unit that is not obtained by creating an offsetting liability. Stated another way, revenue consists of the total amount of money received by a governmental unit that does not represent a recovery or refund of an expenditure, the cancellation of a particular liability, or a decrease in assets or contributions from an enterprise or in intergovernmental service funds. *Receipts* usually indicate cash received, unless stipulated otherwise. Note that this definition of revenue refers to those instances when revenue is recorded on the accrual, modified accrual, or cash bases. Some governmental units and other not-for-profit organizations use the term *revenue receipt* to mean *cash*. It should be borne in mind that revenue is synonymous with the operating income of a governmental unit.

Using the Accrual Basis

If a governmental unit billed property owner A for $2,000 in taxes in 2003 and received the $2,000 in 2003, this is revenue for 2003. If the governmental unit billed property owner B for $2,500 for 2003 but the owner did not pay until 2004, the $2,500 is revenue for 2003. Both the $2,000 and $2,500 inflows relate to the 2002 operating activities and the services furnished for that year and to the expenses used for the provision of services. Thus, as of December 31, 2003, the $2,500 is an asset and will be indicated on the balance sheet under "accounts receivable" or "taxes receivable." *Revenue* is made up of revenue and receipts, being generated from a number of sources, grouped, according to the recommendations of the National Council on Governmental Accounting, as follows:

- Taxes
- Special assessments levied
- Licenses and permits
- Intergovernmental revenues
- Charges for services
- Fines and forfeits
- Miscellaneous revenues

Sales Revenues

Not-for-profit organizations such as hospitals typically operate on an accrual basis. Thus, sales of goods and services for a specific period are revenues for that period. Revenues are generated at the time a patient receives services and is charged, which may not coincide with the time when the patient or a third party was billed or when cash was actually received. (To simplify record-keeping, some hospitals recognize revenue only when the patient is billed.) In those cases in which there is a high probability that the patient is not likely to pay his or her bills, revenues are reduced by the amount established through the use of a contra-asset account defined as allowance for bad debt.

Membership Dues

When membership dues become payable, they are considered revenue whether paid before, after, or during the applicable period. Dues that are unpaid after the period become *assets* or *receivables*. At the end of the period, the amount of receivables is reduced for probable bad debt. Life membership is, however, treated differently in most cases: Instead of recognizing only the portion of life membership as it comes due, the total amount is typically identified as revenue when it is received.

Pledges

The principles stated under "Membership Dues" also apply to pledges. Future pledges are revenue in those periods to which the pledged contribution applies, even if the cash is not received during the same time period. Downward adjustments are made to recognize potential bad debts. Some analysts oppose the recognition of pledges as receivable because they are legally unenforceable. Additionally, uncollectible pledges are too unreliable to make reasonable estimates. The term *revenue* and *income* are used interchangeably in not-for-profit agencies. More recently, however, *income* has come to mean the amount remaining after subtracting all expenses, although the United Way uses the term *revenue* to mean money donated or received from any given source.

Funders' allocation of resources to not-for-profit agencies typically coincide with one of the following practices in making payouts to recipient agencies: (1) a prearranged payment schedule (typically quarterly), (2) prearranged payments based on actual expense flow (typically biweekly or monthly), or (3) cost reimbursement based on actual expenses.[10] There are, of course, contributions and special events that generate revenues that follow no specific patterns. Regardless, the funders or contributing organizations have found that they must live with the imposed payment plans.[11]

The Economics of Revenue Raising

The functions of government revenue include (1) the efficient generation of resources to finance the delivery of goods and services, (2) fairness in the distribution of tax burdens, (3) income distribution and redistribution, and (4) a fiscal policy instrument for managing consumer demands. These activities may be referred to as the *revenue*, *redistributive*, and *fiscal policy* (manipulations of the taxing powers to affect consumer demand) functions of taxation.

The decision to pursue any one, or a combination, of these revenue functions involves value judgments—that is, determining *who* will pay and in *what* amounts. Many questions can thus be raised about the revenue function relating to concerns of distribution, redistribution, and equity effects of the cost of government services to the taxpayers. The precise *distributional impact* on the incomes of individuals in a given community cannot easily be determined, although estimates of impacts, referred to as tax incidence, may be derived by a careful study of the components of the tax base and tax rates. Importantly, it should also be borne in mind that the tax burden may not fall on the initial tax base object due to "tax shifting" (the ultimate resting place of a tax impact). For example, the property tax on an owner-occupied residence cannot be shifted, but in those cases in which the owner rents housing units, the tax can partially be, at least, shifted onto the renters.

Taxes may affect the allocation of resources and economic efficiency by distorting economic decisions of individuals and businesses. When taxes are not related to the provision of goods and services, taxpayers will be unable to assess the costs and benefits of the goods and services. Lacking such information, taxpayers cannot effectively formulate demands for public services, creating the likely possibility that their goods and services will be of suboptimal quality. This may result in the faulty allocation of resources between the public and private sectors. Tax differential rates among different jurisdictions may also have the effect of inducing persons, businesses, and even industries to relocate.

Our discussion suggests that taxes and revenue policy have important implications for the stability of the economy. The concerns for stability and growth are mainly national responsibilities, although local government units are keenly interested in stability and in economic growth for their taxing capacity. For example, real property values are largely dependent on the current state of the housing market, a sector heavily reliant on national economic conditions. As real property taxes represent the primary source of revenue for local governments, the nation's economic situation is of keen concern. An individual governmental unit alone has minimal effect on economic output, but where local governmental units provide tax incentives, they can induce some businesses to move from one jurisdiction to another. Tax rates may influence outsourcing or insourcing.

Much attention has been devoted in public sector economics to the importance of distributing tax burdens equitably among taxpayers. A number of sophisticated theories and approaches have been developed to aid in explaining the distribution and equity consideration in taxation. In the discussion that follows, two benchmark criteria for evaluating taxes in public finance are discussed: (1) the application of the *efficiency criterion* and (2) the application of the *equity criterion*.

Tax Efficiency

The *efficiency criterion* accepts the view that different taxes impose varying degrees of distortion on the market economy, creating welfare losses by causing a departure from the Pareto optimality (an inability to allocate resources to improve the well-being or utility of an individual without making at least one other person worse off). Ideally, an objective of a society's tax system is to minimize the excess burden or welfare costs due to taxation when diverting a given amount of resources from the private to the public sector. The efficiency criterion evaluates a tax on the amount of excess burden it creates per revenue dollar collected. The taxes that impose less excess burden are said to be more efficient from an economic perspective. An effective tax is said to be neutral in that it affects consumption, savings, work, leisure, and other important choices only minimally. A tax must keep distortion on market choices to a minimum to avoid potential substitution effects on the economy. Ideally, a tax should transfer resources from the private to the public sectors without affecting the overall efficiency performance of the economy.

Tax efficiency also relates to the way in which a tax is enforced. This is particularly important because tax equity must mean more than a theoretically rational tax system. Hence, there must be equitable enforcement of the tax on all those subject to it so that no one illegally transfers his or her tax burden to others. Also important for the efficient enforcement of a tax is the convenience, simplicity, and compliance cost to taxpayers of determining their tax liability. These factors ultimately affect the cost of collection and hence, the efficiency of the tax.

Equity Criterion

Horizontal Equity. Distributional effects are inevitable in all tax systems. A good tax system must be evaluated not only by horizontal equity, but also by vertical distribution. A tax is viewed as being *horizontally equal* if it treats equals equally. For example, if two persons have equal economic circumstances before a tax is imposed, they would be in the same economic circumstances after the imposition of the tax. That is two people earning the same income should be taxed the same. Tax equity requires that the application should neither be arbitrary nor discriminatory. Horizontal equity requires that taxpayers with the same income should pay identical amounts of tax.

Despite horizontal equity's popularity, it does have some drawbacks. To apply the criteria to a tax system, the point at which two persons have equal economic circumstances or welfare must be ascertained objectively, which is not an easy task. For example, should the size of the family be considered? How are income and wealth to be considered in determining ability to pay taxes? Will a distinction be made between capital gains and ordinary income?

Vertical Equity. According to the concept of *vertical equity*, unequals should be assessed unequally. This criterion suggests that persons of differential tax-paying circumstances or abilities should pay different amounts of tax. Judging the degree to which the tax system is vertically equitable requires that value judgments be made about the desirable or appropriate way to treat people at different income levels. To facilitate an understanding of vertical equity, the *ability to pay* and *benefit* principles are further examined.

The *ability to pay principle* suggests that all taxpayers should bear "equal sacrifice" (based on their financial capacities) in the payment of taxes. Hence, taxpayers with more income would pay more taxes. How large or how small should the differentials be among taxpayers? The tax rates are typically based on three main alternatives: the *regressive, proportional,* and *progressive* concepts.

If the tax paid as a percentage of income declines as income increases, the tax is considered to be *regressive*, as shown in Figure 4.1, part C. The reverse is true of the *progressive* tax (see Figure 4.1, part A). As income rises, the percentage of taxes rises. If the tax paid as a percentage of income remains unchanged as income increases, the tax is said to be *proportional* (see Figure 4.1, part B). Note that regressive, progressive, and proportional taxes rely on percentage of income paid in taxes for computation, so absolute tax dollars paid should not be used in determining the nature of a particular tax.

Of the three types of rates, only the progressive is normally viewed as being in accordance with the ability to pay principle. This is also partially true for a proportional tax, because as far as income goes, the absolute amount of taxes paid increases, even though the percentage does not change. Even a regressive tax system may have a degree of progressivity in its application if people with high income are required to pay a higher absolute amount of taxes, even though the percentage of tax paid of income falls. Only the progressive tax, however, accords with the ability to pay principle

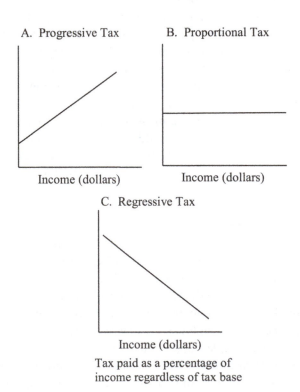

FIGURE 4.1   Tax base relationships: Distributional equity.

and distributional equity after taxes. It should be noted, however, that a particular tax should never be analyzed in isolation from other taxes, because it is the *total* or *combined* effect of the taxes that ultimately determines the regressivity or progressivity of a tax system.

The *benefit principle* is viewed as the primary alternative to the ability to pay principle. Unlike the latter principle, which more directly addresses the concepts of equity, the benefit principle addresses the goal of market efficiency. A major advantage of this principle is that it directly relates the revenue and expenditure sides of the budget with each other. Basically, it provides a good approximation of market behavior in the allocation process of the public sector. The operation of the benefit principle permits individuals to voluntarily exchange purchasing power in the form of fees or the acquisition of government-produced goods, thereby permitting individuals to pay directly for the government-produced goods from which satisfaction or profit is derived. It should be especially noted that the equity is suggested neither by the monetary nor sacrifice benchmark, but by the dual facts that (1) the purchase of the government-produced goods is voluntary, as in the private market sector, and (2) the payments are made according to the benefit received.

In practice, the benefit approach is restricted because of the inherent nature of collective consumption that typically characterizes the public sector—that is, individuals cannot be excluded from most of the benefits generated by government-produced goods, such as defense or police protection. Hence, unless compulsion is involved requiring consumers to pay, they will benefit as "free riders" and avoid payment. For this reason, many public sector goods that are not susceptible to the market pricing mechanism cannot be provided under the benefit principle.

The tax paid as a percentage of income (regardless of tax base) approach, though useful in some cases, involves a benefit principle that is not comprehensive enough in its application to provide the desired benchmark of equity in the distribution of the tax burden. It has been found to be applicable in those cases in which the government applies the user charge approach, such as in the cases of toll roads and garbage collection. Among the reasons why these services should be sold (involving user charges) include the following:

1. Generation of revenue intake approximating the value of the services produced
2. Motivation to determine whether the service is worth the cost
3. Creation of value-consciousness of managers about the service they receive
4. Generation of indicators to assess performance
5. Creation of cost-consciousness with respect to the value of services exchanged, minimizing waste and overuse and promoting productivity[12]
6. Produces equitability as service users pay in proportion to benefits received

7. Minimization of government expansion, because the quantity of service purchased indicates citizens' preferences
8. Use of market mechanism for price determination and service expansion

The popularity of user charges has made it a growing source of revenue in local governments. As the tax burden grows, local taxpayers have viewed user charges as a way of slowing their increase in property taxes. Since the mid-1970s, and especially with the decline of federal aid during the 1980s, user charges have been embraced by all levels of government as a desirable means of financing all services that are divisible and amenable to fees. "For an increasing number of local governments, revenue from charges and fees now exceeds the total revenue from all taxes, including the property taxes."[13]

Tax and Fiscal Disparity

Fiscal disparity provides information about aggregate inequality among political jurisdictions on revenue raising. State and local policymakers are shown the amount and mix of revenue that their governments collect. Policymakers typically ask questions such as the following: What is the capacity to raise revenues versus what is actually collected? Is the revenue capacity adequate to finance the needs for public service? These questions are especially relevant in times when revenue falls short of targeted expectations.[14]

States and localities differ widely on the fiscal pressures they face. Some jurisdictions must work harder to deliver the approximate equal services to residents. Among the factors that affect a state's taxing capacity are the number of residents below or near the poverty line, those needing cash assistance, special education health care, and schooling for children between ages 5 and 18. When there is high demand for these services, the states are said to have high fiscal need, requiring increasing costs to deliver or augment the scope of services that must be provided.[15]

It is useful to draw attention to the concepts that are employed in evaluating fiscal disparity:

- *Fiscal need* is a reflection of high service demands that citizens require to provide adequate services.
- *Fiscal capacity* is access to, and ability to raise, revenue from particular tax sources.
- *Tax effort* is the proportion of tax capacity that is actually used—the ratio of revenue collected to taxing capacity.
- *Fiscal comfort* is the ratio of expressed or identified needs compared to fiscal capacities.
- *Fiscal disparity* is a reflection of the differences across jurisdictions having fiscal discomfort.

"The degree of fiscal disparity among subnational jurisdictions has been a troubling issue among nations including the United States and Canada."[16] Devolution of service responsibilities from the central governments has been an important factor in increasing fiscal disparity. As the central government devolves responsibilities to states and localities, the requisite resources did not accompany the transfer of responsibilities.

If we want to make comparisons among the states, a method called the *representative tax system* (RTS) may be used. The RTS is equal to the ratio of actual nationwide specific tax collection to the nationwide standard base. For example, if the estimated nationwide standard retail sales taxes were $2.65 trillion for all jurisdictions in 1997, and the actual sales collections were $179 billion, the RTS is equal to $179 billion ÷ $2.65 trillion, or 6.74 percent.

If Connecticut sales taxes in 1997 were estimated at $34.4 billion, the RTS would be equal to 1.3 percent of the national standard ($34.4 billion ÷ $2.65 trillion). If Connecticut had imposed the 6.74 percent standard national rate, it would have raised $2.3 billion in revenue, generating a $709 per capita sales tax. Given the $667 national standard per capita sales tax, the Connecticut sales tax capacity was 106 percent ($709 per capita ÷ $667 per capita).

Property Tax

Property tax is the major source of revenue for local governments. It accounted for 73 percent of all local revenue in 1997, whereas states' reliance on property taxes amounted to only 2 percent in the same year. The property tax can be viewed as a tax on wealth levied against the value of property and based, at least partially, on the ability to pay and benefit concepts. Many defects are associated with the property tax, including its (1) regressivity with respect to income; (2) administrative inefficiency; and (3) creation of distortions in economic decision making.

The property tax involves both *real property* and *personal property*. *Real property* includes land and improvements to land. Improvements comprise the addition of such things as buildings and other structures that are permanently attached or fixed. *Personal property* consists of tangible and intangible property. Tangible property comprises, typically, movable objects such as machinery, inventory, furniture, luxury goods (jewelry and paintings), and automobiles. Intangible property includes items that have no inherent tangible value, but that rather represent claims to value such as stock certificates and bonds. For tax purposes, property can be categorized and differentiated by class of ownership (e.g., government, religious, tax-free) and by use (e.g., residential, commercial, industrial, agricultural). Because of the difficulty of administering personal property taxes, most states have abandoned them, either partially or totally. Each state has its own property tax structure. After the base has been defined, each governmental unit applies the tax rates to the base. Among the typical tax jurisdictions are the state, county, municipality, school district, and many other authorities.

There are three steps in the property tax process: (1) *assessment*, (2) *determination of rate*, and (3) *collection*. *Assessment* relates to the discovery and valuation of property (see Table 4.1). It is carried out usually by elected local officials, although some states may conduct this function for statewide property such as railroads. The quality of the assessment activity is not uniform. The associated high administrative cost is a major reason for spacing the revaluation at lengthy intervals, often in five- or ten-year increments. Many local units underassess property but then take the opportunity to apply a higher tax rate to generate the locally needed revenue. Additionally, property owners have the ability to challenge an assessment in court with the hopes of preventing a valuation increase. These challenges are often affirmed by the courts and can significantly reduce the budgeted real property tax base for the local government.

After the *rate is determined*, it is applied to an assessed value to generate a given amount of revenue. The rate may be expressed in terms of dollars per hundred or thousand dollars of assessed value of property or in terms of mills (tenths of a percent) per dollar of assessed value. A tax rate of $5 per $1,000 of assessed value is also equivalent to 50 cents per $100, or five mills per dollar. The formula used to determine the property tax rate is as follows:

$$\frac{\textit{Total budgeted revenue minus anticipated revenues from other sources}}{\textit{The assessed valuation of property within the governmental jurisdiction}} = \textit{Tax rate of assessed valuation}$$

Collection involves the process of applying the tax rate to each property in the tax district (and involving the assessed value of all taxable properties). Tax bills are calculated and mailed yearly, semiannually, or quarterly. The tax is calculated as follows:

$100,000	(market value determination)
× .40	(assessment ratio)
40,000	(gross assessed value)
− 10,000	(exemption)
30,000	(net assessed value)
× .10	(10% tax rate, 100 mills)
$ 3,000	(tax liability)

$$\text{Thus the effective tax rate} = \frac{3{,}000 \text{ (tax liability)}}{100{,}000 \text{ (market value)}} = .03 \text{ (or 3\%)}.$$

TABLE 4.1   Stages of the Property-Tax Cycle

Appraisal determines the value of property for tax purposes, using legally specified standards of valuation.

1. Taxable and tax-exempt property are discovered.
2. Legal owners and taxable site of property are identified.
3. Property is appraised on the basis of use and estimated value as of the appraisal date.
4. Property owners are notified of changes in appraised value.
5. Appeals from property owners are heard by independent board of review.
6. Adjustments to appraisals are reviewed and approved by board and appraiser.
7. Final certified appraisal roll is prepared.

Assessment adjusts appraised value to determine the taxable value of property.

1. Appraised value is multiplied by assessment rate (or ratio) to determine assessed value.*
2. Assessments are equalized by state agency to the same percentage of full value across jurisdictions.*
3. Assessed value is adjusted for partial exemptions, such as homesteads.*
4. Truth-in-taxation notices are prepared and published.*
5. Public hearing is held on proposed tax rate and/or budget.
6. Tax rate(s) is(are) set by governing board.
7. Rate(s) is(are) certified as being within legal limits.*
8. Tax roll is prepared and certified.

Collection involves the preparation and distribution of tax notices to both current and delinquent taxpayers.

1. Tax bills are prepared and mailed to owners of record.
2. Lien is attached to property to secure payment of taxes, penalties, and interest.
3. Current tax payments are received, credited, and distributed.
4. Unpaid taxes become delinquent after due date.
5. Delinquent tax roll is prepared.
6. Delinquent tax notices are prepared and property owners are notified.
7. Court order is sought to foreclose on lien on outstanding delinquencies.
8. Property is sold at a public auction for payment of back taxes, penalties, and interest.

Note: Asterisks indicate activities that are not performed in all states.

Source: Robert L. Bland, *A Revenue Guide for Local Government* (Washington, DC: International City Management Association, 1989), p. 45 (Used with permission of the publisher.)

Economic Effects of the Property Tax

Three criteria are briefly discussed: (1) equity and distribution, (2) allocation and efficiency, and (3) stability. On the *equity and distribution* scale, the property tax scores poorly on both ability to pay and the benefit principles of taxation. It relates to the ability to pay in that property ownership can be equated with wealth and can be employed to generate income, which is an index of the ability to pay. The benefit principle is involved because the owners of the property can avail themselves of a number of public services that are available directly to them, such as fire protection. As presently administered, the property tax is essentially a real estate tax and not a general property tax, and as such does not accord well with acceptable tax principles. For example, retired persons on small fixed incomes may become subject to higher taxes on the appreciating value of a home that was purchased many years earlier or inherited from previous generations. Similarly, undeveloped land that earned no income is taxed as if it did. Another major distributional problem relates to disparities among governmental jurisdictions due to differences in the value of the tax base. Some jurisdictions have high per capita rates, while others have low rates. Jurisdictions with low tax bases are not able to provide the required services that citizens may need. This is a major reason why the California Supreme Court in 1971 held, in *Serano vs. Priest*, that reliance on the property tax for financing education discriminated against the poor. Although this decision was later overturned in 1973 by the U.S. Supreme Court, it acknowledged that the system in most states was inequitable and chaotic.

The property tax produces allocation and efficiency distortions for a number of reasons, including assessment practices and effects on locational decisions by business and industries that take advantage of specified tax breaks. Stability is not a strong factor in favor of the property tax, because it is *relatively income-inelastic* in that property tax collection does not normally move in the same direction as the economy.

Economic Effects of the Income Tax

In varying degrees, all levels of government levy the income tax. The federal government is the most dominant in doing so among the three levels. The personal income tax is a major federal revenue source. It is essentially neutral in terms of allocational effects. Moreover, it acts as a positive economic stabilizer, is easy to administer, and can be adjusted to create equity. Because of the broad-based nature of this tax revenue, its yield (tax rate times base equals revenue) is high. On balance, the personal income tax is viewed as the best among the major tax instruments.

Economic Effects of the Sales Tax

Sales taxes are employed by the federal, state, and local governments, with the major use taking place at the state level. There, two basic types of sales taxes are employed: the *general sales tax* and the *excise tax*. There are numerous variations to be found in each. The general sales tax (a percentage of retail sales) is usually based on a broad range of goods and sometimes services. Excise taxes are imposed on specific goods levied as a percentage of sales, based on some specified unit (e.g., a gallon of gasoline); these taxes are often applied to goods viewed as societal "vices," such as tobacco and alcohol.

The general sales tax, also known as the "broad-based," "gross receipts," or "ad valorem" tax, is based on a percentage of the sales value to the seller. Typically, the seller quotes the tax rate separately from the price of the goods, and it is paid by the customer. The sales tax is politically appealing and is a productive and steady revenue producer at both the state and local levels of government. The tax is easy to administer, and in some cases, local government uses it as a substitute for the unpopular property tax. The general sales tax has an income substitution effect in that it does raise prices for the purchaser or consumer, in essence lowering income. Because not all goods are taxed, it is not easy to generalize about this substitution effect. Additionally, there is a number of means that have been used to reduce the regressivity of the sales tax, including exemptions on such items as food, medicines, and other necessities.

Managing the Revenue Program

Besides the structuring of taxes to achieve an equitable and efficient tax system, the fiscal manager must develop and maintain a tax system that will generate sufficient revenues/resources to meet the community's demand for specified amounts of goods and services. A summary of general guidelines that should be considered in the development and management of a revenue system follows.

Determining Revenue Needs

Revenue requirement estimates are based on expected or proposed expenditure plans. Ideally, the revenue forecast should be carried out as soon as possible for the ensuing fiscal year to permit an evaluation of its adequacy to meet expected needs. When the analysis reveals a gap, the early lead time will permit the design and installation of new or enhanced tax sources. The following are factors that should be considered in developing revenue plans:

- Inflation rate factor
- Political philosophy of the policymaker and relevant interest groups

- Community growth and development
- Expanded and new programs
- Population characteristics and trends
- Nature and components of the tax base
- Stability of revenue over the business cycle
- Tax efforts

Typically, revenue needs in some units of government and not-for-profit agencies are not projected in advance. Instead, the amount of available revenue is surveyed and the agency programs are fitted to them.[17]

Fair and Equitable Distribution of the Tax Burdens

Tax rates are based not only on the benefits received principle but also on the ability to pay basis, as discussed above. As a tenet of good tax administration, the tax should be uniformly and equitably (nondiscriminatorily) applied. No one should be allowed to escape payment because of improper assessment, inefficient tax collection procedures, or an improper exemption allowance.[18]

Shifting the tax incidence may create an inequitable burden and negatively affect vertical equity. Incidence refers to the burden that individuals or group bear following the imposition of a tax. Incidence or the final resting place of a tax occurs, for example, in a situation in which a landlord shifts the increase of property tax to its renters. The person on whom the tax falls suffers a decrease in disposable resources rather than the landlord.

Revenue Base and Growth

A tax should have elasticity in that it should be relatively responsive to growth in the economy. The expansion or growth in programs made necessary by economic growth should be financed directly from the expanded economic activity in the community. The normal assumption is that growth should always be attendant upon expansion in revenues, provided that "the revenue base is tied to sources which are affected by the growth."[19] The lack of responsiveness of the tax base to economic growth, or to elasticity, forces governmental units to increase existing taxes or create new ones. Although the revenue system base should be responsive to economic growth, the tax base should not be so structured that it is subject to widely fluctuating cyclical changes in the economy, which would create conditions of fiscal instability.

Revenue Productivity

A major priority of a tax is to produce revenue. Unless regulation or commitment to some social objective is an overriding concern, each tax is judged based on its potential to generate revenue. Ideally, all governmental entities would like revenue to expand in some direct proportion to population, employment, business volume, and change in personal income. When this relation to tax is maintained, it is said that the revenue is "elastic." This is typically what happens to the federal income tax. For a percentage rise in income, approximately 1 percent of revenue is automatically generated. The operation of this type of elasticity makes it unnecessary to constantly change tax rates. Of course, elasticity can also work in reverse, such as when elastic revenue experiences a proportional fall due to the decline of business activity, creating the need to reduce governmental services. The elasticity factor allows the revenue source to act as an economic stabilizer when a progressive tax system is in place. As the economic activity or prosperity rises, maximum taxes are automatically withheld, thereby serving as a break on the quickening pace of economic activity. Likewise, when the economy begins to decline, less taxes are withheld, helping to slow or cushion the downward trend.

There is always a tradeoff between elastic and inelastic revenue sources. Overreliance on elastic revenue sources may create future potential instability and budget revenue shortfalls, especially when the economy falls into recession. Although a mixture of both inelastic and elastic revenue sources should be maintained, a greater proportion of revenue should come from those sources with elasticity: what precisely would be the optimal mix for a given governmental unit is constrained and determined by the available tax sources and past experience.

Revenue Neutrality

The operating norm of tax neutrality requires that taxes realize *intended* objectives, while minimizing interference in private economic sector decisions. This is not an easy task to accomplish, because most policies tend to positively or negatively affect some individuals and businesses. When government chooses to raise excise taxes on gasoline, it deliberately reduces consumption, thereby affecting both consumers and suppliers. The objective of tax policy is not to have unintended negative effects on industries or businesses by arbitrarily imposing greater taxes on some competitors, producing social loss in the community. The point being made here is that the public interest may justify influencing private economic decisions.

Making It Easy to Comply: Administrative Feasibility

This is one of the basic tenets of public administration. The objectives and structure of any law or regulation should be so administered that they motivate or enhance the possibility of voluntary compliance. Hence the tax procedure and administrative system should be developed to promote the ease and convenience of compliance. This approach minimizes cost and produces the greatest efficiency in collecting revenue. It is said that whenever the cost of administration/collection is high in relation to better-run tax systems, it may be desirable to revamp the administrative structure.

Revenue Collection and Cash Management

Finding ways to speed up the receipt of revenues is one of the principal objectives of effective cash management—a point that is elaborated on in detail in chapter 6. Each governmental unit and other not-for-profit agency should design revenue programs to generate an adequate amount of cash on a timely basis. The objective is to have sufficient cash to meet maturing obligations and other regular expenditures in order to minimize the need to borrow.

Ideally, a governmental agency or other not-for-profit agency should devise a revenue collection system that coincides with its expenditure or payment schedule requirements where state or local laws or funding agencies permit. As far as possible, revenue estimates should be provided monthly or quarterly. Receipts should be maintained on the same basis to facilitate the monitoring and tracking of the collection.[20]

Maintaining Controls over Collections

Basic internal control norms should be observed. The receiving and accounting functions should be separated—a segregation of duties—to minimize the potential for fraud and collusion. Prenumbered written receipts should be required for collection transactions. All receipts should be deposited intact in the governmental or agency's bank account. A procedure requiring the prompt recording of billed revenues to taxpayers' accounts should be adhered to in order to minimize the possibility of errors and misplacement. It is essential to maintain up-to-date taxpayer records. A convenient time and location should be established to facilitate payment; today this is facilitated by the advent of e-filing tax returns and payments via the Internet. Finally, tax statements should be designed to be readily understood, showing *when* and *how much* interest and penalties apply to delinquent taxes. When accounts become delinquent, taxpayers should be promptly informed. Especially in small governmental jurisdictions and other not-for-profit agencies where the separation of duties is difficult to obtain owing to minimal staffs, intermittent audits may be necessary to maintain adequate controls.

A number of indices have been developed to assess collection performance. These include the following: The *collection index*, used to indicate the progress made in reducing outstanding receivables, is calculated as follows:[21]

$$\text{Collection index} = \frac{\text{Collection made during the period}}{\text{Receivables outstanding at the beginning of the period}}$$

The *average collection index* indicates the average length of time for which receivables were outstanding. The index employs the following formula:

$$Average\ collection\ period = \frac{Net\ collection\ period}{Collection\ index}$$

The *past-due index* shows the proportion of all accounts, either in amount or in number, that are past due. This index is calculated as follows:

$$Past\text{-}due\ index = \frac{Total\ past\ due}{Total\ outstanding}$$

Enforcement of Collection

Enforcement comprises three main tasks: "controlling delinquency, discovering nonpayers, and auditing taxpayers."[22] *Delinquency* accounts require time notification and follow-up legal action as the situation may dictate. *Discovery* involves collection investigations to locate and identify businesses and individuals who have failed to report their businesses or change of location. Compliance *audits* seek to ensure that taxpayers are properly reporting and accurately calculating their taxes due. There are a variety of enforcement actions that can be taken before and after delinquency to enhance revenue collection:

- Charging penalties and interest sufficient (higher than short-term loans) to deter potential delinquent taxpayers and bad checks
- Filing warrants to publicly record property on the court docket
- Imposing tax liens on property to induce taxpayers to pay taxes that have been assessed
- Seizing personal and real property (the most aggressive means of securing tax payment)
- Pursuing legal action
- Withholding payments to vendors who owe taxes
- Prompt reporting of delinquent accounts by government agencies to the collection division
- Having regulating agencies withhold or suspend licenses and permits of those individuals and businesses owing taxes
- Discontinuing utility service for nonpayment of taxes
- Denying contracts, loans, and grants
- Withholding or offsetting tax refunds
- Arranging payment plans
- Assessing corporate officers for the taxes owed by the business
- Garnishing wages for taxes owed

- Serving a levy requiring a bank to turn over a taxpayer's account to apply against a tax liability
- Sending collection letters and making telephone calls
- Promoting tax amnesties
- Skip tracing (a system used to follow the taxpayer's whereabouts) to locate delinquent taxpayers
- Enforcing parking tickets by such means as the "Denver boot," which makes cars undrivable[23]

Managing Delinquent Accounts

Traditionally there was a general reluctance (until recent years) to aggressively pursue delinquent accounts, especially in those cases involving unpopular taxes. This attitude has undergone an important change in recent years. The demand for more goods and services, the resistance to paying greater amounts of taxes, and the prolonged economic recession have forced governments to undertake greater initiatives in motivating individuals to pay their taxes.

Increasingly, government officials have been employing new approaches to obtain quicker response from delinquent taxpayers (see, for example, the San Diego approach in Table 4.2). In some communities, delinquent accounts have been farmed out to collection agencies that use procedures similar to those applied in the private sector. In other cases, communities publish the names of delinquent taxpayers in the local newspapers, a form of public shaming. Although this approach has been relatively successful, extreme care must be taken to avoid the erroneous publishing of names.

Revenue Forecasting

Forecasting has never been in wide use in the public or most not-for-profit agencies. The major exception involves the yearly budget, in which revenue is forecasted, planned expenditures are projected, and cash flow projections are made (in some governmental and other not-for-profit agencies). In the private sector, it has become an accepted practice that has been integrated into the regular decision making process. The use of forecasting, especially in a number of local governmental units, has been increasing—not because of the policymakers' desire for rationality, but because of the opportunity to use the forecast as a political instrument to get program directors and interest group advocates, typically, to lower their expectations for expenditure resources. For example, when the forecast is made, advocates for more resources are immediately informed about the constraints and are more likely to limit their requests based on projected revenue availability. Depending on the assumptions that forecasters use, the projected revenue may be shifted either upward or downward. These projected figures can then become guidelines or parameters in budget negotiations.

Forecasts may be classified in terms of the length of time they cover: (1) The *medium-range forecast* may be used to tackle such problems as expected budget gaps or revenue shortfalls before they become crises. (Medium-range forecasting may extend across a budget period, involving problems such as the possible termination of a federal grant or revenue sharing.) (2) The *short-range forecast* relates predominantly to the development of the annual budget and related revenue forecasts and budget projections. (3) *Long-range forecasting* includes a wider range of internal and external macroproblems that must be examined. The past trends and present conditions of the governmental unit are carefully studied. Such factors as population, age, income structure, and employment (types and patterns) are correlated to determine the governmental unit's tax capacity or capability to undertake the projected expenditures.

Preliminary Guide to Revenue Forecasting

The National Advisory Council on State and Local Budgeting (NACSLB) articulated ten recommended practices that should be followed in revenue forecasting:

1. *Fee and charges* should be evaluated to assess the extent to which they will cover the costs of the services they intend to provide.
2. Develop policies to limit the use of *one-time revenue sources*.
3. Identify major unpredictable revenue sources.
4. Adopt a clear policy on revenue diversification.
5. Institutionalize multiyear revenue projections.
6. Monitor the periodic analysis of major revenue sources.
7. Understand and evaluate revenue sources' rates and bases and the effects of potential changes.
8. Periodically examine tax and fee exemptions (including discounts and credits) in assessing the effects of potential revenue lost.
9. Obtain consensus on the revenue forecast employed to estimate budgetary resources.
10. Prepare and maintain a revenue manual on revenue sources that indicates factors that may affect present and future projected revenue yields.

Basics: The Revenue Forecasting Process

The revenue forecasting process (see Figure 4.2) is employed to provide reliable revenue projections on which budget and expenditure plans can be made. Several steps that are involved in this process.[24]

Step 1 establishes the base year. The base year depends on a number of factors, including the revenue's historical date of availability and source. Typically, most revenue forecasts are projected from one to five years.

Step 2 involves (1) the projection of the revenue growth trend and (2) the identification of the revenue source characteristics. The main objective of the forecaster is to calculate the revenue growth pattern and the extent to which it is increasing or decreasing over a specified time period. Additionally, attention is given to the rate of change, demand fluctuation, and seasonal fluctuations.

Step 3 requires the outline of the basic operating policy assumption that undergirds the revenue forecast, such as the economic outlook and demographic and political assumptions. At this point, it is important to have a collective agreement relating to the rate of change, citizen demand, and existing and new policies that will affect the revenue source.

Step 4 attempts to validate the assumptions on which the revenue forecast and projections are made. Because the assumptions will greatly affect the forecasted figures that will be used to make programmatic decisions, care must be taken to ensure not only that assumptions are reasonable and appropriate, but also that they are clearly understood, reflect reality, and are accurately applied.

To aid in assessing the impact and validity of projections, sensitivity analysis should be used by asking "what if" scenarios for given revenue sources. The objective is to demonstrate how revenue projections vary under differing assumptions relating to changes in collection rates, demand, economic conditions, and other relevant factors. "What if" scenario analysis can be utilized to produce optimistic, pessimistic, and most likely situations given the underlying inputs. When the different scenarios generate widely varying revenue amounts, it can be reasonably assumed that the projections have low reliability, suggesting that reconsideration of the assumptions is in order.[25]

Step 5 is undertaken once the validity of the revenue assumptions has been clarified. The forecasting methods are prioritized and the best option selected based on the political and economic environment, consistent with articulated assumptions and predictable maximum revenue yield.

Step 6 involves the collection consistent with the assumptions and projected revenue forecast.

Step 7 requires adjustment of the forecasting model to correct for significant variation between projected and actual revenue yields. Operating assumptions and changing conditions are evaluated to determine the corrections that must be made to the forecasting model.

Finally, in selecting a forecasting model, the comparative utility between the quantitative and qualitative models should be evaluated. Typically, the use of qualitative methods requires less historical and statistical data. This difference can be viewed as a positive opportunity, allowing the forecaster to adjust more readily to dynamic and changing conditions.

TABLE 4.2   Streamlining Delinquent Collection Procedures: City of San Diego

Develop In-House Capability

- Hired experienced debt-collection manager to develop in-house program.
- Treasurer's office brought back all accounts from outside agencies. "Address correction requested" on envelopes allows the post office to put correct address on the letters of anyone who has moved, providing a critical tracing trail to tax-payer's whereabouts.
- Trained existing staff on appropriate collection procedures and how to collect on judgments in small-claims court.
- Program initiated to enforce and collect treble damages and penalty on bounced checks not paid within 30 days. The enforcement of this provision provides significant revenue intake.
- Automated the manual tracking and billing procedures, enhancing the opportunity to produce an array of letters.

Streamlining Regulations and Centralizing Collection

- Payment arrangements are allowed to be set up only by staff of the collection division of the treasury department. This requirement centralizes the credit function, information relating to debtor's credit risk, and reporting to credit services.
- To protect the city's interest, bankruptcy notices were directed to treasurer's collection division to arrange for proper court filings and appearances.
- All actions on write-offs and bad checks are centralized. Writes-offs are made only after all reasonable efforts have been undertaken to collect debt. "Insufficient funds" notices from bad debts are pursued for treble damages up to $500 plus the face amount of the debt.

Relationship with City Attorney

- New regulations require that the city attorney provide quarterly updated reports on all outstanding delinquent accounts in its possession. Though the regulation limits the treasurer's action to small-claims court, the collection personnel prepare the vast majority of the legal actions for the municipality with the necessary document for the city attorney's signature. This has been done due to the mutual trust and confidence that has been developed and the success that has been achieved.
- City attorney refers cases of award of court costs to the city from losing plaintiffs to the treasurer's office for collection.

Credit Reporting

- Collection division subscribes to a credit-reporting service as one important means of prompting debtors to pay. It is the last resort before writingoff their account.
- The credit-reporting system makes it difficult for debtors to obtain future credit, especially unsettled problems on real estate or on automobile loans.
- Debtors designated as "skips" are reported to the city when they seek credit.

- A debtor without assets but with a good credit rating may be counseled to borrow against his/her credit card or bank to settle his/her city account. When the debtor has exhausted his/her borrowing capacity, such an individual would be counseled to arrange a down-payment plan.
- Credit histories reflecting extended amounts of unpaid debt or bankruptcy filings are likely to reveal hopeless opportunities for collection and thus should be writtenoff.

Program Results

- Accounts less than $25,000 have seen a 1,350 percent increase in collections since 1983, for a cost-benefit ratio of nearly 3 to 1.
- Improved documentation of records has resulted.
- Enforcement of appropriate penalties and fees has induced greater payments and generated greater revenue inflow.
- As a further inducement to spur voluntary and early tax payment, it is being recommended that a referral fee be imposed to aid in hiring more personnel for the collection division.

Important Considerations Prior to Program Implementation

- Assess the support from top organization officials. If the required support is not available, the program is not likely to succeed.
- Move slowly to avoid turf battles and friction. The San Diego program used the first two years to train, automate, and professionalize the collection division and to demonstrate its efficiency and effectiveness.
- Departments referring collection are given regularized updating reports and a final report indicating revenue collections that can be matched with the cost of the given program.
- Responsibility for collecting delinquent accounts is centralized, whether located in-house or contracted to an outside agency. Whoever is assigned the collection must be knowledgeable about relevant laws and procedures to be able to assess the agency's capability for effectively carrying on the collection function.

Source: Adapted from Conny M. Jamison, «Collecting Delinquent Revenues: No Stone Unturned in the City of San Diego» *Government Finance Review*, 7, no. 1 (February 1991): 25–28.

Forecasting Methods

What methods should be used in forecasting revenues? Although the answer to this question cannot be completely determined, the degree of desired accuracy, the expertise available, and the available data base significantly influence the end product. A number of techniques have been suggested. They may be categorized into qualitative and quantitative methods. The qualitative side may be divided to include (see Figure 4.3) (1) expert opinions, emphasizing techniques such as *naive, best guess, consensus,* and *delphi;* and (2) sampling, emphasizing:

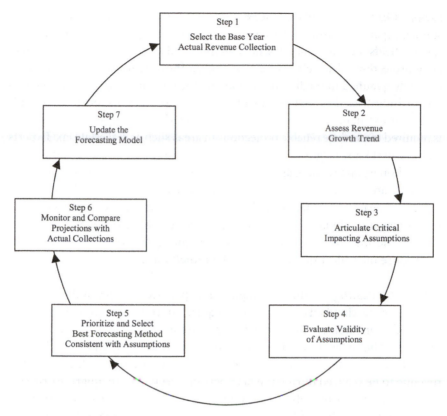

FIGURE 4.2 Revenue forecasting process.

(Adapted from Barry Bloom and Solomon A. Guajardo, Revenue Analysis and Forecasting (Chicago: Government Finance Officers Association, 2001), p. 11.)

internal estimates, and *donor surveys.* The quantitative side may be divided to include (1) causal or regression analysis, employing techniques such as *simple* (least squares), *multiple regression analysis,* and *econometrics*; and (2) time series, focusing on *moving averages, exponential smoothing,* and *classical decomposition.*

Qualitative Forecasting

Qualitative forecasting typically makes revenue projections with minimal or no aid of statistical techniques. Reliance is placed heavily on human judgment. The unarticulated and underlying assumption is that the experienced forecaster can better evaluate historical information and impacting environmental factors that will affect the revenue projection. Although the qualitative forecaster does not necessarily exclude quantitative data, the process involved in producing the revenue projection may not be as rigorous or systematic as the qualitative approach.

Expert Opinions. Unlike consensus forecasting that employs financial personnel, expert forecasting is based on the opinions of specialized individuals in specific fields such as economics, demography, and market research making revenue projections. The belief is that specialized individuals in relevant areas are uniquely qualified to predict trends and environmental changes in specific sectors or industries that are likely to affect revenue sources. Expert forecasting is especially useful in making forecasts when a high degree of technical knowledge is required to produce reliable projections in areas such as real estate tax. Experts with the best knowledge on "inflation rates, interest rates, real estate market, rate of new home construction, and consumer demand"[26] should be employed.

There are some disadvantages associated with this approach. Typically, there is a heavier reliance on judgment than on systematic documentation. Biases may intentionally or unintentionally influence the revenue projections. Finally, the inability to select experts with the appropriate knowledge and experience may affect the accuracy of the projections.

Naive Forecasting.[27] This technique is inexpensive to apply and easy to use because of its simplicity. It does not require more than minimal statistical knowledge or extensive historical data. Naive forecasting focuses on the most recent normal period on which the future revenue yield is projected. Typically, the revenue forecaster uses the prior-year revenue yield as the amount of revenue to be realized during the next period (week, month, quarter, or year).

The underlying operating assumption of the naive approach is that the historical relationship of the recent past will remain constant and thus is a good predictor for the immediate future. When the conditions surrounding the revenue source are stable for revenue sources such as license permits and intergovernmental transfer revenues, the naive technique can be useful. Its disadvantages are that it ignores the possibility that changes might occur in the relationships among relevant factors affecting the revenue source, and because of its limited focus on specific periods, it foregoes the opportunity to obtain revenue trends.

Best Guess. The best guess approach is based on the use of experts who, because of their education, experience, and previous successes, will be employed to determine the forecast. Although the experts may use a given formula, approach, or combination of existing methodologies, the methods used are not made explicit. The forecast is given credibility because of the participants' expert reputations.[28] It is therefore difficult to evaluate whether this approach is correct.

Consensus Forecasting. The consensus approach involves a process by which a group of individuals collectively agrees on specific revenue yields. The consensus technique relies on the group's collective experience, knowledge, and information about past revenue collection patterns in reaching its revenue projections. Through a mutual process of give and take about how existing and prospective conditions will affect revenue sources, experts reach their conclusions about the amount of revenue to expect. This technique is very applicable in situations in which there is no or little reliable historical data and in which the political and economic environment is volatile. Taxes to which the consensus method may usefully be applied include business licenses and personal income. Despite the advantages of the consensus approach, there are some potential disadvantages: It is highly dependent upon the quality of participants and, because the decision is based on consensus, there may be unwarranted enthusiasm about the correctness of the projections. Additionally, "groupthink," whereby a particular projection/assumption becomes more agreeable as more individuals in the group concur with it, can distort economic realities and result in unrealistic consensus forecasting; essentially, individual expertise and knowledge become mitigated.

Delphi Forecasting. The delphi method has aspects that are similar to the consensus approach in that its process leads to a collective and expert consensus decision. The motivating assumption for employing the delphi technique is that informal expert opinion is likely to generate more accurate results. The approach requires the identification and paneling of relevant outstanding experts, qualified to answer pertinent questions relating to factors such as economic, demographic, and political variables that will likely affect the revenue sources. Panelists' responses to these questions are collected, categorized, and redistributed to the panelists for review and critique, allowing them to revise

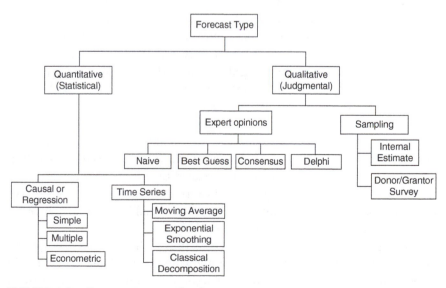

FIGURE 4.3   Forecasting methods.

or defend initial responses. Participants with radically different responses are requested to justify their answers. The process is repeated until consensus is reached. To minimize the influence of group pressures, the identities of the panelists are not revealed.

This technique is very useful as a revenue source forecasting instrument. Delphi results are dependent on economic, political, and demographic factors when there is minimal or no available data, especially in a changing or volatile environment. Additionally, delphi has been used as a useful means in producing accurate assumptions about factors such as employment rates, growth rates, prices, and population growth rate.

There are disadvantages associated with the use of the delphi technique. The selection of appropriate experts is particularly important, because the accuracy of results will be greatly influenced by the participating finance experts. Delphi can be time-consuming and expensive to administer, because it involves written questions. Also, the way questions are written may affect panelists' responses, so the phrasing of questions must be given careful attention so as to maximize the value of the projection.

Quantitative Forecasting

The use of quantitative methods to forecast revenue has been gaining favor, especially in large public entities and in some other large not-for-profit organizations. Quantitative forecasting employs a process that generates estimates of future revenue yields, including techniques such as causal or regression (simple, multiple, or econometric) and time series (moving average, exponential smoothing, or classical decomposition). The utility in using quantitative techniques is that it allows the analyst to explore the mathematical relationship of the historical revenue source data and the factors influencing them. The relationship found is used to project future revenue yields. As long as the relationships remain relatively unchanged, the forecast will be accurate, especially if the underlying assumptions regarding the revenue source data and factors influencing the revenue yield align with reality.

Time Series Model. The time series component approach relies on the recent past as a means of projecting revenue yield. Time series revenue projection is based on historical data, with equally spaced time intervals such as weeks, months, quarters, or years. By graphing historical data, the pattern or trend of a revenue source can be identified. Political and social factors that may influence a revenue source are not considered.

This approach assumes a continuing direction of the time series or growth pattern over an extended period of time, allowing the trend line to fluctuate in a predictable direction. The historical data-based methodology is consistent, simple to understand, and easy to apply. The time series component approach has been used to make relatively dependable projections of local government revenues. The results produced by time series analysis "are affected by long-term trends in underlying economic and demographic variables."[29] Such variables are good predictors, because they indicate whether the economy is moving and in what direction. For example, in a city where the economic activity is sharply declining, the potential revenue intake is likely to follow the same downward path, as was the case with parking meter revenue in Durham, North Carolina, in 1976. As the commercial and business activity began to move out of the downtown business district to other areas, the parking meter tax fell almost 70 percent in just over ten years[30] (see Figure 4.4).

Figure 4.4 reveals a constant upward trend in parking meter collections for the city of Bright. This pattern is in sharp contrast with what Durham experienced and with what Hollywood, Florida, experienced between 1977 through 1993, until dramatic investment in central city districts turned both situations around. Because the variation in the trend line in the figure is small, it suggests that basic trends in determining collection are very significant and that cyclical or other components had only minor effects on collections.[31]

Cyclical factors or wavelike movements occurring irregularly over a number of years affect business activity, which affects revenue. The cycles affecting revenue include interest rate cycles, business cycles, and stock market cycles, with the business cycle having the most effect on revenue stability.[32] In view of the potential effect that cycles may have on revenues in general, an understanding of the conditions of the economy and phases of the business cycle is most desirable. Of particular note is that although the financial manager is not expected to make sophisticated economic forecasts, he or she must be cognizant of the state of the economy on a continuing basis. Past cycles often provide guidelines. For example, cyclical fluctuations in interest rates tend to affect local government revenues in two ways: (1) They affect borrowing costs paid by government, and (2) they influence property taxes by affecting the level of new construction.

Seasonal components typically will not be discerned from annual or cyclical trends; rather, seasonal variations can be effectively identified by examining monthly time series components. An examination of sales tax collections can be used to highlight the effects of the seasonal factor. In examining these collections, it is easily deduced that collections, in the form of sales, excise, and payroll taxes, during the month of December usually rise dramatically due to holiday shopping.

Calculating the Trend Line Using the Least Squares Method. While the least squares method is a form of simple regression, we will discuss it here more as an extension of time series trend analysis and hence postpone our brief discussion of causal or regression analysis until the next section. Calculating the trend line in this manner (see chapter 10) permits us to obtain an

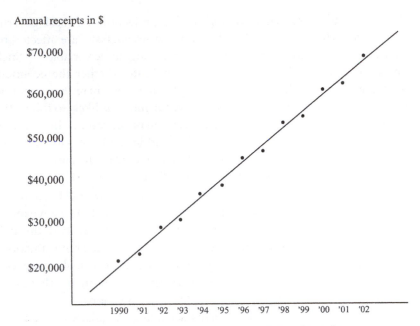

FIGURE 4.4   Parking meter revenue forecast, City of Bright.

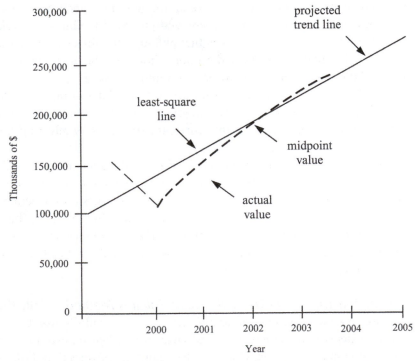

FIGURE 4.5   Graphic view of least squares trend line (revenue).

TABLE 4.3 Least-Squares Formula: Calculation of Future Trend Values

Let x = time deviation of years from middle year

  y = historical level of collection of taxes in dollars

Time Series Data

Fiscal year	Collections
2000	$150,000
2001	125,000
2002	180,000
2003	220,000
2004	250,000

Year	Actual collection (Y)	Time deviation of each year (X)	Square of x deviation (X^2)	(Trend ordinates) (Expended values) XY	XY
2000	$150,000	−2	4	−300,000	126,000
2001	125,000	−1	1	−125,000	155,500
2002	180,000	0	0	0	185,000
2003	220,000	+1	1	220,000	214,500
2004	250,000	+2	4	500,000	244,000
Total	925,000	0	10	+295,000	

Central year average $= \dfrac{\text{Total collections}}{\text{Number of years}} = \dfrac{925,000}{5} = 185,000$

Thus XY/X^2

Let $xy = +295,000$

  $x^2 = 10$

  $= 295,000 = \dfrac{295,000}{10}$ annual increment $= 29,500$ annual increment (slope)

estimate of the slope and level of the trend and allows us to calculate and plot future trend values (see Figure 4.5). A degree of caution is advised in using this method—it rarely produces an exact fit. Indeed, the actual trend may approximate a curved rather than straight line.

To determine the variation of the actual data from the trend line and to adjust the data for trend, the percentage of trend can be calculated by dividing the actual data for each year by the calculated trend value for a given year (times 100), producing the "percentage of trend," as was done in Table 4.4. Any cyclical component effects will show up as high or low percentages of trend value during the periods of contraction or expansion, respectively; when major irregular component effects are present, they will appear as one-time deviations.

In Table 4.4, the percentage of trend suggests that the year 2000 was affected by cyclical factors. Moreover, the greater the cluster of percentage-of-trend values around 100 percent, the greater the confidence in the accuracy of results. This would make permissible the assumption that variations occurring in the actual collection are caused by the underlying trend. When significant variations show up above or below 100 percent, many other factors may be affecting collection, suggesting that caution should be used in interpreting the results.

Trend Analysis. Trend analysis indicates a continuing direction of movement in a time series. It is useful in projecting government revenue sources. This is because many revenue sources are influenced by long-term trends paralleling economic and demographic variables. In trend analysis, the analyst calculates the rate of change for one period to the next (see Table 4.5) or an average rate of change for a specific number of periods.[33] The obtained rate is then applied to the most recent actual revenue yield to provide the anticipated revenue collection for the next year(s). The underlying assumption is that the close recent past period will approximate the next future period. Little is expected to change between the time periods involved. A formula can be developed and used to calculate the rate of change from period to period follows:

$$\text{Change } (\Delta) = \frac{P_2 - P_1}{P_1}$$

where P_1 = the base period and P_2 = the following period.

To calculate the average rate of change for a data set (see Table 4.3), the formula is as follows:[34]

TABLE 4.4   Calculating the Percentage of Trend

Fiscal Year	Actual collections		Calculated trend value			Percentage of trend
2000	($150,000	÷	$126,000)	×	100	119.0%
2001	(125,000	÷	155,000)	×	100	80.6%
2002	(180,000	÷	185,000)	×	100	97.0%
2003	(220,000	÷	214,500)	×	100	102.5%
2004	(250,000	÷	244,000)	×	100	102.0%

$$\text{Average change } (\Delta) = \frac{\sum (P_n - P_1/P_1)}{n}$$

where P_1 = the base period, P_n indicates each following period, n indicates total periods in the data set, and Σ represents the results of summed periods.

Based on the data set, Table 4.5 shows three forecasted revenue levels: 2, 6, and 8 percent, respectively. The 2 percent level represents the most conservative projection, whereas the average 6 percent provides a middle ground and 8 percent produces the most optimistic revenue projection.

Although trend analysis has important advantages such as its simplicity, multiple revenue scenario generations, and consistent methodology, there are some disadvantages that should be noted; all periods are treated equally even though their values may not be representative of the trend; seasonal and cyclical trends are ignored; and economic and environmental factors that may be affecting the projection are excluded.

TABLE 4.5   City of Bright Ice Rink

Year	Revenue period	Actual Ice rink revenue	Growth rate %	Forecast 2%	Forecast 6%	Forecast 8%
1991	1	$ 65,583	0			
1992	2	66,849	2			
1993	3	68,186	2			
1994	4	70,232	3			
1995	5	75,851	8			
1996	6	77,367	2			
1997	7	88,972	15			
1998	8	94,310	6			
1999	9	103,741	10			
2000	10	109,965	6	$ 109,965	$ 109,965	$ 109,965
2001	11			112,164	116,563	118,762
2002	12			114,407	123,557	128,263
2003	13			116,695	130,970	138,524
2004	14			119,029	138,823	149,606
2005	15			121,141	147,152	161,575
Average		$ 72,768	6%			

$$three\text{-}month\ moving\ average = \frac{\$20,000 + \$25,000 + \$30,000}{3}$$

$$= \frac{\$75,000}{3} = \$25,000.$$

FIGURE 4.6 Three-month moving average $75,000 total.

$$three\text{-}month\ moving\ average = \frac{\$25,000 + \$30,000 + \$45,000}{3}$$

$$= \$33,333.33.$$

FIGURE 4.7 Three-month moving average $33,333.33.

Moving Average. The moving average is a technique that allows the number of past periods to be added, thereby producing a projected value (arithmetic average). For a three-month moving average, the amount for the second and third periods are added and divided by three to obtain the moving average. If your monthly donations or collections were $20,000, $25,000, and $30,000, respectively, the moving average would be:

When the next month's actual value becomes available, the moving average is updated by dropping the oldest value. If $45,000 is the new value, the new moving average becomes

This technique is easy to understand and very simple to apply (see Table 4.6). Additionally, it is based on actual and the most current data. If the data is not affected by continuous changes over time, it can provide relatively accurate projections. Of course, the reverse is also true: Because the moving average technique weighs data equally, it does not adapt easily to emerging trends. The longer time periods give the technique greater opportunity for smoothing the moving average over time due to changes. The three-period averages may be expanded to include a data set that covers a longer timeframe (see Table 4.6) to aid the analyst in making a revenue forecast for the expanded future period.

Causal or Regression Analysis. The use of the causal regression method indicates that the analyst knows which factor is influencing the variable being forecasted. The simple regression technique has only one variable. Regression analyses allow us to produce estimates about future revenue source yields. This is done by determining the relationship between one period variable (an explanatory, predictor, or causal variable, such as a tax rate or inflation rate that causes change in outcome of an event) and a dependent or forecast variable.

TABLE 4.6   Moving-Average Time Series for the City of Bright Public Golf Course

Year	Month	Revenue period	Actual golf course revenue	ThreeMonth moving average	Growth trend %
2001	Jan.	1	$13,500		
2001	Feb.	2	13,825		
2001	March	3	14,300	$13,875	
2001	April	4	15,105	14,410	4
2001	May	5	14,672	14,692	2
2001	June	6	15,702	15,150	3
2001	July	7	17,100	15,825	4
2001	August	8	17,301	16,701	6
2001	Sept.	9	18,250	17,550	3
2001	Oct.	10	18,400	17,984	2
2001	Nov.	11	18,651	18,434	3
2001	Dec.	12	19,800	18,950	3
2002	Jan.	13	21,890	20,113	3
2002	Feb.	14	21,775	21,115	5
2002	March	15	20,900	21,522	2
Average					3%

Regression may be employed to "fit" an equation to create a relationship that generates a forecast. In the case of a not-for-profit organization's personal income (independent or causal variable) and charitable donations (dependent or forecast variable), we can set up the equation and make the forecast for expected donations. Let x be the independent variable, and y be the dependent variable. The formula is as follows: $Y = f(x)$. This linear relationship is expressed as

$$Y = a + b(x)$$
where
$Y =$ the predicted revenue yield
$a =$ the value of y when x equals zero
$b =$ the regression coefficient or the amount
    of change when x changes by one unit
$x =$ the value of the independent variable.

In our example, let us forecast donations where personal income is $400,000 and disposable income is $30,000 and the x coefficient is 1.2:

$$Donations = \$400,000 + 1.2\,(disposable\ income)$$
$$= 400,000 + 1.2\,(30,000) = \$436,000$$

It is important to note that the forecast of donations is dependent upon an accurate forecast of disposal income. An inaccurate forecast of disposable income will generate a faulty figure for current donations.

In forecasting revenue source yields using regression analysis, the independent variable (may be quantitative or qualitative) plays a critical role. All relevant independent variables (such as social, political, and administrative) affecting a revenue source should be identified. This attention helps to produce reliable projections. Before employing regression analysis as a forecasting instrument, the analyst should articulate basic operating assumptions: (1) There must be a reasonably strong relationship between past independent and dependent relationships that provide the basis for reliable future projections, (2) data contain normal distributions for all variables, and (3) outliers or extreme values are not represented in the data set.

Unlike qualitative techniques, regression analysis allows the forecaster to test articulated assumptions. Additionally, it facilitates the identification and evaluation of critical factors that impact particular revenue sources. Despite these outstanding positive aspects of regression analysis, there are some disadvantages associated with its application, including the necessity of having an understanding of basic statistics, the requirement of extended, detailed historical data, and the need for keen understanding of identifiable relationships between past dependent and independent relationships to ensure forecast reliability. Finally, many precise assumptions regarding these relationships are required.

Multiple Regression. Multiple regression analysis involves multiple causal factors. There must be at least two independent and dependent variables. Multiple regression is an extension of simple regression by adding one or more predictor variables so that the equation might appear as follows:

$$Y = a + bx + cZ = error$$

In the equation, Y is the predicted variable, whereas a is the value of X where Y is zero and b is the rate of change relative to X. X is the first and Z is the second predictor, or causal variable error estimate—the statistical estimate of the range of error for each given equation. Y varies at the same rate as X and Z. Of note is that the use of more predictors or causal variables has the potential to generate more accurate predictions while reducing the error estimates. Also, the equation can be used to predict the value of Y simply by inserting the X and Z coefficients, allowing the calculation to be made.

Econometric Forecasting. This technique closely resembles regression analysis. Econometric forecasting emphasizes the relationship between a dependable variable and one or more independent variables to predict revenue source yields. Econometric forecasting focuses almost solely on economic factors that affect a given revenue source, such as economic growth, employment, land, property values, interest rates, and tax rates. Additionally, there a number of important assumptions underlie econometric forecasting: (1) All relevant economic variables are considered; (2) all non-economic factors (e.g., administrative, social, and political) remain essentially constant; and (3) the revenue sources being forecasted have a direct relationship with the articulated independent causal variables.

In developing an economic model, the analyst must first identify all the economic factors affecting a specific revenue source before the relationship between specified factors and revenue source yield can be assessed. After the economic variables have been identified, they are put into equations to generate the revenue projection. As noted, the econometric model is especially useful in forecasting revenue sources that are significantly influenced by economic factors. Among the revenue sources that the econometric method may be usefully applied in forecasting are the personal and corporate income tax, real estate tax, sales tax, and user charges.

Econometric forecasting requires the identification of important factors that allow the analyst to gain enhanced understanding, showing how economic activity affects revenue sources. Despite the utility of the econometric approach, there are some disadvantages when it is applied. To be most useful, assumptions must be stated with precision. The complexity of the technique requires that the forecaster have statistical and economic knowledge. The application of the technique requires detailed data relating to economic factors and revenue sources.

San Francisco's revenue forecasting model uses a set of twenty-three econometric equations that are interrelated components consisting of the following: (1) ten equations forecasting San Francisco's tax base; (2) five equations forecasting key local and regional economic variables, including San Francisco's assessed value; and (3) eight equations forecasting revenues produced by the seven major local taxes (property, business, sales and use, utility, property transfer, parking, and transit and occupancy) and one state subvention (the motor vehicle in lieu of payment).[35]

In developing its revenue forecasting model, San Francisco articulated three main objectives: (1) improving the accuracy of its forecasts, (2) providing a policy tool to enable the city to better analyze its tax and revenue policy, and (3) increasing the ease of revenue forecasting while achieving the undertaking within reasonable cost. Thus far, the model has had a degree of success. However, seven of the main revenues were mispredicted by as much as 2 percent, for example, unanticipated business slowdown. The business transfer tax has been the most difficult to predict.[36]

Exponential Smoothing and Classical Decomposition. These methods are beyond the scope of this volume. Information on them may be found in forecasting publications.[37] Basically, these methods extrapolate the past into the future.

Forecasting in the Not-for-Profit Organization

In not-for-profit organizations, the previous activities are typically used in preparing budgets. The manager responsible for making projections examines past trends and other factors considered likely to affect the revenue outlook. Subaggregate factors such as the number of students, patients, and contact hours may be used to make revenue projections. A number of external factors are likely to affect revenue projection. For example, a drop in the birth rate may change elementary school enrollment, resulting in decreased demand for teachers.

Three types of revenue patterns may occur: *regular*, *seasonal*, and *random*. Regular revenue occurs as anticipated monthly, quarterly, or annual payments. Examples are collections in churches, patient billings, and interest on bank deposits. At private schools, tuition may be received twice a year, and fees from sporting events may be generated during certain seasons. Seasonal revenues derive from anticipated revenue fluctuations over a period of time, usually annually. For example, donations to charitable organizations are likely to increase during the holiday season from November to December. Random revenues from charitable institutions, grants, and other special behests may be conferred anytime during the year.

Summary Observations

Revenue is the fuel that runs financial management systems. Accordingly, an understanding of revenue is essential to the financial manager. It is not enough just to have a knowledge of the technical aspects of revenue raising, involving the economics of taxation, forecasting, and administration. Political implications have become especially important as well since the enactment of Proposition 13 in California in 1976. The new consciousness among taxpayers about the desire to raise only necessary taxes and to reduce them when possible has created greater sensitivity on the part of financial managers and political officials to promote more efficient collection procedures. Additionally, it has motivated politicians to use revenue forecasting to obtain budget reductions and seek possible alternatives to taxing sources, such as more use of user fees to finance government services. Revenue management in not-for-profit organizations has many similarities, although there are significant differences in the funding sources. Of course, not-for-profit organizations tend to be subject to greater uncertainties about the timing and predictability of their revenue inflows.

Notes

1. See "The UK and Its Good Tax System: An Analysis Based on the Evolving Criteria," *King's Student Law Review* (June 19, 2013): 1.

2. Robert L. Bland, *A Revenue Guide for Local Government* (Washington, DC: International City Management Association, 1989), pp. 13–15.

3. Adam Smith, *An Inquiry into the Nature and Causes of the Wealth of Nations*, vol. 5 (London: Methuen & Co., Ltd., 1924/1776), v. 2.24.

4. Regina E. Herzlinger and Denise Nitterhouse, *Financial Accounting and Managerial Control for Non-Profit Organizations* (Cincinnati: South-Western Publishing, 1994), p. 321.

5. See *Independent Inquiry into Financial Sustainability of NSW Local Governments* (Sidney, Australia: Local Government and Shires Associations of NSW (LGSA), May 2006), p. 283. http://www.lgnsw.org.au/files/imce-uploads/35/final-report-findings-and-recommendations.pdf.

6. See Tuukka Sarri, "Some Approaches for Assessing the Sustainability of Public Finances," economic master's thesis (Espoo, Finland: Aalto University, School of Economics, 2011).

7. Ales Krejdl, "Fiscal Sustainability—Definition, Indicators and Assessment of Czech Public Finance Sustainability" (Prague, Czech Republic: Czech National Bank, October 2006), p. 2.

8. Tuukka Savvi, "Some Approaches to Assessing the Sustainability of Public Finances," p. 1.

9. See General Accounting Office, *Accounting Principles and Standards for Federal Agencies* (Washington, DC: GAO, 1978), pp. 1–25.

10. Robert D. Winter and Rhea K. Kish, *Budgeting in Not-for-Profit Organizations* (New York: Free Press, 1984), p. 201; United Way, *Accounting and Financial Reporting* (Alexandria, VA: United Way of America, 1974).

11. Winter and Kish, *Budgeting in Not-for-Profit Organizations*, op. cit., p. 204.

12. Robert N. Anthony and David W. Young, *Management Control in Nonprofit Organizations* (Homewood, IL: Richard D. Irwin, 1984), p. 182.

13. Bland, *A Revenue Guide for Local Government*, p. 106.

14. Robert Tannerwald, "Interstate Fiscal Disparity in 1997," *New England Economic Review* (3rd quarter, 2002): 17.

15. Ibid., p. 18.

16. Ibid., p. 19.

17. See Terry Nichols Clark, G. Edward DeSeve, and J. Chester Johnson, *Financial Handbook for Mayors and City Managers* (New York: Van Nostrand Reinhold, 1985), pp. 36–37.

18. Arthur Mendonsa, *Financial Management in Local Government* (Athens: University of Georgia, Institute of Local Government, 1969), pp. 88–89; see also Richard E. Wagner, *Public Finance* (Boston: Little Brown, 1982), pp. 43–52.

19. Mendonsa, *Financial Management in Local Government*, p. 90.

20. Ibid., pp. 90–91.

21. David P. Dolter and Roger Mansfield, "The City as Debt Collector," in *Practical Financial Management*, ed. John Matzer Jr. (Washington, DC: International City Management Association, 1984), p. 71.

22. Ian J. Allan, "Enforcement of Revenue Collections," *Government Finance Review 9*, no. 3 (June 1993): 44.

23. Ibid., pp. 44–45.

24. See Barry Bloom and Solomon A. Guajardo, *Revenue Analysis and Forecasting* (Chicago: Government Finance Officers Association, 2001), pp. 9–12.

25. Ibid., p. 64.

26. Ibid., p. 34.

27. Ibid., p. 30.

28. See Hans Leverbach and James P. Cleary, *The Beginning Forecasters: The Forecasting Process through Data Analysis* (Belmont, CA: Lifetime Learning Publications, 1981); and Steven C. Wheelwright and Spyros Makridakos, *Forecasting Methods for Management*, 2nd ed. (New York: John Wiley, 1978).

29. Charles D. Liner, "Projecting Local Government Revenues," *Popular Government, 43* (spring 1978): 33.

30. Ibid., 35.

31. Ibid.

32. Stephen J. Agostini, "Searching for a Better Forecast: San Francisco Revenue Forecasting Model," *Government Finance Review 7*, no. 6 (December 1991): 13–15.

33. Bloom and Guajardo, *Revenue Analysis and Forecasting*, p. 42.

34. Ibid.

35. Ibid., pp. 15–16.

36. James Gaestner, "Revenue Budgets," in *Financial Management in Non-Profit Organizations*, eds. Tracy D. Connors and Christopher T. Callaghan (New York: American Management Association, 1982), pp. 27–28.

37. See chapter 12 in Terry S. Maness and John T. Zietlow, *Short-Term Financial Management: Text and Cases* (Fort Worth, TX: Dryden Press, 1998).

5

Purchasing and Inventory Management

Purchasing is a crucial function of government. The magnitude of expenditure for the purchase of goods and services is second only to the expenditure for personnel in most government and other not-for-profit agencies. In 1992, state and local governments' expenditures for the purchase of goods and services exceeded $190 billion. By 2012, government purchasing approached $2 trillion dollars, with much of the growth being driven by the outsourcing of certain government services. Because of the sizable allocation of resources to purchasing and procurement, considerable interest has been drawn to the area.

With the new federal drive to reduce or at least slow down the rate of increase in medical-related services, hospitals and other health care and service providers have come under closer scrutiny, and the intensity of the surveillance is likely to continue. Regulatory bodies and third-party intermediaries (e.g., Blue Cross and Blue Shield checks on the reasonableness and validity of costs for the federal government in supported health care programs such as Medicaid) have placed great emphasis on hospital cost containment and efficient purchasing power. At all levels of government, but especially at the federal level, the demand to reform the purchasing function has become a major priority.

To achieve maximum efficiency and effectiveness in purchasing, managers must be committed to more than faddish and simplistic approaches. It is generally accepted almost as an article of faith that the best way to reform and achieve optimal results from the purchasing function is to identify and adopt superior benchmarked practices. Typically, this means implementing competitive commercial or businesslike practices. Agencies of the government such as the Department of Defense (DoD) are viewed as prime candidates for businesslike practices, in part due to their large budgets and significant competition among private suppliers. Without rigorous analysis, when possible, the DoD was induced to adopt purchasing reforms that promised to free up resources for modernization and readiness. Thus far, initial analysis has shown that reform results have not lived up to expectations.[1] The DoD reforms have led to increasing prices for government commodities. The reforms have prevented the DoD from adopting the best practices of large corporations. "The beneficiaries of the reform are not government purchasing entities, or American taxpayers, but instead the private suppliers who now receive the higher prices."[2] Instead of the government using less to achieve more, it may be using more to achieve less. This result suggests that great attention must be given to the management of this critical function in public and not-for-profit agencies. This chapter examines the purchasing function and the emerging emphasis on sustainability. Emphasis is placed on the ways that are used to enhance the administrative structure and improve its efficiency and effectiveness.

Defining Purchasing

Purchasing may be viewed as a *support service*, as shown in Figure 5.1, part A, or as a *management program* as shown in Figure 5.1, part B. From a comprehensive perspective, purchasing is concerned in public and other not-for-profit organizations with the acquisition of all goods and services except those provided directly by employees of an organization. This comprises the purchasing of materials, supplies, equipment, furniture, and all other services performed under contract. Agencies may participate in planning the accommodation and adjustments to new public works construction in addition to executing the regular functions of the agency.[3]

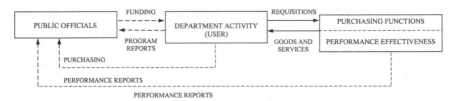

FIGURE 5.1a   Purchasing as a support service.
Source: GAO, Study of Selected Local Procurement Systems, Part I (Washington, DC: General Accounting Office, 1978), p. 24.

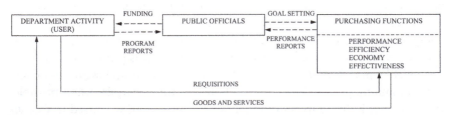

FIGURE 5.1b   Purchasing as a management program.
Source: GAO, Study of Selected Local Procurement Systems, Part I (Washington, DC: General Accounting Office, 1978), p. 24.

Scope and Objectives of the Purchasing Function

Purchasing seeks to procure required goods and services to achieve maximum value for the resources expended. Goods and services should be acquired in the appropriate quantity and quality, at the place, manner, and time desired, and at the lowest cost possible. Although the overriding purchasing criterion relates to the lowest cost possible, it is critical to understand that quality and price go hand in hand. The prompt delivery of goods and services of inferior quality is counterproductive.

A practice that has gained popularity among some governmental units and other not-for-profit agencies, especially when purchasing long-lived assets, is *life cycle costing*. This is used to determine the total costs of goods and services. This approach evaluates not only the initial acquisition costs, but also maintenance, operating costs, energy, and productivity potential, as well as any trade-in or recovery value that may be realized upon disposal.[4] Life cycle costing is similar to the net present value (NPV) techniques used by private entities in capital project valuation. NPV methods determine initial cash outflows, net working capital inflows/outflows, future cash inflows derived from the initial investment, and cash inflows/outflows, resulting in the terminal year of the capital project. All of these values are discounted to their present values, using estimated yields, to determine the NPV of the entire capital project. Owing to the unpredictable nature of interest rates, these NPV values should be viewed with caution and not relied upon as certainties.

As a general rule, purchasing seeks to obtain goods and services at the appropriate time and at the best price from competent suppliers. As a universal expectation, purchasing in public and other not-for-profit organizations must be free from favoritism, arbitrariness, and caprice. Among the duties, responsibilities, and objectives to which a purchasing system should give due cognizance are the following:

- Maintaining adequate supplies of materials at all times
- Developing qualitative performance measures to aid in evaluating the performance function
- Working individually and collectively (with vendors and using agencies) to achieve cost reductions
- Conducting comparative cost–benefit studies to determine whether to undertake work in house or to contract it out
- Automating procedures and processes when doing so promotes efficiency and productivity
- Developing and conducting training programs for buyers and supervisors
- Employing team buying and other appropriate arrangements that facilitate more effective performance
- Arranging for alternative supply systems and sources to minimize or avoid interruption in the delivery of public goods and services.[5]

Attributes of an Effective Purchasing System

A well-run purchasing system should include the following features:

- A written and updated policies and procedures manual
- A purchase requisition system to communicate purchase requirements
- A purchase order system to communicate commitment to the vendor, the accounting department, the person who will receive the materials, and the requisitioner
- An updated list of employees who are authorized to request purchases, including associated specific dollar limits
- A preaudit system with which to compare requisitions before issuing purchase orders
- A well-functioning system for evaluating "bill"-type purchases
- A system to expedite overdue orders
- Maintenance of a system to locate suppliers meeting specified requirements in terms of the most affordable price and delivery schedules

The Purchasing Process

This process comprises the steps concerned with the acquisition of goods and services (see Figure 5.2). It is initiated at the time when a need is identified and continues until the goods have been received and approved for use or the service has been delivered. While the steps required to carry out the purchasing function vary among governmental units and other not-for-profit agencies, typical activities include the following:

- Specifying quantities essential to meet necessary requirements
- Preparing purchasing requisitions
- Selecting sources or advertising
- Soliciting bids
- Conducting informal bidding
- Analyzing bids
- Issuing purchase orders
- Following up or expediting purchase orders (when required)
- Receiving and inspecting goods or services
- Making payment for goods

In addition to these purchasing activities, the process usually includes a provision for storage and inventory control and a clear delineation of responsibility for disposal of scrap or obsolete or surplus inventory. An important point is that purchasing encompasses far more than the mere processing of orders. Because of the magnitude of resources devoted to purchasing, it plays a key role in helping to reduce agency costs.

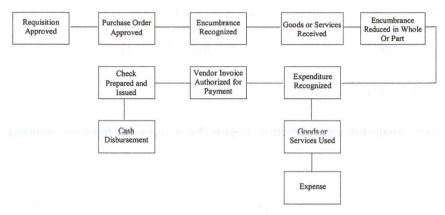

FIGURE 5.2   Phases of a purchase transaction.
Source: Adapted from Ernst and Young, *Introduction to Accounting*, p. 3–2.

Centralized Purchasing

Centralization of the purchasing function is widely advocated in both the public and private sectors. The widely held view is that centralization is an optimal approach to realizing cost-effective procurement for a large number of activities. It does not permit individual entities to follow their own preferences in the selection of vendors or products and in the purchase of common items in small quantities. When the appropriate authority and responsibility are combined with effective management techniques, a centralized purchasing system becomes an instrument that is accountable to the public or clientele for effecting sound procurement policy.[6]

Defining Centralized Purchasing

This may be defined as the concentration of the responsibility and authority for the government- or agencywide purchasing function under the head of a single manager or purchasing agent. In governmental units, authority and responsibility to manage and coordinate purchasing activities are delegated by statute to the purchasing agent.

When Is a Centralized Purchasing Function Needed?

To determine when a centralized purchasing function is needed, a number of questions must be asked: What is the anticipated amount of savings to be gained? How many poor-quality products are being received? What are the needs for standardization and specification? Is there a need for an improved bidding procedure? Is there a need for better expenditure control? What are the costs of existing decentralized purchasing and storage systems versus those of documented benefits? How do the costs and benefits of the decentralized systems compare with the potential benefits from the centralized purchasing system?

How to Establish Centralized Purchasing

Several steps are necessary to effectively accomplish centralized purchasing: First, obtain full administrative support. In government agencies, political support, including that of clientele and interest groups (stakeholders), may be critically important. Second, "sell" the benefits to department heads and other relevant individuals and groups and enlist their cooperation. Finally, establish the purchasing department's credibility by carefully choosing the responsibility centers or departments for initial implementation; carefully map out or schedule other departments for joining the system. The process should begin with those departments with which good relations exist and that are the most disposed to accommodate change and innovation. However, before centralized purchasing is installed in any department, an assessment of the weaknesses and needed improvements should be conducted.[7]

After it has been decided to consolidate purchasing activities within a centralized system, a number of activities are required. First, the basic objectives, responsibilities, and authority of the purchasing function must be determined. It is not enough to establish the scope of authority and responsibility; the regulation should define the degree of accountability desired and how it is to be enforced, and a clear delineation of limits should be placed on the purchasing agent's delegated responsibilities and authority. With the establishment of the centralized purchasing unit and the appointment of the purchasing agent, the procedures necessary to effectively operate the purchasing function are then developed.[8]

Location of the Purchasing Function

The placement of the purchasing unit varies widely throughout governmental units in the United States. At the federal level, civilian procurement is carried out by the General Services Administration, which reports directly to the president. Procurement for the military is done by designated agencies that report to the service chiefs, who in turn have been appointed by the president.

It is interesting to note where the purchasing function is located in Canadian systems. Here "a case can be made for placing the purchasing function under the jurisdiction of the treasurer since purchasing has a greater affinity to finance than to any other central management function."[9] Another model has been emerging in the Canadian local government system whereby the purchasing head reports to a central administrative service group, especially when finance functions are attached to the group (as is the case in Thunder Bay, Ontario).

In a number of places in the United States, such as Chicago, the purchasing office is attached to the mayor's office. Purchasing accounts for a large portion of expenditure for public goods and services, and accordingly it represents an important political investment that can be used to reward political friends/ family (nepotism) and exercise direct financial influence over governmental resources. Thus, to ensure that the purchasing function operates creatively and professionally, due consideration must be given to its placement and authority, the training of its employees, and the mechanisms required for its control.

Advantages of the Centralized Purchasing System

Because the degree of centralization varies from organization to organization, the benefits to be gained will vary, depending on its extent. When a purchasing system is effectively centralized, it makes possible considerable savings and better maintains a system of internal controls over the procurement function. Among the common benefits that may be realized from a centralized purchasing system are the following:

- It induces lower prices of goods and services: (1) Quantity discounts are made possible by consolidating like items to permit bulk buying, and (2) owing to an increased knowledge of the organization's needs, opportunity to participate in group purchasing is maximized.
- It encourages the streamlining of management: (1) Better scheduling and delivery of goods and services at the right place and time are facilitated; (2) surplus stocks and shortages are minimized; (3) a systematic disposal policy for dealing with surplus, obsolete, and scrap materials can be maintained; (4) receiving, storage, and inventory controls are facilitated (for example, fewer orders are processed, reducing recurring cost, inspection time, and record-keeping); (5) better purchasing practices and greater coordination of purchases are promoted; (6) the opportunity to develop in-house purchasing specialists is enhanced, and the chances for attracting high-quality purchasing professionals increased; (7) the number of employees required to perform purchasing activities is reduced; (8) the receiving process is able to operate in tandem with inventory control; and (9) the purchasing manager is held accountable for the purchasing function. The receiving function is responsible for checking the status of incoming goods to ensure their acceptability in terms of condition, quantity, and proper placement. The receiving activity is charged with the following specific responsibilities: (a) assuring that goods and services received correspond to a purchase order on file, (b) examining the goods to determine if they have been tampered with, (c) noting any damage in the packing slip and the carrier's waybill in the presence of the carrier or on the form required for that purpose, (d) checking the carrier's documentation to compare with the number of items actually delivered, and

(e) forwarding a copy of the receiving report to the accounting department and to the appropriate location for use in inventory.

- It improves administrative functions through better planning and control (segregation of duties), standardization of materials, and implementation of improved funding techniques such as contracting and performance measurement.[10]

Competitive Bidding as an Effective Purchasing Tool

The competitive approach is the one most widely acclaimed for the acquisition of goods and services, though it is not always used. In fact, at the federal level, a significant amount of military procurement is achieved through noncompetitive bidding. Typically, the competitive approach requires contracts above a specified monetary level to be submitted to competitive bidding or competitive negotiation. Public competitive contracting in state and local governments falls into three categories: (1) *competitive sealed bidding* (including multistep bidding); (2) *competitive quotation bidding*, also known as *informal bidding*; and (3) *competitive negotiation*.

Competitive sealed bidding is known by a number of names, including "competitive bidding" (the Model Purchasing Ordinance that was developed by the American Bar Association identifying and synthesizing the best elements of state and local procurement systems) and "formal advertising" (the terminology used by the federal Procurement and Acquisition Regulations). Competitive sealed bidding is the statutory approach employed most frequently at the state and local levels. Purchase by negotiation occurs only when competitive sealed bidding is not feasible or practical. Once the need to purchase has been acknowledged, central purchasing initiates the sealed bidding procedure with the issuance of an initiation for bids (IFB). The IFB is intended to encourage competitors to offer the produce or service and to give all potential bidders an equal opportunity to bid. There are other important norms, duties, and responsibilities regarding bids that should be clearly set forth, involving (1) controlling their opening and tabulation, (2) public disclosure, (3) acceptance via telephone and fax, (4) modification or withdrawal, (5) acceptance of late bids, and (6) mistakes. With respect to mistakes, the National Association of State Purchasing Officials has observed: "The essential rule is that no change or correction should be permitted which would prejudice the interest of the public or would be unfair to other bidders."[11]

Multistep sealed bidding is used in approximately 70 percent of state purchasing, typically for purchases requiring the provision of complex goods and services (such as a medical records system including personnel training and alternative approaches to performing the work). Multistep bidding employs the IFB with a two-step approach. Before commencing step 1, potential suppliers may request information (a statement is usually attached indicating that no commitment is intended). Step 1 (the technical proposal) indicates the bidder's experience and resources for delivering the goods or services. Pricing most often comes in the second stage and involves a sealed envelope. The proposals are opened and evaluated and negotiation about pricing follows.[12] If changes are made in the technical proposal, revised pricing is allowed. Where a technical proposal is fully acceptable, negotiation is unnecessary, and "award is made under sealed competitive bidding."[13]

Competitive quotation bidding is a commonly used method to acquire goods and services where the dollar amounts do not require sealed bids. A kind of informal bidding takes place; potential suppliers provide a listing of their prices, which can be compared with those of competitors to facilitate the best price selection. About 90 percent of the states require a competitive quotation.

Competitive negotiation bidding is not a recognized or authorized approach at the state or local levels and has thus been unavailable as a viable alternative procedure except as it may be permitted under emergency conditions.

Competitive Bidding versus Negotiation

Although competitive bidding is the preferable procurement approach, it is not always possible to employ it because of the nature of the goods and services involved. A waiver is allowed in such cases as the following:

- Sources are limited.
- Prices are fixed.
- Services are required to complete ongoing tasks.
- Products are manufactured in correctional institutions.
- Purchase is made from one unit of government to another.
- A needed item is available only for a short period.
- Utility services are purchased.
- A replacement part is available from only one source.

Cooperative Purchasing

Cooperative purchasing takes a variety of forms. Most often it involves arrangements among two or more governments to purchase goods and services under the same contract. The main objective in cooperative purchasing is to receive a cost reduction by making a volume purchase, using potential supplier economies of scale. The cooperative purchasing method provides a number of benefits:

1. It permits small units of government or agencies to obtain sizable discounts that would not otherwise be available, permitting significant savings.
2. It eliminates duplicate effort and improves technical support in defining requirements and soliciting, awarding, and administering contracts.

3. Officials can pool collective knowledge regarding when and where to buy and can share the benefits.
4. It can initiate a large enough dividend to encourage suppliers to produce and market new and modified products that are not commercially available.

Cooperative purchasing tends to encourage the sharing of information among purchasing units about where to get the best deals as they relate to the following:

1. New products entering the market
2. Alternative products located through value analysis
3. Development of cost-effective methods of supplying goods and services
4. Equipment repair experience
5. Breakthroughs in contracting methods
6. Breakthroughs in prices being paid for specific goods and services[14]

Sharing information may also provide valuable insights about the causes of significant price differences of similar items.[15]

It is important to keep in mind that cooperative purchasing will succeed only if it is supported by all participants, especially senior officials of the governmental units or agencies involved. Participation in cooperative arrangements should be based upon the evaluated benefits to be derived by the governmental unit. As a general rule, participants with cooperative arrangements should take turns making the purchase contract, giving all participants an opportunity to benefit from the learning process (except in those cases where the largest participatory unit's lead role permits superior benefits to be gained by all). A key element that must be observed in cooperative purchasing is that once commitments have been made for purchases, no withdrawals will be allowed: "All participating authorities must accept the group decision."[16]

Permission contracts involve those situations in which a third party (such as a local government that is allowed to enjoy the benefits of a state contract) that is not a participant in a contract is permitted to enjoy the benefits when and if it chooses. The contract price of the main contractor (in this case, a state) becomes a "ceiling price against which permissive users of the contract can bargain."[17] The successful bidder of the state purchasing contract permits the third party to use the bid prices as the target bargaining price. Although this practice is unenforceable, it is not typically challenged and is in wide use throughout the United States and Canada.

Measuring Purchasing Performance

A successful purchasing system requires that the function be operated in an efficient and cost-effective manner. This accountability objective can best be facilitated when realistic and measurable goals and objectives are set forth and appropriate systems are developed to permit feedback to monitor and control it. This requires that performance be reported periodically and that internal and external audits be performed from time to time. Performance measures can provide input information to aid management in assessing how the purchasing duties and responsibilities are being discharged and how performance can be improved. The purchasing system can (1) aid management to better determine how well the purchasing responsibilities are being met, (2) be used to evaluate performance against set standards or historical indicators, (3) be used to assess the cost-effectiveness of the purchasing function, pointing possibly to cost reductions, and (4) be useful in showing time and money savings due to the purchasing agent's actions.

Measurement of the purchasing function is not an easy task, because there are no generally agreed-upon standards or indicators for evaluating its performance. Although there are indicators that have been developed to assess the performance of the purchasing function, caution about their use has been expressed. The first concern is that management tends to give too much emphasis to quantitative indicators such as savings, and too little to qualitative aspects such as the maintenance of effective levels of inventory and the establishment and use of a purchasing manual that clearly defines and delegates authority and responsibilities.

The second caution concerns the reliance on a single indicator to measure performance. Among the shortcomings inherent in the single-indicator approach are that it is only a partial performance measure and is subject to easy manipulation to show improved performance that has not really occurred.[18] Despite the lack of consensus about the appropriateness of indicators as a means for evaluating the performance of the purchasing function, they are used in public and other not-for-profit organizations to assist in such evaluations. Among the indicators that may be used are the following:

- The ratio of goods and services purchased to the total expenditure of the governmental unit or agency
- The cost–benefit ratio of making purchases (buying) to total purchases made
- Volume and percentages of purchases rejected due to defects
- The average daily value of orders overdue
- The ratio of price variance to budgeted purchases
- Administrative savings resulting from blanket use of purchase orders
- The ratio of purchasing employees to total governmental unit or agency employees
- Reduction in the frequency of rush orders
- Cost reduction attributable to standardization
- Cost reduction attributable to value analysis

$$\begin{array}{c}
\text{Cost of goods} \\
\underset{(BI)}{\text{Beginning inventory}} + \underset{(P)}{\text{Purchases}} - \underset{(CUS)}{(\text{Units}) \text{ sold}} = \underset{(EI)}{\text{Ending inventory}}
\end{array}$$

FIGURE 5.3   Periodic inventory tracking equation.

Inventory Costing: Perpetual versus Periodic

Preceding our discussion of economic order quantity, it might be useful to discuss two approaches (perpetual and periodic) to determining how an organization keeps track of inventory on hand. *Periodic inventory tracking* can be obtained by the following equation:

If supplies at the beginning of the year are 20 units, and 12 units were purchased and 13 units were sold, what is the ending inventory?

$$BI + P - CUS = EI$$

Accordingly, if $20 + 12 - 13$, then $EI \, \alpha \, 19$.

The *perpetual inventory method* requires that the organization keep a continuous total or end balance at all times. Daily items sold or used are subtracted, and items purchased are added, automatically as each transaction or activity occurs. Thus, at any given moment or at the end of the day, we know exactly the inventory on hand. Although use of the perpetual inventory method may incur more administrative costs due to the constant record keeping required, it provides officials with up-to-date real-time data concerning inventory levels. Such information is vital in procurement decision making.

Understanding Economic Order Quantity

Because inventory represents a large asset in government and other not-for-profit organizations, it is important that it be managed effectively so that it can make its appropriate contribution to the organization's goals. This requires that management strive to achieve an optimum inventory balance and recognize the relationships of one inventory item to another.[19] In addition, management must be continually aware of three very important types of costs that are associated with inventory: (1) the inventory carrying cost (e.g., storage, depreciation, insurance) subsequent to its acquisition, (2) the purchase ordering costs, and (3) stockout, or the cost of running out of inventory.

A *stockout* results in service interruption and dissatisfaction for clientele and constituents. In the case of snow and ice removal, for example, a shortage of salt may increase the time necessary to clean the streets. As a first step in minimizing stockout activity patterns such as the flow and size of inventory orders, the dependability of suppliers and length of time it takes to receive an order should be determined. Once estimates are made of the cost of stockout, the stockout loss probability factor can be determined. A stockout loss function is shown in Figure 5.4. As the size of the inventory grows the stockout probability goes down, and vice versa. The objective of stockout analysis is to pinpoint the time when inventory should be reordered. While avoidance of an inventory stockout is a desirable objective, inventory must be monitored closely, because as the inventory size rises, the carrying costs (e.g., insurance, storage, spoilage, depreciation or obsolescence, opportunity costs) rise directly with it. Figure 5.5 illustrates the inventory carrying cost as a function of inventory size.

Determination of the stockout or running-out cost depends on the specific organization and kinds of inventory items in question. In the case of a hospital, the cost would have to be measured both in terms of tangible cash cost, due to the liability of not providing patient care, and in terms of intangible costs that are very difficult to measure, such as illness, increased pain, and death. Consequently, there are several basic decisions that management is required to make, particularly important being (1) the size or amount of inventory to order at a given point in time, (2) the extra amount of inventory that will provide safety from stockout, and (3) precisely when to initiate or place an order.

Importance of the Size of the Inventory

If the inventory is larger than can be effectively used, it ties up unnecessary amounts of cash that could be employed for alternative organizational purposes or investment options. The longer the turnover period of the inventory, the greater the likelihood is that it will succumb to obsolescence, deterioration, or damage. However, when the size of inventory is too low, it creates impediments, such as shortages. Note that these management decisions suggest tradeoffs between the different kinds of inventory costs. As the size of the inventory increases, the carrying costs increase, decreasing the chances of an inventory stockout. This, in turn, decreases the frequency of orders, effectively reducing ordering costs. Figure 5.6 suggests the tradeoffs that are involved and the level of inventory that is required to minimize total inventory costs. In part B of the figure, note that the optimum safety stock is not at the point where the carrying cost and stockout cost intersect. The assumption is that optimum stock represents the point of an acceptable stockout loss, as opposed to the more ideal situation depicted in Figure 5.6, part A. The same thinking applies in Figure 5.7, parts A and B: The economic order quantity (EOQ) is not at the intersection of carrying costs and ordering costs, but rather at the lowest part on the total cost (TC) unit. This is the point where we will obtain the lowest cost.

Management's Operation of the Organization

Rush purchase orders reduce efficiency and increase cost. These problems are compounded due to the perspective of the different department heads. The fiscal department views the lowest level of inventory possible as desirable because it permits greater cash flow. The operating or user departments typically insist on having the highest possible level of inventory to meet all departmental needs, irrespective of the cost. The purchasing officers take a balanced view of the situation in wishing to maintain low inventory, appropriate safety, avoidance of stockout loss, minimal orders, low costs, and rapid inventory turnover.

When considering the quantity of inventory to maintain, two opposing factors must be borne in mind: (1) As reduction in the quantities of inventory items purchased occurs, the carrying costs fall and ordering costs rise, but (2) as the amounts of inventory items ordered rise, the situation is reversed. A critical concern in an organization is to find a way to satisfy material needs in the most economical manner.[20] Hence, a way must be found to order and reorder inventory at the most appropriate points in time.

Many approaches have been used to aid in establishing the optimum order volume for inventories and the minimization of costs. The approach most widely used when just-in-time (JIT) cannot be applied is the EOQ approach, which is used to manage ordering and carrying costs and as a means to achieve optimal balance among cost objectives. EOQ tells the manager the optimal number of units to order of a specific item and when to do so. The total costs of the inventory include three main components, as follows:

- Purchase price of the inventory
- Carrying costs:
  - Capital costs: required inventory plus safety stock inventory to minimize risk of running out of inventory
  - Out-of-pocket costs, such as insurance, taxes, inspections and obsolescence, telephone, utility, personnel, damage, loss, and pilferage
- Ordering costs:
  - Time required to place orders
  - Shipping and handling; storage
  - Ordering mistakes

When the inventory objective at minimum (total) cost is reached, EOQ has been achieved.

Examining the Inventory Cost Components

Let S represent the carrying cost of one unit of inventory per year, comprising both the capital and out-of-pocket costs. When we multiply the carrying cost for one unit for a year times the number of units available or on hand for the year, we obtain the carrying cost. The inventory on hand will vary, being low at the time of ordering and high shortly afterward; accordingly, to determine the

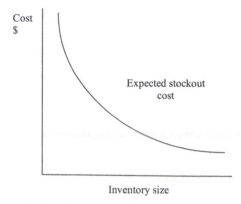

FIGURE 5.4 Estimated stockout as a function of inventory size.

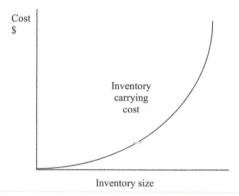

FIGURE 5.5 Inventory carrying cost as a function of inventory size.

carrying cost, we must multiply the cost of carrying one unit, S, by the average number of items in inventory for the period.

If Q represents the number of inventory units we order at any given point in time, Q units will be used until all are gone. Additional units of Q will be ordered. If inventory is assumed to be used evenly on a periodic basis, the Q average is Q ÷ 2 (or Q/2) units of inventory. The assumption is that there is no lead time involved in obtaining the inventory. Because this pattern is repeated during the period with no allowance for safety stock, the average inventory level is Q/2. Hence, if we order 80 items and use on average 80 per period before we receive the next shipment, our inventory on hand will be 80 ÷ 2, or 40. The carrying cost can be calculated by multiplying the average inventory Q ÷ 2 × S, the carrying cost of one unit of inventory:

$$\text{Carrying cost} = \frac{Q}{2} \times S = \frac{QS}{2}$$

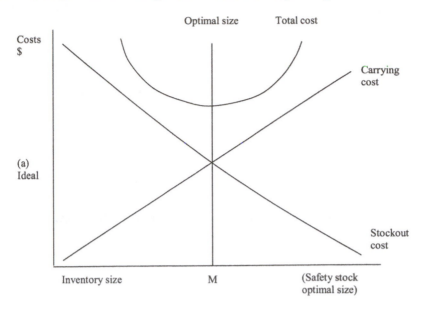

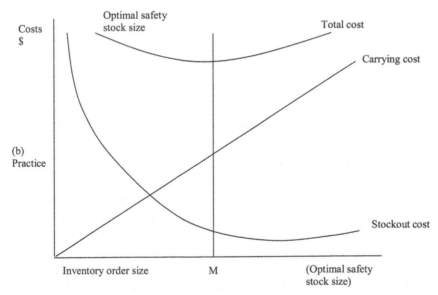

FIGURE 5.6 Optimum inventory as a function of stockout costs and ordering costs.

The ordering cost is obtained by multiplying the number of orders placed by the cost per order. If we let A represent the total number of units needed in a year, then $A \div Q$ will indicate the number of orders that must be placed. If we let P represent the cost of each order placed, we can then obtain the total

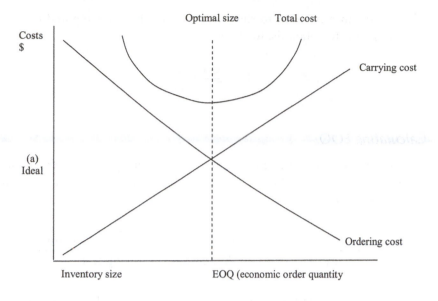

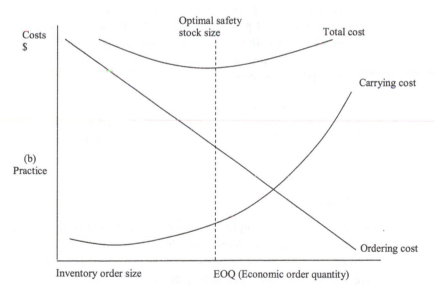

FIGURE 5.7 Optimum ordering quantity in relation to carrying and ordering costs.

ordering cost by multiplying the number of orders times cost per order as follows:

$$\text{Ordering cost} = \frac{A}{Q} \times P = \frac{AP}{Q}$$

We are now in a position to show how to combine carrying and ordering inventory costs to obtain the total cost (*TC*):

$$TC = \frac{QS}{2} + \frac{AP}{Q}$$

Calculating EOQ

Our objective in calculating EOQ is to order (inventory items) at the point in Figure 5.6 where total cost is at a minimum. The formula used for this optimal point (EOQ) is as follows:

$$EOQ = \sqrt{\frac{2AP}{S}} = \sqrt{\frac{2 \times Annual \text{ usage} \times \text{Purchase order cost}}{\text{Unit inventory carrying cost}}}$$

Let us examine an example: Assume a hospital uses 2,000 surgical clamps per year at $20 per clamp. The applicable interest rate is 8 percent of the $20, or $1.60. If an additional out-of-pocket cost is $0.60, the total carrying cost would be $2.20 ($1.60 + 0.60). The total estimated ordering cost is $14.83 per clamp. What is the optimal number of surgical clamps that should be ordered? The optimal size is obtained as follows:

$$EOQ = \sqrt{\frac{2 \times 2000 \text{ units} \times \$14.83}{\$2.20}} = \sqrt{26964} = 164.2 \text{ or } 165 \text{ surgical clamps per order.}$$

When to Place Orders

Placing orders can be relatively simple to calculate when we know our approximate periodic usage. If, for example, we use 300 units over a 30-day month, we are using inventory at a rate of 10 units per day. Assuming that it takes 12 days to receive shipment, orders should be placed 12 days before the end of each month or when 120 units are left on hand.

Just-In-Time (JIT) Purchasing

Just-in-time purchasing (JIT) provides a significant contrast to the EOQ technique for managing the purchasing and inventory functions. JIT was developed in Japan as a means of reducing inventory storage, improving quality, and allowing purchase orders to be driven by customer/clientele expectations. JIT aims to minimize costs associated with handling, storing, and obsolescence that do not add value to the product.[21] The objective is to have only the right materials and products on hand at the right place and right time, something that can be achieved by the gradual removal of non–value-adding activities. This approach has been adopted in a number of private sector manufacturing firms. In the not-for-profit sector, hospitals have been most active in experimenting with JIT.[22] An important observation that should be borne in mind is that the ideal, optimal theory of JIT can seldom be realized. However, the aim should be to approximate it as close as possible and continually strive toward optimal JIT purchasing.

Before an organization embarks on the implementation of JIT, it should assess the potential payoffs from a well-designed operating system. This would require the identification of all costs associated with inventories, including ordering, storage, and interest costs. These costs should then be compared with a well-working JIT system, including the cost of special "rush orders" that will occasionally be necessary, even with an efficiently operating JIT system. Before making comparisons, particular points should be borne in mind: (1) A number of benefits from the JIT system will not be realized during the early years owing to, among other things, the time necessary to develop relationships and experience, (2) the startup of the system inevitably will have unforeseen problems, (3) unexpected supply/distribution problems will arise, (4) unforeseen bottlenecks will potentially cause dissatisfaction among customers and clients, and (5) JIT works best where activities are repetitive. After the direct and indirect costs of the ideal JIT system have been estimated as far as possible, comparisons between the ideal and current operating system can be made. If possible significant savings are indicated, then JIT should be given serious consideration.[23]

Unlike the traditional purchasing system described in Table 5.1, JIT involves far more than simply unloading materials onto a loading dock. The effective implementation of a JIT system requires maximum cooperation, communications, and synchronization of an organization's needs and production/service scheduling between the organization and its suppliers. The system must ensure that products are not only delivered safely but also properly labeled, delivered in a timely manner, and available in the quantity and quality desired. This requires that both the supplier and vendee firms have a clear understanding of the consumer/clientele expectations. To minimize confusion and maximize precise coordination, the number of suppliers must be kept to a minimum. This often means that long-term contracts must be signed and partnering relationships developed and maintained. Becoming a dependable world-class supplier may require that suppliers tailor their systems to make them compatible with the organizations they serve. To achieve this objective typically means that suppliers can focus on only a limited number of products and processes (specialization). To enhance efficiency and maximize the synergy of the organizations, the supplier often installs its own software within the organization. In this new arrangement, the role of the purchasing function changes "from placing orders to managing and monitoring a supplier's management, technical, and process capability."[24] Purchasing managers hold the view that the best way to achieve the optimal product quality while simultaneously promoting continuous improvement. Because of the demanding criteria, including time constraints, proximate location of suppliers is an important factor permitting the supplier to more easily adjust to the organization's operations.

Among the benefits that accrue from the JIT system include the following:

- Reduction in operating costs
- Improvement of cash flow
- Enhancement of quality
- Reduction in number of vendors
- Reduction in inventory obsolescence
- Improvement in space utilization
- Enhancement of productivity
- Empowerment of organization personnel

Purchasing as Innovation: Electronic Purchasing

Electronic purchasing, also known as electronic procurement or supplier exchange, was introduced at the same time when JIT began to gain acceptance both in the public and nonprofit sectors. Meanwhile, the utility of the Internet as an instrument to aid the purchasing function emerged. As the development of the Internet became more widely known, governmental units began to embrace it and apply the technology to achieve noteworthy innovations, especially in the purchasing function. "E-purchasing" has been accepted as one important means of improving the efficiency of the traditional purchasing process by reducing cycle time, reducing haphazard and unplanned buying, lowering prices, improving vendor relationships, and improving strategic sourcing. E-purchasing's objective is "to include all participants in the supply train as one virtual organization via the Internet. The virtual organization establishes a common base of information and opens the door to efficiencies gained from business-process engineering and . . . removing paper and human interfaces between the steps in the process."[25]

Three models have been identified to facilitate the development of a $1.1 trillion government procurement market: (1) *independent exchanges*, (2) *government-led consortium exchanges*, and (3) *industry-led exchanges*.[26] The *independent exchanges* are private entrepreneurs who want to link governmental purchasers with private sector suppliers of goods and services. These private entrepreneurs are the instruments bringing the government buyers and the suppliers together. For a fee, the entrepreneur "creates governmental procurement portals, marketspaces where procurement officers and suppliers meet, with the reward being the transaction fee."[27]

TABLE 5.1 Comparison of Traditional and Just-In-Time (JIT) Purchasing

Traditional	JIT
Viewed as a tactical function	Viewed as a strategic function
Buying decision is driven by price	Buying decision is driven by quality
Quality defined by specification	Quality is defined mainly by customer-clientele expectations
Buyer dominates the purchasing function	Dealer dominates the purchasing function
Many suppliers are maintained	Single or few suppliers are monitored and maintained, with close partnership relations
Defects are tolerated as normal expectation	Zero defects are tolerated
Inspection is used as chief means to maintain quality	Prevention is used as chief means to achieve total quality
Quality is a static concept	Quality improves and changes throughout the process
Communication is based on the slow, hand-written-paper approach	Communication is electronically based
Delivery is determined more by supplier constraints than JIT	Delivery is synchronized to JIT requirements

Source: For additional ideas, see Kenneth A. Wantuck, Just-in-Time for America (Milwaukee: Forum Ltd., 1989).

Precisely what form this type of exchange will take depends on the governmental- procurement needs, such as medical equipment, computers, or furniture. "[I]ndependent exchanges could be established by firms desiring to operate across a wide variety of governmental interests and purchasing needs . . .,"[28] perhaps similar to the Priceline and Amazon enterprise models. These entrepreneurs operate predominantly as a "one-stop" shopping for most governmental purchasing needs. This approach gives the potential governmental supplier a single point of entry. The question about independent exchanges concerns their long-term prospects after they demonstrate the viability of producing cost savings: There are likely to be strong incentives for buyers to bring the operation in house to save the fees paid to exchange operators.[29]

Government-led consortium exchanges are the second approach. These are consortia consisting of governmental agencies, typified by the model initiated by Massachusetts in 1998. Because of its potential purchasing size, it constitutes a kind of "blue-chip" buyer. This model allows suppliers a single entry point of contact, thus avoiding dealing with multiple agencies and levels of government.

Industry-led exchanges are the third form. These are expected to be business-led consortia of current potential suppliers to government. In this view, most governments have interests in collaborative arrangements, especially in view of the potentials they offer, but they are not likely to come together for the long haul, given especially in light of Massachusetts' E-Mall experience, in which the participating states withdrew due to competing companies' incentives to leave the consortium. Suppliers that have much to gain are more likely to set up government e-marketplaces in cooperation with private sector support.[30]

In 1998, Massachusetts took the lead at the state level in establishing a purchasing E-Mall, bringing together several states (Idaho, New York, Washington, South Dakota, Texas, and Utah) to realize a number of significant advantages, including

- Economy of scale buying power
- Providing a large market for government services
- Labor savings (of 50 percent) by responding to fewer bids
- Reduction in paperwork
- Access to electronic catalogs
- Reducing purchasing time

Despite the success and efficacy of the Massachusetts-led consortia, at the end of the demonstration or pilot stage period, the other participants opted out to develop their own procurement marketplaces in-house or with private sector support. Massachusetts has, however, continued the E-Mall for its state purchasing purposes.[31]

Electronic Catalogs

Electronic catalogs (e-catalogs) are available over the Internet (connection to one of the search engines is all that is needed). The e-catalog offers a number of benefits:

- It provides up-to-date information on products and services.
- Ordering online simplifies the process and reduces the administrative cost of purchasing.
- It allows emergency purchasing when competitive bidding is not required.
- It permits complete access to contract information.[32]

To be maximally effective, e-catalogs must include product specifications and pricing. They must have a text search capability workflow, requisitioning, and business approval process to maximize efficiency.[33]

Models of E-Catalogs. Three models currently exist for e-catalogs' implementation: *supplier-hosted, third-party–hosted* and *buyer-hosted.* The *supplier-hosted* e-catalog installs and maintains the necessary hardware and software. It requires only that the buyer have a web browser to access the catalogs. The *third-party–hosted* e-catalog provides "a single database amassing all contract suppliers."[34] It provides interfaces among suppliers. A major benefit of the third-party approach is that it gives the buyer a single interface to the internal procurement system. The *buyer-hosted* e-catalog allows the buyer to act as a third-party aggregator. This approach operates like a single database system: The buyer establishes and maintains the Web site, procures and maintains both hardware and software, and administers the Web site and e-catalog content management. "Data must be imported from various suppliers, which requires the establishment of multiple interfaces or other means of electronic means of transfer of data."[35]

E-Catalog: Some Disadvantages. The coming of e-purchasing has not eliminated the control processes that have been established over time to promote integrity, reasonable prices, and quality—all operating in the manual system. The *term contract* (the agreement between the buyer and supplier indicating what specifically can and cannot be purchased and the terms and conditions) provides the link between the buyer operating process and supplier. When an item is desired, the term contract must be examined to determine the details of what can be ordered. If the item is permitted, a prenumbered requisition must be authorized indicating what is to be charged. Once the information is recorded in the financial system, the requisition is approved and encumbered. From the point of initiation to completion the process takes eleven steps, as noted in Table 5.2.

Streamlining E-Purchasing

To overcome many of the problems associated with the existing e-purchasing system, a fully integrated system (see Table 5.3) should be implemented. Among the benefits to be gained from such a system include the following:

- Storage of term contract data in, and access directly from, the e-catalog
- Direct generation of purchase order (P.O.) using e-catalog term contract information
- Electronic distribution of P.O. using EDI XML (via the Internet), facsimile, or e-mail
- Residence of transactions data in one database, thanks to the Enterprise resource planning (ERP) system, facilitating multiple applications
- Storage of redundant data in the ERP system, eliminating the need to reconcile systems
- Ability for the purchasing employee to conduct business with no more than a computer and a web browser, thanks to the ERP system[36]

TABLE 5.2   State Purchasing: The E-Catalog Steps

Steps	Requesting agency	Central procurement	Supplier
1.	Review term contract to locate required item		
2.	Create requisition and forward hardcopy for approval		
3.	Appropriate officer approves		
4.	Data is entered in financial-information system and requisition is pre-encumbered		
5.	Forward requisition to central procurement		
6.		Review requisition and confirm receipt	
7.		Create purchase order (P.O.) and post to term contract	
8.		Encumber P.O.	
9.		Distribute P.O.	
10.			Enter P.O.
11.			Fulfill order

Source: Adapted from Michael Corvino, "Streamlining Purchasing Through E-Catalogs." Government Finance Review, 16, no. 1 (February 2000): 15.

"A fully integrated e-catalog/e-procurement application with a web-enabled ERP system, as an integrated suite of business applications (e.g., financial, procurement, human resources, etc.), provides the platform through which all business transactions are processed and captured."[37]

Enterprise Resource Planning for Purchasing

Fully integrated, and entirely electronic, enterprise resource planning (ERP) systems are applicable to the management of an entity's supply chain and therefore its purchasing functions. For procurement, ERP systems contain e-purchasing order management modules that include contract management, on-time requisition, payment determination, and vendor management. This module works in conjunction with accounts payable, inventory, and cash management modules to prevent discrepancies and data redundancy. Departments, in the past, had completely separate and independent accounting/financial systems that had to be reconciled on a regular basis. This reconciliation consumed valuable personnel time and entity resources, reducing overall organizational efficiency. ERP procurement modules facilitate entities in obtaining the lowest price for a given quality level of a good/service and ensure that the goods/services are distributed when needed.

The purchasing module, as a component of the supply chain management (SCM) ERP module, assists in optimizing an organization's supply chain operations. In conjunction with customer requirement processing, inventory management, goods receipt/warehouse management, and supplier management/sourcing, purchasing with the SCM system can enable entities to reduce inventory levels, deliver goods/services faster and on an as-needed basis, and reduce unused warehouse capacity.[38] Increasingly, SCM and ERP systems are shifting to cloud-based technology (technology using the Internet and central remote servers for data maintenance and applications), facilitating greater organizational flexibility and data integration.[39] The use of cloud-based technology, even for organizations that do not employ SCM or ERP systems, should be considered to reduce risk of losing data and promote data sharing between entity personnel.

Implementation of an ERP should be done using a carefully conducted cost–benefit analysis. Not all organizations, especially small entities with singular purposes, should adopt ERP systems as the cost and difficulty of implementation can prove extremely challenging or unnecessary. ERP vendors, such as Oracle, Microsoft, and SAP, are increasingly offering systems specifically tailored for public sector entities. Such systems are still extremely expensive, but continual software advancements and fierce competition between vendors have reduced the cost of ERPs and made them viable options for larger governmental organizations.

Green Procurement

Sustainable procurement attempts to meet the demand for goods and services based not only on the cost–benefit analysis guidelines, but the effects that these purchases will have on the environment. Thus, the traditional criteria of price and quality are now being considered in terms of how purchasing is enhancing or impairing the environment. The purchasing function is viewed and carried out in more holistic perspective. Many organizations employing procurement follow the "triple bottom" model that considers the economic, social and environmental factors in decision making.

Purchasing can play influential role in the pursuit of sustainability due to the magnitude of resources expended by government on the purchasing function. As a condition of purchasing supplies and services, governments may require an adherence to particular sustainability guidelines, as done by the city of Winnipeg, Manitoba, Canada.

Importantly, governmental entities are facing increased public pressure to more efficiently use recourses; additionally, environmentally concerned constituents assessing public sector activities are stressing the procurement of sustainable, "green" goods and services. In response to these coinciding demands and enhanced environmental regulations, the federal government has implemented the *Green Procurement Compilation* (GPC) to enhance and promote sustainable procurement. This publicly available website helps procurement officials identify pertinent "green" purchasing requirements for products and services. Within the site there is a green products portal that identifies items listed in mandatory and nonmandatory environmental programs. These programs include BioPreferred, Design for the Environment, Energy Star, Comprehensive Procurement Guidelines, Federal Energy Management Program (FEMP), EPEAT, WaterSense, and Significant New Alternatives Policy (SNAP). With the GPC, federal procurement officials have tools necessary to carry out the acquisition of "green" goods and services that not only financially benefit the government, but also enable organizations to reduce operational environmental and societal effects.[40]

Concluding Observations

Because of the large amount of resources allocated to the purchase of goods and services in public and other not-for-profit organizations, the purchasing function attracts significant attention. Obtaining the biggest effect per purchasing dollar requires expertise and professionalism. Although this is possible in large governmental units and organizations, it is often too costly for smaller ones. Various means have been devised to aid these small units, such as

TABLE 5.3   E-Purchasing in ERP Fully Integrated Systems

Steps	Activities
1.	Requesting agency accesses the e-catalog.
2.	The e-catalog identifies the user via log-on, ID shows the useronly contract and items authorized to procure.
3.	Keyword search allows user to locate desired items and places it in the e-catalog shopping cart.
4.	Buyer approves the item within the shopping cart.
5.	Procurement system creates P.O.
6.	P.O. is generated using the e-catalog contract information and default budget.
7.	P.O. is routed through the approval system within the agency hierarchy.
8.	Upon approval through integration with the financial system, the P.O. is encumbered in real-time and distributed electronically to the supplier.

Source: Adapted from Michael Corvino, "Streamlining Purchasing Through ECatalogs." Government Finance Review, 16, no. 1 (February 2000): 17.

cooperative and permissive purchasing arrangements. In large and medium-sized organizations, centralized purchasing has become synonymous with effective purchasing practice. The accepted view is that centralized purchasing is indispensable if the best deals and prices are to be achieved.

Notes

1. Joseph Besselman, Ashish Arora, and Patrick Larkey, "Buying in a Business-Like Fashion and Paying More," *Public Administration Review* (September/October 2000): 422.

2. Ibid.

3. Lennox L. Moak and Albert M. Hillhouse, *Local Government Finance* (Chicago: Municipal Finance Officers Association, 1975), p. 209.

4. League of California Cities, "Life-Cycle Costing," in *Practical Financial Management*, ed. John Matzer Jr. (Washington, DC: International City Management Association, 1984), pp. 166–188.

5. Moak and Hillhouse, *Local Government Finance*, p. 210; Council of State Governments, *State and Local Government Purchasing* (Lexington, KY: Council of State Governments, 1988), pp. 18–19.

6. U.S. Government Accounting Office (GAO), *Study of Selected Local Procurement Systems, Part I* (Washington, DC: GAO, 1978), p. 1.

7. S. Randolph Hayes, "Total Centralized Purchasing: Can It Ever Be Achieved?" in *Hospital Purchasing*, ed. Charles E. Housley (Rockville, MD: Aspen Systems Corporation, 1983), p. 29.

8. Ministry of Intergovernmental Affairs, Ontario, Canada, *Managing Purchasing* (Toronto: Ontario Government Book Store, 1981), pp. 13–14.

9. Ibid., p. 15.

10. Ibid., pp. 13–14.

11. Council of State Governments, *State and Local Government Purchasing*, p. 68.

12. Ibid.

13. Ibid., p. 69.

14. GAO, *Study of Selected Local Procurement Systems, Part I*, p. 17.

15. Ibid.

16. Ministry of Intergovernmental Affairs, Ontario, Canada, *Managing Purchasing*, p. 55.

17. Council of State Governments, *State and Local Government Purchasing*, p. 104.

18. GAO, *Study of Selected Local Procurement Systems, Part I*, p. 21.

19. Bruce G. Haywood, "Understanding Economic Order Quantity," in *Hospital Purchasing*, p. 161.

20. Ibid., p. 165.

21. E. O. Henke and C. W. Spoede, *Cost Accounting: Managerial Use of Accounting Data* (Boston: PWS–Kent Publishing, 1991), pp. 78–79.

22. See Jerry W. Wilson, "Stockless Inventory Systems for Health Care Providers: Three Successful Applications," *Journal of Health Care Marketing* 12, no. 2 (June 1992): 39–45.

23. Henke and Spoede, *Cost Accounting*, p. 79.

24. Greg Hutchins, *Purchasing Strategies for Total Quality* (Homewood, IL: Business One Irwin, 1992), p. 158.

25. Mark A. Abramson and Grady E. Means, eds., *E-Government 2001* (Lanham, MD: Rowman & Littlefield Publishers, 2001), p. 116.

26. Ibid.

27. Ibid, See also: U.S. Public Procurement Markets, https://www.google.com/?gws_rd=ssl#q=total+government+purchasing+size+in+the+usa.

28. Ibid., p. 117.

29. Ibid., p. 116.

30. Ibid., p. 117.

31. Ibid., pp. 117–118.

32. Michael Corvino, "Streamlining Purchasing through E-Catalogs," *Government Finance Review 16*, no. 1 (February 2000): 13.

33. Ibid.

34. Ibid.

35. Ibid., p. 16.

36. Ibid., pp. 16–17.

37. Ibid., p. 17.

38. "Four Fundamental Components of ERP." http://www.techadvisory.org/2012/03/four-fundamental-components-of-erp/. March 28, 2012.

39. "What Is Cloud Computing?" http://www.theguardian.com/cloud-computing/what-is-cloud-computing. Guardian News and Media, June 21, 2010.

40. "Green Procurement Compilation." *Green Procurement Compilation*. http://www.gsa.gov/portal/content/198257. U.S. General Services Administration, January 29, 2014.

6

Cash Management

In recent years, attention has been focused on cash management at all levels of government and in other not-for-profit organizations. There are a number of reasons for this interest. The 1970s and 1990s saw periods of high inflation, recession, and high interest rates. From 2000 to 2008, the inflation rate has been moderating following the Great Recession of 2008. Over the past five years, inflation has remained below the Federal Reserve Bank 2 percent benchmark and is expected to remain contained for the next few years. Although concerns about inflation have remained low, citizens have been demanding greater amounts of goods and services, yet staunchly resisting paying the taxes required to fund them. Donors to not-for-profit agencies are finding it more difficult to maintain or increase their contributions, especially after the Great Recession. A better management of cash is seen as one means of stretching available dollars to meet the expenditure pressures. The process has been facilitated in large part by new computer technology that permits the use of more sophisticated methods of cash management, changes in federal laws affecting banks and financial institutions, and improved communication among cash managers.[1] As the rates of interest have continued to fall during the 1990s to the present, cash managers have had to be more creative and more careful as the options to generate greater returns narrowed. For example, Seattle, Washington, developed a creative cash handling training manual to enhance its cash management system.[2] This chapter reviews cash management practices, the development of the role of the cash manager, and techniques for effecting cash management improvements.

Defining Cash Management

The bank law changes enacted during the 1990s have increased the number of bank services and better defined their costs. In some ways, these changes have added to the complexity of the variables, constraints, and alternatives that must be understood in fashioning an effective cash management program.

Cash management may be defined as a process concerned with two important objectives (1) providing and ensuring maximum cash availability through delaying cash disbursements and expediting cash collections and (2) securing maximum yield on the short-term investment of idle cash. To achieve these objectives, a communication and monitoring system must be in place to identify the point at which revenue is earned and to track when an expenditure payment clears the bank. This action maximizes the cash investment yield, because it minimizes the time lag between the recognition of revenue earnings and their conversion into cash, and it accurately times the dates of expenditures. Cash management is focused on "the conversion of accounts receivable to cash receipts, the conversion of accounts payable to cash disbursements, the rate at which cash disbursements clear a bank account and what is done with the cash balances in the meantime."[3] Cash must be managed to provide required liquidity to meet all maturing obligations, both expected and unexpected. The amount of cash that an entity holds to meet both routine and unforeseen needs involves (1) its willingness to risk running out of cash to meet required demands, (2) its ability to predict cash flows with a high degree of accuracy, and (3) its available lines of credit or reserve borrowing power.

Evaluating and Establishing Long-Term Needs

The cash manager must make certain that the cash management objectives and priorities are specifically defined and consistent with the entity's overall mission. After this is done, these actions should be reflected in the subsequent policies to be adopted.[4] Next, long-term expected cash flow patterns and targets of perhaps three to five years should be set forth. This step provides parameters and general guidelines about revenues and expenditure expectations that will be helpful in developing useful policies. Attention is directed toward those sources of revenues that are subject to wide and unpredictable fluctuations and long-term needs (including borrowing) that must be planned to effectively meet capital expenditure requirements and debt repayments.[5]

The Cash Management System

In the pursuit of maximum cash availability and maximum yield, as noted above, cash management objectives inevitably conflict, since cash that is maintained for use cannot be employed to produce a higher yield. This conflict can be avoided only if an ideal or optimum balance is determined. Although methods for estimating these balances do exist, determining the optimal balance is not an easy task, especially among smaller units of government and other not-for-profit organizations. Patitucci and Lichtenstein have suggested that the availability objective be pursued first, then the yield goal.[6] The effective operation of a cash management system (see Figure 6.1) requires the consideration and understanding of a number of elements, including policies and constraints, bank–institution relations, and investment strategy.

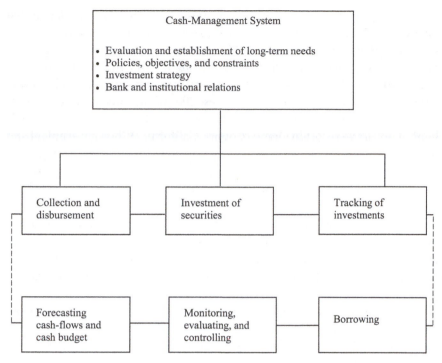

FIGURE 6.1   The cash management system and the operating cycle.

Policy Objectives and Constraints

Policies set the legal and procedural guidelines for facilitating the execution of the day-to-day activities of the cash management program, whereas guidelines typically identify its objectives and criteria for evaluating its progress and achievements. Within the context of the adopted policies, the cash manager should set specific annual objectives such as cash availability levels, desired yield, and the amount of idle cash that will be invested throughout the year. These objectives can be used to periodically assess the performance of the cash management functions.[7]

There are many constraining factors to which the cash manager must give due cognizance, such as local, state, and federal laws that directly affect cash management practices, "determining when monies can be collected, when obligations must be paid, where deposits can be placed, and what securities can and cannot be purchased."[8] Other not-for-profit organizations must conform to the funding agencies' stipulations. For example, the United Way requires that agencies that have free cash or surplus return amounts in excess of $5,000 at the end of a fiscal period. Although the policy is not rigidly enforced, it does create some degree of uncertainty.

The risk related to investment in securities is another constraint factor that public agencies must control. Unlike in private enterprise, government laws and regulations help to minimize this problem. For example, most governments are permitted to invest in relatively safe instruments such as treasury notes and bills. Accordingly, most governmental units are not likely to lose large amounts of their investments unless illegal, imprudent, and unmonitored risks are allowed to operate, as was the case in the early 1990s, when billions of dollars were lost in Orange County, California. When government and other not-for-profit agencies move cash into investments that carry greater risks, extreme care must be exercised. Prudence and due diligence require that the drive for market yield be balanced with a high priority for risk aversion, as the cash used for such investments derives from taxpayers.

In the age of electronic transfer of funds and the numerous investment options that have been created, cash managers often find that brokers, dealers, and banks prefer to maintain control of the securities in light of their need for flexibility to trade and negotiate with other institutions. This practice denies agencies or governments the opportunity to maintain physical control over their investments on the underlying security or collateral. As a measure against this external risk, governments have insisted "that collateral securities be physically delivered to the government as a condition for making the investment," a practice that may reduce yield but provides an important form of protection.[9]

Cash Flow Planning

While cash is important to all organizations, it is especially critical to the not-for-profit organizations in which there is less access to cash—a result of being unable to participate in capital markets as can their like counterparts in the private sector. Thus existing and maturing obligations (bills to be paid) require precision cash management to maintain adequate liquidity at all times. This means the wise management of cash and cash equivalent current assets. In other public, not-for-profit agencies, attention must be given to items such as receivables, gifts, interest income, contribution pledges, dues or fees, delinquent accounts, and, to a lesser extent, borrowings.

With such importance being placed on cash budget management, not-for-profit and government managers must be aware and knowledgeable of prevailing market interest rates. Hoarding cash, even if required by law, results, during times of high interest rates, in an opportunity loss for the organization: The cash could be used to generate higher returns through investment in securities, bonds, and other financial instruments. Although not traditionally used as a source of revenue, investments in marketable securities and financial instruments can provide valuable funding in times of cash shortfalls. Failure to use organizational assets, especially cash reserves, can result in significant opportunity costs and forgone income for not-for-profit and governmental entities.

In the public agencies, focus is placed on some of the same cash flow sources as the other not-for-profit organizations. The greatest attention is placed on inflow cash sources from taxing, permits, and fines. Although the politics of revenue raising can be a difficult barrier to overcome, identified public welfare needs can help to overcome taxing constraints. However, obtaining the approval for revenue still requires that revenue inflows be balanced with expenditure outflows. This requires a close and constant watch on the cash flow.

Purpose of Cash Flow Analysis

Cash flow analysis attempts to answer questions such as "What is the source of cash?" and "Where did the cash go?" The statement of cash flows explains how an organization's cash is generated and how it is used during the fiscal period (see Figure 6.2). Details are provided showing how the cash balance changed during the period and how each transaction affected cash. The cash flow statement provides a comparison of the cash basis and accrual methods. The statement shows why the accrual basis is accepted as a better measurement indicator of periodic income. Cash flow information complements the balance sheet and income statement (in the private sector) and the statement of revenue and expense or expenditure (in the not-for-profit sector), providing a more complete picture of the organization's operation and financial position. The statement directly links the revenue statement and balance sheet, because it analyzes accounts included in these two statements.

Unless accounts are recorded on a cash basis, cash balances cannot be achieved simply by tracking revenue inflows and expense outflows. Generally accepted accounting principles (GAAP) and, to a lesser extent, Government Accounting Standards Board (GASB) standards require accrual accounting. Especially in other not-for-profit agencies, GAAP typically requires accrual accounting, which accurately tracks the actual cash flows. For convenience and clarity, each statement of cash flow is divided into three categories: cash flow from *operating activities*, cash flow from *investing activities*, and cash flow from *financing activities* (see Figure 6.2).

Operating Activities. *Operating activities* are made up of transactions relating to acquisition, or the production of goods and services and distribution of them to residents or clients. This category includes all revenues, fees, contributions, and interest received and all cash paid for resources consumed to provide goods and services. The operating activities category includes the same transactions that go into the income statement in the private sector, but not necessarily the revenue and expenses or expenditures in the public and other not-for-profit organizations, unless they are on the accrual basis (expenses).

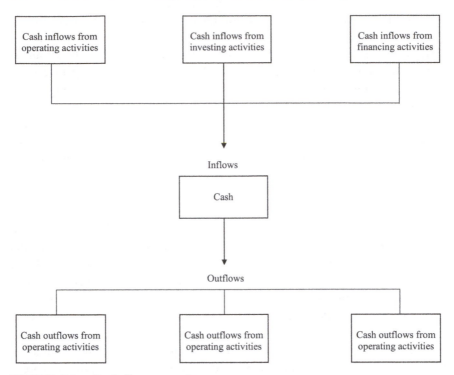

FIGURE 6.2   Cash flow overview.

The operating category simply converts the accrual basis of the transactions to cash. Current assets and current liabilities typically result from operating activities such as prepaid insurance, deferred revenue, accounts receivable, accounts payable, and supplies.

Investing Activities. The *investing* category involves acquisitions of long-term assets during a fiscal period. Depreciation and amortization expenses are not recognized, because they do not represent cash flow. When the direct cash method is used, these items are excluded. Cash flow takes place when fixed and intangible assets are purchased or sold.

Financing Activities. *Financing activities* are transactions that involve long-term obligations to creditors. This category reports cash flows resulting from borrowing or reporting debt. The preparer of the cash flow statement may use either the direct or indirect method. GAAP permit the cash flow statement to be presented in either of these two recognized formats, which differ only in the operating category. The format for the financing and investing activities remains the same.

The Direct Format

The statement of cash flows is divided into three categories: financing, investing, and operating activities. All cash transactions affecting the balance sheet and income statement or statement of revenues and expenditures are placed in the appropriate categories. Operating cash flow includes transactions (see Table 6.1, part A) that affect cash and are associated with operating activities: fees and taxes from clients/residents, purchase of supplies, interest paid (transactions 3, 4, 5, 13, and 14 in Table 6.1, part A). The investing cash flow category includes transactions related to the purchase and sale of long-term assets (transactions 9 and 10). Financing activities cash flow includes the sale of bonds (transactions 11, 13, and 15). The direct method of the cash flow statement includes all transactions that directly affect cash during the period, showing where the cash came from and where it goes (see Table 6.1, part B).

The Indirect Method

In the private and public sectors, propriety activities of large organizations typically employ the indirect method for reporting cash flows. The indirect method reconciles net income on the accrual basis to the cash basis. The indirect cash flow is obtained as a result of changes in current assets, current liabilities, and other accounts. Only the operating category activities of cash flow differ from the direct method. The following summarizes how to obtain cash flow from the operating category:

	Net income/surplus
+	Depreciation and amortization
−	Increase in current assets: accounts receivable and inventory
+	Decrease in current assets: accounts receivable and inventory
+	Increase in current liabilities: accounts payable
−	Decrease in current liabilities: accounts payable
=	Cash flow from operating activities

To obtain differences in the accounts, we need at least two years' data. For example, if accounts receivable is $20,000 in 2013 and $18,000 in 2012, there is an increase in a current asset that will be subtracted from net income/surplus.

The Cash Flow Budget

Once the annual operating and capital budgets have been approved, they should ideally be converted into the cash flow budgets to determine the difference between resource requirements and cash availability. This can be done by preparing a monthly (or a shorter time period if necessary) cash flow budget to pinpoint potential cash shortfalls or surpluses.

TABLE 6.1a City of Falls Tree: Transactions for 2013

Account	Cash	Other Assets	Liabilities + Equity	Statement of Revenue and Expense/Expenditures	
				Revenues	Expense/Expenditures
Beginning balances					
1. Concession sales		10,000		10,000	
2. Dues and donations		180,000		180,000	
3. Cash (taxes receivable)	168,000	−168,000			
4. Cash (fees receivable)	10,000	−10,000			
5. Purchase inventory supplies	−12,000	12,000			
6. Wages payable			20,000		20,000
7. Purchase supplies on account		10,000	10,000		
8. Depreciation expense		5,000			5,000
9. Purchase equipment	40,000	40,000			
10. Sale of equipment	8,000	−8,000			
11. Long-term loan	21,000		21,000		
12. Bond proceeds	50,000		50,000		
13. Interest paid	7,000				7,000
14. General expenses paid	−120,000				−120,000
15. Payment matured bonds	−20,000		−20,000		

Cash budgeting requires a keen understanding of the major and minor sources of cash receipts and disbursements in order to estimate the accurate cash availability. Unlike revenue and expenditure budgets that are based on obligations and commitments, cash budgeting requires the identification of specific receipts and disbursements as well as relevant dates. Owing to the length of time (from 1 to 60 days) between commitment and obligation, which is indicative of the regular/traditional budget, this is not a useful predictor of cash levels.

To achieve a realistic cash budget, the historical experience of the past and prospects of future developments must be carefully studied. The cash budget projection may be made weekly, monthly, quarterly, or semiannually. It requires summarizing the projected sources and application of cash for the coming year (see Table 6.1, parts A and B) from all inflow sources, recognizing the lag times for receivables and pledges, past experience, and best educated guesses. Whatever the projection period, the cash budget must be updated when information and conditions require. When estimates are made for quarterly or longer periods, the need for updating becomes more urgent. For larger governmental units and other not-for-profit agencies, prudence and accuracy may require weekly, or perhaps daily, cash budgets.

Based on the net projection of cash flow, a deficit would require a redesign of the budget to bring it in line with policy objectives that typically maintain a minimum cash balance. Because cash availability is so critical, cash flow must be constantly monitored. This is especially important when particular sources are widely fluctuating from month to month. The need to have cash flow information always available requires that the cash flow budget and accounting system be integrated, giving the organization the opportunity to obtain online computer spreadsheets (see Table 6.2, parts A and B).[10]

The cash budget is not used as an allocating instrument, nor is it concerned with programs or operating functions. Rather, it merely identifies projected expenditures and a revenue stream, usually for periods of six months to a year. These projections will enable the cash manager to determine how much cash will be available or idle at various times during the year, and for how long. An analysis of this information will permit the cash manager to develop an effective basis for making informed investment decisions.

Cash Collection and Disbursement

The *collection* and *disbursement* elements are critical to success in achieving the objective of maximum cash availability and meeting cash and investment needs. If cash collection can be speeded up, the twin aims of increasing cash inflow and enhancing the potential for greater earnings on investment will be achieved. There are a number of impeding or constraining factors, however: For example, various tax due bills cannot be mailed out before a given date,

TABLE 6.1b City of Falls Tree Animal Shelter: Statement of Cash Flow for Year Ended December 31, 2013

Cash-Flow Operating Activities		
Receipts:		
Dues and donations	168,000	178,000
Concession sales	10,000	
Total receipts		
Payments:		
Supplies and materials	12,000	
Interest	7,000	
General expenditures	120,000	
Total payments		139,000
Net cash flow from operations		39,000
Cash flow from inventory		
Purchasing equipment	(40,000)	
Sale of equipment	8,000	
Net cash flow from inventory		(32,000)
Cash flow from financing		
Proceeds from bond sale	50,000	
Long-term loan	21,000	
Payment of mature bonds	(20,000)	
Net cash flow from financing activities		51,000
Net cash increase		58,000
Cash on December 31, 2012		97,000
Cash balance on December 31, 2013		155,000

hospitals may not be able to influence third-party payers to speed up scheduled payments, and cash inflows at universities are limited by registration dates.

There is always lag between when checks are mailed and when funds are credited to an organization's checking account. The period involved in mailing, recording, processing, and clearing is known as the "float time," and its length directly affects the availability of cash. The objective, then, is to find a means to shorten or minimize the float time. A number of methods have been used, such as the *lockbox* system, which allows clients of public and other not-for-profit agencies to send their checks to a post office box. The bank collects the checks daily from the lockbox and deposits them directly to the client's account, reducing the float time and making the money more quickly available (typically two to four days sooner).[11]

Although the lockbox system is a useful innovation, it may not fit the needs of every organization. Before adopting this approach, costs versus benefits should be assessed. Positives include the returns that result from the added

TABLE 6.2a Cash-Flow Budget: Sample Spreadsheet (Governmental Type) for 12 Months

	Jan.	Feb.	Mar.	Apr.	May	June	July	Aug.	Sept.	Oct.	Nov.	Dec.
Revenue/cash Receipts (inflows)												
Tax revenue												
Property taxes												
Sales taxes												
Income taxes												
Nontax revenue												
Charges and fees												
Permits												
Fines												
Intergovernmentalaid												
Miscellaneous												
Total inflows												
Disbursements/ expenditures outflows												
Salaries, wages												
Materials and supplies												
Debt service												
Benefits												
Other												
Total cash outlays/outflows												
Excess (deficits) cash												
Add beginning balance												
Ending cash balance												

TABLE 6.2b   Cash-Flow Budget: Sample Spreadsheet (Other Not-for-Profit) Northeastern Accounting Association for 12 months

	Jan.	Feb.	Mar.	Apr.	May	June	July	Aug.	Sept.	Oct.	Nov.	Dec.
Cash flow												
Revenues/cash Receipts (inflows)												
Member dues												
Associated member dues												
Information service												
Publication sales												
Continuing education												
Annual meeting												
Royalty income												
Interest income												
Corporate donations												
Total income												
Expenses (cash outflows)												
Salaries and payroll taxes												
Retirement and benefits												
Professional fees												
Supplies												
Telephone												
Postage and shipping												
Rent												
Equipment repair and insurance												
Travel												
Meetings and classes												
Marketing												
Purchase of equipment												
Total cash Outlay/outflow												
Excess/deficit of cash												
Cash, beginning of period												
Cash, end of period												

cash, the more rapid inflow of funds, and reductions in costs associated with internal processing; negatives consist of a fixed monthly charge assessed by the bank, plus a per-item processing fee. The following formula aids in assessing the costs and benefits of the lockbox system:[12]

$$BAL = (NUM) \times (AVG) \times (TIM) \qquad (6.1)$$

when
$$
\begin{aligned}
BAL &= \text{usable balances generated due to the lockbox system} \\
NUM &= \text{number of checks per day} \\
AVG &= \text{average value per check} \\
TIM &= \text{reduced number of transit days}
\end{aligned}
$$

Based on the increase in the usable balances (BAL) and the annual interest rate (INT), the annual dollar returns related to the additional funds (ADR) generated from the lockbox system can be determined. They are represented by the following:

$$ADR = (BAL) \times (INT) \qquad (6.2)$$

To find the annual total cost (ATC) of the lockbox system, we need to identify the bank processing cost per check (UC) and the number of checks processed during the year (ANU), generating the following:

$$ATC = (UC) \times (ANU) \qquad (6.3)$$

Finally, the determination of the break-even point, where the benefit generated is equal to the system's costs incurred, is calculated as follows:

$$ADR = ATC \qquad (6.4)$$

Whenever the benefits of the lockbox system exceed the cost, the system should be implemented (i.e., $ADR > ATC$). If the reverse is true, it should be rejected. An application of the lockbox approach may be analyzed from the following example.

The city of Bright is examining lockbox systems for possible implementation in the collection of its water bills. It has been estimated that a lockbox system will reduce float time by four days. The 10,000 water customers in Bright have an average $200 monthly tax bill. The city earns 10 percent on its short-term investments. The bank charges $0.20 for each check it processes. Should Bright adopt the lockbox system?

Assuming that the number of working days each month is twenty and that checks flow at this rate, the number of checks processed per day (NUM) is:

$$NUM = \frac{10,000}{20} = 500 \text{ checks per day}$$

Using equation 6.1 to calculate usable balances:

$$BAL = (NUM) \times (AVG) \times (TIM)$$
$$= 500 \times \$200 \times 4$$
$$= \$400,000$$

Note that the implementation of the lockbox system will provide an additional $400,000 for investing. This amount can be invested at 10 percent to produce an annual dollar return (ADR) as follows (using equation 6.2):

$$ADR = (BAL) \times (INT)$$
$$= \$400,000 \times 0.10$$
$$= \$40,000$$

The $40,000 equals the annual benefit generated as a result of the implementation of the lockbox system. The annual number of checks processed per year (ANU), assuming customers are billed on a monthly basis, is determined as follows:

$$ANU = 10,000 \times 12 = 120,000$$

The cost for implementing the lockbox system is calculated by using equation 6.3:

$$ATC = (UC) \times (ANU)$$
$$= \$0.20 \times 120,000$$
$$= \$24,000$$

Because the ADR is $40,000 and the ATC is $24,000, the benefits exceed the cost by $16,000.

Electronic transfer and *branch deposits* are other means for speeding up cash collection. By means of the Federal Reserve Wire System, banks may electronically move balances from one bank to another. Like the lockbox system, it is used to reduce transit time and speed up check collection. Because the cost of transferring funds ranges between $1 and $6 per transaction, it should ideally be used only for larger transfers. In those states and jurisdictions where branch banking is permitted, deposits can be made in outlying branches to be immediately credited to the individual agency account.

To determine when to use the electronic transfer method, a break-even analysis can be performed to determine the minimum amount that would be required to make this method cost-effective. The following information is needed to calculate the break-even point: unit cost of the transfer, float days gained/saved in transit time, and the annual interest rate on idle balances. Using equation 6.5,

$$Break\text{-}even\ point = \frac{Cost}{Days \times Rate/365}$$

(6.5)

Assume the following scenario for the city of Bright: cost for an *EFT* = $6, days of float gained = 2, and short-term rate = 8 percent:

$$Break\text{-}even\ point = \frac{\$6}{2 \times 0.08/365} = \frac{\$6}{0.0383} = \$13,698$$

This suggests that wire transfers are cost-effective in cases in which receipts are in excess of $13,698.

An alternative way of calculating the break-even point can be achieved by using the following equation:

$$Break\text{-}even\ point = \frac{Cost \times 365}{Rate \times Days}$$

(6.6)

Using the data for Bright, the alternative method generates approximately the same results:

$$Break\text{-}even\ point = \frac{\$6 \times 365}{0.08 \times 2} = \$13,688$$

Preauthorized checks are signatureless checks that can be used to accelerate the collection of fixed payments. Under this arrangement, the client or customer signs an agreement with the public or not-for-profit agency to allow its bank to write a check, for a given amount, on his or her account. By means of a computer file, the agency sends the bank the necessary information to carry out the function, and by similar means, the bank informs the agency of the deposit and availability of funds. This process has the advantage of reducing the float time while creating a greater certainty of cash inflows.[13] Smaller agencies may wish to explore this technique.

A final method that not-for-profit and government entities may use is an *accelerated payment incentive program*, commonly referred to as sales discounts in the private sector. By offering taxpayers incentives to pay earlier than required, possibly through a 1% discount on taxes owed, the receiving entity can obtain cash faster than originally anticipated. Although this expedites the cash collection period, it may reduce the overall taxes received. Again, a cost–benefit analysis should be performed to determine whether such a policy is fiscally prudent and meets the cash needs of the organization.

Collection Procedures

The complexity of collection procedures increases with the size of the government or other not-for-profit organization. Small organizations typically have one bank account to which all the checks and monies are deposited, whereas larger organizations may have many bank accounts and many sources from which cash inflows originate. The objective is to get the cash into the organization's account as soon as possible and to keep it for as long as permitted to increase earnings on investments. Collection can often be facilitated by a number of simple common-sense actions, such as billing outside agencies for services as soon as performance is completed, facilitating citizens' and clients' payments of taxes and fees, and establishing and maintaining good relations with funding agencies. Coordinating and facilitating the achievement of cash management goals involve the following steps:

- Establishment of revenue collection policies and procedures for each major revenue source.
- Provision for special deposit procedures to deal with major revenue processing problems (such problems may result, for example, from the quarterly or annual collection of property taxes).
- Establishment of deposit procedures for each type of revenue base or location.[14]

To aid in the collection procedure, a detailed checklist of each revenue source should be developed, identifying the specific activities to which close attention should be given. Rosenberg, Stallings, and Coe have suggested a good example, as shown in Table 6.3.

Letters of Credit

Streamlining the letter of credit payments system provides communities with the opportunity to better predict the time when federal funds will be available to make disbursements for federally funded projects. Improvement in the letter of credit process does not quicken the speed of the process, but it does enable the entity or agency to accurately time the receipt of the federal funds with the project expenditures and disbursements. This avoids delaying the application of funds (cash) to other projects, essentially avoiding a kind of internal loan. The letter of credit is the federal government's method of choice for disbursing funds to local governments. Typically, the federal government grants authorization to the governmental entities to draw down federal bank accounts as the entity's cash needs dictate in order to meet grant disbursement obligations.

To be eligible to participate in the federal letter of credit system, the grantee must meet specific criteria. It must have had at least a one-year relationship with the federal government, as well as a grant for $120,000 or more. The second condition requires that the grantee agrees to draw down the approved project funds only as needed. The grantee must also file periodic reports on cash and disbursements and balances to the agency that approved the project. Finally, the grantee agency must give the awarding federal agency the opportunity to review the grantee's financial practices and recommend remedial action in cases where the terms of the grant are not being followed. This ensures a degree of accountability and transparency for local governments using federal funding. In those cases in which state and local government laws and regulations prohibit local government and agencies from expending cash before it is physically in hand (in the treasury), the letter of credit system cannot operate efficiently.

Disbursement Procedures

Ideally, cash should be disbursed only when absolutely required and at the last possible moment. Although this practice should be carried out in a manner that avoids fines for late payment and minimizes poor vendor and community relations, efforts should nonetheless be made to hold or delay payments to clients.

Effective disbursement requires that accounts payable be well managed. Invoices should be analyzed and filed according to their dates for payment to permit discounts to be taken and facilitate timely payment. Factors such as the following should be considered: "the discounts available, the standard policies for handling different types of invoices, the past history of the vendor for requiring rapid payment, and the method by which the payment will be made (e.g., mail pickup, electronic transfer)."[15]

A means that is sometimes used to improve the availability of cash is the *warrant*. A warrant is like a non-interest-bearing note payable that the issuer promises to pay upon presentation at some specified future date. The warrant is typically presented to a clearing bank for payment. Subsequent to payment, the clearing bank presents the warrant to the governmental unit and receives payment. The warrant is unlike a check in that there need not be money in the bank when it is written; rather, money does not have to be made available until the warrant is presented for payment. The ability to use the warrant allows the governmental unit to retain the cash for a longer period than might otherwise be the case. (Some opponents say that it denies vendors the opportunity to use their money.) Normally, a higher fee is charged for the extra processing required.[16]

The *wire transfers* system can be used to delay disbursements in the same manner that it can be used to speed collections. Because wire transfers maximize the time for which money can be used in an entity, they reduce the disbursement float time and minimize the need to draw cash from other areas. The wire provides a definite time that permits funds to be invested instead of having to make rough estimates of how long it will take checks to clear the bank. This is very important in cases in which large payments must be made at scheduled times. Moreover, when purchases of investment instruments are executed through brokers in other cities, often involving large sums of money, wire transfers may be the most suitable means. Since banks are required to pass on the cost, it is necessary to calculate the break-even point, as was shown in equation 6.4.

The *automated clearinghouse* (ACH) method is employed mainly to process electronic payments and direct deposits of payroll and, to a lesser degree, pension payments. The ACH method is costly and should be undertaken only if net benefits or savings can be demonstrated. In cases in which the ACH method is likely to positively affect employee relations, a good rationale can be established in implementing it. Although float time is lost in the ACH method, there are some advantages associated with its use, including reductions in check processing charges, account reconciliation costs, employee time lost for cashing checks, and storage costs for canceled checks.

TABLE 6.3   Checklist of Detailed Procedures for the Collection of Revenues in Municipalities

Licenses and permits

- Deposit all monies intact.
- Maintain a list of all delinquent licenses or permits and strictly enforce collection of delinquencies uniformly.
- Require all licensees or permit holders to display their licenses and/or permits. Instruct government offices to look for such licenses and/or permits and notify the collection agency when violators are suspected.
- Utilize reports submitted to other government agencies, such as taxes paid to the state treasury, to verify gross receipts, if fees are based on gross receipts.

Parking lots, golf courses, swimming pools

- Indicate in plain sight at all locations a schedule showing the full range of fees.
- Design a standard format for use at all locations if tickets are used.
- Check all cash-register receipts to ensure that cash and ticket counts reflect recorded frequency and monetary totals.
- Rotate attendants through different facilities and work schedules at frequent intervals.
- Practice close supervision and surveillance.
- Have all keys to lock boxes, cash registers, and similar equipment under control of authorized supervision and not available to attendants.
- Schedule frequent unannounced visits by internal auditors who will review the inventory of tickets, count cash, require authorization for all exemptions, and so on.
- Segregate duties involved in authorization and collection/disbursement of cash.

Parking-meter collections

- Establish, number, and describe meter routes.
- Select coin-collection equipment that will be secure against theft.
- Consider maintaining weight records by route.
- Rotate the schedule of route collection periodically.
- Collect coins at hours that coincide with heavy traffic.
- Safeguard keys to coin-meter receptacles; issue daily to coin collectors.
- Mutilate and destroy worn keys.
- Order new keys only on authorization of responsible persons.
- Require meter collectors to wear distinctive uniforms.
- Supervise the coin-counting process.
- Ensure the security of the coin-counting area.
- Have meter collectors report the location of all broken, stuck, or pilfered meters as they are discovered.
- Maintain dollar and/or weight records to provide for periodic comparisons of collections for each weight.
- Issue receipts daily to collectors.
- Establish procedures to make reconciliations of cash deposits. If coin-counting machines that register total values are used, such values can be reconciled to deposits.
- Schedule periodic unannounced reviews of all phases of operation. Spot-check collection and counting procedures, personnel rotation, revenue comparisons, and so on.
- Consider the installation of meters that accept credit/debit cards, thus reducing the risk of theft and the number of personnel required to physically extract currency from the meter.

Property taxes, parking-and vehicle-code fines, sales taxes, gasoline taxes, cigarette taxes, liquor-license fees, and motor vehicle fees

- Establish written contracts with other agencies as provided by law.
- Test receipts-to-treasury record periodically to verify that all receipts are deposited properly and in a timely fashion.
- Request confirmation from agencies doing the collecting and distributing and compare information received from them with the municipal records.

Federal and state grants

- Prepare status reports for each grant. These reports show such data as:
  - grant description;
  - granting agency;
  - total amount of grant;
  - terms and restrictions concerning the use of the grant; and
  - anticipated payment terms of the grant.
- Bill the granting agency as soon as permitted by grant guidelines.

Source: Adapted from Philip Rosenberg, C. Wayne Stallings, and Charles K. Coe, *A Treasury Management Handbook for Small Cities and Other Governmental Units* (Chicago: Municipal Finance Officers Association, 1978), pp. 54–55.

Consolidating or Pooling Cash

Governmental units and most other not-for-profit agencies use the *fund accounting system*, which tends to negatively affect cost management. The fund accounting practice requires that restricted funds be segregated and that receipts and the disposition of resources be accounted for and reported separately. It is not uncommon to find government and other not-for-profit agencies maintaining separate bank accounts for each fund. The maintenance of separate bank accounts, which is useful perhaps for control, is an impediment to effective cash management because it requires that the cash manager keep track of the individual balances with their separate cash flow patterns. This proliferation of bank accounts leads to a number of unacceptable results: (1) administrative costs rise, (2) the cash manager's ability to make accurate projections of each separate cash flow decreases, and (3) uncoordinated and fragmented investments are produced. Review shows that consolidation and pooling of cash can minimize most of these problems.[17]

A number of methods have been developed to facilitate the pooling of cash while permitting separate fund bank accounts to operate. The *single concentration account* has been gaining acceptance among municipalities because it permits the pooling of all cash receipts while allowing a separate zero balance account for cash disbursement.[18] The operation of a single concentration account allows local banks to automatically transfer funds to it. Several advantages are gained by this method: (1) It permits separate checking accounts to be used for disbursements, (2) it permits cash consolidation, (3) it makes it easier and less expensive to invest idle cash in short-term market instruments, (4) it reduces the problem of maintaining a minimum balance in each account, and (5) it minimizes disbursement float time.[19]

Borrowing

Because debt management affects the flow of receipts and disbursements, it should be given due consideration. Long-term borrowing in public and other not-for-profit organizations is intended mainly to finance capital projects that are expected to have several years of useful life. Usually, the money is received in large amounts and held for specific time periods. During these periods, care must be given to how the money is handled. In governmental units, for example, federal arbitrage regulations should be observed (borrowing at lower, tax-exempt rates and reinvesting at higher rates is also forbidden by most state governments; absence of restrictions on such activities could lead to high-risk investing and potential losses).

Short-term borrowing should be used only during those periods when the shortage of cash inflow causes temporary gaps. Identifying these gaps before they occur and taking appropriate actions to deal with them is one of the principal objectives of effective cash management. Among the most common types of short-term borrowing are (1) tax anticipation notes (TANs), which are issued for a specific period of time, to be repaid upon the collection of a specific tax; (2) bond anticipation notes (BANs), which are short-term notes in anticipation of a bond issue and are retired from the proceeds of a particular issue; and (3) revenue anticipation notes (RANs), which are issued to obtain cash in anticipation of revenue that is not a tax source (e.g. fines, tolls).

Monitoring, Evaluating, and Controlling

The important inflow and outflow accounts such as receipts, disbursements, and balances in cash and investments should be monitored daily, and monthly, quarterly, and yearly reports should be regularly issued. Periodically, or as required, the performance of the cash budget managers is also compared with the predetermined performance indicators. From these assessments, performance reports are prepared and sent to administrators and elected officials. The reports are used as valuable inputs to aid in forecasting and fine-tuning projections for the ensuing fiscal period.[20]

Because of the vulnerability of cash and securities to fraud and abuse, special care should be taken by the internal auditor to ensure that the internal control systems are operating properly at all times to safeguard these liquid assets. This internal control system is also a focal concern of the independent auditor, whose recommendations are important in fashioning future cash management policies and objectives. Internal control framework, like that developed by the Committee of Sponsoring Organizations of the Treadway Commission (COSO), could be used by management and the internal audit department when developing and implementing internal controls within the organization.

Bank Relations

Banks occupy important roles in communities by providing access to primary and secondary markets and by providing essential services (see Table 6.4). In most communities, the local governmental units are large depositors whom the bank usually attempts to attract. Many elements contribute significantly toward achieving the goal of effective cash management, which include the following:

- Keen knowledge of available bank services
- Information about the cost of each bank service provided
- Competition among banks for the deposits of the governmental unit
- Continual evaluation of the banking relations
- Maintenance of day-to-day competition among banks to obtain the best value when making investment decisions[21]

TABLE 6.4   Available Banking and Financial Services

Collection services	Disbursement services
Wire transfers	Wire transfers
Automated clearing-house (ACH)	Payable-through-drafts
collections	Balancing monitoring and reporting
Pre-authorized checks	In-bank services
Lockbox systems	Direct-deposit system
Depository-transfer checks	Account-reconcilement service
Over-the-counter payment systems	Pre-authorized check payments
Armored car services	Automated clearing-house (ACH)
Night depository services	payments
Coin-counting services	Concentration/zero-balance accounts
Special-deposit messengers	Microfilm checks
	Computer services

Investment services	Credit services
Investment advice	Line of credit
Savings accounts	Note purchases
Time deposits	Bond underwriting
Investment instruments certificates of	Bond purchasing
deposit repurchase agreement/custodial	Bond transfer and registration services
arrangements	Short-term notes
Short-term U.S. Treasury securities	Municipal commercial paper
Banks' acceptances	
Commercial paper	
Money-market-mutual funds	

Source: Adapted from Rhett D. Harrell, "Banking Relations Part I," in *Cash Management For Small Governments,* ed. Ian J. Allan (Chicago: Government Finance Officers Association, 1989), p. 65.

It is especially important that banks give attention to *community involvement.* Policies such as providing loans to individuals and businesses in the local community and participating in local government bond issues provide both tangible and intangible benefits to the community that cannot easily be expressed in quantitative dollar terms.[22] When a bank's community involvement policy is active and positively oriented, the bank may occasionally justify sacrificing a higher potential yield to foster its continuance. The sacrifice of potential higher yield may be offset by repeat customer business from local government and businesses as well as overall community financial growth.

Banking Policies

Public and not-for-profit agencies' bank relations may not typically be able to escape political influence. Every effort should be made to minimize such influence, however, because it may impede competition in procuring banking services at the best prices.[23] Banking policies that can economically permit the maintenance of bank accounts in all banking establishments within the community and require periodic rotation of banking services to each financial institution will likely minimize the political influence that may take place. This approach has its drawbacks, though. The maintenance of the minimum deposit approach is not preferred for the following reasons: (1) It reduces the opportunity to pool cash and increase investment earnings; (2) it increases processing costs; (3) it reduces the flexibility to respond to emergencies; (4) degrades accuracy in making a cash forecast owing to the large number of accounts that may be involved; (5) it increases handling fees, especially in large communities; and (6) determining the size and length of time of deposits in a variety of banks can present problems.

Selecting Banks on a Competitive Basis

Law or precedent may dictate that the entity can only conduct business with the bank that provides it with the most competitive prices for timely and comparable service quality. Typically, the competitive approach will involve competitive bidding that specifies the services desired in a request for proposal. Returned bids are reviewed and analyzed and a contract award is made (see chapter 21 for details).

The *cost of bank services* is normally determined in two ways. The first is based on the cost accounting system of the bank. This information provides the bank with a basis for imposing a monthly service charge according to the number and kinds of services provided (for example, the number of checks processed or the number of coupon redemptions for a local jurisdiction's bonds, disbursements, and account reconciliations).

The use of compensating balances in non–interest-bearing accounts such as demand deposits is the second approach. These deposits represent "free money" to the bank, which invests them to generate earnings for itself. In those cases where banks pay interest on amounts in checking accounts, such interest is significantly lower than what the deposits actually earn. Banks sometimes use the float time to earn money that helps to defray their costs. The compensating balance may be calculated by using the following formula:

$$
\begin{array}{l}
\textit{Required} \\
\textit{compensating} \\
\textit{earnings factor} \\
\textit{balance}
\end{array}
\quad = \quad
\begin{array}{l}
\textit{Annual charges} \\
\textit{for services} \quad \div (1 - \textit{reserve requirement)} \\
\textit{(return bank expects} \\
\textit{to earn on deposits)}
\end{array}
$$

For example, for the city of Bright, assume annual charges of $4,500, an earnings factor for bank of 5 percent, and reserve requirements of 15 percent of deposits:

$$\textit{Required compensating balance} = \$4,500 = \frac{0.05}{1-0.15} = \frac{\$90,000}{0.85} = \$105,882.35$$

When banks cannot or do not furnish an analysis of their compensating balance costs and minimum requirements, a third approach for paying banking services may be considered: Many business firms and governmental entities avoid the problem of computing an amount as a compensating balance by the simple expedient of agreeing with the bank that the account will return a profit. To this end, the bank is asked to provide a monthly analysis of the account. The bank analyzes and records earnings from account balances, less the cost of all transactions, and subtracts costs from earnings, indicating either profit or loss.[24]

Investing in Short-Term Securities

Engaging in short-term investment is necessary because of the uncertainty about how much cash will be needed to fully meet operating needs. The instruments used most for government investments are bank certificates, money market funds, U.S. Treasury obligations, time deposits, repurchase agreements, and U.S. agency securities. Collectively, these investments are known as *marketable securities.* They are relatively risk-free, interest-bearing paper assets, having a high degree of liquidity in that they are easily sold. To make the maximum contribution toward the achievement of cash management goals requires that the cash manager be knowledgeable about the characteristics of different investment securities, including their yields, determined by prevailing market interest rates, and primary and secondary market statuses.

Treasury Bills

Treasury bills (commonly known as "T-bills") and *Treasury certificates* are U.S. government short-term instruments. Treasury bills are initially issued in $10,000 denominations having 91- to 182-day maturities, while certificates are issued with 9- and 12-month maturities. Since T-bills bear no interest, they are sold at a discount. The interest return or yield is the difference between the purchasing and selling or maturity prices of the notes. A testimony to the liquidity of the T-bill is the very active secondary market that exists. T-bills may be bought and sold at any time between the issuance and maturity dates. This is a major reason why they are so attractive as an option for idle cash investment. For the same reason, however, T-bills carry the lowest yield of all money market instruments because they are essentially a risk-free investment.

Government Agency Securities

A number of U.S. government agencies, such as the Farmers Home Administration, the Federal National Mortgage Association, and the Export–Import Bank, issue securities that are fully guaranteed, whereas organizations such as banks of cooperatives, the Federal Home Loan Bank, Tennessee Valley

Authority (TVA), Federal Land Bank, and Federal Intermediate Credit Bank issue securities that are not fully guaranteed. There is a large secondary market for these securities, but their liquidity is not as great as that of Treasury bills. This accounts in large part for the yield spread between Treasury bills and government agency securities.

Certificates of Deposit

These consist of negotiable and nonnegotiable receipts for monies normally deposited in large commercial banks for a specified period of time with a specified rate of interest. *Certificates of deposit* (or "CDs," as they are commonly called) are, in essence, time deposits. CDs issued by larger banks usually have greater liquidity than those of smaller institutions. Like Treasury bills, they are traded on the secondary markets, though not as actively. Typically, CDs trade in secondary markets in $1 million amounts or multiples of $1 million, although odd lots can be obtained in multiples of $100,000 and $250,000.

Commercial Paper

These are business promissory notes specifying a future payment date. They are usually sold at a discount and are supported by the general credit of the agency or company. In most cases, only companies with very high credit ratings (AAA or Aaa) can confidently issue commercial paper. Well-known, highly solvent companies that issue commercial paper include General Electric, Coca-Cola, Wal-Mart, and Citigroup. Maturity dates range from 30 days to 9 months, with a yield one-quarter to one-half greater than that of Treasury bills. Laws in many states prohibit local governments from participating in this type of investment.

Repurchase Agreements

A *repurchase agreement* is a type of short-term investment that permits governments to invest cash for short periods of time, typically between one and seven days. The governmental unit or agency enters into an agreement to purchase Treasury bills from banks that agree to repurchase the securities at some specified date for a specified higher amount. This type of investment is virtually risk-free.

Money Market Funds

Money market funds are mutual funds that invest in marketable securities. This involves the pooling of cash from a number of investors to purchase different types of market securities such as CDs and Treasury bills. The return from the investment is shared proportionately. Although no commission is normally charged, a small management fee is permitted. Money market funds have grown over the past 20 years in large part because of their returns, which have been significantly higher than the rates on passbook savings accounts. For public and other not-for-profit organizations, these funds offer a number of attractive features:

- They permit small organizations to obtain expert management of their idle funds.
- They provide yields that are much higher than those obtainable from savings banks.
- They provide virtually risk-free investments, because most instruments are Treasury securities, CDs, and commercial paper.
- They provide flexibility for entering and/or withdrawing funds.
- They don't require large investments.

Tracking of Investments

An important function of cash management is the maintenance of accounts online, using an up-to-date tracking system of all outstanding investments. This system must be capable of providing information on the amount and source of money invested, the maturity schedule, and the yield each investment is generating. As an important risk management practice, collateralized investment values should be checked daily to compare them with market value. This minimizes the possibility that the collateralized investments will fall below the required market value without it being recognized. Additionally, maturity dates must be constantly tracked to ensure that the appropriate interest and principal on investment are paid when due. Monthly and periodic reports, as required, are sent to the departments responsible for the funds.[25]

Investment Strategy

The *investment strategy* is an important element in the cash management program in that it provides guidelines for determining "what will be purchased, when, and for how long, and what the target investment mix should be on specific dates."[26] An investment strategy should ideally be written and aimed at assisting the cash manager to best invest available funds for the time period covered by the strategy. In preparing the strategy, consideration should be given to the following:

- Explicit assumptions about prospective market conditions, cash availability, and the desired mix of securities
- Guidelines and timetables for purchasing specific types and amounts of securities

- A clearly delineated system for selling or pruning securities if destabilizing conditions so demand
- Clearly defined procedures for accelerating investment when excess cash is available to expand purchases
- Development of specific performance indicators to assess the cash manager's achievement[27]

Determining the Optimum Cash Balance

To collect, process, and disburse cash in the most efficient manner, it is most useful to know the *optimum cash balance* required. Because of uncertainties related to cash inflows and outflows, it is difficult to determine this. A rule-of-thumb approach has been suggested: that the governmental unit or not-for-profit organization may hold cash sufficient to cover the expected average expenditure likely to be incurred for a specific period, such as a week (the shorter time period, the more advantageous the organization's cash position). This amount is held as security against running out of cash. Amounts above this imposed level will be invested, and amounts below will trigger the selling of securities. When this rule is used jointly with an accurately projected cash budget, it provides a reasonable basis for meeting cash needs, especially those of smaller public and other not-for-profit organizations.

Concluding Observations

Attention to cash management is a recent phenomenon that developed in response to the high interest rates and inflation of the late 1970s and early 1980s, the low interest rates of the 1990s, heightened taxpayer resistance toward higher taxes, and decreasing donations to not-for-profit organizations. Improved cash management is viewed as one way to increase available resources. Effective cash management requires the coordination of many factors, among them a well-thought-out investment strategy, an efficient and timely collection and disbursement system, an effective short-term securities investment program, and timely and strategic monitoring.

A successful cash management program requires that a way be found to accelerate the collection of cash while slowing down its disbursement as much as possible. The objective must be perceived within the context of the organization's policies and implemented in a way that limits the impairment of client services and vendor relations. A number of improved procedures have been introduced to speed the availability of cash, such as the lockbox system, the electronic transfer of cash, the single concentration account, and the zero balance account. Finally, the pursuit of greater earnings on idle cash should be carried out with prudence to avoid unnecessary risk.

Notes

1. Michael Dotsey, "An Investigation of Cash Management Practices and Their Effects on the Demand for Money," *Economic Review 70*, no. 5 (September/October 1984): 3; see also Raymond L. McCabe, "Electronic Funds Transfer as a Cash Management Tool," *Governmental Finance 10*, no. 4 (December 1981): 9–14.

2. See Lloyd Hora, "Bucks: Better Understanding of Cash Control Systems," *Government Finance Review 8*, no. 2 (April 1992): 17–19.

3. Frank M. Patitucci and Michael H. Lichtenstein, *Improving Cash Management in Local Government: A Comprehensive Approach* (Chicago: Municipal Finance Officers Association, 1977), p. 4.

4. Paul L. Shinn, "An Overview of Cash Management," in *Cash Management for Small Governments*, ed. Ian J. Allan (Chicago: Government Finance Officers Association, 1989), p. 13.

5. Ibid.

6. Ibid.

7. Ibid., p. 15.

8. Ibid.

9. Ibid., p. 6.

10. Jody Blayek, *Financial Planning for Non-profit Organizations* (New York: John Wiley, 1996), p. 114.

11. Dotsey, "An Investigation of Cash Management Practices and Their Effects on the Demand for Money," p. 11.

12. Ronald Braswell, Karen Fortin, and Jerome Osteryoung, *Financial Management for Not-for-Profit Organizations* (New York: John Wiley, 1984), pp. 150–152.

13. Dotsey, "An Investigation of Cash Management Practices and Their Effects on the Demand for Money," p. 4.

14. Patitucci and Lichtenstein, *Improving Cash Management in Local Government*, p. 27.

15. Ibid., p. 29.

16. Ibid.

17. See Walter P. Berg, "Selecting a Municipal Depository," *Municipal Finance* (November 1969): 94.

18. Dotsey, "An Investigation of Cash Management Practices and Their Effects on the Demand for Money," pp. 4–5.

19. Ibid., p. 4.

20. Shinn, "An Overview of Cash Management," p. 18.

21. Patitucci and Lichtenstein, *Improving Cash Management in Local Government*, p. 32.

22. Ibid., p. 33.

23. Rhett D. Harrell "Banking Relations, Part I," in *Cash Management for Small Governments*, ed. Ian J. Allan (Chicago: Government Finance Officers Association, 1989), pp. 62–63.

24. Berg, "Selecting a Municipal Depository," p. 94.

25. Shinn, "An Overview of Cash Management," p. 18.

26. Pattitucci and Lichtenstein, *Improving Cash Management in Local Government*, p. 40.

27. Ibid., pp. 40–41.

7

Risk Management

Until 1978, risk management aroused little interest in public sector and other not-for-profit organizations. This has radically changed due in great part to the erosion of sovereign immunity of governmental units as a municipal defense following the case of *Monell vs. City of New York* (1978), in which the court extended the right of citizens to sue the government for negligent acts of their employees. Because of this ruling, governmental entities became vulnerable to a number of suits. The erosion of governmental immunity, the public's proclivity for litigation, and the potential liability exposure have forced public and not-for-profit organizations to give greater priority to risk management.

From the mid-1970s through 1982, the insurance industry was able to obtain extraordinary earnings on its cash investments due to prevailing high interest rates. Simultaneously, the industry was experiencing low demand for its services, inhibiting it from aggressive pricing policies. However, as interest rates fell and market demand firmed in 1984, the insurance industry, mindful of its huge losses in 1983, instituted major increases in insurance premiums. Increases of 100 percent or more became widespread. It is significant that these sizable increases were taking place while deductibles were rising and the amount of liability coverage was falling.[1] (Whenever uncertainty and demand is high for a service, as in the case of the present desire by organizations for terrorist insurance, prices are likely to be very high.)

The repercussions of *City of New York* made increases in insurance premiums inevitable. The number of suits and the magnitude of awards could not be sustained on the old premium structure. Suits and awards such as the following have occurred since 1978:

- In Newport Beach, California, the court awarded $6 million to a man who became paraplegic after diving into the water and hitting a sandbar.
- Merill, Michigan, with a population of 1,710 and a budget of $250,000, was ordered to pay its former police chief $250,000 for wrongful discharge.
- An award of $2.6 million was granted to a woman in Torrington, Connecticut, "because the police failed to protect her from her estranged husband."[2]

Dallas, Texas, reports that when it solicited bids for insurance coverage in January 1985, it expected that its insurance would increase in cost by perhaps 100 to 200 percent and that a number of insurers would bid. The city received a sole bid asking for $1.5 million in premiums, compared to $154,000 only the year before.[3] It was events such as this that forced governmental entities to seek alternative options, such as intergovernmental risk pools and self-insurance, as a more economical means of protecting themselves. Because of this, successful means (sometimes known as the "alternative market") developed to meet the public sector's insurance liability during the 1980s. Instruments such as risk pools provide enhanced aid and services to members. Risk pools provide "workshops, loss control site visits, claims administration, and manuals illustrating risk-management tools and technologies."[4] Unlike during the 1980s, when the few options for liability insurance were expensive, commercial carriers now offer a greater variety of liability insurance options at more reasonable prices. As an aid to keeping insurance prices at acceptable levels, the Public Risk Database Project (PRDP) has been initiated to collect nationwide data on losses from public sector entities. The aim is to standardize data on losses to facilitate better risk program analysis and comparisons among governmental entities to aid in identifying cause, frequency, severity of claims, patterns, and best benchmark practices.

Risk management is more difficult for governmental units because, unlike businesses, their experience is less than two decades old. The potential negative effects and financial loss have forced public and, to a lesser extent, not-for-profit organizations to develop expertise in risk management. Yet a number of governmental units need to streamline their fragmented risk management programs. The risk management crisis of the 1980s has been forcing government and other not-for-profit agencies to recognize the desirability of a systematic, centralized approach to protect themselves against loss. Thus, risk management has been gaining significant recognition in both the public and private sectors.

As greater recognition of risk management is being given by public and other not-for-profit agencies, a broader scope of managing risk is emerging in the private sector, where it is known as *holistic* or *enterprise risk management*. It encompasses all potential risk that might affect the organization, including both operational (the traditional focus) and financial (managed separately as part of the financial management functions). Financial risk management may typically involve policies relating to short- and long-term (pension) investment, the maintenance of diversification strategies (to minimize risk investment in different classes of securities), and the institution of effective internal control procedures to protect assets (physical and human) and minimize liability.[5]

Stakeholders' demands and expectations are not satisfied simply by cutting cost or achieving efficiency. In business, organizations must achieve competitive advantage and product superiority. In both government and business services must not only be enhanced and timely delivered, stakeholders require organizations to demonstrate and report on responsible sustainable practices. To achieve enhanced outcomes from sustainability, "organization must be able to recognize, manage and respond to both the opportunities and risks."[6]

If the organization wants to maximally accomplish its objectives, the system should understand and develop a framework that breaks strategies and objectives with four interconnected but distinct categories that create a strong context for risk identification and consideration, as follows:[7]

1. *Strategic risks* prompt the organization to focus on what can go wrong, allowing the organization to think proactively about what can go right.

2. *Operational risks* require that organizations deal effectively with the volatility that takes place in the business environment. These relate to changing weather patterns that may create natural disasters such as the 2011 Japanese Fukushima earthquake and tsunami, and the U.S. East Coast Hurricane Sandy. In Japan, the Nissan and Toyota companies' productions were significantly affected for many months.

3. *Compliance risks* are increasing at international, national and regional levels creating new regulatory risks. Governments are implementing new regulations in coastal areas in response to sea level rise. Among the regulatory actions include health and safety, human rights, antibribery, and environmental regulations.

4. *Reporting risks* have been mounting for greater transparency, making it necessary for many organizations to provide sustainability reporting to meet the triple bottom line (TBL) expectations. TBL refers to stakeholders of an organization who focus attention on how an organization gives recognition to social, economic, and environmental factors (known as the three "Ps" or people, profits, and planet) in achieving its goals such as profits, return on investment, or a particular targeted outcome.

Sustainability and Risk Management

How we think about sustainability has changed. No longer can sustainability be compartmentalized: It is now the responsibility of everyone in the organization. We have a public/constituents who are now more sophisticated: Thanks to wider availability of information, and the visibility of organizations, people have a better understanding of the interconnectedness of organizational actions. This development has created a groundswell of support and demand for the acceptance of sustainability principles. Physical and financial assets, once viewed by businessmen and accountants as the greatest determinant of organizational value (83 percent thought so in 1975), are so seen by only 23 percent of businessmen today. Now the largest component of value, in the view of businessmen and accountants, is identified as intangible assets, such as human capital, intellectual capital, and external stakeholders.[8]

Defining Risk Management

Risk is unavoidable. Value is a function of risk-generated return. Thus, each decision enhances value or decreases it. Organizations seek to minimize risk exposure, the organization incur only the kinds and magnitude of risk that allow it to successfully pursue its goals. This is what sustainability calls the "sweet spot," or the optimal risk-taking zone, as shown in Figure 7.1.

The pursuit of the sweet spot requires an assessment process that is simple, understandable, and sustainable. The risk management process involves the following activities:

- Definition of goals, objectives or outcomes desired
- Identification of risk
- Development of criteria to assess vulnerability to risk
- Assess/analyze the risks
- Prioritize the risks in terms of significance and likelihood of occurrence
- Determination of the method(s) required to manage the risks
- Development of mitigation strategies to respond to the potential risk such as preventative controls (forestalling the risk event before it happens) or detective controls (dealing with and minimizing the effect of the event before it occurs)[9]

Until quite recently, risk management in the public sector was oriented around "insurance management." The manual on risk management by Charles K. Coe (*Understanding Risk Management*, 1980) is indicative of this continuing approach. Although the author indicates that risk management is not insurance management, the manual reads that way. Today, the practice has moved away from this single focus.[10]

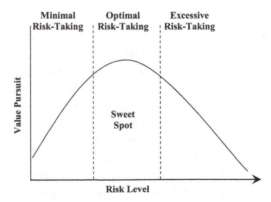

FIGURE 7.1   Sustainability sweet spot.

(Adapted from COSO, Risk Assessment in Practice (Durham, NC: CSCO), p. 1.)

Risk may be defined as an organization's exposure that creates the potential for loss. The process that is used "to assess the causes and effects of uncertainty and risk on an organization"[11] is called *organization risk management* (ORM). The purpose of all risk management is to protect the organization from catastrophic losses and to minimize the total cost of accidental loss. In reality, organization risk management is a comprehensive and systematic approach aimed at identifying, measuring, and controlling an entity's exposure to accidental loss, theft, and liability involving human safety, financial, physical, and natural resources. Examples of these types of loss include (1) damage or loss of property, (2) income loss due to destruction of records, (3) expense incurred in replacing damaged property or repairing a broken water main, (4) liability due to wrongful acts by an entity's employees or officials, and (5) personal liability due to job-related injuries resulting in loss of productivity.[12] Minimizing the organization to risk provides the public and other not-for-profit organizations with predictability about the availability of budgetary resources for allocation. This chapter attempts to convey an understanding of risk management and the alternative options that are being used to achieve maximum safety at a reasonable cost.

Risk Management Policy

A constructive initial step in risk management is the development of policies to guide governments' and not-for-profits' actions. Among the aspects that organizations should consider before articulating risk policies include the following:

- Prioritized risk management program goals
- Clear articulation of the authority and responsibilities of the risk manager
- How the risk management activities are to be coordinated among departments
- Clear guidelines relating risk retention through the use of deductibles or self-insurance
- Whether and, if so, how insurance purchasing responsibilities are to be centralized
- The extent of management support for loss reduction and prevention rather than reimbursement for loss

Importance of Risk Management

To be most effective, risk management must be understood and accepted by the highest level of leadership and every employee must buy in. Leadership must set the tone and demonstrate its continuing and unwavering commitment to risk prevention. The organization should adopt an education and training program about policies, procedures, and ways and means of developing positive attitudes toward safeguarding assets and the prevention of loss. There must be a system that clearly identifies and prioritizes risks. Where resources permit, a safety officer or risk manager should be appointed in all areas. In summary, an assertive risk management program requires the following:

- Recognition of the value of risk management by top-level management
- Clear articulation of risk management roles and responsibilities
- Top-down delegation of risk management responsibilities through the hierarchy of the organization
- Regularized inspections and prioritization of vulnerable areas within the organization
- Regularized review of the risk management program
- Creation of a loss prevention or safety committee
- Development of a system for investigating accidents and claims
- Implementation of safety orientation programs for new employees[13]

Risk Management Process

The goal of the general risk assessment process (see Figure 7.2) involves scanning environmental hazards/risks that are creating exposure threats, producing both perils and opportunities, leading to varied outputs and specific consequences. Although there are slight differences regarding the sequence or specific steps of the risk management process, general agreement exists of five basic elements: (1) discovery and identification of risk, (2) measurement and evaluation of risk, (3) risk control, (4) risk financing, and (5) risk administration.

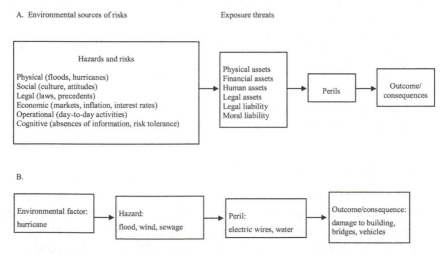

FIGURE 7.2   Risk assessment process: A general overview.

Discovery and Identification of Risk

An important first step in risk determination requires the identification and inventory of the resources of an organization that are exposed to potential loss (see Figure 7.2). It would be useful initially to scan the environmental risk sources that create hazards and cause government and other not-for-profit entities to jeopardize their financial and nonfinancial assets by their possible consequences. This involves (1) an examination and analysis of items such as liquid assets (cash, checks), capital assets, budgets, contracts, leases, organizational charts, policy and procedure manuals, annual reports, capital projects, property records, human resource records and crime records, and other financial records; (2) regular or periodic inspection of premises owned or leased by the governmental or not-for-profit agency; (3) use of well-conceived risk-discovery questionnaires identifying major types of possible losses; and (4) use of reputable insurance brokers to aid in exposure analysis.[14] "Large-scale and long-term hazards have become increasingly prevalent in our economic system."[15] The consumer market has made available a number of products, such as fen-phen and cigarettes, that may produce harmful results and liability. External environmental disasters include the Exxon Valdez oil spill, nuclear power plant accidents such as occurred at Three Mile Island, and toxic waste dumps that present hazards to local communities' water supplies.[16] Attention should be focused on those items or situations that have the greatest potential for financial loss.

Measurement and Evaluation

After the exposure has been identified, measurement and evaluation are the next logical steps. Measurement assesses the potential effects of the risk on the organization: They may be quantitative, relying heavily on the present records of insurance carriers. Assessment may be subjective, relying more on qualitative analysis. In measuring risk, a thorough review of an organization's past loss experience and the frequency and severity of each exposure must be carried out. This is not an easy task: "[M]easurement of identified risk exposures is the most difficult and least precise step in the art of risk management."[17]

Data should be organized for each identified exposure and coverage as follows: (1) The frequency of a particular incident for a specified time period, perhaps four to six years; (2) the amount of claims resulting from the incident during the same time period; and (3) the type of incident involved (e.g., injury to foot, leg, back) during the same time period.[18]

Risk Control

This step is essentially an analysis of the relevant alternatives that might be selected to reduce or eliminate the identified exposure. This is perhaps the most critical step in risk management. A decision must be made to determine whether the risk can be eliminated entirely, reduced significantly, absorbed partially or totally by the governmental unit or organization, or transferred to insurers.[19]

Risk reduction in many local governmental organizations is complicated owing to fragmentation among different departments that share the responsibility for risk management. This is a major problem operating against efficient management of risk control. The National Safety Council statistics for 2011 demonstrate this point in showing the total cost resulting from loss of time worked due to personal injury amounted to $188.9 billion, or $18,891 per disabling injury. Per 100,000 deaths of working-age people, industries such as agriculture, manufacturing and transportation, registered 24.6, 2, and 13.9, respectively, while the government sector rate was 1.9. Except for transportation, these figures represent a significant decline between 2010 and 2011.[20]

If improvements are to be realized, governmental units and others must reduce the frequency and possible severity of loss by eliminating hazards and unsafe conditions. This necessitates greater coordination than has been usual to date in local government. Achieving the risk reduction objective requires actions such as the following:

- Identify risk control areas, and policies and procedures relating thereto.
- Assist each department in interpreting and applying the rules.
- Monitor compliance of the policies and procedures periodically.[21]
- Establish safety and training programs (both in-house and external courses).
- Develop effective record-keeping systems.
- Centralize responsibility for risk management.
- Involve all levels of employees in helping to identify unsafe conditions.

Risk control should ideally be viewed as a preventive measure in that the potential for exposure to loss is recognized and dealt with before it materializes. The principal ways for eliminating risk are to change the way things are being done or else to discontinue the risky activity or service.

Risk Avoidance

Ideally, risk avoidance compares the tools and techniques that allow an organization to be completely shielded from exposure to potential risks. This option is typically not available to governments, because they are required to provide essential services such as police and fire departments. The ideal avoidance suggests that an effective prevention system be in place that inhibits or eliminates risk from materializing. This means that the organization must comprehensively and clearly understand environmental hazards' risk factors that create liability (legal and moral) and asset (physical, fiscal, and human) exposure to perils (see Figure 7.2).

Risk Assumption/Retention/Funding

Risk assumption/retention may occur in two ways: by unexpected or by planned assumption. Unexpected assumption occurs most often because of ignorance and neglect, or because the risk manager failed to thoroughly understand the implications of the actions taken, as indicated by the following examples:

- Ignorance that unless specifically stated, *actual value* (ACV) means current replacement less accumulated depreciation
- Failure to carry the required insurance amount or percentage of coverage to meet the co-insurance clause stipulation
- Failure to properly state or identify risks
- Failure to take timely action to insure against risk exposure[22]

Because of the public or other not-for-profit agency's difficulty in obtaining insurance coverage, risk retention has been pursued as a viable option. Before a final decision is made, a thorough evaluation of the governmental unit or agency's ability for risk retention should be undertaken.

Three basic principles are viewed as being essential for an effective loss financing program:

- The governmental unit or organization should have the financial capacity to meet its anticipated losses while accommodating its ordinary operating and capital needs.
- There should be exposure distribution across the entire organization sufficient to have an economy of scale that provides a relatively stable loss exposure.
- The entity should insure against losses. "Layers of insurance above the self-retained levels must be purchased so that the risk of loss greater than the entity is capable of absorbing is transferred to a commercial insurance carrier."[23]

The size of the governmental unit or organization is a particularly important consideration, because the larger the organization, the greater its ability to absorb claims against it. Small and predictably recurring claims can be more economically handled by the entity, thus avoiding the extremely high cost of insurance carriers.

Once the conditions and basic criteria for evaluating the organization's capability for reducing risks are known, a decision can be made regarding the assumption of risks. To aid in this endeavor, a frequency/severity matrix or protective pyramid may be used. An examination of Figure 7.3 suggests that the left side of the matrix containing the high-frequency/low-severity and low-frequency/low-severity loss can be assumed by the organization, because one is predictable and the other has a low risk factor. On the right side of the matrix, the low-frequency/high-severity condition provides a situation in which risks are such that the organization should obtain commercial catastrophic insurance. In the high-frequency/high-severity case, the situation is more problematic. Because of the high risk both in terms of occurrence and severity, the price and availability of such insurance may be too high to pay. Therefore, an evaluation of the situation will heavily influence which risks might have to be retained or transferred.

The protective pyramid (see Figure 7.4) is analogous to the matrix approach in that the large number of exposure cases of high frequency/low severity are found at the base of the pyramid (capable of being handled by individual self-insurance). The smaller number of cases of low frequency/high severity is viewed as being at the top of the pyramid (requiring catastrophic insurance). In the middle of the pyramid are myriad possibilities, such as pooling and harmless agreements.

Several types of risk insurance typically available to municipalities and other not-for-profit organizations include the following:

- Damage to property, including automobiles and machinery, by fire, water, earthquake, flood, or radiation
- Business interruption because of data processing equipment;
- Loss of property due to criminal acts by employees or private citizens
- Liability coverage for actions such as automobile-related accidents, workman's compensation, professional errors and omissions, and medical malpractice or public official liability
- Loss of income-producing properties or increased costs due to fire to property, bridges, tunnels, boilers, machinery, and the like

Self-Insurance

Before choosing the self-insurance option, the government/organization should conduct a thorough analysis of its cost and risks in light of alternatives. An indispensable requirement for a successful self-insurance program is

High frequency Low severity	High frequency High severity
Low frequency Low severity	Low frequency High severity

FIGURE 7.3   The frequency/severity matrix.

a strong safety and loss program. Attention and study should be devoted to the types of actual and potential losses over a five-year period, to existing safety and loss and control programs, and to the potential effect on employees when planning to self-insure a workman's compensation program.

When the governmental unit employs the partial or total self-insurance option, there are two ways it may be used, involving large deductibles or co-insurance. Under the partial or total self-insurance approach, an insurance fund is set up and managed to provide payment for unexpected losses. If the fund is professionally managed, it has the potential of replenishing itself and perhaps in time may even become a source of income. Under the co-insurance approach, amounts are budgeted and appropriated each year. Co-insurance is essentially a pay-as-you-go concept. Although this approach is widely used, it has some possible negative aspects, such as that if the amount of liability fluctuates widely, it can present a problem for governmental units and organizations that have rigid budgets. This may also occasion steep rises in insurance premiums.

It was the drastic increase in insurance premiums for governmental and other not-for-profit agencies during the 1980s that generated pressure to find better alternatives ways to induce the insurance industry to cover risk at more reasonable costs. Self-insurance and pooling became the only options for some governmental units if they wished to maintain risk coverage and avoid termination of private insurance policies during the 1980s. "There are 15,000 public entities being covered in these [municipally sponsored self-insurance pools] and other intergovernmental pools."[24]

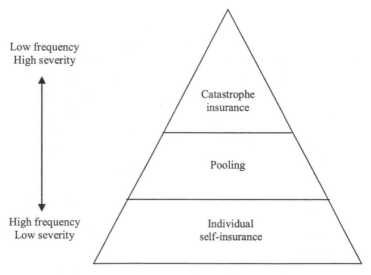

FIGURE 7.4   Protective pyramid.

In an effort to limit awards for damages, Colorado has attempted to specifically define its Governmental Immunity Act by listing the areas for which it will be liable, including the following:

- Operation of state motor vehicles
- Operation of public hospitals, parks, and correctional facilities
- Dangerous conditions that interfere with the movement of pedestrian or vehicular traffic
- Operation and maintenance of any public facility, including water supply plants, electrical, gas, and other power facilities, sanitation plants, and swimming facilities[25]

Monitoring Claims

Although the Public Risk Database Project (PRDP) is developing a standardized reporting format for governmental entities, many have additionally developed internal monitoring systems to keep abreast of what claims are being paid and the potential amount that may be paid in the future. Once estimates of open claims have been made for potential payments, the equivalent amounts should be reserved, pending final settlement. Governments' own tracking reports should include tracking numbers, incident descriptions, dates of claims, causes, type of claims, amounts paid to date, and amounts reserved for claims.

Risk Transfer

Risk avoidance/loss prevention are necessary parts of the risk management function. Inevitably, all governmental agencies and other not-for-profit agencies will, at some time, experience financial loss. To minimize the effects of these losses, insurance has been the traditional means of transferring risks. As noted above, intergovernmental risk pools have emerged as alternative competition to the liability insurance provided by the insurance industry. Of particular note is that there are varying types of pools: Some may transfer all of the risk or simply spread the risk among pool members. When contracting out work, especially construction, the governmental agency or organization may accept only those contractors or subcontractors that are willing to assume the liability for incidents that could occur. This risk transfer takes the following forms:

- Insurance: *property* (damage and loss of property), and *liability* (negligence in performance of operations)
- Workman's compensation: pays medical bills, disabilities, and lost income from job-related injuries
- Risk pools: the same as insurance (transfer risk) and allowing for spreading of risks

Risk Administration

In large units of government, risk management is likely to be a separate and distinct function headed by a risk manager; in smaller units of government, this function is performed by the financial officer. Clearly written policies and procedures should be an indispensable requirement. The main objectives are to oversee the implementation of the risk management process, which involves identifying exposure, evaluating risks, controlling and funding risks, and other duties and activities related to the risk management. These would include evaluating and reviewing important leases and contracts, maintaining a risk management information system, and allocating costs, losses, and premiums. Finally, the risk manager acts as a communication channel for disseminating risk-related information, which is reported timely throughout the organization.[26]

Risk Management and Quality Assurance: The Case of the Medical Industry

The skyrocketing liability insurance premiums experienced by doctors, hospitals, and other medically related functions have forced the industry to take a closer look at its risk management activities. Traditionally, hospitals have long practiced quality assurance as the routine way of maintaining quality in the delivery of medical services. When the need arose to streamline the risk management function, it was found that many of the activities required under "quality assurance" paralleled those of risk management. The Joint Commission of Accreditation of Hospitals (JCAH) felt that "the integration of risk management and quality assurance made good business sense as a means to improve patient care, reduce liability, and maintain harmony in the labor force."[27] When the crisis in malpractice insurance became a major concern more than two decades ago, commercial insurance carriers indicated that if hospitals developed acceptable in-house risk management programs, they would be granted favored treatment. The "promise of reduced premiums based on in-house risk identification, evaluation, reduction, or elimination and consequential favorable-claims history . . . provided"[28] the motivation for boards of trustees and administrators to take aggressive steps to manage risk.

Incident Reporting

In an effort to reduce its exposure to risk, a psychiatric center introduced "incident reporting." After 3,293 incident reports were reviewed, it was found that accidental injuries generated one-third of the incidents, with major categories including "leave without consent, patient fights, and assaults."[29] This manual count led to analysis of the incidents and identification of possible trends, convincing the center's officials that these reports had considerable potential to explain why incidents were happening, especially if more detailed information (for example, type of incidents, nature, frequency, witnesses, sex, ages of patients, and particular days and hours of occurrences) was made available. It was felt that if this data could be collected, it would aid in achieving two important objectives: (1) improving patient care while minimizing risks to patients and staff and (2) realizing an insurance savings due to claims reduction, because the hospital would have its factual investigation report available to shield the institution from unfounded and unsubstantiated claims. Although judgmental factors still play a part in determining when a specific event should or should not be considered an "incident," the following criteria will aid in correctly identifying them: actions contrary to plans for the best-quality patient care, actions that place patients or staff at risk, and actions that put the program or facility in a tenuous legal or political position.[30]

After the test year, a computerized incident reporting system for the center, containing over thirty types of incidents (ranging from biting and assault to incorrect medication) was instituted, permitting answers to be obtained for a variety of questions. So far, the system appears to be producing the intended results: reducing liability and producing a better utilization of resources in delivering cost-effective patient care.

Pooling Insurance

Because of the insurance's rising costs, a number of units of governments have been moving to *pooled risk*. Pools are especially useful when a unit of government lacks clout with the commercial insurance industry to negotiate terms that fit its particular needs. When specialized coverage needs arise, traditional insurers typically write a separate policy or issue an endorsement and add the applicable cost increases.

This pooling approach has been instrumental in bringing about useful changes to risk insurance in governmental units. Pools have developed expertise and negotiating power to better provide customized coverage for needs that might have previously been unattainable. These pools may be exposed to such areas as the following:

- Employment-related claims such as discrimination, sexual harassment, and retaliatory discharges
- Discrimination in the provision of services, creating potential liability emanating from such laws as the Americans with Disabilities Act (ADA)
- Environmental liability relating to pollution coverage resulting from court decisions, lead paint, leaking underground tanks, and other factors, creating first- and second-party cleanup claims
- Special services, including recreational activities such as festivals and skateboarding ramps[31]

Before participating in a pool, an entity should thoroughly evaluate its benefits versus commercial insurance: the integrity and professionalism of the pool, its contractual agreement, the security it shall provide, and the costs. The contractual agreement requires particular scrutiny. The potential pool member must recognize that it is taking ownership within the program. Typically, the enrollment document makes the entity liable for additional charges that may become necessary owing to unforeseen excess costs that the pool may incur. Alternatively, members may receive dividends or rebates when pool costs are lower than anticipated. This system of assessments and dividends tends to bind entities into longer-term relationships than otherwise with most commercial insurance programs.[32]

When pools are not tailor-made to the individual entity's needs, care must be taken to ensure that the entity understands the implications of its pooling arrangements. This caveat should be well heeded: Joining pools often involves the acceptance of a packaged program that does not permit room to modify the coverage to meet the entity's specific needs. For example, coverage may be required that is not desired. It is probably that commercial insurance allows more flexibility—often, it permits self-insured extensions and deductibles.[33] As tighter budgets constrain public entities, insurance costs are likely to tilt the scale toward pooling arrangements. A careful assessment of the benefits, costs, and needs should always be undertaken.

Summary Observations

Emphasis on risk management is a recent development. The erosion of the governmental unit's sovereign immunity was occurring at the same time when insurance premiums were skyrocketing for liability coverage in the medical profession during the 1980s. Because of both developments, better risk management has been viewed as one way to minimize the high cost of risk exposure.

The risk management problem has changed since the 1980s. The insurance industry no longer exercises the leverage it once did over risk premiums for governmental agencies. Unlike during the 1980s, public and other not-for-profit agencies now typically view risk exposure as a major priority to be effectively managed and controlled. "Risk pooling" developed as an effective alternative to meet the high insurance costs required to cover risk. Commercial insurance rates have fallen to more reasonable levels. Now insurance carriers are again actively competing for the public sector and other not-for-profits' business.

Notes

1. Dean G. Phelus, *Risk Management Today* (Washington, DC: International City Management Association, 1985), p. 1; Eric Wiesenthal, "Public Liability Woes Threaten Localities," *Public Administration Times* (November 1, 1985): 1, 12.

2. Wiesenthal, "Public Liability Woes Threaten Localities," p. 12.

3. Ibid.

4. Nicholas Greifer and Brennan L. Schwartz, *An Elected Official's Guide to Risk Management* (Chicago: Government Finance Officers Association, 2001), p. 18.

5. Peter C. Young and Steven C. Tippins, *Managing Business Risk* (New York: American Management Association, 2001), pp. 16, 180–182.

6. Ibid., p. 2.

7. Ibid.

8. Committee of Sponsoring Organizations of the Treadway Commission (COCO), et al., *Risk and Reward: Demystifying Sustainability Risk* (Durham, NC: COCO, 2013), pp. 1–2.

9. COSO, *Risk Assessment in Practice* (Durham, NC: COSO, 2013), pp. 1-3; and Paul Wallis "Risk Management: Achieving the Value Propositions," *Government Finance Review 28*, no. 1 (February 2012): 36–42; and Rodney J. Taylor, "*The Case for 'Integrating Sustainability and Risk Management: Why Sustainability Must Be a Priority for Corporate Risk Management,'*" (Windmere, FL: 2009), pp. 1–6. http://one.aon.com/files/integrating_sustainability.pdf.

10. See, for example, Greifer and Schwartz, *An Elected Official's Guide to Risk Management*; Young and Tippins, *Managing Business Risk*; and Peter C. Young, *Managing Risk in Local Government* (Austin, TX: Sheshunoff Information Services, 1999).

11. Young and Tippins, *Managing Business Risk*, p. 19.

12. Phyllis Sherman, *Basic Risk Management Handbook for Local Government* (Darien, CT: Public Risk Management Association, 1983), pp. 5–10.

13. Jo Ann Hankin, Alan Seidner, and John Zeitlow, *Financial Management for Non-Profit Organizations* (New York: John Wiley, 1993), p. 539; Greifer and Schwartz, *An Elected Official's Guide to Risk Management*, p. 29.

14. Charles K. Coe, *Understanding Risk Management* (Athens, GA: Institute of Local Government, 1980), pp. 13–14.

15. Al H. Ringleb and Steven L. Wiggins, "Institutional Control and Large-Scale Long-Term Hazards," in *Government Risk Bearing*, ed. Market S. Sniderman (Boston: Kluwer Academic Publishers, 1993), pp. 1–2.

16. Ibid., p. 2.

17. Institute for Local Self-Government, *Public Agency Liability: The Law and the Risks; Management, Avoidance and Transfer* (Berkeley, CA: Institute for Local Government, 1978), p. 58.

18. Jesus J. Pena, Alden N. Haffner, Bernard Rosen, and Donald W. Light, "Combining Risk Management and Quality Assurance," in *Hospital Quality Assurance*, eds. Jesus J. Pena et al. (Rockville, MD: Aspen Corporation, 1984), pp. 256–268.

19. Coe, *Understanding Risk Management*.

20. Laurence C. Cragg and H. Felix Kloman, "Risk Management: A Developed Discipline," in *Risk Management Today*, eds. Natalie Wasserman and Dean G. Phelus (Washington, DC: International City Management Association, 1985), p. 13; and National Safety Council (NSC), *Injury Facts* (Washington, DC: NSC, 2013), pp. 9, 58. http://www.mhi.org/downloads/industrygroups/ease/technicalpapers/2013-National-Safety-Council-Injury-Facts.pdf.

21. Ibid.

22. Coe, *Understanding Risk Management*.

23. Institute for Local Self-Government, *Public Agency Liability*, p. 96.

24. Wiesenthal, "Public Liability Woes Threaten Localities," p. 12.

25. Ibid.

26. Cragg and Kloman, *Risk Management*, p. 21.

27. Pena, Haffner, Rosen, and Light, "Combining Risk Management and Quality Assurance," p. 253.

28. Ibid., p. 254.

29. Ibid.

30. Ibid., p. 255.

31. Betsy Kutska, "Pools Rush In . . ." *Government Finance Review 9*, no. 1 (February 1993): 15.

32. Daniel S. Cullen, "Pooling and Insurance—One and the Same?" *Government Finance Review 9*, no. 1 (February 1993): 14.

33. Ibid.

8

Borrowing and Debt Management

The responsibility for long-term borrowing and debt management is critical in public and other not-for-profit agencies. Particularly in smaller agencies, imprudent decisions can lead to serious financial problems. Because of this, it is very important for the officials who oversee borrowing and debt management to have a general understanding of, and a degree of familiarity with, the different types of debt, the structure of debt, debt instruments, and the process by which bonds are bid and sold. This chapter examines the critical role of the management process in the sale of long-term debt, mainly as it takes place in governmental units. Attention is focused on the types of debt instruments and their proper uses, the functions and responsibilities in the debt management process, and the many potential problems to avoid in the debt issuance process.

NACSLB's Recommended Practices

The National Advisory Council on State and Local Budget's (NACSLB) recommended budget practices provide useful guidelines for debt management and capital planning. Six of its practices have particular interest for us:[1]

- Policy should be adopted on debt issuance and management.
- Policy on debt capacity should be set forth, specifying the maximum amount of debt service that should be outstanding at any given time.
- Develop options for meeting capital needs that are consistent with programmatic and capital policies.
- Develop system to measure and evaluate capital program implementation.
- A capital improvement program (CAP) should be developed identifying priorities, the financial plan, and the timetable for implementing selected capital projects:
  - How do you plan to pay for it?
  - What is the right combination of pay-as-you-go versus debt financing?

- To aid in achieving the maximum coordination of financial policies and fiscal health (see chapter 19), a governmental entity should implement a system to monitor and evaluate financial conditions.

Debt Policy Development

Because the issuance of debt instruments can be a major and critical function of public and other not-for-profit agencies, a clearly defined and well-articulated policy on debt is indispensable. Debt policy provides a long-term planning framework that facilitates and improves rational decision making. It allows governments and agencies to synchronize their long- and short-term needs with planned resource use and revenue outflows. It demonstrates to the public and rating agencies a well-thought-out plan for incurring debt, responding to problems as they may arise and how required payments will be effectively met. Carefully defined and articulated debt policy should include the following:

- Identification of the allowable method of sales, such as competitive, negotiation, or private placement
- Specific compliance requirements with state and federal tax laws, such as debt limits and arbitrage requirements
- Indication of how capital budget, planning, and debt financing are linked
- Specifying how the bond proceeds will conform to the intended purpose
- Articulation of the debt refunding requirement
- Specification of the structural features of the bonds such as debt maturity, use of zero-coupon bonds, and redemptions
- Defining the types of individuals (e.g., CPAs, lawyers, registered municipal bond advisors) and entities with whom the organization may conduct debt issuances and transactions
- Outlining the different types of debt that are allowed to be issued, such as general obligation debt, revenue debt, and leaseback debt[2]

The Size of Debt Issuance

One approach is to use the intertemporal budget model (IBC) constraint model to determine budget and debt sustainability or equilibrium condition:

$$B_t = \sum_{i=1}^{\infty} (1+r)^{-i} PB_t + i,$$

Assume that B_t is the stock of public debt, r is the interest of the public debt, and PB_t is the primary balance (government revenues minus government expenditures, excluding interest expenditure):

$$B_t = \text{sum } [(1 - r)^{-i}] \times (PB_t + i)$$

Initial debt level = Present value of primary
Balance surpluses/deficits

As an example, assume the following:

$r = 3\%$

$i = 10$ yrs.

P_v factor (3%, 10 years, annuity) = 8.53020

Primary balance surplus = $10,000,000 annually

$B_t = [(1 - 0.03)^{10}] \times (\$10,000,000 \times 8.53020)$

$B_t = \$62,952.87$

Under this initial debt level, with municipal bond interest rates at a low 3% (typical for AAA-rated municipalities), the ten-year bond issuance will maintain intertemporal budget equity if the bond amount does not exceed $62,903,752.87 issuance amount. The primary balance surplus is assumed to remain constant at $10,000,000 annually.

In Example 2, assume the following:

$$r = 3\%$$

$i = \infty$ (no retirement date/assumed perpetuity)

Primary balance surplus = $10,000,000 annually

$B_t = (1 - 0.03) \times (\$10,000,000/0.03)$

$B_t = \$323,333,333.30$

Under this assumption, with municipal bond interest rates at 3%, the infinitum bond issuance (no expected date for retirement) will maintain intertemporal budget equity if public debt does not exceed $323,333,333.30 issuance amount. The primary balance surplus is assumed to remain constant $10,000,000 annually. Because there is no debt issuance retirement date, the $10,000,000 surpluses are treated as perpetuity asset flows.

Revenue Debt: What Are the Indicators?

If a debt management program is to be effective, the organization must be aware of its liabilities that must be satisfactorily managed and discharged based on revenue availability. Debt indicators usually include the following:

- *Accrued pension liability* is the amount of pension obligation that is required to be paid from general revenues, normally disclosed in the general *government liability long-term debt account group* (GLTDAG). Typically, the accounting pension liability estimate is significantly lower than the actuarial estimate.[3]
- *Legal debt limitation* is defined for all local governments, except in some states, such as Pennsylvania, where a home rule charter leaves the matter up

to local voters. The difference between existing debt and the limit requirement is the allowable amount of debt that is left that can be issued (known
as the "debt margin").

- *Direct debt* consists of all the government's long-term obligations (including
  debt instruments such as tax increment finance [TIF] bonds, special assessment bonds, capital leases, and certificates of participation [COPs]) that are
  directly backed by general revenue and taxes.[4] Although rating agencies
  exclude obligations such as the accrued pension liability and landfill costs,
  they should be considered part of the direct debt. Exclusion of such obligations leads to liability understatement.
- *General obligation (G.O.) debt* is made up of long-term debt warrants, certificates of obligations, and enterprise fund debts that taxpayers guarantee
  through "full faith and credit" of the taxing authority.
- *Bonded debt* includes all bonded G.O. debt and enterprise bonds, consisting
  of all debts that must be regularly paid and serviced.
- *Total debt service* is the annual debt service, excluding the enterprise fund,
  that is required to be paid from the general revenue and taxes.
- *General obligation (G.O.) service debt* is the amount paid annually for G.O.
  debt instruments, excluding the enterprise fund that is paid from operating
  revenues.
- *Bonded debt service* is the total G.O. and enterprise debt service that a government unit pays annually.

Debt financing takes place at all levels of government. Even so, misunderstanding about the scope and nature of public debt is common, perhaps
because of the minimal amount of information exchanged about public financial undertakings. Another contributing factor is the unwise attempt to equate
public and private debt. Additionally, there has long been antipathy against
borrowing, suggested by the following comment: "[Borrowing] is a system
which tends to make us less thrifty—to blind us to our real situation."[5]

Borrowing is a substitute for taxing citizens immediately, replacing present
taxes with future taxes or alternative cash flows, thus necessitating the payment of interest on the debt. In essence, "public borrowing is a means by which
people with relatively low preference for present consumption lend to those
with relatively high preference for present consumption."[6] Until the late 1930s,
government borrowing was considered a very unusual event. It was referred
to as "extraordinary finance," suggesting that "it was a method that was used
only during extraordinary times such as war and depression."[7] Government
borrowing can be classified as either *current* or *capital*, depending on the purposes for which the money is being used. Goods and services to be consumed
in a period of a year or less are viewed as current, whereas those that will be
consumed over longer periods are capital expenditures, typically intended for
long-lived physical assets such as schools, utility plants, and highways. Because

of the long time span for capital projects, the benefits generated and outlays made cannot be easily synchronized.

Although the federal government and a few states may run deficits as a permissible policy to fund current spending, this option typically is closed to local governments and most other not-for-profit agencies. Borrowing for current operations is not permitted for periods longer than a year, which typically coincide with tax revenue inflows for the period or with grants from other governmental units. Short-term debts so created are known as *tax anticipation loans* or *revenue anticipation loans*.

Besides the restrictions on current borrowing, most states have constitutional provisions limiting their debt-creating capacity. More than half require a constitutional amendment to borrow beyond a specified debt limit. Most state constitutions require that a special tax be levied to cover debt service and stipulate that the state may not lend its credit to individuals or corporations.[8] State restrictions on local government debt are quite specific and stringent. Usually, there are stipulations regarding (1) the purpose of the borrowing, (2) how the debt should be incurred, (3) the amount of local debt, (4) the interest rate, (5) the term of the debt, (6) the retirement provisions, and (7) the form of the debt. The most common stipulation relates to the amount of allowable debt versus the assessed value of the local jurisdiction. In most cases, different assessment ratio debt limits are applied to the various types of debt. The greatest restrictions are placed on the smallest communities; less stringent provisions apply to school districts. Such provisions ensure that jurisdictions do not become "overleveraged" or "thinly capitalized," terms used in the private sector to describe corporations that have very high levels of debt to equity. High levels of debt, relative to underlying assets, can prove disastrous in periods of poor operational performance/inadequate cash inflows, potentially leading to insolvency.

Debt limitation requirements have not been without their detractors. Property taxes, which constitute the major source of local revenue and on which the tax limitation is predominantly based, vary significantly among communities, thereby permitting differing degrees of limitation. To compensate for this disparity, local governments have manipulated the assessed valuation of property to raise their debt limitation ratio. The assessed valuation of the property is raised, and the tax rate or millage is reduced. Particularly significant is the fact that the use of the property tax as the determining factor ignores that an increasing source of local spending are grants from other governments.[9]

Types of Debt Financing

A number of avenues are open to public and other not-for-profit organizations to finance borrowing needs, typically for long-lived assets or capital projects. The financing option pursued will be influenced by a number of factors, among them the financial strength of the governmental unit or organization, the nature and scope of the project being financed, and the predictability of the cash financing flow. Among the general options available to organizations are to (1) pay cash, (2) set aside cash reserves for the prospective acquisition, or (3) borrow. Before selecting from financing options, a thorough analysis of the costs and benefits of each should be made. Generally, a sound approach will involve a combination of all three and minimize the overall cost of financing.

The payment of cash or pay-as-you-go approach (see chapter 12) is essentially self-financing, allowing interest payments to be avoided; it enhances the borrowing capacity of the organizational unit. Although very popular, it has distinct shortcomings. This approach assumes that a community or organization will have sufficient revenues to meet current operations, plus an excess to meet capital facilities requirements. "Pay-as-you-use" is a related concept, suggesting that the payment of the borrowed funds will be returned as people pay user charges for the services rendered.

Short-Term Debt

This comprises obligations that will mature within a year. Most often, short-term debt is assumed to provide temporary or interim funding. It may be used for the following purposes:

- To provide cash to initiate or begin a project
- To provide cash as an interim financing means to await improved market conditions before issuing long-term debt
- To provide startup cash for initial construction
- To provide cash as a stopgap measure while resolving financial problems
- To provide cash to accommodate underbudgeted expenditures
- To minimize cash flow fluctuations[10]

A number of *short-term instruments* are used to generate cash to meet expected spending needs. The following are three important instruments with which financial managers should familiarize themselves:

- *Tax anticipation notes* (TANs) are used to meet shortfalls occasioned by lags in tax collection; the anticipated revenue is used as security or pledged for the bank's advancing the loan (see the discussion in chapter 6).
- *Revenue anticipation notes* (RANs) are used to provide cash to overcome lags involved in the receipt of intergovernmental revenue. The anticipated revenues are pledged as security for the cash advance. Upon receipt of the revenues, the loan is repaid (see chapter 6).
- *Bond anticipation notes* (BANs) are used to generate funds to initiate a capital project, especially in cases in which interest rates are volatile. In such situations, it may be necessary to wait until interest rates stabilize for long-term debt issues.

Long-Term Debt

This is typically used to provide permanent financing for major capital improvements, construction, and the acquisition of capital facilities. As a general rule, long-term debt should not be used to fund current expenditures as this places the debt burden on future generations and fails to adhere to interperiod equity. It is important that the term of the bond issued be at least equal to the life of the asset being financed. There are several categories of long-term bonds.

The General Obligation (G.O.) Bond. This bond indicates that the security standing behind it is the total credibility and unrestricted resource of the government unit or other not-for-profit agency. The bond is said to be issued with the "full faith and credit" of the issuer. In a governmental unit, the general tax revenue provides the ultimate source of funds. Although at one time general obligation bonds were the only tax-exempt debt that was issued, this has changed significantly. Now, a large amount of tax-exempt debt is represented by revenue bonds.

Revenue bonds. These bonds are obligations issued to finance a revenue-generating project or enterprise. Both the principal and interest of revenue bonds are required to be paid exclusively from the generated earnings. The massive growth in revenue bonds has come about as a way of shifting the burden away from taxpayers to users, thus avoiding referendums and imposed debt ceilings. Typical uses of the revenue bond include financing of sewer and water systems, airports, toll roads, hospitals, parking facilities, and industrial developments.

Industrial bonds. These are issued by governments to construct facilities for a private corporation that makes lease payments to the government to service those bonds. Such bonds may be general obligation bonds, combination bonds, or revenue bonds. The state legislature enacts enabling legislation to permit local governments (typically municipalities) to finance the acquisition or construction of industrial facilities. The major purpose of these bonds is to encourage local economic development efforts. Originally, industrial bonds were used almost entirely to attract, expand, or retain industrial facilities within a community. However, their uses have expanded in recent years to include financing of sports facilities/stadiums, hospitals, transportation, pollution control, and industrial parks.[11] The 1986 Federal Tax Reform Act severely restricted the use of industrial bonds. However, in 1993, the restrictions were repealed and the exemptions restored.

Unique borrowing vehicles. These have been developed in recent years "to take advantage of the expanded public role in the delivery of goods and services [and] the desire of the private sector to capture the benefits of tax-exempt financing."[12] Among the activities that have been undertaken are (1) resource recovery involving a privately owned waste disposal plant; (2) mortgage finance, permitting tax-exempt bonds to be sold by a governmental unit or authority, which uses the proceeds to make low-interest mortgage loans; (3) joint action allowing governmental units to cooperatively own a power plant; and (4) municipal assistance corporations, permitting a city to issue tax-exempt obligations supported by special revenue sources; this approval may be used especially in situations in which the city's credit does not make the debt issuance possible. The receipts obtained from the bond issue may be used for governmental purposes, as they were during New York City's 1975 fiscal crisis.

Public-Private Partnerships

A recent debt reduction/risk mitigation strategy being implemented by states and municipalities has been to shift a significant portion of the cost for large capital projects to private investors via public-private partnerships (PPP). Private companies or investors partner with governments to design, build, operate, finance, or maintain highways, transit systems, bridges, and other high-cost capital projects. This entails government and private sector management and employees working side by side to complete the intended project. One caveat officials must consider when entering into PPP is the potential of conceding significant portions of future revenue to the partner private investors/companies; therefore, a careful cost-benefit analysis is crucial. With municipal/state revenues falling and expenditures such as health, debt interest payments, and education rising, shortfalls for capital projects are becoming more common, and PPP may provide a viable solution. Contrary to some opposing arguments, recent evidence shows that PPP do not displace government employees or raise rates on citizens that use the completed projects, but rather reduce anticipated costs/prevent project cost overruns and enhance service delivery.

A recent PPP example that highlights the potential success for this alternative form of public capital project funding is the I-495 Capital Beltway HOT Lanes. This $2.068 billion project is a partnership between the Virginia Department of Transportation (VDOT) and Capital Beltway Express, LLC (a joint venture between the Fluor and Transurban companies), begun in 2008 and completed in November 2012. The previous four-lane Capital Beltway received improvements, including fourteen miles of two new lanes in each direction, high-occupancy vehicle (HOV) lanes, replacement of aging infrastructure, construction of carpool ramps, and a congestion-free network for carpools, vanpools, transit and toll-paying motorists. Sources of funding for this PPP included private activity bonds (PAB), a TIFIA loan, Commonwealth of Virginia grants, VDOT change order funding, interest income, and private equity. [13] Capital Beltway Express, LLC was given an eighty-year toll concession to operate the highway with revenue sharing with the Commonwealth of Virginia based upon meeting or exceeding a predetermined internal rate of equity. The project was completed on time and within budget and has been a major success, contributing to a significant reduction in traffic congestion in northern Virginia.[14]

Debt Carrying Capacity

It is important to know the precise debt carrying capacity of a governmental unit, because this indicates how much that unit may reasonably borrow. In such a unit, debt capacity is dependent upon the quantity and quality of available resources that can be legally (statutory debt limit indications to the borrower the size of the maximum credit line) and practically drawn upon to meet the articulated needs. Looked at from another perspective, debt capacity may also be self-imposed policy limit on outstanding indebtedness. Before the *debt capacity* can be determined, the *debt burden*—the legitimate obligations that a governmental unit or agency is responsible for liquidating at some time in the future—must be calculated. The debt burden can thus be compared to the amount of taxes or monetary resources that taxpayers are required to provide in order to finance outstanding debt service. Debt burden can be quantified on a per capita basis to determine the share of debt each taxpayer is allocated, which can aid officials in establishing the reasonableness of future debt issuances. When overlapping governmental units (e.g., school districts, public authorities, special-purpose districts) extract taxes from the same taxpayers, those analyzing debt capacity must be cognizant not only of debt obligations in an individual unit, but also of the composite debt responsibility in all the units concerned. Among the main components that may be evaluated in determining the relative tax capacity before bond issuance are the following:

- Examining the reliability of revenues dedicated to pay debt service
- Revenue trends evaluation and expenditure trends evaluation
- Debt burden (including debt per capita—debt as a percentage of personal income)
- Debt affordability or having sufficient cash flow to pay debt service
- Property value per capita
- Human resources in terms of age, employment, education, and type of occupation
- Debt to personal income
- Per capita personal income
- Per capita disposable income
- Productivity of the tax system (indicators include per capita tax collections and per capita taxes as a percentage of per capita income)
- Political, legal, and administrative constraints against expanding or broadening the tax base
- Debt to assessed value on estimated value of taxable property

- Property tax base
- How much annual budget is consumed by fixed debt service
- Stability of the tax system
- Tax base growth rate
- Potential effects on credit rating[15]

An underlying premise for evaluating fiscal capacity is that—in ordinary conditions—the debt of a governmental unit or agency parallels the size and growth of the governmental unit's tax base. It is important that schedules of debt repayment be prudently arranged to avoid excessive pressures on operating expenditures, thereby minimizing the possibility of impairing the governmental unit or agency's credit rating. To aid in monitoring changes in the debt structure, which has implications for both short- and long-term solvency, the Financial Trend Monitoring System (FTMS) (discussed in chapter 19) is most useful. The FTMS follows the change in debt, the scope, the cost of capital items that will be purchased, and overlapping debt.[16]

Debt Margin

Like debt carrying capacity, the *debt margin* is a useful indicator to the entity regarding its ability to assume additional debt. The debt margin is the difference between the amount of debt outstanding (based on legal requirements) and the amount of debt allowed. If, for example, a government's debt is limited to 10 percent of its assessed property value, assuming that the assessed value of property is $20 billion, then the government can issue a maximum debt of $2 billion. If the government has $1.5 billion of debt outstanding, then the legal debt margin is $500 million (25 percent of the debt limit).

Useful Common Ratios and Past History

Investors, stakeholders, and interested groups use a variety of indicators and bond-related data to assess an entity's ability to pay bond principal and interest and avoid defaulting. The following are notable examples:

- *Debt service costs* as a percentage of total general fund and debt service fund expenditures is an important measure. This measure is similar to the times-interest earned ratio that has been widely used within the business sector. When this ratio exceeds 20 percent of total general and debt service expenditures, it is viewed as being too high, and the debt level unsustainable.
- *Debts per capita* as a percentage of taxable property are ratios that measure *fiscal capacity*. They relate bond indebtedness to the sources of government revenue. It is important to know what components of debt outstanding are included. For example, is the debt limited to G.O. debt, or does it also include revenue debt?

- The *credit history* of the bond issuer is very important in determining the borrower's credit standing.

Planning a Bond Issue

An initial activity in planning a bond issue involves the determination of the purpose for incurring debt, its scope, and the cost of capital items that will be purchased or contracted. Ideally, bonds should be issued as part of a governmental unit's capital improvement program (CIP), involving physical improvements required to meet community service needs (see the discussion of this in chapter 12). It is in the CIP that the definitions of the quantity and quality of services to be delivered are indicated.

Carefully determining the cost of the project to be financed is critical. If the costs are overestimated, unnecessary interest and associated costs will be incurred. Underestimating the cost of the project is likely to be even more expensive, because it may necessitate a supplemental bond issue that may necessitate using higher interest rates. This requires that a bond be issued for an optimal amount.[17] To aid in selecting the means of obtaining the necessary financial resources for funding the decided-upon project, the governmental unit or agency should seek expert assistance from consulting agencies, financial advisors, and bond counsel to minimize costs and legal problems and facilitate document preparation. Recent regulations concerning municipal bond advising are discussed in detail in chapter 21.

Once a decision has been made about the amount of resources needed, the available options other than incurring debt must be explored, including existing revenue sources, federal and state grants, and bond funds from prior issues. It should be determined how advantageous it would be to sell bonds through public bid versus private negotiations (where this option is legal). The bond debt option should include a consideration of selling general obligation versus revenue bonds. A choice between the two options requires an assessment of the following:

- Prospective beneficiaries (direct and indirect) over the expected life of the project
- Potential alternative revenues obtainable from user charges
- Legal authority to issue general obligation bonds
- Potential for the bond being approved by voters
- Political and legal authority to raise or increase taxes
- Implications and effects of the bond issue, especially demands on general obligation versus other financing priorities
- Comparative costs of general obligation and revenue bonds[18]

Table 8.1 provides essential debt management terminology related to the issuing of bonds.

General Obligation and Revenue Bonds: Particular Considerations

In cases in which revenue bonds do not require voter approval, fewer problems are encountered than with general obligation bonds, but revenue bonds typically carry higher rates because they are not secured by the "full faith and credit" of the issuer. The structure of the bond issue depends on whether it is of the general obligation (G.O.) or revenue type. A critical consideration by a prospective purchaser relates to the degree of coverage for the debt service from revenue pledged in support of the debt. As a general rule, the purchaser/investor will be more comfortable with a high coverage ratio than a low one. If possible, a comparative check of similar projects in other jurisdictions should be made. Another concern is the patrimony (undepreciated value of the facility or the net asset value) that may have been negotiated in earlier years but is not likely to provide enough security for interest payments in later years. This position accords with the view that the maturity of a debt should not be allowed to extend beyond the useful life of the facility financed.[19]

Unlike the revenue bond, which depends on revenue generated from a specific project, the G.O. bond relies on the revenue or total estimated annual revenue of the governmental unit. Because the same pool of revenue must be used to serve all G.O. bonds, it is important that current expenditure in any given year not exceed the project revenue.

Call Provision

When a bond has a *call provision*, the investor may be required to redeem the bonds at some time other than the specified maturity date. The call may apply to a portion or all of the outstanding bonds. If the optional payment of principal is not specified in the bond contract, the call option can be used only with the consent of the investor. The decision to include a call provision requires a comparative probabilistic analysis of the costs versus benefits. Typically, a call provision is considered when interest rates are high by historical standards.[20]

TABLE 8.1   Debt-Management Terminology

Bond counsel. The bond counsel's main objective is determining if there are conflicts with constitutional and other constraints such as monitoring/limitations, arranging required elections, reviewing bond-related statements for conformity with the law, ensuring that competitive sales are advertised and that an underwriter is secured for the negotiated sale, rendering opinions on the status of tax-exempt bonds, and answering questions posed by prospective purchasers and public officials.

Callable bond. This is a type of bond that permits the issuer to call in and pay the obligation before the stated maturity date by notifying the purchaser of the redemption in the manner specified in a bond contract.

Consulting engineer. This is one who provides technical advice and conducts feasibility studies in areas such as designing and constructing roads, water and sewer facilities, and public buildings, making revenue and operation cost estimates.

Debt service. This is the required amount of money necessary to pay interest and principal for a given year or years. When the term "debt-service payment" is used, it refers to the service of all bond payments that mature at some specific time.

Debt-service charge. It is an organization's ability to service its debt. Typically, it is measured by a ratio called "debtservice ratio" (see chapters 2 and 18).

Financial advisor. This is an individual who provides a wide spectrum of services to a debt issuer, including assessing the borrowing capacity; assembling an array of financial statistics and economic data such as tax rates and overlapping debt; making user-charge estimates; projecting revenue-flow estimates; advising on marketing methods; writing call-provision features; assisting in preparing and distributing notice-of-sale and bid forms; determining the need for rating services; arranging analysis of creditworthiness; coordinating delivery of bonds; and ruling on acceptability of bids. The Dodd-Frank Wall Street Reform and Consumer Protection Act of 2010 has brought more regulation and accountability to this profession; please see Chapter 21 for more details.

Maturity date. This is the date on which the principal amount of security becomes due and payable.

Municipal bond underwriters. It is the process in which bond dealers buy entire new bond issues from the state and local entities and then resell them in smaller blocks to investors. Typically, new issues are underwritten by syndicates or a group of dealers who go together for each particular sale. By forming the syndicate, the dealer members share the risk of buying and owning an issue. This facilitates their cooperating to distribute the bonds to their customers in an effort to make a profit on their markup.

Municipal Securities Rulemaking Board (MSRB). Bond dealers and syndicates operate under MSRB rules with the approval of the Securities and Exchange Commission (SEC). The rules are self-enforced by the National Association of Security Dealers (NASD).

Negotiated sale. This is a method that is used for selling securities in which the terms of the sale are arrived at through negotiation between issuer and purchasers without formal competitive bidding. This may include sales of securities directly to commercial banks or consortiums of commercial banks, investment banking firms or syndicates, and private placements by issuers.

Series bond. This is a bond whose principal is repaid in periodic installments over the life of the issue.

The call provision is usually included to permit the issuer to achieve a number of objectives, including the voluntarily reduction of outstanding debt; reducing debt in accordance with the bond agreement (indenture); reducing interest costs by refunding; and reorganizing the debt voluntarily.[21]

The call provision provides flexibility in unstable markets. It also provides the issuer with the option to reduce the bond's interest rate when interest rates decline, allowing the issuer to reduce costs but also reducing the earnings potential of the investor. To compensate for this, the investor usually requires higher interest returns on callable bonds than on noncallable ones. Investors may also require a period of time by which the bond may not be called after issuance, known as the *deferment period*. When the bond is called, the difference between the call price and its par value is referred to as the *call premium*.

Advance Refunding

In those cases in which a deferment call provision exists but interest rates decline significantly before the deferment period, the issuer may issue bonds before the callable date when the outstanding bonds become due or callable. The proceeds from the advance funding are deposited in an escrow account and invested in securities, typically U.S. Treasury bonds or other authorized securities, to be used to redeem the underlying bonds at the maturity or call date and to pay interest on the bonds refunded. It is important to note that refunding is normally desirable only when interest rates are high enough to generate a benefit.

Credit Rating Agencies and Investors

The concern about incurring and management of government debt has become a widely debated topic. The 2008 financial crisis that created the Great Recession has seen the aggregate world debt grow from $23 trillion in 2007 to a projected $48 trillion by the end of 2015. This would increase the ratio of world debt from 44 percent of GDP in 2007 to 59 percent by 2015.

A major portion of the debt increase has come from advanced economics (AEs), increasing from $19 trillion in 2007 to a projected $42 trillion by 2015 (see Table 8.2). The ratio of aggregate debt to aggregate GDP for AEs moved from 48 percent in 2007 to a projected 85 percent by 2015.[22]

The two biggest AEs are the United States, contributing 35 percent of the increase in 2007 (and 39 percent by 2015). Japan accounted for 26 percent in 2007 and a projected 22 percent in 2015.

The United States spent $831 billion to help bring the country out of the Great Recession. The American Recovery and Investment Act of 2009 (also known as "the stimulus bill") allowed states to continue many services and aided a number of people needing food stamps and unemployment benefits. Although policymakers knew that the deficit was increasing, they felt that it was needed to maintain government services and a modicum of consumption buying power. There are some who think that the debt is too high and who

TABLE 8.2   Public Debt of Selected Countries Exceeding .05% of World Debt, 2012 Estimate

Country	Public Debt (billion USD)	% of GDP	Per Capita (USD)	% of World Public Debt
World	56,308	64%	7,936	100%
United States	17,607	73.60%	36,653	20.61%
Japan	9,872	214.30%	77,577	17.53%
China	3,894	31.70%	2,885	6.91%
Germany	2,592	81.70%	31,945	4.60%
Canada	1,206	84.10%	34,902	2.14%
India	995	51.90%	850	1.75%
Mexico	629	35.40%	5,416	1.2%
Greece	436	161.30%	40,486	.77%
Russia	308	12.20%	2,159	.55%

Source: CIA Facebook 2013.

worry about the prospect of our passing too much debt to future generations, making them pay our costs without receiving the benefits. There is concern that too much of our debt obligations are held by overseas governments and investors, as shown in Figure 8.1. Of the total national debt held by federal accounts, Figure 8.2 shows the distribution.

One of the most crucial factors influencing the success or failure of a debt offering is the governmental unit or agency's credit rating, regardless of whether the sale of a major bond issue rating is obligatory. *Credit rating* is used to designate the quality of governmental bonds and hence directly affects the interest rate that is required to be paid. Standard and Poor's Corporation (S&P), Moody's Investor Service, Fitch Investors Services, Duff & Phelp Credit Rating, and Sheshunoff and Co., Inc., are the five main rating firms in the United States that provide professional judgments or opinions concerning the quality and security or creditworthiness of debt issuers. Each rating service charges a fee for its services based on rate schedules that vary according to the size and extent of the analysis desired. Many factors are considered by investors and rating agencies, as shown in Table 8.3.

Moody's and Standard and Poor's are by far the most dominant in the rating business. Moody's has been in operation since 1918 and rates approximately 15,000 municipal bonds and 4,500 new issues per year. Standard and Poor's began its municipal bond rating in 1940 and presently has 7,000 ratings outstanding. Each year it rates approximately 1,500 new issues.[23] As can be seen

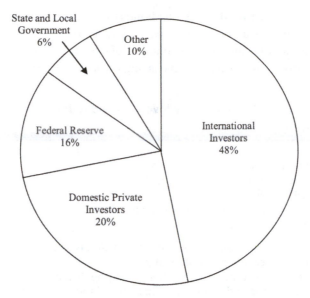

Figure 8.1   Owners of the U.S. federal debt, June 2012.

Source: National Priorities Project, Borrowing and the Federal Debt, http://nationalpriorities
.org/buget-basics/federal-budget-101/borrowing-and-federal-debt.

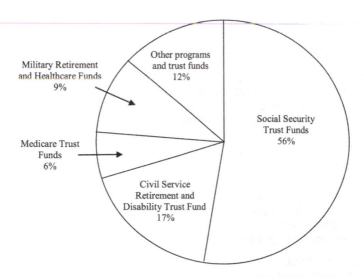

FIGURE 8.2   Federal debt maintained by federal accounts, January 2013

Source: National Priorities Project, Borrowing and the Federal Debt, http://nationalpriorities
.org/budget-basics/federal-basic/federal-budget-101/borrowing-and-federal-debt.

from Table 8.4, Standard and Poor's rates bonds from AAA (highest-quality, with extremely strong capacity to pay principal and interest) to CCC (highest degree of speculation) and D (indicating a bond in default). Moody's Investor Service ratings range from Aaa to Caa, with Ba having the lowest investment grade.

TABLE 8.3   Factors Considered by Investors and Rating Agencies in Determining Rates

The amount and nature of the debt and debt-service requirements:
- Total amount of debt and per-capita debt levels
- Purposes for which debt has been created
- Rate at which debt has increased
- Debt-repayment schedules and overlapping debt
- Degree of reliance on short-term debt

Economy of the community and the region of which it is a part:
- Geographical area and past history of growth
- Educational and income characteristics of the population
- Location of area served and general character of future potential
- Sources of economic activity—employers, diversification, and dependence
- Maintenance of the economic plant
- Leadership
- Wealth of the community—taxable property, resources, transportation

Social factors:
- Educational opportunities
- Cultural opportunities
- Recreational facilities
- Community record for handling social unrest
- Housing stock
- Characteristics of the population

Management of local government:
- Overall governmental structure—professionalism vs. balkanization
- Degree to which the government is well-administered
- Organization of financial administration
- Effectiveness of capital planning and programming
- Quality of revenue administration—passive collector of taxes vs. active
- Revenue base—new reliances
- Revenue calendar out of sync
- Reputation for prudent financial management
- Conditions of the physical plant
- Contingent liabilities
- Sinking fund management

Other considerations:
- Debt limitations—higher regulatory controls
- Capacity of government to deal with local problems
- Security of deposits—guarantees of banks
- Bondholder's remedies—explicit or implied
- Subdivision controls—poorly planned expansions
- General regulatory codes

TABLE 8.4   The Major Rating Systems: Standard and Poor's and Moody's

Fitch	Standard and Poor's Corporate and Municipal Rating	Moody's Municipal Rating	Descriptions: Credit Worthiness
AAA	AAA	Aaa	Highest quality, unquestionable ability to pay interest and principal.
AA+ AA AA-	AA+ AA AA-	Aa1 Aa2 Aa3	High quality and very strong capacity to pay interest and principal.
A+ A A-	A+ A A-	A1 A2 A3	Upper-medium quality, strong capacity to pay principal and interest, but is more susceptible to adverse changes in economic conditions.
BBB+ BBB BBB-	BBB+ BBB BBB-	Baa1 Baa2 Baa3	Medium quality with adequate capacity to pay interest and principal, though subject to adverse economic conditions over extended periods, weakening its capacity to meet financial commitments.
BB+ BB BB-	BB+ BB BB-	Ba1 Ba2 Ba3	Predominantly speculative quality with low insurer's capacity to pay principal and interest. It faces major uncertainties and exposure to adverse business conditions.
CCC	CCC	Caa	This is highest degree of speculation and is highly vulnerable. It is dependent on favorable business, financial and economic conditions to keep commitment.
CC	CC	Ca	Obligor is very speculative and highly vulnerable.
C	C		Obligor is so highly vulnerable to nonpayment, may be used where bankruptcy petition has been filed.
D	D	C	Obligor has failed to pay one or more of its financial obligations as they came due.
Expected	Pr	e,p	Preliminary rating may be assigned pending receipt of documentation and legal opinion.
	Unsolicited	Unsolicited	Rating was initiated by the rating agency and not the issuer.
NR	NR	NR	No rating has been requested or there is insufficient information to make a rating determination.

Role of Rating Agencies

Rating agencies as objective arbiter? During the period leading up to the Great Recession, a large number of subprime housing mortgages were given questionably high ratings by the big security rating firms (Fitch, Moody's, and Standard & Poor's), which pooled them and gave them much higher ratings than they deserved. Because of this, the rating firms played a significant role at various stages leading up to the subprime mortgage crisis of 2007 to 2008, which ushered in the Great Recession of 2007 to 2009.

The rating agencies acted as great enablers. Most of the mortgages could not have been sold without the rating agencies. Importantly, many of the nation's pension funds are restricted by law not to buy securities unless they have been rated as high-quality by one of the top rating agencies. Pools of over $3 trillion poor-quality mortgages were given the highest rating. By 2010, billions of these highly rated securities were downgraded as junk, culminating in the collapse of three major investment banks—Merrill Lynch, Bear Stearns, and Lehman Brothers.

The lack of due diligence by these pillars of the financial community created a crisis of confidence about who can be trusted. Can these rating agencies be trusted to do the right thing in light of their conflict of interest? The entities that they evaluate also pay them for their rating services. The participating destructive role of the raters is clear. "The rating agencies acted as advertising copy writer and publicist for bad paper."[24] More than 10,000 collateralized questionably highly rated debt obligations were sold around the world. (Table 8.5 shows that the credit rating agencies' influence stretches across the world.) The risk assessing system of the rating companies were either flawed or compromised. Although there has been much debate about conflict of interest and objectivity of these rating agencies and the need for reform, nothing has been done.

TABLE 8.5   Credit Rating: Fitch, Moody and S&P Rate Selected Countries January 3, 2013

Country	S&P Rating	S&P Outlook	Moody's Rating	Moody's Outlook	Fitch Rating	Fitch Outlook
Argentina	B-	NEG	B3	NEG	CC	
Australia	AAA	STA	Aaa	STA	AAA	STA
China	AA-	STA	Aa3	POS	A+	STA
France	Aa+	NEG	Aa1	NEG	AAA	NEG
Greece	B-	STA	C		CCC	
Russia	BBB	STA	Baa1	STA	BBB	STA
Saudi Arabia	AA-	STA	Aa3	STA	Aa-	STA

Singapore	**AAA**	STA	**Aaa**	STA	**AAA**	STA
Spain	**BBB-**	NEG	**Baa3**	NEG	**BBB**	NEG
Sweden	**AAA**	STA	**Aaa**	STA	**AAA**	STA
United Kingdom	**AAA**	NEG	**Aaa**	NEG	**AAA**	NEG
United States	**AA+**	NEG	**Aaa**	NEG		

Legend:
Top Notch: AAA, Aaa
Under Observation: AA+, AA-, Aa+, Aa-, Aa3, Aa1, Aaa, A+, BBB, BBB-, Baa3, Baa1
Junk: B3, B-, CCC, CC, C
NEG - Negative
POS - Positive
STA - Stable

The investing public relies on credit ratings as a means of assessing credit quality. Issuers sell bonds that carry a variety of security pledges. The various rating agencies publish their ratings on an array of debt instruments. The value of credit rating is based on belief that rating agencies have highly qualified and experienced professionals who employ rigorous criteria and analyses that confer validity and reliability to their assessments.

Credit rating agencies regularly communicate the criteria they employ. Standard and Poor's uses *Credit Week Municipal, Credit Week,* and *Credit Wire,* S&P's electronic rating dissemination of information. To enhance credibility and objectivity to their functions, the major credit rating agencies such as S&P do not invest resources for their own account, nor do they serve as underwriters, financial advisors, or managers of funds.

In the decision making process, the credit rating agency carrying out the credit risk evaluation function does not make recommendations on securities. The evaluator (rating agency) attempts to restrict itself as follows:

- The rating is not a recommendation to purchase, sell, or hold a given security; because confidential information is provided by issuers, it would be improper to make recommendations.
- Rating agencies that also make recommendations must obtain data only from public sources.
- Typically, ratings relate primarily to specific security, not to general-purpose evaluation.
- The rating agency process does not include an audit of the issuer, nor does it attest to the authenticity of information that the issuer provides.
- Because of the lack of or insufficiency of the information, the rating agency may change, withdraw, or place the issuer on a credit watch.
- No legal basis exists that constitutes a fiduciary relationship between the rating agency and issuer.

To achieve the highest possible rating, the issuing agency organizes and structures financial information to parallel the credit criteria of the rating agency. The issuer and advisor have responsibility for structuring a particular issue. S&P and Moody's often react to an issuer's proposed financing, including publishing and clarifying criteria and making interpretations and evaluation. Last, rating agencies do not act as investment bankers or financial advisors.

Standard & Poor's Rating of Municipal Debt

Standard & Poor's municipal debt rating process is complex. For this reason, S&P advises that at least three to four weeks' lead time be given when requesting a rating decision. Frequent issuers with a history of using S&P can normally obtain a shorter timeframe for ratings or review decisions. The rating process usually requires meetings with the issuer's representative. Meetings typically have at least two staff members and a member of the issue committee. After the decision is made on an issue, continuous updating on the issue is provided. The rating remains in effect until the next debt sale. Among the data that is provided to S&P include annual financial reports, budgets, capital planning, major changes in taxpayers, and the type of businesses and aid from state and federal governments.

Moody's Rating of Municipal Debt

Moody's Investor Service stresses four primary factors in assessing credit quality:

1. *Economic factors* tend to be the least controllable but are viewed as critical to credit analysis. Therefore, to gauge future expectations, the analyst must understand the forces that are likely to contribute to specific economic strength and weakness such as demographic trends, employment rates, income levels, and the community's overall level of wealth, the region's largest employers and the diversity and viability of its largest taxpayers.
2. *Debt factors* involve the evaluation of debt to assess the increased effects on all outstanding debt or credit quality. Various key debt ratios (see Table 8.6) are considered. When the same taxpayers are subject to overlapping debts, the applicable share must be considered in determining the overall tax burden. A key factor that is given attention is the issuer's rate of *debt repayment or payment*, which indicates the speed or rate of principal retirement, suggesting the willingness and ability of the issuer to pay. Rapid repayment is viewed as a positive indicator, whereas a slow payout may be given the reverse interpretation.[25]
3. *Financial factors* involve an analysis of financial position (balance sheet) and operating results from expenditure outflows, revenue inflows, and affecting forces emanating from expenditure and revenue volatility, taxpayer

demands, legislative action, and programmatic pressures. Close attention and analysis are given to the diversity of tax sources, the degree of reliance on the issuer's own sources for expenditures, and the general fund balance as a percent of revenues. A larger balance provides flexibility, especially when expenditures are economically sensitive and relatively difficult to forecast. Additionally, large reserves of at least 5 to 10 percent should be maintained to provide a cushion for unplanned contingencies.

4. While *management strategies/administrative factors* are difficult to assess, it is essential to understand the division of responsibilities, degree of professionalism, expertise, and power necessary to carry out functions such as effective tax collection, budgeting, and implementation of sound debt practices consistent with voter preferences. Additionally, it is important to establish a well-developed economic policy that is responsive to prioritized needs and resource constraints.[26]

Moody's has identified five major credit factors that drive rating changes, as shown in Table 8.7.

Changes in Ratings

Before rating changes, there are a number of potential signs of distress that will draw the attention of rating agencies, especially regarding those issuers that maintain continuous, confidential, updated information on their financial conditions. The following represent potential indicators of financial distress:

- Wide fluctuations of economically sensitive tax collection sources such as sales and income
- Continued downward trend of fund balance due to operating losses

TABLE 8.6   Key Debt Ratios

Ratios	How determined
Net Direct Debt Burden (excludes sinking fund and self supporting debt)	Net direct debt divided by the estimated full value of taxable property
Net Overall Debt Burden (includes overlapping debt share)	Net overall debt divided by the estimated full value of taxable property
Net Direct Debt per capita	Net direct debt divided by total population
Net Overall Debt per capita	Net overall debt divided by total population
Full Value per capita	Estimated full value of taxable property divided by total population

Source: Adapted from Linda Hird et al., "The Determinants of Municipal Credit Quality" *Government Finance Review*, 15, no. 6 (December 1999): 35.

TABLE 8.7   Factors Driving Rating Changes

Credit factor	Potential rating-change driver
Economy	• Significant development in the local tax base driving continued growth in total property values • Increased or decreased diversification of the local economic base • Loss of key industry or employer with no articulated alternative
Finances	• Expected augmentation or loss of financial flexibility • Expectation that significant growth or decline of reserves will continue
Debt	• Significant increase in debt obligations without correlating developments to offset tax-base leveraging • Utilization of debt structure not appropriately matched to assets' useful lives
Administrative/ management strategies	• Implementation of new strategies that are expected to augment or detract from operating flexibility • Change in political environment that affects ability to react to unanticipated events

Source: Adapted from Linda Hird et al., "The Determinants of Municipal Credit Quality" *Government Finance Review*, 15, no. 6 (December 1999): 38.

- Operating transfers becoming greater portion of operating budget
- Steadily rising fixed costs as a percent of budget
- Steadily significant increases in employee benefits, especially pension fund costs
- Regularly selling assets to cover operating budget costs
- Debt obligations not paralleling assets' useful lives

Bond Insurance

This is a relatively recent development, arising from the need to insure government-related bonds against the possibility of default by issuers. In such an event, the insuring company assumes the obligation to make all necessary payments for the coupons and maturity amounts required for investors. The initiating insurer in 1971 was the American Municipal Bond Assurance Corporation (AMBAC), whose objective was to reduce the interest cost to the issuer.

For a one-time premium ranging between one-third of 1 percent and 3 percent of the total interest and principal amount of the bond, the issuer can receive insurance protection for both principal and interest.

In 1974, the Municipal Bond Insurance Association (MBIA) was created as a competitor to AMBAC. Unlike AMBAC, whose ultimate backing consists only of its net worth, MBIA is comprised of five underwriters: Aetna Insurance Company, Aetna Casualty and Security Company, Fireman's Insurance Fund, Travelers Indemnity Company, and Continental Insurance Company. As with AMBAC, premiums are determined on the basis of size of the total interest payment and principal and may be paid by either the issuer or the bond underwriter. Although Standard and Poor's rates both AMBAC- and MBIA-insured bonds as AAA, Moody's assigns no ratings to them.[27]

Disclosure

Typically about a month before a bond sale, the issuer publishes a preliminary official statement or prospectus that describes the contents of the bond issue to enable potential investors to effectively price the bond. Subsequent to the bond sale, the final official statement is developed, providing details relating to the issue and coupon rates. Governmental units are not required to comply with the regulations of the Securities and Exchange Commission and other federal agencies.

The events of 1974–1975 relating to the financial crisis of New York City and the problems of a number of other cities, including Cleveland, raised the concern that the problems created were due in part to faulty reporting systems or manipulated reporting. Because of these developments, agencies, states, and a number of professional associations began calling for better disclosure guidelines. In some cases, legislation was introduced at the state and federal levels stipulating minimum disclosure guidelines. The Governmental Finance Officers Association (GFOA) published perhaps the most influential document, *Disclosure Guidelines for Offering of Securities by State and Local Governments* (1976). Two years later (in 1978), the GFOA issued *Guidelines for Use by State and Local Governments in the Preparation of Yearly Information Statements and Other Current Information*. The GFOA also offers a certificate of conformance based on how well a governmental unit's financial statement conforms to generally accepted accounting principles (GAAP), but it should be noted that this certificate does not verify the accuracy of the financial information contained within the statement.

Negotiated versus Competitive Sales

The issuer has the option to sell competitively or by negotiated sale in revenue bonds, whereas most states require general obligations to be competitively bid. The competitive sale permits underwriters to bid against each other to buy an issuer's bonds. Acceptance of the competitive approach is widespread, because there is a general feeling that it removes the possibility of favoritism, resulting in lower interest rates to the issuer.

In a negotiated sale there is no formal bidding—the underwriter is chosen beforehand. Typically, the issuer contacts a number of underwriters to solicit information regarding the expected interest rate or underwriter's spread (profit). The usual practice is that issuers exchange information on their proposed sales with underwriters with whom they have had satisfactory dealings in the past. The underwriter that is selected usually assists the issuer in a number of activities, including putting together the issue in terms of maturity date, maturity amount, and call provisions; preparing the official statement; assigning a credit rating; pinpointing the market timing for the issue; cultivating potential investors; and complying with legal requirements. After the selection is made, the issuer and underwriter work together to determine the structure, timing, and price of the bond for the underwriter itself. The negotiated bond approach is considered suitable when interest rates are high and volatile and the issue is complex. Since 1973, the number of revenue negotiated bond sales has increased sharply—from 25 percent to more than 75 percent of the dollar value of municipal revenue bonds in 2002. For the same period, the total short-term expenditure negotiated bond sales have averaged 30 percent of municipal bond sales.

In both the negotiated and competitive methods, the underwriter is the focal participant who buys the bonds from the issuer and in turn sells them to investors. For smaller issues, the underwriter buys the entire issue; larger issues are handled by a syndicate for later resale. Whether the sale method is competitive or negotiated, the underwriter assumes complete risk and responsibility for selling the bonds. Because of the negotiated underwriter's ability to time the sale and investigate the demand beforehand, its risk is limited.

When the underwriter decides to make a bid, it needs to determine the yield that will be necessary to attract investors, in conjunction with its own minimal requirements for making a profit. It is most important that the underwriter make an accurate assessment of the market for the bond, because miscalculations will result in the bond's offering price being lowered, thereby minimizing or eliminating the underwriter's profit. An important point here is that the underwriter's costs for searching and preparing the bid are recoverable only if it is successful in being awarded the issue. Thus, the potential of not recovering out-of-pocket costs restricts the underwriter's search and preparation efforts.

There are a number of options available to the negotiated sale underwriter that are not available to the competitive underwriter. If the former recognizes that it can sell the offering at a lower interest rate or that investors want different amounts of bonds than had been planned, the underwriter can modify the terms of the issue to reflect the changed circumstances.

Precisely what types of bond sale are desirable for a given issue depends on a number of variables. Among them that might affect the choice of type of sale are the following: the stability of the market, the experience of the issuer in the bond market, the size of the issue, the complexity of the issue, and administrative regulations in the state and/or local governmental unit. In selecting a negotiated bond sales approach, the cost and benefits of six factors should be evaluated:[28]

- The significance of the scope of the issue for the geographic tax-exempt market should be reviewed.
- Determining the lowest possible interest will make market timing critical. When the number or volume of tax-exempt issues is high or there is an unstable "roller coaster" market, the negotiated financing approach can be an advantageous means to pinpoint a window of market entry.
- When the issue is complex or innovative, the negotiated route is likely to provide the greatest opportunity to explain and make the case for the issuer in the marketplace.
- When there is concern about the rating process and potential downgrading, the expertise involved in a negotiated sale should be considered.
- In those cases where the issue requires a great deal of explanation because of significant economic or political developments or newsworthy or complicated building projects, the issuer may find the negotiated approach beneficial.
- A new issuer concerned about creating a positive image during its emergence, monitoring a strong position in the secondary market (in the case of reselling bonds of the issuer), and a contrasting style of management, ideology, or philosophy vis-à-vis a previous administration, may want to consider the negotiated sale option.

Notice of Sale

When an issue is prepared to be sold, advertisements are placed, usually in national and local media, announcing it. The traditional advertising document used is known as the "official notice of sale." Active issuers will normally send copies of the notice of sale to prospective bidders and financial and legal publications. The information in the official notice of sale includes the following:

- Amount of issue, including maturity and call features
- Authorization for the bond sale
- Type of bond (e.g., revenue, G.O.)
- Names of the bond counsel (may be more than one)
- Bid form and basis of award
- Amount of good-faith reliance, if required
- Denomination and registration privileges of investors
- Time, place, and date of bid acceptance
- Maximum interest cost permitted
- Statement of purpose of bond and security

Basis of Award

When the issue is to be bid competitively, it is important that the issuer determine the basis on which the decision to award will be made. The best-known bases for this are the *net interest cost* (NIC) and the *true interest cost* (TIC). The NIC is derived by determining the total interest payments for a debt issue and dividing them by the dollar amount of the bonds outstanding times the number of years they are outstanding. When bonds are issued at a discount, the latter is added to the interest payments. Conversely, when the bond is issued at a premium, the latter amount is subtracted from the interest payments. The formula for calculating the NIC is as follows:

$$NIC = \frac{Total\ interest\ payments + discount\ (-premium)}{Number\ of\ bond\text{-}year\ dollars}$$

For example, the interest payment equals $500. An amount of $50 is paid out for final maturity, due in one year and each year thereafter for the life of the bond:

TABLE 8.8   Bond Maturity Table with Total of $4,000

Years to maturity	Par value	Coupon	Coupon payment per maturity	Bond year (dollars)
1	$1,000	5%	$ 50	$ 1,000
2	1,000	5%	100	2,000
3	1,000	5%	150	3,000
4	1,000	5%	200	4,000
Total	$4,000		$500	$10,000

There are no premiums or discounts. The bond year dollars equal $10,000. The NIC is 5 percent:

$$NIC = \frac{Total\ coupon\ payments}{Bond\text{-}year\ dollars} = \frac{\$500}{\$10,000} = 0.05 = 5\ percent$$

A more involved example will help to clarify the NIC calculation. An issuer sells $20,000 of bonds with five separate maturities and no discount or premium. The serial maturities and coupons are as follows:

TABLE 8.9   Bond Maturity Table with Total of $20,000

Years to maturity	Par value	Coupon	Coupon payment per maturity	Bond year (dollars)
1	$1,000	5%	$ 50	$ 1,000
2	1,000	5%	100	2,000
3	1,000	5%	150	3,000
4	1,000	5%	200	4,000
Total	$4,000		$500	$10,000

$$NIC = \frac{Total\ interest}{Bond\text{-}year\ dollars} = \frac{\$2,715}{\$48,000} = 5.65\ percent$$

If the issue had been sold at a discount, the interest rate would be higher. For example, if the issue had been sold for an average price of $96, the issuer would have received $400 less. The NIC with the $400 discount added to the total interest payments is as follows:

$$NIC = \frac{\$2,715}{\$48,000} + \$400 = \frac{\$3,115}{\$48,000} = 6.48\ percent$$

The TIC method is considered a superior alternative to the NIC. A major criticism of the NIC approach is that it ignores the present value or the timing of interest rate payments—thus it misleads the issuer into choosing a higher bid than otherwise. The TIC accounts for the time value of money or present value.[29] It recognizes the interest rate that must be paid on the actual purchase price, which is the face amount minus the premium or plus the discount, to yield the bond coupon, thereby giving a more accurate picture of the costs involved.

Electronic Bond Bidding

Technology has made it possible to bid on bonds electronically. Websites presently provide comprehensive data on municipal bond sales. These sites provide bond calendars and contain such information as municipal news; extensive information on retail bond sales; listings of winning syndicates and bidding accounts; maturity information, such as coupons, rates, yields, concessions to Committee on Uniform Securities Identification Procedures (CUSIP) insurance and ratings; and historical postsale worksheets.[30] A large portion of historical information is free, and the remainder can be purchased at minimal cost. The electronic medium provides investors with timely and critical information; moreover, the cost of issuing bonds is accomplished at significantly reduced savings. By means of the CUSIP bureau, the electronic application and receipt of new issues are now possible, allowing for total automation of the syndication process: "The book-running manager and accountant or selling group members can use automation to define deals (terms, pricing, account, collect and verify order, create allocations and group sales, process trades, and handle accounting, close outs, and disbursement of monies)."[31]

Benefits of Automation

A number of monetary saving objectives that can be achieved using the electronic technique of bond bidding and sales:

- Processing transaction costs are decreased.
- Staff costs are reduced, because fewer employees are required.
- Errors and associated costs are reduced.
- Processing time is reduced by eliminating redundancy/repetitive actions such as retyping the same data on multiple forms.
- The automated process permits bid "issuers to view bid results in their rank order as they are submitted."[32]
- It allows potential bond bidders to view statistics online while enabling issuers to monitor bids for possible violations.
- Within a few minutes of the sale, the winner can be known.
- All participants (bidders) have access to information from a central database.
- Bidders can make changes up until the sale.
- The process causes the dramatic shrinking of profit margins, because it induces participants to find ways and means to constantly reduce costs.[33]

Concluding Observations

Debt management, which was once relegated to relative obscurity, became a front-burner issue during the 1970s owing to financial crises in a number of cities, among them New York and Cleveland. To be effective as a financial manager (and, to some extent, as a chief executive) in a governmental unit or not-for-profit organization requires a degree of understanding that will improve the chances of recognizing potential problems and the ability to seek advice to avert them. Because debt represents a significant portion of spending in many governmental units, it requires close attention and substantial understanding.

Notes

1.   National Advisory Council on State and Local Budgeting, *Recommended Budget Practices: A Framework for Improved State and Local Government* (Chicago: Government Finance Officers Association, 1998), pp. 19–20, 28, 30, 52, 65.

2.   See Rowan Miranda and Donald Picur, *Benchmarking and Measuring Debt Capacity* (Chicago: Government Finance Officers Association, 2001), pp. 6–7.

3.   Ibid., p. 15.

4.   Ibid.

5.   David Ricardo, *Principles of Political Economy and Taxation* (Homewood, IL: Richard D. Irwin, 1963/1817), p. 140.

6.   Richard E. Wagner, *Public Finance* (Boston: Little Brown, 1982), p. 308.

7.   Ibid., p. 303.

8.   Alan Walter Steiss, *Local Government Finance* (Lexington, MA: Lexington Books, 1975).

9.   Ibid., p. 75.

10.   U.S. Conference of Mayors, *A Mayor's Financial Management Handbook* (Washington, DC: U.S. Conference of Mayors, February 1980), pp. 111–119; Lennox L. Moak

and Albert M. Hillhouse, *Local Government Finance* (Chicago: Municipal Finance Officers Association, 1975), p. 250.

11. See U.S. Congressional Budget Office (CBO), *Small-Issue Industrial Revenue Bonds* (Washington, DC: CBO, 1985).

12. Ibid.

13. "FHWA Releases Draft P3 Model Contract for Public Comment." *NCPPP*. National Council for Public-Private Partnerships, n.d. http://www.facebook.com/thencppp?fret=np.

14. Ibid.

15. Moak and Hillhouse, *Local Government Finance*, pp. 391–396, Davenport & Co., "Debt Capacity: Setting the Standard," Virginia Government Finance Officers Association, 2009.

16. See *Evaluating Financial Conditions Handbook 2* (Washington, DC: International City Management Association, 1980).

17. A useful approach has been identified by Philip M. Low Jr. in *How to Calculate the Size of Your Bond Issue*, Special Bulletin 1976B. (Chicago: Municipal Finance Officers Association, June 1, 1976).

18. George Kaufman, "Debt Management," in J. Richard Aronson and Eli Schwartz, ed. (Washington, DC: International City Management Association, 1981), p. 308.

19. Lennox L. Moak, *Municipal Bonds* (Chicago: Municipal Finance Officers Association, 1982), p. 232.

20. Duane Stock, "Analysis of Call Feature on Municipal Debt," *Government Finance Review*, 15, no. 6 (December 1999): 13–14.

21. Ibid., p. 14.

22. Eswar Prasad and Mengjie Ding, *Financial Times*, October 31, 2015.

23. Public Securities Association, *Fundamentals of Municipal Bonds*, rev. ed. (New York: Public Securities Association, 1982), p. 40.

24. Martin Mayer, "Credit Ratings in the Crosshairs," *Brookings* (August 2010), p. 1.

25. Linda Hird et al., "The Determinants of Municipal Credit Quality," *Government Finance Review 15*, no. 6 (December 1999): 35.

26. Ibid., pp. 36–37.

27. Ibid., p. 64.

28. Mark S. Farber, "A Negotiated Sale," in *The Price of Advice: Choosing and Using Financial Advisors*, eds. John Peterson and Patt Ulatt (Chicago: Government Finance Officers Association, 1986), pp. 105–106.

29. See chapter 12 for the method for computing present value.

30. Renata Morgenstern, "Electronic Bidding for Municipal Innovation for Competitive Bond Sale" *Government Finance Review 16*, no. 1 (February 2000): 23.

31. Ibid., p. 23.

32. Ibid.

33. Ibid., pp. 24–25.

9

The Budgeting Function

Public budgeting grew out of the political and social necessity of sharing power. It was through the budget that the English aristocracy, in Article 12 of the *Magna Carta* (1215), obtained both symbolic and substantive control over the king's absolute power of the purse. In this way, the barons obtained the power to say no to the king's revenue-raising objectives. Before engaging in domestic or foreign activities, the king was now required to consult the barons and follow a recognized procedure before resources could be raised. The budget is thus "the product of the institutionalization of the rules and processes wrested from a sovereign, excessively jealous of his prerogatives."[1] Over time, the budget evolved as a formal instrument guaranteeing accountability and an important means of control in the modern democratic state.

Whatever our political ideologies, the scope and significance of the budget cannot be ignored. Budgets are essential to every type of organization. Their effect on the fortunes of governments and agencies has long been recognized. British statesman William Gladstone remarked: "Budgets are not merely affairs of arithmetic, but in a thousand ways go to the root of prosperity of individuals, the relations of classes, and the strength of kingdoms."[2] This chapter provides the reader with a brief overview of the components and issues that are essential to the understanding of modern budgeting techniques and philosophy. It also provides an introduction to chapters 10 through 15, which examine the uses of budgets and the different types found in practice.

Perspectives on Budgeting

The budgeting function represents the third sequential step in the financial system. The budget makes specific and concrete the potential implementations of the planned programs . Budgeting is a process involved in developing a plan, implementing it, and instituting a monitoring system to control outputs and effects, aiming to conform or exceed planned expectations. Budgeting is basically a component of cost accounting, because most of the planning efforts relate to costs to be incurred. Budgetary planning forces management to look ahead to anticipate problems and develop means or options to overcome them. To be most effective, budgetary planning must be viewed as a continuing effort.

Budget and Planning

All budget-making involves planning. The articulation of goals, objectives, strategies, and priorities is indispensable to the development of a sound budget. Community needs, priorities, challenges, stakeholder concerns and opportunities are assessed. It is the *planning* function that sets the stage for all subsequent activities in budget preparation, thus its importance cannot be underestimated. Figure 9.1 presents an expanded conceptual view of the linkage of planning and budgeting. Note that the budget amount of the prior period becomes a major input of the new planning cycle. Existing programs are evaluated, desired programs are identified, environmental or external factors are assessed, changes in the government/agency are determined, strategic

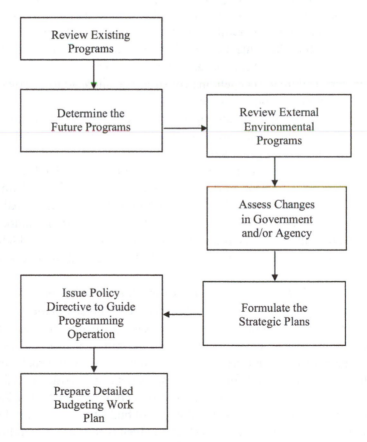

FIGURE 9.1   Planning and budgeting.

plans are formulated, and the policy directive necessary to guide program development (program planning) and the detailed work plan (budgeting) are put together.[3]

What Is a Budget?

The budget is the key policy document. The budget must be comprehensive, including all revenue and expenditure to facilitate the necessary tradeoffs between policy options.

The *budget* is a concrete road map indicating where an organization is going. A budget is a statement of the allocation of scarce resources designed to realize the organization goals and objectives for a specific period. As a financial plan, the budget details how the organization will collect and spend resources for a given fiscal period. A well-conceived, well-applied, and well-implemented budget allows the organization to realize its goals and objectives with maximum efficiency and effectiveness. Alternatively, a budget that is poorly conceived for anticipating needs and problems will cause the organization to stumble along from crises to crises. The very nature of budgets forces managers to recognize constraints. Every responsibility center manager must manage daily within the context of specific spending limitations. Budget limitations are agreed upon to keep manager spending within resource constraints or parameters. Failure to set spending constraints could lead to negative consequences for the entire organization.

A budget is an economic, planning, political, legal, and social document. It is a comprehensive financial work plan covering a specific period of time. The plan outlines the services and activities or projects to be provided and indicates in quantitative terms the necessary expenditures and available resources. The plan takes into account community preferences' competing claims and indicates how the resources will be allocated to satisfy these claims. All those whose preferences count are represented in the budget in dollar amounts—in other words, all groups or individuals receiving the benefits, which may be subsidies in the form of welfare, tax relief, day care, and the like—will be included.

The budget links the financial resources and human behavior necessary to accomplish policy objectives. Because the budget is an instrument (Table 9.1) for allocating scarce resources, it is an *economic* instrument. It is a *political* instrument because it settles conflicts in determining *who* will get *how* much of the available scarce resources and *when*. Finally, it is a *social* instrument, because it is a device for distributing benefits and costs according to community preferences.[4] Every budget is a reflection of a particular kind of accountability, as shown in Table 9.2. The type of budget that is used is directly dependent upon the user's desire to achieve a given type of accountability that reflects the goals and objectives, or value preferences, being sought.

TABLE 9.1   The Budget as an Instrument

Planning Instrument—sets goals, priorities, and strategies and coordinates the community/agency resources into an expenditure plan identifying what programs or activities will take place and at what levels.

Political Instrument—involves competing interests attempting to influence a government/agency to form policy favorable to them.

Social Instrument—provides a vehicle to grant and deny privileges and disburse burdens and benefits to individuals and businesses.

Economic Instrument—offers powerful potential for affecting the growth and productive capacity of the community and its citizens.

Legal Instrument—grants authoritatively the rights, responsibilities, power, and guidelines that regulate the budget format, timing, and process.

Source: Adapted from Jerome B. McKinney and Lawrence C. Howard, *Public Administration: Balancing Power and Accountability*, Second Edition (Westport, Connecticut, 1998), p. 361).

Sustainability Budgeting

When we speak about sustainability budgeting, we should give cognizance to the fact that we may be referring to two different perspectives that may produce distinctly different outcomes. One perspective emphasizes the ecological reality or the environment in which the social and economic sphere interconnect and operate so as to enhance or minimize environmental harm. In the triple bottom approach, there is a continuous and unyielding pursuit, as discussed in chapter 1, to achieve the mutual interest or the common ground. The objective is to promote intra and intergenerational equity, passing on an environment that is as good as or better than the one inherited by the current generation.

The other perspective of view sustainability is solely a fiscal or financial pursuit to maintain the following:

- *Solvency:* having the ability, both in the short and long terms, to pay government financial obligations
- *Growth:* the ability to maintain continuous economic prosperity
- *Stability:* the ability of government to maintain existing level of tax burden and spending while meeting all future obligations
- *Intergenerational equity:* allowing only those liability or obligations with equal or greater benefits to be passed on to future generations[5]

This well-articulated view of fiscal sustainability totally ignores the environmental aspect on which the economic and social dimensions depend. The main or only objective is the maintenance of government's taxing and

TABLE 9.2 The Budget Accountability Continuum

1 Line-Item ──▶ Budget	2 Performance ──▶ Budget	3 Zero-Base ──▶ Budget	4 Program ──▶ Budget	5 *Budget for Social Purposes and Change (Emerging)*
Objective: inputs control accounting for object of expenditure – Fiscal/Financial – Dollar accountability – Conformance to legal and procedural requirements – Units of input: staff hours, materials used	Objective: achieving desired standard outputs while minimizing inputs relating amount of input units to output units – Emphasis on efficiency/ economy/productivity – Using workload (no. of units of work to be done) as output – Input dimension of efficiency, cost or some proxy measure such as man-hours worked – Examples of efficiency-measure indicators: • Cost: input/output ratio such as solid waste collected per dollar spent or per employee hour • Volume and quantity such as number of lunches served	Objective: achievement of articulated goals/ result objective at the lowest cost possible for identified clienteles and constituents, creating the opportunity to reallocate resources from lower to higher priorities – Emphasis on efficiency, productivity, and economy for accomplishing targeted objectives – Resource use constrained on the basis of benefit to be achieved – Examples of program-measurement indicators – Resource allocation based on priority ranking – Cost-effectiveness: specific acceptable costs and benefits as a condition for acceptance or rejection – Incentives for inducing managers to exchange quality information up and down the hierarchy	Objective: measured needs, demands, results, impact, effectiveness, outcome, relevance, sustainability, and significance, determining congruence between stated goals and objectives to achieved results; and delivering the goods at the time, place and manner, and in the quantity and quality desired to target clienteles and constituents – Examples of program-measurement indicators: • need: quantifiable conditions or problem areas which require action if maximum welfare of the general public is to be served, requiring the identification of priority relationships among needs • demand measures: identifying the need for a given public service measuring the dimension or scope of work to be performed in an entity such as miles of streets to be cleaned, number of businesses requiring protection, and so on • workload measures: indicating amount of work to be performed in a department or responsibility center linking with demand measures such as number of garbage pickups and number of patrol hours to be completed • outcome: number of illnesses prevented due to vaccine	Objective: determining the extent to which programs make target groups or population better off over time than they were prior to the intervention – Generating sustainability: percent of target group who failed to develop diseases after a vaccination, percent of school-age children whose nutrition level improved as a result of school lunch program – Extent to which recipients transformed no longer depend on the program

Source: Jerome B. McKinney, "SEA Reporting: Linkage with Public Budgeting and Accountability," delivered at Government Standard Accounting Board, Service Efforts and Accomplishments Reporting Concepts, Vancouver, BC, Canada, May 5, 1993.

spending policy balance in the long run and the ability to meet all current and future obligations. The two perspectives are entirely mutual. The sustainable environmental objective and the fiscal sustainability objective can be pursued and achieved simultaneously as the governments such as Sweden, Winnipeg Manitoba, and numerous corporations around the world have done.

Contrasting Public and Private Budgeting

The pricing and market systems act as the strategic resource allocation mechanism in the private sector, whereas the budget performs this function in the public sector. In the private sector, expected revenues are directly tied to the quantity and quality of goods and services produced and sold. Revenues are a good indicator of whether planned levels of activity have been realized. Unlike in the private sector, public and nonprofit agencies must determine in advance the amounts to be raised to achieve projected levels of activity, and the means to raise them. A failure to collect expected fees does not mean that the expenditure plans can be changed to match revenue intake. The public agency can resort to supplemental appropriations, but this is often viewed with hostility. Similarly, the nonprofit agency must rely on its reserve funds or on its funding sources. The latter most often do not like to provide additional funds, so agencies whose revenues are under budget must learn to live with their mistakes. In both public and nonprofit agencies, yearly budgets are fixed and all funds provided are expected to be spent. Not spending the funds typically results in expenditure reductions according to the amount unspent. Because the system does not provide incentives for the workers to conserve, the approach is "counter-productive and weakens the sensitivity of the budget as a measure of performance."[6]

The *control aspect* of the budget is far more critical to public and nonprofit organizations than it is to private ones. Several reasons may be advanced for this phenomenon. Particularly in private manufacturing companies, most costs are engineered costs. Accordingly, in these companies most costs can be identified with the products produced. In nonprofit agencies, however, most costs are discretionary, because the amounts to be spent typically vary widely depending on management decisions.[7]

Unlike the fixed budgets of the nonprofit organizations, the budgets of profit-oriented companies tend to be tentative, and management is expected to adjust to the changing conditions that affect sales or outputs. Managers are expected to revise plans so that the profit objective can be maximally achieved. However, conditions in government and nonprofit agencies are viewed as essentially stable and predictable. For example, the number of miles of road to be built and maintained, the number of hospital beds, or the number of students enrolled at a university, are not likely to change significantly from one period to the next during a single year.[8]

Purposes of Budgeting

One unarticulated objective of a budget is to minimize uncertainty and make the future more predictable by identifying what is wanted, how much of it is available, and when it is available.[9] The budget quantitatively articulates planned intentions and priorities. Ideally, every proposed dollar of expenditure is specifically identified with an organizational unit known as a *responsibility center*, the manager of which has control over the use of that dollar.

Of all the components of the financial management system, budgeting is perhaps the most important. The continuing pursuit of the balanced budget enhances stability in financial management, because it fosters a matching of revenue (intake/inflow of resources or money) with expenditure (outflow/spending of resources or money). As a detailed work plan, the budget provides direction for the implementation of articulated policies and significantly facilitates the achievement of organizational objectives.

Policy Direction

Being a plan, the budget indicates a specific policy direction to be followed for a specific period of time. It contains a set of coordinated choices aimed at achieving articulated or implied goals and objectives. Some specific elements of budget policy should include statements relating to the following:

- *An operating budget* should identify the funds to be included, the sequence of preparation of the operating and capital budget and required budget reserves, authority for budget guidelines, and preparation.
- *Revenue policies* indicate proposed changes in tax rates, guidelines for allocating and spending one-time grants and windfall taxes, and reviewing and setting fees and charges (see chapter 5).
- *Budget implementation* guidelines should articulate how enterprises or self-perpetuating funds are to be supported, how interfund borrowing and payments are to be made, how accountability is to be maintained for balancing expenditures with appropriation, and the required standard that will govern accounting reporting and auditing.
- *Debt policies* are standards and conditions for issuance and using short- and long-term borrowing (see chapter 8).

The Budget as Marketing Instrument

The budget attempts to identify citizens' needs and values. The rebudget is used as a means to obtain the necessary resources to respond to citizens' needs and desires. The point is made that the budget is used to promote and enhance understanding. It should be an instrument to induce citizens to participate in government processes. Citizens should be able to see the extent to which the budget reflects their values, thereby providing a rationale for them to accept and support budget choices.[10]

The view is expressed that *budget marketing* is imperative today, as confidence in government, business, and civic leaders to "do the right thing" has fallen significantly. Thus, government by "proxy" or "blue ribbon" committee that made decisions for the community in the past is not as easily accepted now. The committee approach to solving problems tends to create an "insider/outsider" mentality. The increasingly sophisticated information, technology, and electronic networks can be used to survey citizens' views about the budget.[11] Surveys have become quite practical, such as the operating Public Electronic Network that has been established in Santa Monica, California, to monitor citizens' satisfaction. Other media include "community briefing budget road shows" and "town hall meetings," wherein regularly scheduled briefings are held to update community groups.[12]

Mutual Contracts

The budget may be considered a *mutual contract* between the provider of resources and the deliverer of goods or services. This makes it especially important to involve those who will implement the budget. In spite of this desired norm, a number of nonprofit agencies exclude service deliverers from the budget process when crucial decisions are made. There have been many cases in which the budget submitted to the resource providers has been sharply reduced but the service provisions left intact.[13]

In the public sector, the legislature and chief executives agree to provide the executing agencies with funds, with the understanding that they will expend them according to the previously agreed-upon objectives. In like manner, the governmental budget can be viewed as a contract between the legislature and citizens of the governmental unit. The citizen implicitly agrees to pay taxes on condition that the government provide certain general and specific services.

Communication

A budget should communicate the objectives and standards of performance expected of all decision makers. Externally, it can detail the costs and expenditures of operations by identifying the inputs, such as materials and equipment, and the outputs of specific goods and services, such as miles of road built or repaired, number of patients treated, or number of manuscripts submitted for publication. When management is concerned not only with inputs and outputs, but also with results or effectiveness—such as in the percentage of patients successfully treated (health care or welfare organizations), the number of degrees and diplomas awarded (universities), or a reduction in the crime rate (police departments)—the budget can be a useful instrument in providing such information. It is also a useful means for communicating changes in priorities and providing a rationale for undertaking particular programmatic objectives. The budget process can be an effective instrument to help voters and clientele better understand the reasons for making policy changes. Today, many governments and organizations use town meetings and other forums, especially interactive websites, to facilitate citizen participation and improve budget communication.

Motivational Control

The budget can be used to motivate employees by dispensing or withholding rewards. The use of the budget as a means of control over departmental and functional expenditures has dominated much of the history of budgeting. The traditional line item and incremental budgets (discussed in chapter 13) were designed to control administrative discretion in the spending of agency funds. In fact, the orientation of line item budgets is so directed at limiting specific expenditures (e.g., personnel and materials) that it has been referred to as the "dollar accountability budget." Furthermore, each spending organizational unit is treated as a cost center to which responsibility can be specifically assigned and from which accountability can be obtained.

Monitoring of Service

The budget can be used to monitor and assess the performance of various constituent units and programs by providing continuing feedback on progress. Variance analysis of performance at timely intervals permits corrective action to be taken. For example, analysis of wages may show variance because of an increase in pay rates subsequent to the preparation of the budget, poor deployment of staff (e.g., the use of more highly paid workers than planned), or both (see Figure 9.2).

Like labor, materials may be analyzed for variance because of price increases, excessive use of materials, or both (see Figure 9.2). The same conceptual approach employed for labor can be used to calculate materials variance:

- Budgeted quantity − actual quantity × budgeted rate per unit of output = materials variance)
- Budgeted rate per unit quantity − actual rate per unit quantity × actual quantity used = variance because of price of materials input
- Budgeted cost of materials − actual cost of materials = net materials price variance

In government and most nonprofit agencies, the budgeted cost is a substitute for the standard cost, which represents the amount that a procedure

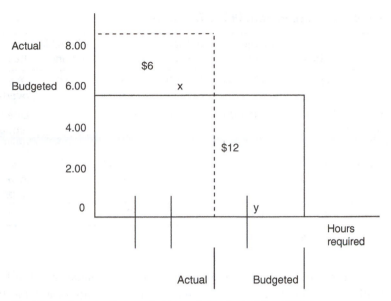

The information equation needed to analyze a budget is as follows:

	Budgeted	Actual
Hours	5	3
Wages	$6	$8
Labor	30	24
Variance		6

- Budgeted Hours (5) – Actual Hours (3) × Budgeted Rate ($6) = Labor-Use Variance ($12).
- Budgeted Wage Rate ($6) − Actual Wage Rate ($8) × Actual Hours (3) = Wage-Rate Variance ($6).
- Budgeted Labor Cost ($30) – Actual Wage Cost ($24) = Net Wage Variance ($6).

FIGURE 9.2   Labor cost variance.

or service should, ideally, cost. Although the development and use of the standard cost are infrequent in the public sector, they are widely used in private industries and some nonprofit organizations such as hospitals. Standard costs are valuable aids in budget preparation because (1) they are objectively predetermined; (2) they can assist management in measuring performance by comparing actual costs with planned standard costs, therefore providing information that permits management to isolate and explain variations from plans; (3) they provide a useful means of valuing or costing inventory that is transferred out or carried from one period to the next; and (4) they provide a dependable basis for pricing goods and services.

Whether the objective standard (determined by rigorous engineering requirements) or the budgeted standard (amount appropriated by the authorizing body) is used, the responsibility center may regularly conduct variance

TABLE 9.3   Variance Report: Police Department

Activity	Item	Budgeted costs	Actual costs	Variance	Allowable variance	Remarks
Field inspections	Personnel	$ 100,000	$ 130,000	$ 30,000 (UF)	10%	Due to overtime
Community service	Materials	45,000	35,000	10,000 (F)	15%	Due to reduced price
Downtown patrol	Supplies	5,000	7,000	2,000 (UF)	20%	Due to increased price
	Totals	$ 150,000	$ 172,000	$ 42,000		

Note: F = favorable; UF = unfavorable.

analyses. A threshold point is established to permit top management to focus its attention only on those variances that exceed its limits (see Table 9.3). This approach is similar to the management practice known as *management by exception*, except that only a deviation above a given threshold level (for example, amounts that exceed 20 percent for supplies in Table 9.3) is reported to management.

Resource Allocations

The allocation of resources to the most worthy uses is a major goal of budgeting. The allocation criteria determine how limited resources are to be divided among the various and competing uses. If these criteria are defective, it is likely that a misallocation of government resources will result. Resources will go to some centers that should not receive them, whereas units that do need them may not get enough. This outcome denies the organization or government the best potential use of its scarce resources.

Accountability Instrument

The budget sets forth, in dollars, an agreement or compromise between the legislative and executive branches on the one hand and the administrative officials and relevant members of the community on the other. In the nonprofit sector, a budget sets forth an agreement between the governing board and officials of the agency. The programs provided for in the budget are targeted implicitly or explicitly to clientele and constituents over a specified period. By means of the performance indicators included within the budget, assessments can be made to determine whether the promised services and goods have been delivered at the times and places specified and in the manner, quality, and quantity desired. By means of performance indicators (see chapter 11), the budget permits managers to know whether they are perhaps using the same amount of resources to achieve more and better benefits for their clients and constituents, or whether perhaps they are using a reduced level of funding to realize the same or better results.

In the final analysis, accountability can be most effectively accomplished only when the controlling instruments of performance measurement (e.g., the accounting, auditing, efficiency and economy, and reporting and evaluation systems) are directly linked to responsibility centers, which are then linked to the key personnel responsible for delivering specific goods and services to the target group. Take, for example, the manager of dietary services in a hospital. He or she oversees the performances of subordinates responsible for patients' food service, the kitchen, the cafeteria, and so on. The manager of dietary services is, in turn, accountable for his or her performance to the head of administrative services.

It may be useful at this point to summarize the attributes of a good budget. A budget is a device to do the following:

- Indicate the direction of financial policies for a specified period of time
- Explain the effects of budget requests on tax rates or charges
- Explain the effects of intergovernmental relationships
- Explain the proposed expenditures of estimated revenues
- Identify the level of services to be produced based on the projected revenue
- Specify the amount and charges for goods or services that will be provided and show the short- and long-range consequences of reducing or eliminating goods and services
- Facilitate control over expenditures
- Communicate the objectives and expected standards of performance that will be compared with results
- Motivate employees to achieve articulated objectives in their individuals units
- Aid in maintaining a monitoring system to assess performance of the various units and provide timely feedback on their progress
- Assess the affects of goods and services on the target population

The executive budget system requires that agencies prepare requests. Inputting the final recommended requests, as elaborated below, can be a highly involved process. Decisions have to be made about what programs should be maintained or expanded or reduced, what new programs can be initiated and at what level. All of these decisions take place in the pluralistic U.S. context characterized by a web of competing demands—often greater than allowable resources would permit.

While the integrated executive system is preferred by administrators and proponents who wish to effectively fix accountability, there are other models operating. At the county level, fewer than 10 percent employ the executive model. In some instances, legislative staff is allowed to observe executive budget hearings, providing the opportunity for feedback to legislators before the proposals reach the legislature for formal review. It has been long accepted that executive and legislative staffs continually meet to exchange informal views on existing and proposed policies.

Functions of the Budget Office

Whatever the structure of government, an officer or individual is given responsibility for collecting and receiving the budget requests before passing them on to the executive or appropriate legislature, board, or council. The budget office carrying out the review function has been changing. Traditionally known for its budget cutting, local government budget officers have been evolving into a role that attempts to educate, "helping departments rather than opposing them; explaining budget constraints . . . , and presenting the budget to the public, media, and financial community."[14]

The budget office carries out three main functions: *coordination*, *policy guidance*, and *supervision and implementation*.[15] Despite its less conflictual role, the budget office is expected to perform a number of tasks:

- Acts as chief articulator and interpreter of the government's or chief executive's priorities. An aim is to explain and clarify the priorities to minimize the preparation of proposals that are likely to be rejected.
- Revenue estimation (see chapter 5). Especially in local governments and other not-for-profit organizations, this is the starting point in the budget preparation and approval process. This conservative revenue budget approach helps to constrain requests, while creating the opportunity for a surplus, or at a minimum, a balanced budget.
- Budget requests are put together to form the "budget proposal."
- Proposed expenditures are continuously compared with estimated revenues, thereby ensuring that spending requests do not exceed revenue.
- It integrates estimates to bring them in line with executive policy priorities. The zero-sum game agencies that employ strategies in justifying every dollar when submitting requests are pared to conform with executive priorities.
- It analyzes and critically reviews agency requests and financial plans, focusing on past performance evaluation, service needs, relative cost effectiveness, efficiency analysis, and relevant groups' supporting agency programmatic demands.

In articulating the priorities of the chief executive, the budget office's educating role requires the dissemination of financial policies. The office must clearly communicate to all participants in the process the parameters and limits of budget requests. It is expected to demonstrate both internally and to the financial community a commitment to professional financial management practices. Additionally, the budget office enhances its statute, credibility, and integrity by earning the reputation for making accurate revenue estimates and discouraging the view that there is maneuvering room for negotiating in budget requests. All of this suggests that the ability to communicate effectively is indispensable in today's budget office.

Because all inflows and outflows affecting an agency are reflected in the budget, the budget office requires continuous interaction with key departments affecting financial matters, such as treasury, accounting, and information technology: "The budget office typically becomes the strongest voice for updating computing capabilities."[16]

Developing the Budget

Budgeting is an ongoing and dynamic process that is typically marked by regular phases: (1) planning, needs assessment, and priority setting (in local governments and other not-for-profit agencies, preparing and updating revenue projections may be the first step or phase); (2) preparation, including developing budget guidelines, expenditure forecasting, requesting estimates from departments, reviewing departmental estimates, and the development of performance measures; (3) legislative reviews of agency requests and appropriations (adoptions); (4) the execution of proposed programs (implementation, including spending and disbursement of funds); and (5) audits and evaluations of agency expenditures. The budgeting phase takes place in a context that is characterized by "deadlines, reports, hearings, policy reviews, and work experience and is deeply immersed in politics."[17] Figure 9.3 provides a schematic view of the dynamic context of budget-making. Five phases in budgeting

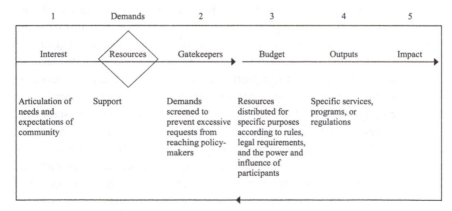

FIGURE 9.3   Budgeting resource allocation.

resource allocation are indicated below, each of which will be discussed later in this section.

1. The community (the general public, clients, constituents, and other relevant groups) expresses what it wishes the government or agency to do and not do.
2. The gatekeepers (these are the people who typically decide what requests will or will not be seen by the policymakers, screening or rejecting demands made on the system to obtain scarce resources) receive the reports and compare them with available resources. Basing their conclusions on perceptions and consultations with policymakers (executive and legislative officials), the gatekeepers accept, modify, or reject the requests.
3. The policymakers review the existing resources and evaluate the power and influence of the participating interest groups. Through a process of bargaining and mutual compromise, policymakers determine the distribution of available resources as a balance between the vote that they are likely to obtain during the next election and what they feel is in the best interest of the public. Nonprofit agencies attempt to obtain the largest amount of resources that the funding agencies can provide and the largest amount of fees that can reasonably be collected from users. The objective is to expand resources or at least get by on what is available.
4. The compromises become the basis for the allocation of resources, resulting in a policy that specifies services, programs, and regulations.
5. The effects (i.e., benefits and costs) on the target population are assessed and fed back into the system.

Despite the dynamics taking place in the allocation of resources, the emphasis is on maintaining the status quo. Few significant changes or innovations ever occur in budget-making.[18] At the national level, neither the chief executive nor Congress has significant discretionary control over yearly expenditures, because most of the budget is determined by previous mandatory commitments. These include programs such as Social Security and veterans' benefits. Additionally, there are required payments on outstanding contracts for public works and defense, as well as interest payments on the national debt.

Because in the budgets of nonprofit agencies there tend to be no ironclad agreements that the funding agencies will continue to support recipient agencies, these budgets are controllable. Once relationships have been established and the incremental budget system has been adopted, however, nonprofit agencies tend to be funded as a matter of policy. Like public sector agencies, recipient nonprofit agencies, especially those funded by United Way, cultivate relationships with volunteers, review committees, clientele, and corporate opinionmakers in an effort to gain support for their claims for pieces of the budget pie.

The approach to budget preparation has not been marked by a high degree of uniformity. Typically, budget projections tend to represent historical priorities. Resource allocation is based less on planning than on control, as noted earlier. If nonprofit and public sector agencies hope to improve their budget decisions, they must find answers to questions like these: What amount of service is needed? What level of service can be produced? What is the desired level of service? How can the available resources be used efficiently to achieve the stated objectives? Can the service be better provided by in-house staff or by contractors? To enhance the results of the answers to these questions, the planning process should precede the budgeting phase.[19]

In initiating budget development, a consideration of factors such as the following should be included in the information base: (1) the analysis of elements that affect public demand; (2) the constraints and limits on fiscal resources; (3) the extent to which federal, state, and other resources are available; (4) the adequacy of the current level of service; (5) the implications of population changes; (6) the political sensitivity of contemplated programs; and (7) the minimum standards of goods and services to be delivered to clientele and constituency.[20] To aid rational decision making in the budget-making process, *needs assessment*, *cost projection of services*, and *priority setting* should be considered.

Needs Assessment

Needs assessment is the examination of the aggregation of observed and articulated desires, needs, and expectations of individuals, groups, and the community. Needs may be reflected in each community. Data may be obtained by observing conditions such as poverty, the deterioration of bridges, and crime and by evaluating inquiries obtained by direct feedback from clientele and constituents.[21]

To obtain reliable information on current needs, these procedures should be followed: (1) The quality of available data at all levels—federal, state, and local government—should be examined and the criteria for identifying the need established. (2) The policy statements of legislative and executive officials, position papers, the census, demographic information available from various planning agencies, departmental files, special studies on the target population, records of public hearings, and surveys conducted by other agencies (public or private) that may provide information regarding like or similar services should be analyzed.[22] This data should then be converted into specific demands for goods and services, suggesting the level and quality of services to be provided.

Cost Projection of Services

The needs that have been identified become the inputs for forecasting service activities to meet client demands. The aggregation of service activities (demands) reflects the goals and objectives of the organization's strategic plan. When the planned and costed activities have been accepted, the process results in the annual activity budget.

When estimating service costs, the individuals charged with the function should be knowledgeable about the resources that are required. Different methods for calculating the costs might typically be used in practice. One approach is the "line item" that simply lists things to be acquired such as salaries, fringe benefits, supplies, and facilities (see chapter 15). The method can be easily applied by using past history and add a "growth factor."

This popular approach for estimating costs fits the needs of some organizations but may have drawbacks for others. Because focus is put on inputs or items bought such as supplies, utilities and salaries, it is difficult to assess the accuracy of the costs. The method does not provide assurance that incorporates efficient use of resources, making this type of budget difficult to defend.

The drawbacks associated with the line item approach have stimulated the search for better ways to estimate costs. The difficulties are many in developing an alternate model that ideally captures the variables affecting cost factors in organizations. To be most useful, the model should attempt to approximate directly or indirectly variables such as inflationary trends, labor market fluctuations, technological changes, the quality of the decision making, and policy changes.

The *cost volume analysis* model is a second approach that requires a different way of thinking. It emphasizes how costs behave in relationship to changes in the volume of service activity. Costs are viewed as variable, fixed, or semivariable (see chapter 2). *Variable cost* changes in direct proportion to the volume of activity. For example, assume that a state department of welfare provides direct payment of $300 per month per child. As the number of children increases, the total monthly reimbursement increases in direct proportion. Thus, if the number of children in a facility is twenty per month, the resource outflow from the welfare department would be $6,000 ($300 × 20).

The flexible budget (allows budget to vary from a given volume, facilitating benchmark evaluation) is a third model of estimating the cost of activities when fixed and variable costs are defined. A common form of showing how changes in volume affects cost is reflected by using the equation for a straight line as follows:

$$y = a + b\,(x)$$

where

y = the cost at specified volume.

a = the cost where the dollar axis (y-axis) at a zero activity level. This is the estimate of fixed costs.

b = the amount of change in cost varies with volume. The rate of change in straight line is the average variable cost per unit of volume.

x = the measure of volume, or activity level.

Assume that a state-run children's home has the following:

$$\text{Salary } y \quad = \$200,000 \ + \$0 \ (x)$$

$$\text{Food } y \quad = \$0 \qquad + \$400 \ (x)$$

$$\text{Maintenance } y \ = \$300,000 \ + \$200 \ (x)$$

Calculate the three listed costs when the number of residents in the state home is equal to 100. The cost for the children's home is as follows:

$$\$260,000 \ [\$200,000 + \$6,000 \ (100)]$$

The flexible budget can be used both "before the fact" to estimate the cost and "after the fact" to aid in undertaking performance evaluation and control. For example, if we had 130 residents rather than 100, the 100 residents that were estimated, due to increased referrals from the courts, the additional residents caused maintenance costs to increase to $323,000.

The original flexible budget allowance cost amounted to $320,000 or [$300,000 + 200 (100)]. The difference between the budget estimate and the actual cost gives an unfavorable spending variance of $3,000 ($320,000 − 323,000). When the flexible budget is adjusted to the actual activity level, it shows an adjusted amount of $320,000 (300,000 + 200 (130). When the adjusted budget amount is used as the benchmark, the spending variance would be favorable in the amount of $3,000 ($326,000 − 323,000). This use of flexible budget shows how it can be used to enhance the performance budget analysis.

Priority Setting

Priority setting is a process by which an agency or entity articulates the functions or programs that are considered most important to the attainment of service objectives to be pursued during a coming fiscal period.[23] Priority setting is critical because of the scarcity of resources and the desire to optimize benefits. The director or manager of each responsibility center is responsible for identifying those programs that have the highest priority. This identification process may result in the shifting of resources among programs to improve an agency's objectives. For example, a district police station that experiences a sharp drop in crime or a hospital trauma center that has a significant decline in patients cannot continue to justify the same level of staffing; personnel should be shifted to other areas where they can be better used.

Priority setting is deeply immersed in values, especially in the public and nonprofit sectors, where resource allocation is not based on the profit criterion. Priority setting may be an exceedingly difficult process. Its outcome is greatly influenced by the ability to mobilize power and exercise influence. The allocators determine what individuals, groups, or organizations will benefit, when they will benefit, and to what extent. Priority setting is easier when there are generally agreed-upon norms and perceptions of the clients' and constituents' needs.

If economic rationality is a desired objective, the priority-setting process can be facilitated when participants in organizations or communities agree in advance to abide by allocations made on the basis of cost-effectiveness or a ranking process similar to the one employed in zero-base budgeting (ZBB) or a predetermined, objective rating scale. Such a scale could rate the functions of the agency in order of importance (with the numerals 1 to 6 representing a descending order). Next, each function may be rated numerically in order of importance, as shown in Table 9.4. If equity is the main objective to be maximized in the table, it is given the highest rating—1. Similarly, the importance of community development permits it to be rated 1. Maximizing the equity objective while pursuing community development gives a matrix score of 1 (a number 1 equity rating × a number 1 community development rating), the highest priority rating possible. On the other hand, the rating of the neighborhood improvement objective as 6 and the rating of the transportation function as 5 provide a total matrix score of 30. When priorities are articulated in public and nonprofit agencies, they can be most useful in executive budget-making.

Executive: Prelegislative Submission

Once the budget requests have been prioritized and costed, the executive decides the strategies that are best to gain approval of the financial plans with the least changes. This requires that the executive consider a number of factors, including the following:

- The relevant stakeholders and interests who are likely to be most influential in getting priorities enacted
- The extent to which legislators, citizens, and relevant groups are interested in solving the problems addressed
- Dealing with groups or audiences whose problems are not given priority
- Gauging the communication required to attract the maximum attention to those interests who matter the most in getting the program enacted and enhancing changes for reelection

TABLE 9.4 Priority-Setting Matrix

Maximizing outcomes or objective		Government functions					
	Rating	Community development	Human resources	Environmental resources	Health and safety	Transportation	Legislative and citizen participation
		1	2	3	4	5	6
Equity	1	1	2	3	4	5	6
Economy	2	2	4	6	8	10	12
Standard of service	3	3	6	9	12	15	18
Service improvement	4	4	8	12	16	20	24
Service coordination	5	5	10	15	20	25	30
Neighborhood improvement	6	6	12	18	24	30	36

Source: Adapted from Barry M. Mundt, Raymond T. Olsen, and Harold I. Steinberg, *Managing Public Resources* (Stamford, CT: Peat Marwick International, 1982), p. 33.

Executives in other not-for-profit agencies do not have to be concerned with the diversity of interests as those in public agencies. However, they must give due cognizance to the board-relevant interest groups and clientele groups. Therefore the executive must articulate messages to meet these expectations.

Ballot Box Budgeting

The regularized and predictable budget-making process described thus far is not the only means for allocating scarce resources within the American federal system. California has shown that direct democracy may play a significant role when easy access to the initiative process is permitted. This process, if used prudently, can aid in promoting public accountability and participation. Alternatively, it can be an exceedingly constraining and disruptive instrument in the allocation of public resources.

Despite a projected deficit of near $20 billion for fiscal year 2003–2004, public opinion showed that Californians continue to believe their taxes to be too high. Governor Gray Davis was recalled in 2003 when he raised unpopular taxes in his attempt to solve the state budget deficit. During the budget crisis in 1976, it was not until the deficit reached $14.3 billion that public opinion swung in favor (70 percent) of an increase in the state's income taxes. Since 1976, this receptivity to taxes has been rare in California. The ability of California's policymakers to resolve the state deficit crisis has been greatly hampered by the emergence of *ballot box budgeting*. Californian's easy access to the initiative process has produced many referendums that dictate fiscal policies.[24]

Between 1977 and 1989, tax-relief measures reduced potential state revenues by $178 billion. Proposition 13 accounts for nearly $120 billion of this amount. Initiatives now obligate approximately 70 percent of the state budget to local governments. No tax may be passed in the state unless it receives a two-thirds majority. Additionally, between 1976 and 1992, tax indexing led to a $40.1 billion revenue lost to the state, and the phaseout of inheritance taxes and rent credit cost $6.4 and $2.6 billion, respectively.[25]

Today some Californians believe that despite its flaws, the initiative referendum is still effective. Yet others worry that the initiative process no longer works as the designers intended. Special interests monopolize the process that meant to limit them. Collecting signatures has become a regularized and costly process, coordinated by professional consultants. Proposition 30, tax increase to fund education, cost both sides a total of $120.5 million ($67.1 million in donations for, $53.4 million in donations against). The ban on labor contributions, Proposition 32, cost a combined $133.8 million ($60.5 million in donations for, $73.3 million in donations against).[26]

Any tax or expenditure issue may be put on the ballot as long as the supporters can obtain the required number of signatures. There are essentially no constraints on those proposing the initiative. No financial statute is safe from the initiative. Thus legislators must always anticipate a potential initiative challenge. In 2012, five propositions directly affecting taxes or the budget system were proposed, two of which passed.[27]

The Executive Role

The executive role in budget-making in the public sector has been influenced by a cultural fear of executive power and a concern for accountability. These influences caused the establishment of a system of checks and balances that led to fragmentation in financial management until the reform movement during the late 1800s. The movement culminated in the introduction of state and local executive budgets (which make the chief executives of these governments directly responsible for preparing budgets, submitting them for approval, and administering the approved budgets). The *executive budget* placed the chief executive in charge of reviewing agency submissions. The executive may cut or modify requests or do whatever is required, especially at the local level of government, to balance the budget. With the passage of the Budget and Accounting Act of 1921, Congress instituted the executive budget at the national level. The act created the Bureau of the Budget, which is now known as the Office of Management and Budget (OMB), to serve as an arm of the chief executive and assist in preparing the budget. The act provides the chief executive with significant coordinating powers.

Further expanding the powers of the chief executive, Congress passed the Employment Act of 1946, which created the Council of Economic Advisors as a direct counselor to the president. The main aim of the council is to assist the president in forecasting and controlling fiscal policies. Under this act, the Joint Economic Committee was also established to provide Congress with additional means for examining the premises on which the annual budget is prepared.

Over the past four decades, many efforts have been made to improve the quality of the information used by the chief executive in making rational decisions. The introduction of the planning, programming, and budgeting system (PPBS) during the 1960s was the first major attempt at all levels of government to introduce analysis as an aid to decision making in the executive branch. This was followed in the 1970s by the introduction of the concept of management by objectives, ZBB, target-base budgeting, total quality management (TQM), the reinvention of government (late 1980s to 1990s), and the Government Performance Results Act of 1993. This performance management movement is being widely adopted in public and nonprofit organizations. Like PPBS, ZBB is aimed at assisting central management to better allocate scarce resources and control their use. An examination of the attributes and functions of the executive budgets of chief executives at the federal, state, and local levels (as shown in Table 9.5) reveals few divergences. Thus, it would be logical to conclude that

TABLE 9.5   Comparative Executive-Budget Functions and Responsibilities

Attributes/functions	Federal	State	Local	Nonprofit
Balanced-budget requirements	no	yes	yes	yes
Staff is required to provide information/intelligence for better budget decision-making	yes	mostly yes	mostly no	Mostly no
Budget is an effective coordinating instrument/extension of executive personality	yes	yes	yes	mostly yes
Executive is the most visible political official	yes	yes	yes	no
Executive has exclusive power to prepare budget	yes	yes	yes	mostly yes
Executive authority to exercise item vetoes over approved budget or appropriation, including:	no	yes	yes	no
– Allotment powers	yes	mostly yes	no	no
– Executive has problem with career bureaucrats	some	some	minimal	minimal
– Power over program execution	yes	yes	yes	yes
– Budget staff exercises strong management-efficiency role	no	yes	yes	no

the structure and operations of the executive budget at all levels of government are marked more by similarities than differences.

Although seldom discussed, the physical location of the budget office holds particular symbolic and substantive implications for the allocation and control of available resources. At the federal level, the OMB is located in the executive office building. In some states, the executive budget office is located in departments of administration directly responsible to the governor. The state constitution of Missouri places the budget office in its department of revenue, but relatively early in the state's history it was moved to the governor's office, where it remains to this day. Local governments have experimented with a number of budget office locations. In some cities, it is directly under the authority of the chief executive officer or in a department under the authority of a controller, a department of finance, or a division of a department of management. In all cases, however, the responsibility for control and decision making resides with the chief executive or, as in metropolitan Toronto, Canada, with an executive committee.

In the nonprofit sector, the executive budget is the norm, although it is not easy to make broad statements about this practice because of the variety of models found. Most often, the executive director of the agency is given executive powers similar to those found in governmental units. He or she exercises those powers under the scrutiny, whether close or minimal, of a finance committee. The interest, expertise, and activism of the committee members and the board determine the degree of vigilance. If an executive budget is the norm, executive influence over the budget process is pervasive. The chief executive's authority to recommend expenditures and revenues provides a powerful means for establishing the agenda and focusing attention on his or her preferred use for budget resources. Because of the dominance of the chief executive and his or her budget staff over budget matters, the chief executive exercises a monopoly over the information that is released to relevant constituents and various participants in the budget making process. The budget provides the primary tool with which to effect coordination and integration of agency or governmental activities. By means of the central administrative budget's establishment, planning, and management studies, the accounting control and personnel system become closely integrated.

Functions performed by the executive budget establishment include the following: (1) establishing policy direction guidelines and service levels; (2) overseeing the preparation of the budget; (3) reviewing, critiquing, adjusting, and approving expenditure reports; (4) developing revenue estimates; (5) conducting economic research studies and salary surveys; (6) presenting proposals before the legislative or review committees or boards (the latter in nonprofit agencies only); (7) overseeing the administration of the budget; and (8) designing and implementing financial performance reports.[28]

The first phase provides the chief executive with an opportunity, via the "call for estimates" and the transmittal letter, to put forth budget policy as specifically as possible. This will include at least the following: (1) a general budget outlook that reviews the economic, social, and other critical factors likely to impact on the agency or the governmental unit; (2) assumptions about revenue from general and other funds, indicating tax rates, and about projections, indicating budget targets; (3) projections of expenditures (especially those from the general fund), indicating "the likely increment and opportunities for program substitution and displacements";[29] (4) suggested changes and modifications in budget procedures; (5) contemplated changes in debt service policy and requirements; and (6) projected capital programs and special programs. The budget timetable and specific procedures of budget-making may differ significantly among units of governmental and nonprofit agencies. All these agencies perform essentially the same functions in developing the budget document.[30]

Hospital-Generalized Budget Process Steps

The following are the steps involved in making a hospital's budget:

1. The authorizing board of trustees sets the goals and objectives that will guide the institution during the coming period.

2. The hospital budget committee identifies budget guidelines, which are then approved by the hospital administration. Within this context, the preparation of a number of internal and external factors, such as the following, are considered relevant to planned activities: how economic factors such as inflation may affect the budget; statistical assumptions regarding patient days; changes in building requirements; the introduction of new services; the number of procedures that must be followed by the laboratory and major departments, such as radiology; outpatient visits; and proposed government legislation and regulations.

3. Budget packages are distributed to department heads or responsibility centers. They are also given technical assistance in preparing their individual budgets.

4. Departmental hearings are conducted. The budgets of responsibility centers are coordinated and reviewed, summarizing the hearings and promises agreed upon to assist controllers in future monitoring.

5. The budgets are approved and distributed to all department heads and responsibility centers.

The Executive Budget Cycle

Timetables for the completion of particular activities are especially important in public budgeting, because designated times are typically established by statute and thus are legally binding. In addition, actions to be completed can have significant implications for resource allocation. For example, economic forecasts and revenue estimates may determine the level of spending within a program, or determine whether the program can be undertaken at all. At the federal level, the executive budget cycle timetable is as shown in Table 9.6.

The Legislative Role

By identifying policy direction and preparing and formally presenting the budget to the legislature or authorizing body, the executive limits and determines the legislative fiscal policy agenda. The budget-making process is essentially the same at the legislative and executive levels of government and nonprofit organizations. Typically, the presentation of the budget contains a budget overview—namely, major economic and social assumptions and a summary of major issues. The budget document is presented in a clear and understandable manner: (1) Revenue estimates are broken down and identified by source. (2) Statements of proposed expenditures are detailed. The budget format is designed to set forth the purpose, cost, and expenditure source of each service. (3) Amounts requested by each department or responsibility center and recommended by the chief executive are identified. (4) Finally, narrative statements justifying supporting requests are included.

At the federal and state levels and to some extent in local governments, department heads are usually present during budget discussions to respond to legislative questions. However, department heads, especially those of local government units, may as a matter of strategy be asked to stay out of sight unless requested to attend. The apparent operating premise is "out of sight, out of mind."

The participation of citizen and interest groups in public hearings is an operating norm at all levels of government. Indeed, most states require local units to hold open hearings on the budget. However, while some local

TABLE 9.6 The Budget Cycle of the Federal Executive

Actions to be completed	Dates
Develop economic assumptions (by Council of Economic Advisors); review forecasts of international and domestic situations; issue policy guidelines regarding the preparation of materials for review. Determine initial-planning figures and cost projections for the coming year; compare total proposed-outlay estimates with revenue estimates; present fiscal policy, program issues and budget levels of the president.	March–May
Establish general guidelines and agency targets for annual budget; issue internal annual budget estimates. President (through OMB) provides agencies with policy assumptions and budget-planning target for each agency.	June
Assist agencies in developing detailed estimates.	July–September
OMB holds hearings to review agency budget requests. Economic assumptions and fiscal policies are reexamined in cooperation with the Council of Economic Advisors and Treasury Department. Assumptions are discussed with the president and recommendations to the president are made. Agencies are notified and recommendations are revised to reflect the president's decisions.	September–November
Again, review economic and fiscal outlook with the president in cooperation with the Council of Economic Advisors and the Treasury Department. Draft president's budget and transmit recommendations to Congress within 15 days after Congress reconvenes in January.	December–February
With the approved appropriations, the Treasury Department and General Accounting Office sign appropriation warrants and forward them to agencies.	August–September

governments encourage citizen participation in budget discussions via town hall–style meetings, many make little effort to build a well-designed system that works, despite the opportunities to build and promote better policies that such a system would offer. If due care is taken in designing and implementing a system of citizen participation, disruptions and delays in proceedings can be minimized.

Until recently, the legislatures at all levels of government were unable to influence and participate in budget-making and fiscal matters to the same extent as elected chief executives (especially in systems operating on the executive budget model). Because of minimal intelligence gathering and lack of expert staff, members of these bodies have been limited to routine review and oversight. Except in a few states such as California, there is no single head to coordinate and lead the legislative staff. Also, in only a few states (and in most local governments), there is no systematic coordination of revenue and spending bills. Typically, revenue and spending measures are parceled out to a number of different subcommittees. The vacuum created by the legislature's fragmented management of fiscal policies has given the chief executive a dominant role in fiscal policymaking. In most units of government, as much as 75 to 85 percent of all budget proposals are initiated by the chief executive or the executive branch, over which the chief executive exercises control.

At the national level, the Congressional Budget and Impoundment Control Act of 1974 attempted to address this unequal influence exercised by the president vis-à-vis Congress. Until the act's passage, uncertainty and virtual chaos characterized the congressional process. A major feature of the act was the creation of the Congressional Budget Office (CBO), which attempts to add greater rationality to the legislative policymaking process (see Table 9.7). Before this act, there was no coordinating committee in the House of Representatives or Senate that was capable of considering the president's budget as a whole. When the executive budget reached Congress, it was broken up and sent to a number of committees. Budgeting decisions were made without regard to their effects on the general economy: "No systematic procedure existed for resolving conflicts among authorizing, appropriation, and tax committees on the basis of conscious congressional decisions related to the national goals and priorities."[31] As can be seen in the congressional budget cycle in Table 9.7, the act created budget committees in both the House and Senate that are responsible for developing priorities.

The CBO is headed by a nonpartisan official who coordinates the congressional budget staff in its functions as a research arm and as an aid to Congress in evaluating the president's executive budget. Congress is thus provided with the means to examine the premises on which the president's budget is based and of making independent projections regarding deficits, employment, and the general state of the economy.

TABLE 9.7 The Congressional Budget Calendar (Based on the 1974 Budget Act)

Actions to be completed	Dates
CBO submits first-year projection of current spending.	October 1 or soon thereafter
President submits current-services budget, indicating projected spending for existing programs.	November 10
Joint Economic Committee provides budget committee with analysis of current-services budget.	December 31
President submits his budget.	15th day after Congress meets in January.
Budget Committees conduct hearings and commence work on first budget resolution.	Late January–March
All legislative committees submit estimates/reports to the budget committees.	March 15
CBO submits report to budget committees.	April 1
Budget committees report first concurrent resolution.	April 15
Congress completes action on first resolution, providing new budget authority and new spending authority. (Until the resolution is adopted, neither the House nor Senate may consider new budget or spending-authority bills, revenue changes, or changes of the debt limit.)	May 15
Congress completes action on first appropriation and concurrent resolution on the budget.	May 15
House Appropriations Committee completes action on all bills.	June 10
Congress completes action on all reconciliation matters.	June 15
Congress completes action on bills and resolutions providing for new budget authority and new spending authority.	7th day after Labor Day
Congress completes second concurrent resolution. Neither the House nor Senate may thereafter consider any bill, amendment, or conference report that increases budgeting authority amounts or decreases revenues beyond amounts agreed to in the second resolution.	September 15
Congress completes action on reconciliation bill or resolution. Adjournment of Congress takes place only after it completes action on second resolution and reconciliation measure.	September 15
Fiscal year begins.	October 1

The Budget Adoption

Three major activities typically characterize the adoption of budgets: *authorization*, *appropriation*, and *revenue decisions*. Ideally, these three activities should be effectively linked, but in practice this is not easily achieved owing to political constraints and lack of agreement about the best way to achieve linkage.

The first step toward making the budget proposals a concrete reality is the *authorization* activity. Authorization defines the substantive power and responsibilities of all its actions when creating an agency or program. Sometimes an act of authorization may specify the limits and scope of its actions—such as, for example, the number of personnel an agency may employ, the number of outreach centers that may be built, or the length of trucks that may be driven on federal highways.

Appropriation is a critical facet of budget-making that grants the legal authority to obligate and make payments from general or specific sources of funds. Because the budget authority to spend money must normally be known *before* commitment, the authorization activity typically precedes appropriation.

Revenue decisions are the function that all governments and not-for-profit agencies must undertake (see chapter 5) if they want to implement programmatic objectives. The required resources must be raised by levying taxes, charging fees, or borrowing. Whatever the sources of the funds, they must be clearly identified and be consistent with community expectations.

Concluding Observations

This chapter provided an overview of the functions, structures, and purposes of modern budgeting. Budgets are multipurpose in that they can be used to achieve accountability/control, and political, social, planning, and economic ends. The interplay among the executive, legislative, and relevant interest groups in the budget process was examined. Throughout the chapter, emphasis was placed on the interplay of theory and practice.

Notes

1.   Jerome B. McKinney and Lawrence C. Howard, *Public Administration: Balancing Power and Accountability* (Oak Park, IL: Moore Publishing 1979), p. 319.

2.   Mark Mills and George Starr, eds., *Readings in Public Finance and Taxation* (New York: Macmillan, 1932), p. 763.

3.   Michael J. Boskin and Aaron Wildavsky, eds., *The Federal Budget: Economics and Politics* (New Brunswick, NJ: Transaction Books, 1982), p. 22.

4.   Jerome B. McKinney, *Understanding ZBB: Promise and Reality* (Chicago: Public Policy Press, 1979), p. 2.

5. Allen Schick, "Sustainable Budget Policy: Concept and Approaches," *OECD Journal of Budgeting 3*, no. 1 (2005): 108–110, 120–125; see also William D. Eggers and John O'Leary, "Sustainable Government Is Attainable Government," http://www.governing.com/columns/mgmt-insights/sustainable-government-attainable-government.html.

6. Charles L. Harper, Curtis P. McLaughlin, and John W. Bartley, *Financial Systems for Community Health Organizations* (Belmont, CA: Life Learning Publications, 1981), p. 122.

7. Robert N. Anthony and Regina Herzlinger, *Management Control in Non-Profit Agencies*, rev. ed. (Homewood, IL: Richard D. Urwin, 1980), p. 328.

8. Ibid.

9. In many public and nonprofit agencies, goals are not articulated but rather are implied based on the allocation of the budgeting resources.

10. Frank Benest, *Marketing Your Budget* (Washington, DC: JCMA, 1997), p. 56.

11. Ibid., p. 18.

12. Ibid., p. 32.

13. Harper, McLaughlin, and Bartley, *Financial Systems for Community Health Organizations*, p. 130.

14. S. Duncombe et al., "Factors Influencing the Politics and Process of County Government Budgeting," *State and Local Government Review* vol. 24 no. 1 (1992): 19.

15. See Gregory Michel, *Organization and Design of an Effective Budget Organization* (Chicago: Government Finance Officers Association, 2002), p. 11.

16. Robert L. Bland and Irene S. Rubin, *Budgeting: A Guide for Local Governments* (Washington, DC: International City Management Association, 1997), p. 65.

17. McKinney and Howard, *Public Administration*, p. 322.

18. Ibid.

19. Philip Rosenberg and C. Wayne Stalling, *An Operating Handbook for Small Cities and Other Government Units* (Chicago: Municipal Finance Officers Association, 1978), p. 40.

20. Lennox L. Moak and Kathryn W. Killian, *A Manual of Techniques for the Preparation, Consideration, Adoption, and Administration of Operating Budgets* (Chicago: Municipal Finance Officers Association, 1963), p. 131.

21. Keith A. Neuber et al., *Needs Assessment: A Model for Community Planning* (Beverly Hills, CA: Sage Publications, 1975), p. 10.

22. Barry M. Mundt, Raymond T. Olsen, and Harold I. Steinberg, *Managing Public Resources* (Stamford, CT: Peat Marwick International, 1982), pp. 24–25.

23. United Way, *A "PPBS" Approach to Budgeting Human Service Programs for United Ways* (Alexandria, VA: United Way of America, 1974), p. 18.

24. James D. Savage, "California's Structural Deficit Crisis." *Public Budgeting and Finance 12*, no. 2 (summer 1992): 88–89.

25. Ibid., pp. 87–89.

26. See California 2012 ballot propositions, http://ballotpedia.org/California_2012_ballot_propositions.

27. Ibid.

28. Moak and Killian, *A Manual of Techniques for the Preparation, Consideration, Adoption, and Administration of Operating Budgets*, p. 29.

29. Edward A. Lehan, *Simplified Governmental Budgeting* (Chicago: Municipal Finance Officers Association, 1981), p. 62; see also State of Massachusetts, *Approaches to*

Budget Preparation and Presentation (Boston: Massachusetts Division of Community Services, 1980), p. 23.

30.   Hospitals may often break down their budgets differently, developing revenue, expense, operating, and cash budgets. More detail about this is provided in chapter 11.

31.   Committee on Economic Development (CED), *The New Congressional Budget Process and the Economy* (New York: CED, 1975), p. 2.

10

Expenditure Forecasting

Because of the many types of expenditures that must be projected in both the public and private sectors, there is no single, all-encompassing approach to their forecast. No exotic mathematical model or analysis can be used to project expenditures with a high degree of accuracy. There is considerable evidence to support the view that simple approaches are as effective as the more sophisticated methods.[1] This chapter examines a number of approaches that are employed in forecasting expenditures. First, traditional approaches used in budget development are examined, after which expenditure components, standard costs, the least squares method, multiple regression analysis, and controllable and uncontrollable costs are considered.

Projecting the Cost of Current Services

Projecting the cost of existing activities is based on factors typically outside the agency's control, such as population changes; inflation rates (which affect items such as salaries, wages, benefits, materials, supplies, and contractual services) government mandates; existing staffing levels; discretionary and non-discretionary expenditures emanating from policy commitments such as the funding of pension benefits and subsidies; equipment replacement and repair schedules; capital costs, meaning expenses associated with construction, operation, and maintenance; debt amortization; and volatile cost centers subject to unpredictable cost changes, such as municipal convention centers, which are typically affected by the cycle of the economy. The projections are guided by assumptions and constraints set down by top management (the president, mayor, or manager in the public sector; the board of governors or trustees in the nonprofit sector).

The cost projection of current services serves several useful purposes. It provides continuity between present and future costs and promotes the development of a dependable database from which projections in each responsibility center can easily be made. Finally, it provides a dependable basis on which to evaluate whether future services should be improved, expanded, or reduced.

Approaches to Budget Development: General Guidelines

Moak and Killian have suggested several orientations that may be used as general guidelines in budget development.[2] These methods may be used singly or in combination.

Open-ended Budgets

Managers who are given no explicit guidelines regarding budget amounts are allowed to submit whatever amounts they consider necessary to run the optimum program for the agency. This method can provide an optimal funding baseline but is increasingly unrealistic, as fiscal constraints have become intensified in recent years at all levels of government.

Fixed-Ceiling Budgets

Unlike the open-ended budget, the fixed-ceiling budget (akin to the target-base budget that is discussed further in chapter 14) is constrained by a dollar amount that is specifically stated for each department prior to the preparation of the budget. Thus, the budget may fall below the fixed ceiling but may not exceed it. Often this ceiling is based on prior years' actual expenditures and incentivizes managers to prioritize expenditures.

Work Measurement and Unit Costing

This approach requires that a measuring criterion be established to determine the number of products or service units to be generated. Based on the number desired, the cost per unit can be determined and the budget projected.

Increase versus Decrease Analysis

This method is closely related to the popular incremental approach to budgeting. Cost projections are made by identifying the costs to be increased or decreased in comparison with the previous year's costs. The items so determined are analyzed and projected.

Priority Listings

This approach, especially the ranking phase, is akin to the zero-base budgeting (ZBB) approach (discussed in chapter 15), and requests that projects be ranked in order of priority.

Shared Management Method

This approach encourages top and bottom managers in the middle and lower levels to share information and perceptions, collaborate, about the factors that are likely to affect expenditure projections.[3] The shared approach allows top management to contribute its overall strategic perception of the organization, whereas middle- and lower-level managers in, for example, a health-care institution, contribute insight acquired through their greater sensitivity toward physicians' needs, desires, and priorities relating to such activities as laboratory tests, changes in radiological procedures, and the physical condition of facilities. Additionally, middle- and lower-level managers will typically have knowledge about top management's short- and long-range plans and strategies, especially if the management style in the organization encourages some degree of their involvement in the shared decision making system. Shared decision making requires that both top and operating (middle) managers study and exchange their knowledge of the following key resources:

- Historical data and trends relating to inpatient and outpatient days
- Departmental goals and strategies
- Governmental and third-party decisions; for example, changes in federal law that alter Medicare reimbursement amounts, affecting the number of allowable inpatient days and types of patients serviced
- Outside competition; for example, the establishment of neighboring health care facilities (hospitals, health maintenance organizations, and clinics)
- Other known facts or rumors[4]

Item-by-Item Control

Like the priority-setting method, this approach contains come of the attributes of ZBB, particularly as it relates to the emphasis on questioning and justifying the necessity and desirability of each item. However, the item-by-item control method is more in line with the line item/object budget focus that is prevalent in most governmental budgets.

Alternative Proposals

Attributes of the ZBB system are very evident in this approach. Emphasis is placed on the basic or base budget (indicative of the ZBB minimum-level practice, as discussed in chapter 15) and on the analysis of the consequences of pursuing each alternative (the ZBB consequences of not undertaking a level of service).

Historical Analysis

Requests for nonpersonal service items are evaluated in terms of past experience and current trends.

Factorial Estimating

Making budget projections by this method involves virtually no discretion or judgment. Program units are clearly defined and tables of organization and equipment are made up, providing a basis from which future requirements can be estimated.

Marginal Productivity Analysis

This approach emphasizes the optimal use of scarce resources. The application of this method shows that successive resource increments yield increasing benefits only up to a point. Beyond this point, each increment produces successively smaller (marginal) benefits or satisfactions, demonstrating that unlimited income is an inadequate reason for allowing unlimited expenditure on a large number of programs. The greatest total utility or satisfaction is realized when the application of resources is limited to a smaller number of uses (programs). Allocation of resources to alternative uses should be continued until the last additional increment of expenditure yields the same amount of additional satisfaction; marginal benefit derived equals the marginal cost. The *principle of marginal rule* yields the following conclusions: (1) Given available resources, the magnitude or scale of an activity should be expanded as long as its net marginal yield is positive, and up to the point where its net marginal yield is zero; and (2) when resource constraint does not permit an activity to be expanded to the zero yield point, the activity should be expanded to the point at which its marginal yield is equal to the marginal yield of the alternative.

An application of the marginal rule principle may be demonstrated in the case of police assignments. Assume that a study of the records of two police department districts reveals the data shown in Tables 10.1 and 10.2. Assume additionally that a citation represents a reasonable output benefit (surrogate). A total of nine officers are to be assigned to districts X and Y. Applying the marginal rule principle, district X would receive four officers; district Y, five officers. Note that the five officers of district Y would yield a marginal benefit of 8, whereas district X's would yield a marginal benefit of 6. Thus we assign five officers to district Y and four to district X, basing our decision on the marginal rule principle.

Applying Cost–Benefit Criteria

This approach, though not widely used, has potential, because in the typical social service agency it is very difficult to identify any single factor that may be used as the criterion for making program selections. Since selection decisions must be made, a basis for making them while maintaining a degree of uniformity among decision makers is therefore required.

The establishment of decision rules or selection criteria can be most helpful. Before the selection basis can be determined, the costs and benefits relevant to the programs must be estimated. An identification of the costs and benefits permits the display of data relating to each program, as shown in Table 10.3, which depicts program alternatives, estimated costs, estimated benefits, the benefit–cost ratio, the decision rationale, and selection constraints for each decision. In light of the constraints, alternative A is eliminated because it does not meet the minimum benefit constraint, and alternative C is accepted because it meets all the constraint factors.

The development and application of a particular criterion must depend on each individual situation, but after a decision–rule system has been established as shown in Table 10.3, it provides a useful method that permits a degree of decentralized budget making and decisions while maintaining a measure of central control.

TABLE 10.1 Marginal Cost Analysis: Police District "X"

Number of officers assigned	Total citations	Average citations	Marginal citations
0	0	–	–
1	15	15	15
2	40	20	25
3	54	18	14
4	60	15	6
5	60	12	0
6	54	12	-6
7	49	9	-5

Source: Adapted from James Snyder, *Fiscal Management and Planning in Local Government* (Lexington, MA: Lexington Books, 1977), p. 245.

TABLE 10.2 Marginal Cost Analysis: Police District "Y"

Number of officers assigned	Total citations	Average citations	Marginal citations
0	0	–	–
1	12	12	12
2	26	13	14
3	39	13	13
4	48	12	9
5	56	11.2	8
6	60	10	2

Source: Adapted from James Snyder, *Fiscal Management and Planning in Local Government* (Lexington, MA: Lexington Books, 1977), p. 245.

Expenditure: Analysis of Major Components

Personnel Services

These are the most important costs in public and not-for-profit organizations, amounting to more than 90 percent in some cases. Close consideration and analysis must therefore be given to this input. Estimates of personnel services typically are based on one or more of the following: (1) experience in prior years; (2) workload trends; (3) staffing patterns, as shown on the current organizational chart; and (4) "guesstimates."[5]

Additional factors to be considered in estimating the cost of personnel services include (1) departmental staffing tables (an assessment of the tasks, functions, and duties of the personnel in each unit or responsibility center), (2) classification plans (defining position duties with the aim of reclassifying or allocating the duties to existing or new positions in the classification plan in cooperation with the central personnel unit and with the appropriate operating line official), (3) estimates of salary savings, (4) use of overtime and premium time, (5) management studies (conducted to coincide with the budget hearings to provide information that will assist in evaluating personnel requests), (6) sick leave and annual leave, (7) quality of the workforce, and (8) effects of new capital facilities.[6]

Although staffing tables are confined to larger organizations, workload data are quite useful in smaller organizations because of the close relationship between the workload and personnel needed for a particular job. Other factors that affect workload trends are (1) new policies or changes in existing ones, (2) commitments to program changes, (3) workload consolidation, and (4) changes in systems or procedures. Simple spreadsheet applications should be adequate for smaller governmental entities when developing staffing tables for input and expenditure analysis.

Salary Savings

For several reasons, the budgeted and actual salary figures seldom coincide. Examples of reasons for this are vacations, vacant positions, turnover, and time lags in hiring for approved positions.

This lack of coincidence has led to the common practice of adjusting the salary amounts downward at periodic intervals. Historical data, the experience of prior years, is the major determining factor in calculating the current percentage of gross and unused personnel services, adjusted for any known changes.

Overtime and Premium Time

A hallmark of effective management is the efficient use of human resource components: "Few operations move in such measured cadence that management

TABLE 10.3   Programs: Benefit–Cost Estimates

Alternative	Estimated Cost (input)	Estimated Benefits (output)	Benefit–cost ratio	Decision rationale
A	$100,000	$150,000	1.50	Eliminated due to minimumbenefit constraints
B	$250,000	$225,000	0.90	Does not meet minimum efficiency constraints
C	$295,000	$475,000	1.61	Meets benefit and efficiency constraints
D	$295,000	$310,000	1.05	Does not meet efficiency constraints
E	$125,000	$190,000	1.52	Meets minimum-cost constraint and benefit constraints
F	$340,000	$510,000	1.50	Exceeds maximum cost
G	$125,000	$175,000	1.40	Does not meet benefit or efficiency
H	$299,000	$511,000	1.70	Provides maximum benefit and meets efficiency constraints
I	$280,000	$490,000	1.75	Provides maximum efficiency and meets other constraints

Constraints: Maximum budget = $300,000; minimum benefit must be at least as great as program E; minimum efficiency must be greater than program A.

Source: Adapted from James Snyder, *Fiscal Management and Planning in Local Government* (Lexington, MA: Lexington Books, 1977), p. 245.

can avoid some nonproductive time or can avoid the necessity for overtime to help meet peaks in workload."[7] Many view overtime as an evil to be avoided. However, it has long been associated with well-managed operations, providing an effective solution during times of unforeseen high service demands. The problem is determining how to keep it in proper proportion and under control.

Contractual Services

The purchase, or outsourcing, of personnel services has become increasingly important in public and not-for-profit agencies. Some of the reasons why services are purchased are summarized by the following objectives: (1) minimizing costs, (2) obtaining task specialization/expertise, (3) controlling the growth of permanent staff, and (4) lessening the pressures brought on by seasonal and unplanned increases in workloads. Overreliance on contractual services for some operations can put an organization at a disadvantage, as hiring additional staff would be the more cost effective solution.

Materials, Supplies, and Equipment

Efficient management of an agency's materials, supplies, and equipment requires that acquisition, maintenance, and control systems be instituted that facilitate achievement of the organization's purpose. Several key factors should be considered in assessing an agency's materials and supply needs: (1) existing inventory and agency policies in relation to current conditions, (2) price levels, and (3) changing patterns in the use of materials and material requirements in view of changing rules and methods aimed at producing the best results. Budgeting for equipment from operating funds is done primarily for equipment replacement; however, some portion of the annual equipment budget for many departments represents a net increase in equipment inventory. These two aspects should be considered separately at all stages of the budget process. Of course, the line of demarcation becomes obscure when the replacement item is a substantial improvement over the item being replaced.[8]

The following should be established when the type, quantity, and quality of equipment necessary to achieve an agency's objectives need to be determined: equipment replacement schedules, along with a dependable inventory system that includes the following information: (a) description and quantity of equipment on hand, (b) purchase data, (c) location of equipment, (d) condition in terms of number of operating hours and maintenance costs, (e) life expectancy, and (f) classification and code number.

Finally, the most efficient equipment replacement practices can be best achieved by clear policy development, which should consider the definition of the work to be performed (e.g., planned maintenance schedules), permanent inventory and service records, and inspection procedures to ensure and validate that an item definitely needs to be replaced.

Expenditure Forecasting Using Standard Costs

It is generally agreed that the critical category in expenditure forecasting is personnel service costs, because this category is the largest and most frequently affected by changes in such items as salary, fringe benefits, and authorized versus actual levels of staffing.[9] Because each personnel position is assigned an identification number, all cost data can be used to control personnel service costs, determine seniority pay, and permit the development of a longevity profile. The latter can be used to "tailor seniority pay as an incentive to minimize turnover to reduce salary costs by granting increases to groups that are projected to turn over frequently."[10]

Positions can be used as the centerpiece for accountability information on all related personnel costs, providing a high degree of versatility, and the data can then be organized to serve a number of objectives. Unlike the traditional line item categories (travel, material, and personnel costs), which conceal information about specific kinds of costs that are important to management decision making, the position technique permits identification of any costs that are of interest. Examples of such costs are costs that vary directly in proportion to the volume of products or services produced, such as tons of concrete needed to build a street; semivariable costs; costs that vary, but not directly, in proportion to the volume or level of activity, such as the cost of maintaining equipment that requires varying amounts of periodic upkeep in quantities disproportionate to the volume or number of service units produced by the equipment; and fixed costs, which stay the same regardless of the volume or activity level, such as depreciation and rent expenditures. After cost has been identified and separated out, a standard cost system (one that determines the most desirable cost of completing an activity, given normal conditions) can be developed, and from this system a budget projection can be made.

Standard costs projection may be developed as shown in Table 10.4. Assume that a police department wishes to create three or more new beats. One police vehicle is required for every three officers or any portion thereof, at a cost of $21,000 plus $4,000 a year for maintenance. Additionally, the instruction fee per officer is $29,610. Up to forty new officers can be trained for the fixed cost of $72,000. A beat consists of twenty-four hours a day, seven days a week, and six officers are required for each beat. The component costs projection is shown in Table 10.4.

TABLE 10.4   Calculating Variable Costs

Personal service:		
Salary	$24,000	
Cost of Living	4,400	
Hospitalization	3,600	
Pension Contribution	4,600	36,600
Other expenses:		
Supplies	800	
Uniforms	700	
Physical examination	500	
Administration	600	2,600
Total		$39,200

(Continued)

TABLE 10.4   (*Continued*)

Type of cost	Units			Standard cost per unit		
Variable	6 Officers	x	29,610	=	$177,660	
Semivariable	2 Cruisers	x	25,000	=	50,000	
Fixed	Classroom instruction		72,000	=	72,000	
			Total		$299,660	
Three beats required:						
Variable	12 Officers	x	29,610	=	$355,320	
Semivariable	4 Cruisers	x	25,000	=	100,000	
Fixed	Classroom instruction		72,000	=	72,000	
			Total		$527,320	

The standard costs approach offers much potential and can be used to effect service reduction or expansion. If care is taken in projecting individual items, it provides reliable projections with greater ease than other methods. "Additionally, if elements of budget preparation are decentralized, this approach allows the central budget staff to quickly check the expense estimates developed by the operating units."[11] Perhaps the greatest asset of this standard approach is that it enables management to change plans quickly in response to altered situations that often occur, especially in local government.[12] The organization can adapt to service output changes and set aside necessary encumbrances to pay for the unplanned expenditures.

Calculating the Standard Costs Requirement for a Laundry

The objective of creating any standard is to make it useful to those for whom it is intended. Consequently, it is important that the standard be accepted by the users. The participation of the potential users in the design and development of a standard is, therefore, a crucial factor that should not be ignored. By participating in the design and development process, the future users are unconsciously selling themselves on the acceptability of the standard.

In determining staffing requirements, managers must contend with both full- and part-time employees. Additionally, employees never work at 100 percent capacity. Part- and full-time employees can be converted into *full-time-equivalent* (FTE) *employees* (one FTE equals 2,080 work-hours per year). However, because employees cannot be divided, the employee staffing patterns must be determined in a step variable or production range, as shown in Figure 10.1. The calculation of the normal annual hours of the step variable range, in an example of a laundry worker who averages 90,000 pounds of laundry per year, is as follows:[13]

a.	Paid hours per week	40
b.	Weeks per year	52
c.	Annual paid hours (a × b)	2,080
d.	Less benefit hours:	
	10 holidays × 8 hours	80
	20 vacation days × 8 hours	160
	7 sick days × 8 hours	56
	Total benefit hours	296
e.	Normal annual work-hours	1,784

The hourly production standard for the average employee can be determined in the following manner:

$$\frac{\textit{Total annual units per employee}}{\textit{Total annual normal work-hours per employee}} = \textit{standard per work-hour}$$

$$= \frac{90{,}000 \;\; \text{pounds laundry per year}}{1{,}784 \;\; \text{normal annual work-hours per year}}$$

$$= 50.45 \;\; \text{pounds per hour}$$

The production standard calculation may be summarized as follows:

TABLE 10.5

Description	Yearly standards	Weekly standards
Pounds of laundry	90,000	1,731
Total weeks	52	1
Actual hours worked	1,784	34.31
Benefits allowed	296	5.69
Paid hours	2,080	40.00

Applying the data indicated above, we can convert paid hours into FTEs as shown in Table 10.6. Once standard rates are determined, the calculation of the budget becomes a simple matter as shown in Table 10.7.

Least Squares Method (Simple Regression)

This is the most commonly used mathematical method for forecasting the expenditure level or volume. The method is based on the assumption that if a straight line is fitted to time series data or a graph, it produces a trend line that can be used to project future years' volume. Hamburg has indicated that the least squares method permits a line to be drawn through a series of plotted points in such a way that the sum of the squares of the deviations from the observed actual points above and below the trend line is at a minimum.[14] Thus, when the straight line is fitted to a set of data, the least squares method provides the "best fit," because the squared deviation is less than it would be for any other possible straight line (see Table 10.8). Figure 10.2 uses a solid line to show the actual tons of garbage collected, and an unbroken straight line to show the least squares trend. Examination of the graph reveals that the further the forecast extends beyond the middle year, the less accurate the trend becomes. Figure 10.2 and Table 10.8 illustrate the least squares fit to a progressive or advancing trend.

The least squares method is based on historical data and simply projects the trend line according to the available information. Attention is not given to other factors or variables, such as holidays, weather conditions, and vacations. Weaknesses such as these must be compensated for in each individual situation by the manager's experience and judgment. The annual forecasts must be broken down to reflect monthly variations and seasonal trends as needed by each organization.

TABLE 10.6   Weekly Laundry-Staffing Workload

Pounds of laundry processed	Actual work requirements	Paid hours requirements	FTE requirements
1,731	34.31	40	1
3,462	68.62	80	2
5,193	102.93	120	3
6,924	137.24	160	4
8,655	171.55	200	5
10,386	205.86	240	6
12,117	240.17	280	7
13,848	274.48	320	8
15,579	308.79	360	9

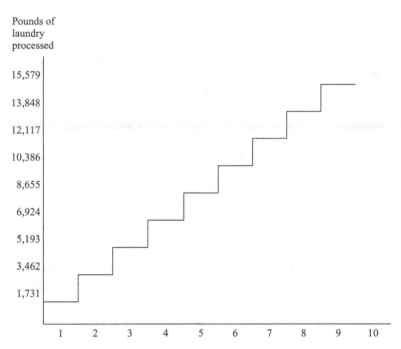

FIGURE 10.1 Weekly staffing: laundry department.

TABLE 10.7 Projecting a Dietary Budget Using Patient Days and Standard Rates, Bright Memorial Hospital

Cost component	Standardized rates	Computation	Budget*
Inpatient days	NA	NA	$ 95,000
Patient meals served	3.25 patient meals served per patient day	Patient days × standard = meals served 95,000 × 3.25	$ 308,750
Person-hours paid	1.65 patient meals served per person-hour paid	Patient meals served/ standard = person-hours paid 308,750/$1.65	$ 187,121
Salary expense	$3.15 average hourly rate	Person-hours paid × standard = salary expense 187,121 × $3.15	$ 589,431
Food expense	$1.15 per patient meal served	Patient meals served × standard paid expense 308,750 × $1.15	$ 355,063

(Continued)

TABLE 10.7   *(Continued)*

Cost component	Standardized rates	Computation	Budget*
Other nonsalary expense	$0.30 per patient meal served	Patient meals served × standard = other nonsalary expenses 308,750 × $0.30	$ 92,625
Total expense	$3.35 per patient	Patient meals served × standard = total expenses 308,750 × $3.35	$ 1,034,313

Notes: *Numbers are rounded to the nearest dollar; NA equals "not applicable."

Multiple Regression Analysis

Many of the problems associated with the least squares method (most of which are caused by the use of only one variable and the omission of other factors from analysis) may be overcome by the more sophisticated method of multiple regression analysis. Many variables that are likely to affect future volume can be included in this method. A projection of tons of garbage, for example, might include time series data such as the number of garbage trucks, the condition and age of each truck, the number and efficiency of garbage collectors, the weather conditions during collections, the population density served, and the economic and educational background of the population served.

The multiple regression analysis method holds much potential for sophisticated analysis, but a thorough examination of it is beyond the scope of this book. Moreover, it cannot be overstressed that the objective of forecasting is not sophistication, but rather the ability to make accurate projections based on costs, benefits, political factors, and other constraints. Managers should be focused on substance rather than form when forecasting.

Controllable and Noncontrollable Costs

For both program management and budget forecasting there must be a clear understanding of the specific costs that can be controlled and the specific times for controlling them. A *controllable cost* is one that can be restrained or changed by a responsibility center head. Ultimately, all costs are controllable in a relative sense at some level of the organization where the specific authority to do so resides. Because we cannot directly affect uncontrollable costs, the discussion will focus only on the controllable components.

Controllable and uncontrollable costs provide varying degrees of restraints and freedom of choices. Uncontrollable costs typically define what the organization must do or cannot do.[15] These restraints and degrees of freedom emanate from statutes, regulations, federal, state, and local laws, funders' requirements, union contracts, and professional ethics. Usually, controllable

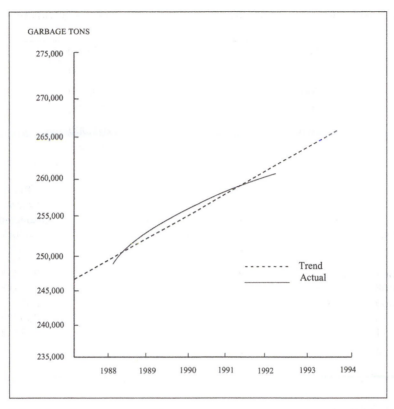

FIGURE 10.2   Fitting a trend line to a progressive trend using the least-squares method.

costs provide the greater leeway to exercise discretionary decision making. Among the factors that constrain controllable cost decisions are the following:

- Agency goals and policies
- Program objectives
- Accountability and evaluation requirements
- Sound fiscal procedures
- Local situations: similar agencies and competition
- Professional practices[16]

Controllable costs also offer opportunities to ameliorate restrictive factors. Discretionary decisions may be used to enhance program objectives and improve efficiency, working conditions, and staff and community relations. Before cost projections are made, it may be helpful to identify all line item costs in terms of three categories: those that are fully controllable, those that are partially controllable, and those that are fully uncontrollable. After these identifications have been made, a strategy for influencing costs may be devised.

TABLE 10.8 Projection: Garbage Expenditure, Progressive or Advancing Trend

Year	Tons of garbage
2007	250,000
2008	255,000
2009	258,000
2010	261,000
2011	263,000

Year	Actual tons of garbage	Time deviation of each year from middle year	Square of deviation		Trend ordinates (expected Y value)
X	Y	X	X^2	XY	Y
2007	250,000	−2	4	−500,000	251,000
2008	255,000	−1	1	−255,000	254,000
2009	258,000	0	0	-0-	257,400
2010	261,000	+1	1	261,000	260,000
2011	263,000	+2	4	526,000	263,000
Total	1,287,000	0	10	32,000	
Average	257,000				

Sum of XY divided by sum of X^2:

Let XY = + 32,000

X = 10

$$= \frac{32,000}{10} = 3,200 \text{ annual increment}$$

The midpoint year, 2009, equals Q, with the average of 257,400 and annual increments of 3,200. Thus, to determine the trend ordinates, use the following method.

Year					
2007	257,400	+	(3,200 × −2)	=	251,000
2008	257,400	+	(3,200 × −1)	=	254,200
2009	257,400	+	(-0-)	=	257,400
2010	257,400	+	(3,200 × 1)	=	260,600
2011	257,400	+	(3,200 × +2)	=	263,800
2012	257,400	+	(3,200 × +3)	=	267,000
2013	257,400	+	(3,200 × +4)	=	270,200

Indexing for Inflation

A problem that is often associated with historical data is the unadjusted effect of inflation. If the data are expected to be the most accurate and useful, data need to be adjusted or indexed to neutralize the distortion or impact of inflation. Managers must be cognizant that a dollar today is worth more than a dollar tomorrow: The time value of money cannot be overlooked. The Consumer Price Index (CPI) reports price changes monthly.[17] The CPI measures the change in a basket of commonly used consumer products. Labor unions employ it in negotiations, and many organizations use it to make cost of living adjustments. In the health care industry, the use of indices is regularly employed. Most hospitals receive a portion of their revenues from Medicare patients for inpatient care, based on diagnosis-related groups (DRGs). According to a given hospital market basket annual index, DRG rates are adjusted.

Since we constantly engage in making cost projections, the use of historical costs will not provide a base on which to make sound decisions about cost predictions and cost savings. You need first to factor in the adjustment that most closely resembles the sector or industry that your organization approximates and most closely reflects the product being estimated. For example, if you are in the medical industry, you will find the following CPI breakdown: medical—prescription drugs and nonprescription drugs and medical supplies; medical care services—professional services made up of physicians, dentists, and other professional services; and other medical services such as hospital and other medical care and hospital rooms and charges.

Inflation Adjustment Calculations

In the city of Bright, the kilowatt rates for electricity during the past six years and the rate approval for the upcoming year are as follow:

TABLE 10.9   City of Bright–Kilowatt Rates Per Hour

Year as of December 31	Rate per kilowatt hour
1	.0862
2	.0957
3	.0968
4	.0979
5	.0986
6	.1342
7	.1561

To create an index that allows us to convert the electricity rate for the seventh year in terms of the first year, each year must be calculated by using the following formula:

$$Index = \frac{Base\text{-}year\ (year\ 7)\ rate}{Historical\text{-}year\ rate}$$

Using this formula, we can convert the year 1 rate to year 7 dollars by dividing the year 7 rate of .1561 by the year 1 rate of .0862, thus generating an index of 1.8190. We must now multiply this rate by the year 1 costs of $165,121 to give year 1 adjusted costs of $299,018:

$$Index\ (year\ 1) = \frac{.1561}{.0862} = 1.8190$$

$$
\begin{aligned}
Adjusted\ year\ 1\ cost &= index \times year\ 1\ original\ cost\\
&= 1.8190 \times \$165,121\\
&= \$299,018
\end{aligned}
$$

The results indicate that the electricity that cost $165,121 in year 1 will cost $299,018 in year 7, after adjustment is made for the change in price levels or inflation. If we repeat the process for price level changes for the other years, the results are as indicated in Table 10.9.

Of particular note is that the calculations are based on year 7, reflecting the effect of inflation during the next year. Because the CPI will not be known until the end of the next year, the fixed and variable costs projected for year 7 would be in year 6 dollars. This would require that the year 7 budget be adjusted for the expected rise in inflation. When costs are declining because of

TABLE 10.10   Electricity-Rate Index

Year	Historical cost ($)	Rate per kilowatt hour ($)	Index base = year 7	Adjusted cost ($)
1	165,121	.0862	1.8190	300,355
2	175,210	.0957	1.6311	285,785
3	178,910	.0968	1.6126	288,510
4	203,218	.0979	1.5945	324,031
5	226,597	.0986	1.4347	325,099
6	273,100	.1342	1.1639	317,861
7		.1561	1.0000	

volume (for example, patient stays in hospitals have been decreasing owing the DRGs' application by health insurers) but inflation keeps costs going upward, the organization needs to segregate the impact of inflation to permit the cost–volume relationships to be clearly understood and controlled.

The Implicit Price Deflator (IPD)[18] that is compiled by the U.S. Department of Commerce's Bureau of Economic Analysis is another index that is better suited to local government. The IPD contains the goods and services that state and local governments typically purchase. It is published throughout the year in the U.S. Department of Commerce's *Survey of Current Business*. The IPD may be calculated by identifying the base-year rate or the current-year rate:

$$Index = \frac{Base\text{-}year\ rate}{Historical\text{-}\ or\ current\text{-}\ year\ rate}$$

For example, we may convert the 2009 IPD of 107.05 to the 2007 IPD of 102.06 by assuming that the City of Bright Recreation Department has total expenditures of $1,496,093 in 2009:

$$Index = \frac{102.06 = (2007\ \text{base year})}{107.05\ (2009\ \text{current year})} = .9534$$

Adjusted year 2009 $= .9534 \times \$1,496,093$
Converted to 2007
constant dolla $= \$1,426,395.$

Concluding Observations

There is no one best way to project the expenditures of public and other not-for-profit organizations. To date, the sophisticated quantitative methods that have been devised to project expenditures have not been notably more successful than the manual, incremental, and piecemeal approaches still in wide use. A major reason for this concerns political realities to which budget decision makers must give due cognizance. If politics could be excluded from the expenditure equation, the calculation for each service unit would be a simple matter: *Service unit output measure times unit variable costs plus service fixed costs equals forecasted dollar amounts.* Finally, in public and other not-for-profit agencies, the understanding of controllable costs is an important input in making cost projections.

Notes

1. Charles Harper, Curtis P. McLaughlin, and John W. Bartley, *Financial Systems for Community Health Organizations* (Belmont, CA: Life Learning Publications, 1981), p. 131.

2. Lennox L. Moak and Kathryn W. Killian, *A Manual of Techniques for the Preparation, Consideration, Adoption, and Administration of Operating Budgets* (Chicago: Municipal Finance Officers Association, 1963), pp. 128–129.

3. Allen G. Herkimer Jr., *Understanding Hospital Management* (Germantown, MD: Aspen Systems Corporation, 1978), p. 112.

4. Frank Maple, *Shared Decision Making* (Beverly Hills, CA: Sage Publications, 1982), ch. 4.

5. Moak and Killian, *A Manual of Techniques for the Preparation, Consideration, Adoption, and Administration of Operating Budgets*, p. 134.

6. Ibid.

7. Ibid., p. 135.

8. Ibid., p. 142.

9. Robert M. Cramer, "Local Government Expenditure Forecasting." *Governmental Finance*, 7, no. 4 (November 1978): 4.

10. Ibid.

11. Ibid., p. 7.

12. Ibid.

13. Herkimer, *Understanding Hospital Management*, p. 100.

14. Morris Hamburg, *Statistical Analysis for Decision Making*, 2nd ed. (New York: Harcourt Brace Jovanovich, 1977), p. 368.

15. Robert D. Vinter and Rhea K. Kish, *Budgeting for Not-for-Profit Organizations* (New York: Free Press, 1984), p. 173.

16. Ibid., p. 175.

17. For a useful discussion, see David N. Ammons, *Tools for Decision Making: A Practical Guide for Local Government* (Washington, DC: CQ Press, 2002), ch. 12.

18. Online information can be obtained from the U.S. Bureau of Labor Statistics at http://bls.gov/cpihome.htm. (Online IPD information can be obtained from the U.S. Bureau of Economic Analysis at www.bea.doc.gov/bea/pub1100cont.htm.)

11

Budgeting as a Management Tool

The history of modern budgeting has been marked by a keen desire on the part of management to tightly control the expenditure of resources. In the private sector, the control orientation was once marked by emphasis on financial accounting (concerned primarily with preparing and reporting financial information to various groups, including investors/stockholders and creditors, outside the agency). This contrasts with the more recent emphasis on *management accounting*, aimed at providing information that is useful and pertinent for internal management decision making.

In public and other not-for-profit agencies, the control orientation emphasizes compliance with legislative and administrative mandates and with the mandates and regulations of other oversight bodies. The widely used line item budget was developed to meet the control need. The emphasis in this type of budget is on accountability in the narrow sense. Attention is focused on items such as travel, supplies, utilities, consulting, and personnel expenditures. The major objective is to prevent allocated funds from being stolen or expended for unauthorized purposes. Although the control orientation is still important in public and other not-for-profit agencies, the demand for better use of scarce resources has forced these agencies to seek more innovative approaches to the conservation of available assets. Al Gore's national report on performance review and the report, *Serving the American Public: The Best Practices in Performance Measurement*, that followed echo the view that public agencies must go beyond present efforts, because government can work better for less cost.[1] The Government Accounting Standards Board (GASB) has indicated its desire (in its Concepts and Statement No. 2, *Service Efforts and Accomplishments Reporting Managing for Results, Strategy Map for Results-Based Budgeting: Moving Theory to Practice* and *Managing for Results: Analytic Challenges in Measuring Performance*) to press for greater use of performance measurements in reporting government results.[2] The International City Managers Association (ICMA) has helped pioneer the idea of benchmarking. In its journal *Public Management*, among other publications, it has kept the issue in the forefront.

The Government Finance Officers Association (GFOA), with its focus on local governments and elected officials, and the Urban Institute, with its many volumes on performance measurement, have contributed significantly to performance measurement development. This chapter emphasizes ways in which the management decision making role can be enhanced in allocating and managing scarce resources in the public and other not-for-profit agencies.

The issue of performance in government has become an important priority. Major interest has developed in assessing government and other not-for-profit performance. By 1990, benchmarking became the new focus of attention as a means of improving productivity. Benchmarking seeks answers to the following questions: "Where do we stand in relation to others' delivering a particular program or service? Who is doing something better than we are? What are they doing better that we are not, and how can we change to mirror their performance?[3] Obtaining the answers to these questions shall tell us how effectively results are being achieved and how efficiently (lowest cost) activities are producing the service.

When comparing two service organizations and one scores higher, something accounts for the difference. Performance measurement is the means that is employed to assist in determining what makes what difference, but it should be noted that some factors might not be ascertainable. To ascertain the variable or factor causing the difference, performance indicators must be quantified using specific measurement criteria. The criteria used to assess the performance becomes the benchmark.[4]

Difference between "Performance Measurement" and "Benchmark"

Although the concepts are sometimes used interchangeably, they are not the same. *Performance* precedes *benchmarking*. Data must first be assembled on specified criteria to identify the performance of a program or activity that leads to performance measurement. Benchmarking requires an understanding of the process involved in carrying out the function or activity that has been measured. It is the understanding and insight gained from the performance measurement process that reveals the best practices. It is a standard of excellence against which like organizations must be measured and compared. A goal of benchmarking is to facilitate comparisons developed through performance measurement against organizations found anywhere in the world.[5] In benchmarking, consideration should be given to the following:

- Determine where improvements are desired.
- Examine how the benchmarked organization achieved its standard of excellence.
- Use the information obtained to enhance performance.

Benchmarking is concerned with measurement that emanates directly from mission, goals, and objectives leading to production of service outputs or performance indicators that can be compared with identified best practices by organizations that excel in accomplishing particular activities. Benchmarking describes a process that allows an organization to compare its performance with others that are known for their outstanding performances. The aim is to find new, fresh, creative, and most importantly effective approaches and new ideas. Benchmarks are standards or performance measures from which one can identify the best among those performing a particular task. Best practices are identified and analyzed for adoption or adaptation by organizations that seek to improve their own activities.[6] Best practices organizations can be identified by defined activities and processes that exhibit the following:

- Are known as leaders in the application and effective use of performance measurement
- Have been using a performance measurement process over an extended period
- Have an effective measurement system that is communicated throughout the organization
- Clearly link strategic plans' performance results and accountability
- Link compensation rewards and other incentives to performance measurement systems
- Have effectively integrated management information systems (MIS) and performance measurements
- Use performance measurement to facilitate and drive continuous improvements[7]

The end objective leads to enhanced process (efficiency) and quality (effectiveness) improvement. The efficiency component increases productivity and reduces costs, and the quality component promotes competitiveness and responsiveness to clientele and customers. The belief is that benchmarking allows organizations to gain more "bang for the buck," forcing participants to work smarter and more efficiently. Greater public value is created while simultaneously promoting greater accountability in the application of scarce public resources.

The idea for assessing service performance had its inception in 1938 when ICMA published *Measuring Municipal Activities*.[8] The publication suggested various types of information that local governments may use to monitor and assess how well the services were being delivered. The concept suggested was the *benchmark*—a standard or point of reference that had to be used to measure and/or judge the quality or value of government services. After World War II, Japan refined and adopted the benchmarking methodology as the cornerstone of its economic rebuilding.[9] Rather than reinventing the wheel,

Japanese companies identified and adapted *dantotsu* (the best of the best fitness to standard), saving time and cost and giving Japan a head start over its competitors. Japanese companies such as Toyota, Sony, and Mitsubishi are world-renowned for operational efficiency, quality, waste management, and responsiveness.

Performance Measures

Performance measurement can be a very useful means for understanding public and other not-for-profit agencies' performance when a process is put in place to manage results. As noted in Figure 11.1, it is a comprehensive system that focuses on an organization's mission, goals, and objectives. To realize the potential of this system, goals and objectives must be accepted as critical priorities and a systematic method for realizing them must be established.

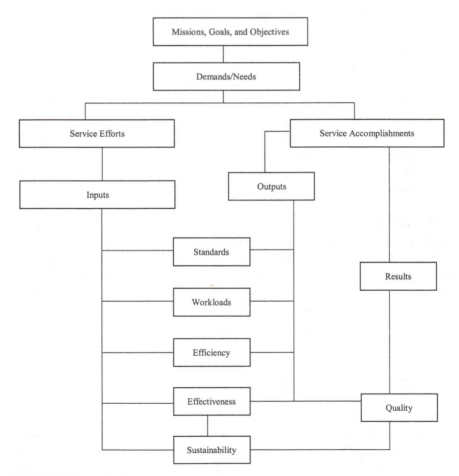

FIGURE 11.1 Linkage among performance measures.

Figure 11.2 shows another view of the operational stages involved in linking and measuring management activities.

The National Performance Review report identified eight findings that it suggested that organizations wishing to be successful follow:[10]

- Clear and consistent support of top management is indispensable to the establishment of a successful performance management system.
- There must be a clear performance measurement framework, understood at all levels of the organization.
- There must be effective internal and external communication with employees, process owners, clientele/customers, and stakeholders.

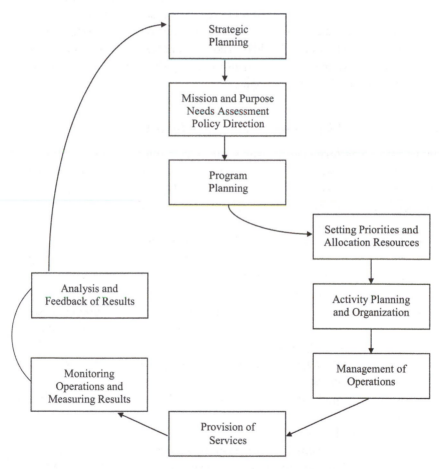

FIGURE 11.2   Managing for results.

Source: Adapted from GASB, "Performance Measurement for Government: Managing for Results," p. 13 (see http://accounting.rutgers.edu/raw/seagov/pmg/resultsmgmt/results .gif).

- Accountability for all results must be clearly assigned so that managers and employees know exactly what they are expected to achieve.
- Performance measurement should provide appropriate decision makers at all levels of the organization with relevant, concise, and timely information that facilitates the opportunity to relate strategic organizational goals and objectives and assess the progress toward achieving the articulated goals.
- Compensation, rewards, and other incentives should be effectively linked to performance measurement.
- Performance measurement should always stress the positive aspects of achievement as opposed to emphasizing shortcomings or failures.
- Results and progress of program achievements should be shared in a timely and open manner with employees, clientele/customers, and stakeholders.
- Program managers should be required to set targets for performance measures, and to use these measures to regularly assess progress.[11]
- Management should set the "tone at the top" regarding performance and accountability, which should be a component for compensation evaluation. Setting an example for the organization is critical in creating a conducive and effective internal environment.

Developing and Updating Performance Measures

In developing performance measures, the analyst must be clientele-/customer-focused and must ensure that quantitative and qualitative measures capture the characterization of the strategic mission and goals as closely as possible. To aid in this endeavor, the following criteria should be followed:[12]

- Ensure that all measures relate directly to the articulated mission.
- Limit the goal measures to a strategic few (see Figures 11.1 and 11.2). All performance measures must be linked to strategic and operational planning, as shown in Figure 11.2.
- Before specifying particular measures, the analyst must thoroughly understand the process or results to be measured, facilitating measurement of only the right or appropriate things.
- Keep the goal always in focus, developing only those performance measures that maximally achieve the goal.
- Keep in mind important categories when developing performance measures:
  - Financial measures
  - Customer/clientele satisfaction indicators
  - Internal operations of the organization
  - Employee satisfaction indicators
  - Community interests and other stakeholder satisfaction indicators

- In implementing a system to create good organizational performance, it is important to keep several criteria in mind:[13]
  - The measure is acceptable and meaningful to clientele/customers.
  - The measure links and describes how well goals and objectives are being met.
  - The measure provides effective linkage.
  - The measure identifies only key results.
  - The measure is simple, understandable, logical, and repeatable.
  - The measure provides opportunity to understand trends.
  - The measure allows economic data collection
  - The measure is collected on a timely basis.

The development of performance measures (see Figure 11.1) is essential before monitoring can be established as a basis for effective performance evaluation. The development of performance measures is dependent on what the controllers (those in authority, whether individuals or groups) view as important or useful in assessing the implied or articulated mission, goals, and objectives of the budget. For example, in most budgets, the mission, goals, and objectives are seldom articulated, and even when they are, they often remain unclear. When a budget identifies funds for a particular organizational or responsibility center and makes allotments for supplies, travel, repairs, and utilities, the implied objective is to control the amount of money to be spent for each item. This control orientation is known as *dollar accountability*. Once the goals and objectives have been established, the development of performance measures is the next logical step in determining how well the goals and objectives have been articulated. This facilitates the formulation and design of performance measures.

Performance measurement implies an evaluation of the possible consequences of directing resources to one use rather than another; it highlights tradeoffs inherent with the appropriation of limited resources. It promotes effective resource allocation, because it allows decision makers to predict what different uses of resources are likely to achieve. For example, the achievement of a welfare agency's goal to remove unemployed fathers from welfare dependency and the achievement of a health care agency's goal to reduce the incidence of lead poisoning among children can be measured using information showing the welfare agency's costs and its success rate in removing fathers from welfare dependency versus the health care agency's costs and success rate in reducing the number of children hospitalized and the mortality rate from lead poisoning. Policymakers are thus provided with a rational basis on which to make decisions. Performance measurement can be used to promote the improvement of operations and output, to develop and control budgets, and to effect individual and organizational accountability. There are several general types of performance measures. The most common include need or demand measures, workload measures, efficiency/productivity measures, effectiveness measures, and sustainability measures. The attributes of these performance measures are shown in Figure 11.3.

Needs Measures

Needs are quantifiable conditions or recognizable problems that require attention and action if the public's welfare is to be maximally served.

Demand Measures

Demand measures are articulated or implied recognition of the need for a given public good or service. This measure indicates the scope and magnitude of a problem. Examples of demand measures include the number of restaurant inspections required, the expected number of citations and (based on past historical records) arrests to be made, the number of patient days, the number of people to be served, the number of manuscripts to be submitted for publication, the number of school children in need of inoculation against childhood communicable diseases, and the number of burglaries in residential districts. Demand measures provide responsible officials with an important aid in understanding why particular services are needed.

Workload Measures

Workload measures can easily be developed from demand measures. While demand measures identify what needs to be done, workload measures indicate the amount of work to be performed or actually executed on a given activity for a specific period of time. Based on the required workload, resources needed to realize the activity can be determined. Workload measures are the most widely used performance indicators in public and other not-for-profit agencies, because they are easily quantifiable and readily understood by the public and by service recipients.

In normal operations planning, workload measures are used to project staffing requirements, develop plans, prepare budgets, and "establish work schedules and measure and evaluate operational output and efficiency."[14] Workload measures can assist management by showing trends in work performance from one period to the next and gradually over an extended period of time. For example, take the night patrol activity of a police department. Knowing the number of hours spent on patrol from period to period provides a basis for ascertaining and monitoring the amount of work being done by particular patrol teams. Moreover, for the preparation of standard budgets and

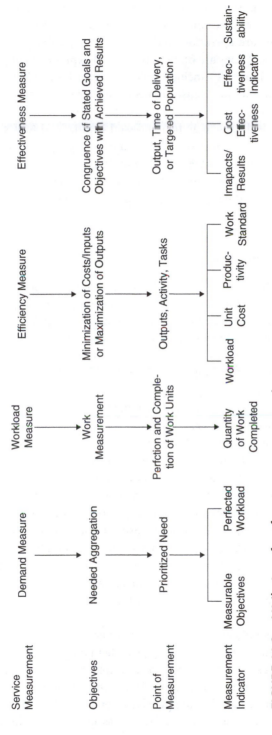

FIGURE 11.3   Attributes of performance measurements.

Source: Some ideas are drawn from Alan Walter Steiss, Management Control in Government (Lexington, MA: Lexington Books, 1982), p. 221.

work schedules, the work performed can be compared with standard hours to determine what unit amount of time each officer or team needs.

Workload measures are *operations indicators* that typically provide little qualitative information.[15] They are often nonfinancial expressions of products or services produced. Examples include miles of street built within a given period, number of automobile licenses issued, number of welfare recipients visited, number of garbage pickups made, or number of examinations administered. An operation indicator may be expressed in financial terms such as the amount of federal assistance to minority business programs, including grants, loans, and gratuities, from x in 2010 to x in 2011. Workload measures are not very useful in determining to what extent stated needs are being met, but they are often used nevertheless, because they are simple and easy to understand.

Efficiency/Productivity Measures

Efficiency measures define the relationship between resources (money, personnel, materials, and capital) and outputs. The concept suggests the organization of resources for the purpose of carrying out a program, activity, or function at minimal cost. When the maximum possible output is produced with the given supply of resources, technical efficiency is obtained and any reduction in input would reduce the volume of the output. A second kind of efficiency is referred to as *allocative efficiency*, meaning that "the cost of any given output is minimized by combining inputs in such a way that one input cannot be substituted for another without raising the costs."[16]

Once an agency has reached its limit or output frontier in the use of its input resources, no additional outputs can be produced, since efficiency is already at 100 percent. Any attempts to add inputs would generate lesser amounts of output, because the technical efficiency level would be breached. In view of this reality, management should keep two dimensions of efficiency in mind: (1) minimizing inputs to produce a greater quantity of output (input efficiency) and (2) maximizing output with a given level of inputs. The output efficiency measure is a comparison of actual or achieved output with expected or standard output based on a given set of inputs. Similarly, input efficiency is a comparison of expected or standard inputs with actual inputs, given a specific output.[17]

Efficiency measures indicate the amount of service output in comparison with the input required to produce it. They provide managers with insight on how allocated resources are being used. For example, the number of inspection hours per health inspector, the number of nursing staff hours (inputs) per patient, or the number of patrol hours per patrol officer indicates how much time the personnel is spending on administrative assignments or duties other than main tasks.

A major problem in the use of efficiency measures is that they are often considered interchangeable with workload measures. Hence, it is not uncommon to find workload measures used to justify budget requests. The additional brief descriptions of types of efficiency measures that follow may aid in understanding how they are applied.[18] (1) The efficiency measure most widely used in public and other not-for-profit agencies is the *input–output ratio*, which permits the use of workload as a unit of output–for example, the number of tons of garbage collected per employee. (2) The *output–input ratio* (emphasizing effectiveness), although helpful, is seldom used. This indicator not only reports the cost of producing a product or delivering a service, it also tells whether the product or service is acceptable or satisfactory. For example, it is not enough to arrest suspected burglars; it is also important to know the percentage of burglars convicted. (3) The *equipment and personnel utilization ratio* shows the extent to which an important resource is in service. Typically, this ratio indicates a resource's available hours versus the hours it is actually in use or the percentage of time it is used. (4) The *relative change measure* permits the tracking of the percentage of increase or decrease in productivity from one period to another or from a selected base period (usually given a value of 100), thereby providing a measurement of relative rather than absolute change. For example, suppose 3,000 potholes were patched in the base year and 3,500 during the succeeding year. This gives a productivity index of 3,500 divided by 3,000, or 16.67 percent. Assuming that there was no change in resource inputs during the base period and succeeding years, the change reflects a 16.67 percent increase in productivity. (5) *Input efficiency ratio* (in which one input, such as the cost of labor, is compared to total staff hours) is used widely, especially in public and other not-for-profit agencies that have a large personnel service cost. For example, the input efficiency ratio for a mental health/mental retardation program would be the total costs divided by total staff hours, compared to a standard.

Effectiveness Measures

Effectiveness measures show the degree to which program objectives have been achieved in terms of quality. *Effectiveness* indicates the congruence between legislative intent or policy objectives and the actual achievement of the program or function designed to achieve them. The measurement of effectiveness includes the concepts of adequacy (how well the identified needs are being met) and responsiveness (how the services are provided and whether they are convenient and timely). Effectiveness measures are the most critical factors in program evaluation and cost–benefit analysis. Their objective is to measure directly the benefits or service delivery to the target population. Examples are the percentage of reduction in air pollution following a new enforcement program, the degree to which the rate of rearrests of individuals enrolled in a criminal justice rehabilitation program has decreased, the average amount of time and minimum number of errors involved in operating a computer system, and the average police response time to emergency calls.

Effectiveness measures have a number of functional uses: (1) program planning (e.g., defining the intended results of a given use of resources); (2) defining management operation (e.g., showing to what degree services are achieving their objectives); (3) evaluating, analyzing, and developing program standards with which performance audits can be compared; and (4) establishing targets that enable the monitoring of employees, organizational units, responsibility centers, and contractors.[19]

Sustainability Measures

Sustainability measures measure the duration for an extended time period over which the impact or efficacy of a program endures. Ideally, all relevant performance indicators should be used to evaluate each activity. Because this will not always be possible, especially in human service activities, it is highly desirable that performance measures be related directly to needs as much as possible. It is clear from the foregoing discussion that all performance measures are logically linked, as also shown in Figure 11.4.

As environmental and societal impacts of operations become more important to stakeholders, both in the public and private sectors, sustainability performance measures are encompassing more than just the ability of the organization to sustain operational efficiency and effectiveness. Measures can include energy usage compared to previous or baseline years, greenhouse gas (GHG) emissions, green building certifications such as the Leadership in Energy and Environmental Design (LEED) designations, water use efficiency, and compliance with green procurement standards, both voluntary and compulsory.[20] Her Majesty's (HM) Treasury, the United Kingdom's department of treasury, issues annual guidance concerning sustainability reports for government entities that include specific metrics to evaluate performance. Some of these metrics include emissions, waste, finite resource consumption, and water usage. These measurements can help organizations and oversight bodies evaluate performance in a more holistic manner that takes into account externalities caused by operations that are often ignored.[21]

Inputs → Efforts → [Money (funds), Labor (skills), Materials and Supplies] → Program Management → [Planning, Programming, Controlling, etc.] → Output → [Services, Goods, Rules, Regulations, etc.] → Evaluation → [Imapact, Outcome, Results, Benefits, Achievement]

FIGURE 11.4   Schematic Input/Output linkage of performance measures.

Accountability Focus on Performance

All performance measures are accountability focused. As was noted in chapter 9, every type of budget points to a particular kind of accountability being sought. For example, a line item budget stresses dollar accountability by identifying the dollar amount of inputs such as personnel, supplies, or equipment that can be bought and used. Unlike a line item budget, the program budget stresses output and impact results. Because performance measures direct managers' attention to the things that are given priority and value, it is important that performances capture the priorities that are desired, otherwise unintended and inappropriate outputs and results or accountability will be achieved. These unintended consequences cause the wrong things to be produced, leading to a lack of congruence between the desired strategic goal and what is actually achieved.

Budgeting and Productivity

Defining Productivity

The most generally agreed upon definition of productivity views it as a ratio of outputs (goods and services produced) to inputs (money, materials, and labor). Productivity measures show how well resources are expended in accomplishing stated objectives. According to Mali, "Productivity is a measure of how well resources are brought together in organizations and utilized for accomplishing a set of results. Productivity is reaching for the highest level of performance with the least expenditure of resources."[22] Because productivity focuses on means or ways of delivering goods and services at the least possible cost, the process (the precise way by which resources are transformed into outputs) is a major concern in pursuing it. For example, a gas-guzzling Rolls Royce could be used to deliver meals on wheels to elderly residents over a four-block area—but although this use of a resource achieves the mission effectively, it misallocates resources because of the unnecessarily high unit cost of delivering the meals.

Productivity may be viewed as a combination of effectiveness and efficiency when there is equal concern for the quality and quantity of services or goods to be produced. In this situation, productivity, efficiency, and effectiveness are inextricably linked. In determining how well resources are being used, a comparison can be made between the volume of the results produced (output effectiveness) and the volume of resources consumed (efficiency). The following is a formula for determining the productivity index:

$$productivity\ index = \frac{Output\ obtained}{Input\ expended} = \frac{Achieved\ performance}{Resources\ consumed} = \frac{Effectiveness}{Efficiency}$$

To enhance productivity improvement, it is necessary to develop measurable indicators for output (performance achievement) and input (resources consumed). When measures cannot be developed for outputs and inputs, the organizational process should be reorganized to facilitate measurement.[23] Calculating the productivity ratio requires the identification of the output and input measures. When these two measures are lacking, productivity cannot be analyzed and the productivity index cannot be developed. To calculate the productivity index, assume the following: Setting priorities and establishing a performance measurement system provides a solid basis with which to effect productivity improvement. Demand or need, workload, efficiency, and effectiveness are used to determine productivity. Although Figure 11.4 is a general schematic representation of input/output linkage, Table 11.1 shows a more specific measurement linkage among the social services, police control, and fire protection functions.

TABLE 11.1   Examples of Performance-Measure Linkages

Function	Demand/need	Workload	Output
Social services	No. of cases requiring services	No. of cases to be served	No. of cases served
Police protection	Emergency calls and no. of burglaries	No. of patrol hours beat-driven; no. of arrests made (clearance)	No. of patrol hours; no. of arrests
Fire protection	No. of places requiring inspection	No. of inspections to be made	No. of inspections made

Efficiency	Effectiveness	Sustainability	Goal
Cost per case served	Percentage of eligible cases satisfactorily served	Extended period over which cases were satisfactorily served	Ability to provide for individual needs
Cost per inspection made	Dollar amount lost due to fire	Duration over which dollar losses continued to decline	Fire prevention
Cost per patrol hour; cost per citation issued	Dollars lost due to crime; cost per degree of security experienced by residents	Period over which loss due to crime continued to climb Period over which residents continued to express increasing degree of insecurity	Crime prevention

Examination of the table reveals the following: (1) Demand/need indicates quantitatively how much work clients and constituents require to meet their articulated needs and desires. (2) Workload indicates quantitatively the amount of work necessary to carry out a given activity. (3) Output represents the amount of goods produced or services provided in the day-to-day activities of an agency without considering the quality of the work performed. (4) Efficiency is the ratio of inputs to outputs. It identifies the cost required to achieve identified objectives. In an examination of efficiency, attention is directed to such questions as the following: What is the cost per fire inspection? What is the cost per patient examined by the outpatient department? What is the cost per ton of garbage collected? Emphasis is directed to the process of converting inputs into outputs. (5) Effectiveness attempts to match the stated goals with the achieved or actual results. The greater the match (or congruence), the more effective the result. In Table 11.1, if all the social service clients are satisfactorily served, the match between stated and actual results is perfect and effectiveness is maximized. In the case of fire protection, no losses from fire mean that maximum effectiveness has been reached.

To be most useful as a productivity instrument, the budget must be closely linked to the management decision making process. The development of a performance measurement system, as shown in Tables 11.1 and 11.2, produces an important framework that can be used to enhance productivity. The management decision making process involves (1) articulation of community needs and goals and the specification of policies to meet those needs, (2) specification of service objectives designed to meet the service level, (3) determination of the desired organizational and procedural changes, (4) provision for a performance monitoring system, and (5) evaluation of results and initiation of the action necessary to bring about the improvement (see Figure 11.5).

After management decides that it will use the budget to actively promote productivity, the process must be institutionalized. The management information system (MIS) must be designed to generate the kind of performance measures that will be emphasized in the controlling, monitoring, planning, and management decision making processes. The performance measures thus developed can be used to aid budget justification and facilitate variance analysis.[24] To enhance decision making, management must develop performance indicators that will meet management needs at given levels of responsibility within the organization.

To be able to develop the most desirable performance indicators in public and not-for-profit agencies, managers must recognize the reality that there are no clear-cut and precise data to permit easy measurement. The linkage between resource allocation and performance result can seldom be directly and explicitly determined. This often requires that public and other not-for-profit agencies' services be measured along a number of dimensions, which

TABLE 11.2 The Goal/Objective of Performance-Measure Linkages

Department: Traffic Safety

Program: School Guards

Goals:

1. To provide for the safety and welfare of all school children walking or riding buses or bicycles to school.
2. To maintain order at school bus stops and to file written reports on motor vehicle violations that threaten the safety of school children.

Objectives:

1. To provide each schoolguard trainee with at least 20 class sessions.
2. To provide total safety and control of children entering and leaving school buses.
3. To provide 150 bicyclesafety talks at local schools.
4. To reduce reported motor vehicle violations involving school children by 10 percent.

	Objectives		
	Prior year	Current year	Projected budget*
Demand Measures			
Number of complaints from concerned parents about the lack of school guards at unattended school crossings	100	90	140
Number of accidents involving school children entering and leaving school buses	115	192	200
Number of dangerous street crossings at new school location	475	510	580
Number of safety-prevention classes to be conducted for school children			
Workload Measures			
Number of school-guard training classes conducted	150	165	192
Number of school guards attending the training classes	NA	NA	NA
Number of hours spent watching children entering and leaving school buses	105	110	90
Number of hours in hearings	250	375	420

Efficiency/Productivity Measures

Number of school-guard training sessions conducted per officer	10	11	12
Average cost per training class	$410	$400	$390
Number of bicycle talks presented per officer	29	25	28
Average cost per bicycle talk	$96	$100	$86
Average number of accidents involving children entering and leaving buses	14	15	10
Average cost per report filed	$106	$150	$90

Impact/Effectiveness

Degree of satisfaction with school-guard training classes	NA	NA	NA
Number of accidents reported involving school children entering and leaving school buses	5	6	1
Percentage of increase or decrease in bicycle accidents reported	15%	20%	5%
Percentage of decrease in motor vehicle violations involving school children reported	75%	85%	95%

Sustainability

Extended period over which satisfaction was expressed about schoolguard training classes.	NA	NA	NA
Duration over which accidents involving school children decreased	15 months	27 months	39 months
Period over which bicycle accidents decreased	25 months	7 months	9 months
Extended period over which motor vehicle violations involving children decreased	26 months	38 months	50 months

Prior year	Current year	Projected budget	Over/under current year explanation
$378,000	$451,040	$503,040	$52,000, mainly for new officers' training and overtime report writing

Note: NA = not available.

*All these amounts can be broken down by objects of expenditures.

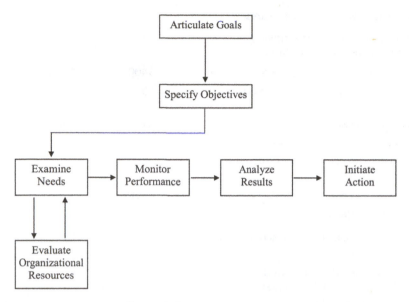

FIGURE 11.5 Activity flow of the management process.

may be imperfect and incomplete, with multiple proxies or surrogate indicators. The development of performance measures that meet a given agency's or responsibility center's needs will depend on the measures' utility (in terms of relevance and significance) to each decision maker.

Using Performance Information

If performance measures are to have maximum utility, they must be effectively linked with mission and goals to final delivery results. The lack of linkage of performance measures creates ineffectual decisions and wasteful application of scarce resources.[25] Therefore, if an organization hopes to achieve a high-performance impact, performance measures must play a strategic linking role:[26]

- They must link resource allocation, strategic planning, and performance measurement.
- They must find effective ways of linking employees and management evaluations, compensation and other incentive systems to hold management accountable for its performance. This implies using both short-term and long-term performance metrics.
- They must identify gaps between the articulated annual plan's specific goals and objectives and actual achievement.
- They must be used both as an internal and external benchmarking instrument and methodology to maintain the comparative best practice or world-class performance.

- They must make continuous upgrading changes in internal processes to enhance the efficiency and quality of the organization's output and results.

Instituting Performance Measures: Some Practical Concerns

Because adopting the use of performance measures in government and non-profit agencies typically means giving up old habits and modes of decision making, the timeframe for the implementation of productivity measures should be based on each organization's situation. Some agencies may take several months to implement productivity measures, whereas others require five years or more. The introduction of a productivity system may take place as follows: (1) An agency or unit that appears to be most receptive and capable is singled out. (2) Line managers are integrally involved in the development of appropriate productivity measures. (3) The central staff is allowed time to assist managers in formulating performance measures. (4) Performance measures are linked to specific services identified in the budget.

Besides the benefits that performance measures offer, they can also produce other unintended consequences. They tend to make managers concentrate their energies more on those programs that are easy to measure. Because the effectiveness of final results or other quantitative factors are harder to measure, much emphasis in both public and other not-for-profit agencies is placed on intermediate output, such as the number of food inspections made by a health department inspector, the number of contacts made by an individual infected with a sexually transmitted disease, the number of inoculations given, and the number of grant proposals completed. Performance measures are often resisted by managers, who fear being evaluated on the basis of results over which they have little or no control. Often managers fail to understand the linkages among the different kinds of measures. For example, a fire department that inspects buildings with the aim of minimizing or eliminating fire may fail to accept responsibility for buildings that are subsequently burned. If the linkage cannot be made in a case such as this, then no more resources should be provided for carrying out the inspection activity.[27]

The passage of the Government Performance and Results Act and Modernization Act of 2010 (GPRAMA), represents a major federal policy commitment to performance measurement. As discussed in chapter 2, GPRAMA forced federal managers to implement strategic planning and performance management as a condition for receiving annual budget appropriations.[28] Each federal agency is required to submit yearly strategic plans with specifically articulated goals and annual performance plans, describing how each agency will implement these agencies are required to provide annual reports on the progress they have achieved.

The GPRAMA brought about a major shift in federal agencies' focus. Unlike the previous fragmented approach to spending programs, the GPRAMA ushered in a new discipline that required the development of performance data that must be linked with the agency's strategic goals. Emphasis is now put on results and effects rather than input or what money buys, such as supplies, travel, and utilities. The new system requires performance measurement linkage for all levels of resource use, making it easier to hold managers accountable for such use. The GPRA induced agencies to develop a performance measurement system that provides a mechanism for reporting on program performance, thus requiring management to set goals and standards; detect and correct problems; manage and improve processes; and document accomplishments.[29]

Linking Performance Measures to Resource Allocation: A Case Example

The example of Dallas County (Texas) shows how the development of performance measures can be effectively used even in a highly decentralized organization in which there is no hierarchical management structure and the county commissioners operate both as full-time managers and legislators. Half the county's budget is controlled by the state. The chief accountant (known as "county auditor") reports to the district judges.[30] Although many organizations still deal with performance measures on an ad hoc basis, Dallas County has developed a *progressive pressure system* (see Table 11.3) that makes performance measurement and comparison with targets a daily instrument of shared management concern in a nonthreatening, nonpunitive way.[31]

Despite the dispersion of responsibilities and the forces operating to minimize cooperation, Dallas County is achieving remarkable results: low taxes, superior bond ratings, and high public trust. "Dallas County commissioners have become results-oriented, not because government was perceived as ineffective, but rather because they sought continually to improve."[32] When the county began its performance measurement implementation in the early 1990s, the reports emphasized workloads and financial measures without involvement or inputs from operating departments. Unlike the typical approach that requires clearly defined mission and goal articulation *before* performance measurement implementation, the Texas state law establishes most missions. This norm does not allow local county officials to set policy agendas.

By 1997, four quarterly reports had been developed. Two of them containing specialized results (outcome) indicators were prepared by the Office of Budget and Evaluation, focusing on specific problem areas of the county. The first performance report dealt with the Juvenile Department's mission of rehabilitating youthful offenders by using the recidivism division rate as the performance measurement (outcome) indicator of success. This performance indicator tracked data (including demographic, social, and educational) on the offenders after release for twenty-four months, aimed at providing officials

TABLE 11.3   Progressive Pressure to Achieve Outcomes

Weakest

- Preparation of objectives and measures
- Establishing/negotiating targets
- Annual compilation of data and public disclosure
- Quarterly gathering of data and public disclosure of interim results
- Preparation of written narratives for each measure
- "Grading" of results by outside agency such as Office of Budget and Evaluation
- Preparation of quarterly "watch" list by outside agency
- Preparation of quarterly "question" list by outside agency
- Written invitation from governing body to explain interim results
- Presentation/discussion of response at public meeting
- Consideration of measures and targets along with resource allocation of compensation decisions
- Specific contract for service with "automatic" consequences in staffing, gain-sharing, and/or compensation

Strongest

Source: Philip B. Scheps, "Linking Performance Measures to Resource Allocation" *Government Finance Review*, 16, no. 3 (June 2000): 12.

with information to allow them to make changes to the programs that were not meeting targeted performance expectations. As plans were being put together to double the county's "Youth Village," the report revealed a high level of recidivism. The planned county expansion of the program was shelved. The program was turned over to the private sector with "cash recidivism guarantees."[33] This was the county's first use of performance measures that affected resource allocation.

Judicial system internal benchmarking was instituted in seventy-two districts for those offices that are dependent on the commissioners for their budgetary resources. Efficiency indicators were developed for each judge and justice of the peace, allowing for judge-to-judge comparisons. The efficiency comparisons were made available to all county districts. Each judge and cost-per-case disposition with other judges hearing a similar docket were identified. This approach allowed the internal benchmarking of similar processes. Although there were apprehensions that were expressed initially about the fairness of the comparisons, the judges subsequently became supporters of the reports and have made numerous contributions to the data presentation technique.[34] To enhance their efficiency indicators, some judges began using part-time court reporters, replacing full-time reporters as a means of cost savings.[35]

In addition to the two specialized reports and the general report on management, a report on output and another, the Capital Projects report focusing on scheduling milestones for capital projects, were prepared. All these reports were the cornerstone of the performance reporting system until 1997, when the full result, outcome-oriented performance measurement system was introduced. Once the system was implemented, every department was trained in performance management. By 1998, all department budgets were required to have results (outcome) measures. Since the introduction of the full performance system, continuous improvements have been integrated and used to enhance it.

The operating environment in which results are constantly reviewed and made available for everyone to see, even throughout the development stage, creates positive and progressive pressure (see Table 11.3). By means of the Internet, managers can look at and review their peers' quarterly reports. Sensitive reports are labeled "draft" until all participating managers have been given the opportunity to add appropriate footnotes and narrative explanations.

The goodwill and trust in Dallas County have motivated managers to want their operations to be visible and efficient—the keys to transparency—and those that prepare the budget want to spend their limited resources where they feel they will produce the greatest benefit. The Office of Budget Evaluation (OBE) informally grades quarterly reports, giving a visible check mark where the reports "appear to be on course."[36] As shown in Table 11.4, when seasonal fluctuations or extraordinary events appear to influence the articulated target, the OBE factors them in and gives each item due consideration. Additionally, the budget analyst and submitting departments are given an opportunity to comment regarding the mitigating circumstances.

Based on the OBE reviews and graded performance report trends (those that can be controlled by management, and those that cannot be controlled are made available to commissioners) are highlighted quarterly. The former relate to troublesome trends such as missing expected targets or results (outcomes). These might include falling rates in successful prosecutions or reductions in distributed child support. The latter draw attention to performance data that shows a worsening or deteriorating external environment. This list represents an early warning signal that events unrelated to the county's management might likely generate future problems. Examples might include increasing referrals to the truancy courts or an increasing share of the state prison population being housed in county jails. The troublesome list is further identified on an "active" or "positive" list. The OBE prepares recommendations, for the commissioners' approval, for correcting the troublesome trend. A "watch" list is held on the table until the next quarter, at which time items on the list may be dropped, new ones added, "or old items may be escalated to the next level of pressure."[37] Based on the commissioners' assessments, the OBE notifies departments on the list indicating that the performance measure(s) has reached watch list status and increased attention is expected.

TABLE 11.4 Dallas County, Texas: Using Performance Measures to Assess Results

Health and Human Services Foreign-Travel Vaccination Clinic

	FY98 actual	FY99 actual	FY2000 1st quarter	FY2000 2nd quarter	FY2000 3rd quarter	FY2000 4th quarter	Annual estimate	Target	Target met?
Work Outputs									
Doses administered	16,401	20,370	6,272				25,088	22,000	×
People seen	8,220	10,773	3,766				15,074	11,000	×
Efficiencies									
Revenue per dose administered	$28	$29	$30				$30	$30	×
Effectiveness (Outcomes)									
Annual revenue received	$464,700	$582,964	$136,388				$545,552	$600,000	
Results of quarterly customer survey (% satisfaction)	N/A	N/A	92%				92%	90%	×

Explanation of significant changes: The increase in the number of doses administered and people seen is the result of extending the clinic's hours.

Source: Adapted from Philip B. Scheps, "Linking Performance Measures to Resource Allocation." *Government Finance Review,* 16, no. 3 (June 2000): 13.

Items that the commissioners determine to be most troublesome are identified. A letter with five signatures is then sent to the department head concerned, suggesting that he or she may wish to discuss the matter with the commissioners to better understand the ramifications and to enable them to evaluate the problems. The letter also asks that the commissioners be provided with additional information, if it is deemed necessary. In every case, department heads have responded and welcomed the opportunity to explain the issues involved as early as possible in a noncompetitive environment.

On a quarterly basis, following the submission of reports, a public hearing called the "Performance Forum" is held, based on the agenda made by the OBE. The commissioners focus only on items in the quarterly performance reports by which the active and watch lists are determined. After the commissioners agree with the lists, they may authorize that congratulatory letters be sent to particular departments with outstanding performance. Additionally, the OBE provides a list of "county functions experiencing external workload pressure, or early warning"[38] of items to be discussed at a later date.

For two months after the Performance Forum (now replaced by the annual budget workshop), time is devoted to discussion and performance reports from departments that have trouble or some performance trends have caused targets to be missed. These place tacit pressure on departments to deal with their problems early and on a timely basis: "Often a shared strategy for correcting the problem will emerge from the informal session."[39]

Summary Observations

This chapter presented the steps involved in the development and use of performance measures within the budgetary context. Throughout, attention was focused on how the budget performance measures are linked to one another and on how these measures provide useful insights in assessing program results and accountability in public and other not-for-profit organizations. Managers of government entities must be aware of the ever-changing criteria used to evaluate performance, including an increased emphasis on sustainability.

Notes

1. See Al Gore, *Creating a Government That Works Better and Costs Less* (Washington, DC: U.S. Government Printing Office, 1993).

2. See Government Accounting Standards Board (GASB), "*Service Efforts and Accomplishments Reporting*" (draft, September 15, 1993); Paul D. Epstein, "Get Ready: The Time for Performance Measurement Is Finally Coming." *Public Administration Review*, 52, no. 5 (September 1992): 5, 13.

3. Richard Fischer, "An Overview of Performance Measurement." *Public Management* (September 1994): 8.

4. Ibid., p. 10.

5. Ibid., p. 11.

6. National Performance Review, *Serving the American Public: Best Practices in Performance Measurement—Benchmarking Study Report*, p. 3; see also http://govinfolibrary. unt.edu/npr/library/papers/benchmark/nprbook.html.

7. National Performance Review, *Serving the American Public*, p. 6.

8. Ibid., p. 10.

9. Ibid., p. 4.

10. Ibid., p. 3.

11. Ibid., p. 4.

12. National Performance Review, *Serving the American Public*, p. 10.

13. Ibid.

14. Barry M. Mundt, Raymond T. Olsen and Harold I. Steinberg, *Managing Public Resources* (Stamford, CT: Peat Marwick International, 1982), p. 14.

15. Robert G. May, Gerhard G. Mueller, and Thomas H. Williams, *A Brief Introduction to Managerial and Social Uses of Accounting* (Englewood Cliffs, NJ: Prentice-Hall, 1975), p. 72.

16. Jack Diamond, "Measuring Efficiency in Government: Techniques and Experience," in *Government Financial Management: Issues and Country Studies*, ed. A. Permchand (Washington, DC: International Monetary Fund, 1991), p. 142.

17. Ibid.

18. Mundt, Olsen, and Steinberg, *Managing Public Resources*, p. 16.

19. Ibid., p. 21.

20. "Public Sector Taking the Lead in Environmental Sustainability." http://app.e2singapore.gov.sg/Programmes/Public_Sector_Taking_the_Lead_in_Environmental_Sustainability.aspx, June 11, 2013.

21. "Public Sector Annual Reports: Sustainability Reporting." *nationalarchives.gov. uk.* https://www.gov.uk/government/publications/public-sector-annual-reports-sustainability-reporting-guidance, HM Treasury, March 2013.

22. Paul Mali, *Improving Total Productivity* (New York: John Wiley 1978), p. 6.

23. Ibid., p. 7.

24. John R. Hall, *Factors Related to Local Government Use of Performance Measurement* (Washington, DC: Urban Institute, April 1978).

25. Allan R. Drebin, "Criteria for Performance Measurement in State and Local Government," *Governmental Finance*, 10 (December 1980): 4.

26. National Performance Review, *Serving the American Public*, p. 21.

27. John R. Allen, "The Uses of Performance Measurement." *Government Finance Review 12*, 4 (August 1996): 11.

28. National Performance Review, *Serving the American Public*, p. 24; see also Office of Management and Budget, Government Performance Results Act of 1993; http://www. whitehouse.gov/omb/mgt-gpra/gplan2m.html.

29. National Performance Review, *Serving the American Public*, p. 26; see also Clinton T. Brass, Changes to the Government Performance and Results Act of 1993 (GPRA): Overview of the New Framework of Products and Processes, http://www.fas.org/sgp/crs/misc.

30. Philip B. Scheps, "Linking Performance Measures to Resource Allocation," *Government Finance Review 16*, no. 3 (June 2000): 11.

31. Ibid.
32. Ibid.
33. Ibid., p. 12.
34. Ibid.
35. Ibid., p. 13.
36. Ibid.
37. Ibid., p. 14.
38. Ibid.
39. Ibid.

12

Capital Budgeting

The need for capital budgeting arises in public and other not-for-profit organizations because it is not always possible to find sufficient revenues to accommodate capital needs. Factors that have contributed to this condition include the increased demand for services, participation and transparency, the cutback/retrenchment movement in the public sector, revenue raising limitations, fiscal constraints and slow recovery associated with the recent Great Recession, the prevailing no-tax syndrome, and resistance on the part of donors to providing adequate resources to other not-for-profit agencies.[1] The heavy expenditures that are usually needed for capital outlays cannot always be met by the popular "pay-as-you-go" or "pay-as-you-use" methods, which encourage a governmental unit or agency to spend no more than the revenues available for a specific fiscal period. This principle minimizes the unwise or premature commitments of resources and avoids the interest payments and other related costs associated with debt financing, thus enhancing the entity's credit rating.[2]

Nonetheless, despite the public's acceptance of the "pay-as-you-go" approach, a number of problems are associated with it. For example, current taxpayers pay for projects or investments from which they will benefit only partially. On the other hand, the argument can be made in the interest of equity that people should pay for capital facilities during their lifespan only as they benefit from them. When public agencies engage in long-term borrowing, current taxpayers are relieved from paying portions of their immediate tax burden, instead transferring it to future generations.

Unlike in the business world or other levels of government, the federal government does not manage its capital facilities. There is a total lack of an effective national capital improvement plan. In fact, the federal government maintains no capital budgeting system or procedure. As a result, most federally owned facilities "are deteriorating and the Government is faced with the prospect of either repairing or rehabilitating them, or risking a staggering replacement burden in the future."[3] Additionally, if the existing deteriorating situation is not addressed, sooner than later, the economic competitiveness of the United States could be significantly degraded.

The chapter examines the capital budgeting processes, financing approaches, and techniques for ranking and selecting capital projects. Throughout, stress is placed on both successful and unsuccessful practices.

Defining Capital Budgeting

A number of terms are used interchangeably to refer to capital budgeting, such as public works planning, capital improvements planning, capital facilities planning, and capital outlay planning. The use of so many terms creates an increased opportunity for misunderstanding the definition of *capital budget*. Most often, the term refers to the legislative plan for proposed capital outlays and the means of financing them for the coming fiscal period. The capital budget is often a part of the regular budget. When a capital facilities or capital program improvement is in operation, the capital budget will be the first-year component.

Capital Budget's Critical and Indispensable Role

The importance of capital budgets in local government cannot be overstressed. Capital expenditure is a major component of most local budgets and plays a significant role in the delivery of public services and the economic welfare of local communities. It is in the capital budget that many of the most critical policy issues are articulated. Capital budgeting is typically responsible for bringing together many different departmental personnel and technical specialties or disciplines. "It also provides opportunities to involve the public—and particularly special interests such as developers, neighborhood associations, business groups, and taxpayer associations—in defining and creating the community's future."[4]

Capital Facilities/Program/Improvement

This is a plan made up of the capital expenditures (the purchase of assets to provide service for many years) to be incurred over a specified number of years to accommodate capital improvements set forth in a long-term work program. Each project or planned expenditure is sequentially and specifically identified according to a schedule of priorities that sets forth the full estimated resources available to finance the projected expenditures. Typically, the projects are large, permanent, or fixed, with a lifespan of fifteen to twenty years, and involve non-recurring expenditures aimed at providing new or additional services. The construction of a public health clinic or swimming pool is an example of a capital expenditure. (Salaries, supplies, or minor equipment replacements are operational expenditures and can be included in the yearly operating budget.)

All recurring expenditures should be excluded from the capital improvement plan (CIP). The following are suggestions to guide financial managers in developing the CIP: (1) Capital items should have a lifespan of three years or more.

TABLE 12.1 Capital Improvement Budget Scoring Matrix

Criteria	Possible Scores		
	0	1	2
Consistency with Community Goals and Plans	Project is inconsistent with city's comprehensive plan or does nothing to advance the City Commission's strategic goals.	Project is consistent with city's comprehensive plan but does little to advance the City Commission's strategic goals.	Project is directly consistent with the city's comprehensive plan and advances the City Commission's strategic goals.
Public Health and Safety	Project would have no impact on existing public health and/or safety status.	Project would increase public health and/or safety but does not address an urgent, continual need or hazard.	Project addresses an immediate, continual safety hazard or public health and/or safety need.
Mandates or Other Legal Requirements	Project is not mandated or otherwise required by court order; judgment, or interlocal agreements.	Project would address anticipated mandates, other legal requirements, or interlocal agreements.	Project required by federal, state, or local mandates, grants, court orders, and judgments; required as part of interlocal agreements.
Maintains or Improves Standard of Service	Project not related to maintaining an existing standard of service.	Project would maintain existing standard of service.	Project would address deficiencies or problems with existing services; would establish new service.
Extent of Benefit	Project would benefit only a small percentage of citizens or particular neighborhoods or areas.	Project would benefit a large percentage of citizens or many neighborhoods or areas.	Project would benefit all of the citizens, neighborhoods, or areas.
Related to Other Projects	Project is not related to other projects in the capital improvement plan (CIP) already underway.	Project is linked to other projects in the CIP already underway but not essential to their completion.	Project essential to the success of other projects identified in the CIP already underway.

(Continued)

TABLE 12.1 (*Continued*)

Criteria	Possible Scores		
	0	1	2
Supports Economic Development	Project would discourage or directly prevent capital investment, decrease the tax base, decrease valuation or decrease job opportunities.	Project would have no impact on capital investment, the tax base, valuation, or job opportunities.	Project would directly result in capital investment, increased tax base, increased valuation, or improved job opportunities.
Environmental Quality	Project would have a negative effect on the environmental quality of the city.	Project would not affect the environmental quality of the city.	Project would improve the sustainability of the environment.
Feasibility of Project	Project is unable to proceed due to obstacles (land acquisition, easements, approval required).	Minor obstacles exist, project is not entirely ready to proceed.	Project is entirely ready to proceed, no obstacles exist (no land acquisition, easements, approvals, etc. are required).
Opportunity Cost	If deferred, the increase in project costs would be less than the rate of inflation.	If deferred, the increase in project costs would be equal to inflation.	If deferred, the increase in project costs would be greater than the rate of inflation.
Operational Budget Impact	Project would significantly increase debt service, installment payments, personnel, or other operating costs, or decrease revenues.	Project would neither increase nor decrease debt service, installment payment, personnel, other operating costs, or revenues.	Project would decrease debt service, installment payments, personnel, or other operating costs, or increase revenues.

Source: John Fishbein and Christopher Cawley, Capital Program Considerations in Challenging Times, *Government Finance Review*, Vol. 25 #3, p. 16.

(2) Acquisition costs should be $5,000 or greater. (3) All capital items "paid for from the proceeds of long-term debt [should be] included."[5] Unlike in the public sector, the business world tends to favor putting as many items in the capital area as possible to take advantage of tax breaks, such as deductions for depreciation.

Capital Budget Process

The capital planning and capital programming role of the chief executive varies according to statutory requirements and the size and type of government. Typically, the chief executive guides the capital planning and capital programming process and makes recommendations to the legislature. However, requests for projects are initiated in the operating departments. The guidelines for preparing and submitting the capital plan are determined by the legislatures, which establish the timeframe on activity, extent of citizen participation, and planning and administrative responsibilities for the capital planning process.[6] In recent years, outside experts have been used to advise agencies on financing options. Additionally, interdepartmental committees have been used to review and rank projects, whereas citizen advisory committees and citizen surveys, such as conducted in Dayton, Ohio, are used to facilitate community input into the capital planning process. Dayton polls its citizens on their priorities for capital improvements and their willingness to finance them, including through taxation, bond issuance, and public–private partnerships (PPP).

Implementation of the capital planning process has been traditionally carried out by the planning departments or central budget staff. These departments normally play the lead role because of their access to data and information (concerning, for example, population, land use, transportation, and the economic base). This provides the basis on which to establish community plans. Infrequently, the public works department may be given the responsibility of the capital planning coordination. The authority to analyze the financial implication and effects of the capital program on the operating budget and to make recommendations on financing approaches is assigned to the finance department. When a planning commission exists, its main responsibility is to review the capital project requests and make recommendations.

Benefits of a Capital Improvement Plan

A number of important results flow from an effectively planned and executed capital improvement plan (CIP):

- It forces communities to systematically examine their goals and needs capabilities.
- It allows communities to schedule, plan, and finance capital undertakings to promote cost effectiveness and conformance with the established policies.

- It allows a jurisdiction to measure the effects of capital spending and capital financing sources and how they affect its total spending.
- It promotes greater efficiency in the use of tax resources.
- It provides an important guide to aid the growth and development of the community.
- It encourages governments or organizations to improve their administrative systems.
- It is an important means for promoting regional cooperation.
- It facilitates and promotes sound financial management, providing a positive view to credit rating agencies.
- It provides the opportunity to forecast future capital demand on current revenues, the need for borrowing, and the amount of outside financing that will be necessary, allowing projects to be moved forward or back as expected revenue sources dictate.
- It offers an effective, systematic, and orderly way for replacing or repairing capital facilities.
- It enhances the governmental unit or organization's opportunity for citizens' participation because of the many programs that federal and state governments maintain to aid in the planning and construction of the infrastructure.

There are many differences among governmental units, as the General Accounting Office (GAO) found in its assessment of capital budgeting in public and private organizations throughout the country. The GAO stated that it could not find a comprehensive, precise discussion of the critical elements of a capital budgeting process anywhere in the literature. Thus, the process described here is a compression of a number of suggested processes. Among the basic steps that should be followed in the formulation of the capital budget are the following:

1. Take an inventory of and assess the existing condition of the infrastructure, establishing the short- and long-term physical needs.
2. Develop alternative projects to meet short- and long-term needs.
3. Select alternatives and establish priority classifications for the short- and long-term needs.
4. Estimate the required resources and short-term funding allocation.
5. Assess the effects on the governmental organization's financial policies.
6. Establish a monitoring system, control work schedules, and financing.
7. Initiate a replacement and maintenance strategy.

Although the governmental procedures among jurisdictions differ, the chief executive traditionally oversees the capital budgeting and capital planning process and makes recommendations to the legislative body. The guidelines for preparing and submitting the capital plan are determined by the legislature.

The capital budget process begins with the development of the capital improvement program. This involves the identification of projects that will meet the entity's needs for a specified number of years. The vast majority of projects are identified by government agencies, though private organizations may make suggestions. Each project submitted is accompanied by a supporting analysis and rationale setting forth the cost data and a justifying narrative.

Planning departments or central budget offices typically direct the process of capital budget planning. Although these departments sometimes review the initial submissions, planning commissions usually perform these functions and make recommendations. In carrying out the review of the proposals, interrelationships are determined, costs are evaluated, and priorities are identified. As part of the review of the screening process, schedules for the proposed implementation of the projects are synchronized with one another to minimize the wasteful use of resources (e.g., surfacing streets *before* laying the sewage and drainage system). In addition, projects that can be reasonably postponed are identified.[7]

The Capital Improvement Plan

This may be viewed as an instrument through which a community lays out its short- and long-term physical growth and development plans. Ideally, the CIP is linked to the community's master and fiscal long-term (ten- to twenty-year) plans, identifying public improvement needs.[8] The CIP is essentially "a schedule listing capital improvements, in order of priority together with cost estimates and the proposed method of financing them."[9] The CIPs are subject to constant changes and should be reviewed each year and updated with regard to the changing needs and priorities of the community or organization. By means of the CIP, the following activities are undertaken:

- Capital needs are assessed.
- Affordability capacity is analyzed.
- Projects (e.g., library, community center) are scheduled over a five- to six-year period.
- A budget is developed for high-priority projects.
- A revenue policy is developed for projected improvements.
- Departmental activities are coordinated to meet project schedules.
- A system is developed to monitor, evaluate, and inform the public about the proposed capital improvements.
- Update capital programs.

There are three documents that emanate from or are closely related to the CIP. First, the *long-term operating budget plan* is set forth. The second is the *capital budget,* representing the first year of the CIP as approved by the appropriate legislative body or board that authorizes required funding to defray the cost of the improvements. The third is the *annual operating budget,* whose relationship to the CIP is significantly influenced by the way in which projects are implemented. The CIP is usually adopted before the completion of the annual operating budget to allow the capital improvement budget to be incorporated into it. This facilitates the linkage "between the CIP and the annual budget and appropriation process used by the community," as shown in Figure 12.1.[10] Note that the CIP programming approach is not a mandated process in most communities. Hence, although it is not desirable to ignore the CIP programming approach, most communities may institute a capital project's plan so long as they meet the legal requirements.

Priority Setting

Priority setting is a necessary activity, because the scarcity of resources does not permit a community or organization to undertake all the projects that it would like to implement. The agency charged with developing the capital budget can provide invaluable assistance to operating department heads in pinpointing cost projections. The agency staff can stress the importance of long-range needs, interpret instructions, and complete the required forms necessary to promote a uniform application of policies and procedures. In addition, a number of officials (e.g., budget director, city engineer, and city attorney) may be needed to answer such questions as the following: In what

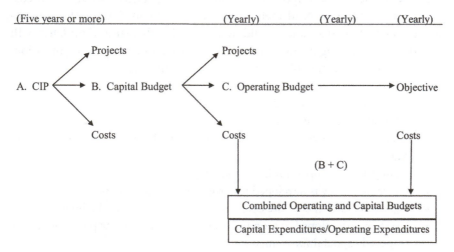

FIGURE 12.1   CIP linkage with capital and operating budgets.

ways and to what extent will the proposed project affect general city or government development?

- What is the fiscal impact in terms of (a) current and future years' capital costs, (b) yearly cost additions or reductions in operations and maintenance, and (c) potential legal liability costs that may be incurred in undertaking or rejecting the project?
- What are the potential environmental, aesthetic, and social impacts of the project?
- What are the implications if the project is deferred?
- Who will benefit from or be hurt by this project?
- Is this project a replacement of an existing structure or is it a new, added responsibility to government?
- Will the project expand the taxable property and economic base of the community? That is, what will be the yearly effects on existing flow revenue (increase? decrease? neutral)?
- What effect will the project have on the efficiency and cost-effectiveness of service performance?
- Can the city or governmental unit afford the proposed capital improvement?
- Will the project be a revenue producer?
- What is likely to be citizen and political opposition?[11]

Public Hearings

Some time before the projects to be undertaken are decided upon, and before legislative consideration, public input should be solicited. To encourage timely public participation, the CIP may be combined with the annual operating budget hearings. Whenever the hearings are scheduled, they should allow time for public comments to be considered on a timely basis to permit changes to be incorporated into the CIP.[12]

In the priority setting process, an initial review should be conducted to eliminate proposals that appear to be obviously impractical to implement during the ensuing period. After this has been done, a simple and precisely defined selection criteria should be established to enhance the community's or organization's present and future financial viability. Perhaps general criteria for a CIP priority system may be employed, as indicated in Table 12.2.

In recent years, a numerical rating system has gained popularity. For example, a specific number of points (e.g., 0–50) are given based on conformance to such factors as economic development, environmental quality, revenue generation, potential for revitalizing neighborhood, citizen neighborhood participation, and useful-life expectancy. Jurisdictions where the rating system may be found include Dade County, Florida; Dayton, Ohio; Montgomery County, Maryland; and St. Paul, Minnesota. In Table 12.3, a university uses the

TABLE 12.2   General Criteria for a CIP Priority System

Rank	Center	Applicable criteria
1	Urgently needed (one year or less)	Immediate implementation to relieve danger to public health, welfare, and/or safety.
2	Necessary or essential (two-to-three years)	Complete projects to bring about major improvements and to remove existing deficiencies and/or impediments.
3	Desirable improvements	Project identified to meet anticipated or projected future needs.
4	Deferrable improvements	Foreseeable needs for projects cannot be effectively supported as part of the present CIP.

rating system to allocate proposed new construction space based on academic mission priority, integrating planning and university considerations, existing building conditions, and expenditure and revenue factors.

Table 12.4 shows how the Spearman's rank (Rho) correlation can be used to assess the degree to which project priority ranks and resource allocation priority ranks are aligned—meaning the extent to which the projects and resource allocations parallel the corresponding rank positions. A Spearman correlation coefficient (r_s) of 0.0 indicates no alignment between projects and resource allocation priority, whereas a correlation coefficient (r_s) of +1.00 indicates that the projects and resource priority are perfectly aligned. Negative correlation coefficients indicate disalignment—meaning that project priorities and resource allocation intentions are not matching. A Spearman correlation coefficient (r_s) of −1.00 shows a perfect disalignment between projects and resource allocations. Ideally, projects having high ranks should receive the largest resource allocations. Table 12.4 reveals a moderate and positive alignment $(r_s = 0.55)$ between the civic center's projects and resource allocations, suggesting that projects and resource allocations need to be reconceptualized. The utility of Spearman's rank correlation is as an index of the strength of alignment between projects and resource allocations, which ranges from 0 (no alignment) to ± 1.00 (perfect alignment or disagreement).

In summary, there are six specific activities that should be sequentially considered when officials attempt to establish project priority:

1. Development of clearly defined selection criteria
2. Development of a point system to permit the assignment of points to each criterion
3. Comparison of each project with the identified criteria
4. Assignment of an appropriate score and ranking to each project
5. Preparation of a priority listing of the projects
6. Analysis of the projects

TABLE 12.3 Evaluation Criteria Matrix for a University Complex

Criteria		Proposals									
		1	2	3	4	5	6	7	8	9	10
1. **Academic Mission of the University**	Ratings: 0–3 does not directly enhance mission 4–7 partially enhances mission 8–10 directly enhances mission										
a. Student training and research (closer proximity to labs and professors in own and related disciplines)											
b. Classroom teaching (improves access to teaching labs, equipment, audio-visual, computers, etc.)											
c. Research (creates opportunities for new or expanded research endeavors, especially sponsored projects)											
d. Public service (upgrades provision and quality, attractiveness, and visibility of public and community services)											
e. Quality enhancement responsive to/compatible with provost's priorities											
f. Recruitment and retention of faculty and students											
2. **Integrative Planning and University-wide Considerations**	Ratings: 0–3 not consistent 4–7 somewhat consistent 8–10 consistent in all ways										
a. Consolidation of units located in multiple, nonadjacent sites; meets long-term/permanent space needs											

(Continued)

TABLE 12.3 (*Continued*)

Criteria	Proposals									
	1	2	3	4	5	6	7	8	9	10
b. Department/unit move consistent with existing understanding with the community										
c. Request consistent with building plans/limitations (accommodates parking, classroom, square footage, labs, etc.)										
d. Vacated space needed to solve other critical space problems										
3. Assessment of Existing Conditions Ratings: 0–3 suggests adequacy/acceptability 4–7 average to below average adequacy 8–10 extreme inadequacy/unacceptability										
a. Lack of adequate space to carry out required functions (implicit and explicit university commitments)										
b. Fragmentation and/or lack of proximity impeding use of department and university resources										
c. Need for general infrastructure improvement (sufficient staff, support facilities, etc.)										
4. Expenditures/Revenues Ratings: 0–3 does not meet expectations 4–7 meets some expectations 8–10 meets all expectations										
a. Reduces expenditures of existing (recurring) maintenance costs; reduces expenditures for deferred maintenance renovations; or reduces rental costs										
b. Provides for operating savings through consolidations										
c. Generates added revenues										
TOTAL POINTS:										

TABLE 12.4   City of Bright, Civic Center: Project and Resource Allocation Analysis (Thousands)—Spearman's Rho Correlation for Ranked Data

Projects	Project Rank (r_1)	Resource Allocation (y)	Resource Rank (r_2)	$r_1 - r_2$ d	d^2
A	1	250.0	5	−4	16
B	7	500.0	3	4	16
C	3	350.0	4	−1	1
D	9	100.0	6	3	9
E	2	700.0	1	1	1
F	8	150.0	8	0	0
G	5	125.0	10	−5	25
H	6	175.0	7	−1	1
I	10	135.0	9	1	1
J	4	650.0	2	2	4
N=10	$\Sigma(r_1)=55$	$\Sigma(y)=3135.0$	$\Sigma(r_2)=55$	$\Sigma d=0$	$\Sigma d^2=74$

Spearman's rank (Rho) correlation

$$r_s = 1 - \frac{6\Sigma D^2}{N(N^2-1)}$$

$$r_x = 1 - \frac{6(74)}{10(100-1)}$$

$$r_s = .552$$

Since the Spearmanrank correlation coefficient is 0.55, the projects and resources are moderately positive aligned.

Spearman's Rho correlation coefficients*

0.90 – 1.0   = Projects and resource allocations are properly aligned.

0.75 – 0.89 = Projects and resource allocations are highly aligned.

0.60 – 0.74 = Projects and resource allocations are strongly aligned.

0.45 – 0.59 = Projects and resource allocations are moderately aligned.

0.30 – 0.44 = Projects and resource allocations are somewhat aligned.

0.15 – 0.29 = Projects and resource allocations are slightly aligned.

0.00 – 0.14 = Projects and resource allocations are not aligned.

Note: *Spearman correlation coefficients range from negative 1.0 to positive 1.0.

Capital Budgeting: Elements Contributing to Success and Failure

In its extensive study of both public and private organizations' capital budgeting practices, the GAO identified elements that either contribute to or jeopardize success. The elements found in a successful organization can be ranked on a continuum of critical to helpful attributes (see Table 12.5). Similarly, the elements found in an unsuccessful organization range from harmful to destructive attributes.

TABLE 12.5   Elements Contributing to Organizational Success and Failure

Elements Found in Successful Organizations	Elements Found in Unsuccessful Organizations
Critical	**Destructive**
Extensively links planning to budgeting.	Does not link planning to budgeting when planning takes place.
Concerned about long-term effects.	Pays little attention to long-term effects.
Incorporates up-to-date information on physical capital into decision-making process.	Does not consistently feed information on the condition of physical capital into the decision-making process.
Important	**Damaging**
Recognizes the effect of deferred maintenance and minimizes it to the extent possible.	Has limited, if any, controls; misses many financial and work targets.
Protects capital-investment funds from being used for operations.	Defers structural maintenance; focuses on cosmetic repairs.
Considers related operations and maintenance costs when making capitalbudgeting decisions.	Cuts budgets with "closed eyes."
Considers alternative methods of meeting the objectives of capital.	
Monitors capital investments and the condition of physical capital.	
Does not have internal conflicts that disrupt capital-budgeting activities.	
Sees individual projects as modernization, revitalization, and investment.	
Uses funding mechanisms to protect priorities.	
Uses incentives to meet work and financial targets.	
Helpful	**Harmful**
Figures out ways to allocate something for everyone (keeps things even, moves on all fronts).	Lets funding mechanisms drive priorities.
Uses categories for decision-making that are important to the organizations, (e.g., productivity items).	Sees individual projects as "pork barrel."
Routinely assesses physical capital and adherence to a maintenance schedule.	Lets special-interest groups operate without control.

Source: U.S. Government Accounting Office (GAO), *Federal Capital Budgeting: A Collection of Haphazard Practices* (Washington, DC: GAO, 1981), p. 40.

The successful organization is able to minimize the effects on its service delivery system when operating conditions change its environment. The GAO stated: "A successful organization is one that can, even under adverse conditions, acquire and/or maintain physical capital without jeopardizing its mission or its clientele. By adverse conditions, we mean declining resources, political instability, or severe conflict among interest groups."[13]

Financial Analysis

Although the pay-as-you-go approach (discussed in chapter 8) has been exceedingly popular in government and other not-for-profit agencies, most governments have not been able to adopt this option and still meet the needs of their citizens. Older communities (especially those with relatively stable recurrent expenditures) having most of their infrastructure in place are in a better position to adopt the pay-as-you-go approach, in contrast to newer communities and those experiencing rapid growth and development. The approach does have two particularly appealing features: (1) In the long run, it is more economical, because financing costs are eliminated; and (2) there is a generally held view among public finance experts that greater efficiency is attained when taxpayers feel the burden/cost of the undertaking immediately.[14]

When the pay-as-you-go approach cannot be followed, a number of modified approximations may be pursued: (1) Adopt a policy requiring that the length of all future debt instruments be successively shortened as they are issued; (2) make an initial down payment from current revenues and increase the portion until the capital outlay can be easily accommodated by current revenues; and (3) declare a moratorium on issuing debt until all outstanding debts are substantially reduced.[15]

When Pay-as-You-Go Is Appropriate

Despite the constant call for the pay-as-you-go approach, it may not always be desirable. Some reasons for this are that (1) it should not be followed when capital projects expand the tax base, (2) it should be avoided when capital expenditures will materially distort the entire tax structure of the governmental unit, and (3) when real interest costs are negative, as during the latter 1970s, it may be fiscally more prudent to borrow. (During that period, it was possible to borrow at rates lower than inflation costs.)[16]

A critical part of the CIP process is the development of the financing plan. The governmental unit or agency must determine how much can be spent, the sources from which the money will come, and the people and entities who will bear the burden. Satisfying the projected capital needs requires the identification and scheduling of funding sources (known as *financial programming*). Action must be taken regarding (1) tax rates, (2) the desired balance between debt service and expenditures, (3) available aid from state and federal governments, and (4) new revenue sources.

Analysis of Revenues and Expenditures

A review of the past five years of the revenue collection and expenditures record is an important first step, as it provides a benchmark against which future revenue and expenditure can be measured. On the revenue side, special attention should be given to recurring items such as property taxes, user fees, and proposed changes affecting valuation of the tax rate, special limitations on property tax prospects for the local job market, inflation, trends in population, and other important changes that might be discernable.[17]

As was illustrated in chapters 4 (see Tables 4.1 and 4.3) and 10 (see Table 10.7 and Figure 10.2), least squares regression models can be used to make revenue and expenditure projections. For revenue projections, the least squares model estimates the slope and level of the trend. More important, this method allows one to calculate and plot future revenues. To make the most accurate projections, the following underlying assumptions must be satisfied: (1) The time series must be linear (i.e., the data must increase progressively over time with an increase that can be plotted by a straight line), (2) past patterns must persist in the future, and (3) past patterns must be regular. More sophisticated regressions models that control for changes in population, industry growth, and other variables can also be used to obtain more precise trends and projections. Regardless of the regression model used, the precision of the projections depends on the extent to which the past revenue data are consistent with the assumptions. Assuming that the underlying assumptions have been satisfied, Table 12.6 shows that the civic center can expect an increase of $22,417 ($b = 22.417$) in summer concert revenues over time. Accordingly, the civic center can expect to obtain $613,335 in summer concert revenues for 2002. The utility of the least squares regression model is that it provides a statistical tool for assessing and quantitatively estimating revenue trends and projections.

When using data from the same period as the revenue review, the expenditures should be categorized as follows: recurring operating expenditures, capital expenditures, and debt service payments. Aspects such as changes in the workforce (especially new employees), salary and benefit trends, and types and terms of existing bonded indebtedness should also be considered. Least squares regression, along with more sophisticated regression procedures, can also be employed to make expenditure projections. Again, assuming that the underlying assumptions have been satisfied, Table 12.7 indicates that the civic center can expect an increase of $19,417 in expenditures over time. More important, the civic center can project expenditures to be $516,460 for 2001.

TABLE 12.6 City of Bright, Civic Center: Summer Concert Revenue Projections (in Thousands)—Least Squares Regression Model

Years (X) 1	Revenues (Y) 2	Coded Time Value (x) 3	Columns (2) by (3) (xY) 4	Column 3 Squared (x²) 5	Trend Value For Revenues (Y_t) 6
1986	375.0	−4	−1500	16	411.582
1987	450.0	−3	−1350	9	435.949
1988	475.0	−2	−950	4	456.416
1989	500.0	−1	−500	1	478.833
1990	550.0	1	550	1	523.667
1991	485.0	2	970	4	546.084
1992	575.0	3	1725	9	568.501
1993	600.0	4	2400	16	590.918
$N = 8$	$\Sigma(Y) =$ 4,010	$\Sigma(x) = 0$	$\Sigma(xY) =$ 1,345	$\Sigma(x^2) = 60$	$\Sigma(Y_t) =$ 4,010

$$Y_t = a + b(x)$$

$$a = \frac{S(Y)}{N} = \frac{4,010}{8} = 501.25$$

$$b = \frac{S(xY)}{S(x^2)} = \frac{1,345}{60} = 22.417$$

$$Y_t = 501.25 + 22.417(x)$$

TABLE 12.7 City of Bright, Civic Center: Expenditure Projections (Thousands)—Least-Squares Regression Model

Years (x) 1	Revenues (y) 2	Coded Time Value (x) 3	Columns (2) by (3) (xy) 4	Column 3 Squared (x²) 5	Trend Value For Revenues (y_t) 6
1986	350.0	−4	−1400	16	341.707
1987	375.0	−3	−1125	9	361.124
1988	345.0	−2	−690	4	380.541
1989	400.0	−1	−400	1	399.958
1990	475.0	1	475	1	438.794
1991	450.0	2	900	4	458.209
1992	435.0	3	1305	9	477.626
1993	525.0	4	2100	16	497.043
$n = 8$	$\Sigma(y) = 3355$	$\Sigma(x) = 0$	$\Sigma(xy) = 1165$	$\Sigma(x^2) = 60$	$\Sigma(y_t) = 3355$

(Continued)

TABLE 12.7   *(Continued)*

$$y_t = a + b(x)$$
$$a = \frac{S(Y)}{N} = \frac{3,355}{8} = 419.375$$
$$b = \frac{S(xY)}{S(x^2)} = \frac{1,165}{60} = 19.417$$
$$Y_t = 419.375 + 19.417(x)$$

Future Revenue and Expenditure Projections

With the completion of the past revenue and expenditure review, revenue and expenditure for the duration of the proposed CIP may be forecasted. This permits the linkage of the CIP with the community's resource capability. Whatever methods are used in making revenue and expenditure projections, various assumptions must be clearly defined. These assumptions involve changes in variables such as population, residential, commercial, and industrial growth. Once the new revenue and expenditure projections have been made, the capital facility plan for each year can be completed. The difference between projected expenditures and projected revenue represents the amount that the governmental unit or agency will need to generate to finance the proposed capital improvements.[18] Numerous options are available to a governmental unit or agency to obtain sufficient funds to carry out its CIP:

- *General obligations (G.O.) bonds* are legal obligations of the organization issuing the bonds. These are used to build public facilities, such as jails, sewers, and bridges.
- *Limited* or *special obligation bonds* are unlike G.O.s in that they do not carry the same statutory and constitutional security. They do not enjoy the "full faith and credit" of the issuing unit, although they have priority over all non-project creditors. In many states, specific sources of taxes are designated to pay limited bond obligations. A few states do not permit bonds to be general obligations unless they are pledged by the property tax; others make a bond a general obligation if any revenue not generated from the project is pledged to pay for its repayment.[19]
- *Revenue bonds* are a type of limited obligation bond and include those issues on which governmental units "promise to pay debt service . . . exclusively from the revenue derived from user fees and charges from the project constructed."[20] Examples are turnpikes and major public improvements, including special-assessment bonds.
- A *lease purchase agreement* involves a facility built by a private or not-for-profit organization.
- *Joint financing with other governmental units* may be arranged.

- *Private development funds* may be used, as in cases in which new infrastructure is required in new developments.
- *Sources of government revenues*, including taxes, special assessments, and user charges, may be employed.

The public sector pays for virtually all the country's infrastructure (roads, bridges, mass transit systems, sewers, water, and so on). The resources to fund most capital facilities were obtained mainly through federal sources and long-term debt issued by state and local governments. Historically, general obligation bonds have been the chief capital financing source for state and local governments. (General obligation bonds are secured by the units promising to pay the principal and interest from general revenue resources.)

Because of public resistance, the financing source for capital improvements has been declining in recent years. More popular are revenue bonds, which permit the debt service (principal and interest payments) to be paid from the revenue produced by the specific project in the future. Although the revenue bond financing approach is likely to enjoy popularity as a means of financing capital improvement, there is a distinct limit as to how many capital improvements can be self-financed. Limitations are caused by resistance to the amounts of user charges that people may want to pay. The demands on state and local governments to provide increased resources to finance improved capital facilities are likely to rise appreciably. Nonetheless, the major financing source (the federal government) has already begun to decrease the available funds in this area.[21]

Capital Budget Analysis

Because government and other not-for-profit organizations have limited resources or revenues, the costs of desirable programs and projects always exceed available revenues. If the best possible use is to be made of scarce revenues, only those projects providing the maximum social gain to the community should be undertaken. Capital budget analysis comprises techniques used for evaluating the social benefits of alternative uses for available scarce resources. Stated another way, the process consists of an orderly sequence of steps organized to produce relevant information for choosing investments. The steps involved require the following:

1. Identification of relevant investment alternatives.
2. Estimation of the cash flow for each alternative.
3. Selection of the appropriate choice criteria to apply to the projected cash flow to facilitate a measure of comparison.
4. Arrangement of data for each alternative (project), the interpretation being consistent with the specified criteria, and selection of the projects with maximum social gain.

Identifying Alternatives

This step demands that the various decision choices be clearly understood. The benefits to be gained from a project should be compared with the benefits that can be achieved from alternative applications of a resource.

Estimating the Cash Flow

Because the accounting system allocates costs on a responsibility or departmental basis, there may be confusion about which costs are relevant to decision making. Therefore, a few useful rules have been suggested to aid in deciding which costs should be included in capital decisions:

- Include only those inflows and outflows that can be directly related to the project; exclude those that would occur irrespective of the project. A capital expenditure is a cash outlay over a number of years that is intended to produce a flow of future benefits. A capital expenditure may be viewed as consisting of three distinct elements: expected future benefits, the time factor, and the risk related to the realization of the expected benefits.
- Focus only on future cash flow, because all past cash flow discussions are *sunk costs* and cannot be changed.
- Pay close attention to cash flow and not to accounting reports, which may differ because of the accrual accounting system. (The cash system and the cash flow approach will usually produce nearly identical results.) It is important to keep in mind that the data on costs and benefits are determined at this stage—that is, cost and benefits in dollars must be identified for the entire life of the project or program.

Applying Capital Budget Criteria: Techniques for Project Analysis

Decision makers in most not-for-profit agencies find it easier to identify costs (the input factor) than to estimate benefits. The situation is even more difficult when the explicit intention of an expansion is to increase service capability or quality. It is critical to select the criteria that will generate information that is useful for ranking in order to enable the decision maker to accept or reject different investment objectives. Five criteria occasionally used in public and other not-for-profit organizations are as follow:

- Simple rate of return/average rate of return
- Payback period
- Net present value
- Excess present value
- Internal rate of return

The simple rate of return (SRR) expresses the average net profits generated yearly by an investment as a percentage of the original investment or as the percentage return on investment over its expected life. The following is one of a number of ways to calculate the simple rate of return:

$$SRR = \frac{Y}{I}$$

Where Y is the average annual profits (minus depreciation) projected for the new investment, I is the initial investment, and SRR is the average annual or simple rate of return. Each investment is ranked according to the relative size of its SRR. Its profitability is then judged by comparison with the investor's required rate of return (RRR). After due consideration of the risk, liquidity, and other relevant factors, use the following decision rules: When SRR exceeds RRR, accept the investment. When SRR equals RRR, be neutral or indifferent. When SRR is less than RRR, reject it.

Table 12.8 shows the projected average annual rates of return for investments X, Y, and Z. Applying the simple rate of return criterion, investment X would be the first choice, followed by Y, and last, Z. Because 8 percent is the required rate of return, the three projects are profitable. Note that the simple rate of return does not consider the time element related to the different cash flows. When each flow pattern has large differences, the simple rate of return may lead to erroneous conclusions.

The Payback Period

This is a very simple quantitative technique and is widely used for evaluating investment opportunities. It provides an estimate of the time required to recover the cost of an investment:

$$Payback\ period = \frac{Original\ investment}{Annual\ cash\ flow}$$

TABLE 12.8   Simple Rate of Return: Three Hypothetical Investments

Project	Net costs Plus Depreciation	Investment	Net Average Annual Inflow	Simple Rate of Return
X	31,000	20,000	2,000	10%
Y	30,000	20,000	1,800	9%
Z	29,000	20,000	1,600	8%

In not-for-profit organizations, two approaches (see Table 12.8) are used: (1) The annual cash flow may be the actual inflow generated by the investment of a piece of equipment, or (2) the amount of savings produced as a result of the investment may be substituted for the annual cash flow. Either approach is acceptable. By way of illustration, assume that a hospital wants to purchase one of two comparable X-ray machines. Machine X costs $108,000, with an annual cash inflow of $12,000. Machine Y costs $120,000 and generates $16,000 in savings annually. The application of the payback criterion would require that machine Y be chosen. The payback for the machines may be computed as follows:

$$\text{machine } X: \frac{108,000}{12,000} = 9 \text{ years}$$

$$\text{machine } Y: \frac{120,000}{16,000} = 7.5 \text{ years}$$

Because of the ease of the payback calculation, it may be conveniently used at lower levels of management to approve small-expenditure projects. The chief advantage of the payback period approach is its ability to pinpoint the time it takes an investment to pay for itself. In addition, it is easy to calculate and understand.

Specific investments are ranked according to their relative payback periods, the projects with the shortest payback period being most favored. The criterion for acceptance or rejection is based on the investors' required payback period (RPP). The decision rule is applied as follows: When the payback period is less than RPP, accept the investment. When the payback period equals RPP, be neutral or indifferent. When the payback period exceeds RPP, reject the investment.

A major disadvantage of the payback period approach is that it ignores all cash flows beyond the payback period. In the X-ray machine example, machine X continues to generate cash inflows for three more years after the payback period, whereas the savings on machine Y stopped at the payback

TABLE 12.9 Three Investment Cash Flows

Year	Investment X	Investment Y	Investment Z
0 Present	−$20,000	−$20,000	−$20,000
1	2,000	6,000	10,000
2	4,000	6,000	8,000
3	6,000	6,000	6,000
4	9,000	6,000	4,000
5	10,000	6,000	1,000

period. When all this information is considered, machine X will be selected rather than machine Y. Because the payback period technique does not consider the time value of money, it is not accepted as a valid means of determining the economic feasibility of projects that will have long lives.

Time Value of Money

This approach is known as the "discounted cash flow method" when applied to capital budgeting decisions. Unlike the payback period and simple rate of return approaches, the time value of money recognizes that the use of money has a cost. Interest is analogous to rent that one pays for the use of a piece of equipment or building. The discounted cash flow method recognizes that $10 to be received or spent in the future does not have the same value as $10 received or spent today. For example, if you deposit $100 in a bank at 8 percent interest, at the end of the year you will have $108, assuming that the interest is compounded annually. If the individual feels that $100 today or $108 one year hence are equivalent, then the 8 percent interest rate constitutes the *opportunity cost of time*—that is, the one-year wait for the money. The 8 percent rate measures the willingness to exchange $100 today (*present value*) for $108 at the end of a year (*future value*). The present value is computed as follows:

$$Present\ value = \frac{Future\ value}{1 + Interest\ rate}$$

or, in this case,

$$100 = \frac{108}{1 + 0.08}$$

Note that the cash flow method is concerned only with *cash* inflows and outflows. This is in sharp contrast with the accounting method (e.g., the simple rate of return), which is affected by depreciation and other noncash transactions.

Net Present Value

Net present value (NPV) indicates the extent to which an investor will be better or worse off when accepting a given project, as opposed to investing in other available options. The net present value (assuming a given rate of interest) is equal to the discounted inflow minus the discounted outflows. When the present value is greater than the outflows, the positive net present value is said to be the excess present value return that is earned on the project.

In evaluating NPV options, the size of an investment's present value influences its ranking and acceptability. When all investments being considered are income-generating, the one that has the largest NPV is given the highest ranking. The following decision rules apply: (1) When the NPV exceeds zero, accept the investment. (2) when NPV equals zero, be neutral or indifferent. (3) When NPV is less than zero, reject the investment.

When the investment options are cost-reducing, the projected cash outflows reflect outlays (i.e., expenditures). Cost-reducing comparisons require that the chosen criterion be based on the minimum net present value of each of the outlays. To calculate the NPV, five types of data are required:

IN = the initial capital investment

P_N = the annual net cash flows attributed to the investment that can be withdrawn periodically or yearly

V_N = any salvage or other terminal investment value

N = the time horizon (N) or the summation for $n = 0$ to N

i = the interest rate or required rate of return.

The formula is set up for a nonuniform series of payments as follows:

$$NPV = -INV + \frac{P_1}{(1+i)} + \frac{P_2}{(1+i)^2} + \cdots \frac{P_N}{(1+i)^N} = \frac{V_N}{(1+i)^N}$$

If projected cash flows are a uniform series of payments (an annuity), USPV is designated as a simplified notation for the *uniform series present value* over N periods at interest rate (i). The formula is then as follows:

$$NPV = -INV + A[USPV_{i,N}] + \frac{V_N}{(1+i)^N}$$

Assuming that an investor is evaluating investment X, Y, and Z and requires a 10 percent rate of return, as shown in Table 12.7, the NPV of investment X can be determined:

$$NPV = -20,000 = \frac{2,000}{(1.10)} + \frac{4,000}{(1.10)^2} + \frac{6,000}{(1.10)^3} + \frac{9,000}{(1.10)^4} + \frac{10,000}{(1.10)^5}$$

The conversion factors $(1.10)^{-n}$ are found in Appendix 2, Table A.1; $i = 0.10$ and values of n range from 1 to 5. The NPV is

$$NPV = -20,000 + 2,000(0.926) + 4,000(0.856) + 6,000(0.794)$$
$$+ 9,000(0.735) + 10,000(0.681)$$
$$= -20,000 + 1,852 + 3,424 + 4,764 + 6,615 + 6,810 = \$3,465$$

An alternate way for computing the net present value requires determining the following:

1. Estimated annual cash flows (determined directly from each investment)
2. Estimated number of years or economic life for which the investment will generate cash flows
3. Net amount of costs associated with the investment
4. The required rate of return

The net present value may then be calculated using the following formula:

Net present value = (Cash flow × Present value factor) – Investment

$$NPV = (CF \times pvf) - 1$$

Using the data in Table 12.2, investment Y above, and Appendix 2, Table A.2, the net present value is calculated as follows:

(1) Annual cash flow   = $6,000

(2) Economic life   = 5 years

(3) Net investment amount   = $20,000

(4) Rate of return   = 10 percent

$$NPV = (CF \times PVF) - 1$$
$$= (\$6,000 \times 3.791) - \$20,000$$
$$= \$22,746 - \$20,000$$
$$= \$2,746$$

This suggests that the investment is financially feasible. Following the same procedure, the calculated net present value investment for Y is $2,746 and for Z, $4,443. Although all three investment alternatives are acceptable, according to the NPV decision rules, investment Z is preferred over X and Y.

Internal Rate of Return

Although the term *internal rate of return* (IRR) is perhaps the most widely known, a number of other names are also used: discounted rate of return, the marginal efficiency of capital, or the yield of an investment. The IRR refers to the rate of interest equal to the net present value of a projected series of cash flow payments at zero.

To find the IRR for an investment, apply the NPV formula with the appropriate projected cash flows (INV, P_n, P_N, V_n), set NPV equal to zero, and solve:

$$0 = -INV + \frac{P_1}{(1+i)} + \frac{P_2}{(1+i)^2} + \ldots \frac{P_N}{(1+i)^N} = \frac{V_N}{(1+i)^N}$$

The interest rate that satisfies the equation is the internal rate of return.

As an illustration, determine the IRR for an investment requiring an initial payment of \$1,000, yielding \$1,300 one year hence. The IRR is calculated as follows:

$$0 = -1{,}000 + \frac{1{,}300}{1+i}$$

Transposing the equation, the yield is

$$1 + i = \frac{1{,}300}{1{,}000} = 1.30;$$

$$i = .3$$

Thus, the IRR equals 30 percent. Assume that the \$1,300 payment was received after two years rather than at the end of only one. The IRR is then calculated as follows:

$$0 = -1{,}000 + \frac{1{,}300}{(1+i)^2}$$

Transposing the equation, the yield is

$$(1 + i)\ 2 = \frac{1{,}000}{1{,}300} = 0.7692;$$

Thus i equals 0.14.

Note that the conversion factor is determined by using Appendix 2, Table A.2 to find the value of i, given that $n = 2$, and providing the conversion factor of 0.7692. In using the table, find the number of periods equated with n (in this case, two). Then move along to the right side of the table until you find the conversion factor exactly or nearest to 0.7692. For this example, the conversion factor for $n = 2$ and $i = 0.14$ occurs exactly at 0.7692. Thus, the IRR is exactly 14 percent. When the factor for i falls in between two interest rates in the table, the best estimate of IRR may be determined through interpolation.

To find the IRR for a series of payments, consider the IRR for $30,000 with a series of payments of $6,000 per year for five years. Appendix 2, Table A.2 is used to find the value of i, where $n = 5$, given a conversion factor of 2.941. When $n = 5$, the value for $i = 0.21$ is 2.991, while for $i = 0.20$ it is 2.926. Thus the IRR for the investment falls between 20 and 21 percent. To obtain a more accurate approximation of the interest rate, interpolate as follows:

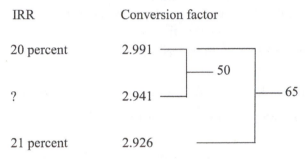

FIGURE 12.2   IRR and conversion factor.

The estimate for the IRR is 50/65, or 20.77 percent. Like the capital budget evaluation techniques discussed previously, the IRR method can be used to accept or reject investment alternatives. The ranking system is based on the relative sizes of the IRR, with the investments having the largest IRR being those most favored. Each investment acceptability is dependent on a comparison with the investor's required rate of return (RRR). The following decision rules apply: When the IRR exceeds RRR, accept the investment. When the IRR equals RRR, be indifferent or neutral. When the IRR is less than RRR, reject it. It is important to remember that these decision rules are subject to considerations of risk and liquidity.

It should be observed that the net present value is closely linked to the IRR; each calculation uses the same discounting approach. However, whereas the NPV specifies a given interest rate, the IRR identifies the interest rate that yields a zero NPV.

Excess Present Value

This approach calculates the positive or negative percentage of streams of inflows over outflows of a project. By means of this approach, an index is calculated as follows:

$$\text{Excess present value index} = \frac{Present\ value}{Required\ investment}$$

This index can be used to compare and rank competing projects. Because it shows the present value of a project per dollar of investment, it provides a means of ranking projects of different sizes. This greatly simplifies finding the optimum solutions for competing projects when the budget for capital outlays have been arbitrarily determined. The criteria for selection and rejection are simple. Projects are ranked in order of profitability based on indices above 100 percent. Projects below 100 percent are undesirable, because the cost of capital would exceed the adjusted rate of return.

To illustrate this, look at the example of a machine to process mail brought at a cost of $22,000. Assume that the money cost is 16 percent and that the machine generates a cash flow of $5,000 per year for ten years:

Present value = $5,000 × 4.833 (using Appendix 2, Table A.2) = $24,165

Excess present value = $24,165 − $22,000 = $2,615

$$\text{Excess present value index} = \frac{Present\ value}{Required\ investment}$$

or

$$\frac{214,165}{22,000} = 109.8\ \text{percent}$$

Determining the Discount Rate

Although seldom discussed, the determination of the discount rate to be used in calculating the net present values and benefit–cost ratios is critical. Two general ways have been used: (a) examining the cost of obtaining funds for the project and (b) examining the return on alternative investments. At the federal level, the Office of Management and Budget has endorsed 10 percent as a rate that may be used in government programs.

Concluding Observations

Capital budgeting has great potential as a tool for public and other not-for-profit organizations. If effectively carried out, it can aid a community's economic development and generate confidence in a governmental unit's ability to wisely manage its resources. Similarly, in other not-for-profit agencies, the appropriate selection and good management of capital equipment can facilitate a better allocation of resources and minimize the possibility of fiscal strain.

Given the magnitude of resources required to fund capital projects, it is difficult for all but a few governmental units to use the popular pay-as-you-go funding approach for such projects. Therefore, capital budgeting requires that decision makers give serious thought to optimal methods for selecting a capital program mix to yield the greatest payoff for the amounts of dollars expended. The method of financing is especially critical, because the selection of a particular option can result in either significant savings or additional costs.

Unlike in the past, a large number of public and not-for-profit organizations have begun applying varied techniques for analyzing and choosing among capital projects. Techniques such as the internal rate of return, net present value, and excess present value have been successfully applied.

Notes

1. John Fishbein and Christopher Cawley, "Capital Program Considerations in Challenging Times," *Government Finance Review 25*, no. 3 (June 2009): 14.

2. Alan Walter Steiss, *Local Government Finance* (Lexington, MA: Lexington Books, 1975), p. 4.

3. U.S. General Accounting Office (GAO), *Federal Capital Budgeting: A Collection of Haphazard Practices* (Washington, DC: GAO, 1981), p. i; see also Thomas M. Downs, "Restoring Public Confidence in Infrastructure Investment," *Intergovernmental Perspective 29*, no. 1 (fall 1993–winter 1994): 15–16.

4. Susan G. Robinson, "Capital Planning and Budgeting," in *Local Government Finance: Concepts and Practices*, eds. John Peterson and Dennis R. Strachota (Chicago: Government Finance Officers Association, 1991).

5. International City Management Association (ICMA), "Planning for Capital Improvements," *Management Information Service Report 16*, no. 18 (August 1984): 5.

6. GAO, *Federal Capital Budgeting*, pp. 17–18.

7. ICMA, "Planning for Capital Improvements," op. cit., pp. 2–3.

8. John L. Mikesell, *Fiscal Administration* (Homewood, IL: Dorsey Press, 1982), pp. 100–101.

9. Ibid., p. 3.

10. Ibid.

11. Steiss, *Local Government Finance*, p. 35; see also ICMA, "Planning for Capital Improvements," p. 13.

12. Robert L. Bland and Irene S. Rubin, *Budgeting: A Guide for Local Governments* (Washington, DC: ICMA, 1997), p. 195.

13. GAO, *Federal Capital Budgeting*, p. 39.

14. Steiss, *Local Government Finance*, pp. 104–105.

15. Ibid.

16. Bernard Smith, "The Pay-as-You-Go Concept in Municipal Financing," *Government Finance Review 6*, no. 3 (June 1990): 21–22.

17. ICMA, "Planning for Capital Improvements," p. 8.

18. Ibid., pp. 8–9.

19. Dillon, Read, and Co., "Infrastructure Financing: An Overview" (November 1963): 4.

20. Ibid.; ICMA, "Planning for Capital Improvements," p. 10.

21. Dillon, Read, and Co., "Infrastructure Financing," pp. 1–2.

13

Line Item and Performance Budgeting

Although the previous two chapters dealt with concepts and uses of budgets in general terms, this chapter examines two types of budgets that are found in practice: line item and performance. Emphasis is focused on how each of these budgeting approaches allocates scarce resources among desirable courses of action. The development of the line item and performance budgets is examined, as well as ways in which they are used for allocating, maintaining, and controlling financial resources.

Line Item Budgeting

The *line item budget* (also called the *object of expenditure budget*) was the earliest type of budget format to be used in public and nonprofit institutions. It came into being hand in hand with the development of modern budgeting. Its introduction was considered an innovative development by financial reformers at the turn of the 20th century and replaced the lump sum budgeting approach. The reformers sought to improve the economy and efficiency of organizations and ensure the legality of expenditures in an effort to control graft and corruption in government. The line item budget took prominence with the establishment of the executive budget, which reposed responsibility and accountability for government spending with the chief executive. This gave the chief executive a powerful instrument for controlling agency demands for money.

Defining the Line Item Budget

Line item budgeting is a technique in which *line items* (also known as *objects of expenditure*) are the main focus of analysis, authorization, and control. The individual financial statement items are grouped according to cost centers or departments (as shown in Table 13.1). Typical line items include supplies, personnel, travel, contractual services, and capital outlays. These are the items upon which major attention is focused and financial resources are controlled. Although there is no way of determining what the line item budget will accomplish, it is easily understood. Table 13.1 clearly indicates the services or commodities to be purchased and total amount of money that the city of Bright will spend for police services. The budget identifies items that administrators and elected officials can relate to in terms of their own experience. The fact that the line item budget presents specific items that can be easily increased or reduced without debating the merits or demerits of a program enhances the opportunity for compromise.

A number of control objectives can be achieved with the line item budget: (1) Scandals can be avoided scandals by making sure that funds are spent for authorized purposes; (2) the legislature's programmatic objectives can be

TABLE 13.1   City of Bright Police Department: Simplified Line-Item/Object Expenditure Budget, FY 2012 (Classified by Organizational Unit and Object of Expenditure)

Police department	Rate		
Salaries and wages			
1 – Chief	$80,000	$ 80,000	
1 – Assistant chief	60,000	60,000	
3 – Captains	50,000	150,000	
2 – Sergeants	40,000	80,000	
20 – Patrolmen	30,000	600,000	
4 – Radio operators	25,000	100,000	$1,070,000
Supplies/materials			
Stationery and related supplies		3,000	
Janitorial and related supplies		1,600	
Gloves		800	
Gasoline and oil		10,000	
Uniforms		12,000	
Other		2,000	29,400
Other service charges			
Telephone		4,000	
Out-of-town travel		8,000	
Parking tickets		2,000	
Utilities		8,000	
Other		1,000	23,000
Capital outlay			
2 – Motorcycles		20,000	
4 – Patrol cars		80,000	
Communication equipment		20,000	120,000
Total Police Department			$1,242,400

accomplished; and (3) the a balanced budget and interperiod equity can be maintained. Of these objectives, the third one and—particularly—the second are the major concerns of the line item/object budget.[1]

Line item budgeting is the most widely used budgeting system today. It has wide appeal because of the type of accountability (narrow, with legal control) that it emphasizes. Attention is given as means for ensuring fidelity—preventing funds from being stolen and expended for unauthorized purposes. Emphasis is placed on things or commodities to be bought rather than on the type and quality of services to be produced. For example, in a typical department such as that shown in Table 13.1, there are separate lines for wages and salaries; purchase of automobiles; equipment and supplies; and expenditures for other services such as utilities—and the list of items is limited only by the number of items or services requested. A typical monthly budget report includes the budget category, the approved budget amount, the amount expended in the current month, the amount expended in the current year, and the percent of budget expended, as well as outstanding encumbrances that have yet to be incurred (see Table 13.2).

The development of the line item budget system involves the following steps:

1. The first step requires that categories of responsibility for expenditures be clearly defined. This action facilitates the development of an effective budget process, establishing clear lines for individual responsibility for each activity.
2. The amount of work and the kinds of skills required for each activity should be determined.
3. The budgetary unit desired to facilitate planning and controlling of expenditures should be defined.
4. A calendar is prepared specifically identifying individual or group responsibility and the target dates for completion.
5. Review of the object of expenditure classification chart should be undertaken to standardize and permit the consolidation or summary of like items within departments.
6. Account codes should be examined and revised when necessary to make them consistent with the budgetary classification system.

The line item process requires that agencies submit requests to the chief executive in terms of types of expenditures to be made according to established line items. The chief executive modifies these requests and submits them to the legislature or appropriate board. The latter then reviews, modifies, and appropriates funds on the line item basis.

Once the budget is appropriated, the executive sets up the accounting system to record the line item amounts as specified by the legislature or board. Additional controls are instituted for personnel hiring, transferring funds

TABLE 13.2 City of Bright Police Department (Patrol): Monthly Budget Report, August 31, 2012

Budgetary Category	Approved Budget	Amount Expended This Month	Amount Expended This Year	Amount of Unexpended Budget	% Budget Unexpended	Outstanding Encumbrances*
Salaries and Wages	$256,000	$22,000	$176,000	$80,000	31.2	-0-
Fringe Benefits	64,000	5,000	40,000	24,000	37.5	-0-
Supplies/Materials	17,200	2,000	6,000	9,200	53.5	$5,000
Equipment	72,000	44,000	44,000	28,000	38.9	5,000
Total	$409,200	$73,000	$266,000	$141,200		$10,000

Note: *Obligation or liability for amount of goods or services ordered but not yet delivered.

among intra-agency and interagency accounts, and regulating the amounts permitted to be spent from period to period. To facilitate the latter, an allotment system is set up to accommodate individual agency expenditure needs, based on past practice and the projection of likely expenditures during the fiscal period. Typically, each agency's appropriated funds are allocated on a monthly or quarterly basis (or whatever period is considered acceptable). The allotment system provides a direct control device: Amounts may not be increased without specific permission from the controlling budget official, who has the power to review fund appropriation requests.

Whereas the allotment system tends to be used in larger agencies and governmental units, an expenditure plan (a less formal system) may be used by smaller agencies and governmental units. In this latter system, the budget or staff official who has the responsibility for monitoring expenditures on a monthly or quarterly basis works with the spending units to develop projections based, typically, on a five-year quarterly or monthly average corrected for any unusual events of the past and any expected abnormal occurrence during the coming fiscal period. When units or departments report that spending levels are higher than anticipated in the expenditure plan without an acceptable reason, prompt corrective action can be initiated. Among the actions that may be taken are transferring funds among activities, modifying work plans, reducing service levels, and cutting back expenditures on nonessential functions.

Advantages of the Line Item Budget

The line item budget assigns expenditures on the basis of the existing organization rather than on the responsibility center. There are a number of advantages associated with this type of budget:

- It permits hierarchical authority to control inputs before the expenditure is made or obligated.
- It constrains the exercise of discretionary powers by operations' managers.
- It helps curtail the number of personnel positions, salary increases, and purchases—the largest cost in public and nonprofit agencies.
- It provides for uniform controls throughout an agency.
- It provides for the comprehensive control of all financial transactions and permits easy compilation of financial data, facilitating financial accounting and auditing systems and minimizing computational costs (records are collected in the everyday course of administrative activity with information being derived directly from vouchers, purchase orders, and other documents in use).
- It promotes clear-cut controls, minimizing the opportunity for circumvention of hierarchical controls (the controls can still be flexible for favored agencies, and stringent for others that engage in unacceptable practices).

- It facilitates budget reductions; when agency spending exceeds revenues, cuts can be made without concern for impairing the program objectives.
- It avoids the possibility of making large and costly mistakes.
- It provides continuity between past, present, and future policy.
- It allows managers to operate with a greater degree of certainty.
- It permits legislators to affect easier accountability and confirmations on dollar amounts rather than requiring agreement on program outcomes, thereby reducing or minimizing the potential for political conflict and deadlock in the political system.

Incrementalism and the Line Item Budget

Incrementalism and line item budgeting go hand in hand. Incremental budgets focus on limited alternatives that differ slightly from existing policy. Prior levels of expenditure become the major decision criterion for allocating resources. Typically, the budget-makers accept amount X from the prior year's budget and add a small increment, amount A, which is a percentage of X. The budget formula thus becomes $X + AX$.[2] The incremental budget method has a built-in upward bias. Small changes, when added together over successive years, can become significant. The incremental approach is accommodative to user advocates because it allows recurring programs to continue their growth with minimal scrutiny. Caution should be used when applying this method, as resource allocation increases should be warranted and subsequently scrutinized rather than permitted automatically.

The Incremental Syndrome. The general orientation of budget-makers directs them to add or subtract a percentage to the previous year's budget. When times are good, there is reasonable expectation that more money will be available. Additions are routinely made "to all line-items or selectively whenever it seems to make the most sense."[3] Likewise, in bad years, small increments are added or subtracted, depending on the revenue outlook.

Decision rules (rules of thumb, generally agreed upon benchmarks, or criteria for facilitating decision making) typically characterize traditional incremental budget preparation. Once an amount is granted to a program or activity, it becomes the base or part of the basic budget from which "fair share" increases or decreases are added or subtracted.[4] Only amounts proposed above the "fair share" amount need to be justified, while expenditures for programs already in existence that do not exceed the fair share guideline go unquestioned and unchallenged.

Marginal or incremental changes constrain attempts to redirect social objectives. Policymaking tends to be short-range and tactical rather than long-range and sustainable. Because no comprehensive analysis or weighing of cost and benefits of objectives is undertaken, no effort is made to make the best decision among available alternatives. The present budget is a mirror of the past, and the future is a projection of the present.

Disadvantages of the Line Item Budget

The main shortcomings of the line item budget include the following:

- There is a total preoccupation with material acquisition or inputs.
- Accountability is focused on a narrow concept of what money can buy, and not on output and impact (e.g., changes produced as a result of the program).
- Little attention is given to organizational and program goals, making it difficult or virtually impossible to provide information for evaluating the efficiency and effectiveness of an agency's activities.
- Most budget items require no justification.
- After a program has been funded, it is likely to continue indefinitely—barring major adverse publicity.
- It provides fragmented historical cost data that are not useful for program execution and evaluation.
- Reports based on the line item budget produce very little financial data that can be used in planning, programming, and evaluating an agency's activities.
- Input planning decisions are made at the lower levels of the organization.
- Goals and objectives of the organization are made on the basis of dollar amounts allocated to the different activities. Operating procedures become policy. Thus, purposes are not consciously considered, and the achievement of objectives is due more to chance than design. (Pittsburgh's Department of Lands and Buildings budget provides a good illustration: The line item budget has six responsibility areas. However, although there are no stated objectives for any activity, performance statistics are included in the budget, providing no basis for effective evaluation.)
- Neither the executive branch nor the legislature is given information permitting the wise allocation of available resources.
- Although it facilitates compromise, it promotes poor decision making.
- Emphasis is placed on what is bought, failing to address policy or management issues.

Politics and the Line Item Budget

Even though line item/incremental budgeting is viewed as stable, predictable, and conservative, the politics that surround its preparation, particularly in the public sector, may permit small increases to explode into unmanageable programs with huge costs overruns. The estimate for the Mark 48 torpedo provides a classic example. Proponents of the torpedo made the initial cost estimate look small in comparison to the benefits to be gained. The program cost was revealed as a series of increments during the development of the prototype. The torpedo was sold to Congress as an almost invulnerable torpedo at a total cost of $680 million. A combination of participants, including the

U.S. Naval Ordinance Division, Westinghouse, and Penn State University, were selected to build the torpedo.[5] To minimize the possibility of cost over-runs, Congress hired Peat, Marwick, Mitchell, and Co. to monitor program costs. Between the time the project commenced in 1963 and its completion ten years later, the costs ballooned from $680 million to $4.5 billion, a fourfold increase. Initially, the torpedo system was estimated to be low in cost but high in terms of effectiveness. The expenditure increments continued for several years before a more accurate cost for completing the project was initiated. If at the outset the real cost had been estimated to be $4.5 billion, the project might never have been initiated. This is a constant problem in public administration, especially in government contracting, in which payment to the contractor is based on cost plus fee arrangement.

The political practice undergirding incremental budgeting has generated several rules that are used in preparing and submitting budgets:

- Avoid asking for sums smaller than the current appropriation.
- When an implementing agency wishes to avoid close scrutiny and review, increases are put in the basic budget. Because new requests are subject to close scrutiny, it is good strategy to identify them with the basic budget or high-priority areas whenever possible.
- Never give the appearance that you are making fundamental changes from existing policies. All necessary increases must be made to look small, appearing to grow out of existing operations.
- Make it possible to permit budget reviewers to look good by leaving something for them to cut. This allows the budget reviewer to act, while you nonetheless achieve your objective.[6]

Like the budget preparers, the reviewers or gatekeepers also employ decision rules such as the following:

- When new personnel are requested, decrease or eliminate the request.
- Renovate or repair facilities rather than replacing them.
- As a general policy, avoid cutting safety or health-related requests, especially those programs that have substantial public support.
- Decrease requests of departments that have poor or bad reputations.
- Reduce or eliminate by some fixed percentage all nonoperating requests.[7]

Target Base Budgeting: The New Orthodoxy

Many of the governmental units (e.g., the state of New Jersey, the city of San Antonio) that dismantled their zero-base budgeting (ZBB) system have reverted to line item budgeting or a variant of it called *target-base budgeting* (TBB). This budgeting approach establishes a departmental or responsibility center spending ceiling. Within the prescribed limits, some shifting among expenditure functions or activities is permitted. The ceiling targets are set on the basis of projected revenue estimates. Thus the target amount or percentage approved varies according to expected changes in revenues; the budget will be balanced and interperiod equity is maintained.

In some jurisdictions, such as Cincinnati, Rochester, Tampa, and Palatine, Illinois, where innovative TBB has been implemented, creative features of ZBB and performance budgeting can be found. Target base budgets are prepared in two parts: the first includes the funded service that is accommodated within the target, and the second part contains the prioritized, unfunded list of service items. Because the targets are set at conservative levels, often a pool of resources is left "to allow for add-backs, new or expanded projects, and political priorities."[8]

Advantages

Target-base budgeting is attractive because it is very adaptable to the regular budgeting cycle flow and is based on a conservative and eclectic philosophy. The operating norm allows it to borrow from other innovations such as ZBB, program budgeting, management by objectives (MBO), and performance budgeting as each situation dictates. As a "hold the line" budget, it is a budget approach that champions fiscal responsibility. It virtually banishes deficits while tending to generate savings or surpluses. Budgets can easily be reduced or maintained during recessions and increased during times of prosperity. Target-base budgeting provides politicians with the opportunity to affect priorities on short notice without creating undue problems. Agency managers are given strong incentives to improvise and take necessary action to enhance their chances to live within their prescribed resource constraint. This forces managers to develop decision rules to allow them to make hard choices and prioritize when faced with crises. Therefore, although targets are centrally determined (top-down), any tradeoffs, specific allocations, and changes among line items and programs are decentralized.[9] Lastly, target-base budgeting allows for retargeting during the year. This forces managers to think about priorities early in the budget cycle.

Disadvantages

Target-base budgeting is revenue-driven, typically not by articulated goals and objectives but by revenue projections, which are subject to changes as revenue sources are affected by the economy, intergovernmental fund transfers, plant closings, and a host of other factors. This reality tends to institutionalize a conservative orientation that leads to underestimation of revenues, which in turn, may lead to ill-advised staff reductions; such staff reductions can have profound negative effects on organizational morale. Because targets are often given in percentages, decisions tend to be ad hoc. The path of least resistance is to cut across the board. This may induce responsibility center managers to play gamesmanship by cutting popular and high-priority programs, knowing that they are likely to receive supplemental resources from the pool of savings to fund them when reallocation is made.

TBB is essentially an emphasis on orthodoxy unless it is implemented and practiced as a hybrid budget, allowing the adoption of innovative features from systems such as ZBB and PPBS. While a number of governmental units have adopted this approach, a far greater number have reverted to the traditional-ceiling line item budget. As a budget that is revenue-driven, there is no direct and systematic linkage between prioritized needs and the services/goods that are delivered. Traditional TBB is a tactical, ad hoc, stop-and-go resource allocation system that does not look toward the future but that rather maximizes budget balancing and stability. This is a virtue that is definitely needed during recessionary periods and in declining communities but that is likely to be counterproductive in growing or stable environments. However, when the more innovative form of TBB is practiced, it has much to offer.

Performance Budgeting

At the national level, the Taft Commission of 1912 advocated a functional work-based classification approach to budget expenditures. This became known as *performance budgeting* (also identified as the *cost data budget*). It was first implemented in the borough of Richmond, New York City, before World War I. Few units of government gave performance budgeting serious consideration until it was popularized by the Hoover Commission in 1949. The commission report stated: "We recommend that the whole budgeting concept of the federal government should be refashioned by the adoption of a budget based on functions, activities, and projects: This we designate the 'performance budget.'"[10] It was widely talked about and practiced throughout the 1950s. In 1956, the American Society for Public Administration held a symposium on budgetary theory that brought together the most prominent individuals to discuss performance budgeting.

Defining Performance Budgeting

The National Committee on Governmental Accounting defines *performance budgeting* as a budget that is "based primarily upon measurable performance of activities and work programs."[11] Stated another way, performance budgeting comprises specific techniques directing attention to the service to be provided and the required work that should be performed. Services are broken down and described in terms of required inputs and projected outputs. The analysis of the efficiency of existing operations is a main objective. Its main tools are cost accounting and work measurement. The budget account is clas-sified by organizational functions, activities, and objects of expenditure, for example, public safety (function), department (police), activity (patrol), and object of expenditure (personnel services, materials, and so on).

Performance budgeting requires that standard unit costs be established. These permit budget projections to be determined by multiplying the unit costs by the number of work units in a given activity for the coming fiscal period. Each budget has a narrative description of proposed activities that are supported by cost estimates, with expected accomplishments identified in quantitative terms. Input and output resource and total costs are clearly identified (see Table 13.3). The major focus of the performance budget is on economic and efficiency accountability. Emphasis is placed on the identifica-tion of activities (output) units for each activity, the estimate of workload (out-put units) to be accomplished for each activity, the determination of input (resources) required to accomplish the projected output for each activity, and the projection of unit costs and expenditure budgeting.

The performance budget is used as an important instrument to assess and improve service efficiency. It is most useful at the program planning level that is staffed by middle management. To facilitate work measurement compari-sons with pre-established work standards and unit costing, expenditures are categorized by function and activity. Performance budgeting is most useful as a means for matching work to be done with the skills and training of the avail-able workforce. To minimize waste and create greater predictability in the pur-suit of the goal of efficiency, the installation of a monitoring system is required.

The workload indicator is a critical component in the performance budget system. It allows management to plan work units, assess unit costs, and pro-duce measurable outputs. The development of the workload requires (1) clear definition, (2) periodic updating of the entity's information system, (3) deter-mination of activities/programs' susceptibility to workload measurements, and (4) locating the process for identifying workload measurement develop-ment within the responsibility center charged with carrying out the activity.

After the organization has committed itself to the implementation of the performance budget system, it must decide at an early stage which comparative benchmark or yardstick will be employed to measure performance. The three most frequently used types of benchmarks involve one of the following: a his-torical standard (comparison of past performance), a budgeted standard (the budget office benchmark), or an engineered standard (based on a rigorously and empirically determined standard, which can be derived from regression analysis). To illustrate the performance budget format for one function, the city of Bright's budget for the community education subfunction (activity) of crime prevention is presented in Table 13.4, which focuses on work activity (commu-nity education), work units (hours worked), unit cost, cost per unit of output, number of output units, and total costs for the completed education activity.

TABLE 13.3 City of Bright: Sample Performance Budget

FUND:	General
DEPARTMENT:	Police
ACTIVITY:	Patrolling

PROGRAM AND PERFORMANCE FUNCTION:

The Patrol Division of the Police Department provides prevention, suppression, and detection of criminal activity, traffic law enforcement, and general public safety to residents of the City of Bright.

PROGRAM COMMENTS:

The Patrol Division responds directly to calls for service received at its headquarters and through the county-wide emergency number 911. The program proposes twenty full-time patrolmen and two sergeants. This year's budget includes $20,000 to expand patrolling downtown. An increase of $24,000 is requested in this FY 2012–13 budget.

PROGRAM MEASUREMENTS:

	Actual 2012–13	Estimated 2012–13	Proposed 2012–13
1. Patrolling Residential Areas (hrs.)	9,825	10,927	11,308
2. Patrolling Business Areas (hrs.)	10,570	10,925	12,215
3. Issuing Citations (no.)	6,514	7,528	8,721
4. Issuing Citations (hrs.)	1,500	1,800	2,312
5. Appearing in Traffic Court (hrs.)	1,395	1,556	2,217
6. Patrolling Special Events (hrs.)	2,007	2,500	2,715
7. Patrolling Events (no.)	31	43	59
8. Arresting D.W.I. (no.)	573	841	733
9. Patrolling for Crime Prevention (hrs.)	3,500	2,900	3,182
10. Patrolling School Crossing (hrs.)	2,967	3,100	3,300
11. Patrolling Supervision (hrs.)	2,537	3,528	4,176
12. Vacation, Sick Leave (hrs.)	513	795	897

WORK DESCRIPTIONS:

1. Patrolling Residential Areas			
Unit: Hours	9,825	10,927	11,308
Unit: Cost	$13.571	$13.651	$13.885
Total Cost	$133,335	$149,164	$157,012
2. Patrolling Business Areas			
Unit: Hours	10,570	10,925	12,215
Unit: Cost	$13.726	$13.866	$13.707
Total Cost	$145,084	$151,486	$167,431

3. Issuing Citations			
Unit: Hours	1,500	1,800	2,312
Unit: Cost	$13.902	$13.991	$13.893
Total Cost	$20,853	$25,184	$32,121
4. Overseeing Traffic Accidents			
Unit: Hours	1,125	2,189	2,531
Unit: Cost	$14.229	$13.789	$13.774
Total Cost	$16,008	$30,184	$34,862
5. Appearing in Traffic Court			
Unit: Hours	1,395	1,556	2,217
Unit: Cost	$13.887	$13.728	$13.757
Total Cost	$19,372	$21,361	$30,449
6. Patrolling Special Events			
Unit: Hours	2,007	2,500	2,715
Unit: Cost	$14.937	$13.941	$14.120
Total Cost	$28,172	$34,853	$38,336
7. Arresting D.W.I.			
Unit: Hours	380	580	701
Unit: Cost	$13.900	$14.100	$14.21
Total Cost	$5,282	$8,178	$9,961
8. Patrolling for Crime Prevention			
Unit: Hours	3,500	2,900	3,182
Unit: Cost	$13.75	$13.82	$3.91
Total Cost	$48,125	$40,078	$44,262
9. Patrolling School Crossing			
Unit: Hours	2,967	3,100	3,300
Unit: Cost	$14.037	$13.982	$13.941
Total Cost	$41,648	$43,344	$46,005
10. Patrolling Supervision	2,537	3,528	4,176
Unit: Hours	$15.25	$16.10	$16.43
Unit: Cost	$38,689	$56,801	$68,940
Total Cost			
11. Vacation, Sick Leave			
Unit: Hours	513	795	897
Unit: Cost	$13.52	$13.71	$13.87
Total Cost	$6,936	$10,899	$12,441
Grand Total	$503,504	$571,532	$641,870

Crime Prevention: Community Education Budget

One full-time officer and one part-time assistant (equivalent to half a full-time officer) have been assigned to this activity. Four objectives have been established, as shown in Table 13.4: (1) the provision of 720 hours of community crime watch education, (2) a reduction of reported "911" calls by 10 percent,

(3) the distribution of crime prevention brochures (420) to community residents, and (4) lecturing (550 hours) in schools and other inviting places. The unit cost average is $10.50 (projected and actual). The number of hours projected and revised number of units in 2012 and 2013 were 3,120 units and 3,040 respectively (see Table 13.4).

A performance budget seeks answers to questions such as the following: What are the agency's objectives and purpose? What services are being provided to justify the agency's existence? What activities are required for realizing the agency's objectives? What volume of work is required to achieve each activity? What are the level of expenditure and the unit costs for both inputs and outputs for the items requested? Note that attention is focused on major functions and work activities such as street cleaning, inspecting, and tree trimming. Each activity must be identified in terms of work or output unit—for example, a mile of street cleaned or an inspection completed. All major resource *input units* for items such as materials and supplies used and personnel hours worked are specifically identified. The cost per unit of input and cost of output per unit of things produced are determined by dividing the cost of resources used by the level or volume of items involved (e.g., 200 personal hours were worked at a cost of $1,000 or a per-unit input cost per hour of $5; thirty miles of streets were paved at a cost of $30,000, or at a cost per output mile completed of $1,000).

TABLE 13.4   Projected Performance Budget for Community Education, FY 2013

	Objective	Projected 2012	Revised 2012	Projected 2013
Workload Measures: Community Education				
1. Number of hours on crime-watch education and related activities	1,2	720	700	710
2. Number of hours lecturing at schools and institutions	4,2	550	510	550
3. Number of hours of in-house community relations	1,2	450	440	420
4. Number of hours distributing materials	3	420	460	410
5. Number of hours preparing materials	1,3	360	360	370
6. Number of hours responding to 911 calls	1,2	320	300	270
7. Number of hours of general seminars	1,2	300	320	310

Efficiency Measures: Community Education				
1. Cost per hour of crime watch	1,2	$13.54	$13.49	$13.15
2. Cost per lecture at schools and institutions	4,2	13.49	13.61	13.15
3. Cost per in-house communityrelations seminars	1,2	13.32	13.49	13.15
4. Cost per hour of distributing materials	3	13.49	13.49	13.15
5. Cost per hour of preparing materials	1,3	13.50	13.50	13.15
6. Cost per hour responding to 911 calls	1,2	13.49	13.49	13.14
7. Cost per hour of general seminars	1,2	13.47	12.54	13.14

Projected 2013

Activity	Work Unit	Unit Cost	Number of Units	Expenditure
Community Education	Hours	$13.50	3,040	$41,040

Successful performance budget development requires a lengthy period of strong leadership. In the initial implementation phase, attention should be given to the development of the budget structures, cost centers, performance measures, and account coding system. Next, the recent past performance history of the agency should be organized. Given the new structure and information on cost performance, the budget estimates can then be developed. The development of a performance budget involves seven steps:

1. Define individual work activities in terms that are measurable and that can be related to resource requirements.
2. Inventory the work units and the kind of work that must be performed on each.
3. Develop quantity standards for each activity to permit an estimation of the amount of work required during the year, expressed in terms of annual number of units of work (tons, cubic yards, gallons, acres mowed, and so on). Quantity standards are used to define the workload to be undertaken and the minimal acceptable quality of work necessary to carry out an activity.
4. Determine the number of work units per activity. This task is made easy after the quantity standards and inventory of the amount of work to be done on each activity has been established.

5. Establish production standards. The efficiency with which work is performed is a function of how the workers are assigned and equipped and the methods used in performing work activities. Responsibility should then be assigned to investigate and evaluate alternative methods for accomplishing each activity.

6. Compute resource requirements by applying production standards to the defined work program. For example, the production standard for premix patching stipulates the following conditions:

TABLE 13.5

Crew size:	3 persons or workers
Equipment:	1 dump truck
Accomplishment/crew day:	3.75 tons premix
Production rate:	6.4 person-hour/ton

Activity	Quantity standard	Work to be done	Work units
Mowing	3 mowings × acres	2,500 mowable	= 7,500 acres
Pothole-patching with gravel	2,500 cu. yds. × gravel/mile	400 miles	= 1,000,000 cu. yds.
Patching with premix	7.5 tons × premix/mile	100 level miles	= 750 tons premix

Assuming the activity called for 750 tons of premix patching, the resource requirement would be:

crew days   =   750 tons − 3.75 tons/day = 200 days

person-hours   =   3 persons × 8 hours/day × 200 days

                =   4,800 personhours

                or

person-hours   =   6.4 person-hours/ton × 750

                =   4,800 person-hours

equipment   =   200 days × 8 hours

                =   1,600 hours for dump truck

materials   =   750 tons of bituminous premix material

7. Collect cost data and convert the performance budget resource requirements into financial terms. The procedures for each work activity would be developed as follows for premix patching:

TABLE 13.6

Object of expenditure	Resource requirements	Average unit cost	Annual cost
Labor	4,800 per hour	× $8.00/hour =	$38,400
Equipment	1,600 dump-truck hours	× $3.00/hour =	4,800
Materials	750 tons of premix	× $12.00/ton =	9,000
Total			$52,200

Uses of the Performance Budget

Performance budgeting is intended to help administrators assess and improve the efficiency of an agency. It is management-oriented and is especially useful at the middle management level to aid in monitoring performances and coordinating work activities and in providing useful information for the review of operations. Additionally, it promotes accountability to top management and improves work planning and scheduling.

The advantages of performance budgeting are that it (1) allows the relaxation of control over inputs, (2) de-emphasizes external control and places greater stress on internal control, (3) shifts the focus from budgeting control to administrative control, (4) regularizes postaudit and postcontrol, (5) promotes better work planning and scheduling, (6) enhances the responsibility and acceptability of management, and (7) facilitates the use of variance analysis and performance reporting as an important management control device.

Perhaps a major reason for the lack of success in the adoption of performance budgeting in public and nonprofit agencies has been due to a number of problems inherent in it. These problems include (1) input and output unit costing, (2) accounting and cost data requirements, (3) diffused organizational responsibility/decentralization, and (4) emphasis on the volume of work done rather than quality and effectiveness. These disadvantages are discussed below.

Input and Output Unit Costing

The unit costing feature, which is an integral part of performance budgeting, has a number of potential problems. Factors such as inflation, strikes, and transportation delays may impact on unit costs, causing them to change. Hence, some opponents of performance budgeting advocate that unit costing be replaced by *work measurement* (the person-hours or physical number of units used) in budget development. The use of person-hours makes especially good sense in public and nonprofit agencies, since it represents about 80 percent of input cost factors.

Accounting and Cost Data Requirements

Most human services organizations present particular problems with output unit cost measurements. In both government and, to a lesser extent, nonprofit organizations, accounts are maintained on the expenditure, or modified accrual, basis rather than full cost basis. This makes it exceedingly difficult to collect cost data that can be used to determine the unit output costs. To overcome or minimize these problems requires extensive accounting and data gathering facilities, which may be too expensive for small municipalities and nonprofit agencies.

Diffused Responsibilities

Since the identification of work activities and unit (input and output) measurements are the critical components of performance budgeting, attention is focused on the contribution of each activity and little attention paid as to how activities relate to specific organizational units. Table 13.7 shows five possible combinations of activities. Although the matrix indicates four activities (numbers 2, 3, 4, and 5) contributing to one another, activity number 1 provides no input or assistance to the others. This is a typical problem associated with performance budgeting: It does not facilitate integration or coordination among activities. These problems must be overcome if public and nonprofit agencies are to be effective instruments in providing the public with goods and services and in accomplishing their organizational missions.

Performance budgeting has enjoyed far less success than line item budgeting, because it demands a greater investment in time and skill. Performance budgeting demonstrates a method by which government and nonprofit agencies could develop techniques to measure performances. Its emphasis on measurement and efficiency is its greatest strength. Performance budgeting's pursuit of efficiency is a narrow focus emphasizing the quantity and unit cost of things produced but not the impact or results they achieve. Minimal attention is given to the budget policy decisions, limiting the effectiveness of performance budgeting in decision making.

TABLE 13.7   Activity Grid or Matrix Reporting

Unit	Activity #1	Activity #2	Activity #3	Activity #4	Activity #5	Total
A	$100,000	$ 25,000	$ 16,000	$ 14,000	$ 40,000	$195,000
B	---	80,000	5,000	12,000	35,000	132,000
C	---	10,000	70,000	30,000	5,000	115,000
D	---	6,000	8,000	4,000	25,000	43,000
E	---	13,000	21,000	90,000	20,000	144,000
Total	$100,000	$134,000	$120,000	$150,000	$125,000	$629,000

Lack of Emphasis on Effectiveness

Performance budgeting focuses attention on process rather than on end purposes and results. Output units measure volume or the amount of work performed. Stress is placed on quantifiable quantities of things (e.g., miles of paved streets, tons of garbage removed, number of library books loaned). The measures do *not* indicate the quality factor of the goods and services produced (e.g., quality of the road paved, cleanliness rating obtained as a result of the garbage removal, number of books requested but not available at the library). However, in a number of cases, the quality attributes can be identified without too much difficulty. By incorporating the quality factor, performance budgeting proponents can blunt the criticism that the budget tends to concentrate on activities that are easily susceptible to output measurement while excluding or minimizing those that are not.

During the last few years, the identity of performance budgeting has become confused due to many commentators' and some practitioners' calling "results–oriented" or "program budgets" *performance budgets*. Accordingly, when someone refers to performance budgeting, we need to make sure exactly which budget is being emphasized.

Summary Observations

Although line item budgeting has many admirable points, it also embodies many weaknesses. Its simplicity, practicability, and understandability are major reasons why it has endured with great popularity. On the whole, however, the shortcomings of line item budgeting outweigh its strengths. Its preoccupation with inputs, narrow control, and dollar accountability and its lack of issue and policy orientation are serious impediments. These problems must be overcome if public and nonprofit agencies wish to use their budget as an effective instrument for the delivery of public goods and services.

Notes

1. Thomas J. Kane Jr., "Budget Directors View Budget Control," *Public Budgeting and Finance 2*, no. 2 (summer 1982): 44.

2. Edward J. Luksus, "Strategic Budgeting: How to Turn Financial Records into Strategic Assets," *Management Review 70* (March 1981): 44.

3. Robert Leduc, "Financial Management and Budgeting," in *The Nonprofit Organization Handbook*, ed. Tracy Daniel Connors (New York: McGraw-Hill, 1980), pp. 6, 51–52.

4. These amounts are the resources designated as being necessary to minimally carry out the functions of a program to prevent it from falling below an agreed-upon acceptable standard.

5. Daniel Guttman and Barry Willner, *The Shadow Government* (New York: Parthenon Books, 1976), pp. 42–44.

6. See Thomas Anton, *The Politics of State Expenditures in Illinois* (Champaign: University of Illinois Press, 1966), pp. 6–51; and Aaron Wildavsky, *Budgeting* (Boston: Little, Brown, 1975), p. 24.

7. Wildavsky, *Budgeting*, p. 24.

8. Irene S. Rubin, "Budgeting for Our Times: Target Base Budgeting," *Public Budgeting and Finance 11*, no. 3 (fall 1991): 5.

9. Ibid.

10. Commission on the Organization of the Executive Branch of the Government, *Budget and Accounting* (Washington, DC: GPO, 1949), p. 8.

11. Municipal Finance Officers Association, *Governmental Accounting, Auditing and Financial Reporting* (Chicago: Municipal Finance Officers Association, 1980), Appendix B-70.

14

The Planning, Programming, Budgeting System

The *planning, programming, budgeting system* (PPBS) was developed in response to dissatisfaction with traditional line-item budgeting and traditional performance types of budgeting. U.S. Defense planners initially and later forward-looking state and local budgeting officials felt that line-item budgeting was overly preoccupied with control and too little concerned with policy and results. Performance budgeting, which was expected to overcome many of the weaknesses of the line item budget, produced problems of its own by focusing on things or work completed and unit costing. It draws attention away from alternative costing approaches that link organizational goals and objectives. Emphasis is placed mainly on things that are measurable or countable. Thus, although there is concern for output, little effort was made to link it with policy goals and objectives.

This chapter focuses attention on the theory and practice of PPBS. The reader is provided with the basic philosophy and techniques that underlie the PPBS approach to the allocation of scarce resources.

Early Program Budgeting

The early development of program budgeting represented a bridge between performance budgeting and the PPBS. Because of the different emphasis of program budgeting and PPBS, they are discussed separately. Like PPBS, the *program budget* (which closely parallels what is now being called the *performance results budget*) emphasizes results.[1] The approach focuses on information that is more usable to the administrator than the accountant. The program budget includes a more comprehensive view of the budget process than either the line item or performance budgets.

Program budgeting has the following attributes: (1) It encourages identification of the program purpose, program development, and commitment to planning. (2) It brings considerable order to masses of detail in terms of understandable issues and specific plans. (3) Like PPBS, it emphasizes multi-year planning and periodic re-evaluation of program results. (4) Unlike PPBS, it begins below top management—at the middle and operating levels—thus guarding against overcentralization. (5) It gives less attention than PPBS to the systematic consideration of alternatives. (6) It stresses the input–output linkage, facilitating cost–benefit analysis.

Program budgeting is an extension of performance budgeting in that it defines program objectives and obtains measures (output) to assess these objectives. However, it differs from performance budgeting because its emphasis is more on program planning and assessment of output results. It is unlike PPBS in that it gives less attention to alternative analyses in making program selections. The definition of "program" is essentially the same in both systems, referring to a combination of resources, manpower, materials, and facilities (e.g., equipment, capital, and skills) that are put together to achieve a common set of objectives within a specified period of time.

Planning, Programming, and Budgeting System

Definition

A planning, programming, and budgeting system (PPBS) is a planning, implementing, and control system. As a comprehensive decision making instrument, it is designed to accommodate and integrate multiple functions (see Figure 14.1). It provides an important link between strategic planning (long- and medium-range) and operating plans. The PPBS is a systematic effort concerned with the integration of planning, programming, and budgeting. It requires the articulation of explicit goals, purposes and objectives from which strategic output–oriented programs are identified. In turn, it generates output budget information from which effective resource allocations can be made. Viewed as such, the PPBS is a subsystem of system analysis. After the program outputs have been specified, expenditures can then be converted into the traditional line item requests.

A major focus of the PPBS is the purposes for which an agency is requesting funds. As a policy-oriented and decision making system, the PPBS seeks to improve resource allocation by helping agencies make the best selection among competing alternatives in the pursuit of organizational goals and objectives. It is thus an important analytical tool designed to help decision makers achieve their assigned responsibilities with optimal results.

The underlying premises on which the PPBS is based are perhaps best revealed in the answers to the following questions: (1) What are the basic goals and objectives being pursued? (2) What are the alternative means for achieving articulated goals and objectives? (3) What are the costs (present, future, and

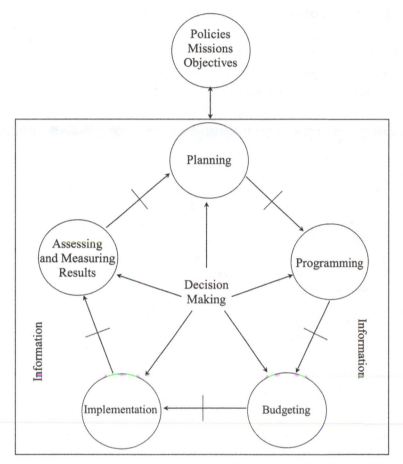

FIGURE 14.1   The PPBS as an integrative decision-making process: A conceptual view.

Note: Crosshatches indicate analyses.

full) of each alternative in both financial and nonfinancial terms? (4) What are the benefits to be achieved from each alternative, and how effective will each aid in achieving articulated goals and objectives? (See Table 14.1, "Factors in Cost-Effectiveness Studies.")

Before the PPBS can be initiated, an agency must develop an analytical capability to examine in depth its objectives and the programs identified to achieve them (see Figure 14.2). There will be a need to create an improved budgeting mechanism to facilitate broad program decision making and translate it into budgeting outcomes to be presented to the chief executive and legislative or board officials for action. The schema in Figure 14.2 shows the steps that may be involved in developing a PPBS budget. Based on an assessment of

TABLE 14.1 Factors in Cost-Effectiveness Studies

The cost-effectiveness study should result in a written document that contains all of the basic elements of good analysis:

1. A clear definition of the problem or problems.

2. Identification of the basic objectives involved.

3. Selection of "criteria" or "measures of effectiveness" that will permit an estimation of progress in relation to the basic objectives. These should not be limited to only those criteria that are believed to be quantifiable. So-called intangibles, if pertinent to program selection, should be included.

4. Identification and description of the key features and of the alternative ways of attempting to meet the problems. Alternatives may be in the form of different programs or different levels of a program, or both.

5. Estimates of the full cost implications of each alternative, including future as well as immediate implications.

6. Estimates of the full effects of each alternative (relative to each of the criteria identified as being important) to include future as well as immediate implications.

7. A clear presentation of the trade-offs among the alternatives considering the costs and effects as estimated in (5) and (6). Charts, graphs, and tables are useful presentation devices.

8. Identification of the major uncertainties and the quantification of the uncertainties, to the extent possible. Some uncertainty, and often considerable uncertainty, can be expected to be present in any realistic analysis. The efforts of these uncertainties on the potential decisions should be estimated.

9. Identification of the major assumptions made in the study with an indication of the degree to which program choices may be sensitive to these assumptions.

10. Documentation of the study in such a manner as to permit others to understand and evaluate what was done in the analysis and to obtain a feeling for how accurate the basic data and the findings can be expected to be. A cost-effectiveness analysis may use, if applicable, many of the techniques of mathematics, operations research, economics, and so forth. They may also draw upon various previously done technical and nontechnical studies that are pertinent to the study at hand. The cost-effectiveness analysis treats such problems as those identified in individual-issue papers or perhaps will examine one category of the program structure or a group of interacting categories.

Source: Adapted from George Washington University, "State-Local Financial Projects," in *Management Information Systems*, ed. Ralph G. Caso (Nassau County, NY: Fiscal Administration, 1971), pt. 3, p. 7.

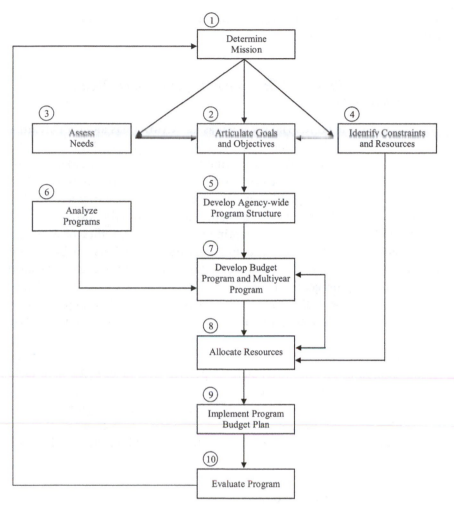

FIGURE 14.2   Schema of the PPBS process.

needs and evaluation of resource constraints, goals and objectives are articulated. Next, an agencywide program structure is developed. Programs are fitted into the structure and analyzed, after which a multiyear program budget and financial plan are constructed.

Figure 14.2 clearly indicates that a budget is an instrument for implementing long-range plans. Unlike traditional line item budgeting in which budget decision making is primarily done upward, the PPBS decision making is mainly a downward aggregative process of information flow. In contrast to traditional budgeting systems that take a retrospective view in assessing what was done with resources, the PPBS takes a prospective focus about the future impact of resource application. An unarticulated but implied premise of the PPBS is that it is better to implement the right decision inefficiently than implement the wrong decision efficiently.

Comparing the PPBS and Government Performance Results Act Modernization Act[2]

The passage of the GPRA (now known as GPRAMA) has aided in creating some degree of confusion about performance budgeting and the PPBS. The GPRAMA avoided identifying a specific type of budget that federal agencies must follow. However, the process it requires closely parallels the PPBS. The GPRAMA put emphasis on program performance reports/results/ planning, and performance-based management. The GPRAMA interpretations by the U.S. General Accounting Office (GAO), Office of Management and Budget (OMB), and commentators' discussions on budgeting sometimes interchange performance budgets and PPBS budgets. Because of this emerging usage, the type of budget being referred to is not always clear without knowing the context. Comparisons on selected categories (see Table 14.2) will help clarify the degree of parallel between the GPRAMA and the PPBS.[3]

There are variants of early program budget in practice such as priority budgeting, accounting for approximately 21 percent of budget systems in local governments. The analytical and administrative efforts are more than traditional budgeting but there is less planning programming budgeting and system (PPBS) and zero-base budgeting. Performance measures are used to aid decision makers analysis. The attributes of the priority budgeting include the following:

- The planning process is defined.
- Organization-wide goals are articulated.
- A general assessment of community needs is made.
- Programs are defined and prioritized.
- Resources are allocated.
- Tradeoffs are then made among programs and service levels.[4]

From Table 14.2 GPRAMA has a number of significant differences than PPBS. Besides indicating the strategic framework for planning and executing their duties, Congress identifies policy, performance, and accountability personnel who must constantly oversee the accomplishments of agency functions. Agencies must not only report to Congress, but they must also provide updated performance progress information on their websites. Congress has moved oversight and transparency to another level, perhaps over rigid in its control requirements.

TABLE 14.2   Comparing the PPBS and GPRAMA Performance Budget

Category	PPBS	GPRAMA
Strategic planning	Yes	Yes
Impact	Yes	Yes
Alternative analysis	Yes	Yes
Input–output linkage	Yes	Yes
Require analytical capability	Yes	Yes
Required programmatic structuring	Yes	No
Integrative decision-making	Yes	No
Managerial-accountability emphasis	No	Yes
Performance reports	No	Yes
Comprehensive mission statement	Yes	Yes
Identification of external noncontrollable factors	No	Yes
Required training	Yes	Yes
Focus on stakeholders	No	Yes
Sustained leadership commitment and accountability for results	No	Yes
Engaging and keeping Congress informed of management and performance issues	No	Yes
Transparency oriented	No	Yes
Coordinated crosscutting approach	Yes	Yes
Results/outcome focus	Yes	Yes
Focus on opportunity to reduce duplication	Yes	Yes
Identifying vulnerability to fraud, waste and abuse	No	Yes
Focusing weaknesses in major management functions	No	Yes
Emphasizing usefulness and use of performance information in decision making	No	Yes
Timely information at decision points	No	Yes
Disclosure of accuracy and validity of information	No	Yes
Performance improvement in each agency	No	Yes
Quarterly reporting on priority goal programs	No	Yes

The PPBS: Analyzing the Concepts

The PPBS comprises concepts, systems, processes, techniques, and formats. It is a management decision making instrument that ties long-, medium-, and short-range plans into budgeting. The PPBS approach is designed to accommodate and integrate multiple management functions into an operating plan of action. Figure 14.1 schematically depicts the four main concepts (planning, programming, budgeting, and systems) in the PPBS decision making system. The schema shows policies, missions, and objectives as the major input into the PPB system, which is held together by a decision making network. This network links a dynamic and interactive process that must be maintained among the major components in the existing information system.

Planning

Planning is the most fundamental activity in program budgeting, because it is based on planned programs that give it a unique identity vis-à-vis other types of budgets. Since the PPBS is a mission- and management-oriented system, *planning* (the first "P") is the focal point and ingredient that facilitates the effective clustering of activities around objectives. Thus, planning begins by defining objectives or outcomes to be achieved, and concludes by suggesting the optimal way to realize these objectives. It is the formulation of a future course of action; it specifies and classifies long- and short-range goals. It is an important means for coping with a dynamic environment that generates uncertainty, a changing mission, evolving goals and priorities, and changing procedures.[5]

Planning does not take place in a vacuum; rather, it is undertaken to achieve some goal or objective. Examples include welfare planning, comprehensive health care, and education planning. All organizations have goals and objectives—planning is the means that is used to achieve them. Typically, organizational goals and objectives are identified in a structure that may be broken down into subgoals (a goal objective structure). Goals may be viewed in a hierarchical structure as indicated in Figure 14.3, in which goals are subdivided, becoming more specific and quantitative at each succeeding level of division.

Planning Constraints

Figure 14.2 indicated constraints as an important factor to be considered in the analysis and selection of program alternatives. What may appear to be a theoretically sound alternative might not be feasible in the real world owing to operating constraints. Therefore, constraints should be considered early in the planning stages so that they may be used as guidelines in the development of goals and development of alternative methods of achieving them.

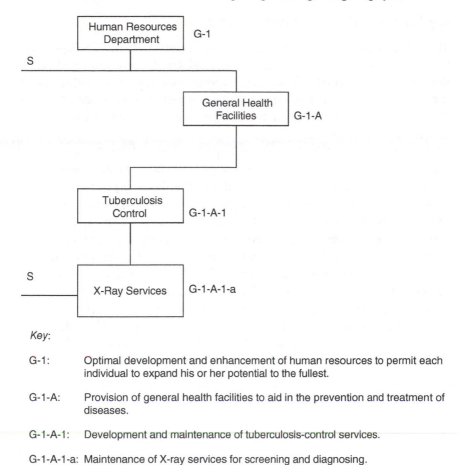

Key:

G-1:   Optimal development and enhancement of human resources to permit each individual to expand his or her potential to the fullest.

G-1-A: Provision of general health facilities to aid in the prevention and treatment of diseases.

G-1-A-1: Development and maintenance of tuberculosis-control services.

G-1-A-1-a: Maintenance of X-ray services for screening and diagnosing.

FIGURE 14.3   A hierarchical goal structure in a large organization.

Program analysis is an important factor during the planning stages. It is especially critical during this stage in which selection must be made among alternative courses of action in the pursuit of articulated organizational goals. Program analysis requires the establishment of selection criteria. The latter permits the elimination of clearly unfeasible alternatives without resorting to detailed analysis. After these initial eliminations have been made, detailed analysis is undertaken to identify the alternative program that meets the established criteria. The analysis typically focuses on three aspects: (1) monetary and other resources needed for the program, (2) the kinds of benefits that will accrue from the program, and (3) comparisons of the total program costs with total benefits. A completion of these actions permits selection of the more suitable and implementable program.

Implementing Points to Consider (Planning)

Three PPBS planning activities should be kept in mind: (1) the development of budgeting guidelines, (2) the identification and definition of goals, and (3) the development of needed information. Budgetary guidelines are indispensable if the budget request is to be more than an incremental resource allocation. The guidelines should contain three important components: assumptions, constraints, and priorities.

Assumptions identify the economic, political, social, and other external factors likely to affect the agency. It is important that both assumptions and constraints be dealt with as early as feasible in the planning process, because it is vital to know the conditions that may impede or limit the scope and method of an agency. For example, it would be unwise to request an expansion of a program at a time when an influential group with direct access to policymakers feels that it should be cut back or abolished. Finally, the articulation of priorities shows the importance of the rank ordering that the agency or community attaches to the allocation of resources for the coming year.

An explicit, clear, and precise definition of goals is critical to program budgeting. The goal statement indicates to the public the kinds of problems that the government or other not-for-profit agency is mobilized to solve, the conditions to be ameliorated, and the extent to which articulated desires and expectations will be realized.

Programming

Programming enters the picture after the mission, purpose, objectives, and broad program outlines have been determined. It identifies program components, tasks, or activities and fits them into a timeframe specified in the goal and objective structure. Programming aids in the generation of alternative approaches to the achievement of program goals and objectives. Perhaps the most essential step is the identification of activities surrounding program objectives and the development of operational plans (e.g., the assignment of resources such as personnel, materials, and facilities) to achieve them. Programming occurs during the program analysis stage or after the program selection has been made. Importantly, programming acts as a bridge between planning and budgeting, ensuring that all strategic decisions and projected expenditures are integrated into the program format for the fiscal or planning period. Answers should be sought to the following questions: In light of the political, economic, and social reality, is the alternative feasible at this time? What are the legal constraints, if any, to this program? Considering the available resource constraint, can this program achieve the most effective and efficient outcome for the resources applied? In light of the lifespan of the program, what will be the financial requirements to continue the program in future years? Is alternative funding available for this program?

A critical opportunity is present in the *programming phase*. This is the phase that permits the manager to consider whether changes in the agency programs are desired. The decision must be made to add new programs and/or to eliminate existing ones or modify them. Obviously, the action taken to add, eliminate, or modify programs must be based on a comparative analysis of benefits in which the advantages and disadvantages are clearly identified.

Implementing Points to Consider (Programming)

Through a process of self-study analysis, programming facilitates the best choicemaking among alternative programs. Through this process, programming is able to determine the extent to which existing or proposed programs complement or overlap other programs. The main activities undertaken to aid the programming process involve the examination of current programs, analysis of feasible alternatives, and identification of desired programs. This step requires: (1) a brief description of each program, (2) a review of the kinds of personnel employed in executing the programs, (3) a detailed description of the target groups or clients served and the time span over which the services have been operating, (4) materials and equipment required, and (5) the total and different types of costs (direct and indirect).

Budgeting

A program budget is much more than a listing of expenditures by program. Instead, all dollars are systematically related to goals and objectives within the program structure. Based on the cost or expenditure allocations, a budget indicates where the emphasis and priorities of the agency are being placed. The dollar amounts are incorporated into both the current-year program budget and the multiyear financial plan involving a projection of alternative programs for several years (usually five).

Implementing Points to Consider (Budgeting)

The budgeting phase has four steps that must be considered. These are the specification of financial support, the budget request review, budget modifications, and allocation of available funds. The completion of the programming phase, specifying of the financial support or resources needed to implement the program selected, permits the budget implementation phase to begin. The quantity of the resources needed are estimated and required dollar amounts are entered in the agency books according to the standard chart of accounts. (Whatever system the agency uses—such as object of expenditure, functional, or program—the dollar amounts are expressed in terms that can be accommodated by the system. Depending on the system required, the budget amount may be broken out to show salaries, health and retirement benefits, and other items needed to implement the program.)

The design of the system requires that participants, other than the proposers, review the budget requests. Unlike other budgeting systems, however, the review is conducted in terms of program goals and objectives and program costs. This is done to ensure that the purpose of the program matches budgetary guidelines and that the identified accomplishments match accepted and articulated goals and objectives. Additionally, it must be determined whether the proposed size of the program will adequately serve the target population and if the best alternative has been chosen. In those cases where program changes have been requested, it must be determined if they make sense within the budgetary guidelines. An examination is made to determine if the dollar amounts requested are adequate or exceed required limits; the amounts requested must be accurately calculated.

The completed budget requests are compared with projected revenues to determine if and where budget modifications may be necessary. In those situations in which modification is required, the following options are available: (1) total or partial elimination of a program, (2) reduction of services in one or more programs, (3) identification of areas where resources could be shifted to effect efficiencies, or (4) available sources from which to borrow funds or that provide access to external grants (in the case of government, tax increases; in nonprofit organizations, access to foundations, business donations, or campaign drives).

System

The *system* concept implies that there are different parts in a network. These are organized to act interdependently in achieving a common purpose. In the PPBS, planning, programming, and budgeting are interdependent activities that are synchronized to optimally achieve articulated goals and objectives. This requires that the mission, goals, and objectives be directly linked to programs and subprograms, objectives, activities, output, impact, and their costs, direct and indirect. In summary, the system approach suggests that an organization is (1) focused on a set of objectives aimed at satisfying a predetermined plan, (2) used to convert resources (inputs) into outputs, (3) viewed as having elements and components that are interactive and interdependent, and (4) devised to maintain a monitoring system to determine deviations from targeted objectives.

Program Measures

Table 14.3 shows different types of measures that may be developed for the city of Bright for the Department of Housing Development. From this table, we can see the linkage of a program mission, activities, and performance measures.

TABLE 14.3 City of Bright, Department of Housing Development: Suggested Program Budget*

Department Mission/Goal: To provide adequate, safe, and sanitary housing conditions for all residents in the City of Bright

Objectives:
1. To make it easier for private builders to construct new housing and rehabilitate old housing.
2. To present Bright neighborhoods as good places to live.
3. To protect the sound housing in the community through timely and effective repair-and-maintenance programs.
4. To develop and implement programs to prevent housing abandonment.
5. To rehabilitate or demolish already abandoned units.
6. To develop long-range plans for housing involving the public and private sectors and neighborhood residents.
7. To create a professionally and efficiently run housing department, responsive to the changing conditions and circumstances.

Program Area: **Housing Development**

Goal: To create a healthier development climate in the city, making it easier for private developers to obtain block-grant funding, construct new housing, and rehabilitate old housing.

Objectives:
1. To encourage private developers to construct 25 percent more new homes.
2. To encourage private developers to rehabilitate 20 percent of the old and aban-doned homes.
3. To obtain 25 percent block-grant funding.

Demand:
1. The number of requests made to rehabilitate homes.
2. The number of substandard homes in need of rehabilitation.
3. The number of requests for block grants.

Workload Measures:
1. Number of housing units rehabilitated.
2. Number of rehabilitated units sold.
3. Number of new home buyers attracted to the city through its program.
4. Number of community block-grants distributed.
5. Number of man-hours targeted for implementing each phase of the program.

Efficiency and Productivity:
1. Cost per unit of homes rehabilitated.
2. Numbers of homes rehabilitated per worker.
3. Number of community block grants processed per worker per period.
4. Number of home buyers attracted per marketing staff per period.

Impact/Effectiveness Measures:
1. Percentage of abandoned homes satisfactorily rehabilitated.
2. Percentage of substandard homes satisfactorily rehabilitated.
3. Number and percentage of people actually buying substandard homes.
4. Amount of community development block grants effectively allocated for rehabilitating homes.

Sustainability:
1. Extended time period over which rehabilitated homes are satisfactorily maintained and/or enhanced.

Note: * Normally, a fiveyear budget is projected for each program.

Developing the Program Budget Format

High priority should be given to the program budget format. There are two main elements: the program structure, and the cost structure. Each program is broken down into subcategories, with the presentation of cost estimates projected over the planning time horizon, typically five years (see Figure 14.4).

Program Structure

The program is the basic framework and building block in program budgeting. Accordingly, great attention must be given to program structure, because

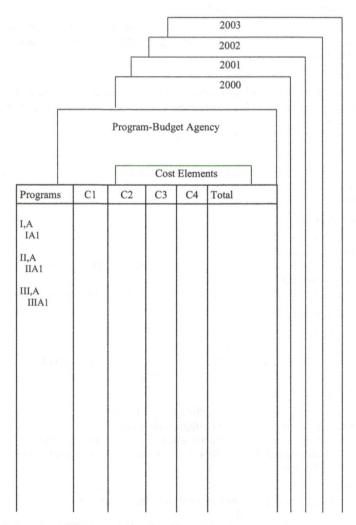

FIGURE 14.4   Program budget format.

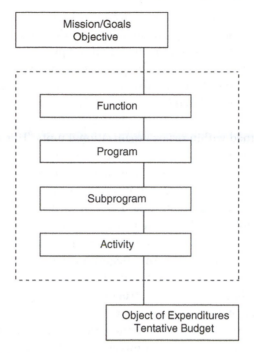

FIGURE 14.5   Program classification system.

it plays an important role in the success or failure of the program budget. The program structure translates an agency's fundamental mission, goals, and objectives into a program hierarchy, ranging from the largest program to the basic constituent or element. The program components are subdivided as desired by management to facilitate planning, budgeting, controlling, and reporting (Figure 14.5).

The program structure should ideally be a link between an agency's goals and objectives and the financial control system of the traditional object of expenditure budget, as shown in Figure 14.4. An agency's output should be directly linked to articulated goals and objectives. The key aim in the PPBS is to develop appropriate classifications that will permit the measurement and evaluation of performance in relation to assigned responsibilities. The program is the highest level of work performed by an agency that carries out assigned responsibilities. All programs are directed at producing some product that is definable and measurable.

Some programs do not conform to existing organizational structures. For example, a state program (see Figure 14.6) dealing with alcohol-related problems may involve many other agencies such as health and welfare, the highway department, youth and adult corrections, departments of employment and education, and the attorney general's office. The question is how these overlaps should be handled. Two approaches have been suggested. The first is simply to define programs across organizational boundaries—thus all related activities contributing to the program goal and taking place in other departments are grouped together. The funding for the program is therefore allocated to a number of departments. By means of a matrix or grid, resource allocation and responsibility can be displayed (see Figure 14.6).

Perhaps the most practical approach is the second, which requires that programs be defined within major organizational units. This approach sometimes results in additional programs, but it enhances control and responsibility reporting. In addition, it provides sufficient information to permit program analysis to modify or eliminate duplicating activities.

An important and continuing question is how detailed the program and subprogram should be. Although there are no specific criteria, each situation should dictate the precise subdivision of a program budget hierarchy. A few observations may aid in clarifying this. Beginning with the mission of the organization down to the smallest subdivision of the program, there must be a logical linkage throughout the program structure. For example, once the mission/ goal and objectives have been stated for an agency, each functional area must be consistent with them. Additionally, there must be as many functional areas as necessary to achieve the agency's mission/goal. Similarly, there must be as many programs as required to achieve the goal and objective of the function. At the program level, the number of subprograms identified is determined at the point at which the program goal and objective have been recognized. Note that for each objective stated, there should be at least one impact/effectiveness indicator to determine how well the objective was achieved. If there are, for example, five objectives but only two impact indicators can be identified, it means that the other objectives are not important or that there is confusion about their logical relationships.

It is thus critical early in the program structuring stage to define precisely the legitimate services to be provided and their likely recipients. This gives an approximate idea for relating the program goals and objectives with impact indicators and the particular intended clients. It provides answers to the questions of "what" the program does and of "for whom" the program is intended. As far as possible, each program should be broken down to answer "what" and "to whom" until the point at which the question of "how" the activity is to be performed can be answered.

A basic function of PPBS is to relate the cost of the government or agency to the services provided. All program structures relate operating organizational units to functional areas, programs, subprograms, and activities. The functional areas identify the major purposes of an agency. The size of the functional area increases as we move from small to large organizations; for example, Wisconsin divided state operations into five functional areas: commerce, education,

ORGANIZATION	PROGRAMS																	
	I. Prevention of Alcoholism	A. Education	B. Law of Economics	C. Research	II. Restoration (Early Stages)	A. Detection	B. Diagnosis	C. Treatment	D. Rehabilitation	E. Research	III. Care (The Chronic)	A. Detection	B. Diagnosis, Evaluation, Referral	C. Treatment	D. Rehabilitation	E. Domiciliary Care	F. Research	Etc.
Dept. of Welfare																		
Employment																		
Dept. of Education																		
Police																		
Youth and Adult Correction																		
Atty. Gen. Office																		
Highway																		

FIGURE 14.6   Expenditure for alcohol treatment program.

Source: Adapted from C. W. Churchman and A. H. Schaimblatt, "PPB: How Can It Be Implemented?" Public Administration Review, 28, no. 2 (March/April 1969): 182.

environmental resources, human relations and resources, and general executive functions.

A program is a division of a functional area providing services for an identifiable group or target population to achieve a specific purpose. The program combines a homogeneous group of services to meet similar needs, disabilities, or attributes. Stated another way, a program "is a clustering of activities and resources around one or more objectives focused on the production of similar outputs."[6] The home repairs loan program in the Department of Housing of the City of Bright provides a good example:

TABLE 14.4

How	What	For Whom
Program	home repairs loans	home owners
Subprogram A	home insulation	home owners needing insulation
Activity 1	processing applications	
Activity 2	applying cut-off criteria	
Activity 3	approving matching grants for insulation	
Subprogram B	emergency home-repair loans	home owners having code violations
Activity 1	processing applications	
Activity 2	applying cut-off criteria	
Activity 3	granting loans to eligible homeowners	

As can be noted from this example, a subprogram is a breakdown of a program into more specific segments of the services being provided for a specific segment of the target population. Similarly, the activities are specific actions and techniques applied to implement the programs.

Issue Analysis

Issue analysis (see Table 14.5, "Outline of Issue Paper") attempts to identify, clarify, and analyze significant problems facing a government agency. Sometimes called *special study analysis*, issue analysis is an important supplement to PPBS. It provides the analytic foundation for the PPBS and aids decision makers in making policy regarding program additions, rejection, or confirmation, or may simply provide vital input to the strategic planning process. Two kinds of issue analysis have been used: one for resolving the budget or fiscal-year

TABLE 14.5   Outline of Issue Paper

The issue paper is a written document that attempts to identify and describe the major features of a major problem facing the government. It essentially attempts to define the problem. It may either stand by itself as a description of the problem area in order to gain an improved perspective or, more importantly, can be used to set the framework, to act as the first phase, of an in-depth cost-effectiveness analysis of the issue.

The issue paper should address such questions as:

1. What is the real problem?
2. What are its causes?
3. Who are the population groups affected? (that is, if other than the general public, identify characteristics such as age group, race, income class, special handicaps, locations, and so on.)
4. What is the magnitude of the problem? How widespread is it now and how large is it likely to be in future years?
5. Toward what objectives should programs for meeting the problem be directed?
6. How can estimates of progress against these objectives be made?
7. What activities are currently being undertaken by this government that are relevant to the problem?
8. What other sectors of the community, or other levels of government in addition to this government, are involved?
9. Are there major constraints, including political ones, that seem to affect the problem?
10. What are the types of alternatives that should be considered for meeting the problem?

Note that answering such questions does not answer what should be done to meet the problem. Answering "shat should be done?" is *not* a function of the issue paper, but rather of a cost-effectiveness-type analysis that ideally should follow the issue paper. The issue paper rather attempts to define the problem and direct attention to the specific information that will need to be obtained and examined before deciding what to do about the problem.

Some quantification might be attempted in the issue paper, such as providing estimates of the number of persons in the target groups that are affected by the problem (question no. 4 above) and providing estimates of the costs and pertinent outputs of current, relevant government activities (question no. 7). A government should *not* be surprised if the problem that is identified by the time the issue paper is completed is not the same as the problem that was conceived at the beginning.

Source: Adapted from George Washington University, "State-Local Finances Project," in *Management Information Systems*, ed. R. G. Caso (Nassau County, NY: Fiscal Administration, 1971), pt. 3, p. 6.

issues and one having a time frame that extends beyond a budget year and is aimed at aiding future development and resource allocation decisions. It is the issue analysis input that makes planning, programming, and budgeting substantive and dynamic.

Crosswalk and PPBS

A number of names, such as *grid* and *matrix*, have been associated with the term *crosswalk* in program budgeting. *Crosswalk* has come to mean the design of a program budget system that allows data to be converted from the program system to traditional line item budgeting, providing both a management and control orientation. Typically, this conversion is made only for one budget year at a time.

The need to make the budget conversion or classification occurs when the program budget differs from the existing budget structure. By use of the crosswalk, the program budget is transformed and regrouped from a policymaking format to one concerned with program implementation and control. With the use of computers, the conversion process has been made less difficult than it otherwise would be. An important requirement is the establishment of a coding method to facilitate ready reclassification of the budget items.

By means of the crosswalk system (Table 14.6), flexibility is increased to enable the provision and use of the traditional budget data to meet administrative, operations, and performance requirements. Significantly, it provides the integration of planning, analysis, and budgeting.

PPBS: Summary Observations

The PPBS is an accountability instrument and well-organized management information system that compels continuing self-study as a means of generating innovation and self-renewal. It is used for examining the financial implications of programs over their expected lifespans. This typically requires the examination of the consequences of expanding or contracting a program, as well as its spillover impacts. The PPBS provides a framework for planning and

TABLE 14.6   Expenditure Crosswalk for Year 1

Account	Object categories	Totals	Program I	Program II	Program III	Program IV
X2	Salaries	$ 75,000	$ 30,000	$10,000	$15,000	$20,000
X3	Materials	85,000	40,000	5,000	20,000	30,000
X4	Travel	20,000	8,000	2,000	5,000	5,000
X5	Utilities	25,000	10,000	2,000	8,000	5,000
X6	Rent	25,000	15,000	5,000	2,000	3,000
X7	Consulting	110,000	50,000	1,000	4,000	10,000
X8	Maintenance	35,000	15,000	2,000	10,000	8,000
	Totals	$375,000	$168,000	$36,000	$64,000	$81,000

facilitating the organization of information so that planners can systematically analyze the fiscal and nonfiscal consequences of proposals and then select the best possible course of action.

Advantages

The advantages of the PPBS are that (1) it can help decision makers focus on objectives and overall goals of an agency, indicating how it is linked with intra- and/or interagency programs and how it can be reached; (2) it links planning, programming, and budgeting into an integrated system; (3) it makes long-range and multiyear planning routine; (4) it promotes an efficient means for allocating resources; (5) it provides understanding that enhances interagency coordination and cooperation; and (6) it provides the required information and data necessary to permit in-depth analysis of alternative courses of action, creating the potential for conflict.

Disadvantages

The PPBS requires massive amounts of data, expertise, and staff time—thus making it time-consuming and costly to undertake. Its great emphasis on goal clarification and goal setting is highly conflicting, because it forces a more explicit value identification and operating philosophy, which may not be compatible with the philosophy of many participants within the budget process. The charge is made that the PPBS minimizes politics—on which budgets heavily depend.

Additionally, because of the PPBS emphasis on rationality, the demand for performance, the requirement of policy impact, and the focus on an explicit statement of objectives, the system is not likely to be consistent with participants' expectations in the budget-making process. Most participants prefer a more general articulation of objectives, because they believe that it provides a better means for protecting their resource bases and minimizes conflict.

Finally, PPBS requires commitment to resources at the outset to develop programs, plans, goals and objectives.

Notes

1. Harry P. Hatry and John F. Cotton, *Program Planning for County and City* (Washington, DC: George Washington University, 1967), p. 16.

2. The act was changed to the Government Performance and Results Act Modernization Act of 2010.

3. Office of Management and Budget (OMB), *Government Performance Results Act of 1993*, http://www.whitehouse.gov/omb/mgmt-gpra/gplan12m.html; and U.S. General Accounting Office, *Executive Guide: Effectively Implementing the Government Results Act of 1993* (Washington, DC: GAO, 1996).

4. GFOA, *Zero-Base Budgeting: Modern Experiences and Current Perspectives* (Calgary, Alberta, Canada, 2011), p. 25.

5. Jerome B. McKinney and Lawrence C. Howard, *Public Administration: Balancing Power and Accountability* (Oak Park, IL: Moore Publishing, 1979), p. 76.

6. Stephen Kenezevich, *Program Budgeting (PPBS): A Resource-Allocation Decision System for Education* (Berkeley, CA: McCutchan Publishing, 1973), p. 48.

15

Zero-Base Budgeting and Total Quality Management

Interest in zero-base budgeting (ZBB) did not become widespread until the 1970s as proponents began to articulate its efficacy for effective resource allocation. Despite this development, the widespread practice of traditional incremental budgeting, with its built-in bias for continuity and growth, became ever more entrenched, and efforts at implementing PPBS and management by objectives (MBO) during the 1960s to achieve a more rational allocation of resources failed to make headway in the public budgeting process. Reformers turned to ZBB. This chapter examines these practices and explores the forces that gave rise to the impetus for ZBB and total quality management (TQM).

Background and Development of the ZBB Approach

The economic, social, and political philosophies that shape priorities were undergoing radical change. By the early 1970s, the long duration of the Vietnam War, a continuing high level of unemployment, unmanageable inflation, a deep recession, and the apparent end of cheap and plentiful energy ushered in a period of conservation. People began asking for a greater degree of certainty, and it seemed irrational to continue to make choices by the traditional incremental, muddling-through approach. This was particularly true at a time when demands for government services were rising even as available resources were falling, thus necessitating contraction and retrenchment rather than expansion.

As government attempted to cope with these problems, emphasis shifted to control by (1) direct citizen input, (2) reorganization, (3) legislative input (sunset laws), and (4) ZBB. The citizen input approach attempted to limit spending and revenue raising through referendums. For example, in 1976, Proposition 13 cut property taxes by nearly 60 percent in California.[1] As McCaffery and Bowman have indicated, however, although direct citizen input may have good intentions, it does not necessarily produce the most desirable outcomes. Unintended results such as reduced federal aid and greater dependence on state government often occur, and subsequently did take place in California.

Because of the ineffectual history of reorganizations (structural changes that de-emphasize substantive social and political problems), the process of direct citizen input gained few supporters. Sunset laws and ZBB received the greatest attention. The sunset approach (initially adopted by Colorado in 1976 for evaluating its forty-one regulatory agencies) is a legislative instrument employed to control the cost and quality of government programs. Government programs, accordingly, are evaluated before a terminal date and are kept functioning only if the evaluation demonstrates satisfactory performances and continuing need for the services. The concept and practice of the sunset approach are commendable, but if inappropriately applied, the approach engenders opposition rather than support toward legislators for their policy-making. For example, in 1977, Alabama state representatives were expected to vote "yes" or "no" on 207 agencies in three hours. It is also said that if true sun-setting were practiced, high-quality individuals would be discouraged from entering government because promises could not be made about the tenure of an agency.[2]

Zero-base budgeting is in some ways similar to sunset laws, but it permits a more comprehensive set of continuing controls and is executive-oriented. In addition, it focuses yearly attention quantitatively on allocative, administrative, and economic efficiency, and qualitatively on effectiveness. The emphasis shifts to control, not only of dollars expended, but of performance and achievement of the greatest policy outcome for the fewest number of dollars. This requires that social changes be undertaken only as they are understood as tradeoffs between benefits to be gained and costs to be incurred. This approach is important to governments, especially in those geographic areas that are experiencing a general economic decline. It is in this context that the potential application of ZBB may be viewed.

Defining the ZBB Concept

Unlike traditional budgeting, "with ZBB nothing is assumed. Every function of every department is questioned. Existing programs are scrutinized as much as expanded or new programs. The entire budget is viewed as a series of supplemental requests with a theoretical base of zero and each supplement must be analyzed."[3] ZBB requires that managers defend every activity under their control before funds are allocated. To qualify for any allocation of funds, every programmatic activity or function to be performed must be identified, evaluated, and ranked in terms of costs and benefits. ZBB is the only budget system that examines a budget request below its base. It aims to cut dollars, not service. Attention is drawn to the harm that cutbacks may entail, yet the greater emphasis is placed on decremental, in contrast to incremental, orientation (which is standard practice in the traditional line item budget).

ZBB is mainly a short-range tool employed in a managerial process to achieve objectives in the most cost-efficient manner. It is a bottom-up approach involving participation from all management levels. The approach has built-in flexibility, because managers are given a range of choices to facilitate priority setting and the establishment of funding levels. Subordinates do not send their budgets up to higher management on a take-it-or-leave-it basis. Clear choices and options are an integral part of the ZBB approach: every proposal presented to management for decision making must have at least three options. According to Leininger and Wong, "ZBB is a management tool which provides a systematic method for evaluating all operations and programs, current or new, allows for budget reductions and expansions in a natural manner, and allows the reallocation of resources from low- to high-priority programs."[4]

A key consideration in ZBB is the search for alternative ways for achieving articulated objectives. The ZBB manager is expected to "start from scratch" by assuming that an activity (any activity that may be considered for implementation) does not exist. The manager can then reconstruct the operation from zero, asking the following questions: Should things be done the way they are now? Would the manager reorganize, consolidate, centralize, decentralize, subcontract, or implement the activity in an entirely different way? By employing this process, it is believed that more goods and services will be delivered at the same or lower cost. Innovative thinking is promoted, thereby enhancing productivity and improving economic performance. Contrasting ZBB with the traditional line item budget vividly highlights the differences between the two approaches, emphasizing ZBB's changes from the status quo (Table 15.1).

Where Should ZBB Be Implemented?

ZBB should be implemented in any organization or unit where a cost–benefit analysis can be developed and that does not presently have a standard cost system. Most governments and nonprofit organizations fall into this category. Typically, most service and overhead areas such as personnel, counseling, accounting, legal, management service, and research also fall into this category. ZBB is most suitable for people- and capital-intensive activities where productivity standards are not easily obtainable to apply in making cost projections.

The ZBB process is used in organizations that have a desire and commitment to achieve speedy, favorable financial results and improve the effectiveness of managers. It is also used in communities and agencies when there is a concern for reallocating resources to meet new and changing priorities, when

TABLE 15.1   Contrasting Traditional Line-Item Budgeting with ZBB

Incremental Budgeting	ZBB
1. Operating budget is estimated.	1. Operating budget is developed by evaluating current activities and alternatives.
2. Accepts existing base and estimates costs of new activities.	2. Assumes a "clean slate" and estimates all costs associated with activities.
3. Estimates costs and benefits for new activities.	3. Identifies and evaluates costs and benefits for all activities including alternatives.
4. Emphasis is put on dollars as the main initiating concern in preparing detailed budgets.	4. Initiating emphasis is put on purposes and activities and on priorities.
5. Little or no effort is made to examine alternative ways of accomplishing activities.	5. New approaches are explicitly examined.
6. Process results in "take it or leave it" budget.	6. Process results in trade-off options/choices for different levels of service and costs.

there is the need to improve productivity and cost-effectiveness in program implementation, and when there is a need to reduce or minimize costs. In communities and agencies in which the manager's attention is focused on specific objectives to be pursued and related to activities and resources required to realize the objectives, managers are encouraged to develop and reassess factors and constraints impeding performance; these managers are given the encouragement to carry out operational planning, better identify priorities, and improve organizational communication.[5]

The matrix in Figure 15.1 shows how we may conceptualize the extent of potential change and degree of impact of ZBB implementation on an organization. The vertical arrow indicates minimal (very stable conditions) to extensive changes. This suggests that the success of ZBB in an organization depends on the prevailing conditions existing in the management environment. An examination of the latter will indicate how burdensome or how attractive the ZBB process is likely to be for the organization.

As can be readily seen from Figure 15.1, the greater the forecasted change (e.g., the likelihood of large budget cuts, high inflation, a large drop in the client casework, a sharp decline in revenue sources, a perceived lack of efficacy by clientele and constituency, deteriorating public usage), the greater managers will be disposed to reassess and readjust their operations and programs. When this situation obtains (significant impact and extensive change), change can easily be imposed from the outside. When minimal change/high stability is the prevailing state, the environment for the implementation of ZBB is

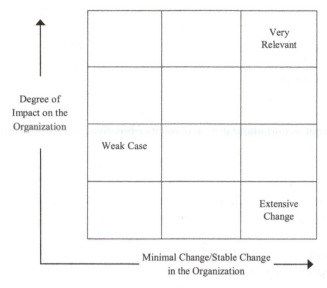

FIGURE 15.1   Evaluating the impact of ZBB on an organization.

Source: Adapted from Henry C. Knight, Zero-Based Budgeting Process: A Practical Guide to Evaluation, Implementation and Use (Hamilton, ON: Society of Management Accountants of Canada, 1979), p. 11. Reprinted with permission of CPA Canada.

less attractive, creating the inclination to more easily revert to a traditional incremental budget. It is not enough to want to install ZBB just because it is a good idea; there must be a defensible rationale for its implementation, which requires in-depth study of the organization's environment.

ZBB: Recent Implementation

Recent adoptions of ZBB have been significantly modified. ZBB "is often applied to budgeting methods that borrow elements of pure ZBB but do not conform to the theoretical ideal."[6] Users tend to fall into two categories: one focuses on inputs such as personnel dollars indicating how reasonable or unreasonable it is based on targeted output goals. The second approach develop a series of service levels for a department from which decision makers may choose, given a particular amount of resources. Department or responsibility centers are provided with what might be referred to as decision packages with various measurement indicators.

In this line item focus departments are given blank budget requests form allowing amounts to be filled in for each line item. These become the starting point instead of using the prior-year amount. As the line item amount changes departments might be asked to identify factors driving the cost (also known as cost drivers). In the city police department in O'Fallon, Missouri, the specific amount of expenditure for each piece of equipment must be identified for each input item such as "portable radio replacement parts, flashlight parts, digital voice recorders, polygraph, and Taser cartridges . . . ."[7]

Rex Hospital in Raleigh, North Carolina adapted ZBB to fit its situation. Despite Rex's long practice of giving high quality of service for relatively low prices, it was forced to increase prices by 15 percent. Because of Medicare costs containment, revenue inflow was expected to continue to decline. To compete for skilled workers and maintain its technological edge, Rex was forced to find a method that would allow it to achieve its objectives with minimum impact. This demanded major cost reduction. Rex's search to find the instrument or technique to reduce its hospital-wide cost led to adoption of ZBB.[8]

One of the attractive features of ZBB was its flexibility in dealing with cycles in the economy. Because of the different options or levels of service that ZBB offers to decision makers, Rex made changes in its budget without the need to replan. This is perhaps an important reason why, in 2009 during the Great Recession, 44 percent of GFOA financial respondents indicated that they were considering adopting ZBB.[9]

Examining the ZBB Process

Before the ZBB process can begin, an organization needs to clearly identify (1) its goals and objectives and (2) its structure. There must exist a framework for linking operations planning (identification of short-term objectives) and long-term planning (or what is called *strategic planning*). Answers to the following questions with short-term implications should be sought: What outcomes are desired from ZBB? What kinds of technology will be used? Who will be the main users of the information for which the ZBB process is being designed? What is the appropriate linkage between the present management information system and the ZBB process? What implementation strategies will be followed? The relevant questions about long-term implications include the following: Where is the government or agency now? Where should it be headed? Is it moving in the right direction? An organization should not attempt to apply ZBB without a clear understanding of its own structure and support, as suggested in Figure 15.1. For this reason, it is essential to know at the outset whether the existing organization is viable for the installation of ZBB. If the organization is not, what programmatic changes are presently being considered, and what changes are planned for the future?

The ZBB process may be viewed as having four essential steps, as shown in Figure 15.2. The process begins with the development of planning assumptions and articulation of goals and objectives. The planning assumptions, goals, and objectives are the major inputs to the operating departments to aid in budget preparation. (As in the case of traditional budget-making, managers also need to know the projected inflation rates, salary increases, and service level requirements.) The next important step is the definition of *decision units*.

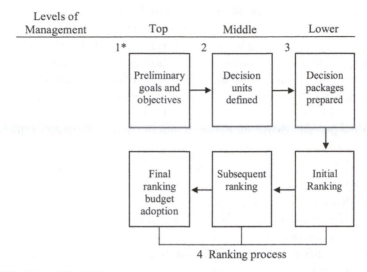

FIGURE 15.2   The ZBB process: An overview.

Note: *Numbers indicate steps or stages in the ZBB process.

(A *decision unit* is an organizational responsibility center for which a manager can be held accountable but for which budgets are required to be made.) The decision unit facilitates the grouping of activities and the analysis of inputs/costs and outputs/benefits. Typically, a decision unit is a program or organizational entity with common and measurable objectives for which budget requests are prepared and to which individual or specific accountability can be assigned.

With assumptions specified and planning goals and objectives defined, top management is in a position to identify agency activities/responsibility areas and the person responsible for performing each activity. The middle- and lower-level managers can now sit down with the program managers and define the decision units. The latter may be projects, training, maintenance, client service, budget units, specific activities, or a grouping of existing or proposed activities (a program) that management views as meaningful for planning and budgeting purposes. (A specific activity might be, for example, street paving, whereas a grouping of closely related activities, or program, would be street maintenance.) Since each decision unit is viewed as a *responsibility center*, there must be a manager who can make important decisions about spending and the quality of work. Hence, a decision unit may be a line item, a project, an activity, a program, or an entire organization, depending on the level of management responsibility for the preparation of the decision package.

In most cases, decision units are formed within the existing organizational structure. This is especially true in those cases in which PPBS has been operating, for it provides a logical structure that can easily accommodate ZBB. The fit or correspondence with the existing structure has the advantage of maintaining the linkage with the accounting system. Where a new decision unit must be designed, the accounting linkage must be incorporated and continued.[10]

Setting decision unit objectives is a function given to the unit managers in the initial implementation of ZBB. The pyramid of objectives is identified with the concurrence of superiors. As the ZBB system evolves and develops, unit goal setting is more closely integrated with the higher-level planning processes that set the overall organizational goals and objectives. Because of the conditioning role that the objectives play in the ZBB system, the organization that practices MBO will find its process readily accommodative with ZBB.

Developing decision packages is the third step in the ZBB process. It is through decision packages that goals and objectives are translated into concrete plans. A *decision package* is a request document (indicating in monetary terms the amount of resources that a manager would like to have) identifying, describing, justifying, and providing information on a specific activity, program, function, or operation to permit managers to make informed judgments about the allocation of scarce resources. The information provided in a decision package should allow management to rank it with competing activities.

Decision packages contain the projected outputs that a manager believes are achievable and the required resources to realize them. A decision unit set, or package, should be complete, whole, and discrete. The activities of each decision unit should provide sufficient information to identify results, evaluate options, analyze costs, and assess benefits. It is important to note that a decision package is considered to be effectively prepared only when management is able to rank it with other packages. A schematic view for developing decision packages is presented in Figure 15.3. It should be recognized that the number of levels of effort (n) typically equals three, whereas the number of options (m) is independent of the number of levels of efforts and may often exceed three.

Decision packages constitute the basic building blocks in the ZBB subsystem. Every unit has at least three or more decision packages except in those cases in which the cost of the program or activity is mandated (for whatever reason). In such cases, only one package is prepared. There are normally three decision packages: (1) *minimal level* or *base*, (2) *current level*, and (3) *advanced* or *enhanced level* (see Figures 15.4 and 15.5). Each decision unit package is prepared at the lowest operating level, where the best cost–benefit information can be obtained.

Several related steps are involved in the formation of the decision package: (1) Define the purpose or goal of the particular activity or function; (2) describe and document existing operations and resources, determining what will be done as well as when and how; (3) evaluate alternative ways or means of achieving objectives; (4) identify benefits to be achieved from specific funding levels (also known as *levels of efforts*) and the consequences that

FIGURE 15.3   Schematic view for developing ZBB decision packages.

are likely to result from nonfunding (if funding for a described activity cannot be obtained, this information should be clearly outlined); and (5) define the performance measures upon which the activities will be evaluated (see Appendix 1).

Where capital outlays can be specifically identified with a particular program improvement, this information should ideally be included in the decision package. For example, if the snow removal maintenance crew needs a new truck, this should be assigned a cost and be included in the budget as a separate package. In those cases where direct identification of capital outlays cannot be identified with a program, individual or consolidated packages are developed. Therefore, before decision packages are funded, such items as debt service must be examined.

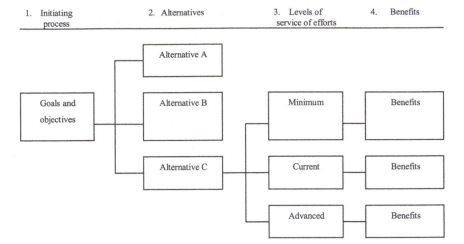

1. Initiating process	2. Alternatives	3. Levels of service of efforts	4. Benefits

FIGURE 15.4 Decision package preparation process—perspective #1.

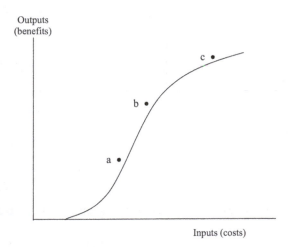

FIGURE 15.5 Graphic view of levels of service/efforts and the concept of diminishing returns—perspective #2.

Note: Point "a" represents the threshold minimum level of effort. From point "a" to point "b" there is a marked acceleration of the increasing benefits. This point ("b") may be considered the current level of effort or service. After point "b," benefits continue to increase but at a decelerating rate until point "c," the advanced level, is reached, producing the maximization of benefits. Most activities should operate at point "c" when possible, because from that point onward there is rapid deceleration of benefits.

The Ranking Process

Once the decision package has been prepared, the stage is set for the final step in the ZBB process, priority ranking. Properly done, this step allows management to achieve the most productive and cost-effective allocation of its scarce resources. Because of its multiple and hierarchical character, ranking allows managers with budget responsibilities to participate in determining the decision unit and overall agency priorities.

Ideally, the person responsible for subsequent rankings (all ranking above the decision unit) should make a concerted effort to be familiar with the lower-level managers' submission. It may be necessary for ranking managers to meet individually with unit managers to obtain a clear idea. Additionally, all cost–benefit information, program measures, and evaluative materials that can sharpen the critical and analytical focus of the ranking manager should be provided. The ranking process permits the separate decision packages, representing the various levels of service for a given alternative, to be ordered to determine which proposed work item will be funded during the next budget year. The process then places a *program function*, or activity, in a descending order of priority based on the benefits to be gained from each undertaking at the various spending levels.

Decision unit managers rank the decision packages for which they are responsible. These rankings are then placed in competition with other decision units. Rankings within one division or between divisions or departments of an organization are shown in Figure 15.6. The consolidated decision packages are reviewed at different management levels until a final ranking is made. At some point during the process, top management will generally know (based on the best revenue projection) the budget cutoff point—that is, the total funds that will be included in the budget—and can determine which decision packages will be funded. For each level of service, the resulting benefits must be specified, because they relate to profit margins in the private sector and to particular target populations in the public sector.

Ranking systems and criteria vary widely among governmental units and nonprofit organizations. The City of Mt. Lebanon, Pennsylvania, provides a good example (see Table 15.2). Decision managers are typically given a number of votes equal to the number of packages prepared and having a ranking value of between 1 and 6, with the highest-priority decision packages given a value of 6. Using the same voting system, Mt. Lebanon uses a municipality-wide ranking committee "composed of all department heads, the finance officer, the personnel and purchasing officer and a student intern who ranks the decision packages, prepared and initially ranked by decision unit managers."[11] Mt. Lebanon's manager participates but does not vote. He reserves the right to make changes in the decision packages' ranking before they are submitted to Mt. Lebanon's township commission. The department heads are given an

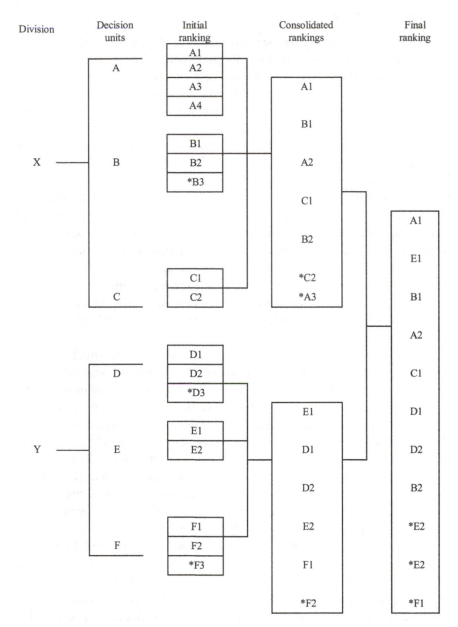

FIGURE 15.6   The ranking process: A consolidation of decision packages (with budget cutoffs).

Note: *Budget cutoff points represent nonrelevant packages not sent upward.

opportunity to discuss their concerns with the commission, which determines the final funding priorities.

In ranking, we cannot take a myopic view that seeks to maximize the short-run gain while ignoring long-term applications. Lowering taxes by one

TABLE 15.2   Criteria for Vote Casting

1. Importance of service levels in terms of perceived health, welfare, safety, and satisfaction of the township's residents;
2. Statutory, charter, and contractual commitments met by the service level;
3. Potential consequences (including political) if the service level is not provided;
4. Federal and/or state funds received dependent on a particular expenditure or match of funds;
5. Informal assessment of the quality of the service provided;
6. Cost-effectiveness of the service level.

Source: City of Mt. Lebanon, Pennsylvania, *1979 Budgeting Manual* (Mt. Lebanon, PA: Finance Office, 1979), p. A-8.

or two mills to win an election (because of the insignificant material gain to most taxpayers, this is a symbolic gesture at best) but failing to plan to replace crumbling bridges is a dramatic example of shortsightedness.

Monitoring Performance

Once the ZBB budget has been approved, the development and implementation of a clearly defined and understood monitoring system are indispensable. Typically, the monitoring system will be established and integrated with the normal management review cycle.

ZBB as a Means for Dealing with Recognized Problems

Once serious thought is given to the potential implementation of ZBB, there needs to be an evaluation of the extent of, and need for, ZBB. Simultaneous with the examination of the ZBB system, the benefits and costs of other methods that are capable of achieving the organization's identified needs should be explored. This is especially important when one realizes the changes in forms, relationships, procedures, and attitudes that may be necessary with the installation of the ZBB approach.

Among the factors that may indicate the need for the ZBB system is a desire to improve the effectiveness of managers. This may require a reallocation of resources involving a reduction in both costs and expenditures. Importantly, there may be a recognized need to improve operations owing to unclear lines of authority, unclear policies and procedures, and poor channels of communication.

The Status of ZBB: Federal, State, and Local Levels

ZBB has undergone significant changes during the past ten years. Government units such as the city of Garland, Texas, have incorporated a hybridized budget system (a different budget system is integrated into ZBB to make it more relevant and usable). Many entities have reverted to traditional budgeting or to various forms of performance budgeting and a type of ad hoc total quality management (TQM). In most of the systems in which ZBB has survived, as in Mt. Lebanon and Rex Hospital in Raleigh, North Carolina, a modified or simplified approach has been adopted. The requirement that ZBB analysis be initiated from scratch has been discontinued. Unlike was once the case, after goals and objectives are decided upon, no specific number of decision packages is required. Greater flexibility is left to program or responsibility managers to determine the programs that need to be undertaken to implement the goals that have been agreed upon. In many instances, only the final decision packages are entered into the formal system. Governments have modified their ZBB systems to enhance their efficiency and adapt to the changing environment to reduce rigidity and improve policy outcomes. Surviving ZBB systems have succeeded because participants are better trained, institutional influences are given greater recognition, and the legislative and executive branches of government have given increased support to the ZBB system.

By adopting ZBB, Rex Hospital rescued its organization from increasing costs and declining revenue inflows due to a clientele/customer base made up of a significant percentage of Medicare patients. To reclaim its competitive edge and remain the preferred provider for a number of major medical plans within its serving area, Rex implemented ZBB. Thereafter, the hospital was able to make large cost reductions and keep it 85 percent below the medical consumer price index for its region.[12]

During the Reagan administration, ZBB was allowed to be phased out at the federal government level, the traditional line item budget becoming the norm once again until 1993, when congress enacted the Government Performance Results Act. This new orientation requires agencies to incorporate five-year planning, programs, and results (see the discussion of the act in chapters 1 and 9).

The Rise of Total Quality Management

The late W. Edwards Deming popularized the practice of total quality management (TQM) in Japan after World War II. Deming was sent to Japan as an advisor to help the Japanese improve their shoddy image for products made in the country. Even though the TQM method and concepts were developed in the United States, it did not receive visibility in America until Japan began to surge ahead in many commercial and industrial areas during the late 1970s and early 1980s.

By the late 1980s, TQM had become the rage throughout America in both the public and not-for-profit sectors. At conventions and meetings, TQM seminar rooms were overflowing. Advocates promised governments would save

millions, cut budgets by 20 percent, and reduce deficits and constituents' complaints to all-time lows.[13] In the 1990s, Governmental units such as New York
City; Ft. Collins, Colorado; Palm Beach, Florida; Madison, Wisconsin; and
Erie, Pennsylvania, as well as the state of North Dakota, have been implementing or examining TQM. Successful budget managers expressed the view that if
the right situation is matched with the right problem, TQM does seem to work.
Unfortunately, it is not easy to execute well. "Despite the success stories, it is
no magic formula for instant government rejuvenation."[14] A direct by product
of TQM has been development of intense interest in clientele/customer focus
satisfaction, and performance management and accountability.

What Is TQM?

TQM is a philosophy or way of life comprising a set of principles, tools, and
procedures for operating an organization to maximally achieve its articulated
goals and objectives. Everyone is expected to be mutually induced to participate in controlling and continuously improving the quality of the work that
must be done to satisfy customer/clientele expectations in every way possible.
The TQM organization is characterized by constant change, teamwork, flexibility, sensitivity, and responsiveness to its environment. It is future-oriented
and mission- and goal-driven. To achieve continuous improvement and
innovation, the organization must (1) plan for the change, (2) implement the
change, (3) observe and evaluate the change, and (4) take action based on what
is learned. These actions constitute what is sometimes referred to as the *planning, doing, checking,* and *acting cycle.* This process (see Figure 15.7) is expected
to lead inevitably to maximum improvement in the quality output of product
or service, decrease costs, increase productivity, lower prices of outputs, and
increase the satisfaction of customers, clientele, or constituents.

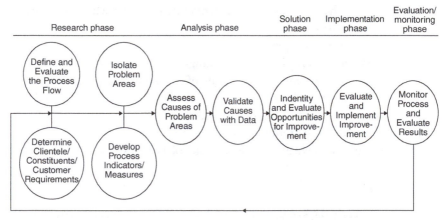

FIGURE 15.7   Continuing process and quality improvement.

The Deming View of TQM

The greatest success will come only from an organization that has a process-obsessed management culture that harnesses the know-how and natural initiative of its employees. This orientation is capable of fine-tuning the organization to achieve the highest standards of excellence and innovation. In the United States, it is exceedingly difficult for private firms to realize these goals, because the heartbeat of the marketplace has been replaced with the singular pursuit of return on investment (ROI). Similarly, in government, the re-election objective at any cost has replaced the drive to achieve the best-quality outcome for constituents.

In Deming's view, it is critical that decisions be made on the basis of data that is undergirded by required practical and theoretical knowledge and not on the basis of instinct. Of all problems in organizations, 85 to 90 percent can be traced to systems or process; only 10 to 15 percent are directly related to humans. When a blemished car rolls off the assembly, "gut reaction" may lead the worker to adjust the machinery. If the problem is embedded in the machinery, the change may actually throw the machine out of adjustment. This might lead to more severe problems. Thus, it is critical that training be an accepted norm in every TQM organization as an indispensable ingredient to achieve maximum process improvement and innovation.[15] Deming set forth fourteen innovative TQM rules or "commandments" that must be followed if the greatest end product results are to be realized:

1. Articulate purpose and pursue it steadfastly.
2. Improve systems constantly and forever.
3. Avoid the use of MBO-type goals and quotas.
4. Eradicate fear in the organization.
5. Create leadership that coaches rather than bosses.
6. Allow quality, not just price, to guide all bids.
7. Maximize the communication potential between departments by breaking down barriers.
8. Provide for ongoing job training.
9. Ban annual personnel evaluation ratings and the merit system.
10. Create and institutionalize a program of education and self-improvement.
11. Ban slogans and exhortations.
12. Avoid dependency on traditional inspection.
13. Inculcate the new TQM philosophy.
14. Expect management to be the driving force of the new system if it is to succeed.

TQM and ZBB

Not unlike the early days of the introduction of ZBB into the U.S. government, TQM is viewed with great expectations. It has an added advantage in that it promises results without elaborate structure. Additionally, public officials view TQM as a cost-reducing instrument that simultaneously enhances the quality of services it delivers to clientele and constituents.[16]

The enhanced quality and cost savings that TQM promises do not provide budget linkage to enable us to effectively cost out programs. Project selection criteria are determined by a team committed to process and outcome improvement. The critical linking role of the budget is missing. An examination of Figure 15.7 reveals that TQM is silent on the budget requirement. Ideally, the budgeting phase should follow the identification of improvement opportunities before initiating the next phase. The fact cannot be overlooked that most improvements have some cost constraints that is unexplained in TQM.

Summary Observations: Theory and Practice Concerns

Although ZBB is expected to be innovative and rational in practice, it tends to be status quo–oriented and highly political. Although decisions are expected to be made based on a cost–benefit analysis, in practice this is seldom the reality, and the generally perceived view that ZBB is an integrative planning tool is seldom obtained. The requirement that ZBB be initiated by goal clarification and goal setting by top management is not accomplished; instead, most agencies permit goal articulation to be done at the department level.

The ranking process requires the greatest amount of trust and commitment to the ZBB objectives, because it permits the exercise of a high degree of discretion; most critically, it is a focal point for determining the allocation of scarce resources. This discretionary element, the lack of quality information, and the significant influence exercised by the decision unit manager have permitted the ranking system to be used as a means for political manipulation. The reasons for this outcome include the following: (1) the haphazard ways in which decision units tend to be defined within individual departments, making comparability difficult, (2) unspecific ranking criteria, (3) inadequate trust and lack of continuous feedback between upper and lower levels of management (decision unit managers fear that the explicit identification of alternatives transfers control over their programs to potentially unsympathetic others), (4) lack of monitoring devices to check on ranking practices, (5) lack of an incentive system to encourage managers to minimize the manipulation of information and priorities, (6) lack of emphasis on productivity in the ZBB system, (7) lack of coordination between legislative sunset laws and executive-oriented ZBB, and (8) loss of vitality to initiate change due to easy adaptation to traditional budget routines. (For a contrast between theory and practice problems in ZBB, see Table 15.3.)

When implementing ZBB, it is useful to avoid viewing it as a set of specific techniques to be mastered and religiously implemented in every specific detail. Instead, it should be viewed as a philosophy—a way of thinking that gives

TABLE 15.3   ZBB: Theory and Practice

Category	Theory	Practice
Planning		
1. Budget base	None, minimum base	All programs have a base; true zero not considered; arbitrary service levels
2. Overall	Explicit; expenditure-related	Not explicit; seldom considered
3. Decision-package objectives	Explicit; output and productivity measures	Not always explicit; seldom have links to productivity or output
4. Policy determination	Exhaustive consideration	Minimal; little consideration
5. Preparation of alternatives	Short-range and comprehensive; cost–benefit	Little or no cost–benefit analysis; no systematic criteria
6. Levels of effort (service levels)	Cost–benefit for each level; zerobase identified	No explicit cost–benefit analysis; no systematic criteria
7. Programming	Not explicit	Nonexistent
8. Integrated	Not explicit	Nonexistent
9. Depth of analysis	In-depth	Minimal; superficial at best
10. Timespan	Short-range; tactical	Short-range; tactical
Organization Theory and Management		
1. Organizational structure	Decision-unit oriented; responsibility unit	Decision units generally conform to existing organizational structure
2. Programmatic	Well-developed	Well-developed
3. Ideology	Innovative; dynamic; neutral	Conservative; status quo; highly political processes
4. Value agreement	Managerial efficiency	Minimal or totally lacking in practice
5. Managementlevel involvement	Middle and lower	Minimum at top; maximum at bottom; inadequate feedback between levels
DecisionMaking		
1. Focus of decision-making	Participation at all levels	Focus on lower-level managers
2. Decision-making flow between management levels	Bottom-up	Bottom-up, with high degree of reduction of information upward

3. Ranking identified	Comprehensive; explicit; rational	Unsystematic political rationality and expediency; minimal information
4. Administrative documents	Moderate	Many more than PPBS

Productivity, Monitoring, and Evaluation

1. Emphasis for Measuring objectives	Measures output	Heavy reliance on workload measures; unsystematic
2. Evaluating results	Required; precontinuing, and postanalysis	Haphazard, unsystematic
3. Evaluating ongoing programs	Continuous	Seldom or not done at all; very unsystematic
4. Staff and time requirements	Minimal to moderate	High

life and substance to the technique that may be usefully employed to effect resource allocation. Goals and objectives must be clearly understood and collectively agreed upon. The information system must be designed to meet user needs and be closely integrated into the accounting system. From the outset, it should have the wholehearted support of top management.

The status of ZBB in governmental and other not-for-profit agencies has declined significantly since the 1980s. It is no longer practiced at the federal government level. Many states and local governments have reverted to traditional budgets. In most instances in which ZBB has survived (such as in the states of Tennessee and Missouri and the cities of Garland, Texas, and Wilmington, Delaware), modified approaches have been adopted. The continuing uses of ZBB can be attributed to a number of reasons, including the following: Attention was paid to demand; a simplified system and unified philosophy were established; patience was exercised; factions involved in institutional politics were given an opportunity to participate meaningfully in resource allocation; and monitoring and evaluating systems were successfully implemented to permit the selection of high-visibility activities for closer scrutiny.

Among the reasons that have been given to explain the demise of ZBB in government units are that many viewed ZBB as an instrument for quick budget reduction; ZBB was used to demonstrate a unit's commitment and priority to innovation, but the type of accountability (results) being sought was not clearly articulated or understood; and minimal support prevented ZBB from taking root strongly enough to replace traditional line item and incremental budgeting.

The move to TQM reveals no clear theory, methodology, or practice. TQM philosophy and practice do not provide a bridge or linkage between theory and practice, as shown in Figure 15.7. Unlike ZBB, which is heavy

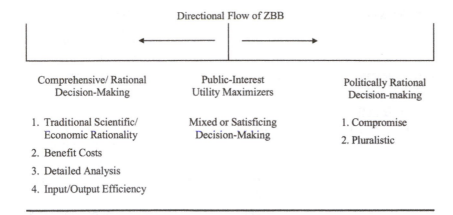

Directional Flow of ZBB

Comprehensive/ Rational Decision-Making	Public-Interest Utility Maximizers	Politically Rational Decision-making
1. Traditional Scientific/ Economic Rationality	Mixed or Satisficing Decision-Making	1. Compromise
2. Benefit Costs		2. Pluralistic
3. Detailed Analysis		
4. Input/Output Efficiency		

FIGURE 15.8   ZBB and decision making.

on structure, TQM minimizes structure. Nonetheless, both systems involve mission-driven, bottom-up management that is costly to introduce and maintain.

Many advocates like TQM because it does not require change or modification to the existing budget structure. This view should be accepted with caution and reflection before attempting to apply TQM. In the long run, TQM will not succeed unless total human, political, and monetary commitments are given to it. The cultural change that TQM requires is not easy to achieve. Thus, the quick payoff that public officials typically expect is not likely to materialize.

Last, it should be borne in mind that ZBB is not installed in a vacuum; rather, it must compete with entrenched ways of doing things. Whenever a new system is installed, participants want to know what it means to them individually. Placing emphasis solely on efficiency and productivity measures will produce anxiety—and this may exacerbate latent fears. Perhaps decision making in ZBB should be tempered by the view implied in Figure 15.8: that the most acceptable and best decision outcomes lay in compromise between the political rationality and economic rationality producing the mixed "satisficing [sic] decision."[17]

Notes

1. Jerry McCaffery and John H. Bowman, "Participatory Democracy and Budgeting: The Effects of Proposition 13," *Public Administration Review* (November/December 1978): 533–536.

2. Jerome B. McKinney, *Understanding ZBB: Promise and Reality* (Chicago: Public Policy Press, 1979), p. 54.

3. City of Mt. Lebanon, Pennsylvania, *1979 Budgeting Manual* (Mt. Lebanon, PA: Finance Office, May 1, 1979), p. 84.

4. David Leininger and Ronald C. Wong, *Zero-Base Budgeting in Garland, Texas,* Information Report 8/4a (Washington, DC: International City Managers Association, April 1976), p. 2.

5. Henry C. Knight, *Zero-Based Budgeting Process: A Practical Guide to Evaluation, Implementation and Use* (Hamilton, ON: Society of Management Accountants of Canada, 1979), pp. 25–33.

6. Shayne Kavanagh, "Zero-Base Budgeting: Modern Experiences and Current Perspectives", *Government Finance Review 28*, 2 (April 2012), p. 9.

7. Ibid, p. 11.

8. Jerome B. McKinney, "Implementing and Managing Zero-Base Budgeting," in Aman Khan and W. Bartley Hildreth, eds., *Case Studies in Public Budgeting and Financial Management* (New York: Marcel Dekker, 2003), p. 141.

9. Ibid., p. 9

10. For more discussion, see U.S. Executive Office of the President, Office of Management and Budget, *Zero-Base Budgeting 77–79* (Washington, DC: U.S. GPO, April 1979).

11. Jerome B. McKinney, *Understanding ZBB and TQM* (Clinton, MD: Public Policy Press, 1995), p. 69.

12. See Matthew M. Person III, *The Zero-Base Hospital* (Chicago: Health Administration Press, 1998), pp. 3–4.

13. David K. Carr and Ian D. Litterman, *Excellence in Government: Total Quality Management in the 1990s,* 2nd ed. (Arlington, VA: Coopers and Lybrand, 1993), p. 2.

14. Jonathan Walters, "The Cult of Total Quality," *Governing* (May 1992): 38. See also Total Quality Management: Performance Management, http://www.referenceforbusiness.com/encyclopedia/Thir-Val/Total-Quality-Management-TQM.html15. Andrea Gabor, *The Man Who Discovered Quality* (New York: Times Book/London House, 1991), pp. 4–5, 7.

16. See Al Gore, *Creating a Government That Works Better and Costs Less* (Washington, DC: U.S. Government Printing Office, 1993); and David Osborne and Ted Gaebler, *Reinventing Government: How the Entrepreneurial Spirit Is Transforming America* (Reading, MA: Addison-Wesley Publishing, 1992).

17. Herbert A. Simon, *Administrative Behavior,* 3rd ed. (New York: The Free Press, 1976), pp. xxviii–xxxi

16

Information Needs and Financial Management

There is a growing need for information management in government and not-for-profit agencies (see Figure 16.1). In the delivery of social services, the demand for greater efficiency and effectiveness of programs, the internal reporting requirements, and the availability of new information technology have made the management of information a critical, as well as difficult, undertaking. These circumstances also point to the compelling need for the development of a coherent *management information system* (MIS). Despite this reality, a large number of government and other not-for-profit organizations have not given the problem adequate attention and resources. This situation, however, has been changing, especially with the advent of the Internet revolution, citizen and client demands for greater stewardship and accountability. This chapter focuses attention on the continuing changes taking place within the narrow, traditional financial management information system and examines the new, more integrated user-oriented approach to financial management. The operations of networks and the server concept (software that can be easily downloaded to serve other machines) have created the opportunity for maximum flexibility, decentralization, and manager- or user-oriented systems. Data can be retrieved from farflung places if the decision maker knows what is desired and understands the capability of the system. Thus designing the information system to meet expectations and knowing how to use the system capabilities are important factors.

Information technology has become a significant instrument in the conduct of public affairs. Since governments' introduction of kiosks in the early 1990s to aid the conduct of business with citizens, information technology has been changing.[1] The Internet is now being used in novel ways to enhance government and nonprofit agencies' decisions. These entities operate web sites allowing citizens to communicate directly with officials and conduct many business activities. Citizens can pay parking tickets and utility bills and renew driving, occupational, and business licenses over the Internet. A large number of taxpayers pay income taxes through the Internet via electronic funds transfers or debit/credit card payment.

Today government information technology in many areas goes beyond simple transactions. For example, geographic information systems (GIS) mapping is being applied in a number of activities such as assessing present and prospective business development, construction projects, and the mapping of emergency evacuation routes. *Biometrics* is another growing application. This technique allows governments to use innovation to improve security involving activities such as retinal scans, fingerprinting and voice recognition. Biometrics is replacing older and costly technology with greater reliability. Finally, there are a number of other administrative and support functions where information technology has been having positive effects. The activities include bond sale bidding, centralized state/local cash management, and purchasing and procurement.

In April 1993, Maryland began providing Aid to Families with Dependent Children (AFDC) benefits via kiosks. The state installed 1,800 automated teller machines at 3,000 grocery stores. The reduction of administrative costs was the main motivation for the implementation of the project. According to Betts, the traditional system cost the state $5.10 per client each month, while the electronic system costs $4.35 per client each month, a savings of $0.75. This was 20 years ago that the electronic system saved the state $1.2 million annually.[2]

States such as Arizona, Colorado, and Hawaii have also installed kiosks to provide basic services. In Colorado, kiosks have been used for obtaining citizen input to the budgetary process. In New Jersey, the Motor Vehicle Service has used kiosks for vehicle registration. The Pennsylvania Bureau of Motor Vehicles has deployed kiosks to improve its vehicle registration services. The use of kiosks can improve service delivery and reduce administrative costs. State agencies can provide routine services effectively and efficiently without increasing their staffs. Moreover, state agencies can reduce waste, fraud, and abuse through the use of kiosks, as the hardware and software that comprise the kiosks contain significant internal and physical controls.[3]

While many management information systems have been developed around computers, others are not computer-based. Effectively operating MIS dependency on sophisticated data processing hardware varies according to the particular needs of each organization. In fact, there are some qualitative types of management inputs that are not readily amenable to computerization. When excessive attention is given to the computer hardware and how data is processed, it may negatively affect the design of the MIS. Typical is this observation by Litechy and Wilson: "All too often, hardware vendors short-circuit the preferred approach by selling their own immediate solution to data-processing problems."[4] The hardware aspects of the MIS should follow the initial determination of the user's information and organizational needs. Although certainly not unimportant, computer hardware needs should be relegated to a secondary position.

Defining the Management Information System

Although many tend to define MIS as an electronic data processing or computer system in which the information flow is automated, this is not a complete definition. In fact, MIS is much more than a computer system. Essentially, it is a process for ordering information and communicating it on a timely basis to aid management in identifying and solving specific problems as they arise. What a management information system is may be better understood by considering each element in its name.

Management comprises activities that are concerned with resource use. These activities or functions involve planning, programming, organizing, budgeting, accounting, implementing, controlling, and evaluating the use of resources in accordance with stipulated guidelines and practices. A characteristic of effective managers is their ability to enhance the capacity and flexibility of an organization to respond to changing demands and conditions. The efficacy of the MIS can be evaluated in terms of its ability to facilitate management to effectively achieve its objectives—the communication of information for decision making.

Information and *data* are used interchangeably, but they are not the same thing. Data are facts and figures that have not been organized for specific use; they are nonsensical when presented individually. Examples include accounting transactions, files, and reports. Data do not become information until they are organized to permit comparisons to be made and to identify relationships that can aid management in making decisions. Information, therefore, is data that are purposefully compiled and interpreted for management's use. The continual storage of information provides the MIS with valuable resources for potential use by management in the future.

A *system* consists of two or more elements that come together to collectively achieve a common purpose. Systems typically possess a set of subsystems arranged in a hierarchy from large to small. For example, the judicial system in the United States extends from the federal Supreme Court (the apex of the hierarchy) to the justice of the peace in a given locality. The effective operation of the judicial system requires that all courts consistently apply the procedures and rulings of the higher courts. This drive toward unison and the pursuit of the common goal of justice may be described as "synergy," meaning that the elements of the system work better and more efficiently together than independently. Hence the MIS generates information that helps management to make improved decisions because of the synergistic context in which the information is derived and used.

The Financial Management Information System

Most financial management activities, especially in local governments, tend to be highly fragmented. A historical examination of the development of the financial information system reveals that it typically has had an independent beginning, arising almost entirely from within each independent financial function. Accounting personnel created systems to satisfy particular reporting requirements, while budget personnel developed systems to meet their needs such as expenditure estimating and budget control. Over time, such diverse systems, with their own terminologies and procedures unconstrained by imposed or agreed-upon criteria and guidelines, were found to be duplicative, inconsistent, and counterproductive.[5]

In chapter 1, the definition of the fiscal management system was given as consisting of three core financial processes: (1) *financing*—raising required financial resources; (2) *budgeting*—developing a work plan stated in both financial and nonfinancial terms; and (3) *controlling*—which is concerned with assuring adherence to the articulated budget plan. The operation of these financial components requires three basic, substantive management processes: (1) *planning*—defining the goals and objectives to be pursued; (2) *programming*—selecting the appropriate activities to achieve the goals and objectives that have been stated and planned; and (3) *evaluating*—assessing the quality and usefulness of the articulated goals, objectives, and activities that have been implemented. These six different processes, ideally, should be incorporated and built into each organization as standard operating procedures. Transactions relating to such activities as payroll, purchasing, inventory, receiving, and disbursing should be guided by uniform procedures. To be effective, these processes must be serviced by an information and reporting system under the continuing surveillance of designated responsibility center officials who are empowered to identify and address issues as they arise.

Because this fiscal management system (FMS) follows essentially a rational approach, the following question may be asked: Doesn't every organization use such a system? In varying degrees, the answer is definitely yes, even though management may not always be aware of it. The point is that each organization requires a FMS for its operations, regardless of whether the need for one is clearly understood.

The financial process has both financial and nonfinancial effects. The information generated from the financial system relating to both financial and nonfinancial activities must be stored and maintained. This is the job of the financial management information system (FMIS), which organizes and converts the financial data into information that enables management to monitor, control, and effectively direct the operation of the organization. This is what is traditionally referred to as the *integrated financial management system*. It is essentially a system that is coordinated to bring relevant financial information together to help develop policies and practices for raising, storing, applying, and evaluating the use of monetary resources.

More recently, the view and meaning of what constitutes an integrated financial management system have been changing. The new emphasis is no longer on planning, programming, and financing.[6] Instead, stress is placed on three aspects of controlling—budgeting, accounting, and auditing—and on *performance management*. Performance management is a by-product of these components. Note that unless the budget process incorporates planning and programming, these aspects are likely to be minimized. This leaves accounting (a record-keeping and expenditure control instrument) and the financial statements derived from accounting records as the key information provider to managers and legislative oversight officials.

An integrated financial management information system should include information that will facilitate executive, legislative, and staff decision making about the allocation, administration, control, and evaluation of resource application (see Figure 16.1). The kinds of information useful to decision makers include the following:

1. *Budget*
   a. Comprehensive listing of all the funds expended by programs, functions, activities, and organizational units, including objectives, functions, and activities
   b. Description of and qualitative data on service outputs of program functions and activities
   c. Benefits increased or decreased at each service level
   d. Cost–benefit analysis of existing and alternative methods for delivery of services
   e. Established procedure for updating revenue estimates
   f. Future expenditure of proposed programs
   g. Breakdown or listing of financial data for capital budget improvements and the projection of future program impacts on the operating budget
   h. Multiyear financial plan

2. *Budget/Accounting Implementation*
   a. Definition of periodic allotments (e.g., monthly, quarterly, annually)
   b. Appropriated funds allocated to organizational units/responsibility centers
   c. Budget modification criteria
   d. Comparison reports of actual expenditures, encumbrances, and revenues versus approved budget
   e. Maintenance of accrual accounting data for enterprise activities
   f. Flexible accounting structure permitting the recognition of encumbrance for any given program or activity
   g. Common data system to permit the recognition of expenditure and revenue programs, activities, and so on, to permit performance data to be collected
   h. Ability to determine full costing of all undertakings

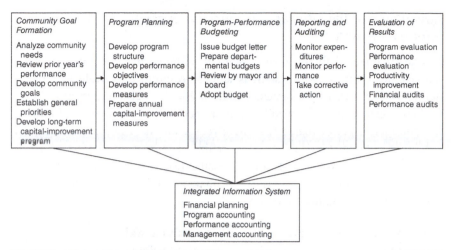

FIGURE 16.1   Financial information and resource management (FIRM) system: City of San Francisco.

Source: Adapted from San Francisco, Office of the Mayor, Program Measurement Handbook (San Francisco: Resources Management Program, City and County of San Francisco, Office of the Mayor, February 1980), fig. 5, p. 33.

3. *Performance Management*
    a. System for assessing performance of activities, programs, projects, and responsibility centers for measuring indicators, such as workloads, output, effectiveness, and quality of performance
    b. Periodic system for setting and reporting on planned performance targets with annual performance plan to the chief executive, clientele, or public
    c. Indicators showing performance measurement linkages to the budget
    d. Reporting of performance analysis with budget expenditure data and comparison of performance targets with recommended appropriations

4. *Auditing*
    a. Maintaining results data on important problems and recommendations emanating from independent audits and others deemed necessary
    b. Maintaining important findings and recommendations of performance audits
    c. Identifying systems for showing response and corrective actions taken due to audit recommendations
    d. Identifying systems, plans, and guidelines to be followed before each audit is undertaken
    e. Process for selecting activities and/or programs to be audited[7]

Advantages of the Integrated Financial Management Information System

Unlike fragmented financial management systems, the integrated financial management information system is able to respond effectively to citizens' demands. It generates performance data to enable decision makers to better evaluate agency and responsibility center accomplishments, and it facilitates the conduct of performance and effectiveness audits. The integrated system enhances policymakers' ability to organize data around significant issues instead of the expenditure or object classification, which is the norm under the existing, fragmented systems. In summary, the following benefits are associated with the integrated system model:

- Information can be presented in a relevant framework.
- Data can be better analyzed and categorized before they are reported and disseminated.
- Information has greater opportunity for reaching decision makers on a timely basis.
- The opportunity to design the system to produce data to meet users' needs is facilitated.
- The opportunities for data analysis and conducting cost–benefit analysis are enhanced.
- There is greater opportunity to standardize, centralize, and increase the consistency of information.
- Greater computerization can be justified.
- The agency or governmental unit must train and upgrade staff. Typically, local governments and other not-for-profit agencies tend to hire consultants rather than developing in-house capability.
- The integrated system minimizes duplication and jurisdictional problems in exchanging information and facilitates efficient information sharing.

Disadvantages of the Integrated Financial Management Information System

Despite the many benefits to be gained from the integrated system, there are disadvantages as well:

- It tends to be expensive and difficult to design and build.
- When a system is large, the problems associated with it tend to be bigger and more complicated.
- Because these systems are highly coordinated and operate to produce synergistic results, subsystem failures may disrupt the entire system.
- Maintaining accessibility, privacy, and security of information becomes more difficult.

- Personnel may resist the implementation of an integrated system on the grounds that it is unnecessary and burdensome for the organization. Employees may also view the additional training required to properly use the system negatively.

Designing an Information Management Needs System

In developing an information system (see Pittsburgh's example in the appendix to this chapter), two critical points should be observed at the outset in determining information needs: (1) Existing processing problems should be identified, and (2) the new types of information needs should be developed to enhance management decision making.[8] Also, it cannot be overemphasized that early in the design of the financial information system, key players (all major operating officials with financial responsibilities—for example, the mayor, city manager, chief executive, legislative officials, and relevant financial officials)—should be substantively involved.

A four-phase approach to designing the financial information system has been suggested. Phase 1, *organizational assessment*, requires three activities: (1) needs determination, (2) assessment of the government or organization's capacity, and (3) system selection. Phase 2, *implementation*, requires that management be alert and sensitive to personnel and other organizational problems attendant on potential changes. Documentation and testing are important in this phase. Phase 3, *operation*, involves ongoing training, determining and delegating operating responsibilities, and planning for system enhancement. Phase 4 is the *preparation of a control plan* setting forth policies and procedures aimed at directing, controlling, and monitoring performance against plans. Since our focus here is on needs determination, our discussion will be limited to this aspect.

Organizations' Assessment Phase

The most important first step in system development is the definition of financial information needs, which typically fall into four basic management responsibility areas: planning, organizing, controlling, and external reporting/record-keeping requirements necessary to aid management decision making.[9] A major objective of this phase is the definition of policies and objectives aimed at overseeing the acquisition and use of resources, ensuring that they are effectively used in achieving objectives and ensuring that the required activities are carried out with maximum efficiency and effectiveness.[10] The needs determination may be carried out by any method deemed appropriate, although the small committee approach seems to be the one most often preferred. When this approach is used, a consultant may be employed in an advisory capacity.[11]

A review of the existing information should be undertaken to determine what needs are being met, as well as those that should be given more urgent attention and those that are not being adequately met. For example, if the payroll component is operating effectively while the expenditure control component is performing below minimal expectations, attention should be given to the latter's problems before any attempt is made to upgrade the payroll system. It is particularly important that both current and future needs be projected when the needs assessment is being made. Planned improvements will help to prevent problems from arising in the future.

During the needs assessment determination, decision flow analysis may be used to reveal the interrelationships among decisions, identifying decisions that are required to be made and those that have no applicability to current problems. Decision flow analysis can be used to aid in showing "interdependent decisions that are being made independently," as well as responsibilities, organizational structures, and performance measures that should be modified.[12] Organizational charts depicting the personnel hierarchy and delegation of authority can facilitate this analysis.

As will be pointed out in chapter 18, there are differing information needs for different management levels and users. Needs of different kinds of users must be given due recognition if optimal decisions are to be made. Thus the design of the information system must provide flexibility to generate the appropriate information for each management level in the organizational hierarchy. In a given organization, let us assume four levels: At level 1, the information is routine and standardized. The processing involves mainly collection, record-keeping, and storage of data. Level 2 is characterized by low-level decision making. The decision criteria and rules are specific and clearly definable; for example, notifying delinquent taxpayers and determining eligibility for a tax exemption. At level 3, information is needed to exercise greater discretion in decision making such as revenue estimating and applying the tax laws and administrative rules. Finally, level 4 requires information to plan broad strategy and forecast needs such as the analysis of the budget's effects on the poor and unemployment.

There are fiscal users, both internal and external, for whom the information system must be designed to respond on a continuing basis. Drebin, Chan, and Ferguson have suggested five information categories that potential users may need for aid in making informed decisions, especially as they relate to accounting statements:[13]

1. Current financial conditions and flows of short-term financial resources. This relates to information about liquidity and the ability to convert assets into cash in a reasonably short period of time. It is also concerned with solvency, or the ability to meet current and maturing obligations as they come due. Cash and equivalent items and other resources available for specific uses are identified.

2. Economic condition and changes in economic condition. Information about the health, the taxing base, and the economic stability of the entity or community is identified. The purpose is to indicate the entity's ability to deliver regular services, meet future maturing obligations, and maintain acceptable levels of capital improvements.

3. Legal, fiduciary, and contractual assurance. Information is included to permit "interested parties to monitor the execution of contractual and legal requirements."[14] It permits public officials to discharge their accountability by reporting on the resources entrusted to them. The recent implementation of more stringent compliance standards, such as Dodd–Frank, has increased the importance of this information user category.

4. Planning and budgeting. The planning and budgeting system provides information to permit those responsible for it to make alternative analyses to effectively allocate resources to those options offering the best effects or results.

5. Management and organizational performance. This information relates to the efficiency and effectiveness with which management achieves articulated and implied organizational goals and objectives.

These information categories are directed toward two types of internal users and eight types of external users: *internal information users*—management; employees; and *external information users*—voters; taxpayers; executives; legislative bodies; service recipients; oversight bodies; vendors; and grantors.

Changing Systems: System Selection Process

The system design and system selection involve essentially the same activities as was explained earlier (see the above definition and discussion of the MIS). Important is the fact that management is seeking to modify or change from one automated system to another. A host of reasons may account for the decision to change, including the following: outmoded technology; inability of system to meet present, evolving, and expanding information needs; excessive turnover in personnel; and failure to involve management and principal users to appropriately influence information need changes. Wold suggested a method that provides useful guides.[15]

The Integrated System: The Database Management System versus the Data Management System

An important question to be asked sometime during the needs determination phase concerns the type of software to be installed to aid in retrieving information from the system. The debate centers around the choice between the database management system (DBMS) and the data management systems (DMS).

The *database management system* contains data and procedures that permit a process to be added or subtracted. Such processes can be manipulated to modify or change/convert the raw data to produce desired information. The internal management operation of DBMS minimizes users' efforts to make the system responsive to their needs. The database approach minimizes data redundancy by maintaining centrally stored data that can be collectively input and shared by a number of users and used for applications such as the enterprise resource planning system (EPR).

Enterprise Resource Planning System: A Variant of DBMS

Although there are many emerging information systems, such as Extensible Markup Language (XML) and Executive Information Systems (EIS), Enterprise Resource Planning System (ERP) has been garnering considerable attention in the public sector because of its potential for reducing transaction costs and streamlining processes for citizens, employees, and suppliers.[16] ERP is a software preconfigured system that facilitates integration of traditional financial management applications such as accounting, budget control, accounts payable, and payroll and a broad range of nonfinancial applications such as human resources, purchasing, and inventory management. These functions are achieved through a common database standard accessible on a real-time basis. The ERP system provides information integration and the facilitation for re-engineering processes' improvement consistent with the best benchmarked business practices. Because of its common database standard and infrastructure capability, it is a useful instrument for electronic commerce (e-commerce) and Web-based delivery of services to citizens (e-government).[17]

As an infrastructure capable of effectively processing large volumes of transactions, the ERP system acquisition and installation are considerably more expensive than the traditional system. Despite this reality, it is contended that it is less costly to maintain than the traditional system. Importantly, ERP has allowed governments to reduce fragmentation and the need to customize development.[18] The large investment that ERP requires makes it important that the organization be prepared to incorporate and adapt to major changes necessary in the organizational environment and structure. Additionally, because ERP drives major changes in responsibilities, job roles, and increases in the quantity and quality of information, it is imperative for management to initiate macrochanges aimed at positively influencing the affected stakeholders.[19]

Some Benefits of ERP

There are a number of contributions that ERP provides, including the following:[20]

- Easy budget and revenue forecasting
- Access to budget or work plan from any location
- Ease of use
- Empowerment of front-line managers to participate in the financial and budget process
- Provision for financial managers to focus on more strategic issues such as "what if" modeling of revenues and budget
- Provision of maximum control for "check ins/check outs" with maximum security
- Facilitation of better use of administrative time
- Minimization of paper trails and facilitation of both internal and external audits

Because of expected large changes in converting to ERP, a needs assessment and cost–benefit must be undertaken. ERP may not be the best option for all governments, especially small, single-purpose entities.

Needs Assessment

The rationale for moving to ERP should be made on sound cost–benefit bases. The system should not be implemented simply because private sector businesses are doing it. Because of the government's operating within a goldfish bowl, it is very difficult to write off large expenditure failures without incurring repercussions. With its massive initial cost outlay and the need for a long-term horizon, implementers cannot hope to obtain reasonable comparative costs with their present systems. There must be strong commitment and patience for change, especially since studies show mixed results to date.[21] ERP implementation is long, arduous, and stressful. It is thus imperative that the process be exceptionally well organized.[22] Of the 117 private firms that have been surveyed, a majority of the users were "satisfied" to "somewhat satisfied." The source of greatest satisfaction with the ERP system was its core financial and accounting function.[23]

A six-step assessment process has been suggested as one way of obtaining the required information prior to making the decision about ERP:

- *Definition of the problem.* This involves articulating the ideal system that is critical to constituents (e.g., *internal*: department heads, technology analysts; *external*: citizen groups, vendors, banks, rating agencies, investors, grantors, and the media), stakeholders, and groups that want to support or use it. Identify present and future information needs and the extent to which the current system meets those needs. This requires the critical evaluation of people, processes (policy and procedures), technology, financial and nonfinancial functions, and adequacy and quality of staff training.

- *Identification of relevant alternatives.* Identify and evaluate the pros and cons of the available acceptable software for the public sector. The evaluation should show how the Web-based system will significantly overcome present deficiencies, while also showing the present desired practices and features that the system provides such as activity-based costing, vendor registration, purchasing accounts payable status, and permit/license acquisition. Market research will help to provide information about off-the-shelf software packages that may meet the desired need and vendors' experience and ability to implement and customize the system to meet specific needs.

- *Selection of viable options.* The overriding criteria relates to the extent to which the option can demonstrate improvement over the existing system. Parameters of the desired system are compared in terms of costs, benefits, and risks. Before selection, a "trial balloon" may be initiated by intentionally leaking options to stakeholders to obtain reaction about the feasibility and implementability of the system.

- *Final decision.* After evaluation of the options has been completed, the department responsible for procurement is determined. An ERP is then developed with or without outside consultation. The implementation process is ideally coordinated by a staff member who is likely to be the future project manager.[24]

Application Service Providers

Application service providers (ASPs) are the firms that have emerged that have the capability to deliver ERP software over the Internet. These vendors have the capability to provide ERP to the small- and mid-size governmental units that could not otherwise afford it. There are three models that the ASPs typically employ: the traditional, managed service, and provider (MSP). The three approaches vary depending upon who is responsible for the communication link between the ASP data center and governmental unit. Each governmental unit is responsible for the internal service and LAN/WAN (local area network/wide area network) and all problems related to it.[25]

Under the traditional, less expensive model, ASP is responsible only for the problems that originate inside its data center. The government contracts directly with the telecommunications company or cable provider. Because neither the government nor the ASP has direct control over the telecommunications link, concern may arise about its reliability in solving problems.[26]

The managed services approach requires that the ASP installs a router at the ASP point of entry at the government local network system. This gives the ASP complete control over the connection between the router and ASP. Because the ASP has continuous control between the router and its data center point of entry, the managed service is viewed as being more dependable than the traditional model. However, this added service and control carries a higher cost.

The MSP model has many parallels to the managed service approach; however, a third party controlled by the ASP maintains the link between the government and ASP. Perhaps the critical factor determining the comparative results between the MSP and managed service depends on how the ASP manages the model. The installation and operation of MSP costs more than the conventional model.[27]

The data management system (DMS) has a broader and more comprehensive scope than DBMS. It consists of a combination of software programs that automatically generate and update fields. In addition, it selects, sorts, and retrieves data. From these data, it has the capability to generate different kinds of reports. Perhaps the main differences between DBMS and DMS are the organization of the DMS files, users' access to the system, and the language used.[28] DBMS permits users greater freedom "to search, probe and query files' contents in order to extract answers to nonrecurring and unplanned questions that are not available in regular reports . . . [and] to 'browse' through the data until they have the needed information."[29] DMS permits less user interaction and is guided by structured programs to process information capable of satisfying user demands.

DBMS enable users to conduct what is referred to as "data mining." Data mining, also known as "knowledge discovery," is the analysis of large amounts of data contained within a database in order to determine previously unidentified patterns or trends. This form of analytics is becoming increasingly important in the private sector as companies are examining massive amounts of data concerning operations and customers to identify ever-changing consumer purchasing trends and macroeconomic conditions. Public sector organizations can also benefit from data mining analysis to stay ahead of the changing needs of the citizens they serve and identify potential organizational synergies that could make operations more efficient. Additionally, data mining can help explain anomalies contained within data sets. Quickly identifying and resolving such deviations is essential to correctly interpreting and using the data stored within the database.

Cloud Computing: Virtual ERP and Database Management

Advancing information systems to the next level beyond an ERP system and server warehouse involves putting the organization in the "cloud" (on the Internet). Having data and software applications, like those used in ERP systems, located on the "cloud rather than in physical database server warehouses enables entities in different locations to use the same databases and software. One such example of effective cloud computing system implementation is the shared services partnership in Pueblo County, Colorado. In response to significantly declining revenues in 2007, small municipalities in the county were searching for ways to reduce the cost of their enterprise software systems, the largest IT expense for the governments. The county assessor developed a plan to consolidate and combine each municipality's information system into a single large one that could be developed in-house. This system, rather than being implemented on multiple, separate, server locations would be accessible via the "cloud"; it would essentially become a virtual infrastructure environment. The cloud computing partnership included services for "property assessment management for assessor offices, property taxation management for treasurer offices, geographic information services (GIS) data warehousing, GIS application server hosting, and Web-based query for the public to access information from the property management systems and the GIS system."

By sharing these services, the small municipalities were able to use both Pueblo County's already existing disaster recovery abilities and relational database infrastructure backup capabilities with almost no additional investment. With the small municipalities on board, the county hired additional software developers and upgraded virtual desktop capacity by 50 percent, essential for high-volume cloud computing. In conjunction with a $250,000 grant from the state and the putting of other less important projects on hold, the county was able to implement the system without exceeding the annual IT budget.

The cost savings from this IT project were immediate and have been significant to date. The county no longer has to purchase and support multiple and expensive database servers, IT purchasing power has been combined to use economies of scale resulting from buying in bulk, and Pueblo now operates database system software licensing on an unrestricted basis rather than limited for each municipality; all participating governments have access to the same enterprise software suite and support services, some of which had been too expensive for the municipalities to afford on their own.

In addition to cost savings, processes have been approved across the board. Analysis techniques are now uniform for the municipalities, facilitating information sharing, collaboration, and innovation. Smaller counties now also have access to automated features under the unlimited licensing agreement that had been too expensive to purchase individually. An economic development benefit was also a residual effect, evidenced by the county hiring three additional full-time employees to support the service partnership program. Finally, the system data is open and accessible to the public, which facilitates transparency and accountability for all government entities involved. The cost savings, process improvement, and increased public accountability make cloud computing a logical next step in advancing government information systems.[30]

Information Technology Asset Management

Once information technology (hardware and software) has been implemented and is being used by an organization, proper management of the IT assets is essential. Failure to identify and mitigate IT threats or adopt necessary process/technological improvements could have significant financial and regulatory consequences for the entity. The government finance officer, rather than officers from the organization's IT department, should lead the planning, adoption, and implementation of an information technology asset management (ITAM) program. IT department officials typically have other priorities that supersede cost savings; their primary goal is to maximize the effectiveness of IT operations and capabilities. Government finance officers are responsible for financial treatment of assets and have the authority of procurement; purchasing the optimal IT assets at the lowest cost is a primary concern. However, collaboration between the finance department, IT department, and other potential users of the IT is essential before procurement to determine the exact needs of the organization and facilitate agreement on what software and hardware should be purchased.

Since few government entities have the ability to develop software in-house, it usually must be purchased from vendors via software licensing agreements. Often, organizations purchase software ill suited for them or have insufficient knowledge about how to use the IT effectively. Performing due diligence before making IT purchases and training personnel adequately to effectively use the assets can produce tremendous cost savings and reduce organizational waste. After IT software and hardware has been procured and the ITAM objectives defined through collaborative efforts, the government finance officer can choose from three options to assess and implement IT asset management:

- Perform the assessment and remediation processes internally
- Collaborate with outside ITAM experts
- Outsource the process

Large organizations may be fully capable of assessing and implementing an ITAM program internally, but for smaller entities, collaboration or outsourcing to knowledgeable private sector firms present itself as the best option. If the ITAM plan is assessed and implemented effectively, the benefits can include immediate savings from renegotiating software licensing agreements, immediate savings by retiring/selling unused or underused hardware or software, reductions in future IT spending, increased accuracy and completeness of data for internal and external reporting purposes, improved controls over IT, increased productivity from well-trained personnel, and the ability to use usage-based decision making. With such cost saving and operational optimization potential, a proper ITAM system that is overseen by a government finance officer has the ability to significantly reduce financial and regulatory risks for governmental entities.[31]

Budget and Accounting Information

The budget and accounting systems are normally required to act in concert with each other. To do otherwise would present the possibility of losing control over the raising and spending of resources. Therefore the code of accounts used to identify accounting transactions typically parallels the codes that keep track of budgeting expenditures. The budget amounts serve as the standards that the accounting system uses to track deviations from actual expenditures and allowed expenditures. When the accounting system recognizes deviations from a standard, it sends signals to appropriate officials to take corrective action. Viewed in this context, accounting is a powerful subsystem in not-for-profit organizations. In many local governments and other not-for-profit organizations, the accounting system is the only information system.

In the past, when recommendations were made to revamp and improve the effectiveness of the total information system in the public sector, the accounting system was usually ignored. Consequently, accounting, rather than being designed as an effective and integral subset of the total information system, has generally been designed only to meet operating, legal, and other budgeting control constraints. As was shown in chapter 2, it focuses on aspects such as the liquidity of assets their and availability to meet maturing obligations, as well as operational accountability by generating information to assess results or program performance.

Conceptually, in an information system, accounting must be viewed as a strategic part of the total system with an impact on all other areas. It must be recognized, however, that the conventional accounting system is not itself sufficient to assess program performance. To assess more than narrow financial or dollar accountability, which conventional financial accounting permits, a variety of information is needed. It is important that the system be user-oriented and designed to produce both financial and nonfinancial information. Examples of nonfinancial information metrics include number of constituents served, employee turnover, demographics and satisfaction with services provided. This requires that each entity organize its information system to capture information that will have multiple and comparative capabilities and applicability to the governmental entity.

Ideally, the accounting, budgeting, and management information system should be integrated as indicated in Figure 16.2, which shows the interconnection of all the processes of management that are tied into the accounting system. The planning, programming, financing, and budgeting phases represent future orientation, while the controlling, evaluating, and accounting phases represent the past and present state of things.

Budgeting and Information Requirements:
A Brief Look at Connecticut

Budgeting (see Figures 1.1 and 16.2) is part of the continuous financial management system process and must respond to ad hoc program analysis requests and to new and changing fiscal situations. These necessities demand that governmental units and other not-for-profit organizations create "an organized, consistent and reliable, timely set of data-bases to support decision-making."[32] Because of this critical requirement, budget personnel should participate in the design and implementation of the financial management system to ensure that the budget function adequately meets the varied and changing needs of the organization.

The continuous budgeting function affects all phases of the financial management systems: (1) the policymaking stages—budget formulation and enactment of appropriations; (2) administration—budget expectation and expenditure monitoring; and (3) evaluation and reporting, including performance auditing and evaluation. If a program's efficiency and effectiveness are to be institutionalized, enhanced data are needed to be aggregated for multiple users, giving due recognition to both line and staff requirements.

Connecticut found that automating involved incremental or successive stages in moving toward a system that provides a programmatic format capable of generating timely and useful performance measurement data. Connecticut integrated payroll and eighty-two personnel and accounting systems "before expanding to more sophisticated approaches to budgeting."[33] In creating its automated budget system (ABS), a number of guiding objectives were established:

- Creation of a common database that was usable statewide
- Creation of an integrated, diverse, and flexible information base
- Provision of information to meet the needs of all levels of management
- Provision of oversight that minimizes microcontrol and detail control
- Enabling agencies to decentralize decision making and accountability
- Planning for budget growth
- Establishing systems to enhance productivity and accountability
- Improving information to better justify budget decisions

The *cost center* "is the core feature of Connecticut's ABS." The cost center is the lowest level in the expenditure hierarchy directly identifying fund, organization, program, or project.[34]

Because of the specificity of the cost center, it can serve as a linkage for responsibility management allowing the organization to hold individual managers accountable for the execution and performance of their financial duties. Additionally, it provides high-level managers with needed information to carry out evaluation planning and policymaking.[35] To minimize implementation problems, the Connecticut ABS suggests the steps shown in Figure 16.2.

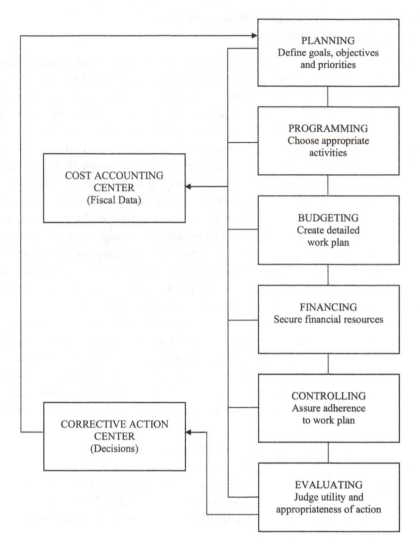

FIGURE 16.2   Financial information system.

Concluding Observations

Fragmented and traditionally oriented information systems, though tolerable in small not-for-profit organizations, have limited usefulness in larger organizations. Because of the many demands to which these organizations must respond, essential information can no longer be collected, maintained, and compartmentalized in individual units. Public demands for efficiency and effectiveness in the delivery of public goods and services require that a whole range of substantive financial information needs be coordinated and integrated into one system. The narrow objects of expenditures or dollar accountability control data are still useful, but there is a greater need for data that are organized around issues that facilitate better decision making.

Too often, managers in not-for-profit organizations equate an information processing system with computer hardware, leading many organizations to acquire expensive computer equipment that has produced unacceptable payoffs. This need not be so. The computer is just one important element in the development of an information system and should be considered only after the information needs and context of the organization, including of the support staff, have been carefully considered. It should be kept in mind that "computer magic" does not happen by chance, but only through well-conceived and well-designed plans developed to achieve specific objectives.

Notes

1. Mitch Betts, "States Redefining Public Service," *Computerworld 27*, no. 16 (1993): 1, 20.

2. Ibid.

3. Ibid.

4. Charles R. Litechy and Earl R. Wilson, "Systems Development for Small Governments," *Governmental Finance 10*, no. 3 (September 1981): 11.

5. Frederick O'R. Hayes, David A. Grossman, Jerry E. Mechiling, John S. Thomas, and Steven S. Rosenbloom, *Linkages: Improving Financial Management in Local Government* (Washington, DC: Urban Institute Press, 1982), p. 182.

6. David A. Grossman and Frederick O'R. Hayes, "Moving toward Integrated Fiscal Management," *Public Budgeting and Finance 1*, no. 2 (summer 1981): 41–42; see also Hayes, Grossman, Mechiling, Thomas, and Rosenbloom, *Linkages*, pp. 12–20, 131–37.

7. Hayes, Grossman, Mechiling, Thomas, and Rosenbloom, *Linkages*, pp. 12–20.

8. Litechy and Wilson, "Systems Development for Small Governments": 11.

9. Rhett D. Harrell, *Developing a Financial Management Information System for Local Government: The Key Issues* (Washington, DC: Government Finance Research, Municipal Finance Officers Association, 1980), p. 2.

10. See Geoffrey H. Wold, "Information Systems Planning," *Government Finance Review 5*, no. 3 (June 1989): 23.

11. William J. Kettinger, *Information Resource Management and the Use of Information in Local Government: A Policy Guide* (Columbia: University of South Carolina Press, 1980), p. 31.

12. Alan Walter Steiss, *Management Control in Government* (Lexington, MA: Lexington Books, 1982), p. 123.

13. Allan R. Drebin, James L. Chan, and Lorna C. Ferguson, *Objectives of Accounting and Financial Reporting for Governmental Units: A Research Study*, vol. 1 (Chicago: National Council on Governmental Accounting, 1981), pp. 101–104.

14. Richard A. Bassler, "Data Bases, MIS and Data Base Management Systems," in *Computer Systems and Public Administration*, eds. Richard A. Bassler and Norman L. Enger (Alexandria, VA: College Readings, 1976), p. 203; Jeffrey D. Ullman, *Principles of Data Base Systems 9*, no. 3 (Rockville, MD: Computer Science Press, 1982), pp. 1–5.

15. See Geoffrey H. Wold, "The System Selection Process," *Government Finance Review 9*, no. 3 (June 1993): 25–27.

16. Leo Yonghong Laing and Rowan Miranda, "Dashboards and Scoreboards: Executive Information Systems for the Public Sector," *Government Finance Review 17*, no. 6 (December 2001): 14.

17. Ibid.

18. Dubos J. Masson, "Treasury Management Software: ERP or the Best of the Breed," *Government Finance Review 18*, no. 5 (October 2002): 28.

19. K. Nicole Fontayne-Mack, "Managing Enterprise Financial System Projects: The City of Detroit Experience," *Government Finance Review 15*, no. 1 (February 1999): 21; Rowan Miranda, Shayne Kavanagh, and Robert Roque, *Technology Assessment: Evaluating the Business Case for ERP and Financial Management Systems* (Chicago: Government Finance Officers Association, 2002), p. vii.

20. Steve Hornyak, "E-Budgeting: How Web-based Solution Simplified Budget Development," *Government Finance Review 15*, no. 1 (February 1999): 25–26.

21. Rowan Miranda, "Needs Assessment and the Business Case for Analysis for Technology Investment," *Government Finance Review 18*, no. 5 (October 2002): 12.

22. David Boyer, "ERP Implementation: Managing the Final Preparation and Go-Live Stages," *Government Finance Review 17*, no. 6 (December 2001): 41.

23. Miranda, "Needs Assessment and the Business Case for Analysis for Technology Investment": 13.

24. Ibid., pp. 13–15; see also Boyer, "ERP Implementation": 41–44.

25. Shayne Kavanagh, "Application Providers (ASPs): Can ASPs Bring ERP to the Masses?" *Government Finance Review 17*, no. 4 (August 2001): 10.

26. Ibid.

27. Ibid., p. 11.

28. Richard F. Schubert, "Basic Concepts in Data Base Management," *Datamation 18* (July 1972): 42–47; James Martin, *Computer Data-Base Organization*, 2nd ed. (Englewood Cliffs, NJ: Prentice-Hall, 1975), pp. 4–7.

29. Norman L. Enger, "Data Management System," in *Computer Systems and Public Administration*, eds. Bassler and Enger, p. 205.

30. Dan Mauro, "Cloud Computing: Pueblo County Shared Services Partnership," *Government Finance Review 26*, no. 3 (2010): 24–28.

31. Rober Meehan, "The Need for Financial Leadership in IT Asset Management," Government Finance Review *23*, no. 1 (2007): 34–38.

32. John R. Fadoir, "State Financial Management System: The Connecticut Experience," *Public Budgeting and Finance 10*, no. 3 (fall 1990): 79.

33. Ibid., p. 82.

34. Ibid., p. 83.

35. Ibid.

17

Auditing

Auditing has been with us since antiquity. Records show that the Egyptians employed it as far back as 2000 BC to carefully control shipments in and out of the royal treasury (government storehouses): Containers of grain destined for the storehouse were accepted only if filled in the presence of overseers and a scribe, who duly recorded them. The effective delivery of the grain was made only after its receipt was recorded by a scribe stationed at the storehouse. Note that the activities performed by an individual were independently checked and confirmed (in a sense, *audited*) by another. Brown has observed: "Whenever the advance of civilization brought about the necessity of one man being entrusted to some extent with the property of another, the advisability of some kind of check upon the fidelity of the former would become apparent."[1] It is management's responsibility for preventing error or fraud:

- Errors are unintentional mistakes, including arithmetical or clerical mistakes, misapplication of generally accepted accounting principles (GAAP), and the oversight or misinterpretation of information.
- Intentionally committed error is fraud. Typically the commission of fraud involves the misappropriation of assets. When comparisons are made to records, fraud can be detected unless the records have been changed to conceal the shortage.
- Unlike the loss of assets, which is fraud that requires access to assets, *distortion fraud* may involve access only to accounting records that have been changed to misrepresent a financial position or results.

The main purpose of government and not-for-profit auditing throughout history has been to detect fraud or error and, to a lesser degree, attest to the fair presentation of an agency's financial condition and detect technical errors and errors of principle.[2] Most individuals, due to lack of time or expertise, are unable to assess the credibility of financial statements or management's representation and assertions made therein. The auditor's report is intended to fill this gap by providing an expert's independent evaluation of financial reports and convey that opinion to reliant parties (stakeholders). An important point to keep in mind is that the auditor seeks to provide reasonable assurance that there is an absence of material misstatement of the financial statement. The auditor can provide only reasonable assurance about accuracy—not certainty that statements are correct. Typical auditing techniques may be incapable of revealing fraud or forgery when there is collusion between management and employees, as management has the ability to override many internal controls put in place to prevent fraud.

Like the preceding chapter, this chapter is also concerned with information. Auditing tests and validates the information generated by the financial management system (see Figure 17.1). This chapter examines the processes, scope, and contrasting features and nature of the different types of audits found in public and other not-for-profit organizations. Audits provide feedback information (see Figure 17.1) to those in authority (executive and legislative officials) for the purpose of reinforcing and strengthening control systems. Those who are reviewing audit reports will find three categories of information useful: (1) Audits may be used to assess the reliability of subordinate officials' reports developed to meet stipulated accountability requirements aimed at providing the verification of information. Such audits may focus on financial, program, or other performance indicators. (2) When officials need to be informed about existing conditions or results not included in submitted reports, the audits are concerned with information acquisition. (3) When the assurance need emphasizes adequate and appropriate controls for safeguarding and protecting resources and ensuring faithful, efficient, and effective performance, the audit may be referred to as *independent assurance*.[3]

Sustainability Auditing

Sustainability auditing parallels many of the objectives sought in performance auditing. Like the latter, sustainability auditing takes an extended time horizon or long-term view of the goals and objectives of the management system and procedures as they relate to the functioning or execution of programs in achieving credible and sustainable economy, efficiency, and effectiveness targets.[4] Based on the targeted goals and objectives and clearly articulated criteria about due condition given to environmental care and preservation, sustainability allows management to determine the extent, if any, of gaps that exist and why between articulated expectations and auditing findings.

A major pursuit of sustainability audit is the use and maintenance of the best practices to realize optimum benefits for all stakeholders. This requires that the organization's planning strategy, organizational structure and accountability requirement must be aligned and be capable of revealing new initiatives and achieving competitive advantage, lower cost, and innovative approaches going forward.

Specific sustainability auditing practices have been developed—for example, showing an organization's commitment to humane conditions in the working

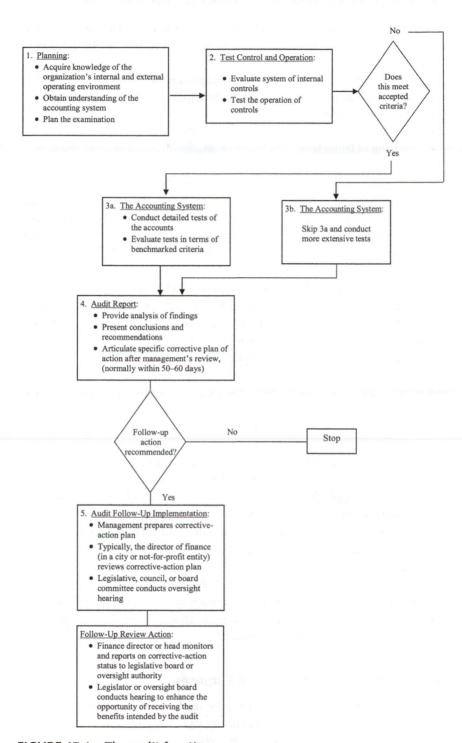

1. Planning:
- Acquire knowledge of the organization's internal and external operating environment
- Obtain understanding of the accounting system
- Plan the examination

2. Test Control and Operation:
- Evaluate system of internal controls
- Test the operation of controls

No

Does this meet accepted criteria?

Yes

3a. The Accounting System:
- Conduct detailed tests of the accounts
- Evaluate tests in terms of benchmarked criteria

3b. The Accounting System:
Skip 3a and conduct more extensive tests

4. Audit Report:
- Provide analysis of findings
- Present conclusions and recommendations
- Articulate specific corrective plan of action after management's review, (normally within 50–60 days)

Follow-up action recommended?

No → Stop

Yes

5. Audit Follow-Up Implementation:
- Management prepares corrective-action plan
- Typically, the director of finance (in a city or not-for-profit entity) reviews corrective-action plan
- Legislative, council, or board committee conducts oversight hearing

Follow-Up Review Action:
- Finance director or head monitors and reports on corrective-action status to legislative board or oversight authority
- Legislator or oversight board conducts hearing to enhance the opportunity of receiving the benefits intended by the audit

FIGURE 17.1   The audit function.

lives of people in organizations across the world. The Ethical Trading Initiative (ETI) Base Code has articulated principles to use in sustainability auditing:[5]

- The extent to which employment was chosen freely
- Freedom of association and right to participate in collective bargaining
- The use of child labor
- The allowance of harsh and inhumane treatment
- Payment of living wage

Auditing suggests a basic responsibility and accountability relationship between top officials (recipients of audit reports) on the one hand, and subordinates (auditees) on the other. This principle directs subordinates to report all relevant information required to review and assess their performance.[6] This view was articulated by the former U.S. Comptroller General Elmer Staats:

A fundamental tenet of a democratic society holds that government and agencies entrusted with public resources and authority for applying them have the responsibility to render a full accounting of their activities. This accountability is inherent in the governmental process and is not always specifically identified by legislative provision.[7]

The public's drive for accountability has created a greater demand for information on the implementation of public service programs. The U.S. General Accountability Office has set forth basic premises underlying audit standards:

- Audits include both financial and nonfinancial or performance audits.
- Resources given to public and other not-for-profit organizations are expected to apply the resources efficiently, economically, and effectively.
- Identify compliance requirements and devise a system to realize them.
- Develop an effective control system to safeguard entrusted resources.
- Resource recipients are accountable to both the public (constituents) and other branches of government.
- Audits must provide credibility and conform to generally accepted government auditing standards (GAGAS) and applicable laws and regulations.
- To enhance accountability, audit reports should be made available unless ethical or legal restrictions prevent it.[8]

Auditing: Defining Its Nature and Purposes

There is no uniform meaning for the term *auditing*. Agreement on a single definition has been made more difficult by the changing nature, forms, and scope of auditing during the past forty years. Examination of Figure 17.2 shows that an audit is comprised of four parts: (1) the actors—auditors, the

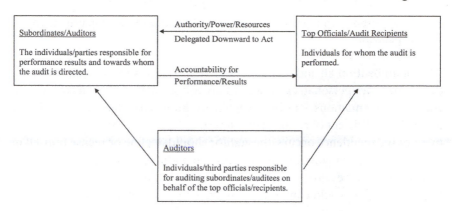

FIGURE 17.2   Actors in the audit process.

auditees (subordinates), and higher officials (audit recipients); (2) the accountability relationship between subordinate and higher officials (audit recipients); (3) the maintenance of independence between the auditors and subordinates (auditees); and (4) the auditors' review and examination of subordinates' execution of the higher officials' delegated duties and responsibilities.

Participants in the audit process seek answers to several basic questions: Why is the audit being conducted? (The typical objective is to achieve accountability and management control.) What is the scope of the audit (it may be financial, compliance, performance, and so on)? Who are the parties (auditor, auditee, higher officials) involved? How is the process to be applied? (The audit process consists of preparation, conduct [examination and evaluation], reporting [communicating], and settlement.)

Auditing, in general terms, may be defined as "a process concerned with the collection and thorough analysis of the underlying information or evidence designed to render an independent, informed, and professional opinion about the representation and assertions made in management reports and supporting documents." Auditing is thus a means for independent verification and assurance about the completeness and creditability of financial and related records attesting to "the correctness of a calculation, the existence of an object, the accuracy of a statement, the reliability of a report, or the occurrence of an event."[9] As the size of many organizations renders evaluation of every minute detail impractical, if not impossible, auditing verifies items that have a material effect on the assertions made in the financial reports.

Auditing Independence

"In all matters relating to the audit work, the audit organization and individual auditor, whether government or public, should be free both in fact and appearance from personal, external and organizational impairments to independence."[10]

It is incumbent on all auditors and audit organizations to maintain independence (includes personal, external, and organizational) so that all conclusions and recommendations will be accepted by knowledgeable third parties as impartial and absent of conflicts of interest. When actual or apparent impairment of independence occurs, the auditor should decline or recuse himself or herself from the situation. Before inviting an audit, the auditing organization should internally evaluate the auditor(s) for potential personal independence impairment that would compromise impartiality. Personal impairment would include the following:

- Having a close or immediate family member as a director or on the board or as an employee who might be in a position to exert influence on behalf of the organization being audited
- Holding preconceived ideas toward an individual, group, organization, government, politics, or goals of a program that may bias the audit results
- Seeking employment with the audited organization while conducting the audit

In the conduct of nonaudit services (mainly management functions) the following principles should be observed: Auditors should not perform management functions or make management decisions, and auditors should not audit their own work or provide nonaudit services in situations where the amounts or services involved are significant or material to the subject matter of the audit.[11]

The Auditing and Accounting Linkage

While there may be qualitative or effective audits without accounting records, there can be no financial- or expenditure-related audits without supporting accounting data.[12] In fact, most audits conducted today in state and local governments and not-for-profit organizations are based on accountants' prepared records and financial statements of funds and account groups (records of nonfund accounts such as land, buildings, and equipment) for the purpose of determining whether the financial statements fairly present the financial position and results of an organization in conformity with generally accepted accounting principles (GAAP) articulated by the Government Accounting Standard Board for local government (GASB), the federal government, the Federal Accounting Standards Advisory Board (FASAB), and other not-for-profit organizations such as the American Institute of Certified Public Accounts (AICPA). Agencies are required to conform not only to GAAP, but also to applicable local, state, federal, and other governing authorities' mandated accounting rules and regulations.

In the typical nongovernmental, not-for-profit agency, the accounting and budget systems are linked by conforming the budget account exactly to the code of accounts, and vice versa. For example, expenditure, appropriation, and revenue are used for both budgeting and accounting purposes. These accounting transactions usually provide the basis for audit reviews in determining whether obligations and expenditures have been accurately recorded. It is important to note that the auditor evaluates the internal control systems that agencies use for authorizing and recording financial commitments.

Finally, the test of an adaptable accounting system is that it leaves audit trails to permit transactions to be easily traced through accompanying supporting documentation. Adaptable accounting systems have clearly drawn procedures and guidelines indicating the lines of accountability to aid auditors in ascertaining how the accounting system is intended to operate. Accounting systems that lack these basic components provide an insufficient base upon which to perform informed and complete audit reviews.

Types of Audits

Audits in Terms of Time

The preaudit is used to determine the propriety of proposed financial transactions and to control the accuracy of collecting and accounting for revenues and accounting for expenditures and disbursements. Postaudits occur at the end of the accounting period—after events have taken place and transactions have been recorded or approved for recording by appropriate officials. While preaudits are conducted by individuals internal to the organization and accountable to higher-level management, postaudits are conducted by individuals, usually certified public accountants (CPAs), external to the organization. Because the independent postaudit is what is usually meant when people talk about audits, it will be the focus of attention in this chapter.

Preaudits

The preaudit function is perhaps the most important type of audit carried out in an organization (see chapter 20), yet it typically has little visibility. Unlike the postaudit, which deals with activities that happened in the past, the preaudit permits action to be taken before the event or problem occurs. It thus may be viewed as a preventative instrument.

Whenever the use of resources is to be initiated, a series of affirmative questions such as the following should be asked: (1) Is the action consistent with articulated or implied policies? (2) If so, is the action approved by the appropriate authority? (3) If so, is the action approved to be undertaken now reflected in the budget? (4) If so, is the amount requested approved in the allotment agreement in the expenditure timetable? (5) If so, is the quality of the product or service consistent with the approved criteria? (6) If so, is there sufficient cash available to expend the funds requested?

Internal and External Audits

Internal audits have all of the characteristics and attributes of preaudits but are much broader in scope and focus. They are independent appraisals (free of organizational constraints and pressures so as to avoid compromising objectivity) of the activities or operations performed within an organization to facilitate management and other controls. Indeed, the persons conducting the internal audits (internal auditors) have been referred to as the "eyes and ears" of management and as impartial providers of information to management. Additionally, internal audits may be conducted during or at the end of an accounting period. They may be used to assess employee compliance with managerial policies, to evaluate the effectiveness of various control systems, and to help members of an organization better discharge their responsibilities. Internal audits furnish management with analyses, appraisals, recommendations, counsel, and information relating to the activities reviewed. In summary, internal audits appraise the soundness, adequacy, and application of accounting, financial, and operating internal controls. Internal auditors

- Act as independent appraisers of important control functions
- Perform advance planning, ongoing, and post-control functions of the organization
- Help members of the organization effectively carry out their duties and responsibilities
- Provide managers with timely analysis, approvals, and recommendations on all matters reviewed[13]

The external audit is synonymous with the postaudit. The individuals conducting these audits are independent and owe their allegiance to officials outside the agency. In government, they report to the legislative body, the public, or some authorized statutory official. In nongovernmental not-for-profit agencies, the auditors report to a governing board or individual designated by the board. External postaudits may be divided according to scope—general and specific (special). General audits include a review of all financial operations pertaining to an agency at the close of an accounting period. Special audits are restricted in scope or time in that they include only a portion of an agency's financial transactions and records or else cover all the transactions and records for a period shorter than a year. It is important to note that internal audits and independent external audits are not substitutes for each other: They are complementary.

Three kinds of groups perform independent external audits: (1) elected audit officials of the governmental unit being examined, (2) officials appointed or elected by a governmental agency other than the one being audited, and (3) independent public accountants providing the service for a negotiated fee. Most states and a small number of municipalities elect an independent auditor or have one appointed by the legislative body. If appointed, the auditor reports directly to the legislative body. Elected auditors report directly to the people and are typically the chief accounting officers within their jurisdictions. The effectiveness of these officials has been mixed. This is especially true when auditors are elected as a result of political connections with elected executives or when only minimal qualifications are required for them to hold office.

In some states, elected or appointed state audit officials may audit selected state agencies, local governmental units, and not-for-profit agencies receiving government funds, either by request or not. Although most local audits are executed by independent certified public accountants, state agencies have increasingly participated in prescribing standard minimal audit procedures, reviewing independent audit reports to ensure compliance with statutes, and conducting spot checks or tests when audit systems and procedures appear weak.

Audits According to Purposes

As an overriding objective, each auditor's opinion assesses whether statements fairly and consistently present (in relation to prior years) the financial position and results of an agency's operations in conformity with generally accepted accounting principles. These objectives may be combined with others to achieve particular audit purposes. Figure 17.3 shows a schematic view of the four basic types of audits on which management relies: (1) the financial data found in the budget; (2) financial statements, and reports comparing actual with planned targets; (3) a report on the efficiency measures, including nonfinancial output data; and (4) a report on the actual data on the effectiveness or accomplishments of the agency. These control reports are intended to aid management decision making. Although economy and efficiency are shown separately, they are bridged by a connecting arrow: The economy component tracks the countable inputs, whereas the efficiency component oversees the system required to convert the inputs into outputs.

Financial and compliance audits or *fiscal audits* assess whether financial operations are properly conducted. They evaluate whether an entity's internal control financial statements are presented fairly and in compliance with applicable laws, policies, procedures, and regulations. A determination is made

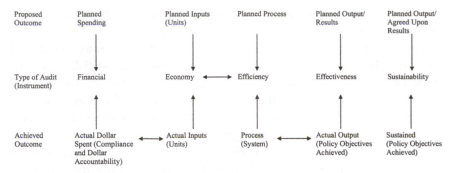

FIGURE 17.3   Schema showing different types of audits.

Source: Adapted from Henry A. Butt, "Values for Money Auditing Local Administration." Public Budgeting and Finance, 5 (summer 1985): 68.

about the adequacy of accounting records and procedures and the financial stewardship of the agency. Recommendations for improvement are usually made. This type of audit serves as an accountability and control device that aids in preventing misuses of public funds through errors, inadequate security, and fraudulent practices.

Program results or *effectiveness audits* assess whether articulated or implied results and benefits as established by the legislature or other authorizing body are being attained and whether an agency is giving ample consideration to alternatives that might be employed to produce acceptable results at lower cost. This may require an analysis of the activities suggested in the statutes to determine if they have been properly developed or designed to achieve the legislative intent.

Program results audits are essentially a form of program evaluation. The implementation of program evaluation, like the audit, is designed to ensure a high degree of independence for the auditors or evaluators vis-à-vis management. This type of evaluation, while very appealing conceptually, often has difficulty assessing congruence between expected and achieved results. A major reason for this problem is that "programs are conceived, justified, and operated under assumptions that are never verified."[14]

Economy and efficiency audits determine whether an agency is managing or using its resources such as personnel, property, and space in an economic manner to achieve its legislative and administrative objectives. Explicit examination is made of the causes of any inefficiencies in agency practices, including inadequacies in management information systems, inefficiencies in administrative methods, defect in work procedures, and ineffectiveness in the development, application, and use of automation and organization structure. Stress is placed on economical acquisition and efficient use of materials and human resources. The economic aspect suggests minimizing expenditures, whereas the efficiency aspect implies maximizing benefits produced for the resources expended.

Responsibility and accountability on the part of public officials are at the heart of each type of audit. Few governments or other not-for-profit agencies use all types at any given point in time. Instead, audits are typically designed to achieve the specific articulated needs of an agency, its investors, the regulatory agencies that oversee it, or public interest groups. Usually, attention is focused on one type of audit, whereas the others, if considered at all, are considered only to a much lesser degree. The greatest number of audits conducted are of the financial and compliance (fiscal) variety, although an increasing number emphasize economy, efficiency, and program effectiveness owing to increasing budgetary constraints. The financial and compliance audit opinions, moreover, are retrospective in orientation, whereas economy, efficiency, and program results audits render present- and future-oriented judgments, conclusions, and recommendations.

Audits and Internal Controls

One of the important objectives of an audit is the examination of an agency's internal control system to (1) determine the reliability and accuracy of the accounting data and information system in general, (2) assess compliance with laws and regulations, (3) promote efficient and effective operating procedures and policy implementation, (4) evaluate methods designed to safeguard assets, and (5) encourage adherence to managerial policies.

In determining the adequacy of internal control systems, several critical characteristics must be examined. These include (1) segregation of duties sufficient to safeguard an agency's resources, involving a prescribed system of authorization and record maintenance to obtain effective accounting control over assets, liabilities, revenue, and expenses; (2) a system guiding the execution of duties and functions in each unit or responsibility center of an agency; (3) staff ability to effectively implement the responsibilities charged to it; and (4) a defined system of internal review. These basic characteristics are so mutually interdependent that the absence or impairment of any one will impede the effectiveness of the internal control system. It should be noted, however, that detailed and minute specification of the internal controls can be prohibitive in terms of cost compared to available resources. Accordingly, each audit should emphasize only those controls that are relevant to the items being audited (see chapter 3).

The reliability of the internal control system provides an important input in determining the extent and scope of an audit. That being so, an internal review auditor should give due attention to the process of the internal control system before commencing the audit. It is important to bear in mind that no one particular pattern of internal control can be specified for all governmental units:[15] For example, the state of Ohio has developed a risk-based methodology for financial audits.

Risk-Based Audit Methodology

Traditional financial audits have been procedure-driven. Certain standardized tests are used, sometimes, without considering the context of the environment in which the audit is taking place. This might not be the most efficient way to carry out an audit. The Ohio risk model "requires the auditor to analyze the risks associated with auditing each particular government and to design a test procedure based upon those assessed risks."[16] The risk-based auditing approach is initiated with an overall audit risk assessment, placing emphasis on three kinds of risks:

- The first attempts to prevent errors from occurring *prior* to action by eliminating *inherent risk* due to unintentional errors (mistakes) or an intentional act—involving, for example, the misstatement of financial information (a government may want to hide revenue by overstating expenditures when adversarial union negotiations are about to take place).
- The second stresses *control risk* in determining the extent to which controls are in place to timely prevent and detect the problems associated with inherent risks.
- The third designs a system that combines the inherent and control risk assessments to test account balances, thereby minimizing the possibility of overlooking something significant. This is known as minimizing *detection risk*.

When the combination of inherent and control risks are low the auditor can accept a high degree of detection risks, since the chances of missing a material account balance are reduced. Conversely, when inherent and control risks are high, the acceptable detection risk must be low. Risk assessment (the inherent, control, and detection risk, as shown in Figure 17.4) sets the parameter regarding the extent of the scrutiny that will be necessary to render the appropriate opinion of an entity's financial records.[17]

Strategic Risk-Based Auditing

The risk-based methodology that we have just discussed is very useful and constructive when conducting traditional audits. *Strategic risk-based auditing*, however, provides an innovative, powerful, and inclusive approach for enhancing an organization's growth and viability.

The typical traditional risk-based audit (emphasis on unauthorized expenditures, dishonesty of subordinates, faithfulness of the organization's profit or surplus and financial position) that focuses on the auditor's assessment risk is seen through a narrow lens that directs attention to classes of transactions to assess the risk whether financial statements are materially misstated. This disaggregative "bottom-up" approach inhibits the auditor's ability to gain an

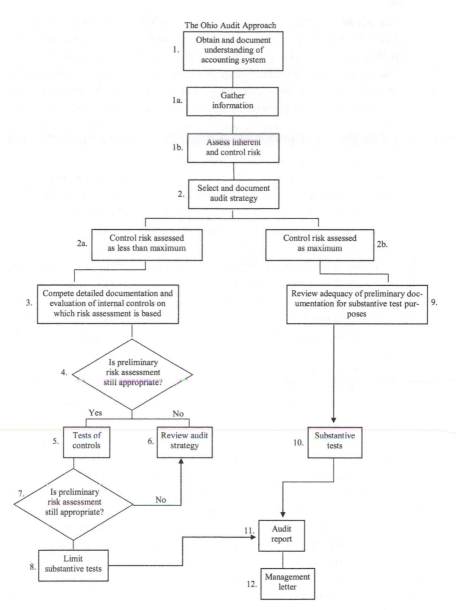

The Ohio Audit Approach

1. Obtain and document understanding of accounting system

1a. Gather information

1b. Assess inherent and control risk

2. Select and document audit strategy

2a. Control risk assessed as less than maximum

2b. Control risk assessed as maximum

3. Compete detailed documentation and evaluation of internal controls on which risk assessment is based

9. Review adequacy of preliminary documentation for substantive test purposes

4. Is preliminary risk assessment still appropriate?

Yes   No

5. Tests of controls

6. Review audit strategy

10. Substantive tests

7. Is preliminary risk assessment still appropriate?   No

11. Audit report

8. Limit substantive tests

12. Management letter

FIGURE 17.4   Risk-based audit methodology.

Source: Michael Howard, William Reidy, and William C. Serverns, "The Audit Approach: Ohio's Risk-Based Audit Methodology." Government Finance Review, 7, no. 2 (April 1991): 17 (reprinted with permission of the Government Finance Officers Association).

understanding of the entire or holistic perspective of the organization or entity needed to judge the entity's ability to produce value: profit or net income in the private sector, surplus or a balanced budget in public and other not-for-profit entities. This narrow lens forces auditors and management to focus on the mechanics of accounting, diverting attention from important consider-ations about the roles transactions play in realizing the organization's strate-gic goals.[18] To minimize this problem, a "government measurement process" (GMP) focus should be adopted.[19] GMP is a risk-based strategic systems audit approach that uses a wide lens, directing auditors' attention beyond account-ing transactions to factors affecting the organizations both internally and externally. For a business organization, an auditor needs to assess potential external economic effect factors such as customers, supplies, investors, and regulations, as well as any other factor that may negatively effect or impair the achievement of the organization's objectives. For a government organization, potential factors that may impair the viability of the organization's ability to achieve its objectives include emerging new political coalitions, declining tax bases, population demographics, executive election of candidates commitment to downsizing governments, and privatization and outsourcing functions.[20]

The GMP focus facilitates a "top-down" approach to the audit, allowing auditors to view the organization and its transactions holistically. Having a GMP focus in conjunction with a traditional risk assessment, "bottom up," approach enables auditors to examine the entity in its entirety and ensure that relevant factors are identified and subsequently examined during the audit procedures.

To achieve maximum success and minimize impairment of value creation, all organizations must be viewed from a system or holistic perspective facili-tating integration and understanding of relationships: "[T]he system approach emphasized basic principles of organization—how the parts are inter-related and coordinated into a unified whole."[21] The practice of the GMP strategic auditing orientation allows us to take advantage of the function of the orga-nizational learning. We are able to obtain insight about the broader economic web of interrelationships that enhance the organization's "ability to create value and generate cash flow needed to sustain growth"[22] and its level of desired per-formance. For example, a not-for-profit organization's ability to understand the forces operating in its environment allows it not only to maintain effec-tive internal accounting and bookkeeping, but also to gain knowledge about donor support, supporting interests, and the inclination of clientele toward support existing and higher fees for services, thereby creating the opportunity for growth and superior service improvements.

When the strategic goals, the wide lens, and organizational learning are kept in view, it makes it more difficult to conceal material facts. Because the auditors who conducted the audit of the Lincoln Savings and Loan Bank (LSL) focused on the transaction or narrow lens, attention was directed at (1) the adequacy of loan reserves, (2) the recording of gains on securities, and (3) the appropriate recording of gains on "real estate undeveloped land." The audi-tor wanted to know whether the transactions conformed to the criteria for accrual accounting. The auditor properly sampled LSL land sale transactions, but he or she did not integrate accounting data with the environmental economic evidence of the LSL.[23] Only the *accuracy* and not the *reasonableness* of the transactions were evaluated. If the LSL business conditions were genuinely understood, it would likely have led to different revenue recognition conclusions. The auditor did not focus attention on how recently purchased remote and undeveloped land could be sold for prices ranging from 400–500 percent above cost in the LSL operating economic climate.[24] A strategic perspective or analysis would have forced the "auditor to consider the LSL current business-operating environment." At the time of the audit, at the place where the land transactions occurred construction was decreasing and real estate values were declining, savings and loan banks (S&L) had recently been massively deregulated, regulators were concerned with LSL's unorthodox business practices, LSL changed from a savings and loan establishment to a real estate speculating organization, the previous auditor resigned over disagreements, LSL's major profit source was undeveloped land, and LSL was at the minimum reserves required by regulation. Because the auditor viewed his actions from a narrow lens and mechanistic accounting perspective, the oversight of the broader implications was inevitable. The GMP strategic system environmental scanning audit model's holistic focus both on the strengths and weaknesses affecting the organization would have made it less likely that problems would go undetected, thereby enhancing the opportunity to promote continuous value creation. This new orientation is called *risk-based strategic systems auditing.*[25]

Inspectors General and the Audit Functions

Since the passage of the Inspector General Act of 1978, attention has been focused on the Inspector General's (IG's) office to provide leadership in auditing in federal agencies. Although a few state and local governments have adopted some aspects of the federal IG model, attention here will be briefly focused on the federal IGs. Under the 1978 act, the IGs were given two main functions: (1) consolidation of the scattered audit and investigation units with a unified agency or department-wide responsibility and (2) pursuit of the reduction of fraud, waste, and abuse. Staffed by nonpolitical, knowledgeable professionals (in both auditing and investigation), the IGs report to both Congress and the president. The IGs are expected to maximize the achievement of three types of accountability. The first is compliance, which promotes conformance to laws, rules, and regulations. The IG applies mainly negative sanctions (e.g., publicizing violators' infractions) to individuals inside or outside the government agency, including contractors or other recipients of government resources, aiming at achieving compliance by visible displays of censure. The objective is to correct the existing problems and deter future occurrences. Performance accountability stresses incentives and rewards to accomplish desired outcomes. Capacity- or capability-building accountability attempts to create organizational competence by enhancing or investing in people skills and upgrading systems and structures.[26]

The view is expressed that the IG needs to place less stress on audits and investigations, because these efforts do not obtain the largest amount of results for the resources expended. Instead, the greatest emphasis should be placed on performance accountability based on carefully defined indicators aimed at achieving the articulated or implied goals and objectives of policymakers (see Figure 17.5, showing the IG performance measurement model and identifying three focused areas and major goals and objectives). This will require a significant reallocation of resources away from audits and investigations.

The performance requirement model will necessitate a new orientation involving at least six steps:

- Articulating mission goals, objectives, and target identification
- Indicating indicators and measurement identification
- Measuring achievement
- Analyzing results
- Interpreting results
- Reporting performance results

It is believed that the orientation performance will pay big dividends in the future by enhancing performance by all concerned.

Selecting the Auditor

The requirement to audit and the precise procedures for auditing an agency are different among state governments, local governments, and not-for-profit agencies. Typically, the responsibility for selection of the independent auditor rests with the legislative body or the governing board of a nongovernmental, not-for-profit agency. Although many governments attempt to select an auditor on the basis of competitive bidding, this approach is not generally accepted as a sound practice. Accountants have expressed the view that the competitive bidding method exerts unprofessional pressures on the auditor. This selection process may not permit the best auditor to emerge. It is thought that the qualitative factors required in an audit cannot be as easily measured as commodities, for which prices can be specified and allowable profits easily determined.

The undue influences of competitive bidding manifested in the private sector during the fraud scandals that occurred during the late 1990s and early 2000s. Enron, WorldCom, and other conglomerates had their choice of auditor and based their decisions almost entirely on price. Large accounting houses, such as the now defunct Arthur Anderson, engaged in price wars with one another for audit and consulting services. The competitive bidding forced

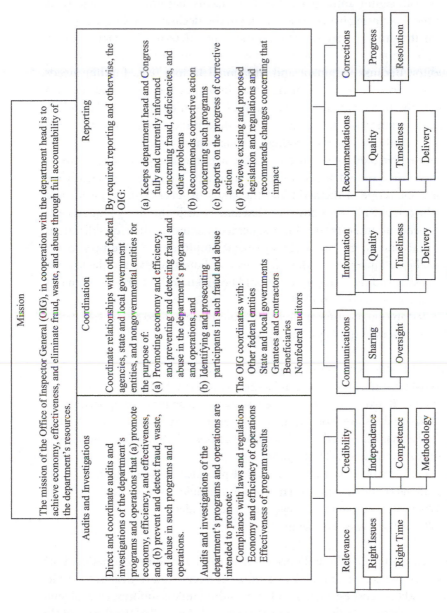

FIGURE 17.5 The IG performance measurement model.

Source: Adapted from Dennis J. Duquette and Alexix M. Stowe, "A Performance Model for the Office of the Inspector General." *Government Accountants Journal,* 42 (summer 1993): 38.

these accounting firms to reduce the scope and comprehensiveness of their audits to remain within budget and, in extreme cases, engage in fraud collusion with management to ensure contract renewals. Additionally, consulting services, with significantly higher fees than audits, became the primary concern of the accounting firms, contributing to the decline in audit quality.

When the profit criterion becomes the major determining factor for the selection of an auditor, it is likely to affect the professional independence of the auditor. Because judgment and situational factors (e.g., funding needs, internal controls, or other problems) may influence the scope and depth of the audit, the independent auditor should be given considerable latitude to explore important leads when necessary to determine whether records are in order and whether the agency's system is functioning effectively.

If competitive bidding is chosen over the negotiated approach, requests for proposals (RFPs) should be sent to potential independent auditors, clearly setting forth the scope of the audit and the kinds of services to be performed. Before the actual RFP, some governments may issue preliminary requests asking independent auditors to submit statements showing their qualifications. Actual RFPs should go only to independent auditors who have been determined to be well qualified. A thorough review should be given to the submitted proposals, and due recognition should be given both to price and quality, as far as these can be determined.

Included among the information that should be obtained before selection is made are answers to the following questions:

- What are the experience and qualifications of the independent auditor?
- What is the time frame for conducting the audit? When the lead time is substantial, it gives both parties (management and auditor) an opportunity to review and resolve problems that may exist before the audit gets under way.
- Will management or the auditor close the books? If the auditor will close the books, more time will be required.
- What kinds of clerical assistance will be provided to the auditor?
- If an internal staff exists, will it be made available to the auditor?
- What recent accounting changes have been made?
- What is the scope of the audit?

In those cases in which the audit price is determined by joint negotiation, both parties need the answers to these questions. In negotiated contracts, the independent auditor's cost estimate should be binding unless unforeseen problems arise, necessitating that the estimates be exceeded. After all of the details of the audit have been determined, the agenda should be specifically identified in a contract.[27] Such aspects as the departments, programs, activities, and funds to be audited, the period to be covered, and the means of handling unexpected problems should be spelled out.

Auditing Standards

Private sector auditing performance standards are set forth by a wide variety of private organizations such as the American Institute of Certified Public Accountants (AICPA) and government agencies such as the General Accounting Office (GAO). The "Standards and Guidelines" enunciated by the GAO basically incorporate and expand the AICPA standards to achieve the specific auditing objectives that are being pursued.

Audit Standards

In the private sector, the AICPA establishes audit standards. Firms falling under the preview of the Security and Exchange Commission (SEC) must follow generally accepted accounting principles (GAAP). Because of the relationship among the SEC, FASB, and AICPA, companies are encouraged to use GAAP. In an effort to obtain financing from investors and creditors and financial institutions, firms attempt to follow accounting practices that will result in their obtaining unqualified opinions. Moreover, auditors have an obligation to apply generally accepted auditing standards (GAAS). To do otherwise would be in violation of professional standards of conduct and could lead to a loss of the CPA designation. The AICPA has three groups of performance standards: *general standards*, *standards of field work*, and *standards of reporting*.

General Standards

Individuals conducting an audit are required to have appropriate and adequate technical training to effectively conduct an audit. The auditor is expected to have internalized values of independence so that they become an operating norm that influences the auditor's way of thinking and acting. The preparation and execution of the audit must be carried out with due professional care.

Standards of Field Work

There must be preplanning and effective supervision of all participants. A review and evaluation of an agency's internal control system is a precondition to all audits to determine the degree of reliance that can be put on the agency's system and the extent of the auditing tests that will be necessary. The authority of the auditor's opinion is based on competent evidence obtained by means of inspection, observation, inquiries, and confirmation.

Standards of Reporting

The report is required to state whether the presentation of the financial statements is in accordance with generally accepted accounting principles. The report states whether GAAP have been consistently followed in the current report and the preceding one. When disclosures are necessary to provide material information concerning the financial statements, the auditor must so indicate. Finally, the report is required to indicate an opinion regarding the financial statement as a whole or an assertion stating that an opinion should be clearly articulated. Whenever an auditor signs his or her name to an auditing report, the character of the auditor's examination must be clearly set forth along with the extent of responsibility that he or she is assuming.

Governmental Auditing Standards

Earlier we examined the various kinds of audits but did not discuss the auditing standards used in conducting public sector audits. Until 1972, when the U.S. Comptroller General issued *Standards for Audit of Governmental Organizations, Programs, Activities, and Functions*, there was no comprehensive statement on governmental auditing standards.[28] The GAO audit guidelines were a response in the early 1970s to the explosion of interest in, and demand for, better assessment of both financial and nonfinancial activities at all levels of government. The guidelines are used by auditors in and outside of government and by both internal and external independent postauditors. The GAO standards were adopted by the federal agencies under OMB Circular A-73, which adopted the GAO audit criteria, and OMB Circular A-102, which was revised in 1979 to include the "single" audit (which forces agencies auditing a program that has multiple sources of funding to conduct one audit on behalf of all concerned). The GAO auditing standards were revised in 1988. In 1993, the GAO provided a revised exposure draft of its 1988 standards for the audit of government agencies that should be completed in 1994. Each kind of audit (e.g., financial, compliance, economy and efficiency, program results) requires specific standards for use in conducting the audit. Many governmental units have incorporated the GAO audit guidelines as law for the conduct of audits within their jurisdiction.

Governmental entities' first requirement is to operate within the constraints of state laws and local regulations. When these entities require practices that do not parallel GAAP, the Governmental Accounting Standard Boards (GASB), or its predecessors, the auditors must conform to the government's stipulated practices. The potential for confusion does exist, but these problems are generally being eliminated, especially as states revise their practices to conform to GAAP. At the federal level, the GAO has incorporated the AICPA audit standards for federal audits unless they are formally excluded.

Single Audits

The pressure to move to the single audit resulted from a number of developments during the 1960s and 1970s. By 1999 nearly $1.5 trillion of federal grants and contracts went to state and local governments, universities, hospitals, and other nonprofit organizations. Federal aid represents a significant funding source for state and local governments. Hundreds and, in some cases, thousands of federal programs (1,100 in the Department of Health and Human Services alone, for example) were administered by different federal agencies. In many instances, each program established its own accounting requirements. A state or local agency that received aid from forty different programs could have been required to have forty or more accounting systems. Compounding the problem was the fact that each federal agency administering a program that awarded funds to a state or local agency had a right to have on-site audits. Thus, keeping track of the accounting, reporting, and auditing demands was a heavy burden to the state and local governments receiving federal assistance.

Efforts to bring about standardization in the 1960s met with minor success. It was not until 1979 with the issuance of Attachment P (*Audit Requirements to OMB Circular A-102, Uniform Administrative Requirements for Grants-in-Aid to State and Local Governments*) that the single audit received formal authoritative support. Attachment P requires that audits be done on an agencywide basis instead of grant by grant.

The review of the results obtained with the implementation of Attachment P led to passage of the Single Audit Act of 1984, which includes as objectives (1) the improvement of financial management systems of federally assisted programs; (2) the establishment of uniform audit requirements for federal assistance programs to state and local governments; and (3) promotion of the efficient or effective use of audit resources, with the stipulation that all programs with revenues of $100,000 or more will be subject to the act as of January 1, 1985. The act was amended in 1996 and implemented by OMB Circular A-133, setting the threshold amount at $300,000, a figure that the OMB is required to review every two years, at which time OMB may increase, but not decrease, the threshold. In 2003, the amount was increased to $500,000. The act permits some exceptions when the grant-issuing agency requires a *program-specific audit* (see Figure 17.6). The law covers both direct and indirect federal assistance programs, including passthrough funds from another unit of government. Direct cash payments to individuals are the only item excluded. Only smaller units of government will not be audited annually. These programs may elect to have the single audit, or be audited as required under the federal financial assistance requirement of the grantor agency or as prescribed by the federal comptroller general.

The audit conducted under the Single Audit Act of 1984 must be done in conformity with generally accepted government auditing and standards applicable to financial and compliance audits. The Single Audit Act does not require economy and efficiency and program results audits or program evaluation unless these approaches are required by plans, regulations, or contracts. Only independent auditors may perform the audits required under the act. All

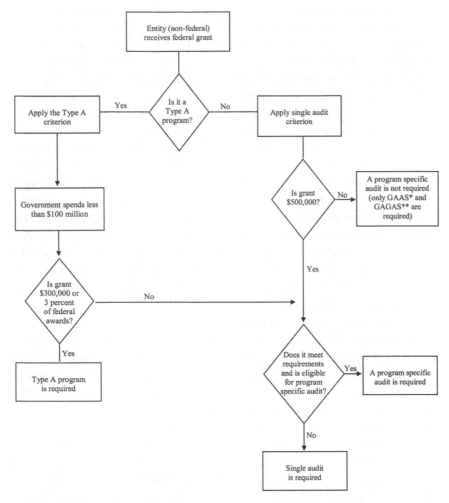

FIGURE 17.6   Applicability of the single audit act and OMB circular 133.

Note: *GAAS: Generally accepted auditing standards.
         **GAGAS: Generally accepted government auditing standards.

audits conducted pursuant to the act must be made available to appropriate federal officials thirty days after their completion and for public inspection. When material internal control weaknesses or noncompliance with applicable laws and regulations are found, the audited agency must submit a plan to the appropriate federal officials for corrective action or else indicate the reasons why corrective action is not necessary.

The Single Audit Act requires that the OMB designate a "cognizant agency" (a specific federal agency) to oversee the implementation of the audit requirement within a given state. The cognizant agency has three main responsibilities:

(1) to ensure that agencies conduct timely audits and conform to stipulations of the act, (2) to make certain that audit reports or corrective actions are transmitted to appropriate federal officials, and, where possible, (3) to coordinate audits done by contract with those required under the act to aid in developing audit continuity and integration. Additionally, the cognizant agency, in the 2003 revised OMB Circular A-133, must now receive more than $50 million in federal awards. It is estimated that the revised 2003 circular eliminates 6,000 government and nonprofit agencies while reducing the assignment of cognizant agencies from 1,000 to 500.[29]

Operational Audits

There is some confusion about precisely what an operational audit is, because it is also a type of performance audit. An operational audit is different from a performance audit in that it is more inclusive. An operational audit comprises not only economy and efficiency audits and effectiveness audits, but also financial audits. The performance audit, it is important to note, refers only to economy and efficiency audits and effectiveness audits as clearly set forth in the International City Management Association (ICMA) special reports on performance audits and *Governmental Accounting, Auditing, and Financial Reporting* (GAAFR).[30]

Operational auditing facilitates decentralized management, because it is designed to keep agency management, top executives, and especially legislative officials informed about whether an agency is using its resources both legally and effectively. Additionally, the operational audit is employed to review and appraise the soundness, adequacy, and application of all accounting, financial, and operating controls. This audit is not focused solely or mainly on accounting, but also considers how an agency's total resources are being applied. The operational audit attempts to determine the congruence among executive or legislatively articulated or implied objectives of administrative activities, functions, and programs that have been assigned for implementation with achieved results. The auditor is basically concerned with how well an agency is managed and the extent to which it realizes its objectives. Much that is presently done as performance auditing was formally carried out by management advisory services or consulting concerns.

Operational audits are more difficult to conduct, because the standards and criteria to be applied are inexplicit. Many are derived from various sources, although legislative statements tend to be an important source, along with professional organizations that set standards of performance levels for specific fields. Typically, there are not explicit management indicators for accomplishments, economy, efficiency, and effectiveness. Additionally, legislative intent is not always clear. A number of general common-sense standards or guides may be used in carrying out operational audits, covering such areas as (1) use of government property for personal benefit; (2) lack of coordination of agencies and/or units implementing related activities and programs; (3) lack of automation and up-to-date techniques; (4) excessive client complaints, unresolved disputes, and unsuitable policies, standards, and regulations; (5) nonadherence to policies, regulations, and procedures; and (6) unreliable reports.

The performance audit procedures parallel those of the financial audit. Financial and operating reports, administrative regulations, laws and contracts, agency policies, financial and operational information, and documentary evidence are examined. The auditor seeks answers to questions such as the following: (1) What are the specific goals and objectives of the audited programs and activities? (2) Under what basis of authority (legal or administrative) is the program being operated? (3) How well are the audited objectives being achieved? (4) How well do the established procedures and practices aid in achieving the agency's goals and objectives? (5) What are the specific causes or reasons why existing procedures and practices are positively or negatively affecting the agency's goals and objectives? Findings are categorized in terms of (1) those favorable to management and (2) those that are unfavorable. For unfavorable findings, the auditor is required to state how widespread or material, using predetermined thresholds, they are and to indicate their direct and indirect impacts on cost. It is not enough to simply identify the problems; alternative solutions for eliminating them must be identified.

Reporting for performance audits is divided into three sections. In section 1, the scope and objectives of the audit are stated. Section 2 contains an explanation of the findings of fact, indicating the causes and effects that management is having on the work environment in achieving the agency's objectives. Section 3 recommends ways to meet the identified problems, indicating the agency's enthusiasm and willingness to contribute to alternative solutions, and stating previous recommendations that have not been implemented and current recommendations with which management disagrees.

Audits of Nonprofit Entities

Generally accepted accounting principles have particular applicability to colleges and universities, hospitals, and other nonprofit organizations. Each of these specialized areas has audit guides peculiar to itself. For example, colleges and universities have *Audits of Colleges and Universities*; hospitals have the American Hospital Association's guidelines and the AICPA's *Hospital Audit Guide*.[31] Voluntary health and welfare organizations (also known as "human service organizations"), which derive most of their resources from contributions, have the AICPA's *Audit of Voluntary Health and Welfare Organizations*.[32]

Other not-for-profit organizations' need for solicitations provides an incentive for them to follow GAAP. Bond-rating agencies have fostered the use of GAAP by these not-for-profit entities that enter the public bond market.

A number of not-for-profit agencies still use accounting practices because they are required to do so by their governing boards.

Access to capital markets is becoming increasingly important for not-for-profit and governmental entities as formerly abundant tax revenues remain stagnant or decline. Globalization is facilitating international capital flow and accessing these funds is paramount to securing favorable interest rates and obtaining adequate returns on investments. GAAP and its global counterpart, International Financial Reporting Standards (IFRS), are widely accepted in international capital markets and allow organizations using these accounting standards to more easily obtain low-cost funding.

The Audit Report

The various types of audits typically follow the same audit report format, although the operational audit tends to be more extensive. The general standards to be observed in writing the audit report have been summarized by the U.S. Comptroller General:

1. Be concise yet complete to facilitate ready user understanding.
2. Present accurately, completely, and fairly all material and factual information.
3. Present findings and conclusions clearly and as simply as the subject matter permits.
4. Include only factual information that can be adequately supported by evidence included in the working papers. Include supporting information only to the extent that it is necessary to make a convincing presentation.
5. Where possible, include recommended actions for operations improvement, providing information on the problems and recommended courses of action to assist management in taking corrective action.
6. Put primary emphasis on improvement, minimize past criticisms, and point out unusual difficulties faced by operating officials.
7. Explain issues and questions requiring study and consideration.
8. Direct attention to noteworthy accomplishments, particularly when the improvements may be applicable elsewhere.
9. Give recognition to the views of responsible officials on the auditor's findings, conclusions, and recommendations.
10. Explain the scope and objectives of the audit.
11. Direct attention to significant and pertinent information that has been omitted because it is deemed privileged or confidential, giving the legal basis for such action.[33]

Audits containing financial reports are required to state the auditor's opinion as to whether the information contained in such a report is presented fairly. When the auditor is unable to express an opinion, the reasons should be indicated in the audit report. (When the auditor cannot agree with the fair presentation of the report, he or she renders a qualified or adverse opinion.) Additionally, the auditor states whether the audit is prepared in accordance with generally accepted accounting or prescribed principles applicable to the organization, programs, and functions or activities audited. Appropriate supplementary explanations about the financial reports are included as deemed necessary for full disclosure, including violations of legal or regulatory requirements and other instances of noncompliance.

Concluding Observations

Auditing serves a strategic role in financial management because it validates and attests to the accuracy of financial statements. In the public sector, it can cost a governmental unit thousands or perhaps millions of dollars in additional interest payments if a negative opinion about its financial statement leads to a downgrading of the unit's credit rating. Auditing can be used as an important management tool. The preaudit is employed to ensure that policies and activities take place in accordance with management policies and administrative procedures. The postaudit typically acts as a legislative or board oversight and accountability instrument when it evaluates the fairness and compliance of financial statements with statutory requirements and generally accepted accounting principles.

Of the different types of audits found in practice, the financial audit is the one most widely used. In recent years, management decision making requirements and public demand have made it necessary to go beyond the narrow dollar accountability approach that typifies the financial audit. Hence, economy and efficiency, effectiveness/results, and operational audits are gaining support.

Notes

1. Richard Brown, *A History of Accounting and Accountants* (Edinburgh: T. C. and E. C. Jack, 1905), p. 74.

2. Robert H. Montgomery, *Auditing* (Chicago: American School of Correspondence, 1909), p. 12.

3. Lennis M. Knighton, "Four Keys of Effectiveness Auditing." *Governmental Finance* 8, no. 2 (September 1979): 3–4.

4. See AA1000 *Account Ability Principles Standard* (2008), pp. 4–7. http://www.accountability.org/standards/aa1000aps.html.

5. Sustainability and Ethical Trading Initiative (ETI) Audits. http://www.sgs.com/en/Sustainability/Social-Sustainability/Social-Responsibility-SR/ETI-Audits.aspx.

6. Ibid.

7. U.S. Comptroller General, *Standards for Audit of Governmental Organizations* (Washington, DC: U.S. General Accounting Office, 1981), p. 1.

8. U.S. General Accounting Office, *Government Auditing Standards: 1994 Revision* (Washington, DC: U.S. General Accounting Office, June 1994), ch. 1.

9. Ibid., p. 4.

10. U.S. General Accounting Office, *Government Auditing Standards: Amendment No. 3 Independence* (Washington, DC: U.S. General Accounting Office, January 2002), p. 6.

11. Ibid., p. 1.

12. Note that the term *expenditure* is used in the not-for-profit sector, whereas *expense* is used in the private sector. *Expenditure* emphasizes things bought or acquired, while *expense* refers to actual consumption or expired costs.

13. See Seth Allcorn, *Internal Auditing for Hospitals* (Germantown, MD: Aspen Systems Corporation, 1979), pp. 4–5.

14. Frederick O. R. Hayes, David A. Grossman, Jerry E. Mechiling, John S. Thomas, and Steven S. Rosenbloom, *Linkages: Improving Financial Management in Local Government* (Washington, DC: Urban Institute Press, 1982), p. 154; for an extensive discussion of effectiveness auditing, see Richard E. Brown, Thomas Gallagher, and Meredith C. Williams, *Auditing Performance in Government: Concepts and Cases* (New York: John Wiley, 1982), pp. 73–101.

15. See Price Waterhouse, *Enhancing Governmental Accountability* (New York: Price Waterhouse, 1983), ch. 3.

16. Michael Howard, William Reidy, and William C. Serverns, "The Audit Approach: Ohio's Risk-Based Audit Methodology." *Government Finance Review 7*, no. 2 (April 1991): 15–20.

17. Ibid., pp. 15–16.

18. Timothy Bell, Frank Mairs, Ira Solomon and Howard Thomas, *Auditing Organizations through a Strategic-System Lens: The KPMG Business Measurement Process* (New York: Peat Marwick, LLP, 1997), p. 2.

19. Ibid., 14.

20. Ibid.

21. Ibid.

22. Ibid., pp. 18–19.

23. Ibid.

24. Ibid., p. 22.

25. Ibid., p. 23.

26. Paul C. Light, *Monitoring Government: Inspectors General and the Search for Accountability* (Washington, DC: Brookings Institution, 1993), pp. 2–3.

27. Municipal Finance Officers Association, *Governmental Accounting, Auditing and Financial Reporting* (Chicago: Municipal Finance Officers Association, 1980), p. 90.

28. U.S. Comptroller General, *Standards for Audits*, revised 1981.

29. Stephen Gauthier, "Single Audit Changes," *Governmental Finance Review 19*, no. 3 (October 2003): 60–61.

30. International City Management Association (ICMA), *Performance Audits in Local Governments: Benefits, Problems, and Challenges*, Management Information Report 8 (Special Report, April 1975); see also Municipal Finance Officers Association, *Governmental Accounting, Auditing and Financial Reporting*.

31. American Institute of Certified Public Accountants (AICPA), *Audits of Colleges and Universities*, 2nd ed. (New York: AICPA, 1975); American Institute of Certified Public Accountants (AICPA), *Hospital Audit Guides*, 4th ed. (New York: AICPA, 1982).

32. American Institute of Certified Public Accountants (AICPA), *Audit of Voluntary Health and Welfare Organizations* (New York: AICPA, 1981).

33. U.S. Comptroller General, *Standards for Audits*, pp. 7–9. See also GAO *Government Auditing Standards* (2011 revision); http://archives.gov/oig/pdf/government-audit ing-standards-2011-revision.pdf.

18

Reporting

Whenever resources are obtained from sources other than the individuals' using or spending them, reporting to some external group or individual to render stewardship and accountability is a normal expectation. Such accountability may be based on law, contract, policy, or moral obligation. *Stewardship* refers to the execution of efficient administration. Importantly, "reporting on management's stewardship . . . is a principal purpose of financial statements."[1]

Private sector financial reports emphasize the ultimate effects of transactions for a given period, whereas governments stress how transactions will affect near-term financing. Most public sector decisions are related to annual or biannual appropriations, emphasizing balances and transactions related to near-term government financing—the operating budget. The business reporting model is thus aimed at showing how business capital (investments by owners and stockholders) is being enhanced and maintained. This is the main reason why the balance sheet clearly separates net assets based on investment generated from capital stock or paid in capital and retained earnings—accumulated value created by yearly undistributed profits. Last, the operating statement of a business focuses attention on transactions that generate earnings (namely, revenues, expenses, gains, and losses) or the creation of net value to the business. Unlike private businesses, whose objective is to maintain and expand capital or create value, the public sector does not seek to preserve capital. Assets are classified according to availability for use (e.g., capital assets, restricted and unrestricted) in delivering goods or services.

Basically, financial statements in not-for-profit organizations must provide information that can be used to assess management's ability to effectively utilize resources to achieve implied or articulated organizational goals. Certain questions immediately arise: To whom should fund users report? What kinds of information should be reported? What should be the format of the reports, and what are the authoritative guidelines and criteria to be followed? Although the answers to these questions appear obvious on the surface, in practice they tend to be difficult to find. Events such as the prolonged recession of the late 1980s, the early 1990s, and the early 2000s, the national spiraling deficit, the total quality management (TQM) movement, the interest in reinventing government, and the Gore report, *Creating a Government That Works Better and Costs Less*, have caused the chief rulemaking body (the Governmental Accounting Standards Board, or GASB) for governmental entities to take a closer look at these questions, culminating in its *Service Efforts and Accomplishments* (SEA) to aid in understanding government performance.[2] In 2008, the financial crisis brought on the Great Recession, which is still affecting us.

The Reporting Entity

The *reporting entity* is the basic element that is used in financial reporting. It indicates which governmental units will be included in the financial statements. The controlling or main governmental unit is called the *primary government*. All other units that are included in the financial report are called *component units*. Typically, cities, counties, or states are examples of primary government, while any parts of these units such as departments of public safety, parks, and recreation and human services are components. Sometimes a special-purpose governmental unit such as a local school board or hospital district may be a primary entity, if the following attributes are present: Component is separately elected; component has separate legal identity; or component is fiscally independent. Component units are accountable to the primary governments; exclusions of the component in financial information would lead to incomplete and misleading reports. In general, the key factor in identifying the component units relates to financial accountability.

The relationship between primary government and component units can be viewed as being similar to the private sector relationship of parent and subsidiary corporations. Parent corporations are legally responsible for gathering, consolidating and preparing financial statements using all relevant information from subsidiary entities. Failure to include information, in its entirety, would result in material omissions from the company's consolidated financial statements, thus misleading the investors to whom the corporation owes fiduciary duties.

All financial reports attempt to provide essential information necessary for the fair presentation of governmental finances. Generally accepted accounting principles (GAAP) are the standard to which all financial reports must adhere. In public agencies (state and local governments) these standards are set by the GASB, while the Financial Accounting Standards Board (FASB) sets the standards for private enterprises and not-for-profit agencies.

Required financial information that should typically be presented within a financial report is as follows:

- Categorized data in financial statements.
- Disclosure notes accompanying the financial statement to provide the best picture possible of the financial statements.

- Useful financial analysis not essential for presentation in financial reports such as extra data required for supplementary information (RSI). Although RSI is not a focus of the independent auditor, the latter may make inquiries about RSI to management regarding measurement and presentation.

This chapter contains an overview of the different types of reports and the suggested general guidelines typically followed in preparing reports on the financial status, emerging sustainability reporting and achievement of public and other not-for-profit organizations.

Emerging Sustainability Reporting

Sustainability reporting is an emerging approach that provides information about economic environmental and social factors affecting an entity's everyday activities. A sustainability report provides information showing comparable short-term and long-term relationships and their relevance for a given entity. Sustainability reporting reflects the linkage of the entity's philosophy and structure with its strategy and long-run mission. This emphasis allows the organization to better measure, understand and communicate its economic, environmental, and social positive or negative long-term performance.

When sustainability reporting provides information on elements such as stakeholders' perspective and employees' participation, a direct link can be shown about good governance and transparency. Because sustainability reporting includes both financial and nonfinancial information, data is expressed in both financial terms (monetary units) and nonfinancial or qualitative terms (for example, clients' expression of satisfaction) and quantitatively (for example, tons or units of greenhouse gas). To be most useful, data is presented in a systematic manner with appropriate measurement to facilitate comparison with the past and the present progress (see Figure 18.1). This requires that measurable performance indicators be developed and be connected to the organization's strategy.

Sustainability reporting is used to describe an organization reporting on its achievements in terms of economic, environmental and social performance. Acceptance is growing as evidence and practice suggests that sustainability issues can materially affect an organization's performance. Additionally, there is considerable demand from stakeholders and the public for greater transparency and accountability, reputation, identification for cost savings and achievement of continuous improvement, encouraging innovation, and aligning of the organization's strategy to reflect the needs and expectations of the audience and drawing attention to potential risks.[3]

Commitment to sustainability requires the institutionalization of a regularized reporting cycle that facilitates the normalization of data collection, communication and ongoing monitoring. Sustainability reporting should ideally be viewed as a very important resource that can be used as a means of

Description	Energy	Waste	Water	Procurement
Financial	Expenditure on transportation/ heating	Disposal costs	Water bills	Price of purchases
Non-Financial	CO_2 tons per person	Waste in tons/ number of collections/ recycle waste	Water consumption (cubic meters)	Share of eco-labeled and fair trade products

FIGURE 18.1   Financial and Non-financial environmental indicators.

Source: International Congress of Supreme Audit Institution (INCOSAI), Sustainability Reporting Concepts, Frameworks and the Role of Supreme Audit Institution and the Working Group on Environmental Auditing, 2013, http://www.environmental-auditing.org.

managing change, maximizing profitability in the private sector and enhancing the delivery of goods and services in the not-for-profit sector with ethical behavior and social justice without damaging the environment.

Sustainability reporting may be viewed as synonymous with nonfinancial reporting (Figure 18.1), triple bottom line (TBL), and corporate social responsibility (CSR). More recently integrated reporting combines financial and nonfinancial performance. A number of benefits are associated with sustainability reporting, including the following:

- Increased understanding of risks and opportunities
- Linkage between financial and nonfinancial performance
- Focus on long-term policies and strategies
- Streamlining processes, reducing cost and improving efficiency
- Mitigating or reversing negative environmental, social and governance impact
- Enabling external stakeholders to understand the organization's true value and tangible and intangible assets

Major providers of sustainability reporting guidelines include the following:

- Global Reporting Initiative (GRI)
- Organization for Economic Cooperation and Development (OECD)
- United Nations Global Compact
- International Organization for Standardization (ISO 26000, International Standards for Social Responsibility)

Historically, the financial reports of both public and other not-for-profit organizations' present funds' flow information. Data are organized to show the sources from which funds are derived and the applications to which they are put within the legal restrictions placed upon each fund, all with the aim of promoting budget and fiscal compliance. Financial reporting is a useful aid, helping public officials to show how they are faithfully discharging their fiscal responsibility to the electorate. The goal of financial reporting is the provision of financial resources to meet the needs of statement users. The information is useful for making economic, political, and social decisions; for assessing government accountability and stewardship; for assessing government's ability to meet maturing obligations; and for providing information that is useful for evaluating managerial and organizational performance.[4] The successor rule-making body to the National Council on Governmental Accounting (NCGA), the GASB, in its Concept Statement No. 1, "Objectives of Financial Reporting," subscribes to the NCGA's position, culminating in the generation of a comprehensive annual financial report (CAFR) or the component unit fiscal report (CUFR), both designed to achieve the objectives.[5]

The GASB established accountability as the critical objective in financial reporting: "Accountability requires governments to answer to the citizenry—to justify the raising of public resources and the purposes for which they are used. . . . It is based on the belief that the citizenry has the 'right to know,' right to receive openly declared facts that may lead to public debate by citizens and their elected representatives."[6] The GASB articulated accountability to be achieved in terms of three components or subobjectives:

- *Interperiod equity.* "Financial reporting should provide information to determine whether current-year revenues are sufficient to pay for current-year services." The report should indicate whether current-year citizens shifted a portion of its cost of services to future-year taxpayers.
- *Budgetary and fiscal compliance.* "Financial reporting should demonstrate whether resources were obtained and used in accordance with the entity's legally adopted budget. It should also demonstrate compliance with other finance–related, legal, or contractual requirements."
- *Service efforts and accomplishments.* "Financial reporting should provide information to assist users in assessing the service efforts, costs, and accomplishments of the governmental entity." This information aids users in assessing the government's operational accountability (economy, efficiency, and effectiveness) and "may help form a basis for voting or funding decisions."[7]

The GASB articulated additional objectives (see Table 18.1) that governmental reporting should reflect in disseminating annual financial information.

Financial reports have been directed predominantly at meeting the needs of administrators, legislators, service recipients, resource providers, accountants, investors, public employees, and observers interested in public finance and

TABLE 18.1   GASB: Financial Reporting, Additional Objectives

Financial reporting should assist users in evaluating the operating results of the governmental entity for the year:

a. Financial reporting should provide information about sources and uses of financial resources. Financial reporting should account for all outflows by function and purpose, all inflows by source and type, and the extent to which inflows met outflows. Financial reporting should identify material nonrecurring financial transactions.

b. Financial reporting should provide information about how the government entity financed its activities and met its cash requirements.

c. Financial reporting should provide information necessary to determine whether the entity's financial position improved or deteriorated as a result of the year's operations.

Financial reporting should assist users in assessing the level of services that can be provided by the governmental entity and its ability to meet its obligations as they become due:

a. Financial reporting should provide information about the financial position and condition of a governmental entity. Financial reporting should provide information about resources and obligations, both actual and contingent, current and noncurrent. The major financial resources of most governmental entities are derived from the ability to tax and issue debt. As a result, financial reporting should provide information about tax sources, tax limitations, tax burdens, and debt limitations.

b. Financial reporting should provide information about a governmental entity's physical and other nonfinancial resources having useful lives that extend beyond the current year, including information that can be used to assess the service potential of those resources. This information should be presented to help users assess long- and short-term capital needs.

c. Financial reporting should disclose legal or contractual restrictions on resources and risks of potential loss of resources.

Source: Adapted from GASB Concept Statement No. 1, "Objectives of Financial Reporting" (1987).

administration. Although the general public's interest in financial statements has increased during recent years due to taxpayers' revolts and the cutback management movement of the 1970s and the private reporting scandals of the last twenty years, the average citizen shows little interest in the principal operating funds that generate deficits or surpluses.

An effectively presented financial statement of a governmental unit should describe the principal facilities and capital improvement program for a period of at least five years, identifying the proposed yearly expenditure application by specific type of asset, planned use, and source of funding. Aggregated original and replacement costs for fully depreciated assets over a five-year period and the replacement policy regarding those assets should be presented.

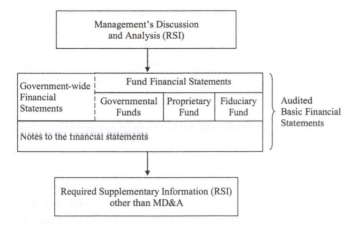

FIGURE 18.2 Minimum requirements for general purpose financial statements: New government financial-reporting model.

Source: Adapted from GASB Statement No. 34, "Basic Financial Statements and Management's Discussion and Analysis—for State and Local Government."

Comparative data showing planned versus actual operating and debt service expenditure, including the presentation of the past four years' actual results, should be described and any recognizable trends should be explained. The report should discuss the past year's accomplishments and the proposed objectives for the ensuing year. Citizens should be told where to obtain available reports, especially those analyzing the efficiency and effectiveness of operations. Although this is an inexpensive and relatively effective way for promoting good relations, it is often handled poorly by most public and other not-for-profit organizations. Although improperly handled by many officials, the Internet is facilitating dissemination of these financial statements via government and not-for-profit websites.

To be eligible for consideration for fair presentation and be in conformity with GAAP before GASB Statement No. 34, "Basic Financial Statements and Management's Discussion and Analysis—for State and Local Governments," many financial reporting models were followed. Now the number of models has been reduced to three: the business enterprise, the not-for-profit organization, and state and local government. Figure 18.2 shows the new government financial reporting model to which reports must now conform.

GASB Statement no. 34

The 1999 Governmental Accounting Standards Board (GASB) Statement No. 34, "Basic Financial Statements and Management's Discussion and Analysis—for State and Local Governments," has profoundly affected the structure and content of state and local governments' financial reporting.[8] Statement No. 34

established a comprehensive new governmental financial reporting model. The GASB did not eliminate traditional financial reporting; instead, it incorporated the popular features of traditional financial reporting into the new model. The expectation is that the new model would not only accommodate existing users of state and local government reports, but also attract new users.

Government-wide Financial Statements and Purpose

The purpose of the government-wide financial statements is to show that government is more than the sum of its individual parts (individual funds). Although the traditional short-term focus on near-term inflows and outflows of spendable resources are important, especially for budgeting purposes, the government-wide financial statement focus provides an overview of the total effects of the long-term effects of short-term financial decisions. Although it is useful to know the cost basis for delivering services, government decisions are not guided or driven by the profit objective. Instead, governments focus on inflows or spendable resources (expenditures), not costs (expenses). The information on costs of activities for governmental funds can only be found in the government-wide statement. The major new features of the new model are the following:

- *Required government-wide financial reporting* (see chapter 2 and Figure 18.2) allows state and local governments to access government-wide financial statements that present an easily understandable overview of government finances as a unified entity. This new government-wide financial statement complements rather than replaces traditional fund–type financial statements.
- *Adds long-term focus for government undertakings,* allowing decision makers to emphasize the long-term perspective in government-wide financial statements while retaining the traditional focus on near-term inflows, outflows, and spendable financial resources.
- *Narrative overview and analysis* presented in the new model provides a report for users: a brief, easy-to-read introductory narrative and analysis of basic financial statements, known as the "management's discussion and analysis" (MD&A). This component is an essential element in private GAAP-conformed financial statements, providing users with a plain, yet essential, overview concerning current operations and industry trends.
- *Focus on major funds,* as opposed to aggregated individual funds, is required.
- *Budgetary reporting* is expanded to include not only the traditional fiscal-amended budget but also the original budget. Additionally, the new model presents the aggregated budget total, such as including total special revenue funds. Comparisons are provided for the general fund and each major special revenue.

New Model Information Reporting for Capital Assets: GFOA Concerns

The new model requires capitalizing and depreciating state and local government's general infrastructure assets such as roads and bridges. Although there is some support for this provision, others, such as the Government Finance Officers Association (GFOA), offer a modified position. The GFOA position is that each government should individually decide how it will comply with the GASB Statement No. 34 infrastructure provision based on an analysis of cost versus benefits. Among the practical guidelines the GFOA suggests are the following:

- Limit the retroactive reporting requirements on infrastructure to classes of infrastructure.
- Define major classes of infrastructure as narrowly as possible.
- Limit infrastructure reporting to assets acquired during fiscal years ended after June 30, 1980.
- Use estimates wherever possible.
- Use composite approaches to calculate depreciation expenses.[9]

Implementation Schedule

Each governmental unit is expected to implement all provisions of GASB Statement No. 34, except for the retroactive reporting of infrastructure assets, as follows:

- Units with $100 million or more starting after the fiscal year ending June 30, 2002, while retroactive reporting of infrastructure assets starting after the fiscal year ending June 30, 2006.
- Units with $10 million to $100 million starting after the fiscal year ending June 30, 2003, while retroactive reporting of infrastructure starting after the fiscal year ending June 30, 2007.
- Units with less than $10 million, starting after the fiscal year ending June 30, 2004, while retroactive reporting of infrastructure assets is not required.

Interim and Internal Reporting Linkages in the Financial Management System

Internal control and public accountability require that timely reports be issued throughout the fiscal year. Depending on administrative needs, daily, monthly, weekly, and quarterly reports may be developed. These interim reports assess ongoing programmatic activities and potential problems that may be developing.

Most governmental units do not publish interim reports; rather, they are produced to assist administrative officials and budget examiners at all levels of the organization or governmental unit. Occasionally, the legislators may find them useful, especially when they provide data showing how budget plans are being followed. Interim reports help management evaluate the extent to which administrative agencies are complying with budgetary, financial, legal, and administrative procedures and programmatic achievements. Such important reports aid in disclosing deviations or variations from operating plans and permit corrective action to be taken. In expressing the need for interim reports, the observations are made that (1) they reflect monthly and quarterly current financial positions comparing financial results with estimates, indicating limitations for the month and/or the year to date, (2) they are mostly for internal use, (3) they exclude general fixed assets, and (4) they provide information on budgetary and cash flow projections aimed at facilitating management control.[10]

Frequency of Reports

Although comparative expenditure reports should be provided to management at least monthly, showing both actual and budgeted expenditures for a given period and the year to date, particular programs or activities may require weekly or even daily reports.

All reporting systems are normally expected to have at least two types of reports: (1) internal reports required for agency use and (2) external reports for administrative, legislative, and other interested parties. Reports should be prepared to meet particular guidelines. Accountability for the achievement of assigned responsibilities must be clearly identified. A measuring system that is capable of comparing preplanned objectives or standards with actual achievements must be maintained. To be useful, the results must be reported with sufficient promptness to permit corrective activities to be taken. If maximum utility of the results is to be obtained, presentation must be consistent for all levels of management from one reporting period to another. Importantly, simplicity should be a guiding objective. Clear and concise presentation will enhance the use and understanding of the report.

Ideally, the reports intended for internal use should provide information to management that will be useful in effectively overseeing the agency operations. These reports should assist management in controlling operations (for example, the use of workload analysis) by monitoring how approved plans are being implemented. The reports will facilitate the management of funds, pinpointing the need for supplementary estimates or adjustments of allocations. The product of each report should typically provide the basis for the development of next year's budget and aid in the review of plans and priorities.

External reports satisfy a number of requirements, among them legal, contractual, and fiduciary ones. Such reports provide information to assist interested parties in monitoring the performance of the agency or governmental unit to determine whether the resources have been used in accordance with requirements. External reports aid taxpayers, grantors, and service recipients in determining whether resources have been applied effectively.

Annual Reporting

Every governmental unit is expected to publish a *comprehensive annual financial report* (CAFR).[11] This activity represents the final step in the financial management reporting system, indicating how well executive officials have discharged their responsibilities. The purpose of the report is to indicate the extent to which there was compliance with appropriations and contractual, legal, and other requirements.

The introductory section of the annual report should contain a letter of transmittal to the mayor and council or legislative body; more recently, a second letter from the mayor or chief executive to the council and/or the general public briefly describing changes in financial policies and the important areas of financial management has become customary. Other materials, such as a description of the reporting governmental entity, an organization chart, and a listing of elected officials, may also be submitted. Recently, additional reports have been appended to the annual one. The opinion of the independent auditor or other required postaudit reports are also appended. When the unit of government has qualified for the certificate of conformance from the Government Finance Officers Association, it is included.

The Comprehensive Annual Financial Report Components

The *comprehensive annual financial report* (CAFR) is also known as the *complete annual report* (see Figure 18.3—the GASB required reporting model). Some CAFR users may wish to compare cost of service versus revenue collection and assess cash flow adequacy, whereas others monitor budgetary compliance. To satisfy the multiple expectations of CAFR's users, the complete CAFR consists of statements that combine and report upon an entity's activities from both a government-wide and fund perspective. This requires the reporting on many individual funds and including an array of statistical data.

The complete CAFR is composed of three main sections (introductory, financial, and statistical) aimed at providing information to satisfy different types of users:

- The *introductory section* includes a letter of transmittal and general information indicating how the government is organized and the key elected officials and administrators. The executive or financial director writes the transmittal letter, also known as the "state of government," giving an overview of

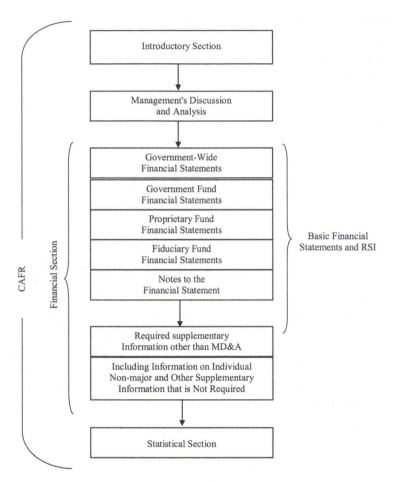

FIGURE 18.3   Comprehensive annual financial report: The new financial-reporting model.

Source: Adapted from Stephen J. Gauthier, New Governmental Financial Reporting Model (Chicago: Government Finance Officers Association, 2000), p. 22.

the financial and economic conditions that the government faces (major initiatives and key budgetary and accounting practices) and a summary of recent financial developments. A great deal of the information presented in the letter of transmittal is incorporated into the required management's discussion and analysis (MD&A), a component of the CAFR financial section. This section may also include a "Certificate of Achievement for Excellence in Financial Reporting" when the CAFR conforms to the standards of the Government Finance Officers Association (GFOA), an independent professional association. Because the GFOA does not audit the entity's having received the certificate of achievement, it does not vouch for the accuracy of the information presented. This point is especially important in light of

Orange County's (California) obvious fiscal mismanagement of billions of dollars—yet the county was subsequently awarded a certificate of achievement. In response, the GFOA observed that investment losses does not necessarily relate to improper financial reporting. The certificate is indicative of conformance to a format and not the endorsement of the underlying financial data.

- The *financial section* is the major component of the CAFR. It is made up of the MD&A and is similar to the MD&A that is a component of the financial statements of businesses. The MD&A in both government and business is a nontechnical overview of financial performance for the year and the financial position at the end of the year. This section contains the basic financial statements, notes to the financial statements, required supplementary information (RSI) other than MD&A, and the auditor's report. The *auditor's report* provides the assurance that statements have been presented fairly in accordance with generally accepted accounting principles. The report is comprehensive, expressing an opinion on the financial statements, but does not include all the information contained in the CAFR. The basic financial statements are the critical focus. Statistical data, individual funds, and supplementary information are often not given audit attention.

- *Management's discussion and analysis* (MD&A) provides a narrative introduction and overview to aid users in interpreting the basic financial statements. MD&A analyzes important data presented in the basic financial statements. By so doing, it provides substance, insights, and comprehensible analysis to the average citizen about the government's economic environment and fiscal health. Statistical data relating to demographic and economic trends have normally accompanied the CAFR. Such data have been presented in tables whose interpretation have been left to statement users.

    Among the type of information included in MD&A are the following:

    1. Description of required financial statements
    2. Summarized information from government-wide statements
    3. Analysis of the government's financial position, importance of economic factors, and results of operations
    4. Analysis of differences between original and final budget and actual and budgeted amounts
    5. Analysis of changes in capital assets and long-term debt
    6. Review and discussion of conditions of infrastructure assets
    7. Discussion of known facts, decisions, or conditions that have or are likely to have a significant or material impact on the financial position of the government

Basic financial statements comprise two main types: government-wide and fund. There are two *government-wide statements* (see chapter 2, tables 2.9 and 2.10, for examples): the statement of net assets (balance sheet) and statement of activities (revenues and expenses). *Fund statements* are required to be prepared for three categories of funds: (1) governmental funds, consisting of the balance sheet and the statement of revenues, expenditures, and changes in fund balances; (2) proprietary funds, composed of the balance sheet, the statement of revenues, expenses, and changes in net assets, and statement of cash flows; and (3) fiduciary funds, comprising the statement of fiduciary net assets and statement of changes in fiduciary net assets.

The new model, unlike the old, requires that statements for governmental and proprietary funds focus only on major funds. The smaller or nonmajor funds are aggregated into a single column. Fiduciary funds do not use the major funds concept; they are typically aggregated into a separate column for each fund type, such as investment trust, private trust, and agency funds.

• *Required notes* are the schedules of statistical data and supplemental information that the government must provide in the CAFR financial section to the basic financial statements. The information includes (1) the actual budget comparisons, (2) the assessment of the infrastructure condition (for governments that choose not to depreciate them), and (3) information relating to pension actuarial valuations.

The GASB has mandated that both the notes and supplementary information be included in the CAFR. The notes are viewed as part of the basic financial statements, whereas the supplementary information is not. In view of this, RSI (required supplementary information) may not be given audit scrutiny.

• *Schedules in the CAFR* may be included to indicate compliance with legal and contractual provisions. Schedules may be necessary to bring together data that are dispersed among several statements, thereby providing an informative perspective to report users. For example, a table (schedule) may summarize investments that are scattered across a number of funds. The GASB lists fifteen statistical tables that a government is required to include in the CAFR unless the information is deemed to be decidedly inapplicable. Table 18.2 indicates these CAFR statistical tables.

Statements of Other Not-for-Profit Organizations

The American Institute of Certified Public Accountants' (AICPA) *Audit Guide* lists several types of financial statements that comprise the annual report of an organization. The *statement of support, revenue, and expenses and changes in fund balance* is essentially a summary of the financial activities indicating all the sources of support and revenues and all expenditures. The AICPA recommends that the statement of changes in fund balances be made part of this statement, showing balances at the beginning and at the close of the year. Important interfund transactions are included and summarized. The *statement of financial expenses* contains a summary presenting an analysis of the

TABLE 18.2   CAFR: Required Statistical Table

1. General governmental expenditures by function—last ten fiscal years

2. General revenues by source—last ten fiscal years

3. Property tax levies and collections—last ten fiscal years

4. Assessed and estimated actual value of taxable property—last ten fiscal years

5. Property tax rates—all overlapping governments—last ten fiscal years

6. Specialassessment billings and collections—last ten fiscal years (if the government is obligated in some manner for related special-assessment debt)

7. Ratio of net general bonded debt to assessed value and net bonded debt per capita—last ten fiscal years

8. Computation of legal debt margin, if not presented in the general-purpose financial statements (GPFS)

9. Computation of overlapping debt (if not presented in the GPFS)

10. Ratio of annual debt service for general bonded debt to total general expenditures—last ten fiscal years

11. Revenue bond coverage—last ten fiscal years

12. Demographic statistics

13. Property value, construction, and bank deposits—last ten fiscal years

14. Principal taxpayers

15. Miscellaneous statistics

Source: Adapted from Governmental Accounting Standards Board Codification, Section 2800.103.

entity's object of expenditure by program, function, and support. This statement, in essence, indicates how the resources (money) were spent in carrying out the agency's *program services* and *support services*. Last, the *balance sheet* presents the assets, such as cash investment, building, and equipment, and the liabilities, such as payables and encumbrances, toward which the assets will be applied. The difference between the assets and liabilities gives a balance—a deficit or surplus.

Integrated Annual Reporting

The American federal system is made up of many layers of governments, often serving the same political community. Not infrequently, a number of governmental units, comprising the county, the city, special districts (e.g., schools), corporations, and authorities, can be benefited if the service delivery performance can be rationally integrated through a single annual report document. The presentation of a clear, comprehensive, and concise overview of local government finance is the principal objective in putting together the integrated annual report. Thus all changes taking place during the fiscal year should be set forth in a section devoted to changes taking place in the operating and capital budgets during the fiscal year.

The Introductory Section

A number of general guidelines may be suggested for integrating such a report. Each of the participating, independent entities, structures, and frameworks may be briefly described, pointing out the formal and informal linkages with the dominant local government. Common features include the accounting structure (such as titles and terminology), accounting basis or bases, and the fiscal year of the dominant local government (and deviations therefrom). It is important to direct attention to "overlapping and underlying local governmental units and authorities."[12]

The Dominant Local Government: Budgeting Processes

The annual financial report of the major unit of local government describes the basic preparation and review process as well as the adoption and administrative processes of the annual operating budget. A comparison of operating budget funds for several preceding years should be included. As far as possible, the linkages between the operating budget and the capital budget and capital program should be reviewed, indicating the support flowing from the operating funds. The authorization and application made on behalf of the capital budget over several years should be indicated.

Cooperative capital facilities planning is the most useful outcome that is likely to result from these undertakings, although integrated planning need not be the only vehicle to bring this about. The integrated budget system may be an important vehicle to provide statistical information on assessed and taxable property valuation, exempt properties, revenue sources, state aid, federal aid, operating expenditures, and capital expenditures.[13]

GASB Service Efforts and Accomplishments Reporting

A main premise of the GASB is that public entities do not presently report on how well resources are being used to enhance the well-being of citizens. Because of the lack of dissemination of SEA-type information (guidelines for developing measurements for assessing programs and activities), the public is denied the knowledge necessary for assessing accountability relating to the delivery of public goods and services. The GASB views the existing provision of information, which emphasizes the acquisition and use of resources, as inadequate. It should therefore be complemented with performance information that shows linkages between resources used and the accomplishments they generate in terms of output, efficiency, and effectiveness/impact (see chapters 11 and 16) in the form of a separate report. This should be a part of all general-purpose external financial reporting (GPEFR) to aid in producing informed citizen decision making.[14]

Characteristics of SEA Information

To provide maximum utility to the public, SEA-type reporting should contain a number of characteristics:

- *Relevance—including* data essential to understanding the extent to which the goals, objectives, and accountability have been achieved
- *Understandability—ability* to make the entity's performance readily understood through means of graphs, charts, and tables
- *Comparability—provision* of a frame of reference for assessing an entity and its subunits and program activities, and the opportunity to compare performance with similar entities
- *Timeliness—provision* of information at the time needed for assessing accountability and to make decisions
- *Consistency—reporting* on the same basis from period to period
- *Reliability—generation* of information from controlled and verifiable data[15]

Popular Reporting

The most prominent organization presently promoting effective government reporting is the Government Finance Officers Association (GFOA), through its certificate of conformance and, recently, its popular reporting award. The Michigan Municipal League, in 1944, and the University of Connecticut's Institute of Public Service, in 1946, both initiated programs to promote better understanding of public financial reports. The objective of both organizations was to promote greater public recognition, acceptance, and comparison of reports with other jurisdictions.

Popular Report Reward

As the financial reporting for government has become more complex, information in the CAFR reports has been increasing in difficulty for the general public to understand. As the reports have become more technical, they have become usable mainly by investors, creditors, and other financial experts. Popular reports are intended to communicate financial status and results of an entity to users who are nonaccountant types or are less technically oriented in governmental GAAP, now administered by GASB for state and local government and the AICPA for other not-for-profit organizations.[16] Because popular reports are not prescribed by any set format, individuals putting them together are constrained only by the limit of their imagination and creativity. But for GFOA eligibility, the reporting entity must satisfy a number of stipulations:

- Be the recipient of the GFOA certificate of achievement of excellence in financial reporting and have CAFR statements for the most recent fiscal year.
- The report must be prepared in conformity with generally accepted accounting principles; otherwise it must give an explanation for nonconformity.
- All U.S. governmental entities must indicate fund types from which report data are derived.
- Financial information should be derived from CAFR.
- Canadians must include the financial reporting award, in addition to the aggregated or consolidated report and an auditor's report that is nonqualified. Moreover, financial information should be derived from a government's general aggregated financial report.

The efforts of the University of Connecticut's Institute of Public Service continue, but the Michigan Municipal League was terminated in 1966. The criteria they used in judging the quality of reports were the following:

1. *Attractiveness.* This indicator is measured by citizens' willingness to examine the report due to the appeal of its external appearance and design and the organization and presentation of the materials inside. Such appeal features include the "practical use of type for text and headings, legibility, and effective use of pictures."[17]
2. *Reader understanding.* This indicator attempts to assess the average citizen's ability to better understand local government undertakings. This is determined by an evaluation of the logic, organization of materials, and clarity of the written text. High marks also go to conciseness, brevity, and creative and informative uses of appropriate charts and photographs.
3. *Content.* An attempt is made to determine how well the report summarizes the governmental undertakings and the perceived contributions toward the public's understanding of the kinds of services being delivered. This section presents data on the financial status of the community's budget, income, and expenditure providing a comparative analysis of costs, volume, and other statistics on fiscal trends.
4. *Utility.* This attribute is assessed by determining if the size of the report permits easy filing, ready carrying, and handling. Facilitative "directory-type" information items include table of contents, lists of government officials and organizations, important telephone numbers, and calendar of important dates.

Although not specifically identified, the audience must be kept in mind at all times. After all, it is the audience that the publication is attempting "to inform, influence, or entertain."[18] Like commercial enterprises, not-for-profit organizations seek to predict, compare, and evaluate benefits and sacrifices in terms of dollars, time, and risks, despite the fact that the results sought are non-monetary. Not-for-profit organizations cannot use the commercial-oriented profit yardstick; rather, they seek to achieve goals whose performance involves indicators such as the reduction in delinquency, improved health care, or reduction in crime. Ideally, financial statements must permit users to assess the attainments of past organization goals, and the ongoing efforts to realize present goals and the probability of future goal attainment.

The AICPA identified seven qualitative characteristics that should provide useful guidelines in preparing financial reports:

1. *Relevance and materiability*. To meet this test, the following question should be asked: Is the information germane, and would its inclusion or exclusion influence or make a difference in the judgment of a reasonable person reading the financial statement? A positive answer indicates that the information in question should be included.

2. *Form and substance*. Substantive economic and program characteristics should govern informative reporting, not the form of the report. Legal and/or technical criteria should establish the guidelines for accounting transactions and other events.

3. *Reliability*. Separate facts from interpretation. Disclose uncertainties and assumptions related to the information presented. The main point is that users of financial information should be informed about the data limitations.

4. *Freedom from bias*. This test does not imply absence of judgment, but rather that neutrality, objectivity, and fairness should be guiding aims. The financial statement should not be slanted to benefit any particular reader or group.

5. *Demographic data*. Analysis of population characteristics provides the kind of information that is especially complementary to the financial data. The following are examples of useful demographic data: (a) changes in the population; (b) per capita income, per capita tax burden, and changes therein; (c) description and stability of industries; (d) comparative growth rate of main local revenue sources, expenditures, and per capita income; (e) taxable and nontaxable property values; (f) average change in long-term per capita debt; (g) discussion of population and age changes, education levels, school-age children, ethnic characteristics, income levels, and unemployment rates; (h) number of government employees funded from own source; (i) percent of employees participating in collective bargaining; and (j) types of clientele.

6. *Comparability*. This guideline suggest that *like* things be reported *alike* and *unlike* things be reported *differently*. This task is made more difficult in

not-for-profit agencies because of the variations that characterize the different kinds of services that are provided. However, if the guideline is followed, these problems will be minimized.

7. *Consistency*. The operating norm is that comparable events should be treated in a similar manner from period to period. For example, after an accrual system is adopted, change to a cash system during the period would be considered a violation of this guideline and GAAP.

Reporting: Some Inadequacies

There are a number of continuing concerns about financial reporting in the public sector and other not-for-profit organizations. The expenditure reporting system used in the public sector emphasizes the acquisition of goods and services rather than the application (how much is consumed) approach employed in business. Expenditure accounting assumes an immediate expiration of resources. The incurrence of debt (e.g., a loan or, especially, the floating of a bond) is viewed as a resource, and the purchase of fixed assets is recorded as the application of resources, irrespective of the useful life of the asset. To maintain some degree of control over fixed assets, a separate general fixed asset group (GFAG) of accounts must be developed. It is generally believed that use of the expenditure reporting system is responsible for poor record-keeping concerning fixed assets in many not-for-profit organizations. Because of the expenditure practice, public sector funds require five governmental funds (general, special revenue, capital projects, debt service, and special assessment), two proprietary funds (enterprise and internal service), two fiduciary fund types (trust and agency), and two groups of accounts (fixed assets and long-term liabilities). The GASB government-wide financial statements attempt to overcome the modified accrual- and expenditure accounting system. Unfortunately, not many governmental units prepare this statement on a timely basis.

Some observers of the public sector financial scene express the view that the present financial reporting system is plagued by shortcomings. They contend that (1) it is not possible to determine the cost of services, (2) there is no system for measuring capital maintenance, (3) there is a commingling of sources and uses of funds with interfund transfers, and (4) the heavy emphasis on budgetary compliance does not facilitate meaningful information reporting.[19]

Disclosure Issues

There is no complete consensus by accountants and agency managers on precisely what should be included in financial statements. This is a continuous problem—deciding whether governments should develop combined balance sheets including all funds while excluding interfund balances. The same could be said about consolidated balance sheets that factor out interfund balances in presenting the balance sheet with one "superfund." The demand for a consolidated balance sheet is based on a number of concerns, including the following: (1) There are too many interfund balances that tend to obscure or distort the financial position of a governmental unit. (2) The present system does not present the true "net worth" of the governmental unit.

Rentals, leases, pensions, fringe benefits, and depreciation and other expenditure items are not always uniformly treated, although there is an emerging convergence of views on this point. The biggest area of concern is related to accrued pension liabilities. The method that accounts for pension expenditures only as they are paid to reserve funds ignores significant benefits that have been earned but not paid. Nonetheless, such benefits are commitments and debt that must be paid out at some future date to present employees. Governmental units that fail to reserve funds at the time they become due can bring about major financial crises, as has been the case in several local governments during the last several years.

One such example of financial crises involving governmental pension funds is the city of Detroit, Michigan. Detroit, a city that has long dealt with high crime and population flight, saw a steady reduction of tax revenue due to a declining population, business closures, and real property devaluation. As city revenue continued to decline, the pension liability owed to then current and former city employees incurred consistent growth. Significant operating expenditures resulted in the city being unable to make adequate payments toward the pension fund. Additionally, city accountants used unrealistic growth expectations, which are permitted given the significant leeway governmental accountants are given when making certain financial assumptions, in regard to the funds already in the pension. These growth projections seldom materialized. All these factors culminated in Detroit's filing for bankruptcy in July 2013, in large part because it was unable to make necessary payments to the city's pension fund. The pension fund burden became too large for the city to fiscally manage.[20]

Summary Observations

An examination of the not-for-profit financial statements clearly shows the basic differences between the for-profit and not-for-profit sectors. The latter organizations require a set of financial statements, unlike those of their commercial counterparts. To whom accountability and/or stewardship must be rendered is a basic principle underlying all reporting. To be acceptable, reports are expected to conform not only to legal, professional, and regulatory standards but must also be readily understandable to specific or general types of audiences. Users to whom financial statements are directed are expected to assess the efficacy with which management is discharging its responsibilities.

Despite the socially oriented objectives of not-for-profit organizations, most reporting is still based on financial accounting. It is a legal "spend-for" concept that emphasizes dollar accountability. Although this approach is changing, it still has some way to go. Last, the kind of financial statement needed is situational in that each organization must find the level of aggregation that fits its needs, as shown in Figure 18.2.

Notes

1. American Institute of Certified Public Accountants (AICPA), *Objectives of Financial Statements* (New York: AICPA, 1973), p. 25.

2. See Al Gore, *Creating a Government That Works Better and Costs Less* (Washington, DC: Government Printing Office, 1993), and David Osborne and Ted Gaebler, *Reinventing Government: Entrepreneurial Spirit Is Transforming the Public Sector* (Reading, MA: Addison-Wesley Publishing, 1992).

3. See SustainAbility and the United Nations' Environment Program (UNEP), "Buried Treasure: Uncovering the Business Case for Corporate Sustainable Development," 2001; and World Business Council for Sustainably Development (WBCSD), "Sustainable Development Reporting: Striking a Balance," December 2002.

4. National Council on Governmental Accounting, *Concept Statements: Objectives of Accounting and Financial Reporting for Governmental Units* (Chicago: NCGA, 1982, Government Finance Officers Association), p. 2.

5. See National Council on Governmental Accounting, *Statement No. 1, Governmental Accounting and Financial Reporting Principles* (Chicago: NCGA, 1979); and Governmental Accounting Standards Board, *The Needs of Users of Governmental Fiscal Reports* (Stamford, CT: GASB, 1985).

6. See GASB Concept Statement No. 1, "Objectives of Financial Reporting," (1987), p. 2.

7. Ibid.

8. Robert J. Freeman and Craig Shoulders, "A Bold Step Forward," *Government Accountants Journal 49*, no. 1 (spring 2000): 8–14; see also John Sacco, "Part of Changing Political and Global Pressures," *Government Accountants Journal 49*, no. 1 (spring 2000): 20–21. Sacco states that GASB Statement No. 34 reflects the ideological views espousing competition, contracting out privatization, and the private business approach.

9. Stephen J. Gauthier, *An Elected Official's Guide to the New Governmental Financial Reporting Model* (Chicago: Government Finance Officers Association, 2000), pp. 3–4.

10. National Council on Governmental Accounting, *Concept Statements*, pp. 18–19.

11. Ibid., p. 19.

12. Lennox L. Moak and Albert M. Hillhouse, *Local Government Finance* (Chicago, IL: Municipal Finance Officers Association, 1975), pp. 428–430.

13. Ibid., p. 432.

14. See Governmental Accounting Standards Board (GASB), *Service Efforts and Accomplishments Reporting* (Draft, September 15, 1993), p. 11.

15. Ibid., pp. 30–31.

16. Barbara R. Hennessy, "Communicating Financial Data to Nonaccountants: A Case for Popular Reporting," *Government Finance Review 7*, no. 5 (October 1991): 7.

17. Hal Peger and Gerald Lonergner, "Popular Financial Reporting in the Public Sector(?)," *Governmental Finance 5*, no. 2 (May 1976): 33.

18. Ibid., p. 36.

19. See Coopers and Lybrand and the University of Michigan, *Financial Disclosure Practices of American Cities: A Public Report* (New York: Coopers and Lybrand, 1976), pp. 9–11.

20. Wikipedia, "Detroit Bankruptcy," January 30, 2014. http://en.wikipedia.org/wiki/Detroit_bankruptcy

19

Evaluating Fiscal Health

Interest and concern for the fiscal health of governmental units and other not-for-profit organizations, especially colleges and universities, heightened in the mid-1970s with the financial crises in New York City and Cleveland. Numerous cutbacks were necessary due to the reduction in revenues at all levels of government. The fiscal problems of the cities followed more than a decade of continuous growth in expenditures. Beginning in the early 1970s, an era of seemingly endless growth throughout the economy was replaced by increasing inflation, a stagnant national economy, rising costs, and declining productivity. Many larger cities that had expanded social and other types of services found them difficult to maintain as the stagnation and malaise in the economy continued.

A number of cities, among them Pittsburgh and Chicago, slowed expenditures significantly, adapting to the changing economic environment. However, other cities such as New York and Cleveland continued their incremental budgeting habits, making no adaptation to the decline in revenues; this led to fiscal strain and, ultimately, fiscal crisis.[1] The experience of a government-supported nonprofit agency such as the Smithsonian Institution shows how an entity can develop effective strategies to deal with retrenchment. Out of a budget of nearly $400 million, the Smithsonian Institution recognized early in 1990 that an impending recession would likely produce of a shortfall of $10 million. The Smithsonian mobilized management to undertake a zero-base review based on clearly defined and articulated priorities. The downsizing and restructuring were carried out within specified time frames. Simultaneous with the recession and downsizing, the Smithsonian adopted total quality management (TQM). To build the maximum momentum for the goals and objectives, visible TQM successes were highlighted.[2]

Although the 1970s, 1990s, and early 2000s saw financial problems in state and local governments, none could have anticipated that major well-known banks and some related businesses would be rescued by the government. The housing boom ushered in massive speculation in housing finances, using "credit default" swap (CDs). These CDs have been designed to transfer credit exposure of fixed income products (usually long-term loans) between parties. The seller of the credit default swap agreement guarantees the payback of the CDs for a fee while the buyer collects the interest on the CDs. The $62 trillion market crashed when a large number of CDs were defaulted. This development created the U.S. Great Recession and an attendant worldwide financial crisis negatively affecting virtually every state and local government.

During the Great Recession of 2007–2009, entities at all levels of government experienced financial strains, some to the point of insolvency. Declining revenues and increasing demand, from both businesses and individual taxpayers, forced governments to make painful spending cuts and take on additional debt to finance to meet mandatory expenditures.[3] Cities such as Madison, Wisconsin, and Irvine, California, weathered the economic downturn relatively unscathed and are among the best-run and fiscally healthiest cities in the country today. Other municipalities, such as Detroit, Michigan, and Cleveland, Ohio, are in economic crisis, with Detroit having filed bankruptcy at the end of 2013, burdened by a staggering $18 billion in debt.[4] This chapter explores the theories and practices relating to the fiscal health of governmental units and agencies. Particular emphasis is placed on the analysis of fiscal strain and the ways that it can be identified, monitored, and prevented.

This chapter is really about fiscal sustainability, the ability of a governmental entity to meet current and maturing obligations and maintain current services from current taxing capacity. This is the maximum level of revenue that a government may raise from its revenue base.[5] To maintain the particular level of sustainability or financial condition, a governmental entity must follow policy and procedures that would allow it to achieve this reality. "Maintaining or restoring sound financial condition requires local officials to adjust to long-term socioeconomic and demographic changes, respond to economic impact of the business cycle, or plan for the future."[6]

A number of states have developed various assistance approaches to help local government achieve their financial condition objective. Among the states, Florida and the state of Washington provide the most useful guides. Although the Washington approach is more comprehensive and detailed, the state of Florida has an approach that is simple and easy to implement. The system has five components:

- Financial indicators
- Date elements
- Guide to analysis of financial condition
- Potential factors that could cause deteriorating condition
- Websites with information useful for assessing financial conditions

Perhaps one of the best in-depth applications of the Financial Trend Monitoring System is done by Kansas City, Missouri. To bolster its FTMS analysis, measures from the Government Finance Officers Association (GFOA) long-term financial planning model are included. GFOA recommends that a long-term planning fiscal analysis of the environment be examined in terms of sufficiency, flexibility, equity, economic demand, and political environment. The underlying assumption is that a sound financial condition depends greatly on an entity's ability to balance long-term demands for service with existing financial resources. The FTMS gives relevant decision makers the opportunity to better focus on identifying potential problems before they occur and allow them to take effective action to prevent or minimize their impact.

Kansas City uses a ten-year time frame to facilitate trend line analysis and poses four useful questions:

1. "How fast is the indicator changing?
2. How does one trend compare to another and is there correlation?
3. How do our trends compare to local or regional trends?
4. How can we effectively use the results for planning, budgeting and policymaking?"[7]

The city developed a scorecard to provide relevant decision makers and stakeholders with a summarized view of what it calls the seventeen "core" or fundamental indicators to provide a snapshot of financial condition, as can be seen in Table 19.1:

- *Positive* if the indicators meet the policy or performance expectations.
- *Watch* if the trend is uncertain. It suggests that that indicator should be given close attention as it may move in a direction that negatively affects the city's financial health.
- *Negative* indicates failure to meet policy or performance or target set by city. It demands corrective action.

Fiscal Strain: Review and Analysis

As an area of study, *fiscal strain* was formerly barren of theories, and analysis of such concepts as fiscal stability, economic viability, decremental budgeting, fiscal monitoring, and fiscal strain was nonexistent. Not until the mid-1970s was serious attention focused on the problem of fiscal strain, after a number of financial crises experienced by local governments. Although the theoretical underpinnings of concepts are beginning to emerge, as evidenced by Clark and Ferguson's *City Money* (1983), Brown's "10 Tests of Financial Condition" (1993), and Wolff and Hughes's "Net Available Assets Is a Proxy for Financial Condition" (June 1998), most of the literature tended to be descriptive.[8] Even so, many theoretical and practical insights can be obtained from these sources.

TABLE 19.1   Core Indicators

Not Rated	4
Population	
Per Capita and Median Household Income	
Employment	
Property Value	
Positive	3
Property Tax Per Capita	
Franchise Fees Per Capita	
Salaries & Benefits as a Percent of Operating Expenditures	
Watch	3
Operating Revenue Per Capita	
Sales and Use Tax Per Capita	
Capital as a Percent of Total Expenditures	
Negative	7
Structural Balance	
Unreserved Operating Fund Balances	
Earnings Tax Per Capita	
Operating Expenditures Per Capita	
Fringe Benefits as a Percent of Personnel Costs	
Debt Service as a Percent of Operating Expenditures	
Annual Pension Payments	
Grand Total	17

Source: Kansas City Missouri, *Financial Trends Monitoring System Report* (2003–2012), p. 3.

A paradox during periods of fiscal strain and retrenchment management is that the greatest opportunity to develop effective management systems (e.g., management planning, internal control systems, fiscal health monitoring systems, and information systems) occurs during periods when resources are plentiful. However, these are precisely the times when such systems appear to be superfluous or irrelevant.[9] Under conditions of abundance, habit, intuition, snap judgments, and other forms of informal analysis and decision making often suffice, because the costs of making mistakes can be easily absorbed without threatening an organization's survival.[10] However, during austerity periods, because resources are restricted, the innovative management systems that were not previously found to be necessary cannot be implemented despite their critical need. Additional problems abound when retrenchment comes along:

- Lack of resources to motivate managers, to seek consensus-building solutions, to provide incentive payments, and to minimize resistance to change
- Lack of resources to provide promotion incentives (necessary to motivate and keep successful managers)

- Lack of resources necessary to expand (especially in the public sector) due to merit and tenure practices that lead to organizational entropy because new and creative talent cannot be attracted
- Lack of resources leading to adoption of inclusionary practices to ensure that participants do not avoid assuming their share of the increased burden (the exclusionary practice is used during periods of growth to exclude people from enjoying benefits unless they share in the burden)[11]

Defining Fiscal Strain

Most writers fail to provide a definition of fiscal strain. One prominent writer in the field, Charles H. Levine, observed that fiscal solvency means the provision of services at a level and with the amount of "benefits that are adequate, equitable and stable."[12] He went on to further define terms: *adequacy*—suggesting the sufficiency of goods and services to maintain individual well-being; *equity*—guaranteeing equal access and opportunity to benefits from goods and services; and *stability*—referring "to the maintenance of goods and services commensurate with the needs and expectation of the citizens."[13] Although intuitively appealing, this collective definition cannot easily be operationalized, because it is too vague. Thus attempts at measurement would be exceedingly difficult. A more useful and operational definition would permit measurement so that it can be determined when the organization is moving toward an acceptable state and when it is experiencing increasing fiscal strain. Perhaps the most acceptable definition is one that permits the matching of private sector resources (e.g., employment or population) to government spending and debt. In this way, fiscal strain can be determined by the degree to which the expenditures of an organization or government are matched against private sector resources. After an acceptable match is decided upon, expenditures may be adapted or manipulated to maintain the desired fiscal balance. This can be done by developing fiscal strain indicators or ratios using an equation, such as the following:[14]

$$Urban\ fiscal\ strain = \frac{Government\ spending\ and\ debt}{Private\ sector\ resources}$$

Note that unless approximate or proportionate changes occur in both the numerator and denominator at the same time, the system will become unbalanced. Hence, when a change occurred in Pittsburgh's denominator factor (a decline in the tax base) in the early 1970s, it reduced spending (the numerator), thereby averting a fiscal strain crisis. Similarly, Cincinnati coped with its fiscal pressure by increasing user fees for a number of functions (e.g., water, parking, and the airport), by reducing demands on the general funds, by reducing the municipal workforce, by regionalizing services (e.g., transferring the University of Cincinnati to the state and the municipal court to Hamilton County), and by reducing planned capital expansion.[15] When the same events occurred in New York City, its government made no effort to reduce spending, which caused a financial strain crisis.[16] The point suggested here is that fiscal strain is determined by two major factors: the governmental fiscal policy output (government spending and debt) and the private sector resources (employment, jobs, and so on) of the governmental entity. If the city leaders or organizational officials are able to adapt to changes that occur in the determinants, the governmental units need not reach fiscal strain.[17]

The Making of Fiscal Policy Outputs

Fiscal policy output is the response to the demand by important relevant groups and individuals for a particular program, project, or benefit. The resultant policy is affected by the philosophy of the participants, who advocate that government spending take a specific direction. Four examples have been suggested: (1) The mid-1960s saw the New Deal Democrats such as Lyndon Johnson in Washington and his imitators in many cities. They were fiscally liberal and viewed government social programs as important instruments for helping disadvantaged blacks and the poor. (2) The ethnic politicians such as the Hispanics, resemble the New Deal Democrats in that they strove to increase social services and expand job opportunities for the unemployed members of their constituencies. (3) Republicans viewed taxpayers as having more legitimacy than labor unions and organized interest groups. They believed in keeping taxes low and minimizing social programs. (4) The new fiscal populism was exemplified by Presidents Jimmy Carter and Bill Clinton and Peter Flaherty, Pittsburgh mayor. Although they were fiscal conservatives, they attempted to respond to the needs of the disadvantaged while attempting to minimize the burden to the average taxpayer.[18]

The making of each policy output typically involves a complex of dynamic, interacting forces. Of the many factors (e.g., citizens' preferences, interest groups, leaders' preferences, and residential choice) affecting the policymakers, it is important for us to know which has the greatest influence.[19] This knowledge can provide insights about the decisions that produce fiscal strain.

Fiscal Strain: New York City

New York City experienced windfall increases in revenue from 1966 to 1970. During this period, revenues increased by about 14 percent per year. This increase was generated by growing local revenues and supplemented with state and federal increases, the latter averaging a 39.7 percent yearly rise between 1966 and 1970. However, during 1971–1975, New York's operating revenues experienced a declining rate of increase.[20] The various periods of revenue decline were characterized by distinct administrative responses:[21]

1. During the initial decline, officials resorted to denial and delay, hoping the increased revenue would mitigate the problem. Denial was complemented by budget manipulation, such as raising operating funds via the capital budget and postponing required maintenance.
2. The second decline was marked by the resistance of agencies and clients to cutbacks and vigorous efforts by agencies to stretch resources. Cutbacks were evenly distributed across departmental programs. Because of an attrition agreement with the labor unions, few layoffs were necessary. At the same time, management instituted a number of improvements, such as automation of the budget to enhance the city's credibility/transparency with the financial community.
3. From 1975 to 1978, across-the-board cuts continued, but few targeted cuts were made.
4. The 1978–1980 period saw the city making deeper, "more targeted cuts," along with significant organizational changes.[22]

It is also worthy of note that maintenance postponement and user fee increases took place during each of these periods.

Change in the level of resources was the most crucial factor (variable) in New York's fiscal strain. Each of the five identified levels of resource changes (moderate continuous growth, windfall revenue growth, no revenue growth, moderate decline, severe decline) affected the political structure and administrative strategies in specific ways. For example, lack of revenue growth generated weak central control and fragmented interest groups within the political structure, thereby negatively influencing demand and delaying administrative strategies. The fiscal pressure was not great enough to force decisive reductive action.[23]

Each level of service produced different types of outcomes at the departmental, program, and client levels—ultimately determining who received and who was denied the benefits of scarce public resources. The macroconsequence manifested itself in areas such as the quality of the physical infrastructure (buildings, sewers, roads, and so on), the city's capacity to deliver services, and the quality of the city's living conditions.

Cause of Fiscal Strain

In the early analysis of fiscal strain (sometimes also referred to as *fiscal distress*), the causes were descriptively and loosely identified. The following are some of the principal symptoms or causes:

- Extended and severe economic decline, including unabated population and employment losses
- Long periods of excessive reliance on supplemental federal aid and static revenue growth for fixed costs

- Decline in public productivity compared to the overall local workforce, perhaps due to unionization
- Deferment of current costs, including maintenance on fixed facilities and incurred pension liabilities
- Financial management practices, including the manipulation of accounting and reporting systems[24]

There is wide disagreement on the specific causes of fiscal strain. A grouping of the causes into three categories has been suggested:

1. The *migration and tax base erosion explanation* holds that population migration has been a dominant factor in creating fiscal strain. Migration into the cities was marked by the influx of poor blacks and Hispanics, which overloaded the capacity of cities, especially in the areas of education, welfare, job training, and health. The migration of upper- and middle-class residents from the city to the suburbs left the cities with a disproportionate number of poor and unemployed residents, thereby eroding the revenue base. The residents moving in required considerably more services than those moving out. Additionally, the residents' moving out caused a significant shift in the base upon which taxes were being levied, creating a revenue gap. Finally, the outmigration movement saw the population moving to the Sun Belt from what is now referred to as the Rust Belt, taking with them industries and technology and hence creating job loss and population and tax base erosion, not only in the city but also in the region.

2. The *bureaucratic growth perspective* relates to the public choice model, which relies on nonmarket economics. Proponents of this model posit that the rapid growth of government has negative implications. The growth of government leads to increases in services. People are willing to pay for some services, but not for those they believe are unnecessary. This model suggests that the services tend to grow larger than required because requests for them are not regulated or restrained by the cost factor—that is, all residents enjoy the benefits of the services produced, whereas only a few may be required to pay for them. The greater the number of residents enjoying these benefits without the tax burden, the greater the number of individuals supporting these services. Likewise, bureaucrats find it in their interest to expand the bureaucracy, enhancing their own career opportunities; thus they help to use their voting power to expand the bureaucracy when the opportunity arises.

3. The *political vulnerability approach* suggests that cities are more likely to reach fiscal strain as political officials (policymakers) are subjected to demands that compel a positive response. Three conditions occur that increase exposure to political vulnerabilities: (a) voter coalition breakdown, in which important political figures such as the mayor are unable to muster

a working majority of groups, making it necessary to spend revenues, at times inefficiently, in order to maintain and attract support and hence leading to fiscal strain; (b) weaknesses in the formal authority structure, in which a strong mayor and machine government are seen as incapable of resisting demands, whereas city managers' reforms, which permit the delivery of efficient services at lower cost, could minimize the potential for fiscal strain; and (c) shifting power among interest groups, in which the strongest ones impose their demands on a vulnerable political leadership, negatively affecting fiscal policy.[25]

Fiscal Strategies That Failed

Intergovernmental revenue and legal reform play important roles in local fiscal policy. The impact of intergovernmental revenues may be significantly affected by the terms of the grant to the local government. Two models that guide grant distribution have been suggested. Under model I, the local governments are passive actors executing the policies determined at a higher level of government (state or federal). In model II, local units play a more active role, using intergovernmental revenues to implement local preferences. The model II approach parallels the traditional decentralized role that most local governments desire. The national government typically favors model I because it permits greater influence for the implementation of national policies and better accounting of the intergovernmental fiscal flows.[26]

Clark and Ferguson have disagreed with the widely held belief that intergovernmental aid is a significant determinant on local policy and that nonlocal revenues typically reinforce local influences.[27] The evidence (from 1960 to the late 1970s) in both Europe and the United States shows that intergovernmental assistance does *not* seem to help local governments avoid the problems associated with fiscal strain. In Europe, the cities receiving the greatest assistance experienced the most severe fiscal strain.[28]

The widely accepted view that the transfer of functions mitigates fiscal strain has not been borne out in studies.[29] In fact, the transfer of functions may have the reverse effect. Moreover, the plea made by cities such as San Francisco and New York to federalize welfare programs involves many thorny issues. Does New York, with its higher welfare payments, move down to the level paid in Mississippi, or vice versa? Because it is more realistic to expect the average welfare payment to move up to the New York level, additional federal resources would be required to finance welfare.

It is generally agreed that the state debt limit on local government does not work unless the debt limit reflects local preferences, because government typically finds ways to get around the limitations.[30] Most communities never reach the debt limit for general obligation (G.O.) bonds, for which they must use their "full faith and credit," because they want to avoid scrutiny by the state legislature. Therefore revenue bonds are floated for facilities such as water; revenues generated by the particular service are earmarked to pay the debt. Subsequently, those revenues are not available for operational or alternative expenditures.

Fiscal Strategies That Work

Policies that are adopted reflect the political ideology of the governing officials (e.g., Democrats, ethnic politicians, Republicans, new fiscal populists). The general policies of the four groups listed may be summarized as follows:[31]

Democrats

Typically, the Democrats are disposed toward identifying new revenue sources and increasing taxes. On the expenditure side, tough cutback decisions are delayed and capital expenditures are reduced only when difficult situations demand it. Reduction of employee compensation is viewed as an option to be followed only when other alternatives have been exhausted. The most influential inputs in the decision making process come from the mayor, city council members, employees, party leaders, relevant neighborhood groups, and service recipients.

Ethnic Politicians

Although their orientation is similar to that of the Democrats, they emphasize the skill enhancement/job training of ethnic employees on the city payroll. Additionally, they advocate the provision of symbolic services, or what is sometimes called "goodwill gestures," for members of the dominant ethnic group. Although similar to the Democrats in their decision making mode, they tend to defer to elected officials and employees and representatives of influential ethnic groups.

Republicans

Reduction of taxes and services, when the situation demands, is the initiating course of action for Republicans. When implementing policies, neither employees nor interest groups are given mitigating attention or special exemptions. Generally, the deepest cuts are made in programs targeted for the poor. If the situation is propitious, a policy for productivity improvement will be pursued. The decision making process favors the individual tax-paying citizen. Unlike the Democrats and ethnic politicians, Republicans typically allow programmatic decisions to be determined by professional staff, with inputs made, in varying degrees, by relevant leaders in the community.

New Fiscal Populists

Although their tactics may appear different, their actions and results parallel those of the Republicans. They give the general appearance of responsiveness to the disadvantaged, but programs targeted toward these groups are usually cut. One of the overriding objectives of the new fiscal populists is to place emphasis on productivity improvement. The populists stress input from citizens as do the Republicans, but unlike them, they give precedence to citizen input over that of the professional staff. Leaders use information such as town or open meetings or polls to assess the preferences of citizens. Knowledgeable experts are consulted and ideas about improving productivity are sought: Essentially, the private sector has significantly more say on public policy decisions and spending.

Cyclical and Structural Stress

Cyclical stress inevitably occurs from time to time in every government and not-for-profit agency because of downturns in the economy. Each time imbalances occur in different sectors or areas of the economy, revenues to the public sector are affected. When the imbalances are due to fast growth, revenues are positively affected. Governments can and should use these periods to increase reserves that may be used as a cushion for when the economic cycle turns sour. Because governments operate in a "goldfish bowl environment," with continuous and intense public scrutiny, increasing fund balance reserves for slowdowns generates pressure to reduce taxes.[32]

Policymakers often do not effectively analyze the factors generating the increases in revenue such as increases due to the prosperity (volume) or the natural growth resulting from tax base expansion. Taxes are prematurely lowered to reduce political pressure and increase popularity among voters.[33] When revenue growth due to prosperity is mistaken for natural or real tax base growth, future fiscal stress and crisis can result. This is the situation in which many state and local governments presently find themselves. The great prosperity and stock market boom of the mid-2000s, driven by the housing market bubble, has been followed by a major downturn in the economic cycle; the severity of which coined the moniker "the Great Recession" to describe the period of 2007–2009. Most state and local governments faced, and continue to face, huge revenue shortfalls. The volume of revenues has fallen dramatically and fund balance reserves have dissipated. The revenue shortfalls have created a budgetary crisis throughout the country with some municipalities, such as Detroit, Michigan, filing for bankruptcy.

Minimizing the Cycle Problem

If governments hope to avoid or minimize revenue shortfall problems, three important factors should always be kept in mind: (a) the understanding of cyclical versus structural defects, (b) the price of government acquisitions, and (c) the expected end results. By knowing the nature of the problem affecting revenue growth (cyclical versus structural defect), policymakers would be in a position to act proactively in minimizing or avoiding problems.

Cyclical defects or downturns in the economy are temporary, whereas structural defects suggest long-term gaps that are likely to arise between projected revenue growth and estimated cuts in services. Because these defects suggest only the direction of revenues, they are not self-executing—they cannot solve the heart of the problem. The magnitude of the fiscal gap can only be known when the potential cyclicality of economic downturns and structural defects are effectively estimated and quantified. This requires substantial planning that involves long- and short-term forecasts of both revenue and expenditures for five years or longer. When the forecasts suggest the insufficiency of funds to meet projected expenditures, long- and short-term changes must be made. Once these changes have been implemented to address the gaps, short-term needs can be met while allowing a more gradual transition or accommodation to the long-term projections.

The average price of government remained steady from 2008 to the present. Most decision makers in government focus on the cost of undertaking activities, ignoring or not fully considering the relation between *price* and *value*. (*Price* is the amount of taxes citizens pay versus the perceived things or *value* they receive.) Financial accountability is the major objective, with minimal concern about the results or impact of government spending.

Especially when revenue sources are volatile and unpredictable, governments should employ the *revenue budgeting approach* (known as the *conservative budget approach*). This requires that availability be known at the beginning or initiating point in the budget process. It forces decision makers' budget requests to conform to the defined revenue parameters. Budget requests can be prioritized and pared down based on missions and goals to meet the needs of the government. One fertile area in which government may achieve productive budget reductions is information technology. The view is that much of what government does involves the collection and processing of information that is cumbersome and expensive. These functions can be better managed by streamlining the system internally or externally and outsourcing.[34]

The use of information technology (IT) has grown exponentially over the previous decade with private and public sector IT investments reaching all-time highs. Much of this growth has occurred due to the implementation of enterprise resource planning (ERP) systems and the establishment of large data warehouses for data mining/analysis purposes. Although information technology is meant to streamline data use, analysis, and communication, the costs of implementation can exceed the benefits, such as the case with many failed ERP systems. If implemented properly and with equipment that facilitates organizational efficiency, IT can reduce costs, slow the hiring of additional personnel, respond to demands/risks more quickly, and most importantly allow the entity to mitigate the effects of unexpected fiscal strains.

To minimize costs over the long and short runs, government must be able to reliably forecast the qualitative effects of cyclical and structural defects. This requires the ability to accurately determine the taxes that citizens will pay and the results that the available resources will produce in satisfying articulated expectations.

Assessing Financial Conditions

In a narrow accounting sense, the acceptable *financial condition* (known also as *cash solvency*) shown in Figure 19.1 may refer to a government's or agency's ability to generate sufficient cash to meet obligations maturing within thirty to sixty days. It may also refer to an agency's or governmental unit's ability to meet all important expenditures accruing within a budgeting period without incurring a deficit, also called *budgetary solvency*.[35] A broader perspective of the financial condition views it as a government's or agency's ability to meet both long- and short-term costs as they come due, such as pension payments, accrued leaves, capital replacements, and deferred maintenance. This is referred to as *long-run solvency*. Ultimately, the financial condition provides a reading of how well a governmental unit is capable of providing "the level and quality of services required for the general health and welfare of a community as desired by its citizens."[36] Stated another way, the fiscal condition suggests the ability to finance existing levels of services, access to reserves, and the revenue base to respond to regional economic disruptions such as the closing of a major local employer, and the ability to meet growth, change, and decline.

In assessing the fiscal health environment and context, each community or organization must be carefully studied. Key features that should be considered in evaluating a government's or agency's fiscal condition include the following:

- Physical condition of the local infrastructure such as roads, bridges, and sewer system
- Dependence on federal financial assistance, particularly regarding the support of regularly recurring operating expenses
- Pension liabilities, especially unfunded obligations
- Employee union demands, especially those that require contractual pay increases without offsetting productivity increases

- Militancy of local taxpayers as evidenced by tax expenditure limitations
- Inflation and its effects on the fixed costs of government
- Bond defaults and the ability to finance long-term debt repayment[37]

The traditional approach in using bond ratings as the main or sole indicator of a governmental unit's fiscal health is unwise and can be misleading, as the New York City financial crisis demonstrated. The city's continued use of short-term debt to meet its chronic budget imbalance was "easily overlooked because of the city's poor accounting and reporting system and its use of long-term debt to finance current operating expenses."[38] An important point is that the possibility of a bond default is typically equated with a government's ability to pay maturing obligations. This does not say anything about the broader fiscal health of the community. Other important factors include not only an evaluation of the likelihood of default, but an analysis of the government's ability to maintain current or acceptable levels of service. Sufficient financial resources must be available to weather economic difficulties, achieve acceptable growth in the local economy, maintain revenue stability, and generate the capacity to respond to increased demands for local services.[39]

Traditional financial statements are insufficient as a basis for evaluating the fiscal health of communities. They do provide information on how financial data conform to generally accepted accounting principles (GAAP) and other regulatory and mandated requirements. Typically, information relating

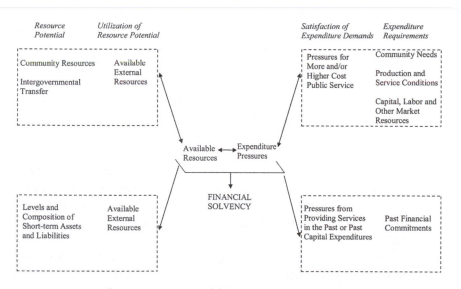

FIGURE 19.1   The components of financial solvency analysis.

Source: Robert Berne and Richard Schramm, The Financial Solvency of Local Governments, in Working Papers in Planning (Ithaca, NY: Cornell University Press, January 1979), p. 18.

to data such as the reliance on outside revenue sources, uncontrollable revenues, industrial growth trends, per capita income trends, capital improvement requirements, and physical plant replacement is not found in financial statements.

Monitoring the Fiscal Condition

The field of public financial management has been preoccupied with such short-term concerns as the availability of cash to meet immediate financial obligations, giving little or no attention to the long-term issues that ensure the fiscal stability of the community. This myopia has been made apparent in the current fiscal crisis afflicting Detroit, Michigan, which was forced to file bankruptcy in late 2013 when it became unable to meet its pension fund obligations. Although the investment community has been concerned with the debt carrying capacity, as noted earlier, it has not developed broad indicators that could be usefully employed to assess the financial condition of particular governmental units.

Many problems militate against the development of an effective monitoring system. Before the financial crises of the 1970s such as that in New York City, there was little interest in developing such systems. Data relating to economic and demographic activities could not be easily obtained; those that were obtainable on governmental functions, revenue structure, and financial reports could not be reliably compared for a host of reasons. Thus it was very difficult to analyze the effects on revenue of a decline in employment or change in the form of a major business (e.g., wholesale to retail). No benchmark indicators were established to guide decision makers on, for example, desirable per capita expenditures, long- and short-term amounts of debt, or levels of reserves.

Accomplishing a *Financial Trends Monitoring System* (FTMS) is not a simple, straightforward task. (FTMS was developed by the International City Management Association during the late 1970s and early 1980s.) Many elements must be considered, such as the state of the national economy, local business and economic conditions, population makeup, and employment trends. Many factors must be isolated, quantified, and evaluated. The most critical and specific pieces of data cannot always be determined until they have all been systematically brought together and meticulously evaluated. Such a process is fraught with problems, but the potential yield is likely to be worth the costs.[40]

The FTMS identifies, analyzes, and measures the factors affecting the financial condition of a given community. It is a means for organizing internal data (budgeting and financial reports) and other relevant external data (demographic and economic) to produce financial indicators that may be used to monitor financial changes within a given community. The FTMS does not provide a single index number to identify fiscal health, but it draws attention to potentially serious problems, suggest hints or clues to the likely causes, and gives time by which to take preventive action. By means of the FTMS, the governmental unit can maintain an information system to indicate its relative financial strength and weakness. It can be used as a basis to reorder internal staff priorities, to chart or modify long-term policies, and to institutionalize strategic planning perspectives in the annual budgeting cycle routines.[41] Twelve factors (the primary impacting forces on a financial condition) constitute the FTMS. These financial condition factors act in concert with thirty-six financial indicators "to measure different aspects" of seven financial factors (see Figure 19.2).[42] The factors have been perfected and can be used to monitor the community's financial condition.

Financial condition factors are classified as environmental, financial, and organizational and are generated from the existence of financial problems within the given community. Taken as a whole, the factors provide a basis on which the financial condition issues are evaluated. The environmental factors are both a source of demand (e.g., an increase in population brings about an increase in service needs) and a provider of resources (e.g., an increased population increases wealth and the tax base). Organizational factors indicate the ways in which governments respond to changing environmental factors. (A rational assumption is that if government officials are given adequate advance warning, they will act to avert a financial crisis.) Financial factors provide a reading of the status of internal finances, which are determined by interaction of the environmental and organizational forces (see Figure 19.2).[43]

The external or exogenous factors (community needs and resources, external economic conditions, intergovernmental constraints, natural disasters and emergencies, and political culture) are filtered through the organizational factors (legislative policies and management practices), producing the financial factors (revenues, expenditures, operating positions, debt structure, unfunded liabilities, and capital plant) that describe "the internal financial structure of the governmental unit."[44] The revenue factor informs about the growth, flexibility, elasticity, diversity, and dependability of the government. The expenditure factor provides insight about the growth, mandated cost, productivity, and effectiveness of government programs. The operating position reveals the liquidity condition.[45]

Indicators

When properly used, the indicators can be one of the strategic means for alerting government about actions that may be taken to mitigate or prevent a financial situation from becoming a problem. Indicators are quantified changes about the environmental, organizational, and financial factors. Thirty-six indicators are identified in Figure 19.3. When assessing financial condition and employing financial trend monitoring, particular attention should be given to the following:

- specific indicators that should be developed
- Indicators that fit the particular community and government
- The importance of interpreting indicators' significance[46]

A Proposed Ten-Point Test of Financial Condition Assessment for Small Cities

Because of the large number of factors, indicators, and data necessary to carry out competent financial condition assessment, doing so can become a burdensome activity for small municipalities. This makes it difficult for assessment to promote the financial condition as "a regular part of financial management."[47] To minimize these constraints and facilitate financial condition assessment in cities with under 100,000 population, the GFOA (Government Finance Officers Association) proposed a "10-Point Test of Financial Condition." It developed ten important financial ratios calculated for each city, and for 750 similar cities throughout the nation. These ratio calculations allow municipal officers to make comparisons in determining where they stand vis-à-vis the

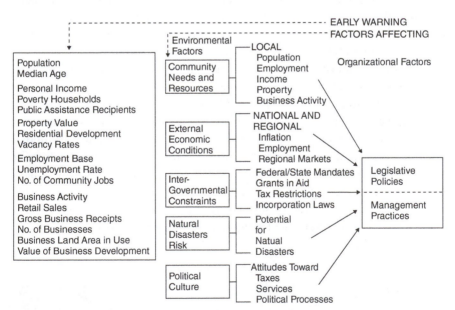

FIGURE 19.2a   Financial trend-monitoring system.

Source: Adapted from Sanford M. Groves and Maureen Goodsey, Evaluating Local Government Financial Condition, Handbook 2, Financial Trend Monitoring System: A Practitioner's Guide. (Washington, DC: International City Management Association, 1980), p. 2

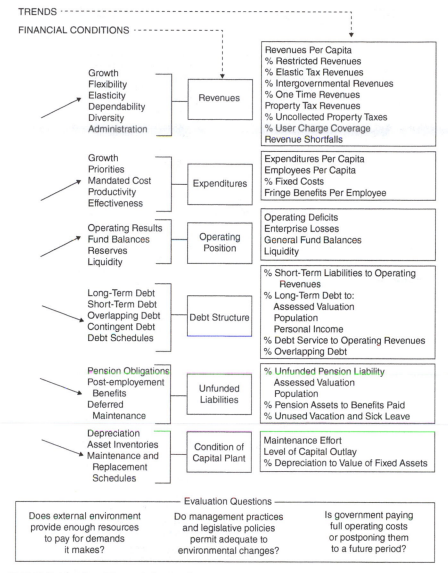

FIGURE 19.2b   Financial trend-monitoring system.

Source: Karl Nollenberger revised text, Sanford Groves and Maureen Goodsey, Evaluating Financial Condition: A Handbook for Local Government (Washington, DC: International City Managers Association, 2003) (reprinted with permission).

financial condition of other similar cities. The test was developed to satisfy the need of cities to have a quick and dependable way of assessing financial conditions and to make use of the comparative Financial Indicators Database that was developed and published by the GFOA in 1992.[48] The ten-point financial

Financial Factor	Financial Indicator	Formula
Revenues	1. Revenue per capita	Net operating revenues in constant dollars / Population
	2. Restricted revenues	Restricted operating revenues / Net operating revenues
	3. Intergovernmental revenues	Intergoernmental operating revenues / Gross operating revenues
	4. Elastic tax revenues	Elastic operating revenues / Net operating revenues
	5. One-time revenues	One-time operating revenues / Net operating revenues
	6. Tax revenuses	Revenues in constant dollars
	7. Uncollected property taxes	Uncollected property taxes / Net property tax levy
	8. User charge coverage	Revenues from fees and user charges / Expenditures for related services
	9. Revenue shortfalls or surpluses	Revenue shortfalls or surpluses / Net operating revenues
Expenditures	10. Expenditure per capita	Net operating revenues in constant dollars / Population
	11. Expenditure by function	Expenditure function / Total net operating expenditures
	12. Employees per capita	Number of employees / Population
	13. Fixed costs	Fixed costs / New operating expenditures
	14. Fringe benefits	Fringe-benefit expenditures / Salaries and wages

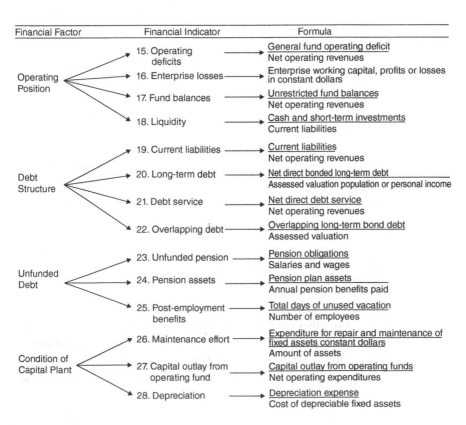

Financial Factor	Financial Indicator	Formula
Operating Position	15. Operating deficits	General fund operating deficit / Net operating revenues
	16. Enterprise losses	Enterprise working capital, profits or losses in constant dollars
	17. Fund balances	Unrestricted fund balances / Net operating revenues
	18. Liquidity	Cash and short-term investments / Current liabilities
Debt Structure	19. Current liabilities	Current liabilities / Net operating revenues
	20. Long-term debt	Net direct bonded long-term debt / Assessed valuation population or personal income
	21. Debt service	Net direct debt service / Net operating revenues
	22. Overlapping debt	Overlapping long-term bond debt / Assessed valuation
Unfunded Debt	23. Unfunded pension	Pension obligations / Salaries and wages
	24. Pension assets	Pension plan assets / Annual pension benefits paid
	25. Post-employment benefits	Total days of unused vacation / Number of employees
Condition of Capital Plant	26. Maintenance effort	Expenditure for repair and maintenance of fixed assets constant dollars / Amount of assets
	27. Capital outlay from operating fund	Capital outlay from operating funds / Net operating expenditures
	28. Depreciation	Depreciation expense / Cost of depreciable fixed assets

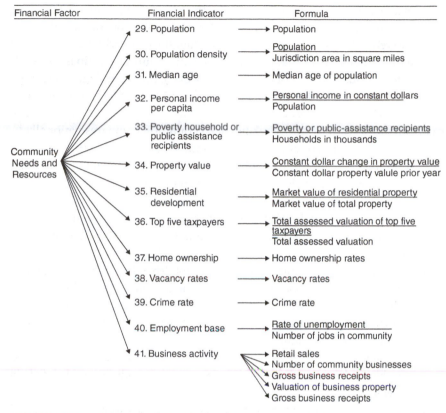

Financial Factor	Financial Indicator	Formula
	29. Population	Population
	30. Population density	$\dfrac{\text{Population}}{\text{Jurisdiction area in square miles}}$
	31. Median age	Median age of population
	32. Personal income per capita	$\dfrac{\text{Personal income in constant dollars}}{\text{Population}}$
	33. Poverty household or public assistance recipients	$\dfrac{\text{Poverty or public-assistance recipients}}{\text{Households in thousands}}$
Community Needs and Resources	34. Property value	$\dfrac{\text{Constant dollar change in property value}}{\text{Constant dollar property valule prior year}}$
	35. Residential development	$\dfrac{\text{Market value of residential property}}{\text{Market value of total property}}$
	36. Top five taxpayers	$\dfrac{\text{Total assessed valuation of top five taxpayers}}{\text{Total assessed valuation}}$
	37. Home ownership	Home ownership rates
	38. Vacancy rates	Vacancy rates
	39. Crime rate	Crime rate
	40. Employment base	$\dfrac{\text{Rate of unemployment}}{\text{Number of jobs in community}}$
	41. Business activity	Retail sales $\dfrac{\text{Number of community businesses}}{\text{Gross business receipts}}$ $\dfrac{\text{Valuation of business property}}{\text{Gross business receipts}}$

FIGURE 19.3   Schema of the financial trend-monitoring system showing financial factors, indicators, and formulas.

Source: Adapted from Sanford M. Groves, Evaluating Local Government Financial Condition, Handbook 2, Financial Trend Monitoring System: A Practitioner's Guide (Washington, DC: International City Management Association, 1980 and 2003), p. 2; and Karl Nollenberger revised text by Sanford Groves and Maureen Goodsey, Evaluating Financial Condition: A Handbook for Local Government (Washington, DC: International City Managers Association, 2003). Reprinted with permission. See also Sanford M. Groves, "An Introduction to Evaluating Financial Condition," in John Matzer, Jr., ed., Practical Financial Management (Washington, DC: International City Management Association, 1984), pp. 24–25.

condition test is focused on four financial factors (see Table 19.2): (1) revenue ratios, 1–3; (2) expenditure ratio, 4; (3) operating position ratios, 5–7; and (4) debt structure ratios, 8–10. The test involves a three-step process: (1) Based on the current financial reports, the financial ratios are calculated. (2) ratios are compared with similar-sized cities. (3) The city's financial condition is graded based on calculations in the second step.

Table 19.2 presents the financial condition worksheet, which can be used to calculate ratios and categorize the 750 cities by population (50,000 to 100,000; 30,000 to 50,000; and 15,000 and under). For each category, the city's score is put in one of four quartiles. Each quartile contains 25 percent of the cities in that category. Quartile 1 shows the ratios of the worst-ranked cities. The second quartile contains the next-best ratios, and the third and fourth quartiles have progressively better ratios. Table 19.3 shows that the cities with populations of 50,000 to 100,000 have per capita quartile revenue figures for ratio no. 1 as follows: The first quartile is $714 or more (the worst), the second quartile ranges from $532 to $713, the third quartile ranges from $429 to $532, and the fourth quartile is $428 or less (the best). From this information, the finance officer can easily identify how his or her city's financial condition compares nationally.[49]

Of the ten financial condition ratios, six (ratios 1, 3, 4, 8, 9, and 10) are viewed favorably if they have low values and four (ratios 2, 5, 6, and 7) if they have high values. The interpretation that is generally given to the ratios are as follows:[50]

- A low no. 1 ratio indicates the ability to generate greater revenue.
- A high no. 2 ratio indicates that the city is not dependent on external sources of revenue.
- A low no. 3 ratio indicates that the city is not dependent on operating transfers to maintain the operations of government from the general fund.
- A low no. 4 ratio indicates the adequacy of the existing infrastructure.
- A high no. 5 ratio indicates that the city has had a greater relative rise in revenue than expenditures.
- A high no. 6 ratio indicates that the city has been generating a surplus that can be used to meet unforeseen increases in expenditure or shortfalls in revenues.
- A high no. 7 ratio indicates the availability of cash to meet existing and maturing obligations.
- A low no. 8 ratio indicates the city's ability to meet short-term obligations from the regular flow of revenues.
- A low no. 9 ratio indicates the city's ability to meet maturing long-term obligations.
- A low no. 10 ratio indicates the city's ability to meet debt service obligations when they become due.

From Table 19.2 (the financial condition worksheet), each quartile is assigned a number from −1 for the first quartile to +2 for the highest quartile. The city that has all ratios in the first quartile will receive a score of −10, whereas the city that receives all scores in the second quartile will have a total score of 0. The following grading scale has been suggested:

- A score of 10 or more is identified as the best.
- A score of 5 is identified as better than most.
- A score of 1 to 4 is identified as average.
- A score of 0 to −4 is identified as worse than most.
- A score of −5 or less is identified as among the worst·

TABLE 19.2 Financial Condition Worksheet

(A) Ratio	(B) Your city's ratio	Quartile 1 (0 to 25 percentile)	Quartile 2 (25 to 50 percentile)	Quartile 3 (50 to 75 percentile)	(C) Points assigned to each quartile Quartile 4 (75 to 100 percentile)	(D) Enter your score circled on the left
1 Total revenue / Population	1 _____	−1	0	+1	+2	_____
2 Total general fund revenues from own sources	2 _____	−1	0	+1	+2	_____
3 General fund sources from other funds / Total general fund sources	3 _____	−1	0	+1	+2	_____
4 Operating expenditures / Total expenditures	4 _____	−1	0	+1	+2	_____
5 Total revenues / Total expenditures	5 _____	−1	0	+1	+2	_____
6 Unreserved general fund balance / Total general fund revenues	6 _____	−1	0	+1	+2	_____
7 Total general fund cash and investments / Total general fund liabilities	7 _____	−1	0	+1	+2	_____

(continued)

TABLE 19.2 (*Continued*)

(A)	(B)	(C) Points assigned to each quartile				(D)
Ratio	Your city's ratio	Quartile 1 (0 to 25 percentile)	Quartile 2 (25 to 50 percentile)	Quartile 3 (50 to 75 percentile)	Quartile 4 (75 to 100 percentile)	Enter your score circled on the left
8 Total general fund liabilities / Total general fund revenues	8 _____	−1	0	+1	+2	_____
9 Direct long-term debt / Population	9 _____	−1	0	+1	+2	_____
10 Debt service / Total revenues	10 _____	−1	0	+1	+2	_____

Source: Ken W. Brown, "The 10-Point Test of Financial Condition: Toward an Easy-to-Use Assessment Tool for Smaller Cities." *Government Finance Review,* 9, no. 7 (December 1993): 23 (reprinted with permission of Government Finance Officers Association).

TABLE 19.3 Quartile Ranges for 750 Cities from the Financial Indicators Database

		Population 50,000–100,000 (162 Cities) Quartile				Population 30,000–50,000 (167 Cities) Quartile			
		1 1–25% (Worst)	2 25–50%	3 50–75%	4 75–100% (Best)	1 1–25% (Worst)	2 25–50%	3 50–75%	4 75–100% (Best)
1.	Total revenues / Population	$714 or more	$714 to $532	$532 to $429	$429 or less	$631 or more	$631 to $493	$493 to $399	$399 or less
2.	Total general fund revenues / Total revenues	80.2% or less	80.2% to 87.7%	87.7% to 96.8%	96.8% or more	77.5% or less	77.5% to 87.4%	87.4% to 96.4%	96.4% or more
3.	General fund sources from other funds / Total general fund sources	7.285% or more	7.285% to 2.083%	2.083% to 0.003%	0.003% or less	6.598% or more	6.598% to 2.438%	2.438% to 0.001%	0.001% or less
4.	Operating expenditures / Total expenditures	95.8% or more	95.8% to 89.9%	88.9% to 81.6%	81.6% or less	94.4% or more	94.4% to 86.5%	86.5% to 77.4%	77.4% or less
5.	Total revenues / Total expenditures	0.878% or less	0.878% to 0.964%	0.964% to 1.038%	1.038% or more	0.864% or more	0.864% to 0.952%	0.952% to 1.034%	1.034% or more
6.	Unreserved general fund balance / Total general fund revenues	0.086% or less	0.086% to 0.180%	0.180% to 0.300%	0.300% or more	0.133% or less	0.133% to 0.211%	0.211% to 0.338%	0.338% or more
7.	Total general fund cash and investments / Total general fund liabilities	0.622% or less	0.622% to 1.539%	1.539% to 3.372%	3.372% or more	0.916% or less	0.916% to 1.909%	1.909% to 3.525%	3.525% or more
8.	Total general fund liabilities / Total general fund revenues	0.245% or more	0.254% to 0.101%	0.101% to 0.069%	0.069% or less	0.193% or more	0.193% to 0.099%	0.099% to 0.063%	0.063% or less
9.	Direct long-term debt / Population	$413 or more	$413 to $201	$201 to $21	$21 or less	$416 or more	$416 to $141	$141 to $15	$15 or less
10.	Debt service / Total revenues	0.134% or more	0.134% to 0.074%	0.074% to 0.041%	0.041% or less	0.146% or more	0.146% to 0.080%	0.080% to 0.025%	0.025% or less

(Continued)

TABLE 19.3 (Continued)

	Population 15,000–30,000 (213 Cities) Quartile				Population less than 15,000 (208 Cities) Quartile			
	1 1–25% (Worst)	2 25–50%	3 50–75%	4 75–100% (Best)	1 1–25% (Worst)	2 25–50%	3 50–75%	4 75–100% (Best)
1. Total revenues / Population	$666 or more	$666 to $481	$481 to $326	$326 or less	$736 or more	$736 to $465	$465 to $368	$368 or less
2. Total general fund revenues / Total revenues	77.7% or less	77.7% to 88.6%	88.6% to 98.3%	98.3% or more	76.4% or less	76.4% to 89.2%	89.2% to 96.7%	96.7% or more
3. General fund sources from other funds / Total general fund sources	5.987% or more	5.987% to 1.157%	1.157% to 0.001%	0.001% or less	8.089% or more	8.089% to 1.270%	1.270% to 0.001%	0.001% or less
4. Operating expenditures / Total expenditures	97.9% or more	97.9% to 91.1%	91.1% to 81.9%	81.9% or less	99.0% or more	99.0% to 92.2%	92.2% to 80.3%	80.3% or less
5. Total revenues / Total expenditures	0.876% or less	0.876% to 0.954%	0.954% to 1.034%	1.034% or more	0.868% or less	0.868% to 0.962%	0.962% to 1.038%	1.038% or more
6. Unreserved general fund balance / Total general fund revenues	0.104% or less	0.104% to 0.218%	0.218% to 0.386%	0.386% or more	0.173% or less	0.173% to 0.278%	0.278% to 0.444%	0.444% or more
7. Total general fund cash and investments / Total general fund liabilities	0.819% or less	0.819% to 1.865%	1.865% to 4.719%	4.719% or more	1.162% or less	1.162% to 2.522%	2.522% to 5.761%	5.761% or more
8. Total general fund liabilities / Total general fund revenues	0.208% or more	0.208% to 0.104%	0.104% to 0.061%	0.061% or less	0.189% or more	0.189% to 0.102%	0.102% to 0.057%	0.057% or less
9. Direct long-term debt / Population	$326 or more	$326 to $133	$133 to $8	$8 or less	$329 or more	$329 to $87	$87 to $1	$1 or less
10. Debt service / Total revenues	0.133% or more	0.133% to 0.063%	0.063% to 0.011%	0.011% or less	0.105% or more	0.105% to 0.039%	0.039% to 0.001%	0.001% or less

Source: Ken W. Brown, "The 10-Point Test of Financial Condition: Toward an Easy-to-Use Assessment Tool for Smaller Cities." Government Finance Review, 9, no. 7 (December 1993): 24–25 (reprinted with permission of the Government Finance Officers Association).

Concluding Observations

The fiscal crises of New York City, Cleveland, and many other cities focused attention on the inadequacy of traditional financial statements to effectively manage a community's or agency's fiscal resources. The bond rating system, though useful as a means of analyzing a governmental unit's or agency's creditworthiness, is too crude and limited in scope to serve as an indicator of the fiscal health or fiscal strain. Early attempts to find a single fiscal health indicator, though not successful, provided insights about the development of a series of indicators and ratios that can provide early warnings, thereby permitting action to be taken before a potential problem arises.

Analyses of fiscal strain throughout the nation reveals that it is not inevitable or restricted to older communities, especially those in the Northeast and Midwest. It can appear in any community that fails to properly manage expenditure and debt (the equation's numerator) and private sector resources (the denominator). If a watchful eye is kept on the changes in these two critical factors, a balance can be maintained and a governmental financial crisis can be minimized or avoided. The Great Recession of 2007–2009 highlighted municipal mismanagement and reaffirmed the need to set aside reserves and prepare contingency plans for times of fiscal strain. Cities such as Madison and Irvine displayed effective planning and adaptation during the recent economic downturn and are thriving even as Detroit suffers from billions in debt and undergoes state conservatorship.

Notes

1. Terry Nichols Clark and Lorna Crowely Ferguson, *City Money* (New York: Columbia University Press, 1983), pp. 5–6.

2. See Nancy D. Suttenfield and L. Carole Wharton, "Seizing the Opportunities of Fiscal Retrenchment," *Public Budgeting and Review 13*, no. 2 (fall 1993): 49–62.

3. The Pew Charitable Trust, *Will the States Be Ready for the Next Recession?* (February 4, 2014), pp. 1–3.

4. Sauter, Michael B., and Thomas C. Frohlich, 24/7 Wall St. "24/7 Wall St.: Best- and Worst-run Cities." *USA Today*. January 3, 2014. http://www.usatoday.com/story/money/business/2014/01/03/best-worst-run-cities/4301919.

5. See Benoy Jacob and Rebecca Hendrick, "Assessing the Financial Condition of Local Government," in *Handbook of Local Government Fiscal Health*, eds. Helisse Levine et al. (San Francisco: Jones Bartlette Learning, 2013), p. 21.

6. New York State Comptroller, *Financial Condition Analysis*, Division of Local Government and School Accountability (Albany, New York: State Comptroller, 2013), p. 2.

7. Kansas City Missouri, *Financial Trends Monitoring System Report*, 2003–2012, p. 2.

8. See Clark and Ferguson, *City Money*; Lance W. Wolff and Jesse Hughes, "Net Available Assets as a Proxy for Financial Condition: A Model for Measuring and Reporting Resources Available for Local Government," *Government Finance Review 14*, no. 3 (June

1998); and Ken Brown, The "10-Point Test of Financial Conditions: Toward an Easy-to-Use Assessment Tool for Smaller Cities," *Government Finance Review 9*, no. 7 (December 1993).

9. Charles H. Levine, "Organizational Decline and Cutback Management," in *Managing Fiscal Stress*, ed. Charles H. Levine (Chatham, NJ: Chatham House Publishers, 198), p. 15.

10. Ibid., pp. 15–16.

11. Ibid.

12. Charles H. Levine, "The New Crisis in the Public Sector," in *Managing Fiscal Stress*, p. 12.

13. Ibid.

14. Clark and Ferguson, *City Money*, p. 6; see also J. Richard Aronson, *Municipal Fiscal Indicators* (Washington, DC: U.S. Department of Housing and Urban Development, Office of Policy Development, 1980); Sanford M. Groves, W. Maureen Godsey, and Martha A. Schulman, "Financial Indicators for Local Government," *Public Budgeting and Finance 1*, no. 2 (summer 1981): 5–19; Lyman A. Glenny and Frank Bower, "Warning Signals of Distress," in *Challenges of Retrenchment*, eds. James R. Mingle et al. (San Francisco: Jossey-Bass, 1981).

15. Nancy Humphrey, George Peterson, and Peter Wilson, *The Future of Cincinnati's Capital Plant* (Washington, DC: Urban Institute Press, 1979), pp. 7–13.

16. Roy Bahl, *Financing State and Local Governments in the 1980s* (New York: Oxford University Press, 1984), ch. 3.

17. Ibid., pp. 4–6.

18. Clark and Ferguson, *City Money*, pp. 4–5.

19. Regarding residential choice, a person will be more likely to move from a locality if the local policies diverge from his or her preferences.

20. Charles H. Levine, Irene S. Rubin, and George G. Wolohojian, *The Politics of Retrenchment: How Local Governments Manage Fiscal Stress* (Beverly Hills, CA: Sage Publications, 1981), p. 31.

21. Ibid., pp. 31–32.

22. Ibid.

23. Ibid., pp. 43–44.

24. U.S. Department of Housing and Urban Development (HUD), *Local Financial Management in the 1980s: Techniques for Responding to New Fiscal Realities* (Washington, DC: U.S. Government Printing Office, 1979); Bahl, *Financing State and Local Governments in the 1980s*, pp. 71–79.

25. See Irene S. Rubin, *Running in the Red State* (Albany: State University of New York Press, 1982), ch. 1; Clark and Ferguson, *City Money*, ch. 1; and Levine, et al. "The Politics of Retrenchment," pp. 16–19.

26. Clark and Ferguson, *City Money*, p. 224; see also Jeffrey L. Pressman, *Federal Programs and City Politics* (Berkeley: University of California Press, 1975).

27. Clark and Ferguson, *City Money*, p. 227.

28. Ibid.; see also Ken Newton, *Balancing the Books* (Beverly Hills, CA: Sage Publications, 1980).

29. See Roy Bahl, "Estimating Equity and Budgeting Effects of Financial Assumptions," *National Tax Journal 29* (March 1976): 54–72; Edward K. Hamilton and Francine Rabinovitz, *Whose Ox Would Be Healed? Financial Effects of Federalization of Welfare* (Durham, NC: Institute of Policy Sciences and Public Affairs and the Ford Foundation, 1977);

Bernard R. Gilford, *New York City: The Political Economy of Cosmopolitan Liberalism*, Annual Report (New York: Russell Sage Foundation, 1977).

30. See Dale Hickam, Robert Berne, and Leanna Stiefel, "Taxing over Debt Limits," *Public Administration Review 41* (July/August 1981): 445–453.

31. Clark and Ferguson, *City Money*, pp. 243–255.

32. Anne Spray Kinney, Peter Hutchinson, and David Osborne, "Funding Opportunities in Fiscal Stress: How to Balance Your Budget and Improve Performance," *Government Finance Review 18*, no. 4 (August 2002): 12.

33. Neal R. Pierce, "Recession Triggers Bitter System Conflict," *Government Finance Review* (February 2003): 48.

34. Kinney et al., "Funding Opportunities in Fiscal Stress: How to Balance Your Budget and Improve Performance," p. 27.

35. Robert Berne and Richard Schramm, *The Financial Solvency of Local Governments*, in *Working Papers in Planning* (Ithaca, NY: Cornell University Press, January 1979), pp. 3–7; and International City Managers Association (ICMA), *Evaluating Financial Condition* (Washington, DC: ICMA, 2003).

36. Sanford M. Groves, "An Introduction to Evaluating Financial Condition," in *Practical Financial Management*, ed. John Matzer Jr. (Washington, DC: International City Management Association, 1984), p. 14.

37. HUD, *Local Financial Management in the 1980s*, p. 27.

38. Ibid., p. 26.

39. Ibid., pp. 26–27.

40. Groves, "An Introduction to Evaluating Financial Condition," p. 17.

41. Ibid., p. 19.

42. Ibid.

43. Ibid., p. 21.

44. Ibid., pp. 22–21.

45. Ibid.

46. Karl Nollenberger revised text, by Sanford Grover and Maureen Goodsey, *Evaluating Financial Condition: A Handbook for Local Government* (Washington, DC: International City Managers Association, 2003), p. 1.

47. Brown, "The 10-Point Test of Financial Condition: Toward an Easy-to-Use Assessment Tool for Smaller Cities," *Government Finance Review*, p. 21; see also Wolff and Hughes, "Net Available Assets as a Proxy for Financial Condition: A Model for Measuring and Reporting Resources Available to Local Government," *Government Finance Review*, pp. 29–31. The authors suggest that their model is another way that may better allow local governments to cope with fiscal stress by suing a standardized reporting format for measuring and reporting fiscal condition.

48. Brown, "The 10-Point Test of Financial Condition," p. 22.

49. Ibid, pp. 22–23.

50. Ibid.

20

Fraud, Waste, and Abuse

Although the problem of fraud, waste, and abuse (FWA) has always existed in varying degrees in public and other not-for-profit agencies, public attention and concern were not focused on it until the latter part of the 1970s. A number of developments helped to raise this consciousness about FWA: (1) Inflation kept spiraling upward during this period; (2) the cost of conducting the business of government kept rising, accompanied by an increase in complaints concerning the quality and quantity of goods and services delivered; (3) there were widespread reports of kickbacks, collusion, and corruption among public officials; and (4) massive amounts of resources were being directed to the military, yet its readiness and fighting efficiency were being questioned and daily reports were uncovering the outrageous prices that the government was paying for materials from nonbid, private contractors.

The public's concern about FWA was a major factor in creating a crisis of confidence in both public and private institutions. Trust in government has reached its lowest point in decades. In a September 2013 Gallup poll, 81 percent of Americans polled reported their belief that the federal government will do what is right only some of the time—or never. Just 19 percent believed that the federal government will do what is right most of the time or just about always. This is the greatest level of distrust polled since 1994. The American public's lack of faith in public institutions arises, in part, from the perception of rampant corruption, misappropriation, and waste throughout all levels of government.[1] Trust in state and local governments is higher, but the U.S. federal government is facing a public image crisis and should take necessary measures to restore public confidence.

The Great Recession of 2007–2009 exacerbated the public's mistrust of both the private and public sectors. Large, private institutions, such as Bank of America and Freddie Mac, experienced massive financial scandals and were subsequently saved from bankruptcy only by government loans—that is, taxpayer money. Many Americans saw this as a misallocation of their tax dollars and as a reward for misleading accounting practices and corporate greed that put the companies in dire fiscal situations.

A Daniel Yankelovich poll performed in 1977 registered a significant rise of public mistrust in national institutions. Trust in government declined from an 80 percent approval rating during the late 1950s to about 33 percent in 1976. In the business sector, approval fell from a level of approximately 70 percent during the late 1950s to 15 percent in 1970. Three out of four people polled felt that too much power was concentrated in the hands of too few people, that federal officials could not generally be believed, and that far too many people were taking payoffs in exchange for favors.[2] Tax money was wasted and misappropriated, many people felt, and when it came to having a say about how things were run, "the little guy did not stand a chance."[3]

A recent poll estimated the number of dishonest Americans at 31 percent of the population (rising sharply from the 12 percent estimated in 1961). Forty percent are identified as situationally dishonest, suggesting that those individuals in this category will be honest or dishonest depending on which situation provides the greatest payoff.[4] Employee fraud costs American businesses approximately $200 billion annually, compared to the $11 billion cost of violent crime. Banks estimate that 95 percent of all losses are caused by employees. In contrast, bank robbery and customer fraud result in only 5 percent of crime losses.[5]

During the last twenty years, FWA scandals both in the public and private sector gained national attention. In the private sector, the ZZZZ Best Company of southern California concocted a scheme that fraudulently put hundreds of millions of dollars of assets on its books. Discovery led to the conviction of the owner and many of his subordinates. The management of one Denver company broke into the auditor's office to obtain work papers and secretly planted evidence to inflate the financial results of the company. In Ohio, the Phar-Mor company's president and chief financial officers were indicted for stealing more than 50 percent of the company's assets.[6] Enron and WorldCom created billions of dollars of fictitious sales to conceal losses causing major bankruptcies. Thousands of employees lost their jobs. Stockholders lost millions, and many retirees lost their pensions. Bernie Madoff orchestrated the greatest Ponzi scheme every, defrauding the public of $65 billion.

This chapter introduces the reader to the problem of FWA in not-for-profit organizations, discussing how it comes about and how institutional controls may be developed or strengthened to minimize it. Particular emphasis is given to examining internal controls and describing vulnerability assessment determinations.

The Grace Commission

Formally known as the President's Private Sector Survey on Cost Control (PPSSCC), the Grace Commission, headed by J. Peter Grace, has been a vocal critic of the federal government's waste and inefficiency. President Reagan charged the commission with evaluating the government's operations as if it were a private sector enterprise, and the commission concluded that $424 billion in annual savings could be realized if recommended procedures reducing waste and inefficiency were implemented. A number of outrageous examples of inefficiency and waste were circulated to the press, including (1) the federal General Services Administration's employment of seventeen times as many people and use of fourteen times as much space as a comparable private sector enterprise; (2) the price tag of $61,250 for a Veterans Administration hospital bed, or about four times that of a similar unit constructed in the private sector; and (3) a $91 price tag for a 3¢ screw.

Although the Grace Commission did much to highlight and direct public attention to waste and inefficiency in government, it oversimplified the problems it was studying. The methods used for conducting the study were ad hoc, unsystematic, and difficult to defend. In fact, most of the outrageous examples of waste and inefficiency that it identified could be explained away for one reason or another. Moreover, the commission's rationale that private sector production of goods and services is superior to the public sector's capability is not entirely defensible.[7]

If the commission were to evaluate J. Peter Grace's own W. R. Grace Company, its rating might be comparable to or perhaps even be worse than that of the public sector. The 1971 purchase of the Mr. Gasket Company of Brooklyn, Ohio, by the Grace Company provides a good case in point. Soon after the $17 million company was purchased, many of the experienced middle- and lower-level managers who had "grease under their nails" were dismissed and replaced by MBA degree holders imbued with the Grace management philosophy and perspective. Ten years after the purchase of the company, the original owner, Joe Hrudka, was offered the opportunity to repurchase the Mr. Gasket Company for $4 million ($13 million less than the original selling price). Within two years of the repurchase, the company's market value was estimated at slightly more than $150 million.[8]

A number of important observations can be made here. Hrudka's reacquisition of the company brought the immediate rehiring of more than 85 employees who were let go by Grace. A Mr. Gasket official expressed the opinion that it was necessary to rehire these former employees and dismiss Grace's MBAs because the Grace managers "simply did not know the business." The point was made that there was virtually no correlation between job requirements and the experience of the people who were hired to fill them. The major indictments of Grace management included the following:

- It failed to establish effective communication links with suppliers and distributors.
- It failed to study and understand its competitors.
- It forced out the people who knew the business when it severed its links with the original owners.

- It suffered from decision paralysis: Corporate headquarters had to be consulted for even the most routine business decisions.
- There was a lack of sound and creative ideas about the business. In addition, the time lag for implementation of ideas for new products continued to lengthen.
- The MBAs, with a push from headquarters, selected a profit level and strove to realize it without understanding how to reach it.
- Only items with big profits were pushed. The "nickel and dime items" were not considered, even though these were where the profits were to be made.
- There was too much preoccupation with time and motion studies and too little focus on finding the right product and appropriate mix at the appropriate time.

The former Westinghouse Electric[9] provides another compelling example showing that the public sector does not have a monopoly on inefficiency. During the 1980s, Westinghouse made clear to its engineering and transportation divisions (as well as others) that they had to produce a minimum profit level of 15 percent. This forced the division managers to dutifully obtain contracts with at least a 15 percent profit margin. The problem with these contracts was that they were more illusory than reality when it came to meeting the agreed-upon profit target. The engineering and transportation division heads were playing the bureaucratic game. When hard times came to Westinghouse, it jettisoned its engineering and transportation division. The data revealed that the division was not meeting Westinghouse's profit target. Transformation from within was viewed as an unacceptable option. The division was sold to AEG of Germany. Within four years of the purchase, the number of workers had been increased from 800 to 1,200, and the division was generating robust profits.

In summary, it can be said that the private W. R. Grace Company was oblivious to the business environment in which it was operating. It moved too slowly and operated like a rigid or mature bureaucracy in an area that required a keen understanding of its environment and the ability to react quickly an ever-changing business environment. Grace's cadre of middle-level managers was inappropriate for the time, place, and business. At the end of ten years, experience had not increased, and the learning curve had not been smoothed. Thus W. R. Grace, to forestall the possibility of the business's falling apart, was willing to resell it for only the worth of its assets. Similarly, Westinghouse could not get its engineering and transportation division to produce targeted profits, because it failed to determine the factors necessary to motivate its workers to produce these targeted expectations.

An important point that might be made here is that the private sector's supposed productive superiority over the public sector has very little basis in fact. Atlanta, Georgia, privatized its water system with the expectation that citizens would get better service at less cost but was soundly disappointed. The private company selected did not deliver on its promises, prompting the city to reassume operation of the water system. It is not an organization's being public or private that determines its efficiency or productivity, as the national report *Creating a Government That Works Better and Costs Less* stresses (see chapter 2).[10] Instead, it is a matter of having effective members of management who can make astute business decisions while motivating workers toward optimal production.

Without question, FWA is a serious problem in the public sector and perhaps also, to a lesser extent, in other not-for-profit organizations. At the federal level of government, the General Accounting Office (GAO) estimates from $5 billion to $50 billion in fraud annually, whereas Donald Lambro suggests that up to $100 billion is lost due to waste and abuse.[11] As noted earlier, the Grace Commission put the figure at $424 billion. A former inspector-general at the Department of Health, Education, and Welfare (now the Department of Health and Human Services) estimated the loss of as much as $8 billion that department alone due to FWA. Hence, the general public feels that government officials waste a large portion of taxpayers' money.

Defining Fraud, Waste, and Abuse

There is no universal definition of FWA. Sometimes the FWA concept is used interchangeably with terms such as *bribery* and *corruption*. Most observers do agree that it involves behavior that violates norms and standards. Obviously, the definition of FWA will be affected by value judgments. Thus its application should, as far as possible, be context-specific. The general attributes that might reasonably be identified with FWA have been summarized as follows:

- It is a violation of public trust.
- It is a conversion of public benefit to private ends.
- It is a perversion of authority and the commission of an unacceptable act.
- It is a failure to enforce laws, rules, and regulations or to apply sanctions to a given situation.
- It is bribing a public official.
- It is making false statements or claims.
- It is the intentional or unintentional misapplication or wasteful use of public resources.[12]

Although the general definition and attributes discussed here are useful, greater specificity is needed to be able to apply the concept of FWA consistently in specific situations.

Fraud involves trickery, cheating, and intentional deception that results in an individual or individuals relinquishing lawful rights or ownership of property. There are two kinds of fraud that cause injury: *actual* fraud and *constructive* fraud. When someone relies on an individual's intentional misinterpretation of material fact, this is called *actual fraud*. *Constructive fraud* is unlike actual fraud in that it is not caused by self-interest or evil design but by the very nature of the act.[13] Fraud is, in essence, an intentional or unintentional illegal and wrongful act employed explicitly for obtaining an asset or benefit from public programs. The conditions that give rise to fraud have been grouped into three categories: (1) situational pressures, such as heavy losses and high debt (see Table 20.1); (2) perceived opportunities encouraging fraud, such as inadequate internal controls, poor accounting records, inadequate authorization for transactions, lack of physical security over assets, and lack of independent checks; and (3) personal characteristics, such as poor moral character, low credit rating, and rationalizing behavior.[14] The Sarbanes–Oxley Act was passed as a deterrence against fraudulent actions that companies such as Enron, Worldcom and Waste Management had perpetrated in the public. The act mandates that public companies have an independent audit of internal controls when reporting financial information. The common forms and methods used to commit fraud include the following:

- Intentional mistakes, such as arithmetical or clerical errors—for example, purposely omitting an entry or making incorrect calculations
- Purposeful misinterpretation of the facts
- Recording of nonexistent transactions
- Intentional misallocation of contract costs
- Embezzlement and theft by means of deceit and suppression of the truth
- Removal of varying amounts of money from cash funds and registers
- Overcharging of clientele or service recipients while pocketing the difference
- Placement of fictitious names on the payroll
- Payment of advances to nonexistent employees
- Receipt of kickbacks from suppliers for overpriced or inferior goods
- Payment for self-completed false invoices
- Taking of agency materials, equipment, and services[15]
- Pocketing of money from delinquent accounts
- Submission of false remittances of electronic claims for payment[16]
- False representation of a material fact by words or conduct
- Illegal acts involving the obtaining of an asset or something of value through wilful misrepresentation[17]
- Overwithholding or underfunding of pension benefits
- Overpayment of doctors, clerics, and hospitals
- Overcharging for travel expenses
- Theft of money from one customer account to pay another (known as "lapping")
- Theft of duplicate payments, especially utility payments

- Creation of bogus credit memos for receipts of payments
- While pocketing portions of the receipts, paying suppliers that should not be paid or that should not be paid as much

Fraud may be motivated by a number of reasons:

- Financial problems, as illustrated by the Montgomerys in Alexandria, Georgia (see Table 20.1)
- Conducive environmental pathology or ethics and lax controls allowing for the appropriation of monetary and nonmonetary assets
- Feeling of underappreciation and lack of rewards for consistent or exceptional work
- Ego gratification for beating the system, sometimes particularly in computer fraud
- Ideological perspectives, including political and religious reasons[18]

Fraudsters can involve different creative approaches. In spring 2009, fraudsters illegally obtained $2 million from West Virginia. Fraudsters studied the West Virginia accounts payable payment system for paying vendors and initiated the following actions:[19]

- West Virginia forms for purchasing and accounts payable were forged based on copies found on the Internet.
- The state was sent paperwork asking for deposits in what appeared to be new legitimate accounts with appropriate documentation to accounts payable personnel.
- These fake documents were then used to sweep funds overseas.

Waste most often comprises unintentional acts that result in inefficient practices or the misapplication of resources, causing increased public costs or reduced benefits to potential recipients.

Waste involves the taxpayers' not receiving reasonable value for money in any funded government program owing to an inappropriate act or omission by individuals who have control over government resources. This relates to executive, judicial or legislative action. Waste goes beyond fraud and abuse, because most waste does not involve violation of the law. It typically relates to mismanagement and lack of oversight.[20]

Abuse involves the violation of agency rules, procedures, and regulations, impairing the effective and efficient implementation of an agency's programs. Often it involves behavior that is deficient or improper when compared to behavior that would be considered reasonable and proper. Acts of abuse typically involve the reduction or denial of goods or services rightfully due to eligible participants. There is an element of ambiguity about abuse, because

TABLE 20.1   Fraud and the Purchasing Director: Alexandria, Georgia

Background

Jason Montgomery had been director of purchasing for 16 years. He bought supplies and secured various services for the city. He was an outstanding employee who had a reputation for integrity and dedication. He was married and had four children. His salary, combined with that of his wife, amounted to $46,000. This allowed the Montgomerys to live a comfortable lifestyle in a middle-class neighborhood in Alexandria. Their level of spending permitted them little opportunity to save.

The Problem

When Jason's oldest son entered college, Jason had enough money to pay the college expenses. A year later, he knew that his second son would be ready to begin college. Jason realized that he would not be in a financial position to send his other children to college. Given his position and his familiarity with suppliers, Jason approached the buyer of one of the local suppliers who had previously offered him favors and asked if he could direct a greater share of the city business to his firm. Jason sought the buyer and gave him a proposal. For a $1,000 monthly honorarium, Jason would increase the volume of city business to the supplier's firm.

Soon after the payments to Jason had begun, the supplier increased his prices and started shipping a cheaper grade of materials. When Jason sought an explanation for the changes, he was told that there were no plans to return to the original prices and quality of products. Besides, there was no way that Jason could go to his supervisors and admit that he was taking kickbacks. By the time a colleague inadvertently discovered the arrangement, the city had overpaid the suppliers approximately $300,000 for paper products.

Jason was a model employee for 16 years, yet he participated in an illegal and dishonest act. He was subject to the three factors (perceived pressure, perceived opportunity to commit and conceal, and an excuse to rationalize the behavior as acceptable) that have been used to explain why people participate in fraud. Jason had fallen victim to financial pressure and the opportunity to conceal.

Source: Adapted from W. Steve Albrecht, "Fraud in Government Entities: The Perpetrators and the Types of Fraud." Government Finance Review, 7, no. 6 (December 1991): 27.

value judgments play a bigger role here than in the case of fraud. The abusive individual may be described as being ineffective or inefficient, or as misinterpreting policies and program guidelines. Abuse is often more insidious than fraud, making it more difficult to combat.[21]

Internal Control Systems and Fwa

If fraud, waste, and abuse are to be minimized over the long run, the establishment of a control system that provides information about the accuracy and reliability of an agency's assets is required. The internal control system must ensure that the agency's accounting transactions are accurate and complete and that procedures for detecting malfunctions are effective.[22] An internal control system is made up of a set of procedures and actions designed by the management of an agency to facilitate policy execution/compliance and mitigate FWA to a minimum. It was noted in chapter 3 that internal controls have two basic elements: (1) *administrative control*, consisting of procedures and records to ensure the implementation of agency decisions as intended, and (2) *accounting control*, consisting of procedures concerned with the safeguarding of assets and reliability of financial records. Internal control provides reasonable assurance that assets are used for government purposes, that public and not-for-profit information is accurate, and that employees comply with laws and regulations. To ensure reliability, an internal control system requires the establishment of a regular internal audit program to monitor the system, evaluate its performance, and provide the agency management with the required timely feedback. An independent auditor audits the entire internal control system on an annual basis.

Internal Control as a System of Action

The federal Office of Management and Budget (OMB) requires that each agency evaluate its internal control system. An effective system of internal controls needs more than administrative and internal accounting controls. It also requires continual feedback of information to management indicating how well agency policies are complied with and financial information activities are being executed. The internal control system aids management in monitoring policy implementation, maintaining the accuracy of financial records, reporting on weaknesses and remedial actions required to improve those deficiencies. "By frequently checking agency performance, the internal audit serves to deter fraud, error, waste, and abuse in government."[23] While the feedback mechanism is an important factor in mitigating FWA, each agency's overall system of internal control still must be audited periodically by independent auditors. Four major components make up the internal control system: *administrative controls*, *internal accounting*, *internal audits*, and *external controls*. The most critical and cost effective of these is the system of internal accounting control, which emphasizes the following:

- *authorization*—to ensure that transactions are executed in accordance with an agency's specified guidelines
- *recording*—to ensure that transactions are recorded to permit the preparation of reports in accordance with generally accepted accounting principles (GAAP) and to maintain accountability over assets
- *access to assets*—to permit only authorized personnel to have access to assets
- *asset accountability*—to compare the records for assets with existing assets on a periodic basis, taking appropriate corrective action when relevant differences occur[24]

"Information on assets, liabilities, revenues, and expenditures must be reliable to meet legal demands and to allow investors, stockholders, and the public to evaluate the organization properly."[25]

Ideally, internal accounting controls, when properly established, become a network of checks and procedures that act as an important barrier and deterrent to improper conduct. A breach or violation is likely to occur only when management is negligent and fails to effectively monitor and maintain the system. Internal accounting controls may be classified as *preventative* or *detective*. Most often, they are employed in combination. *Preventative controls* are implemented before an event's occurrence and may be viewed as instruments of deterrence, whereas *detective controls* function after the event. The former are preferable and result in greater FWA cost savings, but the typical organization should have both types in place. No single type or set of procedures, rules, or organizational controls is applicable to all agencies at all times. Instead, the appropriate type of internal control will depend on the specific nature of each agency.[26]

There are a number of warning signals, or "red flags," that may be precursors to fraudulent behavior and activities affecting the accounting system. Regarding people behaviors, the following should give cause for possible scrutiny and examination:

- Unexplained change in lifestyle
- Close or abnormal relationship with vendors or suppliers
- Constant seeking of loans from fellow employees
- Excessive use of alcohol or drugs
- Unexplained changes in behavior or mood

Regarding the accounting system activities that should be given close attention and review, the following are included:

- Missing documents or gaps in the transaction numbering system
- Unexplained or unusual refunds to clients
- Unbudgeted expenses or unbalanced accounts
- Unexpected decrease in the average time of collection payments
- Increasing backlog in recording transactions

The Preaudit as Preventative Check

The *preaudit check* is a system that determines the appropriateness of a proposed action before it takes place. For example, purchase orders and vouchers are verified and checked before the orders are sent to vendors, and vouchers are carefully reviewed/authorized before any payments are made to vendors (suppliers). Among the objectives of the preaudit are the following:

- Ascertain that forms authorizing the disbursement of funds are complete and accurate.
- Determine that requests for payment are in accordance with administrative rules and procedures and comply with statutory requirements and contractual agreements,
- Determine that appropriations are available for the request for payment.
- Determine that the price and purchase are reasonable.

In the long run, an effective system of internal controls is the most useful means for reducing FWA in government (see Figure 20.1). A strong system of internal controls will help ensure that resources are used in accordance with legal requirements, regulations, and policies. It facilitates the generation of reliable data that are maintained and properly disclosed in reports to aid in safeguarding resources and minimizing their loss due to FWA. Several categories have been used to summarize the general requirements of an internal control system:

- Competent, well-trained employees who are provided with clear lines of authority, effective supervision, and technical training
- Appropriate and effective segregation of duties (e.g., separating the custody of the asset function from the accounting for asset activity, separating the original recording of accounting transactions from posting to the general ledgers, separating record-keeping from operational responsibility)
- Proper procedures for authorization (e.g., preventing the same individuals who authorize the purchase of materials from receiving them)
- Sufficient documentation and records (requiring that forms be used on which all transactions are summarized and entered, including purchase orders, subsidiary ledgers, and time cards)
- Physical control over assets, records, and forms to ensure protection against theft, fire, and other damage
- Independent and unannounced checks on performance by having someone not responsible for the transactions check or oversee the appropriateness and execution of performance

Electronic Data Processing and Control

Electronic data processing and control (EDP) has become an increasingly important part of modern management. Financial management has been especially amenable to EDP application. In fact, instances of computer-related fraud and abuse have been occurring far more, on average, than fraud and abuse through conventional methods, both in the not-for-profit sector and in private organizations. In government, because of improper control, programmers and employees who have access to computers have been able to divert large sums of government money for their own use.

Although EDP has not changed the purposes or objectives sought by internal controls, it has significantly affected internal control systems:

- EDP systems significantly reduce the requirement for clerical employees, limiting the opportunities for segregated functions.
- Information is maintained internally in the machine, retarding the conventional monitoring approach.

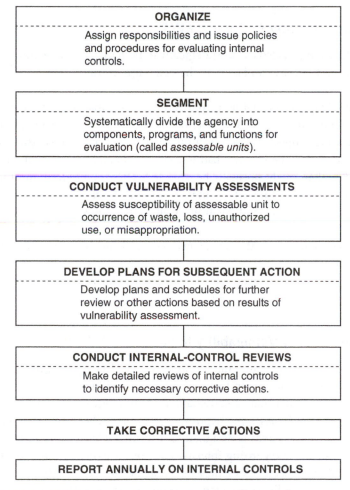

FIGURE 20.1   OMB process to evaluate internal controls.

Source: U.S. Government Accounting Office, Implementation of the Federal Managers' Financial Integrity Act: First Year (Washington, DC: GAO, 1984), p. 3.

- Most transactions, documents, and record-keeping–related transactions are maintained by computer, drastically reducing or eliminating the "audit trail."[27]

At the federal level of government, Congress passed the Federal Managers Financial Integrity Act in 1982, requiring that each agency implement a system of internal accounting and administrative controls consistent with the standards prescribed by the comptroller general. Particularly noteworthy is the requirement that each agency evaluate its system of internal controls, indicating to what extent it is in conformity with the comptroller general's standard in a report to Congress and the president.

Using the Computer to Combat FWA

The EDP system can also work strategically to help management combat FWA. Computer technology can facilitate the detection of fraud:

- Identify unusual activities by purchasing agents that suggest the possibility of fraud. (In this case, a number of small identical orders were placed with the same supplier. By means of the sequence of the invoice, the computer revealed that the supplier had few customers and was receiving far more orders than might normally be expected. These computer indicators initiated an investigation, which, in turn, revealed fraud.)[28]
- Identify Medicaid and Medicare claims that show a pattern suggesting potential fraud.
- Match welfare and other recipients to payroll and death records to identify potential abuses.
- Identify taxpayers who file differing tax returns for state and federal governments.

Assessing Agency Vulnerability to Fwa

When making a fraud vulnerability assessment (FVA), an agency's internal control system is the major focus of attention. Vulnerability assessment is predominantly a quantitative systematic technique for measuring an agency's exposure to FWA. In assessing exposure, an agency relies heavily on how well its internal control system is designed to minimize FWA. Close attention and heightened scrutiny regarding internal controls is likely to improve the reliability of vulnerability assessment, which may be viewed essentially as an analysis of the susceptibility of an agency, or any component thereof, to avoidable loss (including a dissipation of assets and unauthorized use or distribution of resources), inaccurate reports and information, unethical or unlawful actions,

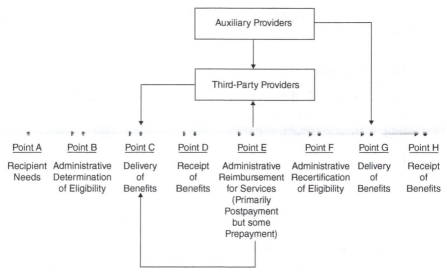

FIGURE 20.2   Program vulnerability points.

and other activities that may adversely affect the public image and standing of an organization.

By means of a survey approach, an evaluation of an agency's potential for or vulnerability to FWA can be determined. Note that the emphasis is placed on the potential for FWA and not on how existing internal controls actually prevent it.[29] FVA is thus an estimate of which units are susceptible to FWA: management, program, activity, project, function, or other units. In Figure 20.2, vulnerability points for auxiliary and third-party providers are identified from vulnerability point A to H. Each vulnerability point carries with it particular risks associated with the program concerned.[30]

In the U.S. Department of Housing and Urban Development (HUD), not only are existing systems evaluated for susceptibility to FWA, but new and substantially revised programs are also subjected to FVAs. "The vulnerability assessment not only identifies the potential for FWA, but it also outlines the risks and abuses that may occur if adequate management controls are not maintained at the frontend."[31] Known past abuse, weaknesses, or failure of management controls are clearly identified. The objective is the maintenance of a fraud vulnerability assessment system that permits programs to be managed without fraud, waste, and inefficiency.[32] Despite the superior FVA system that was established in HUD, widespread FWA took place during the 1980s because effective monitoring and follow-up recommendations were ignored or not enforced in a timely manner. This suggests that no system is self-executing—its success only goes as far as the ability of the people who administer it. Consistently evaluating management actions and responses can help to mitigate instances of overriding internal controls or ignoring systematic FWA opportunities.

The Vulnerability Process

As the first stage in FVA, the structure of the organization should be analyzed in terms of its administrative functions. The organization should be classified according to its various components:

- Programs or functions, broken down by subprograms or subfunctions
- Matrix of the organization, indicating each department's contribution to the operation of the program
- Degree of independence exercised by the program function
- Allocated budget
- Relative centralization and decentralization
- Personnel assigned to each program
- Determination of goals, objectives, and the delivery system
- Management sanctions in place
- Appropriate incentives in place to motivate sound management action against FWA

The degree of centralization and independence is an important factor in carrying out an FVA, because it tends to suggest the intensity of supervision that may be present. When programs have multiple locations, it is usual to perform FVAs at the various different sites.[33]

In the second stage, each program or responsibility center is evaluated for an FVA by considering the factors that lead to FWA, such as inherent risk in the agency functions and in the organizational environment. The important objective at this stage is the development of criteria to produce a ranking of the programs' or functions' vulnerability to FWA.[34] The use of the ranking approach has been gaining wider use. Among the agencies employing it are the U.S. Defense Audit Agency, the HUD inspector-general, and the GAO in its *Framework for Assessing Job Vulnerability to Ethical Problems*.[35]

The *Task Force Report* (Government Accountants Association) on internal controls has suggested a guide (see Figure 20.3) that could be used in vulnerability assessment. The FVA has three main steps:

1. Conduct an analysis of three general control environments. This includes an examination of the personnel's competence and integrity; effectiveness of the delegation and communication of authority; and an overview of the organizational structure, budgeting, and reporting practices, and the organizational checks and balances to financial control and internal auditing.
2. Examine the inherent risk, such as outside pressures on the agency, unclear or convoluted goals and objectives, budgeting constraints, decentralization,

VULNERABILITY FACTORS	RISK VALUE	VULNERABILITY FACTORS	RISK VALUE
Highly Controlled-Little Vulnerability		**Moderately Controlled-Moderate Vulnerability**	

Precise Legislative Authority
Minimal Budget Authority/Outlays
Complete Government Program
  Administration
Ample Administrative Resources Provided
No Commercial Value
Minimal Public Involvement
Extensive Written Procedures
Timely and Adequate Financial Reporting
		Broad Legislative Authority
		Moderate Budget Authority/Outlays
		Joint Third-Party and Government Program
		  Administration
		Adequate Administrative Resources Provided
		Substantial Commercial Value
		Moderate Public Involvement
		Essential Areas Have Written Procedures
		Financial Reports Adequate but Not Timely	

Little Control-Limited Vulnerability		**No Control-High Vulnerability**	
Unspecific Legislative Authority Limited Budget Authority/Outlays Mostly Third-Party Program Administration Minimal Administrative Resources Provided Limited Commercial Value Selective Public Involvement Partially Effective Written Procedures Financial Reports Not Comprehensive		Value Legislative Authority Large Budget Authority/Outlays All Third-Party Program Administration No Administrative Resources Provided High Commercial Value Widespread Public Involvement No Written Procedures Late and Incomplete Financial Reporting	

FIGURE 20.3   Vulnerability assessment grid.

Source: "Federal Executive Reporting on Internal Control—An AGA Study." Government Accountants Journal, 29, no. 3 (fall 1980): 16.

limited age and life expectancy, and potential problems suggested by prior studies.

3. Make a preliminary evaluation of the adequacy of internal controls.[36]

After these three FVA steps are completed, a determination about the vulnerability of the program or function can be made. The results of the FVA provide the input to conduct internal control reviews on each program and administrative function. The flow process for vulnerability determination employed in the Department of Housing and Urban Development is shown in Figure 20.4.

Incentive Mechanisms to Minimize Fwa

Although incentive mechanisms are an important factor in the fight against FWA, the topic has been insufficiently addressed. The establishment of a conducive, accommodative, and effective organizational environment is most desirable. In such an environment, effective controls will be in place and ethical practices emphasized and followed at all management levels. In addition, honesty must be viewed as an indispensable asset to the organization. Among the positive practices that should be observed are the following:

- Maintenance of an open line of communication with employees
- Hiring and promotion only of competent and trustworthy employees

- Close examination of the work of employees on a continuing basis
- Regular review and appropriate changes to weak control areas
- Unannounced inspection tours
- Thorough investigation of public complaints, tips, and rumors
- Careful review of budgetary and MIS reports, giving attention to material deviations
- Clear and early assignment of responsibility
- Prompt issuance of agency policy[37]

Auditors' Independence and fwa

Private sector revelations about the collapse of a number of major corporations such as Enron, WorldCom, and the recent Lehman Brothers bankruptcy have focused attention on the role that the external auditor plays in the dissemination of financial information to users. Because the external auditors' relationships with their clients went beyond the expected norms, their independence was scrutinized by Congress and the public. The appearance of the interactions engendered the view that lack of independence might have played a significant role in creating the ensuing problems. Without independence, the vital credibility that the public attributes to the auditor's opinions as to the fair presentation of financial statements is impaired. "Lack of auditors' independence creates the opportunity to perpetrate fraudulent acts. The opportunity may be intentional (planned and contrived) or it may be situational, arising from the choice created in a passing moment."[38]

Because of the massive accounting scandals that have been publicized about private sector companies, mistrust and lack of confidence have become increasingly pervasive among the public, thus the need for arm's-length transactions (lack of conflict of interest) between government officials and auditors. Confidence requires independence in both appearance and fact. The GAO's *Government Auditing Standards*, or the "Yellow Book," states: "In all matters relating to the audit and work, the audit organization and the individual auditors, whether in government or public, should be free both in fact

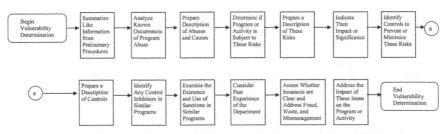

FIGURE 20.4   Fraud vulnerability determination.

and appearance from personal, external, and organizational impairments to independence."[39]

Explaining the Fraud Triangle

The fraud triangle model (see Figure 20.5) allows us to explain the factors that influence individuals to commit occupational fraud. The convergence of three factors influences the fraudulent behavior. If the organization wishes to minimize or prevent fraud, it must attempt to understand the operating factors causing the fraud and to take timely proactive actions to remove one of the elements of the triangle to reduce the likelihood of the crime. Three factors (pressure/incentive, opportunity, and rationalization) have been identified as the interacting forces.[40]

Pressure/Incentive

Pressure or need constitutes the first leg of the fraud triangle. This is the cause of the individual committing the crime. There are a multitude of things

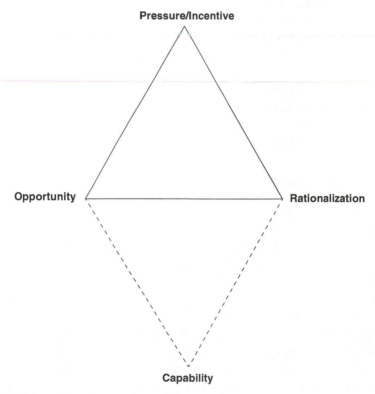

FIGURE 20.5   Fraud triangle and diamond.

involved in the factor, including unsolvable financial problems, addiction, and simply greed.[41]

Opportunity

This is the second leg of the fraud triangle. Opportunity enables fraud to occur, typically from weak internal control processes, poor management oversight, and one's critical position and authority in the organization. This leg provides the method by which the fraud will be undertaken. The individual settles on a means with the lowest risk of detection that can be employed to solve the problem at hand. Because the opportunity leg is the one that management exercises the greatest control, the organization must constantly develop and review its procedures and processes that are vulnerable to fraud always making it less tempting to facilitating employees to commit acts that they would not ordinarily do.[42]

Rationalization

Rationalization represents the third leg of the fraud triangle. It relates to the mindset of the fraudster that justifies the fraud act. The fraudsters do not view themselves as criminal but simply honest people who must deal with bad circumstances. The fraudster finds a way to justify the crime in such a way that he or she views as unavoidable, necessary, and justifiable action such as:

- Action necessary to save family
- No help available from the outside
- Borrowing money for the short term
- Feeling of being underpaid by employer[43]

The Fraud Diamond

Forensic observer suggests that the existence of the element in the fraud triangle may not be enough to explain why fraud occurs. "Often unrecognized and unnoticed is the fundamental reasoning for the fraudulent activity—the element of the human mind and the individual behaviors (i.e., the wrongdoer's "capability to commit the fraud")."[44]

Behavioral scientists have not been able to identify the psychological factors, valid and reliable attributes, or markers that can identify the propensity(s) that cause people to commit fraud. Researchers have, however, identified characteristics and personality traits that may level people to engage in fraud.[45] David Wolfe and Dana Hermanson note: "opportunity opens the doorway to fraud and incentive and rationalizations can draw a person toward it. But the person must have the capability to recognize the open doorway as an opportunity and to take advantage of it by working through, not once, but time and again."[46] Many of the multibillion dollar fraud would never have taken place had it not been where the right person with the appropriate capability was not positioned at the right place at opportune time. When the four elements of fraud are viewed from a collective perspective, the convergence could likely reflect an explanation as follows:[47]

- Pressure/incentive: an urge or desire resulting in the commitment of fraud
- Opportunity: the system, processes, procedures, and oversight manifesting weak links that can be exploited by the person with necessary skills and capability
- Rationalization: Fraudster feeling confident that the very low possibility of detection and the magnitude of benefits is worth the risk
- Capability: High confidence believing that he or she has the right abilities and traits to successfully achieve the fraud objection

Although some of the fraud elements overlap, the real value or contribution of the fourth leg or diamond is that capability is a distinct requirement that is necessary for assessing risk exposure or vulnerability, allowing the fraud to be committed. Viewed in this context, the fraud diamond or the addition of the capability component moves the explanation of fraud beyond the three-legged triangle, which puts emphasis mainly on environmental factors.

To be able to deal effectively with the capability risk or vulnerability, an organization must explicitly assess the capabilities of its top executives and key personnel. It is important to remember that personnel capabilities have significant risk potential, requiring checks and balances, continuing review of and enhanced or expanded audit scope and testing.

Training Programs to Combat FWA

The commitment to the fight against FWA has been given the greatest formal acceptance at the federal level of government. All departments and major agencies of the federal government have an inspector-general whose major objective is to minimize or eradicate FWA. There are a number of places throughout the government where seminars and specialized training in FWA techniques and approaches can be learned. Although these training programs are not yet well organized, some credible efforts have been instituted:

1. The Graduate School of Agriculture in Washington, D.C. (U.S. Department of Agriculture affiliated but an independent entity) conducts a three-day seminar throughout the year from October to September on (1) prevention and detection of FWA, (2) evaluation and reporting on internal control systems, and (3) internal controls in automated systems.

2. The General Accounting Office provides a three-and-a-half-day seminar on fraud awareness for its employees involved in the FWA area.

3. The Association of Government Accountants provides, from time to time, a short seminar on financial investigation.

4. The Federal Office of Personnel Management offers a two-day seminar on evaluating, improving, and reporting on internal controls in federal agencies.

5. The U.S. Defense Contract Audit Agency provides a self-study course for its auditors on the prevention and detection of fraud, waste, and abuse. Additionally, all audit-related training courses stress FWA prevention and detection.

6. In the private sector, the National Association of Certified Fraud Examiners (NACFE) offers training seminars.

7. The John Jay School of Criminal Justice offers a Master's of Public Administration (MPA) Inspector-General program.

Concluding Observations

Special emphasis on the comparative efficiency of public versus private agencies indicates that there is very little, or no, inherent superiority of one type over the other. The systematic problems that must be faced to combat FWA require creative and innovative leadership. Estimates of the amount of FWA in government vary significantly depending on who is making the estimate. Irrespective of the estimates, the public feels that the degree of FWA is extreme and that governmental officials cannot be trusted. Distrust of government also extends to other institutions, including the supposedly more efficient business community. The greatest efforts toward eradicating FWA have been devoted to strengthening the internal control system. This includes paying greater attention to internal auditing and to vulnerability assessments of FWA. It is this author's view that the long-run approach to minimization of FWA requires *resocialization*—a change of the internalized norms and philosophy of public officials.

Notes

1. "Trust in Government." *Gallup.com*. Gallup, September 2013. http://www.gallup.com/poll/164663/american-trust-government-generally-down-year.aspx.

2. Reported in Seymour Lipset, "The Decline of Confidence in American Institutions," *Political Science Quarterly 98*, no. 3 (fall 1983): 379–398.

3. Michael Johnston, *Political Corruption and Public Policy in America* (Monterey, CA: Brooks/Cole Publishing, 1982), p. 1.

4. See Richard C. Hollinger, *Dishonesty in the Work Place: A Manager's Guide to Preventing Employee Theft* (Park Ridge, IL: London House Press, 1989).

5. W. Steve Albrecht, "Fraud in Government Entities: The Perpetrators and the Types of Fraud," *Government Finance Review 7*, no. 6 (December 1991): 27; see also, Joseph T. Wells, "Six Common Myths about Fraud," *Journal of Accountancy 169* (February 1990): 82–88.

6. Werner Grosshaus, "Internal Assessments—Are They Really Needed in Performance Auditing?" *Government Accountant's Journal 40*, no. 4 (winter 1992): 41–43.

7. Steven Kelman, "The Grace Commission: How Much Waste in Government?" *Public Interest* (winter 1985): 62–82.

8. Interview on *60 Minutes* (CBS television, July 20, 1985); author interviewed management of Mr. Gasket Company in Brooklyn, Ohio, August 7, 1985.

9. Westinghouse no longer exists: Various parts of the company were sold to other corporations.

10. Al Gore, *Creating a Government That Works Better and Costs Less* (Washington, DC: U.S. Government Printing Office, 1993).

11. Kelman, "The Grace Commission," pp. 62–66; and U.S. General Accounting Office (GAO), *Fraud in Government Programs: How Extensive? How Can It Be Controlled?* (Washington, DC: U.S. GAO, 1981).

12. Jerome B. McKinney and Michael Johnston, eds., *Fraud, Waste, and Abuse in Government* (Philadelphia: Institute for the Study of Human Issues, 1986).

13. See *Black's Law Dictionary*, rev. 4th ed. (St. Paul, MN: West Publishing, 1968), p. 789.

14. See W. Steve Albrecht, Marshall J. Romney, David S. Cherrington, I. Reed Payne, and Allan J. Roe, *How to Detect and Prevent Business Fraud* (Englewood Cliffs, NJ: Prentice-Hall, 1982), chs. 3–5.

15. See U.S. Government Accounting Office, *Fraud in Government Programs*, p. 2; Martin Calpin, *Understanding Audits and Audit Reports*, 4th ed. (Ottawa, PQ: Canadian Institute of Chartered Accountants, 1984), p. 35.

16. Carrie Johnson, "Medical Fraud Growing Problem," Washington Post, June 13, 2008, p. A-1.

17. See Inspector General, Office of Inspector General, Auditor Fraud Resources, U.S. Defense Department, (2013), p. 1.

18. Peter Jones, *Combating Fraud and Corruption in the Public Sector* (London: Chapman & Hall, 1993), p. 2.

19. AICPA, "Internal Controls: Just the Start of a Fraud, Waste and Abuse Prevention Program," Government Accountability Brief (2009), pp. 1–2.

20. Office of the Inspector General, "Auditor Fraud Resources," U.S. Department of Defense (2014), p. 1.

21. Andrea G. Lange and Robert Bowers, *Fraud and Abuse in Government Benefit Programs* (Washington, DC: U.S. Department of Justice, Law Enforcement Assistance Administration, 1979), p. 16.

22. New York State Legislative Commission on Economy and Efficiency in Government, *Preventing Fraud, Waste, Abuse, and Error: Internal Control Reform in New York State Government* (Albany: State of New York, June 2, 1982).

23. Ibid., p. 10.

24. Ibid., p. 11.

25. Ibid.

26. Ibid., p. 17.

27. Mark W. Dersmith and Abraham Simon, *Local Government Internal Controls: A Guide for Public Officials* (New York: Council on Municipal Performance, 1983), part 2, pp. 30–31; see also Thomas Whiteside, *Computercapers: Tales of Electronic Thievery, Embezzlement, and Fraud* (New York: T. Y. Crowell, 1978).

28. Lawrence B. Sawyer, *The Practice of Modern Auditing* (Altamonte Springs, FL: Institute of Internal Auditors, 1981), p. 724.

29. Pacific Northwest Intergovernmental Audit Forum, *Auditing for Fraud* (Philadelphia: Forum, 1982), p. 16.

30. Lange and Bowers, *Fraud and Abuse in Government Benefit Programs*; surveyed were Medicaid, Aid to Families with Dependent Children, vocational education, food stamps, summer food, service programs for children, the Comprehensive Employment and Training Act (CETA), and unemployment insurance.

31. U.S. Department of Housing and Urban Development, *Handbook: Fraud Vulnerability Assessment* (Washington, DC: Office of the Inspector-General, 1980).

32. Ibid., pp. 2–4.

33. Paul E. Weisenbach, "Vulnerability Assessment and Internal Controls," *Government Accountants Journal 33*, no. 1 (spring 1983): 5.

34. Ibid., p. 6.

35. U.S. Government Accounting Office (GAO), *Framework for Assessing Job Vulnerability to Ethical Problems* (Washington, DC: GAO, 1981).

36. Weisenbach, "Vulnerability Assessment and Internal Controls," pp. 6–8.

37. Pacific Northwest Intergovernmental Audit Forum, *Auditing for Fraud*, p. 14.

38. Andrea Doroca and Frank P. Doroca, "Taking Stock of Auditor Independence," *Government Finance Review 18*, no. 5 (October 2002): 8.

39. U.S. General Accounting Office (GAO), *Government Auditing Standards* (Washington, DC: GAO, 2002), pp. 3–11.

40. The Fraud Triangle, the Institute of Fraud Certified Examiners (ACFE) 2014. http:www.acfe.com/fraud-triangle.aspx

41. Ibid.

42. Ibid. Fraud Triangle, http://www.schools.utah.gov/finance/Professional-Development/UFOMA/2a–UFOMA—Fraud-Triangle.aspx.

43. Ibid.

44. Frank Rudewicz, "The Fraud Diamond: Use of Investigative Due Diligence to Identify the Capability Element of Fraud," http://www.marcumllp.com/publications-1/the-fraud-diamond-use-of-investigative-due-diligence-to-identify-the-capability-element-of-fraud.

45. Ibid.

46. David T. Wolfe and Dana R. Hermanson, "The Fraud Diamond: Considering the Four Elements of Fraud," *The CPA Journal*, http://www.nysscpa.org/cpajournal/2004/1204/essentials/p38.htm

47. Ibid.

21

Financial Advising Functions

As the financial function has grown more complex, the need for expert financial advice has grown along with it. Over the years, various sources have emerged. In the public sector, the major sources have been the state, civic-minded corporations, professional associations, chambers of commerce, foundations, local universities, and paid consultants. Although not-for-profit organizations have access to some of the same sources as local governments, their main sources are the United Way and paid consultants.

This chapter presents a brief overview of the advising function in local governments and other not-for-profit organizations. A discussion follows wherein the three main provider groups (investment bankers, commercial banks, and independent paid advisors) are examined.

Capital Financing

Typically, most local governments seek financial advice when they raise funds for capital financing. This advice is sought either for a specific project or bond sale or for the preparation of a comprehensive financing strategy that involves a package of services beyond a particular debt issue. It is generally recommended when there is a need for advising services that they be secured at the beginning of the undertaking, especially in the case of a capital investment program. "Early participation in the process permits the advisor to develop (or assist in developing) a comprehensive financing plan that articulates the government's need for capital funds, explains alternative sources and structures of those funds, and examines their implications for the future fiscal health of the government."[1]

Involving the advising service early in a debt issue can often influence the financing alternatives available to the governmental unit. For example, the advisor's review of the laws may show existing practices that limit the financing options. Given enough lead time, such limits or impediments (current practices, procedures, or laws) may possibly be removed, permitting sizable cost savings to the issuer.[2]

Types of Advisory Firms

There are three main types of firms from which governments can obtain advisory services: *investment bankers, commercial banks,* and *independent consultants.* Investment and commercial bankers are typically grouped together in terms of the services they provide. Both provide advisory services as part of their normal business of marketing securities and making loans. Independent advisors, on the other hand, do not sell securities, make loans, or underwrite municipal bonds; they sell only their professional services. Most advisory services to governments have been confined to a single area—bond-related financing. In the past, advice on general finance and planning or project feasibility has been more the exception than the rule. However, this situation has begun to change, and in order to cope, many firms have been expanding their capability to respond to this need.

Since the 1999 repeal of the 1933 Glass–Steagall Act, significant deregulation has occurred in the banking industry and the separation of commercial and investment services has essentially disintegrated. Banks no longer have to restrict their operations to commercial loans, fund transfers, and so forth but can now engage in speculative derivatives trading and higher-risk financial activities using funds obtained through commercial banking operations. A result of consolidation of commercial and investment banking has been the offering of a wider range of advisory services by financial institutions such as PNC, BNY Mellon, and Wells Fargo. Customers, including the government, can take advantage of these service offerings and their reduced price due to consolidation/economies of scale.

Advisory firms that provide financial advice and underwrite municipal bonds are regulated by the Municipal Securities Rulemaking Board (MSRB). Under MSRB Rule G-23, an underwriter may operate in a dual capacity as financial advisor on a bond issue and bidder for the same issue only if the following conditions are satisfied: (a) The issue is competitive and (b) the issuer interposes no objections. The MSRB rules are applied differently to negotiated bond sales. When the underwriter is also acting as financial advisor, Rule G-23 requires that a disclosure be made in writing to the client indicating the potential for conflict of interest between the two roles. Moreover, the advisor must resign its financial role before participating in the underwriting activities of the client. This role change has traditionally been viewed with a degree of uneasiness because of its high potential for conflicts of interest. In the new role, the underwriter has two clients who have competing interests: The governmental unit selling the bond wants the lowest interest possible, whereas the purchaser of the bond wants the highest. "Since the underwriter is compensated only if the deal goes through, the underwriter is under considerable pressure to make the bonds as marketable as possible to consummate the sale."[3]

The passage of the Dodd–Frank Wall Street Reform and Consumer Protection Act in 2010 has had significant ramifications on U.S. financial industry oversight, including regulations concerning municipal bonds. Under the act, "municipal advisors" must register with the SEC to engage in the advising municipalities about how and when to issue securities and then how to invest the proceeds from the sales. The SEC issued a temporary registration regime for municipal advisors shortly after the Dodd–Frank Act was signed into law, but this was met by substantial criticism. After three years of deliberation and review, the SEC issued a permanent registration regime for municipal advisors in September 2013. This regime exempts certain professionals (accountants, lawyers, etc.) and appointed officials and limits the scope of advice that will require an individual to register to that pertaining to "the investment of proceeds from the sale of municipal securities rather than all public funds." To date, more than 1,100 individuals have successfully registered with the SEC under the permanent regime.

In addition to registration requirements, Dodd–Frank imposes a fiduciary duty on advisors toward the municipalities they conduct business with. Loyalty and care must be exercised on the part of municipal advisors at all times. This creates a more rigorous standard for individuals engaging in municipal securities advising and facilitates legal action from municipal governments and investors in the case of negligence or malpractice.[4]

Deciding on the Type of Firm to Be Used

The selection of a specific type of advisor will depend on a number of factors such as cost, reliability, experience, and confidence in the integrity of the advice. A number of arguments have been advanced for the different kinds of financial services provided:

- Independent advisors' perspectives tend to be broader in the range of services that are provided. Because advising is the independent provider's primary concern, services can be tailored and attention focused on the specific and overall needs of the client. The advisors' role is not limited to debt financing.
- The MSRB does not regulate independent advisors. This means that the governmental unit must thus rely on a firm's reputation.
- Investment bankers and commercial banks stress that their size and good standing gives them a reputation that they strive to maintain.
- Investment bankers and commercial banks that participate in the underwriting are regulated by the MSRB, which provides a degree of assurance that the organizations are maintaining adequate levels of competency and responsibility.

- Investment banking and commercial bankers acting in dual capacities as financial advisors and underwriters create a potential for conflicts of interest. In addition, because these groups typically participate in many syndicate (group underwriting) cooperative arrangements, they may not be willing to push the interest of a given client for the sake of jeopardizing a good working relationship with fellow bankers with whom they will be collectively involved in future underwriting activities. It may sometimes be necessary to employ financial providers that have integrated services—that is, to permit the financial advisor to act as an underwriter and investment banker, a process that has been greatly facilitated since the repeal of the Glass–Steagall Act. In the case of a negotiated underwriting, the governmental unit or organization deals principally with one investment banker for selling and marketing the bond. This permits the bond counsel to provide "a multiparty advisory role by assisting the issuer, the underwriter, the trustee and the purchaser."[5]

Disadvantages of the Independent Service Advice

Although there are efficiencies to be gained by using an independent advisor, there are also a number of associated disadvantages:

- Costs must be closely controlled to ensure that they do not exceed comparable in-house targets and to minimize the possibility of permitting fast-talking service providers to sell public officials unneeded services at excessive costs.
- Accountability becomes more difficult, since the service provider departs immediately after performance.
- Standards of quality must be clearly identified—an exceedingly difficult task in most public and other not-for-profit organizations.
- Obtaining segmented, independent financial advice is unwise owing to the complication of some financing arrangements. To minimize cost and limit risks, it may be necessary to employ financial providers that have integrated services.
- One-time improvements and ad hoc advice are not likely to endure if there is no continuity to ensure that management will carry out recommendations.[6]

Selecting the Financial Advisory Service

A preferred method for the selection of a financial advisory service is found through the distribution of requests for proposals (RFPs) to obtain a wide array of potential firms (see Table 21.1). This means more than a mere announcement of the RFP. A comprehensive list of advisory firms may be compiled

TABLE 21.1 An Action Plan and Simplified Checklist for Obtaining and Using Professional Services

STEP

1. **IDENTIFY OR CONCEPTUALIZE THE SERVICES DESIRED**
   [ ] Somebody has an idea, an inspiration, or a problem.
   [ ] Vendor makes a proposal.

2. **IDENTIFY INTERNAL PLAYERS AND OUTLINE THE PROCESS**
   [ ] Who will and should participate?
   [ ] Develop a step-by-step agenda.
   [ ] Assign staff to specific tasks and deadlines.

3. **DEFINE THE SCOPE OF SERVICES**
   [ ] What do we want and need? When?
   [ ] What will be delivered?
   [ ] What is done for other governments?
   [ ] How will we benefit?
   [ ] What do we do internally; what are our own capabilities?

4. **DETERMINE QUALITY STANDARDS**
   [ ] Identify professional standards.
   [ ] How is quality determined and described?
   [ ] How do others define quality?
   [ ] How will we enforce quality standards?
   [ ] Do we need professional help to define quality?

5. **EXPLORE ALTERNATIVE PRICING METHODS**
   [ ] Review theoretical options.
   [ ] Which are used in this profession?
   [ ] What is the industry standard in this market?
   [ ] What are our fiscal goals and limitations?

6. **PREPARE A REQUEST FOR PROPOSAL (OR REQUEST FOR INFORMATION)**
   [ ] Prepare staff assignments.
   [ ] Review quality standards and scope of services.
   [ ] Provide standard procurement language.
   [ ] Will a contract be prepared using the proposal?
   [ ] Anticipate the evaluation process and state criteria.
   [ ] Require specific information in standard format.
   [ ] Research RFPs used in other jurisdictions.

7. **IDENTIFY POTENTIAL VENDORS**
   [ ] Contact other jurisdictions.
   [ ] Contact professional associations.
   [ ] Consult the GFOA Directory of Financial Services.
   [ ] Prequalify or screen if necessary.
   [ ] Determine which vendors are inappropriate.

(Continued)

TABLE 21.1 *(Continued)*

8. **DESIGNATE SELECTION COMMITTEE**
   [ ] Find appropriate players.
   [ ] Establish criteria.
   [ ] Determine ground rules.
   [ ] Review proposals.
   [ ] Interview vendors/finalists if needed.

9. **FINAL SELECTION**
   [ ] Is action by governing body required?
   [ ] Who presents report?
   [ ] Can rational criteria overcome political influences?
   [ ] Is negotiation appropriate?
   [ ] What if governing body looks for different criteria?
   [ ] What if proposal exceeds budget?

10. **CONTRACTUAL PROVISIONS**
    [ ] Is a control appropriate?
    [ ] Will the RFP and the formal proposal form the basis of the contract?
    [ ] Are quality standards and timetables included?
    [ ] Is pricing/billing basis clear?

11. **IMPLEMENTATION AND ADMINISTRATION**
    [ ] Who is the government's staff contact person?
    [ ] Are progress payments based on performance?
    [ ] Will performance be measured?
    [ ] Are regular reports provided?
    [ ] Who approves payments and maintains files?
    [ ] How will "change orders" be controlled?

Source: Adapted from Girard Miller, *Selecting Financial Services for Government* (Chicago: Government Finance Officers Association, 1984), pp. 39–40; and Patricia Tigue, *A Guide for Selecting Financial Advisors and Underwriters* (Chicago: Government Finance Officers Association, 1999), pp. 21–22.

using aids such as the *Directory of Municipal Bond Dealers of the United States* published by the *Daily Bond Buyer*. The RFP should clearly specify the type and scope of services desired, setting forth the criteria for selection and the method of compensation.

Sometime before the proposals have been reviewed, the governmental unit should clearly identify the criteria to be applied in evaluating the proposals. Among the criteria that should be used are (1) the past experience of the firm and familiarity with the financial services to be provided, (2) the expertise and experience of its staff to direct and implement the project, (3) experience with other governments within and outside the state, and (4) estimated costs of carrying out the project. After this process is completed, the top two or three applicants are invited to make presentations to provide additional input regarding the applicant's familiarity with the substantive matter of the project so as to obtain a reading and feel for the nature and caliber of the principals and to clarify questions and queries that have surfaced within the written proposals.

Negotiating for Bank Service

Because of the profitable nature of governmental units to banks, the pressure to land the governmental entity's account is high.[7] Competitive bidding has been growing as the method of choice for selecting banking services. Among the benefits attributed to competitive banking are increased yield on investment, enhanced collection services' generating greater amounts of dollars to invest, more economical bank services, and enhanced efficiency of each management operation.

After the commitment has been made to use competitive bidding, the governmental unit makes a thorough assessment of the needs that must be met to satisfy its cash requirements. After this is done, a carefully prepared RFP should be developed and sent to all banks in the region, city, county, or state, as appropriate. Before the banks' submission of bids, the jurisdiction requesting the service holds a prebid conference. Research proposals are evaluated based on the stipulated criteria, after which the award is made and the contract signed. Among the factors that influence which bank will be selected include the following:

- Timing and method of notification and wire transfer;
- Availability of coin-counting services
- Use of a concentration/zero-balance type of account
- Provision of account reconciliation services
- Availability and compatibility of computer services
- Access to check cashing services

Compensation of Financial Advisory Services

There is no set or definable system that can be applied in determining an advisor's fee. Any of a number of methods may be used such as a bond float, an agreed-upon amount on an annual basis or an hourly rate, or a percentage of the total dollar amount of the financing related to the advisor's services rendered. Although there is no accepted right or wrong way to determine advisory fees, it is generally considered imprudent to tie an advisor's fee to the amount of bonds sold. This may provide the advisor with an incentive to sell bonds at rates that might be higher than otherwise, thus increasing the commission received. The method provides no built-in incentive to recommend alternative financing approaches or to postpone the sale of the debt or bonds because of a volatile market.

The scope and content of advisory services differ so greatly that it may be hazardous to speak about comparative costs. Surveys in 1991 indicated that bond floatation advisory fees averaged from $1.50 per $1,000 on general obligation bonds of $5–$10 million and $2.80 per $1,000 on revenue bonds. The point has been made that it is wise for an issuer to exchange informal information with other issuers or to send out RFPs to obtain some realistic ideas about the ranges of out-of-pocket costs.[8] Pricing methods for financial services are discussed in detail below.

The Availability of Different Kinds of Financial Advice

Although the most important governmental advice sought is financial, it is the least-known of all the services provided to government.[9] Attempts to obtain consistent financial answers about the criteria that governmental and other not-for-profit organizations employ in selecting financial service providers seldom meet with much success. The kinds of financial services available from the commercial marketplace, the not-for-profit interest group associations, professional associations, universities, other governmental units, and civic-minded corporations are rich and diverse. In fact, it is this diversity that creates a challenge to the public finance professional. A partial list of the types of financial providers helps demonstrate this point:

- Accountants
- Auditors
- Bankers
- Bond counsels
- Computer services
- Financial advisors
- Leasing services
- Pension portfolio management and advisors
- Property appraisers
- Risk management consultants.

Because finance is so critical, it is important that the particular financial services be carefully chosen; the choice can greatly affect the financial condition and operations of an organization. Selecting the most appropriate or best available service is a difficult task in both the public and other not-for-profit agencies. In public organizations, "managers and elected officials are unfamiliar with varying professional standards of quality,"[10] compounding the difficulty of the problem.

During the preceding decade, climate change has become an issue of paramount importance. Firms are responding to the "green" demands of their consumers, including the sustainable procurement requirements of many government agencies. To satisfy governmental and consumer clients, advisory firms are beginning to offer an array of consulting services concerning sustainability and emission standards compliance. The Global Reporting Initiative (GRI) has created the framework for sustainability reporting used by companies and governments around the world. Financial advisory firms, such as PricewaterhouseCoopers LLP and Ernst and Young LLP, are offering implementation and integration services for the GRI reporting framework. These services are being increasingly tailored to meet the unique reporting needs of governmental and not-for-profit entities.

As climate change and sustainability become key components affecting organizational, including governmental, operations and bottom lines, the advisory services offered and competition in these areas will expand. Government entities will therefore have a wider array of services to choose from at better prices.[11]

Pricing of Financial Advisory Services

Pricing methods for financial services differ among the various professional organizations. Table 21.2 indicates one possibility of categorizing the different methods.

Fixed Price or Lump Sum

In this type of contract, the contractor agrees to carry out some specifically defined work in a given time period for an agreed-upon sum of money. Because there is a single price, this type of contract is viewed as the simplest of all the pricing methods. Note that this method shifts the cost risks to the contractor, because the contractor is paid the agreed-upon price regardless of the costs incurred. Overrun costs do not become the concern of the organization, but rather of the financial service firm. Although simple in nature, this method may result in increased risk for the organization, as the fixed price (lump sum) must be paid regardless of the actual dollar amount of bonds issued/services provided.

Unit Price

This is a variation of the fixed price contract. The contractor agrees to perform a repetitive assignment and bills the client for the unit of work completed. This approach is typically used when the quality or volume of work cannot be easily determined in advance. Unit costing facilitates marginal costing, because each additional unit of output cost can be compared with the prior unit.

TABLE 21.2   Financial Services: Contract-Pricing System

Fixed-Price Type	Upset Hybrid Fixed Price	Cost Reimbursement
Fixed fee (lump sum)	Guaranteed maximum price	Cost only
Unit price	Ceilings on overhead fee	Cost plus fixed
Percentage of total	Incentive clauses	Cost plus percentage fee
Fixed price with escalator	Penalty clauses Escalation clauses	Loaded hourly rate

Source: Adapted from Girard Miller, *Selecting Financial Services for Government* (Chicago: Government Finance Officers Association, 1984), pp. 17–18; see also, Edward Weseman, *Contracting City Services* (Pittsburgh,: Innovations Press, 1981), pp. 60–61.

Percentage of Gross Fees or Revenue

This method has wide use in the financial service industry. It allows fees to be charged as a percentage of the dollar amount of the activity (e.g., a financial advisor may charge $1.65 for every $1,000 of bonds floated). This method has survived because of the imperfect nature of competition and the ability of the service provider to exact charges thanks to its influence and dominant position.

Fixed Price Controls with Escalation

In those situations where the contract covers a long period, and especially during periods of unstable prices, contractors attempt to protect themselves and limit risk by attaching escalation clauses.

Upset Fixed Price

This pricing system has enjoyed a degree of popularity among public managers. It allows the contractor to charge on a per unit or per hour basis but is limited by a maximum price that may not be exceeded. When this method is used, the operating assumption is made that the maximum price will be applied unless favorable conditions occur. In a way, it could be easily argued that the upset or maximum price is really a kind of cost reimbursement approach with the application of a ceiling or cap.

Cost Reimbursement–Type Contracts

The application of this approach to contract pricing permits the contractor to be paid for all allowable costs. The approach is premised on the view that prices are determined on the basis of variable costs that cannot be readily identified in advance. The cost reimbursement method is used when the volume and type of work cannot be easily determined. Effective operation of this pricing procedure requires considerable trust in the contractor. Moreover, there is no built-in incentive for the contractor to control costs or meet schedule deadlines. Therefore, reporting and monitoring requirements should be clearly and specifically spelled out.

Cost-Only Reimbursement

This method is acceptable if the quality of the product produced can be maintained. This kind of pricing is based on direct costs and excludes overhead and profit expenses. A contractor may desire such an arrangement to enhance business relationships, keep the services of critical employees, or undercut competition.

Cost Plus Fixed Fee

This permits the contractor to carry out agreed-upon work within a specified period of time for an amount of money based on itemized costs plus an additional fee known as a *fixed fee*, which comprises the contractor's cost, overhead, and profit. This method is used in those cases where the scope of work in question cannot be adequately defined. A number of problems may arise by using this approach, such as (1) the contractor's rapid completion of work to increase his or her profit ratio without due care being given to quality and (2) the contractor obtaining unreasonable profits. To minimize these types of problems from occurring, many governmental contractors have required close supervision and ceiling clauses, stipulating levels that costs may not exceed. These provisions should be realistic to ensure that undue burdens aren't placed on the contractor that could hinder or delay completion of the project.

Cost Plus Percentage

This is known sometimes as the "overhead" pricing system. This method requires that all costs be explicitly defined. An agreed-on percentage of these costs is calculated, generating the fee. This system has a built-in incentive for the contractor to recapture his or her overhead. Accordingly, it is the contractor's intent to include as much expense as possible in the total cost figure. Because of the potential for abuse, this cost approach is usually avoided and even prohibited in some jurisdictions.

Loaded Hourly Rate

This is the "cost plus percentage fee." It is commonly found in public finance agreements. Charges are determined on the basis of labor services. Worker classifications are defined for each function to be performed. A composite hourly rate (including indirect costs) is then assigned to each worker classification. Because overhead costs are built in, there is some incentive to prolong the contract. Like the other reimbursement methods, imposed deadlines and the continued monitoring of work should be carried out. In cases where this method must be used, it is desirable to include ceilings.

Cost Plus Incentive Fee Contract

This has a built-in factor to reward contractors to control costs and to penalize the contractor for cost overruns. This approach typically requires that targets be set: (1) target cost, (2) target fee, (3) minimum and maximum fees, and (4) formula for fee adjustment. The target cost is the contractor's best estimate of the cost required to complete the work. When the contractor controls the hours applied or charged, an incentive is provided that increases the fees. However, if cost overruns are generated, a penalty is imposed. The operation of the minimum and maximum fees thus protects both sides from widely varying fluctuations in price.

The incentive method may be applied creatively to enhance the benefits for all concerned. Consultants may be given the incentive to find ways of reducing costs or increasing revenues. Based on the amounts involved, a percentage can then be applied to the amount to reward the consultant. When such a system is encouraged, care should be exercised to minimize abuse. For example, a consultant should not be allowed to receive a windfall profit from a recommendation that is general knowledge within the industry. To prevent situations such as this, it is paramount that government procurement officials be knowledgeable about industry/market trends and prices.

Hybrid Costing

Variations of the fixed and cost reimbursement types include the following: (1) The *guaranteed maximum price* establishes a price that a contractor may not exceed. It is very much like the fixed price method (discussed earlier). This type of control is common in the public sector, because legislative bodies pass appropriations that cannot legally be exceeded. (2) The *ceiling on overhead reimbursement* may be applied to the overhead to recapture types of contracts such as loaded hourly rates and the cost plus percentage fee. (3) *Incentive clauses* incorporate aspects of the fixed contract. They are an attempt to motivate contractors toward greater efficiency. Contracts that provide for specific incentives to contractors are seldom found in public and other not-for-profit agencies. (4) *Penalty clause* contracts seek to promote minimum standards of professional quality and timeliness. Typically, a fixed percentage or sum is deducted from the contract for noncompliance. When this is designed to effect compliance, however, it may foster production of an output in which quality is impaired. (5) *Price escalators* (multiyear engagements) are used when stability in price levels is sought. Most often, indices such as the Consumer Price Index (CPI) or the gross national product (GNP) price deflator are used to avoid the possibility of contract price renegotiation. There are a number of benefits to be gained from price escalators, such as (a) technology changes that can lower cost and help the organization, (b) benefits to contractors from spiraling costs, and (c) the governmental unit's avoidance of startup and retraining costs. Procurement officials feel that this approach lacks certainty and thus believe that prices should be negotiated at a fixed rate at the time when the contract is entered into.

Public and Other Not-for-Profit Organizations as Sources of Financial Advice

Other governmental units can often be a ready source of financial information and assistance to local governments. The type and quantity of services vary among the different governmental units. At the local level, the state is a major provider of financial advice, both to other state agencies and to local governments. The advent of the Internet, and subsequently of databases that store pricing and service information, greatly facilitated the transmission of financial advice between agencies and levels of government. Procurement officials can reference these databases to find out market rates and pricing options. Because local governments are more often in greater need of financial advice, attention will be focused on this issue.

Advising takes several forms: (1) legally mandated or prescribed financial requirements that the state closely monitors; (2) provision of model financial management practices set forth in a series of reports, booklets, or pamphlets; (3) provision of seminars, lectures, and short courses geographically dispersed throughout the state at regular and convenient times; and (4) a combination of forms 1 through 3.

For example, Pennsylvania emphasizes forms 2 and 3. At regular times and throughout the state, seminars, lectures, and short courses are conducted for local officials. Among the written materials that have been developed for local officials are the following:

- *Fiscal Management Handbook*, containing basics on revenue sources, budgeting, bookkeeping and accounting guidelines, and municipal borrowing
- *Purchasing Handbook for Local Government*, discussing desired techniques and practices
- *Auditors' Guide*, acquainting elected auditors with their duties and responsibilities, outlining the scope of an audit, suggesting programs for the auditing

of various funds, and explaining how to prepare various required fiscal reports

- *Taxation Manual*, containing simplified explanations of the various kinds of local taxes permitted to be levied within the commonwealth
- *Tax Collectors' Manual*, providing guidance and assistance to elected tax collectors

Georgia has emphasized forms 1 and 2. The Institute of Government at the University of Georgia has been a prolific source of financial information for local officials within the state. Among its publications are the following:

- *Getting the Most from Professional Services: Fiscal Advisor* (Charles K. Coe, 1979), containing sample contract provisions, an evaluation checklist, and a brief description of fiscal services provided by advisors, especially on bond issues
- *Getting the Most from Professional Services: Outside Auditor* (1981), providing a brief introduction to the problems facing public officials when searching for an outsider auditor
- *Understanding Risk Management: A Guide for Government* (Charles K. Coe, 1980), containing a comprehensive overview of the risk management field
- *Getting the Most from Professional Services: Computer Selection* (Charles K. Coe, 1979), indicating some basic options that should be considered in selecting a computer
- *A Basic Budget Guide for Small Cities and Counties* by Arthur Mahor, Jr. (1985), containing steps for preparing and adopting a budget in small governmental units
- *Compliance Auditing in Georgia Counties and Municipalities* by Paul T. Hardy, Richard W. Campbell, and Paul E. Glick (1992), reviewing legal requirements for conducting a compliance audit
- *Cooperative Purchasing: A Guide for Local Governments* (1985), explaining how cooperative purchasing saves money
- *Handbook for Collecting Delinquent Property Taxes* (J. Devereaux Weeks, 1984), describing ways of recovering unpaid taxes
- *County and Municipal Revenue Sources* (J. Devereaux Weeks, 1992), explaining general revenue sources available to local governments

The North Carolina publication *Local Government Finance in North Carolina* has been accepted and used as an authoritative guide for local officials in that state. Colorado emphasizes form 1 and provides a comprehensive *Local Government Financial Management Manual*, regularly updated, that sets forth legal requirements and suggested practices.

Not-for-Profit Professional Associations

This category comprises a wide spectrum of financial service providers. Only the most prominent are included in the following list:

- *The Government Finances Officer Association* (GFOA) publishes a number of handbooks, books, pamphlets, and yearly updates on current research in financial management. To foster better financial reports among local governments, the GFOA awards its Certificate of Conformance to those governmental units that meet the announced reporting criteria. The GFOA provides advisory services to its members through its Research and Consulting Center. Assistance is given on technology and related tasks including needs assessment, RFPs, financial system procurement evaluations, contract negotiations, and project management.[12]
- *The International City Managers Association* (ICMA) provides numerous books, pamphlets, and reports. The ICMA publishes books on virtually every area of financial management. Among its prominent publications are the *Management Information Service (MIS) Report* on timely financial topics and *Financial Monitoring Trend System*, developed to assist governmental units in evaluating the fiscal health of their communities.
- *The Association of Government Accountants* (AGA) intermittently publishes reports, books, and pamphlets. The AGA's strength lies perhaps most in the many "short, timely" seminars and lectures offered, especially to financial managers in the Washington, D.C. area.
- *Public Technology Incorporated* (PTI) is a cooperative research development and technology transfer organization providing services to American cities and counties. It helps local governments develop and improve their financial management systems to increase efficiency, reduce costs, and improve services. It publishes books and pamphlets, conducts workshops and seminars, and offers consulting advice. It provides technical assistance in (1) information management/office automation and (2) operational effectiveness, revenues and expenditure, forecasting, and user charges and fees.

Local Government Academy

The Local Government Academy (LGA) provides services to many counties in western Pennsylvania. The organization's goals are to promote responsive local government, train area leaders, educate officials and the general public, and foster collaboration in the community. It offers many training opportunities, coordinates a range of on-site technical assistance to financially distressed communities, and channels new talent and ideas into communities through its acclaimed Municipal Intern Program. Through the Newly Elected Officials

Course (NEOC), the LGA offers special training opportunities to newly elected officials.

Private Corporations and Foundations

The Pittsburgh corporate community, through the chamber of commerce, has been successful in providing financial advice to Pittsburgh, Allegheny County, and the Pittsburgh School District in western Pennsylvania. It perhaps may serve as a useful model for other areas in the country.

The relationship established between the two large governmental units and the school district (Pittsburgh and Allegheny County and the Pittsburgh School District) has been most beneficial, constructive, and creative. The corporate community has provided timely and useful financial advice. The business community and the governmental units reached an operating understanding regarding the disposition of recommendations resulting from studies carried out on the governmental units' operation. "They agreed on the condition that everyone involved accepted one fundamental provision: that any recommendations made by the business and accepted by the elected officials must be implemented."[13] Among the projects that the corporate community has carried out are the following:

- *The Committee for Progress and Efficiency in Pittsburgh* (COMPEP) examined Pittsburgh's purchasing process and recommended ways for it to be streamlined to more effectively carry out its purposes.
- *The Committee for Progress in Allegheny County* (COMPAC) aimed at improving the economy, efficiency, and effectiveness of county government. Three main objectives were sought: (1) to make immediate improvements in the operation of county government, (2) to put in place self-generating enhancements to facilitate change, and (3) to build bridges between county government professionals and their business counterparts.
- *The Committee for Improvements in the Courts* attempted to streamline administrative systems to enhance the efficiency and effectiveness of the courts.
- *The Systems Program for Interactive Financial Forecasting (SPIFF)* was developed for Pittsburgh, Allegheny County, and the Pittsburgh Board of Public Education to provide two important capabilities: (1) maintaining and displaying historical data of up to fifty years prior, permitting it to be organized into tabular form, and (2) containing techniques and methods for projecting revenues and expenditure.
- *The Local Government Financial Forecasting Project* is a computer-based, in-house, long-range financial forecasting capability for Pittsburgh, Allegheny County, and the Pittsburgh Board of Education.
- *The Local Government Computer Capability Project* (COGNET) is an instrument to promote better management and intergovernmental cooperation

among the 131 municipalities within Allegheny County. The COGNET's goal is the development of a computer network to serve the county's eight regional councils of government (COGs) to facilitate the sharing of services and the capacity-building/improving of management capability.

The COGNET project is a follow-up of the earlier Pittsburgh Chamber of Commerce's municipal involvement. The project is tied into the University of Pittsburgh's AT&T "Campus of the Future" and "County of the Future" and is a collective effort of five different organizations: (1) the Intergovernmental Cooperation Program, based in Pittsburgh; (2) the Pittsburgh Chamber of Commerce (as the main resource provider); (3) the University of Pittsburgh; (4) Carnegie-Mellon University as the joint planning, research, and training arms; and (5) the county of Allegheny as the in-kind provider of administrative support. To enhance the project's capability, the Pittsburgh Foundation granted COGNET resources to develop a number of internships with students from Carnegie-Mellon University and the University of Pittsburgh. In June 1985, the Pittsburgh Chamber of Commerce received the Prudential Citation of Merit for Private Sector Initiatives for its innovative direction and accomplishments with the COGNET project.[14]

The Ford Foundation

To stimulate and share creative approaches to the operation of state and local government, the Ford Foundation initiated a program called "Innovation in State and Local Government."[15] This program is now referred to as "Innovations in American Government." The award is substantial—$100,000—and the competition receives over 1,000 applications annually. The objective is to provide awards to units of government that have successfully applied methods to overcome social and economic problems and improve the quality of life. "The goal of the awards program is to identify and publicize initiatives that exemplify creative inventive thinking about government, managerial climates that encourage innovations, and particular state and local innovations that are worthy of transfer and replication,"[16] with greatest attention given to innovation in such areas as families, health care, education, jobs training, and housing.

Municipal and Economy Leagues

These leagues are professional associations and public interest organizations that offer valuable assistance to local governments. The Maine Municipal Association (MMA) provides an example. It is made up of 495 towns and cities and engages in strategic planning, such as it performed in 1982, when it carried out a needs analysis of local government to identify areas on which the MMA should focus its attention. A result of this strategic planning was the strong recommendation that increased financial and consulting services should be provided to member municipalities. This recommendation led to the hiring of a staff to (1) carry out surveys, (2) collect and review members' inquiries as a service to members, (3) provide consulting to members on specific financial issues for a nominal (below-market) per hour fee, and (4) develop financial workshops and publish articles in the association's monthly magazine on current financial events.

Maine has facilitated the exchange of information on financial management. State-level agencies have developed peerlike relationships with local governments. The advantage of this approach manifests itself in institutions involving state and local creative problem solving. For example, when the Reagan administration signaled its policy intent to reduce funding for wastewater treatment facilities, Maine, in a cooperative response intended to minimize the financial uncertainties among local governments, enacted environmental laws tougher than those of the federal government and provided increased financial aid to this important program area.

The Pennsylvania Economy League of Greater Pittsburgh, which is corporate funded, provides an example of civic-minded corporate leadership support for the improved delivery of public goods and services. The league gives advice and assistance to all units of government. Although it prefers to work with a collective of municipalities, it responds to individual governmental unit calls for assistance as well. For example, the Allegheny League of Municipalities has developed a number of handbooks on various financial topics.

Local Universities/Colleges

Most universities and colleges, especially state-supported ones with programs in public administration, provide an array of services and publications to governmental units, often below cost or free of charge. Many of these institutions seek agencies that will provide internships for their students.

The Not-for-Profit Sector

The most prolific source of financial advice comes from private professional associations and United Way–sponsored agencies. For example, in Allegheny County, the CPA association has been generous with its assistance to not-for-profit agencies. Many of the big accounting and consulting firms, such as PricewaterhouseCoopers and Deloitte, sit on not-for-profit agency boards. Generally, their services provided are gratis or at minimal cost to the not-for-profit agencies.

Community Technical Association Center

The Community Technical Association Center (CTAC) is an example of an agency that was organized to assist not-for-profit agencies. It charges fees according to ability to pay. Among the services CTAC provides are (1) financial management (setting up accounting systems) and (2) computerized accounting, including cost-effectiveness analysis, bookkeeping, development of financial reports, budgeting, and financial planning. These services are available to nonprofit agencies and community development corporations on a nonpartisan basis throughout Pittsburgh.

Summary Observations

Although the financial advising function has become an important and strategic function in government and other not-for-profit organizations, little attention was given to it in the literature until recent efforts by the Government Finance Officers Association in its publications. In the past, many governmental units sought financial advice only when they needed to enter the capital markets to borrow funds. However, this situation has started to change for many reasons, among them regulations and the complexity of the financial management problems faced by governmental units and other not-for-profit organizations.

Most states have developed various ways of responding to the increasing need for financial advice, as shown by the governments of Georgia, Maine, Pennsylvania, North Carolina, and Colorado. These efforts cannot, however, meet all the specific financial advising requirements of the governmental units—hence the need for financial advice from corporations, universities, foundations, and associations. As can be seen from Pittsburgh's experience, the corporate community can be a forceful and strategic source of creative financial advice to communities.

Notes

1. West C. Hough and John E. Petersen, "Selection and Use of Financial Advisory Services," *Governmental Finance 13* (March 1984): 42.

2. Ibid.

3. Ibid., p. 45.

4. "SEC Approves Regulation Rules for Municipal Advisors," *SEC.gov*. Securities and Exchange Commission, September 18, 2013. http://www.sec.gov/News/PressRelease/Detail/PressRelease/1370539817759#.VH1Bu8mwU3k.

5. Girard Miller, *Selecting Financial Services for Government* (Chicago: Government Finance Officers Association, 1984), p. 9.

6. Ibid.

7. Rhett D. Harrell, "Banking Relations: Part II," in *Cash Management for Small Governments*, ed. Ian J. Allan (Chicago: Government Finance Officers Association, 1989), pp. 83–85.

8. Ibid., pp. 46–47.

9. Miller, *Selecting Financial Services for Government*, p. 9.

10. Ibid.

11. "About GRI," *Globalreporting.org*. Global Reporting Initiative, n.d. https://www.globalreporting.org/information/sustainability-reporting/Pages/default.aspx.

12. See Stephen J. Gauthier, Rowan Miranda, and Robert Roque, *An Elected Official's Guide to Financial System Procurement* (Chicago: Government Finance Officers Association, 1999); Rowan Miranda, Shayne Kavanagh, and Robert Roque, *Technology Assessment: Evaluating the Business Case for ERP and Financial Management Systems* (Chicago: Government Finance Officers Association, 2002); and Patricia Tigue, *A Guide for Selecting Financial Advisors and Underwriters* (Chicago: Government Finance Officers Association, 1999).

13. Edward S. Kiely, "Mobilizing Business Resources for Better Government: Pittsburgh's Learned Executive Experience," *Urban Resources 1* (summer 1983): 8.

14. Mellon Institute and Carnegie-Mellon University, *SPIFF User Manual* (Pittsburgh: Pittsburgh Chamber of Commerce, 1985), p. 1.

15. Ford Foundation and Harvard University, "Innovations in State and Local Government" (pamphlet, n.d.).

16. Ibid.

Index